POST MORTEM

THE CLASSIC INVESTIGATION OF THE JFK ASSASSINATION MEDICAL AND BALLISTICS EVIDENCE AND COVER-UP

T0056969

HAROLD WEISBERG

Skyhorse Publishing

Skyhorse Publishing books may be purchased in bulk at special discounts for sales
promotion, corporate gifts, fund-raising, or educational purposes. Special editions can
also be created to specifications. For details, contact the Special Sales Department,
Skyhorse Publishing, 307 West 36th Street, 11th Floor, New York, NY 10018 or
info@skyhorsepublishing.com.

Skyhorse® and Skyhorse Publishing® are registered trademarks of Skyhorse Publishing,
Inc.®, a Delaware corporation.

Visit our website at www.skyhorsepublishing.com.

10 9 8 7 6 5 4 3

Library of Congress Cataloging-in-Publication Data is available on file.
ISBN: 978-1-62636-061-7

Printed in the United States of America

TABLE OF CONTENTS

In too many cases the copies of official documents reproduced are unclear. Some are illegible. These are, however, the actual documents from government files. This is their real condition, in itself a commentary on the care about and concern for preservation of the records of the official investigation into the assassination of the President. I addressed this first in the Epilogue to WHITE-WASH II. Where documents have disappeared, the Archivist has refused to obtain replacements from the agencies of origin. Although the Commission had no need to scrimp, it made more carbons than can be clear instead of xeroxing, which it also did, too often from the least clear carbons.

It has not been possible to redo parts of this book that, while still new in content today, actually were prepared for print-ing almost a decade ago. This and other factors will reduce legi-bility. The fault is not the printer's. It is a by-product of the conditions under which the work was done and the situations that pre-cluded earlier publication of all but the final part.

Harold Weisberg

Frederick, Md.
October 1975

PREFACE

This is a book unique in American history. It reveals more information about the assassination of President Kennedy than any before, but it is not about the assassination. Indeed, it makes no pretense of attempting to solve the crime.

Rather, it is the story of how the crime was left unsolved by those whose responsibility it was to develop all the relevant facts and reach conclusions. It is the Byzantine story of how federal authorities deliberately prevented the truth about a President's murder from being discovered, framed an innocent man, and then conspired to protect themselves against revelation of and accounting for their terrible abuses.

The American public has never believed the conclusions of the Warren Commission that Lee Harvey Oswald was the lone assassin of President Kennedy, that no suggestion of conspiracy could be found. But never before has there been this kind of proof that the government's "failure" was deliberate, that at no time was truth sought, that the responsible federal authorities conspired, committed crimes, to hide the truth about the assassination.

This book presents new evidence - new in that it has never before been publicly exposed - that the federal cover-up was knowing and willful: that J. Edgar Hoover*deliberately suppressed evidence he knew disproved his instant solution to the crime; that the Warren Commission knew it dared not challenge Hoover and planned to issue a report confirming the FBI's conclusions before it began its investigation; that the Commission's staff deliberately excluded from the record the most basic evidence of the crime, evidence in total conflict with the preordained conclusions. Much of the overwhelming evidence presented here, although always available to the Commission, was never even seen by it and never made a part of its files.

This book strips the Commission and its "investigation" of their last threads of innocence.

POST-MORTEM is unique also in its format and the circumstances under which it was written.

Since 1964, Harold Weisberg has been a one-man investigative agency. His work in the area of assassination has encompassed virtually all phases of President Kennedy's murder and, after the first 1968 tragedy, included the murder of Martin Luther King. He has devoted all of his time to researching, investigating and writing about these crimes and their official nonsolutions. The undertaking has been mammoth in both scope and effort, taking him all over the country and often into court, suing the government for release of documents improperly kept secret and acting as the investigator in the habeas corpus proceeding of James Earl Ray, the man falsely accused of killing Dr. King. It is unfortunate to have to report that Harold has been forced to labor, for the most part, alone; he cannot pay for assistance because his devotion to his work has bankrupted him, and he receives no cooperation from most of those "critics" whose chief pursuit is commercialization, not fact-finding. He can fight government suppression in court under the Freedom of Information Act only when he can obtain free counsel (he did once represent himself), and

---

*Died 5/1/72.

in his latest efforts he is indebted to Jim Lesar, a young lawyer who, in rendering his services without fee so that a citizen may exercise his rights under the law, should be regarded as a model for all lawyers. (Jim, whose practice is just beginning and who cannot even afford a secretary or clerk, actually borrowed money from the bank so that a Top Secret executive session of the Warren Commission made public as a result of his and Harold's efforts could be published and thus made available to the public. The transcript is reproduced in facsimile with other once-secret documents and a legal appendix in WHITEWASH IV.)

In the midst of this fantastic amount of investigation, Harold has written over nine books, six of them already published. It is a wonder in itself that one man so situated could be capable of such a literary outpouring. And it is thus not surprising that, under these circumstances, Harold has been unable to write the kind of books to which the public, especially historians, are accustomed. In essence, Harold must write about a breaking story, for he is constantly forcing the release of new information. He writes under circumstances which prevent the tedious and time-consuming work of careful organization and rewriting necessary to achieve a "polished" book with at least the veneer of detachment and "objectivity."

The organization which Harold has thus adopted has been one mothered by necessity. He has simply chosen to tell the story of his quest for evidence, his efforts to dislodge the secrets which the government has so long tried to keep locked away in its vaults. It is within this framework that he presents and analyzes the suppressed evidence. Ideally, the writer of nonfiction assembes his evidence first, organizes it and then presents it in a systematic, coherent manner. Were Harold to refrain from writing until all the relevant evidence could be amassed, he simply could never write, and the information he has been able to develop would be denied to the public, its rightful recipients. The alternative has been to compromise the traditional notion of scholarly writing without in any way compromising the principles of scholarship.

POST-MORTEM is thus a truly scholarly book, far more thoroughly documented, in fact, than most so considered, presented in a truly unconventional form. The reader should understand how it came to be written before he attempts to absorb its voluminous contents.

Most simply stated, POST-MORTEM tells how the federal government suppressed, distorted, lied about and sometimes actually destroyed the most basic evidence in the assassination to substantiate a preconceived and false solution to the crime. As in any murder involving firearms, the basic evidence is the medical (autopsy) and ballistics data; the fundamental goal of truth and justice is served by the fullest possible ascertainment of the cause and circumstances of death. No less was true when President Kennedy was gunned down in broad daylight on November 22, 1963, when Lee Harvey Oswald was accused of the crime, and when the Warren Commission was appointed to fill the void after Oswald's murder in the hands of the police eliminated any immediate possibility of a judicial resolution of the crime.

Part I of POST-MORTEM was written in 1967, based on investigation begun by Harold in 1966. Thus, except where Harold was able to make an occasional updating (e.g., pp.50,70), it represents the fruits of his research as of 1967.

Part II is essentially a detailed analysis of information released by the Justice Department in January 1969 relating to the suppressed pictures and X-rays of the President's body taken during the autopsy at Bethesda Naval Hospital the night of November 22. It was written in early 1969, an instant but remarkably accurate and perceptive analysis of documents that conclusively establish the pervasive dishonesty of all the expert autopsy testimony on which the Commission based its conclusions.

Part III resumes the chronicle of Harold's efforts to unearth

what officialdom has kept buried. It presents for the first time anywhere official evidence which the Commission itself did not have or
see, evidence which establishes the falsity of the official conclusions
beyond any reasonable doubt and further establishes the deliberateness
of what Harold aptly terms the "fake inquest." This part represents
the fruits of his investigation from 1969 to 1971 and was written in
1971.

The "Epilogue," itself an impossibility in a book of this sort,
was written in 1972, primarily to document new governmental improprieties involving the pictures and X-rays and the consequent new dis-
seminations of the most obvious falsehoods. The occasion prompting
this 1972 "Epilogue" was the promise of publication by a man of inherited wealth. He later broke his promise.

Part IV was written in 1975, when for the first time Harold
could see his way to arrange a private publication of POST-MORTEM.
It documents and analyzes the latest government disclosures, begrudg-
ing and usually incomplete responses to his persistent efforts, including a lawsuit for vital scientific ballistics tests so tightly
held by the Justice Department that Congress had to amend the law to
prohibit withholding of such documents. These latest disclosures are
a further irrefutable destruction of the official fictions, the official integrity.

The skeptical reader may ask how information so devastating
could have gone unpublished so long in a country boasting a free and
vigorous press. These books have from the first always been available to willing publishers. That none chose to undertake publication
and accept the risk of a substantial challenge to the federal government which has grown so enormous, so powerful, and so corrupted, is
more a sad commentary on the state of the press in America than on
any flaws in the books themselves.

If the reader finds such a statement untenable, the relevant
documentation on which this book is based is presented, in facsimile,
as a voluminous appendix. Thus, the reader is free to study and form
his own conclusions about the evidence, independent of what Harold or
I may say about it. The courage and integrity of the press must be
judged not by the familiar rhetoric, but by an intelligent evaluation
of what the press had but refused to print. The documentary appendix
allows such an evaluation.

Until now it was impossible for Harold to assume the great
costs of a private printing. A new improvement on the printing process has enabled him to undertake such a private printing, financed
in part by the small income provided by the steady stream of mail
orders he received for his earlier books, including the most recent,
WHITEWASH IV. To pay the full printing cost, he will have to go
deeper into debt.

The long-awaited publication of POST-MORTEM comes at a time of
renewed public interest in the assassination. Unlike so many of the
irresponsible sensationalists exploiting this new wave of doubt and
concern to make a buck, Harold cannot be accused of commercialization
in publishing now. The private printing to which he must now resort
at his own expense cannot yield a profit and could never repay the
enormous investment which went into researching this major work.

However, the timing of publication is not motivated solely by
a desire to inform the people. It is Harold's intent to inform the
people and their representatives, the Congress, so that the legislative branch of government can be in a position finally to do something
about the terrible abuses by the executive presaged by Lyndon Johnson's
appointment of the Warren Commission and commenced when that Commission decided to and did engage in a whitewash.

Presidential commissions have become an integral part of the
growing authoritarianism, the antithesis of democracy and individual
rights, which could no longer be ignored by public and press when
Richard Nixon*applied his heavy hand to the course of its development.
_____
*Resigned 8/9/74.

vii

These commissions have become a device by which the executive avoids or covers up the most important national problems under the guise of doing something about them. The most recent instance of this abuse was President Ford's response to revelations that the CIA had engaged in forbidden domestic surveillance and plotting of foreign assassinations. Ford, a former member of the Warren Commission and the one member boasting the distinction of having stolen its secret files, edited them to his advantage and then commercialized them (all exposed and documented in WHITEWASH IV), appointed a commission of partisans, each of which had obvious conflicts of interest which should have prevented their serving on such an investigative body. For the executive director he handpicked a former Warren Commission staff lawyer and principal architect of a false case against Oswald, and then authorized his commission to "investigate" allegations of CIA involvement in the Kennedy assassination. Predictably, the commission "investigated" only the most outlandish allegations made by what is charitably called the paranoid fringe of those writing or speaking on the subject. It was thus that Ford used a special commission to blunt the impact of the inevitable Congressional investigations of CIA abuses and to pretect himself should he, as a candidate for President, be called to account for his improprieties on the Warren Commission.

It is doubtful that Congress has the authority to investigate President Kennedy's murder per se or that an inquiry so restricted in scope could bear fruit. However, it is unquestionably within Congress's investigative and legislative power to conduct a thorough examination of the executive response to the assassination. Moreover, it is Congress's obligation to investigate when such a monumental and pervasive abuse of the public trust occurs. Congress has already recognized its proper interest in legislation to assure governmental accountability by passing and then amending the Freedom of Information Act. Surely it can and should investigate when presented with proof of the greatest violation of the accountability principle that can happen in this country - the deliberate and systematic dissemination of a false account of a President's murder.

Responsible Congressional action is now essential if there is to be any prospect of correcting the authoritarian course on which the executive is set. Any such action must begin with an understanding of the basic facts.

POST-MORTEM establishes and documents the facts as never before. The story which emerges is one totally the opposite of everything every American is taught to believe about his government; it is thus an inherently incredible story, one which most people would prefer not to believe. But the evidence cries out for belief. It is laid out here, in facsimile, much of it for the first time ever, so that each reader can evaluate it and formulate his own answers to the fundamental questions:

Did the government really want to learn the truth about the assassination?

Did the government conduct the full investigation it claims, with truth as its only goal?

Has the government told the truth about the assassination and its official investigation?

If the reader cannot answer any of these questions in the affirmative, he must then admit the reality, the plain fact of this most serious of governmental abuses. If at that point he is denied any redress by his elected federal representatives, everyone becomes the victim of acquiescence and abdication in the face of democracy's greatest challenge.

Howard Roffman

September 8, 1975

Author's Note

Of those I could have asked to preface this book, Howard Roffman is the youngest. Chronologically, two generations separate us. Actually, we are like brothers.

Because there are those who may take this as an indication of bias, I add that we also disagree and that I have asked no one whose reputation might contribute to the success of this work.

In his own right, Howard is an authentic scholar, a graduate historian who has turned to the law. His first published work is on the JFK assassination, Presumed Guilty, published by Fairleigh Dickinson University Press. His coming book is Understanding the Cold War. He is one of the few I consider genuinely unselfish and expert in this complicated and much obfuscated field. Because of this and because of his independence of mind and spirit, I have also asked him to make the final selection of what appears in the appendix and to provide the independent annotation lacing it together and with the text. Inclusion of all that is relevant is a physical impossibility. Those who may believe that he carries a prejudice into these judgments do not know him and would do him an injustice.

His preface is his own, written without discussion of it with me. I find some of it flattering. But in reading it I have restricted myself to making nine marginal marks in asking him to give further thought. Pleased as I am at what he has written, I have had no more than this to do with it.

This is a subject on which one cannot work without emotion if he has any concern for his country. I have made no effort to hide or disguise my feelings. I believe this an obligation the writer owes his readers.

It is also a subject on which no writer can express the fullness of his debt to others. Of these many I single out my wife, to whom fell the most difficult and publicly least appreciated of work, ranging from the typing to the truly excellent indexing. It seems appropriate after more than a decade to repeat the dedication of my first book:

> To my wife, whose ancestors dreamed of man's freedom, fought the Revolution to establish it, and preserved it by fighting both for and against the Union; who is the living embodiment of their spirit and deep beliefs; and whose great labor made this book possible, with the full appreciation of the value of this inheritance that became mine when my parents emigrated to a land in which their son would be born free, this book is lovingly dedicated.

* * * *

This is what might be called a "specialized" book. It deals with and is a post-mortem on that fake inquest and what is most intimately related to it. It will help the reader to recall the official version of this "crime of the century", that at 12:30 p.m. local time November 22, 1963, Lee Harvey Oswald, alone and unassisted, fired three shots with outdated Western hard-jacketed, military ammunition made for the Italian government during World War II, from an old Mannlicher-Carcano 6.5 mm. rifle. Oswald was, allegedly, in the easternmost window of the sixth floor of the Texas School Book Depository Building at Elm and Houston Streets, at the northeast corner of the small park known as Dealey Plaza.

The road pattern in this plaza is pear-like, bisected by Main Street, carrying traffic both east and west, with Elm, on which one-way traffic goes west, and Commerce, on which it flows east, drawing together at a very wide, three-part system of railroad bridges known as the Triple Underpass. The embankments created when the streets were excavated to eliminate the grade crossing are known as grassy knolls.

Reference is commonly to the one on the north side of the plaza, that on the south usually being ignored, although at the time the shots were fired the President was facing it. Across Houston Street from the Texas School Book Depository Building is the Dal-Tex Building. On the east side of Houston between Main and Elm are two old public buildings known as the Courts and the Records buildings. Since the assassination, the sheriff's offices have been moved from here two short blocks to the new county courts building on the south side of Commerce east of the plaza.

One of these shots is said to have missed entirely. To another is attributed the inflicting of seven non-fatal wounds on the President and on then Texas Governor John B. Connally. This bullet is said to have been found - in close to perfect, pristine condition - at Parkland Hospital, where both victims were rushed. The third shot is claimed to have hit the President only, near the base of the occiput, the rear protuberance of the head, then to have exploded out the right side of his head.

The President was irreversibly dead in Dealey Plaza. He was pronounced dead at about 1 p.m., when pro-forma emergency procedures failed. These measures included surgery known as a tracheotomy. Once the real fact of death became official fact, and over the strong protests of public officials, the corpse was flown back to Washington, with the new President, in Air Force One, the President's personal airplane. The autopsy examination was made at the Naval Hospital, part of the Naval Medical Center, in suburban Bethesda, Maryland.

All three shots, all allegedly fired by Oswald and from that rifle, are said to have been dispatched in not much more than five seconds.

Of course, if each of the essential official representations of fact is not true beyond reasonable doubt, we have no idea who killed the President, how many were involved, their reason or reasons, or almost anything else. If each and every one of these things is not true beyond any reasonable doubt, the one thing about which there can then be no quibble is that the "investigation" was a farce, the "solution" to the crime a fiction, and the Commission and its work require their own autopsy.

PRESIDENT'S COMMISSION
ON THE
ASSASSINATION OF PRESIDENT KENNEDY

CHIEF JUSTICE EARL WARREN, *Chairman*

SENATOR RICHARD B. RUSSELL   REPRESENTATIVE GERALD R. FORD   *Staff Members*
SENATOR JOHN SHERMAN COOPER   MR. ALLEN W. DULLES
REPRESENTATIVE HALE BOGGS   MR. JOHN J. MCCLOY   PHILLIP BARSON
                                                                        EDWARD A. CONROY
                                                                        JOHN HART ELY
                     J. LEE RANKIN, *General Counsel*   ALFRED GOLDBERG
                                                                        MURRAY J. LAULICHT
                          Assistant Counsel   ARTHUR MARMOR
                                                                        RICHARD M. MOSK
     FRANCIS W. H. ADAMS   ALBERT E. JENNER, Jr.   JOHN J. O'BRIEN
     JOSEPH A. BALL   WESLEY J. LIEBELER   STUART POLLAK
     DAVID W. BELIN   NORMAN REDLICH   ALFREDDA SCOBEY
     WILLIAM T. COLEMAN, JR.   W. DAVID SLAWSON   CHARLES N. SHAFFER, Jr.
     MELVIN ARON EISENBERG   ARLEN SPECTER   LLOYD L. WEINREB
     BURT W. GRIFFIN   SAMUEL A. STERN
     LEON D. HUBERT, Jr.   HOWARD P. WILLENS*

PREFACE TO PART I: CONCLUSIONS FIRST

The government never really intended to investigate the assassination of President John F. Kennedy, and it never did.

It never intended to tell us what really happened, and it didn't.

It never at any time sought the fact of this frightful crime, properly called that of the century, searched for the available evidence or followed each clue to the truth, regardless of the consequences.

There never was any let-the-chips-fall-where-they-may inquiry.

Indeed, there never was what reasonable men can call an inquiry, a decent pretense even of an investigation.

From the very first moment there was, at best, what I call a "whitewash", nothing better, and one so thin it was transparent. So overwhelming is this, so total, so unvarying in detail, that now that I have published more than a half million words of my own "Report On The Warren Report", there has not been a single substantiated allegation of error against me, not a single one that has been made to my face, and none supported by any evidence, official or otherwise.

This is and can be true only because that evidence the government did not succeed in avoiding - even after it was twisted, misrepresented, lied about, altered, in too many cases mutilated or destroyed - is so completely opposite to its official representation and cannot be and was not improved by the manufactures that accompanied all of this.

Had there been a deliberate conspiracy to achieve this, it could have succeeded little better. Had all the eminences of the Commission, its staff and the federal personnel assigned to it sat down and deliberately plotted, as in the days of the councils of kings, to fake their work, the result could have no better served the end of a conscious conspiracy than the Report that issued after ten months of what we have been deceived into believing was a thorough, impartial search for the truth.

Had there, in fact, been this kind of conscious conspiracy, it is doubtful if it could have been pulled off as well as what really succeeded, when the vast bureaucracy started pulling itself out of the enormous shock of the tragedy to find itself (without, apparently, ever realizing it) already boxed in, its prerogatives largely preempted by the federal police, then engaged, whether or not deliberately, in a monstrous, all-encompassing cover-up.

Even then, had there not been this Commission of eminences, carefully selected to have a respected representative of most major political camps - all save that of the murdered President, which was without representation - and a sycophantic, complacent press easily seduced or self-seducing, this whitewash could not have stuck.

The formula was simple and straightforward, as I set forth in the introduction to my first book on this subject: The members of the Commission were too busy with tasks they could not delegate really to conduct their own investigation. This they left to their staff, having no other choice; and their staff, by the Commission's own choice, was of investigators whose obligations lay elsewhere. Thus, we had the FBI and the Secret Service investigating themselves, for it was while they were responsible for keeping the President from harm that he was killed.

1

Together, they covered up the involvement of the CIA.

The obvious flaws were veneered with semantics composed by the lawyers, who were equal to every departure from and denial of the requirements of their profession and the law, then polished by the willing press.

Thus it was that we were assured officially, as clandestinely but blatantly we had been assured unofficially all along, that Lee Harvey Oswald was a lone and unassisted assassin. Only later, when I and then the authors of those books that followed proved otherwise, that this, really, is not what the Commission ordained, that elsewhere, ready for convenient invocation, was weasel language acknowledging the Commission could not prove that there had been no conspiracy - only when it was too late to have meaning - was this admitted.

This Commission never considered - never considered the possibility of - a conspiracy with Oswald not its assassin. This was probably the least-secret secret of any secret proceeding in all of history. It was lustily leaked in every conceivable form throughout the ten months of the ripening whitewash. It was banner-smeared across the front pages, on the television tube, and was endlessly dinned from loudspeakers and transistor earphones.

So the unacceptable, preordained conclusions - the conclusions that were built-in and could not be substantiated by solid evidence - were made acceptable; first by an enormous propaganda campaign and then by uncritical approval of a mass of verbiage that could not survive analysis. The Report simply was not analyzed by the press, which instead gloried in the fictions, suppositions and theories that were substituted for fact and touted them as though they were the given word.

Not to believe what could not be believed was somehow equated with a new kind of subversion. Those who saw clearly the Emperor's nakedness were called blind.

Thus a popular young President who had announced policies unwelcome to the most powerful vested interests and a determination to reform and control those forces of government that had been without control - notably, the CIA, which had ringed his nose and jerked him by the tender tissues - could be murdered and, as though the nuclear age of the 1960's was a returned medievalism, consigned to history with this dubious epitaph of a fake inquest.

Once the awful reality can be conceived - once the mind is aware of and the stomach settled to the sickening truth and the Commission's Report and evidence are examined with uncorrupted reason - there remains no question; for, save the conclusion that the President is dead, having been murdered, which required no Commission of eminences for its certification, there is no conclusion that is supported by that evidence and almost without exception by that same means each is destroyed.

If the Commission proved anything, it is that Oswald killed no one - not the President and not Dallas Police Officer J. D. Tippit. It simply says otherwise and demands belief. If it established anything about conspiracy, it is that there had to have been one to murder the President; for his murder, under the conditions it stipulated, was impossible for any one man, more so for the also-murdered accused than for most men. Every effort to prove otherwise established this more irrefutably. It was openly misrepresented, lied about. Where time reconstructions prove Oswald could have been at the scene of neither crime, the Report says the opposite, in one case by falsehood, the other by avoidance - avoidance so open that, like the purloined letter of Poe's tale, it was unseen because it was unhidden.

That this could happen - did happen - in the most advanced society civilization has attained is a disturbing commentary on that society. That it is without remedy when every available indication, such as the repeated polls, shows most of the people do not believe the official dictat and want remedy, says the society is not truly democratic, that government is not responsive to and does not meet the demands and desires of the governed.

That it can continue without remedy is possible only because the press has abdicated its responsibilities and converted itself into an agency of government, assailing those who, having sought the truth, declare it. Were the press under actual government control, the harm would be less, for this would be known and allowed for by citizens in evaluating its message. That it is not an official press but acts as one is subversive in a democratic society, for we expect the press to be the watchdog over government, not its bedmate.

Goebbels never plotted a campaign more carefully than our government did in telling us this enormous lie; nor did he ever repeat more often, seeking acceptance by enormity and endless repetition. First there were the 900 pages of the Report, too large for immediate digestion. Then, the Report accepted although it could not be digested and because the press forced it down, there were the estimated 10,000,000 words of the official evidence, in 26 large and expensive volumes, hard to come by, harder to follow; an organized chaos that defied comprehension by its disorganization, diffusion, obfuscations and sheer vastness. This Report and its alleged backstopping are a literary quicksand in which the unwary is soon engulfed unless he takes the countless thousands of hours required for its safe exploration.

Beyond all of this are the files of the Commission, stored in the National Archives, which has but housekeeping responsibilities, controlled by the orders of others. It is not possible to say what is there suppressed, nor how much by volume or significance. A tremendous amount (by total and by proportion) of the estimated 300 cubic feet of files - and that is an awful lot of paper - is still denied researchers, most of it by the peremptory order of the head of the FBI, upon whom there is no check and who, by his exercise of the raw power he wields, precludes checking. If J. Edgar Hoover says a file must be secret, it is secret, and there is none to challenge him, none who can. He is beyond question or questioning, like a god of his own creation. That he was exercised his power injudiciously is also without question. The problem is merely to have the question heard.

For example, most of the data - which means only that data the FBI did not avoid collecting and then what it chose to let the Commission have of what it did not avoid - about the late David William Ferrie, a central figure in the story of OSWALD IN NEW ORLEANS and the investigation by New Orleans District Attorney Jim Garrison, remained suppressed. The official word is less unpleasant, but it is still suppression. Rightly, this can be done only for certain specified reasons: protection of the innocent, the "national security", and hiding the identities of sources of information (read "Hoover's stoolpigeons").

No rational concept of "national security" is here involved.

And it may be that, to Hoover, hiding his stoolies is more important than the truth of the assassination.

But how can Hoover justify the total absence from the available data in the archive of the fact that at the time of the assassination, in New Orleans and in attendance on federal court, this same David William Ferrie was in the company of agents of his FBI?

Is this "protecting the innocent"? Ferrie is dead. Would public association with FBI agents have contaminated that dangerous psychopath or denied him his rights? Is it only from stoolpigeons that Ferrie's public association with agents of the FBI could be known? Didn't they report on it? They have a large file on him. They "investigated" him, if only because it was made unavoidable when Jim Garrison arrested him on November 25, 1963, in connection with the assassination. Can any save Hoover's own special, perhaps personal, concepts of "national security" and "protection of the innocent" here be involved? With whose "innocence" can he be concerned? Only his own, his FBI's!

This is raw suppression, made possible by the unrestrained exercise of raw power. It is the opposite of proper functioning of government in a democratic society. It certainly is not free and honest investigation of the murder of a President. What we today cannot and do not know is whether the members of the Commission ever knew anything about Ferrie, his connections, activities, arrest - and his relations with the FBI, to whom the investigation of him was entrusted. We do not - indeed, we cannot - know whether the suppressed files disclose that the day of the assassination Ferrie was with the FBI, in New Orleans, and was not the alleged "get-away pilot" the federal investigative reports not suppressed falsely say Garrison suspected him of being. They say this not from what Garrison told the FBI (of which there is not a whisper in any of the not-suppressed documents) but because this same David William Ferrie immediately took over direction of the so-called "investigation" of himself and, knowing it to be untrue, with federal-agent complicity, made it the charge against him!

This, of course, is one way to investigate the murder of a President, the way the murder of this President was "investigated". It is, unfortunately, typical of all of the investigation, one of the consequences of the FBI and Secret Service "investigating" themselves. All of the investigation was in this spirit.

Had the staff work, the performance of the Commission's lawyers who were its eyes and mind, later its mouth, been of minimum competence and integrity, there still could have been an acceptable official investigation of the assassination. The lawyers could have ordered the FBI to get on the ball and, failing this, could have demanded of the Commission that it hire, direct and control its own investigators, beholden to no one else, as it was empowered to do. The sad truth is that the lawyers performed like the FBI, never seeking fact, never going out and looking for evidence.

They are the ones who mixed and spread the whitewash. They were in accord with the FBI, wanted what the FBI wanted, accepting what the FBI did. Wesley Liebeler, the same man who leaked confidential material to Edward J. Epstein and thus emerged heroic in Epstein's book, which became Liebeler's vehicle for self-justification, was sent to New Orleans by the Commission. Liebeler did not call David Ferrie as a witness, did not take testimony from him - and he did know about him.

So, what the FBI did was possible only because Liebeler and the other lawyers allowed it. If a more serious charge is not warranted, is this not in itself too much?

What Liebeler and the other lawyers did they could do, and what they did not do they could get away with not doing, only because the chief of the staff, General Counsel J. Lee Rankin, permitted or wanted these things. Rankin's competence cannot be doubted. He is corporation counsel of the City of New York. He had been Solicitor General of the United States. This alone, because of the intimacy he then had with the FBI, which investigated all the cases he handled, should have been enough to disqualify him in any investigation of impartial original intent. Rankin's own record of suppressing evidence, avoiding it, and guaranteeing its destruction is amply set forth in PHOTOGRAPHIC WHITEWASH: SUPPRESSED KENNEDY ASSASSINATION PICTURES. In that book, over his own name appear the until-then secret documents proving that Rankin saw to it that there would not be and never could be a complete photographic record of the assassination, that the Commission would neither have nor see all the record that did exist, and that the essential pictures would never be in any archive, investigative or historical.

Rankin was really the boss. The buck stopped with him.

In all four of the books I published before beginning this one, I declare, and in various ways prove, that the Commission began with its conclusions and, instead of investigating to learn the truth, sought rather to make these conclusions seem as credible as possible. In my combing of its files, I have come into possession of a simple, basic document that, I believe, should end for all time any doubt of this basic truth honorable men unwilling to believe it may have.

That document is the Commission's "File Classification".

It is an editorial classification, not a factual one, not an

4

investigative one. Its files - the very beginning, the essence of the
organization and direction of its work - were built around the conclusion
of Oswald's singular guilt! Before the Commission did anything - before
it looked, asked or even thought - it had decided Oswald alone was guilty.

For the enormous accumulation of 300 cubic feet of papers - and
countless millions of words can be in a single cubic foot - this classification, at its maximum, required very little space. It is double-
spaced, on 22 sheets of paper, most of which are half or more blank!
One that should have been vital, would have been except for the determination to prevent it, is entitled, "Maps, Photos and Press Clippings
(MP)". It has but a single subdivision, "Film". Here we see the Commission's thinking: Its pictures, of the assassination and others, it
filed with its and/or Oswald's and Ruby's press!

The Commission says it investigated to see if there had been a
conspiracy. It did this without a file on "conspiracy"!

It pretends it investigated to learn what happened, not validate
the fairy tale originated by the Dallas police: that Oswald, the alien-
ated "pro-Communist", was the lone killer. But it has no file of or for
its investigations of this character, and it made none. Instead, under
"Investigation and Evidence (INV)", where there are 29 divisions, only a
single one does not relate to Lee Harvey Oswald. That one is on "other
suspects", on which the Report is barren. This "Investigation and Evidence" file also has no "conspiracy" breakdown.

The files, the organization of which represent the very beginning
of the Commission's work, reflect that before that beginning there had
been a determination of the conclusion that was to have come only at the
end, only following both investigation and deliberation.

The National Archives and Records Service did the actual com-
piling of the "file classification" for the Commission in May 1964.
However, the filing system used by the Commission prior to that time
was organized on the basis of the identical classifications ultimately
assembled by the Archives in May. All of the Commission's records,
including the earliest ones received, were automatically filed along
the lines later officially established in the "file classification."

This includes the identification of a "KP" file, of "Key Persons".
There were alphabetical files on those so considered, including the 552
termed "witnesses". Only these are listed in the "file classification":
Governor Connally, President and Mrs. Kennedy, Lee and Marina Oswald, the
Paines, with whom the Oswalds lived, Ruby and Officer J. D. Tippit.

That even the details of the investigation were "concluded" before
the investigation began is evidence in the "Kennedy, John F." breakdown.
This began with five parts, two subdivided:

1 Trip to Texas (Planning and Initial Movements)
2 Motorcade
3 Shots
    3-1 First
    3-2 Second
    3-3 Third
4 Assassination (Include injuries, treatment at Parkland Memorial
    Hospital, Death)
    4-1 Autopsy
5 Return of Remains to Washington

The fierce determination to "prove" that there were three shots
is evidenced by more than the establishment of a file that says this and
nothing else. The third part of this file, which specifies three shots,
no more and no fewer, was reorganized. The numbers, "3-1, 3-2, 3-3", and
the words after them, "First, Second, Third", have been crossed out.
They are replaced by this notation:

"All material relating to shots in files under '3 Shots'."

From this there is no doubt that the Commission did not conduct
an investigation to ascertain how many shots were fired, essential to

5

any tenable conclusions, but to _prove_ that three shots and only three shots had been fired.

Analysis of the Report, as I show in WHITEWASH, establishes that by volume it is mostly a biography - and a questionable one - of Lee Harvey Oswald. The file classification is consistent with this. Four separate files were established on him, each subdivided, the first three with interesting and revealing editorial reflections, by title and content.

They are "Oswald, Lee H. - Pre-Russian Period", "Russian Period", and "Post-Russian Period" (the fourth is "Murder By Ruby"). So there is nothing in this truly enormous accumulation that is not organized around Russia and the concept of an Oswald-Russian connection and an assassination-Russian connection. All of Oswald's life before he went to the Soviet Union is lumped as "pre-Russian", all of it after he "defected" from this "defection" as "post-Russian". This is the way the Commission thought, the way it worked, the preconceptions with which it undertook its assignment. It is not impartiality, not a lack of bias, certainly not politically neutral.

It also is not accurate. It is propaganda, and it is a conditioning of the staff mind. With this prejudice in advance of the "investigation", there is the deceit and further prejudice continued during it. For example, there is no file to show Oswald's bitter and intense anti-Soviet attitude, speeches and writings. The concept, organization and identification of the file are designed to tell a lie, that Oswald was and remained pro-Soviet, whereas the opposite is abundantly true, beyond any question. In its Report, to the degree it could, the Commission avoided this by referring to Oswald's alleged "dedication to Communism and Marxism" and, despite his "defection" to the USSR, never once referring to any "dedication to the Soviet Union". It could not, for he hated that country with bottomless passion.

Oswald's "Pre-Russian Period" file has ten parts. Five are of special note. Identified as "5" and "5-1" are "Finances" and "Income Tax". The Commission could not make Oswald's finances, as it represents them in the Report, work out the way it said they did. It did not account for all the expenditures it knew he made and it attributed to him funds it could not prove he had (see WHITEWASH, particularly 140-1). This was essential for a number of reasons, but especially to make it seem that Oswald had no help in getting to the Soviet Union. The Commission had a special separate file on his income tax. Yet with these documents in its possession, and with the abundant indications of his connections with the United States government and possession of unaccounted-for funds - with the charge made that he had, in fact, been connected with U.S. intelligence activities - it failed to print his income tax returns. Its use of offset printing to reproduce documents in facsimile and the dreadful collection of trash and trivia that it did print in those 10,000,000 words bracketed with its failure to print these returns does not lead to the belief they support the Commission's representations.

Three parts, 6, 6-1 and 6-2, are "Military Service", divided further into "Undesirable Discharge" and "Court Martial". The simple truth is that Oswald's discharge from the Marines was _not_ "undesirable" but for "hardship" and was honorable, even if at the time of this discharge (said to have been so he could care for his destitute mother) he was also equipped with a certification that enabled him to leave the country immediately (WHITEWASH 124). This placed him in the inactive reserve, and it is from that, not active service, that, in an ex parte proceeding having nothing to do with his military service, he was given an undesirable separation. This file "classification" is propaganda mirrored in the Report, not an unbiased organization of fact.

His "Russian Period", as reflected in the file classification, likewise is interesting because of the evidence it gives of the Commission's determinations and conclusions _before_ it investigated. If one may have expected a file on his relations with the Soviet government, it is not there. Likewise, there is no file on his relations with his own government (there is a file called "Defection to Russia", but he was careful never to renounce his U.S. citizenship) although there was a great mass of material on this. With questions of Oswald's intelligence connections existing before the Commission was created and the fact of it beyond question during its existence, even if neglected in the investigation and denied without proof in the Report, the absence of the appropriate file classifications is no comfort to those who wrongly suspect Oswald had a Russian connection and no reassurance to those who know he had with the U.S. government. Again, it is a sign of the Commission's propaganda rather than fact-finding function and performance.

There are 14 subclassifications under Oswald's "Post-Russian Period". All of his life is oriented in these files around "Russia" and nothing else, not even the assassination with which he was charged. Here, too, there is more than passing interest in the structure alone, again conclusions and dishonesty, propaganda in the names alone.

Five of these 14 parts begin with "2", which has the general heading, "Political and Subversive Activities". Oswald engaged in neither in the United States after his return from the USSR, unless talk is deemed "activity" and his distribution of literature under a fake identification is considered "political" rather than intelligence activity. He invented a non-existent "New Orleans Chapter" of the "Fair Play for Cuba Committee" and distributed locally manufactured literature that had no connection with the national organization as part of his establishment of an intelligence "cover", as detailed in OSWALD IN NEW ORLEANS.

Four additional headings are "Communist Party", "Young Communist League", "Fair Play for Cuba Committee" and "Socialist Workers Party". Now, there is mutual exclusiveness in "Communist Party" and "Socialist Workers Party" as part of Oswald's "Political Activities". (Investigation disclosed that he had engaged in no political activities of these natures and was unknown to those familiar with them despite the FBI's diligent and hopeful search for evidence of this kind.) These two parties detest each other. He could not be part of the political activity of both or in political sympathy with both. Accompanying this is the absence of a file for his relations with the Socialist Party, which was as justifiable as any other, for he also wrote that party unsolicited letters. What is termed Oswald's "Political Activities" might better have been designated what is totally missing from the organization and terminology of the file classification, "Intelligence Activities". His "activities" were not political and were intelligence, consistent with those of an agent provocateur or informant.

The use of the word "Subversive" cannot be justified on any ground. Oswald was never so charged by anyone. His name is on no "subversive" lists, dubious as they are. Again, we have the grim determination to accomplish with bias, prejudice and propaganda what could not be achieved by fact or evidence.

The Commission pretended it conducted an investigation to see if Ruby's murder of Oswald was part of a conspiracy. There are four listings under "Oswald, Lee H. - Murder by Ruby". None is of "conspiracy in", "help with" or anything at all like that. Indeed, there never was any real investigation of any kind of a conspiracy, although an investigation of this one was falsely alleged. There is not even a breakdown for the inclusion of those many evidences of police complicity in Oswald's murder, certainly in making it possible and permitting Ruby free access to the building although he was known, known not to have been entitled to access, known to be violence-prone and customarily to travel armed. The four parts of this section of the files are "Transfer to County Jail", "Murder", "Remains" and, subordinate to that, "Autopsy".

Oswald's autopsy is not printed in the Report, no accident. The obvious reasons are the speed with which it was completed, the scientific precision with which it was performed, the fact that it was immediately circulated, and the total lack of any reasonable question about it, all in the sharpest contrast with that dubious, imprecise, entirely unscientific and incomplete farce of an autopsy that was the President's. It dared not allow this comparison between a real autopsy, that of the accused assassin, and the poor thing palmed off as an autopsy of the President. So that this can be seen and understood, I herewith print the Oswald autopsy.

For reasons not immediately apparent, Ruby's "Activities November 22-24", which certainly includes his murder of Oswald, is not classified as part of the file on his committing the murder but is in the personal files on him, of which it is the first division, with three subdivisions. The Commission is consistent: There is no indication of a file for its investigation of possible Ruby conspiratorial involvements.

The 11 subdivisions of the files on Marina Oswald are lacking in three things that would have been essential in any court proceeding (some may be under different designations in these files) and should have been major considerations in any impartial investigation. These are a study of the propriety of her being a witness against her husband, especially the major witness, even if she was a witness to nothing connected with the crime of which he was accused; her relationship with governments, that of the USSR, of which there is no evidence but which should have been established one way or the other, and that of the United States, of which there is no question; and of federal threats and bribery, the first because she was subject to immediate and automatic deportation, which she did not want, and the second making her independently wealthy. (See also WHITEWASH, "The Oswalds' Government Relations"; WHITEWASH II, "Scheherazade".) The facts of the threats and the rewards disqualify her as a witness and indict the Commission that, knowing these things, was silent about them and, in the face of the clear Constitutional prohibition, nonetheless called her as its main witness and credited her, despite a suppressed staff counsel study showing it to be wrong.

Simplification reached its pinnacle in the "Tippit, J. D." file, instructions for which read, "File here all material pertaining to all aspects of the murder of Officer Tippit". The Commission meant this, for its instructions covering the files under "Investigation and Evidence" read, "File here all material concerning its investigations and pertaining to Lee Harvey Oswald and other suspects (sic) EXCEPT material pertaining to the murder of Officer Tippit". Here there is reference to the "Tippit, J. D." file. The Tippit files have three parts, "Shooting", "Witnesses" and "Autopsy". In practice, this meant two only, for the Commission totally suppressed this autopsy and all mention of it. The Report is so barren on this that it lacks official certification of Tippit's death, having no reference to the autopsy itself or to medical or even ambulance-crew reports of it. Here and elsewhere in the files there are copies of the suppressed Tippit autopsy. (Space alone precludes it here. However, the Commission published 26 large volumes and could have published more. Instead, it suppressed.)

If there were any other possibilities, such as "other suspects" or "conspiratorial aspects", anything aside from what may logically be encompassed by "all material pertaining to all aspects" aside from "Shooting" and "Witnesses", the Commission's file classification does not provide for them, as its doctrine and performance did not require them.

Consistent with the focus on Oswald as a lone assassin and no conspiracy of any kind in any part of the assassination or anything connected with it is the file, "Other Individuals and Organizations Involved or Interviewed". It has no subdivisions, no subject classifications of any nature. It includes "all material concerning individuals and organizations mentioned", with the added instruction, "Arrange alphabetically by name" except for "material pertaining to Key Persons". Where there are "organizations for which files have been established, such as Fair Play for Cuba Committee", there are to be but cross-references in this file.

"Government Agencies Involved" are filed separately. They are federal, state, local and foreign, with "Dallas" and "New Orleans" the only two subclassifications, under "Local". Thus, there are categories but not subjects, a design that disguises even suspicions and denies the identification of those agencies of any kind "involved" in the assassination, something one would have expected, if not in the Report, where it does not appear, at least in the files, if they were to have had any

8

meaning to the staff and purpose in the operation of the Commission. How
"involved" also remains a mystery, consistent with the entirely secret
character of the investigation itself, all of it having been held behind
closed doors, most of it in what amounts to back rooms in Dallas, New
Orleans and Washington, with only the Commission lawyer, empowered to administer the oath and ask questions, the official stenographer and the
reluctant witness, happy to escape attention and even happier to be
avoiding cross-examination, all that were present. If there is wonder
why, to begin with, there was need for six categories of "involvement" of
foreign or domestic government agencies in the assassination and its investigation, that wonder still exists. There is nothing on this brief
file classification sheet, most of which is blank, to indicate the reason
for it, the reasoning behind it, or the fact, if any.

     In housekeeping functions, services rendered and asked, investiga-
tions conducted and correspondence, these categories required the further
breakdowns that, if they existed, are not in the official classification.
This is consistent only with hiding and suppression. The records of requests to the FBI alone must be enormous, without doubt requiring elaborate subdivision for the Commission to have functioned with any efficiency or to have known what it had and had not asked for and had and had
not gotten. It is one of the statistical delights of the Commission and
a statistic equated with evidence by it and its supporters that the FBI
alone conducted 25,000 interviews embodied in 2,300 reports totaling
25,400 pages (Rxii). The Secret Service conducted 1,550 interviews.
There were other needs, such as laboratory studies, tests, photography,
etc. All of this and everything else lumped ingloriously and inaccessi-
bly under the single file designation, "GA-1"? It is hardly credible.

     For the Commission itself the classification lists three sets of
files under three different designations. Under "Presidential Commission"
there is a seemingly administrative file of 26 categories, two of which
were eliminated and stricken through. These are "Receipts", under "Supplies and Equipment", which probably is not an indication that it received
no supplies or equipment or kept no records of them ("Receipts" under
"Correspondence and Mail" (includes form letters) was not eliminated),
and "Progress", under "Reports (Administrative Only)", no indication
"progress" was not made.

     The second of these is "Public Comments and Inquiries", disclosing
an immediate and understandable, yet inadequate, sensitivity to what
might be said about the Commission. It is the only classification of all
to have been expanded and the only one to bear internal indications of
incompleteness or secret parts. It alone of the various classifications
provides for no first subdivision with the number "1". This is hardly
an accidental error never detected in all the Commission's long and active life. The first file is actually No. 2, "Excerpts and Comments in
U.S. Publications". No. 3 is the same for "Foreign", with, inexplicably,
but a single breakdown under that, "3-1 Russian". That is the way it
began, that the way it ended. Why from the beginning there should have
been special interest in only Russian "Excerpts and Comments" and not,
say, British, is not obvious. One would think that, especially at the
very first, this government and its Commission, were this Commission the
body to keep track of such things, would have had a great and unending
interest in what the press, people and governments of those nations al-
lied with it thought and had to say about the assassination and its
official investigation.

     Subcategories of "Hate Atmosphere", the relevance of which to this
rather than an operating classification is not apparent, "Citizens File"
and "General Correspondence Received by the Chief Justice" were added
and are noted by hand.

     Some confusion attaches to the "Reports and Source Materials (REP)"
classification because it appears not to provide for source materials and
not to provide for some of the reports that do seem to meet the instructions, "...all reports identified by a Commission number ... reports and
related materials, not identified by a Commission number under the other
subjects listed below".

These are four, all beginning with "Commission": "Final Report" (and subcategory, "Requests for"), "Preliminary Report" and "Staff Reports". However, aside from the absence of a proper category for any "source materials" and the further limitation of "Commission" before each grouping, there are other reports that do bear Commission numbers, like the first FBI "Summary Report", which is Commission No. 1 and the Secret Service report that is Commission No. 3, among others.

Intriguing also is the "Protection of the President" group of files, code identification "PP", Of its six components, all are logical and predictable and, in varying degree, represented in the Report, the eighth and last chapter of which is entitled, "The Protection of the President", except these two: "3 Reported Threats Against President Kennedy" and "5 Other Assassinations or Attempted Assassinations".

If "5" is assumed to have been historical and discounted, there remains the very pertinent one, "Reported Threats Against President Kennedy". On this the Report is mute. From this it fairly may be inferred that there had been no threats or reported threats against the assassinated President. This, however, is quite false, and their suppression from the Report must be regarded with unlimited misgivings. Two of which I know in particular cannot now properly be ignored and could not have been by a Commission whose purposes and responsibilities were those assigned this one - not if it or the government it served intended a real investigation and an honest Report.

Of one of these I can now say little; of the other I have already written in the chapter of OSWALD IN NEW ORLEANS entitled "Preliminary Postscript from Miami" and in FRAME-UP, especially pages 468-71.

Four days before the actual assassination, President Kennedy went to Miami to address the InterAmerican Press Association. Miami police had learned of a plot to assassinate him and insisted there be no motorcade. The President was flown to the meeting place by helicopter. Miami authorities promptly informed the Secret Service and further discharged their responsibilities by a demand for the safer transportation of the President. He made his speech and, although it was not well received by many in his audience (whom he told the United States would not invade Cuba and, if Castro were to be overthrown, the Cuban people alone would do it), he did survive it and no attempt was made to kill him.

Particularly because in advance of the real assassination the details of this conspiracy which the Miami police gave to the government so completely match those the Commission says were the real details of the successful attempt, even to the type of rifle, how it would be carried, and from where it would be used - including the arranging for a convenient scapegoat - the lack of mention of this in the Report warrants deep suspicion and distrust. The life of this President was threatened, immediately before it was snuffed out and exactly as the government tells us it was, and yet the Commission makes no mention of it? This alone is enough to deny acceptability to the official Report which suppresses it.

The second known threat is in time the first. It was made, not in Miami, where the assassination conspiracy did not succeed, but in Dallas, where it did! It was made before there was public announcement that the President would go to Dallas! It was made by exile, anti-Castro Cubans, exactly those groups involved in the New Orleans aspects suppressed by the Commission and reported in OSWALD IN NEW ORLEANS. I have found no trace of this one in the Commission's files.

It was made in public!

A tape recording of it exists!

It was not investigated and reported by the Commission - even to discount it - yet it was unavoidable by the Commission and the investigative agencies had they really investigated. I learned of it by following exactly those obvious leads and clues I specified in earlier writing that the Commission, FBI and Secret Service avoided but could not properly avoid.

This is not the same threat I brought to light in WHITEWASH (153), that the Commission pretended in its Report did not exist because, it reasoned, it could not have been made by Oswald, one of its never-ending non sequiturs it pretends are answers.

Nor is it a New Orleans threat, not Ferrie's (see OSWALD IN NEW ORLEANS, "Assassination: 'A Colloquial Expression'").

It is a known but hitherto unreported one of which I now say no more in the hope of not endangering those who have the proof and can provide it and of not jeopardizing unofficial - now the only possible - efforts to learn all that may still be learned about it.

But the Commission, despite its silence in its Report, did know of and did have a file on "Reported Threats Against President Kennedy".

Most important of all the file classifications is the 29-part "INV" file, "Investigation and Evidence". One of its parts, 3-9, "was removed" and I know nothing of it. The Commission's fine impartiality, its freedom of mind and lack of preconception, untainted dedication to getting the truth and nothing else, its brave determination to conduct a real investigation of its own and not adopt the conclusions of others, is illuminated by the fact that, except for a single one, all are about and on Lee Harvey Oswald as a lone and unassisted assassin!

How much more impartial, open-minded, thorough-going, unfettered, uncommitted and without preconceived conclusions can a Presidential Commission be? After all, of the 29 categories with which, at the outset, it organized the files of its "Investigation and Evidence", is did reserve one, numbered "4", for "other suspects". What difference does it make that it found none; that in its Report it reported on none - not even those arrested by the police and thereafter officially ignored? Is it not enough that it provided for the possibility in its files, if not its investigation - for the possibility there might be "other suspects" - though it did not seek or want them?

This is true impartiality, real integrity of purpose and incorruptibility of practice, a fitting monument to the sanctity of American law and justice when a President is murdered!

The file may have been empty, as the Report is, but the Commission was not without understanding that there might be "other suspects", just as it was not without knowledge of "other threats".

It is not possible to evaluate the size of the various categories of this "Investigation and Evidence" series of files or the investigation behind each, for the bulk of the parts is unknown. It is, however, possible to indicate the focus and emphasis. All of it is aimed at Oswald, in one or more ways. "Evidence Against Lee Harvey Oswald" has 18 of the 29 divisions.

And thus we know he was not prejudged, that the investigation was honest and without preconceptions, as the Commission's defenders swear, and that the murder of President John F. Kennedy was fairly approached and honestly "solved".

From the time I analyzed the Report, prior to the availability of the 26 volumes of printed data euphemistically but inaccurately described as the "evidence" upon which it was based, there never was any doubt in my mind that the Report was what it was intended to be, least unpleasantly and unacceptably described as a "whitewash", which explains the title of this series of books that are my own "Report on the Warren Report".

What I did not then expect to find and what now, after everything to which this long and painful work has subjected me, still shocks me, is the openness of this recipe for the whitewash that is called the Commission's "file classification". There is no secret ingredient, as there is no disguise in it. The official and public pretense is entirely absent. This is the recipe for a "get Oswald" whitewash, a prescription that behind the scenes eliminated every other possibility or consideration, as happened in the hearings and was formalized in the Report.

The Commission never wanted or intended any other "solution",

11

never conceived any, and did what was required to make this as acceptable as it could and prevent any alternative.

Perhaps we may never know all that is buried in those 300 cubic feet of literary quicksand in the National Archives, for that is an enormous swamp to dredge. I do know that I am the only one of those who have published books on this subject to have plumbed it with care and pain and to have published what came up. At the time of the second book in this series, WHITEWASH II: THE FBI-SECRET SERVICE COVER-UP, I announced WHITEWASH III: THE ARCHIVE as the third. At that time, the end of November 1966, I anticipated that what I had by then added to my files could be contained in a single book, a book that would be a sort of appendix with notes. As my work continued, this became a mechanical and a financial impossibility. Even then, new government actions, the integrity and legality of which were at best questionable, presaged the need to include material other than in the Commission's own files, to which analysis would have to be added.

From this rather large file of the extensive investigation I personally have conducted, I have already completed and published two books, PHOTOGRAPHIC WHITEWASH and OSWALD IN NEW ORLEANS. If the appendix prepared for the latter book were printed - and it exceeded my financial capacity - it alone is more than 300 pages of largely once-secret documents. Inclusion of it in the pocket-size edition of that book would have taxed advanced printing technology and made an encyclopaedia-size volume in a much higher price range. And soon I had trebled that file.

The documentation I have salvaged from Commission oblivion warrants a longer text. It cannot all be contained in the appendix for it is too voluminous. Breaking the book into two so the text might be longer, omitted points included and others that are slighted considered in more detail, is not feasible, for that, too, would tax our physical and financial capacities. We are but two people, without resources or subsidy of any kind. Unknown and unfelt by those professional lickspittles to whom the highest dedication is a misapplied tongue and the lowest crime the quest for truth when a President is murdered is the pain that turns to numbness with the pervading fatigue of body and anguish of mind that are the lot of the writer who applies himself to this awful subject for the thousands and thousands of hours required for the acquisition and recording of knowledge, sees the hideous reality he must never let out of his mind if he is to write it and cannot abide the horror of living with it.

If it is not lived with, it cannot be conceived, especially not by those whose feelings are more lingual than emotional or intellectual, who are not captive of this linchpin to misery as endless as the wheel. There must be an end to such writing, which is as unendurable as it is indescribable to those who have not lived with its sickening realities. Yet for me there is now no end. This is the tiger I ride.

However, I do hope that with this book I can leave the medical aspect of the evidence and what is relevant to it, such as this preface on the Commission's organization of its work. It is the most disagreeable work by its nature and because it required greatest intimacy with the failing of society, the deceit of government and so many in it, and the wretchedness of the detail of the dubious inquest with which a man who would have been a great President was sent into history, his grave publicly tended and honored, his principles, ambitions and life dishonored as they were abandoned.

Fuller understanding of the medical evidence requires exploring other seemingly but not unrelated materials. It is, I think, appropriate as it is unavoidable that miserable official actions spawned by what was already in this evidentiary and archival swamp come first.

1. "THE NATIONAL INTEREST REQUIRES"

Continued suppression of evidence in the name of its revelation is the official action by which the United States Government commemorated the third anniversary of the assassination of President John F. Kennedy.

In an unprecedented action not understood by the press, then Acting Attorney General Ramsey Clark on November 1 aimed a one-two punch that denied important evidence while loudly proclaiming the government was "preserving" what he called "the entire body of evidence considered by the President's Commission on the Assassination of President Kennedy".

"I have determined that the national interest requires" this action, Clark said.

In truth, it is obvious to one intimately familiar with the government's conduct and method in its investigation of this "crime of the century" and its official Report, that this action was motivated by growing disenchantment with that Report, persistent and nagging doubts about the integrity of the inquiry and a desire to put the best possible make-up on its reddening face.

My own personal investigation, more than seven years of the most intensive research into both the assassination and its investigation, convinces me that, while pretending to preserve evidence of the assassination and make it available, the government, in fact, intends exactly the opposite, the perpetuation of its suppressions.

For this it used a temporary, limited-purpose law that expired the very next day.

Regardless of intent, the effect was to bury deeper in secret government caches fundamental evidence that cannot reasonably be denied researchers. Especially important here is the spectrographic analysis of the bullet said to have figured in the crimes and the miscellaneous fragments of bullets found in the bodies of the President and Texas Governor John B. Connally and in the vehicle in which they were riding. This essential FBI analysis has never seen the light of day. It was not seen by the Commission, which went to abnormal lengths to avoid it. J. Edgar Hoover now personally sits on it.

Winding up its second punch while the first was emblazoned on the front pages, the government announced the return of the autopsy photographs and X-rays by the Kennedy family, whose "possession" of them had been widely and publicly rumored. This dramatic release was carefully timed to magnify the impact of the first announcement, which it immediately overshadowed. Thus diverted, no major publication, if, indeed, any at all, has analyzed the content and meaning of the government's so-called "preserving" of "the entire body of evidence". Its announcement was automatically accredited in the excitement over the pictures and X-rays, interest in which had been swelling for weeks. Their return, presented as an act of Kennedy-family generosity, involved that name in seeming endorsement of these actions and the official inquiry and its Report.

In the drama of the Kennedy picture and X-ray return, the mishmash of junk, trash and trivia - what the Acting Attorney General was really talking about - got lost in the 525 column inches of small type in the Federal Register in which such announcements are published.

Meanwhile, by returning the government property, the Kennedy family escaped the pressure on it to make this evidence available. The terms un-

der which the pictures and X-rays were restored to the government can effectively suppress them for more than the lifetime of now-living adults.
For the first five years, access is restricted to those who failed to use
them when it was incumbent upon them to do so, government investigators.
Thereafter, only pathologists who are especially approved by the family's
surrogate may see them. Until then, any question of error would be entirely academic. Certainly, competent pathologists will never take the
great time required to master the enormous mass of the evidence collected
published in 26 large volumes and buried in several hundred cubic feet of
unpublished documents, and the tremendous amount of avoided evidence.
Much of what was gathered is irrelevant. An appreciable quantity is pertinent only were Oswald the solitary assassin, which the government alleges but never proved. Understanding comes only after close and long
study. The medical evidence cannot stand alone, cannot be considered
alone, all that pathologists armed only with their science could do. This
would be meaningless, a mere device, a trick. (We consider the returning
of the pictures and X-rays in the following chapter.)

There remains outside government files and outside the Commission's
record an immeasurable burden of the most significant evidence that was
known to exist, whose existence is acknowledged in the gathered documenta
tion, and which the government resolutely refused to collect, even for
history. PHOTOGRAPHIC WHITEWASH: SUPPRESSED KENNEDY ASSASSINATION PIC-
TURES reveals and describes thousands of frames of pictures of this
description. More are now known to exist.

It now should come as no surprise that this unwanted and disowned
information is all of a character that could and does discount the government's predetermined conclusions. That book and WHITEWASH establish
that the Commission refused to accept in evidence any photographs <u>taken
the moment of the assassination</u> that showed the front of the Texas School
Book Depository Building and the surrounding grounds. This happened even
when witnesses were testifying to and describing literally thousands of
such pictures. They and WHITEWASH II describe additional pictures of
this content, both professional and amateur. The abundance of these
photographs is truly astounding. There are <u>none</u> in evidence, <u>none</u> in
the Commission's exhibits - <u>not a single one</u>!

Yet descriptions abound in the evidence of the contents of these
pictures: The front of the building from which the shots, in the official account, all came, and people entering, leaving and standing
around it. It is exactly such pictures that are essential in any impartial investigation showing who went into or came out of the building immediately after the shots were fired, who was standing around it, and
above all essential to the Commission's case, whether Oswald shows in
any of these. The appearance of Oswald in any of these pictures at a
time when from the Commission's presumptions he could not have been there
quite obviously would destroy its case beyond resurrection.

A single TV photographer, Tom Alyea, of WFAA, took 500 feet of 16-
mm. film <u>inside the building, on the sixth floor, including the alleged
sniper's nest, beginning immediately</u>. The FBI allowed most of it to disappear or be destroyed in normal commercial TV usage without getting
any of it, yet its existence was known while it was being shot! During
the six months before it was belatedly forced on the FBI, <u>at least 80
percent of it disappeared and none of the remaining film is in evidence
or in the files</u>!

So transparent are the government's obfuscations to those who
study the case that when, without prior notice, I was questioned by
Richard Wigg of the London <u>Times</u> about the Attorney General's announcement, my instantaneous reaction, from the few brief words of description
in the wire-service dispatch he read me, was that the national heritage
would be neither enriched nor ennobled by these additions to the National
Archives and that, save for perhaps a very few items (like the rifle),
none would have any evidentiary value or add much to what was known.

The accuracy of this forecast comes not from occult power or remarkable intelligence. It is, rather, an illustration of how predictable government devices and trickery are.

Unpleasant as is the realization and unwilling as is the press to face the reality of the unassailable evidence it will not consider, or grossly and persistently misrepresents, the simple truth is that this is a can of nasty wriggling worms, not the touted pot of gold.

Of what does this then-newest of the government's false assurances consist?

There are seven pages, each of three columns of fine print, listing the items specified by the Department of Justice. They are the most amazing collection of official junk and trivia in government history, very few with any evidentiary value. The list is overwhelming proof that the government never at any time sought any assassin other than Oswald and constitutes an additional proof of the charge I first made in WHITEWASH in February 1965, that the government sought only to make it seem possible that Oswald alone might have been the assassin. There is no "evidence" of any other nature in this official trash-heap.

Among the listings in it are:

Twenty-six different items of empty envelopes alone, probably the most numerous category;

Odds and ends of unused notepaper; unused blanks, for subscribing to Life magazine and post-office address change;

A "no admittance" sign;

An employment service calling card;

Empty boxes;

Hand sketches;

Undestroyed trash, like magazine wrappers;

Miscellaneous employment and household records, as for insurance, utilities, salary, social security, vaccination, and withholding tax statements (those for 1955-6, Nos. 168 and 175, exist in duplicate and in duplicate items);

The birth certificates of both Oswald babies;

Wallets, watches, tieclips (one from the Soviet Union described in elaborate detail while possibly significant items are merely designated "photos" or "negatives") and belt buckles;

New and used Christmas, greeting and post cards;

Playing cards;

The $13.87 on Oswald's person when he was arrested;

Marine Corps memorabilia, including a mess pass;

Library cards;

Marina's embroidery and sewing patterns and instructions, recipes, fashion literature, sewing kit (with religious medal and nailfile), apparently some toilet items, her TV trading-stamp book, child-care

There are numerous books and articles swelling the impressively long listing: Two paperback Ian Flemings, two volumes of H. G. Wells' "Outline of History", George Orwell's "1984" (the anti-Communist classic and favorite of the anti-Communist Oswald), various dictionaries and education aids, a copy of The Nation, some of Jean-Paul Sartre's writing, a Sears catalogue, and item after item of political tracts, a number of which are anti-Russian and anti-Communist.

Oswald's own political writings are included, but in a manner that denies this knowledge to those not intimately familiar with the case. Their anti-Russian character is carefully hidden.

Ruth Paine's Minox camera, which has no connection with the assassination, the Oswalds or the investigation, is among the numerous items of her property illegally and knowingly illegally seized (WHITEWASH 80ff.) The cost of suing the government to recoup the value of such property exceeds its value, with the possible exception of the C-2766 Mannlicher-Carcano rifle, whose purchaser, from the public press, paid Marina Oswald a large sum for it and has gone to court. It is the temporary law Congress passed to block this sale that was invoked, on its last day on the statute books, to effectuate the seizures. Strangely, there was no complaint from those whose political stock-in-trade is the sanctity of private property.

Predictably, the really vital evidence, like the Zapruder film, owned by Life magazine, and other films owned by other wealthy and in-

15

fluential corporations, including the Associated Press and United Press International, were not seized. The government does not want the real evidence of the crime, for that is exculpatory of Oswald and disastrous to its prefabricated case.

His autopsy pictures, not federal government property, were taken by the FBI (item D192). Those of the President, federal property, were given away by the government.

Several boxes of 6.5-mm. ammunition that fit the rifle are listed (items C309-10), together with two empty ammunition boxes (D79). The list indicates the empty boxes were Oswald's property, which is not the case. It does not indicate that the live ammunition was bought by the government and includes generally available ammunition entirely different from the hard-jacketed military type that the government alleges was used that day. It does not say that some was soft-nose ammunition 100 percent consistent with the traces left by some of the assassination shooting. including the "missed" or "curb" shot (WHITEWASH 27-8,158-61,164).

It includes some items as just transferred to the archive when this is false. Months ago I examined some of this evidence in the archive and certify that it had, by then, been carefully altered to suit the government's preconceptions. This is documented in detail in WHITE-WASH II: THE FBI-SECRET SERVICE COVER-UP. Among these items are evidence not considered in the Commission's testimony and revealing vital information suppressed from the Report because it is inconsistent with the Report's conclusions. One of these items is false, others misleading and couched in language that can be intended only to deceive.

There are several listings of empty shells, presumably fitting that Italian rifle and gathered from various places and people. There is no listing of the important 6.5-mm. shells recovered from the sixth floor of the Texas School Book Depository Building.

There is no listing of the bullets used in the Tippit killing. There is no listing of the shells recovered at the scene of that crime.

The most vital ballistics evidence is also not listed. This includes the whole bullet on which the entire case hangs, the one from the hospital; the fragments from the Presidential car; and the fragments taken from the bodies of both victims. Also not listed is the suppressed spectrographic analyses of this bullet and those fragments, which can destroy the entire government case. Spectrographic comparison can show that the samples could have had common origin or, what seems more likely to account for the suppression, that common origin is impossible.

The spectrographic analysis was carefully kept out of the evidence and the Report. What few questions were asked about it were directed to the firearms experts, not the spectrographer. The spectrographer was the Commission's last witness. As I expose in WHITEWASH (p.164), he was asked not a single question about this analysis.

The manner in which these items of evidence can disprove the case is obvious to those who know the suppressed and misrepresented facts (see WHITEWASH, "The Number of Shots"). Simply put, it is this:

The Commission says three bullets were fired. Despite its equivocations, its case rests on three bullets, no more and no less. One of these could not be associated with the motorcade and missed it entirely. Another exploded in the President's head and could not have inflicted any other wounds on him or the Governor. The third, the truly magical bullet with a built-in intelligence and a fineness of control possessed by nothing ever launched at Cape Kennedy, must have inflicted a total of seven non-fatal injuries and must also have remained virtually intact, unmutilated and, the word the government shunned despite the emphasis upon it by the doctors, undeformed. In its history, this bullet must, for the conclusions of the Report to be even tenable, have entered and exited the President; gone through the Governor's chest, smashing 10 cm. of his fifth rib in the process; fragmented his wrist, entered his thigh and, unassistedly - and at precisely the right later moment - worked its way out after embedding a fragment in the thighbone; and to have also left

16

a fragment in his chest, a fact suppressed from the Report (the staff avoided calling before the Commission the doctor in charge of the case, George T. Shires, who informed it of this fragment); and to have left more metal in the wrist alone than can be accounted as missing from the entire bullet. This bullet appears to be perfectly intact, without the marking of a single bone on it, whereas the testimony of Firearms Expert Robert A. Frazier is that had it struck coarse cloth or leather it would have been marked.

All of the doctors, in varying phrasings, described this as impossible (WHITEWASH, "The Doctors and the Autopsy"), but it nonetheless is a central argument of the Report. Without it the government has no case at all. This will be dealt with in additional detail as we examine the suppressed evidence in succeeding chapters.

So, the fragments from the Governor's body - all of them, from all three parts - must have come from the hospital bullet. This spectrographic analysis can prove or disprove. The bullet and the fragments do exist.

There are also the scrapings from the windshield of the car. They must match the fragments belatedly found inside the car. Of these five fragments, the government was forced to concede it could not show they were from a single bullet. The existing evidence is that they could come from as many as five bullets. But for the case to hang together at all, all of these fragments, the scrapings from the windshield and the metal from the President's head, must have come from a single bullet. This, too, spectrographic analysis can prove or disprove. Again, all the fragments do exist.

The failure to question the spectrographer about his analysis and the deliberate exclusion of his study from the printed evidence is one of the most suspect of the unfortunately numerous suspicious shortcomings of the government's evidence, procedures and practices that no court would have tolerated.

There are in excess of 3,200 exhibits by number alone in the record. Of these, many have numerous parts. Some run several hundred pages in length. They include bizarre and exotic items, like cheesecake pictures of Ruby's strippers. The enormous extent of the exhibits alone is millions of words, about 10,000 printed pages. In this vast outpouring of the government presses, in the millions of words of testimony in 15 large volumes of hearings where, for example, dozens of pages were consumed in a futile effort to persuade a sick old lady to testify to things she did not know and specified she had neither been interested in nor observed, there is not a single word of the spectrographic analysis.

With all of the credible evidence proving this fundamental conclusion an impossibility, despite the contrary semantics of the Report, following my exposure of this strange lack in the evidence in WHITEWASH, I searched the files in the archives. Here, in hundreds of cubic feet of space, where evidence not published is also stored, there was also no trace of the spectrographic analysis. Inquiry of officials of the archive confirmed this. I was told it was in the possession of the FBI.

I thereupon wrote Director J. Edgar Hoover on May 23, 1966, calling to his attention certain defects I believe exist in the FBI reports and testimony. He has yet to deny my charge that the FBI improperly withheld evidence which involved neither good taste, the protection of his informants nor, in customary concepts, the national security. I told him that his firearms expert, Robert Frazier, and his spectrographer, John F. Gallagher, had not entered the spectrographic analysis into evidence, and that Frazier's testimony "is merely that the bullets were lead, which would seem to be considerably less information than spectrographic analysis could reveal". I reported the assurance of the National Archives that it was in the possession of the FBI and said, "I call upon you to make it immediately available."

He did not. He has yet to answer this letter. (This is not surprising, for Hoover will not even answer my written request for a copy of a press release he issued because he wanted it printed. Not only

17

would he not answer my letter or send the press release - forgetting he is not God and that I, among others, pay him to do just that - but when I first requested it by phone and one of his assistants promised it, it never arrived.) The reason was then obvious and, in the light of this misrepresented and misunderstood action by the Department of Justice, is now more obvious. He dares not!

On the morning of November 3, I appeared at the National Archives and requested access to the spectrographic analysis of Dr. Robert H. Bahmer, the Archivist of the United States. We had a long and informative conversation about this archive, its contents and condition. Here I must record that I found the staff cooperative. Dr. Bahmer referred me to Marion Johnson, who is in immediate charge of this archive.

Johnson did not have the spectrographic analysis, hence he could not make it available. He phoned the FBI and asked for it. I stood by and waited while he was on the phone.

Cortlandt Cunningham, FBI firearms expert, insisted the spectrographic analysis is incorporated in a book-length report from Dallas Special Agent Robert F. Gemberling. Here there are essentially meaningless quotations, within quotation marks, and I showed Johnson, for his delicate diplomacy with the FBI, that this is not the Gallagher spectrographic analysis and, if that is what is quoted, the quotation marks alone certify its unoriginal nature.*

To the FBI argument that this was all they had, I cited the May 13, 1964, testimony of their own expert, Frazier, before the Commission. Frazier assured the Commission, when it evaded its clear obligation then and there to enter the spectrographic analysis into its record, that this document would remain in the FBI files. The word "permanently" was used with unfortunate applicability. In arming Johnson for his mission, I invoked the testimony on page 69 of Volume 5 where Frazier, when asked of Gallagher's report, "Are his report and your formal report a part of the permanent record of the FBI then," responded, "Yes, sir."

The Commission appears to have accepted this as an unequivocal, official assurance. There is no question about the import of the question or the response. The spectrographic analysis, as though such assurance should be required when the assassination of a President is involved exists.

What remains in doubt is whether the FBI is acting under higher orders, is blindly ignoring its legal obligations and continuing to suppress what it does not want available, or is hiding behind some special interpretation of the Acting Attorney General's October 31 directive. That language also appears unequivocal. Its first sentence reads, "I have determined that the national interest requires the entire body of evidence considered by the President's Commission on the Assassination of President Kennedy and now in the possession of the United States be preserved intact."

The public assurances are that all of this evidence would be freely available to researchers. Were this other than the intent of the directive, what useful purpose other than propaganda was served by moving them across the street, from the Department of Justice on the west side of Ninth Street, below Pennsylvania Avenue, NW, to the National Archives, on the east side?

With or without the support of the Attorney General, this is not the first time that Hoover, its national upholder, has acted in other than the meaning of the law.

The continued suppression of the spectrographic analysis is consistent with the long and unsavory official record of suppressing evidence that only tends to prove Oswald's innocence and the falsity of the official story.

The so-called "re-enactment" made at Aberdeen Proving Grounds was another fake and was so designed. It did not duplicate - did not try to duplicate - the career imputed to this single, wonderful bullet of the seven not-fatal injuries, which also eluded self-injury in its fabled

*See pp. 603-4.

history. Close to exact duplication was possible. No shot was fired
through the replica of both the President and the various parts of Governor Connally's body. Failure to do this, to duplicate what the Commission theorized happened, suggests that it was known in advance that
the duplicating tests would prove the opposite of the theory as, indeed,
those less than replication actually do. The Commission merely misrepresented the results of the limited and invalid tests made for it.

In addition to what appears in WHITEWASH (especially "The Number
of Shots"), a detailed study has been published by Raymond Marcus of Los
Angeles. It is entitled, "The Bastard Bullet: A Search for Legitimacy".
Marcus goes into extensive detail on what the pretended reenactment actually shows. Also, there is hitherto secret data on this in coming
chapters. Briefly, what the limited, really entirely inadequate and invalid Aberdeen mockups actually prove is that it was impossible for these
seven non-fatal injuries to have been inflicted without extensive deformity. Bullets fired through only part of the duplicated human tissue
this one is supposed to have hit were distorted entirely out of shape.
Had such a bullet inflicted the injuries on the President and then been
so deformed, or had it inflicted the non-fatal injuries on the President
and some of those on the Governor, where it next struck the Governor it
would have maimed him horribly, for it would have been an oversized dum-
dum.

In the case of the fragments, the failure - then the refusal - of
the government to make them with their spectrographic analysis public
leads inevitably to the conclusion that the evidence does not support
the Report, which without it rests entirely on supposition, a strange
concept of evidence when the assassination of a President is the issue
and when it is not necessary.

If the five fragments from the Presidential car cannot be proved
to have come from the same bullet, to have caused the damage to the
windshield, and to have also been parts of a single fatal bullet, the
government is without proof of its case. If the fragments recovered
from the Governor cannot be proved to have come from the magical and
seemingly intact, undeformed and unmutilated bullet, Exhibit 399, the.
government on this point alone has its case destroyed. With the Governor's injury, the allegations of the Report are contrary to 100 percent
of the medical testimony.

If in either case, with the fatal bullet or the magical one, spectrographic analysis, extant but persistently suppressed by the government
in violation of its own regulation, proves as it can that the suppositions that replace evidence in the Report are false, then we have the
most monstrous frameup in our history and a prima facie case of a government conspiracy.

Originally, it might have been argued, no matter how foolishly,
that only error was committed. However, once I demanded the evidence,
and I did, frequently, over a span of several years, both verbally and
in writing, such a position could not be maintained. The absolute refusal of the FBI to make this essential evidence available, especially
after being required to by the official directive of October 31, 1966,
permits no other interpretation.

Should a document alleged to be this spectrographic analysis now
be presented, with this history, after my repeated and unanswered demands, it will have to be regarded with suspicion, for there is no extant public record of the contents or conclusions of the genuine spectrographic analysis. With the shameful record of the misrepresentation,
destruction and mutilation of evidence by the government already documented abundantly with its own evidence in my five earlier books, the
precedent is already established.

More, unofficial private efforts to buttress the government's presumptions in substitution for proof also failed miserably and again
proved the opposite. For its series of hour-long TV specials aired in
prime time on four successive nights beginning June 25, 1967, CBS obtained the services of Alfred G. Olivier, wounds-ballistics expert at

Aberdeen and designer of those "tests" (5H74ff.). Knowing full well that faithful reenactment required simultaneous duplication of the seven non-fatal wounds allegedly inflicted by the one bullet, Olivier had not done this for the Commission. He did not for CBS, either. His CBS design called for masonite as a substitute for bone, gelatin for flesh. His creation denied Governor Connally even a masonite rib! Despite this disabling infidelity, all of his shots proved the opposite of the CBS "conclusions" - naturally, those of the Commission - for in not a single case did the bullet have the power to cause the seven injuries - even without the obstacle of a rib! What it really proved is that the single rifle bullet was not powerful enough to penetrate four human-body parts.

Like the Commission, the TV network found it expedient to release no detailed results, no impartial analysis. Like the Commission, CBS simply misrepresented the results of its "test".

And again like the Commission, CBS showed no pictures of its bullets which, inevitably, could not have been in the unmarred condition of Bullet 399. My request for this "evidence", these "results", is unanswered.

CBS did show a picture of Bullet 399. In so doing, it did not show where the metal known to have been deposited in three parts of Governor Connally's body could conceivably have come from with this bullet unscratched!

When shown to witnesses by the Commission, this bullet was carefully jailed in a plastic case and wadded with cotton, on the spurious claim that additional tests were to be made by the FBI. There were no tests that precluded the examination of all surfaces of this bullet by the experts called upon to render expert opinion.

Without this close examination, how valid an opinion could any expert give? How honestly could he swear to the result of an examination he was prevented from making? And how honest is the body and the intent of the body making demands of this sort of its experts?

The Commission did have qualified, expert testimony on what happens to bullets when they strike various objects. For example, FBI Firearms Expert Robert A. Frazier testified that "even a piece of coarse cloth, leather" could have marked the surface with scratches (3H431). The doctors, in one way or another, testified they found the career attributed to this bullet inconceivable. Examination reveals it is virtually unblemished, allegedly after smashing the Governor's fifth rib and right wrist and embedding a fragment in his left thighbone.

Now, I am not a ballistics expert, nor am I a doctor, a pathologist, a prosecutor or a lawyer. But, aside from examining the official photograph of this bullet (WHITEWASH 208) and there seeing how close to perfect it is, I also held it in my hand and with some care examined all its surfaces. The marks of the rifling of the barrel are close to 100 percent perfect, entirely so to the unaided eye. There is no damage to them at all, no scratches across them or any visible deformity.

More difficult to understand is how this bullet could have become slightly flattened at the butt end without in any way leaving a mark on the perfect rifling! More magic! While merrily smashing bones all over the Governor, this bullet is supposed to have been entirely immune to what deforms other bullets, to have been impervious to deformity, mutilation, or even scratching!

Not only is this apparent to the naked eye, but it is confirmed by the microscopic examination Frazier made and testified to (3H430). Asked by Assistant Counsel Melvin Eisenberg, "Were the markings on the bullet at all defaced?" Frazier said, "Yes; they were, in that the bullet is distorted by having been slightly flattened or twisted."

"How material would you call that defacement?" Eisenberg asked.

"It is hardly visible unless you look at the base of the bullet and notice it is not round," Frazier told him, and "it had no effect at all" on his examination "for the purposes of identification" because, even under microscopic examination, "it did not mutilate or distort" the markings to interfere with even <u>microscopic</u> examination!

How this could have happened normally - how a hardened bullet could be flattened at one end without serious marking - is a question not in this interrogation of the firearms expert, obvious as it would seem to be. There is no reason to believe this omission is because the answer would in any way have comforted the interrogator, in any way supported the impossible presumption of the Commission.

Nor is there, from this additional evidence, reason to presume that the forcible suppression of the spectrographic analysis is in any way because it in the slightest degree supports the official fictions. If it did, certainly its contents would have been plastered in the record of evidence, splashed across the front pages, dinned from the loudspeakers and flashed from the TV tubes.

This violation of the Attorney General's order, tolerated on all official levels, is consistent with the Commission's departure from the minimal requirements of evidence and honest procedures in suppressing the spectrographic analysis from its record and making it possible for Hoover to perpetuate the suppression.

It is anything but what the order of the Attorney General promised, that, because he had "determined that the national interest" required it, "the entire body of evidence considered by the Commission", would be transferred to the National Archives.

This hippodroming of the autopsy records of a murdered President cannot be divorced from the Barnum treatment accorded the other tangible evidence, for in its shameful flackery, treating the murder of a President and the evidence of that murder with the delicacy and subtlety of a sex scandal on a tabloid front page, the federal government studiously arranged for both to coincide.

Thus, we have the investigation of the assassination regarded and treated as though it were a deodorant or mouthwash, to be sold with loud, repugnant and inappropriate sales-pitches, an undignified degradation of the men, the office, the government and the country.

Every dishonest act wreaks an additional and unnecessary tragedy, as though the murder in itself were not enough, or the phony investigation not already too much. With the so-called "gift" of the so-called pictures and X-rays of the autopsy carefully staged as a propaganda festival designed to credit the incredible, what for the first time here became public - and was fully exploited by the federal propagandists - is the association of the influential family name of the murdered President with the official "solution" to the crime and in a manner that was made to seem and in fact did seem as though the family did endorse the official explanation.

Until that point, the members of the Kennedy family and their spokesmen maintained a discreet silence, passing no judgment or opinion on fact, saying merely that they had read nothing and intended to read nothing about it, and had no reason not to trust the official accounting. It is understandable that the members of the family would avoid additional pain, as they would trust their government. Indeed, how could the then-Attorney General dream that those under him were worthy of less than his undeviating, total trust? Or that they would so abuse his trust!

This first public Kennedy-family endorsement of the Report, played by the government for all its propaganda worth, is an unfortunate extra tragedy of those that seem to have no end.

What a scandalous official commemoration of the third anniversary of the assassination of the President! What a shocking and disgraceful way to treat his assassination and his memory!

It was an odious event.

21

2. SUPPRESSION IN THE NAME OF REVELATION

Why were the long-missing autopsy photographs and X-rays of the corpse of President John F. Kennedy so suddenly added to the National Archives November 1, 1966, 20 days less than three years after the assassination?

Why did they surface then, only to resubmerge immediately, still unseen and to remain unseen?

Why was this accomplished with brilliant press-agentry, timed for the early editions of the morning papers, which were confidentially tipped off with only enough advance time to plan for the story?

Why did this seemingly independent action key in perfectly with the previous day's revelation of the seizure of a bunch of junk heralded as assassination evidence and its enshrining in the National Archives, an action earlier decided upon, not formalized in a written press release but revealed in a press conference, and a disguised last-minute exploitation of a law that expired the day after the announcement?

Why - if it did - did the Kennedy family possess this government property? How? Did the government have copies?

Why were the autopsy doctors, who had been denied access to these photographs and X-rays when they were the necessary prerequisites of their expert testimony before the President's Commission on the Assassination of President Kennedy, suddenly, mysteriously and privately gotten to examine them, timed perfectly for a third-day story and further public brainwashing?

Why was it possible for the doctors to see these pictures only when the government was in public distress over disclosure that the investigation of the assassination was a whitewash? They knew in advance of their testimony, as first exposed in WHITEWASH (p.180) and here confirmed, that this "best evidence" would be denied them as expert witnesses.

What reason consistent with honor could have been invoked to deny this essential data to the doctors when it was evidence that should not make it unavailable to them when it served as government-needed propaganda?

What does it all mean, why did it happen at just that time, when it was a shamefully inappropriate commemoration of the assassination, and why did the government make a publicity circus out of this last in a series of questionable acts relating to the assassination?

Is it but coincidence this was the week President Johnson was asked a press-conference question (frequently "planted") about criticism of the Report and, basking in this flood of fresh publicity, seemed to reaffirm it without actually doing so?

Most of the answers are revealed in WHITEWASH, which analyzes and discloses the essential Commission evidence of the autopsy and presents it in the context of the evidence on the number of shots. WHITEWASH reveals the destruction of some of this evidence and the willful misrepresentation of other of it; the falsification of some to the members of the Commission by its staff and the substitution of a knowingly false and inapplicable hypothesis as a replacement for fact in the Report.

So shocking is this irrefutable intelligence, entirely from the official evidence, that there was tremendous public pressure to disregard it. Officially, the government pretends it does not exist, although the documentary proof, including the certification of the destruction of the first autopsy report and actual photographic copies of parts of the altered, substituted autopsy report, appear in that book.

I sent copies of the book to the proper government officials, including Commission members and staff and the autopsy doctors themselves, without a single complaint about a single factual error. And in private letters I solicited just this, asking that either I be shown wrong or be joined in my demand for a full and public airing.

Silence was the response, for there is no error in my work. It requires more courage than the government has to confess its error and launch a belated investigation to reveal the untainted truth about the assassination, properly termed "the crime of the century".

So overwhelming is the unassailable proof I have assembled that the lawyer who was in charge of this part of the inquiry declined a dozen requests from radio and TV to confront me, invitations I accepted in advance. He dared not. I did not seek to force him for, if we want the ultimate revelation of truth, we cannot get it by the false fabrication of heroes, which I am not, or the wrongful search for witches; for Arlen Specter is not alone among the staff of the Commission in failing his responsibilities. To single him out for censure would be unfair to him, would protect others equally in need of exposure, and could frustrate truth and justice.

For example, without Wesley J. Liebeler's career as an assistant counsel, Specter's would have been entirely impossible. Liebeler soon loudly proclaimed, from behind the skirts of the University of California, that he, impartial and saintly disciple of the law that he is, had launched a "study" that will tell "both sides", as though the world did not expect this of the Report, part of which he authored. Liebeler also assured us in advance that his study, subsidized by the taxpayers and dignified with the honorable name of the university, will prove the rightness of the Report. He thus adds to his distinctions that of being the fox who got himself hired to guard the chickenhouse.

So much for his impartiality in the present. WHITEWASH II, in telling how and by whom the whitewashing was done, fully explores and explains Liebeler's performance and impartiality. It shows that he made possible the misuse of all the basic photographic evidence belatedly placed in the record, and that he, personally, saw to it that:

None of this evidence was introduced as required by normal legal practice;
None of it was properly identified or authenticated;
None of it was original;
None was untainted.

And the so-called investigation in New Orleans, his show, was a real cover-up that succeeded in telling almost nothing about Oswald's activities there.

Part 2 of WHITEWASH II also fully exposes the gutting of the official file of the autopsy, to which, in this book, I add detail. This only began with the suppression of the photographic evidence. No matter what may now belatedly be done to restore to these files what was improperly removed, that it was done can no longer be denied for I have the documentary proof of it and official certification of what happened.

Of course, I am only presuming that what was taken from the official files still exists in uncorrupted form. I believe that it does. I believe the only way it can be faked is to subject those who alone can do it to further danger of criminal action they will not risk.

It is also a presumption and nothing else that what was returned to government possession by the Kennedy family are the authentic and original autopsy photographs and X-rays. There is no reason to suggest that the Kennedys in any way would or could ever bring themselves to tamper with what they were given, and I do not suggest it. But we likewise do not know, any more than they do, that what they were given to begin with was genuine and complete. Today it is impossible to prove - and the government cannot prove it. Grounds for suspicion already exist.

I begin this hitherto untold account of the history of the missing pictures and X-rays with an example.

On Thursday, November 3, 1966, I presented the government, in writing, a demand for a full exposition of the chain of possession of these pictures and X-rays, under an arrangement previously agreed to that forwarded my request for access to this evidence to the legal representative of the executors of the Kennedy estate. I did this because establishing or disproving authenticity is essential, regardless of what the pictures and X-rays do or do not show, can or cannot show. Without this chain and with the undeviating deception of the government, the evidence itself must be suspected.

Nowhere in the Report or its 26 massive volumes of appended testimony and documents is there a single listing of what pictures and X-rays were taken. Incredible as it seems, this is the grim reality, this is the way the assassination was "investigated" and the autopsy "authenticated" and testified to. The doctor in charge, then Navy Commander James J. Humes (later Captain and now retired), was asked "precisely" what X-rays and photographs were taken. He was permitted to give only the most imprecise answer, that of the pictures "15 to 20 in number were made in total before we finished the proceedings" and that of the X-rays they exposed "10 or 12" (2H349).

With any single picture capable of destroying the entire government case, both the impression that was given and without question accepted and the flexibility in numbers now demand a suspicious regard for what was suddenly suppressed in a secret government cache.

The Commission had the most precise accounting of these exposed films of various sorts. This is not in the unhidden receipts, of which I have copies. It is in an official report that was censored from the Commission's enormous printed record, but is in its files, a report made by witnesses who should have been called - and were not.

The receipts are from the Commission's file numbered 371. The report, rather than standing on its own, is buried in an enormous collection by FBI Agent Robert P. Gemberling. It is in the Commission's seventh file.*

The actual report was made by two other FBI agents, Francis X. O'Neill, Jr., and James W. Sibert, who, despite official obfuscations, were at the autopsy from before its beginning until after its end. On the fifth page of their report they list the photographs and X-rays that were given to the Secret Service, the pictures undeveloped and never see by the doctors:

    11 X-rays
    22 4x5 color photographs
    18 4x5 black and white photographs
    1 roll of 120 film containing five exposures

So the official but censored record reveals a total of 11 X-rays, and, rather than "15 or 20" pictures, 45!

Not a single one of the accounts published after the return of the pictures and X-rays to the government gives either of these figures! Not one that I have seen makes any reference to 120 film!

The Los Angeles Times of November 2 gaves the totals as "14 X-ray: 25 black-and-white negatives and 26 color, 4 by 5 inch transparencies - 65 different pictures in all."

The Associated Press provided the same total and breakdown to its subscribers.

That same morning The Washington Post listed "14 X-rays, 25 black and-white negatives and 26 color transparencies."

The New York Times, through its various editions, listed the same

*See pp. 532ff.

24

identifications and classifications and on the next day repeated the same total.

Both Washington afternoon papers have the same divisions and the same totals, with the Star adding there were "an indefinite number of prints" made from the black-and-white negatives.

Thus there is nothing but confusion and disagreement in both the numbers and the kinds of pictures and X-rays. The doctor's own accounting is farcically indefinite when his function and his qualifications as an expert in forensic medicine are considered. It could be and remain indefinite and imprecise only because Arlen Specter wanted it that way, for it is he who asked for "precisely" what X-rays and pictures were taken, he who knew why he wanted (and the record needed) precision, he who accepted anything but precision, he who failed to insist that the doctor be specific in his testimony, produce the record of film exposed, and who could and should have placed the Sibert-O'Neill reports in evidence or called them as witnesses and, instead, did neither.

The FBI could be wrong. It could be wrong in both the total and the individual listings, and further wrong in each of the three classifications of film and in any combination of the film, for the addition of the unspecified variety of 120 film to either the color or the ordinary film does not equal the number now given for either. But if we assume the FBI erred, can we assume it to have erred in each and every one of these many ways? This assumption is against enormous odds.

Had the Commission, especially its legal staff, met the minimum that might have been expected of it, this and similar questions would not exist today. This failure cannot be dismissed as incompetence or carelessness, for the medical experts were qualified in the legal aspects of medicine, the lawyers were experienced and qualified and under a former Solicitor General of the United States, and the investigation was into the assassination of a President.

Are we also to assume that prints were made of but one category of film, and that the number is unknown when they are in the possession of the government? The Star gave as its source "a Justice Department spokesman". I have seen no correction or retraction.

Who made the prints? For what purpose? Were they distributed in any way? Are copies now outside government possession?

Can we expect nothing but destruction, misrepresentation, inconsistency, incompetence and error in the autopsy of a President, plus the very real question of violation of law, including the possibilities of perjury and the subornation of perjury?

To all this dubious history we add that cheap press-agentry was practiced when announcement of restoration of the film was delayed. It was completed by October 31, the date of the Attorney General's order transferring the accumulation of trivia to the Archives. Announcement was deliberately delayed so it could serve as a dramatic public buttressing of the departmental action with the Kennedy name.

It was also an unbecoming propaganda device to arrange delay in the announcement of a lie - that the doctors had "authenticated" the pictures at an unspecified time. This was released November 2, when it served to support everything else that had been done. All of these things required arranging - negotiations over the film, the drafting and approval of the phrasing of the documents (which also were suppressed), and the inspection by the doctors. It is not accidental that they were staggered like a Madison Avenue production.

This technique is more appropriate to the merchandising of a deodorant than to the disclosure of information about a President's murder. Its demeaning use impugns the purity of the government's intentions.

All public accounts, mysteriously, use the identical word for what the doctors did. They "authenticated" the pictures. It is a fair inference that this is the exact word used by the unnamed officials who transmitted the intelligence to the press. All the news media could not, by accident, fasten upon this single word.

Can the doctors "authenticate" these pictures of inconsistent number, greater in number than they swore to, greater in number than the FBI reported, with or without prints of indefinite number and of no description?

There is no way in the world they can!

Until this mysterious moment, when the doctors pored over the film for an announced three and a half hours - the great length of time it served the government's purpose to emphasize - they had never seen the pictures they themselves had taken!

They could not, therefore, in any way or sense "authenticate" these pictures, had no way of knowing whether these are the ones they took; whether these were each and every one of whatever total is finally seized upon of the various different official totals; each and every one that they had taken, neither more nor less, to the exclusion of any other pictures of this or any other corpse.

The very best the doctors could honestly say, and the very most that could honestly be attributed to them, is that the pictures they examined in late 1966 seem to reflect what they recall, after three years and all the other corpses they had examined in the interval, of what they saw on the President's body beginning 7:35 p.m., November 22, 1963. No more, not a bit.

Only because the autopsy of a murdered president is such a rare thing that would impress itself on the minds of those performing the autopsy can even this much be conceded, for pathologists spend their working lives with cadavers, and three years is a long time and many corpses later.

Why, then, could and did not the government content itself with the simple truth, if that is what it is, that the doctors saw the pictures at such and such a time under such and such conditions and, after study and reflection, say that to the best of their present recollections these pictures are consistent with what they saw during their autopsy examination?

The simple statement that might be truthful would not suit the government's clear purposes. The government was very much on the defensive. It then had and has now no adequate answer to what I expose in WHITEWASH, parts of which have since been affirmed by others. It was under attack from all the books and all the attention given them and their authors. At some time it may launch a diversion or smear. It did, of course, inspire widely disseminated sycophantic and false attacks on the books and authors.

For no other reason does government resort to the cheapest devices of personal-product promotion with the assassination of a President involved. The timing of all those events was too closely meshed, too near to perfect press-agentry, entirely too much to be coincidence.

It coincided with growing and expressed national disenchantment with the official account of the President's murder. Polls revealed an overwhelming majority of the people unsatisfied with or in open disbelief of the official version.

It coincided with an off-year election, but a week away from the first announcement, an election in which the government traditionally loses legislative seats.

It coincided with my effort to avoid an additional private printing of WHITEWASH II, which necessitated that copies be distributed and its content - more shocking even than that of WHITEWASH - thus was no longer my secret. There was no reason to doubt the authenticity or meaning of the until-then secret government documents which I paid the government for Xeroxing. The government had a record of every sheet that had been copied for me. Thus it knew what I had learned and would print.

It also coincided with the release of a three-hour TV program entirely destructive of the government's official story. On it were four of us who wrote about the assassination, its investigation and the strange upsetting of the actuarial tables in the assaults upon, murders and mysterious deaths among, those witnesses and others related to the case whose stories are not helpful to the official account. Invited officials declined to defend themselves before us. They were represented by two unofficial Commission defenders.

It coincided with the then-imminent appearance of the "official" unofficial report on the assassination already beclouded by the ambivalent and contradictory public statements of its author, William Manchester. That is, because of Manchester's sponsorship by the Kennedy family and the vast sums involved, a rare commercialization of the Presidency and its tragedy. This, in turn, subjected the Kennedys, especially those in political life, to tremendous pressure. It had the effect of putting the stamp of Kennedy approval on the work of a man who is but a very fallible mortal. Thus, the Kennedys were in the position of endorsing his opinions, subscribing to what he claims to be fact and truth, and underwriting his unchecked and uncorroborated judgment. This is a liability few intelligent politicians would ever face. It was an insurmountable one for Senator Robert Kennedy, who was Attorney General of the United States during the investigation of the assassination, the head of the Department of Justice, hence in charge of that investigation, whether or not he in any way participated in it.

I have explained on every one of those countless public appearances when the question was raised that Robert Kennedy disassociated himself from this investigation for what I regard as human and honorable reasons. His advance endorsement of Manchester's book was more hazardous, not subject to this explanation, and was not necessary. The slightest Manchester error - and "leaks" of his content presaged, but greatly understated, the all-encompassing, contaminating, serious error - could ruin Kennedy because it put him in the position of supporting untruth about his brother's murder.

Many British and American editors knew my private prediction (then more than a year old) that the Kennedys would disassociate themselves from Manchester's work before it appeared. A sign of its coming, a reaction to adverse public opinion, was the near hysteria, despite the surface calm, with which the pictures were returned to the government, whose possession they should never have left.

While few had or cited proof, it had been no secret that the pictures and X-rays were supposed to have been in the possession of the family. This information came to me early in the spring of 1966. For the previous several months it has been published in varying forms.

When the National Archives informed me, eight months earlier, that the Secret Service still had the pictures and X-rays, I wrote its head, James J. Rowley, asking pointed questions, sending a copy of WHITE-WASH, and getting no response - neither refutation of WHITEWASH, which I invited, nor information about the location of the pictures and X-rays, which I asked for.

Through all of this, and especially because of the misleading efforts of the government's misguided, misdirected and misinformed apologists, whether self-appointed or official (and there were both kind), the meaning of this film record has been exaggerated beyond all reason and common sense. Under the most advantageous conditions and assuming its sanctity, which cannot be done with reason but can for argument, what can it, now, at the very best, reveal?

Only that one less lie was told.

There is nothing that these pictures can prove except that the doctors gave a fair representation of the location, number and description of the President's wounds.

They can in no way invalidate other medical testimony, which is utterly destructive of the government's story. Nor can they in any way address any of the other, really all the other, evidence or corrupted evidence of the crimes.

They cannot, for example, replace the wound in the front of the

President's throat that was cut for the tracheotomy performed under extreme duress in Dallas. They cannot, therefore, show whether, as the doctors in Dallas reported and as, until it was altered, the autopsy report still said two days after the assassination, the President's neck wound was from the front. The government says all the shots were from the back.

Can they establish that the fatal wound was not from the front also? Or that there was only one head shot? The autopsy doctors' testimony is so shaky on this that the Report nowhere gives the precise location and description of the head damage. With the pictures and X-rays denied them, the doctors themselves did not present the Commission with even an artist's representation of the head damage that had any scientific meaning.

These truly astounding omissions in a Presidential autopsy have escaped public attention. It is particularly unpleasant to consider when it is understood that the autopsy of the alleged assassin is a model of scientific exactitude, completed immediately, with copies promptly delivered to a number of public officials. The additional significance of this is that the President's autopsy remained top secret until it was released as part of the Report, where it got lost in the vastness and the precipitated national emotion following release.

Can they reveal the number of weapons used or their caliber? Of course not.

The kind or kinds of ammunition?

The location of the assassin or assassins? Again, negative, even though one of the too-numerous and substantive changes made in the autops report was clearly designed to change the description of the rear non-fatal wound to make it more consistent with a shot coming from that sixth floor window. This change was made two days after the assassination, two days after Oswald was arrested (WHITEWASH 183) - after he was murdered and no cross-examination was likely.

The position of the Presidential car at the time any or all of the shots were fired?

The relationship of the President's and the Governor's bodies to each other and the rifle or rifles?

How many shots hit the Governor, and whether any, or the one alleged, also struck the President?

Who owned, and possessed, and used the rifle or rifles - in fact, whether or not smaller weapons were used?

What kind of rifle or rifles were used - even whether this Italian C2766 Mannlicher-Carcano one was?

They cannot show that the Report is right in saying as one of its many bases, error in any one of which destroys it, that a single shot struck both the President and the Governor. They cannot even show that this is possible. That requires evidence not capturable on film in the Naval Hospital in Bethesda, Maryland.

In short, the utmost that now can be expected of this film record - were it to be proven uncontaminated and that of the President's autopsy which it has not been - is that it not indict the doctors for perjury and others for its subornation.

This in no way authenticates the Report, which remains entirely untenable if the doctors were paragons of testimonial virtue.

And here we have one of the reasons for this spectacular restoration of government property with maximum effort to attract maximum attention to it. The impression given by all the news media is that by this single stroke, by this belated act of presumed generosity, in some magical fairy-tale way all the other wrongs were righted; all the evidence I prove was abused, destroyed and mutilated (especially WHITEWASH 178-87; WHITEWASH II 97-127) was made pristine; and now, thanks to God and the beneficent government, no one need ever again have any apprehension over the integrity of the investigation of the assassination.

What nonsense! The return of the pictures emphasizes the wrong in their ever leaving government possession. It dramatizes the failure of the Commission to examine them, and proves there was no reason the doctors should not have complied with the requirements of the law for "best evidence". Can it now be argued that there was or could have been any question of good taste in the doctors' seeing pictures of what they saw in reality? Can it be believed or alleged that there is something wrong, indecent or evil in their viewing, as a condition and qualification of their testimony, pictures of those parts of the President's body they themselves disassembled as their unpleasant task demanded?

And if this arrant foolishness be argued - the government argued nothing in the Report, where it just avoided the question entirely - how can it then be maintained that, in the moment of the government's great and public distress in November 1966, what was wrong in November 1963 and March 1964 suddenly became right? If the doctors could see the pictures in 1966 without violating good taste or giving offense, why could they not have, in 1963, or when their March 16, 1964, testimony (2H347-84) required it?

There is no need to belabor the obvious. When the government did not want the doctors to see the pictures, the doctors did not. When the government desired that the doctors see them, the doctors did. When the government ordered silence, the doctors were mute. When Mr. Big ordered "Talk!" the doctors said what was expected of them.

What may we now expect of the doctors? Confession of perjury or its subornation? Or of incompetence? This is no longer possible. Events are rushing and are past the point of return. For the doctors to wait more than three years and then say they made a little mistake in one little part is not credible. We shall return to this in the following chapter.

In its effort to cleanse itself, which it cannot do, the government has further befouled itself. It has fooled some of the people again and will maintain pretenses a little longer. The ultimate unfolding of truth will, because of this additional dishonesty and imposition on the trust and faith of its citizens, be more of an explosion than an unveiling

Assuming them to be genuine, neither the government nor the Kennedys have bestowed a blessing upon us with the restoration of the pictures and X-rays, for it was accomplished in a way that makes possible the continued suppression of their contents. There was considerable public pressure on the Kennedys, once it was generally known that they possessed this evidence. This pressure demanded either comment on or revelation of whatever evidence was recorded on the film. Neither suited the Kennedys, nor did the pressure on them and the inevitable interpretations that would be put on their continuing silence. The impending Manchester scandal further endangered their position.

Giving the film to the government got the Kennedys off the hook, at least for the immediate. They no longer seem to be suppressing evidence, although in reality they are. The boon to the government is that it has recaptured the evidence and was able to arrange it in a way that cloaks its continued suppression with the trappings of law. This is not an intellectual and legal Rube Goldbergism; it is the reality.

It is not reality to believe suppression is solely attributable to the professed but not expressed antipathy of the Kennedys at the thought of researchers and scholars seeing what with every other mortal the law would grant them access to. This is not a satisfactory reason for continued suppression.

Just before this fast switch in the unended shell game with the evidence, one garbed in the robes of a judge appointed himself defender of the Commission and undertook to assault me, by ignoring all the fact in my book and by twisting and misquoting several of the very few opinions in it. Judge Arnold Fein, given his forum for an impossible defense of the Commissioners by Norman Cousins in The Saturday Review of October

22, 1966, departed what is expected of either a judge or a reviewer to misrepresent my concern over the abuse of Texas law and authorities (whom those less schooled in the law than a judge may regard as the representatives of the law and its embodiment). He pretends I am worried about only "an abuse of Texas authorities". Thus Fein not only found a legal and/or intellectual figleaf to cloak the nakedness of his avoidance of the unanswerable evidence of the autopsy I mustered; he found it possible to avoid the sentence with which I introduced it.

In acknowledging that I face incurring his wrath by repeating this sentence he found so appalling, I must also acknowledge that I do not, really, fear his wrath, reassured as I am by the certain knowledge it will harm me less than what he intends as friendship does the Commissioners. I am comforted by his failure (not his alone, but one he shares with all those others who perpetuate their abdication of responsibility and leadership at the time of the assassination, and who today seek self-justification in dishonest attacks on those who would not be silent in the face of such monstrous injustice) to debate the facts and issues with me, under conditions and in an environment of his own selection.

That sentence reads, "The law applies equally to the least and the mightiest."

Oswald is certainly the least. The Kennedys are of the mightiest.

At the time the government-Kennedy ploy guaranteed indefinite suppression of this film, it also released from the secret files of the Department of Justice to the public archive what The Federal Register describes as "FBI exhibit No. D192, Color prints made in connection with autopsy of Lee Harvey Oswald".

In the United States we have and recognize no royalty of our own. The law does apply equally to the least and the mightiest. It is only by abuse that it is made to do otherwise. There is no reason for making Oswald's autopsy pictures part of the official archive that does not embrace those of the President. There is more reason for including the President's, for while there is no doubt about who murdered Oswald, or how, there is nothing but doubt about who assassinated the President and why. And he was the President of the United States of America.

The means by which this neat legal trick was played were clearly and accurately explained by Washington Star Staff Writer Lyle Dennison on November 3, 1966. Dennison did not realize what he was documenting. He thought he was explaining how the government can accept a gift for its archives. His source is a Department of Justice spokesman, unnamed:

Such arrangements are authorized, the spokesman said, by a 1950 law. The law permits the General Services Administrator - now W. Lawson Knott - to accept 'for deposit' papers and other historical materials of presidents 'subject to restriction agreeable to the administrator as to their use'. The restriction on use and availability 'may be specified in writing by the donors or depositors' of the material, the law says. The GSA chief is required to abide by those restrictions if he agrees to accept them 'for so long a period' as the donors specify.*
Administrator Knott agreed to the Kennedy condition by signing his name at the bottom of a letter specifying the agreement and the restriction. This is the only document there is, and it will not be made public, the government spokesman said.

That this was officially confirmed to me, as it was, is far from the whole story. The balance of Dennison's story is also correct.

The restriction is for the lifetime of living adults. Only government investigators - those who failed to use the pictures and X-rays when it was required of them - may have access for the first five years. There exists no federal investigation to qualify for access. Congressman Theodore Kupferman was, like me, a private citizen, also refused. Thereafter, and for the lifetime of either of the Kennedy children or of any of the adult close relatives of the late President, who may live longer, only pathologists who are specifically approved may view them. What do any - even the most qualified - pathologists know of the circum-

*See pp. 560-4.

stances and the vast accumulation of fact and unfact of the assassination? May we expect any one of them to spend what is required - more time than demanded in the acquisition of his specialty - to qualify to perhaps get the limited meaning now possible from such an examination?

Stripped of the verbiage, this "contract" guarantees suppression of what evidentiary value the film may have unless an exception is elected. None is likely except, possibly, as another cheap publicity stunt.

As the government misused the about-to-expire special law to cloak its continuing suppressions of other and vital evidence, so it did with this 1950 law, and for the same purpose. This was indeed a remarkable, if improbable, marriage of convenience between the Kennedys and the government, each of whom was faced with the growing demand that this evidence be seen by other than official sources and neither of whom, for different reasons, wanted it.

Once it was out of Kennedy possession, especially when so falsely but fancily clothed, demands could no longer be addressed to them. Yet it is they alone, through their designated agent, who can waive the restrictions, and they do not. Back in government possession, access was hedged with conditions the government could not have imposed had it not first given this evidence to the Kennedys and then accepted these total prohibitions as a condition of the restitution.

Then the new Attorney General, in his great and infinite wisdom, "determined that the national interest requires the entire body of evidence considered by" the Commission be preserved in the Archives, where it can be public. He reached this determination officially on October 31, yet was able, on the following day, to accept the suppressive stipulations which so cozily coincided with the government's desires while avoiding other of his words, "I hereby determined that all of the items of evidence not owned by the United States ..." be made part of the public Archives.

For the moment - and only for a brief moment, let us hope - the government has pulled it off, gotten away with another debasement of popular trust, still another unseemly trick. That it would do so when the assassination of a President is involved may seem beyond comprehension, but it happened.

It is a perfidy that brings the day of truth closer.

Alas, it also, by its desperation, will make that day an even more dismal one.

As it turned out, these carefully staged stunts served to make ready for others in equally poor taste and as opposite to factual when, two weeks later, the anniversary of the assassination was exploited for another campaign. Ordinarily, the anniversary of a President's death is the occasion for fond recollections of his greatness, humanity, accomplishments or. if he had any worthy of mention, his policies. When the third anniversary of John F. Kennedy's murder was imminent, people were instead encouraged to forget it, keep quiet, hate or not listen to those who said the truth of his murder had not been told, and that they were nuts if they did not gulp down the official hogwash without complaint.

Commissioner-Congressman Gerald Ford is not one of those more disposed to decline comment when a headline is in prospect; so he had his customary illogical and unthought-out insults for those who had proved he had not done his job well. He was faithfully rewarded with the kind of press accolade that keeps him doing these things, a reward sufficient for him.

Governor Connally allowed himself to be interviewed by Life and quoted as saying he was, too, hit by a separate bullet (WHITEWASH 4-5) but that the Report is absolutely correct just the same. No one had bothered to tell him both things cannot be true. Promptly and hot as though the hot line ended in Austin rather than Moscow, he was back in the headlines next day with a denunciation of those whose writing had already proved him and the Report wrong. Such insult and falsehood are, strangely, always good copy. Connally added a new twist: Writers who do not agree with government are subversive and ought to be hauled before something, anything nasty and hurtful would do. He set another style in prefacing his remarks with the observation he had not read any of the books whose authors he threatened and libeled. As he spat it out, those who oppose the official fiction are "scavengers". Not those who become millionaires from support of it, or those whose political stock, like his and Ford's, is escalated by well-publicized if ignorant and wrong defenses of it.

The style all the quick-headline artists were soon copying from Connally amounts to this:

"I don't know what I am talking about but ..." and on this basis demanding to be heard and credited. It is a mark of the integrity and discrimination of the press that both happened. There were two pre-requisites: ignorance and a lack of scruple or shame. All that had to be said was these two things: The man-to-be-quoted had to certify that, not having read any of the criticism of the government and its Report, he knew nothing about either; and second, that he did not care, everyone else was wrong, anyway. We shall return to the Connally fiasco.

Least becoming of all is the intrusion of Malcolm Kilduff, one of the press secretaries to the murdered President. As befits a man whose lifetime specialty is public relations, he made a notable contribution: the addition of the word "garbage". Not just plain, ordinary "garbage" but "pure garbage". To publicist Kilduff, sublime in his self-proclaimed ignorance, this is what authenticated, documented and irrefutable disproof of the official fiction about the murder of the President who made some-body of him is, "pure garbage".

If on Kilduff's behalf it is noted that he, almost alone, of the murdered President's staff did not exploit that tragedy for self-aggrandizement, it must also be noted that he acknowledged, both pub-licly and to me privately, that he knew nothing about the fact. He promised to read my books and, unless he could prove them wrong, make a retraction. He did neither. His private career as a Washington rep-resentative for industry, whose concerns are with the government, suf-fered from neither his initial sneakiness nor his subsequent dishonesty. Government rewards sycophancy, not criticism.

It was a Roman Kennedy Holiday. Papers, radio and TV were full of it.

Only it did not work, because too many people understood the Eng-lish they stopped to think about. Too many people had a high regard for that President and a low regard for those who could not cover him fast enough.

This not very nice ploy, of throwing the President's corpse at those who tried to find out how he became a corpse and why, backfired. It attracted more attention to the criticism of the government and its Report.

But, unfortunately, this act of the President's family allowed the improper things they had done and then did with the pictures and X-rays to become a separate propaganda campaign. It was the seemingly legitimate cover for the immediately ensuing additional propaganda cam-paigns. It was as successful as it was wrong. The "gift" was lauded in the press as though it had been a fine and generous thing rather than a new device.

With this unstinted praise in the press the reward of the most prominent and publicized family in the country, that of the murdered President, for its public confession of wrongdoing, is it any wonder some of it rubbed off, as we see in the following chapter, on one of those most responsible for the additional and unnecessary tragedy that followed the assassination?

What put the whole thing in perspective was almost entirely ig-nored. It did not make the headlines, was of no interest to the edi-torial writers or by-line pundits. It appeared November 13, 1966, in but a single paper, as a letter to the editor of the Washington <u>Star</u>.

It confirmed the position I had already taken in demanding access to the pictures and X-rays and came from an authority:

As a physician and medical administrator, I was more than puzzled by the recent article concerning the "donation" by the Kennedy family of photographs and X-rays made by the U.S. Naval Hospital at Bethesda in the course of performing an autopsy on the late President Kennedy. Such records are customarily the property of the hospital or medical organization performing the indicated medical procedure and each hospital must retain the original of such records in its files except as it may be directed to do otherwise by court action. In this case, there is the additional complication that these records were the property of the United States Government and should have been available to the Warren Commission in its investigation.

I cannot see that there is any excuse for the release of these records by Naval authorities to the Kennedy family or for that family to place any restrictions on their use by the Federal Government. The records of medical procedures conducted at a hospital under no circumstances, Government or otherwise, belong to the family nor does any hospital administrator have the right to authorize such release.

John P. Nasou, M.D.

There was then and has been since not a single denial, refutation or allegation that in any way Dr. Nasou is wrong. He is <u>not</u> wrong. This is exactly the position taken by Parkland Hospital in demanding a subpena when the government wanted the pictures and X-rays of the Oswald autopsy. The government honored Parkland's upholding of the law and its requirements with respect to the records of the murdered accused assassin. Only with the President was less than the requirement of the law good enough, only when there was something to be hidden.

Worst of all, when public demand for the truth was finally heard, it is the family of the President that helped stifle that demand and allowed itself to be used for this end.

3.   THE "NEW SCIENCE", THE "NEW DICTIONARY" - AND THE NEW MORALITY

Two weeks after wider distribution of WHITEWASH was initiated, in
May of 1966, I wrote Drs. Humes and Boswell about their autopsy examination and testimony. The letters were virtually identical. I sent them
copies of the book, called their attention to its appropriate chapters,
asked for an interview, separately or together, with or without a tape
recording they or I could make to preclude the possibility of my not recalling correctly what they said, and waited.

Neither responded, then or since.

What I then wrote and what I referred them to entirely discredits
the official story - their stories - of that autopsy. It also raises
the questions of perjury and subornation of perjury in the medical testimony. That these doctors were and are silent about their "error" and
the questions of perjury and its subornation has its own kind of elo-
quence.

Both doctors have been consistent: They have steadfastly refused
to see those who indicated disagreement with their testimony, even those
who merely indicated possible doubt. Although Humes said his silence
was ordered, both have spoken to those they knew in advance would write
what they wanted written and what the government wanted believed. In refusing to talk to me, the doctors nonetheless talked to others because of
me, something not reflected in the stories that appeared the end of November 1966.

A number of staff members of the Baltimore Sun were interested in
my work. At their request, I had driven to that city, met with them,
discussed my findings and answered their questions. Richard H. Levine,
who interviewed Boswell, was not one of them. A. W. (Art) Geiselman, Jr.
was. His interview with me, shortly after the spectacular publicity attendant to the "return" of the pictures and X-rays said to have been thos
of the autopsy, was published November 11, 1966. He then wrote:

The author of a book criticizing the Warren Commission said today
that serious scholars on the topic of the Kennedy assassination
should be permitted to study X-rays and photographs of the late
President's autopsy.
Harold Weisberg, author of "Whitewash," said that, otherwise,
the announcement Tuesday that the Kennedy family had released the
X-rays, negatives and transparencies to the National Archives is
meaningless.
He described the announcement as an effort by a Government under
pressure "to give the impression it has nothing to hide while it is
hiding things."
He said he has gone to the National Archives in Washington to
protest the decision to limit for five years access to the X-rays
and photographs to official Government investigative bodies except
with specific approval of the Kennedy family.
Mr. Weisberg's comments followed the announcement by the Justice
Department that the autopsy data was being released to the custody
of the Government by the Kennedy family at the Government's request
...
"The transfer of the X-rays and photographs is meaningless because of the conditions surrounding them," Mr. Weisberg said today.
"The Government from the very beginning had access to the evidence
in the pictures and has not used them.

34

"What is needed now is access to the X-rays and photographs of the autopsy by those infinitely /intimately/ familiar with the evidence, not beginning five years hence with access by uninformed pathologists who know nothing about the case."

The X-rays and photographs in themselves can add little to the knowledge of the case except to confirm testimony of doctors at the commission hearings, he said. But, he said, in the hands of persons such as himself and others with intricate knowledge of the assassination such data can be placed in their proper context and "be quite valuable."

A look at the X-rays and photographs, Mr. weisberg said, might clear up what he described as "the unresolved conflict of testimony" of pathologists appearing before the commission as to the entrance point of the first of two bullets hitting the President.

He pointed out that a chart apparently made at the time of autopsy showed the first bullet hit the President in the back. Yet, he noted, doctors also presented the commission with an artist's drawing showing that the bullet entered the neck. *

The point of entrance is important, Mr. Weisberg said, because it could, when compared with what some experts believe was the exit hole just at the knot of the President's tie, indicate the height from which the gun shooting the bullet was fired.

The lower the entrance wound in the President's body the less likely was the possibility that the same bullet also hit Texas Gov. John B. Connally, Mr. Weisberg said.

He pointed out that the slug which hit the Governor apparently was moving at a downward angle, hitting him in the back, exiting through the chest, passing through his wrist and striking his thigh.

The matter of how many bullets were fired at the presidential car has been a major question raised by Mr. Weisberg ...

This interested Levine, who discussed it with his associate and my friend, John Friedman. There followed a number of post-midnight calls, each beginning after Friedman and Levine had finished their writing for the morning papers, each getting me out of bed, each lasting a long time.

Levine made clear his singular interest was sensation. His is a jaundiced view of people, reporting, newspapers and life, from the Ben Hecht-Charles McArthur mold of reporters. He had no interest in fact or truth, in helping establish what did happen when the President was murdered or in its official investigation. Scandal was fine, and what difference did it make if he spread misinformation or engaged in propaganda rather than a quest for truth, as long as he got a story.

He fixed upon my comment about the autopsy chart in Geiselman's story.

"What should I ask Humes about that?" he wanted to know.

Mark Lane and a few others then critical of the Commission attributed this chart to Humes. This is a logical but factual error, as reading Humes's testimony reveals, for he swore he had not prepared that chart. I told Levine that Boswell had drafted it.

"Could he have been wrong?" Levine wanted to know.

"He was wrong," I told him, because the indicated measurements did not coincide with the location marked.

If he could get Boswell to say he made a mistake, Levine said, he had his headline. The Levine formula exactly coincided with the government's interest. His interview with Boswell was set and came off as scheduled - and formulated - as unofficial official propaganda. But it was too good a formula, too close to perfect in addressing the government's then acute distress, for its carrying off to be entrusted to a brash reporter unknown to the government, or to a single paper when that device could be spread around the world.

Of all the days in the nine hundred and fifty following the autopsy testimony before the Warren Commission, by one of those remarkable coin-

*See p. 310.

cidences we are required to consider nothing else, the Associated Press just happened - entirely by happenstance - to select exactly the same day Levine had arranged for his interview. It also sought out Dr. Boswell. And about what did it want to interview him? Only those things Levine had indicated to Boswell and, on my phone, to me, he would ask about.

And what story did the Associated Press carry, what did its reporter want to know? Only those things that fit the Levine formula!

With three doctors to seek out, it interviewed Boswell only.

Of all the fact and fiction of the autopsy, it also fixed on this chart.

Its story, a thin transparency of Levine's, contained nothing not in his, but was spread throughout the world. Is it not additionally remarkable that the AP carried only some of what Levine got from Dr. Boswell?

No less remarkable is the world-wide journalistic acceptance of the seeming boast that a President's autopsy was characterized by sloppy work, inaccuracy, carelessness and conjecture rather than the precise science one expects from autopsy surgeons, specialists in pathology and forensic medicine.

Levine's is a morning paper. The AP works around the clock. It "beat" Levine to his own story, circulating it in time for afternoon use the day before.

Levine suspected I had "tipped off" the AP. Quite naturally, he found it difficult to believe it was only coincidence that the AP seized upon the same day to interview the same doctor - and no one else - and ask him the same questions - and nothing else.

This is a part of the history I believe should be recorded, for the papers of that time, November 24-25, 1966, do not disclose this background. They falsely indicate the question was raised first by Edward Epstein. His writing on the autopsy, based not upon the testimony, with which he displayed monumental unfamiliarity, but upon what had been fed him by former Commission staff members seeking self-justification, is so inaccurate he hypothesized that changes made in the autopsy report on November 24, 1963, were made much later.

So, we are told, Boswell proclaimed his own error as the norm of forensic medicine, the commonplace of autopsies, not different when a President is murdered. *

That a pathologist acknowledged error in a Presidential autopsy warranted this headline in the Baltimore Sun, which ran the banner in large type across the top of the front page:

KENNEDY X-RAY DATA RELEASE BACKED

Safe in the knowledge nothing like it would - or could - happen, Boswell asked for examination by "disinterested observers" (read "those who know nothing about it"). **

This error, to the Washington Star, justified the headline, "Doctor at Kennedy Autopsy Explains Sketch Controversy". This is hardly what Boswell did, not at all what the story said ("made a diagram error" was the AP's euphemism).

Even The New York Times, whose well-informed and conscientious reporter Peter Kihss used the same phrase, "diagram error", and without question quoted Boswell as saying, "If I had known at the time that this sketch would become public record I would have been more careful" - as though secrecy justified slovenly science when a President is murdered - headed its own story, "Autopsy Doctor Says Films Back Warren Report".

The Washington Post (which knew much better, its own staff having asked questions about the autopsy of a former staff executive and gotten not a single satisfactory answer) rewrote the AP story to eliminate the direct quotation of error or the indirect acknowledgment of it. "The sketch was drawn quickly, as 'rough notes'," the Post explained, leaving the schizophrenia to its headline writer, whose first bank was "M.D. Bac

* See p. 198. **See p. 139.

36

Warren Report" and whose second used the word the story did not, "Admits He Erred In Sketch".

There was no little journalistic child to say the Emperor was naked, or to ask why the doctor might be expected to say the Report and his testimony were wrong. Less politely: proclaim himself a perjurer.

For all their dilettante attitude, for all their failure to prod and probe, the reporters did come up with what would have been sensational revelations to an honest press and on any other subject. Boswell acknowledged to Levine that:

There were microscopic slides made of tissue "which indicated ... foreign substances ..." in the neck wound and that "there was no mention of these slides" in the autopsy report, even though, he said, they confirm it;

"All marks and scars were noted," although there is no such chart in the printed record or the files;

When the body arrived, "The pathologists /himself and Humes7 had already been told of the probable extent of the injuries and what had been done by physicians in Dallas," thus destroying entirely the flimsy excuse that they did not know a tracheotomy had been performed as an FBI report we shall analyze also does;

When the autopsy examination was performed - but before Humes finished the final draft by revising what he had written - "Oswald was still alive, and it was believed the autopsy information would later be called upon in court proceedings;"

Not until they could not probe the rear, non-fatal wound did the doctors order "complete X-rays of the entire body"! Levine's words are, "At this point", or "when the wound in the back of the neck was discovered and probed, by finger and by metal surgical probe, no bullet could be found."

Although the President's body should have been examined along the possible path of the bullet, there is no reference to any sign of its path, merely to a bruise that could have been caused by the tracheotomy. They did not see a path, and bullets do make them. In fact, bullets cannot go through a body without making a detectable path.

The next day's telephone call to the Dallas doctors - he also refers to but one when there had been two - "confirmed", as Levine put it, "what was already a certainty to the pathologists - that there was a bullet wound in the President's neck at the point of the tracheotomy incision."

Then why was the telephone call made to "learn" this, or the second one made at all?

The answer is in WHITEWASH (p.180): The Dallas doctors were tipped off.

"Later that day, November 23, Dr. Humes and Dr. Boswell went over the rough draft and completed the protocol in its final form." If this is true, Dr. Humes perjured himself before the Commission (WHITEWASH 180, 183) in swearing that, "In the privacy of my own home, early in the morning of November 24, I made a draft of this report which I later revised and of which this /part of Exhibit 3977 represents the revision. That draft I personally burned in the fireplace of my recreation room" (2H373) This, to the Commission and the newspapers ever since, is normal - burn the President's autopsy and suppress the notes and the pictures and the X-rays and the slides of microscopic examination and the organ examination.

Yet of his interview with Boswell, Levine said that "before this", meaning earlier November 23 - when Oswald was still alive and there was the absolute certainty that all the autopsy work and findings would be subject to rigorous cross-examination - "Dr. Humes destroyed" the draft.

Further complicating it is this representation of more drafts of the autopsy than Humes or Boswell acknowledged under oath: "Dr. Boswell said that all the original notes were preserved, as far as he knows, and were turned over to the National Archives." (Of this he can have no knowledge and it is untrue. No such notes are or have been there, nor are they printed where required in the Commission's record.) "He said the things that were burned were copies of the protocol as they were revised."

Aside from the conflict with Humes on the time - and if Humes swore falsely, Boswell was also under oath and supported it, raising again the question of perjury - this language accounts for a minimum of one more burned copy of the autopsy, at least one draft more than, under oath, the doctors acknowledged were made.

Boswell also indicated papers had been prepared that no longer exist. It is proper and normal, as I have pointed out from the beginning, to orient wounds from inflexible points so that the location is precise. Only variables - the shoulder joint and the mastoid - are referred to in the autopsy report. That was rewritten after Oswald was murdered, after it was known there would be no cross-examination. In Levine's language, Dr. Boswell said "that he thought he had used a vertebra as a third reference point, but that this did not appear in the autopsy report or in the sketch."

This is part of the story that delighted the papers, that caused them to vie with each other in joyous hosannahs because there had been error in the autopsy when a President was murdered; that made the papers proclaim the good news throughout the land - the President's autopsy was right because it was wrong - better than Gilbert and Sullivan - and all is right with the government and the world! Never have the great and powerful been so uninhibitedly exultant in praise of error.

Error is what suddenly made the Warren Report right.

Nobody wondered - or asked why - it took Boswell three years to admit his "error", especially because it was months after the autopsy that he and Humes testified under oath. Nobody - not Levine, the AP, the Times or any other paper - deigned to embarrass Dr. Boswell, once he agreed to be interviewed, by asking for comment on the thoroughgoing condemnation of this autopsy months earlier at the annual meeting of the American Academy of Forensic Sciences, which heard it denounced as incomplete, "weak ... cannot establish a chain of evidence ... failed to maintain original notes ... must be taken on faith rather than fact ..."

Mystery about the autopsy now is forever guaranteed, but there is no mystery about why Drs. Boswell and Humes did not answer my letters, did not agree to speak to me, but did agree to be interviewed by those who knew nothing about the fact or, like Levine, cared less. It is as though there were guarantees in advance. From Levine none were needed. The performance of the Associated Press could have been no more satisfactory to Boswell if he had written their story.

Levine got his sensation, leaving the country no better for it, with lies about a President's murder more widely disseminated, more firmly believed by more misinformed people. It did him no good, however, for he left the Sun very soon thereafter.

Only the cause of injustice and untruth profited, only those deserving punishment were protected.

Levine told me he had asked Boswell why he had not responded to my letter, to the challenges I published in WHITEWASH, to my offer to tape record anything he wanted to say so I could quote him accurately. Boswell, he told me, was put out because I did not consult him in advance of publication. On December 1, 1966, I wrote Boswell the following letter, sending a copy to Humes:

It has been reported to me, I hope erroneously, that your failure to respond to my letter of six months ago, with which I enclosed a copy of my book, WHITEWASH: THE REPORT ON THE WARREN REPORT, was due to pique, because I had not consulted you in advance of its publication.
A writer attempting to consult all of the 552 people listed as Commission witnesses and the countless thousands of others in the

38

printed evidence in 27 such massive volumes could never in several lifetimes complete a book.

It is my belief that the autopsy of an assassinated President should be a model of completeness, precision, specification, fact, and accuracy. It is my belief that when a body such as the President's Commission, with a staff of men of such outstanding qualifications, takes testimony from medical experts enjoying the high position and respected status you and your colleagues have earned, all of us, including writers, are entitled to assume and expect that the Commission and its witnesses approached their unhappy responsibilities with unlimited dedication to completeness and truthfulness.

Are you suggesting I should have expected your testimony would be inadequate, incomplete or inaccurate, that the Commission desired this, that the requirements imposed on a pathologist by science and law cannot be met except with the prodding assistance of a writer?

The Commission and the medical experts made their own record. All will have to stand on it.

As always happens with this subject, whenever official persons make statements, they raise more questions than they answer. This is true of your statements to the Baltimore Sun, broadcast widely by the Associated Press.

As in the past, I shall make no effort to force myself upon you or Dr. Humes, no effort to entice you to say anything you do not want to say. Whether or not you elect to see me and answer questions is entirely your decision. My original offer stands: I will make a tape recording and provide you with a copy.

I cannot avoid noting for the present and for history that you and Dr. Humes decline or refuse to see those you have reason to believe seriously question the autopsy and the testimony on it while, for example, seeing Fletcher Knebel, a Commission defender. I note also that you granted an interview to the Baltimore Sun when it was first apparent to you that the reporter had no knowledge of the subject matter at all and had as his sole purpose eliciting from you what you ultimately said, that you erred in the official autopsy chart.

My new book, WHITEWASH II, will soon be available. This time I shall not send you copies. But I do want you to know that among the things I say and prove in it is that the President got an autopsy unworthy of a Bowery bum.

The doctors, apparently, are still piqued for neither has responded to me. They were not totally silent. CBS asked Humes to appear on its Special of Specials, four hour-long apologies for the Report and the government, presented on prime time June 25-28, 1967. These were thinly disguised as "non-partisan". Their conclusions were inconsistent with the filmed information.

Proudly reading the copy carefully prepared for him, Walter Cronkite was blissfully unaware that a line in which he took journalistic delight was a big lie. The more he repeated it - and this he did throughout the shows - the prouder he seemed to be:

Since the X-rays and films were turned over to the Archives, Captain Humes has re-examined them. And tonight, for the first time, he discusses with Dan Rather what is contained in them.

The press widely interpreted this and its fulsome repetition to mean that CBS had been able to arrange for a private examination of the suppressed pictures and X-rays of the autopsy. According to what the Archivist has written me, this is false.

If Humes did not know of this CBS lie when he was filmed, he certainly did after the show was aired. He was and has been silent about it, content to leave a lying record, that he "re-examined" the pictures he had never before seen.

This is consistent with the lie in which he, without protest or demurrer, participated in Rather's first quoted question:

Commander -- now Captain -- Humes, have you had a look at the pictures and X-rays from the autopsy since the time that you submitted them to the Warren Commission?

After the touted investment of a half-million dollars and the extensive time and effort of a large, professional staff, it might be assumed that CBS's researchers knew better. Humes submitted nothing to the Warren Commission and, although it could have and should have, it never possessed the pictures and X-rays. Fully aware that he had never seen these pictures prior to or during his testimony and that he had never "submitted them to the Warren Commission", Humes replied, "Yes."

Likewise is there no question that Humes also knew the members of the Commission were not going to see this film evidence. It is he, personally, who supervised the preparation of "artist's conceptions" as an acceptable substitute, to him and to the Commission, for the available and legally required "best evidence", the pictures (WHITEWASH 181ff.). Assistant Counsel Arlen Specter asked this of him a few days before his testimony, as we shall see.

The lie was repeated:

RATHER: And do you have any different conclusion, any different ideas, any different thoughts now, after seeing them again, than you had at that time?

There was no complaint from Humes that he had never seen them until they were "returned" to the government, more than two and a half years after his testimony, more than two years after the Commission had ceased to exist:

HUMES: No, we think they bear up very well, and very closely, our testimony before the Warren Commission.

If the pictures hold up "very well", Humes does not. It was a lie to say "after seeing them again" of the pictures that Humes had never before seen, as it was for Humes to accept the lie and to pretend by his answer that it was truth.

With this beginning, it is less than surprising that CBS was itself without protest, question, even a raised eyebrow, when Humes announced that the official charts "routinely used to mark in general where certain marks or scars or wounds may be in conducting a post mortem examination ... are never meant to be accurate or precisely to scale".

This shocks us "squares" who labor under the apparent misapprehension that there should be nothing less accurate than man and science can make it in the autopsy of a murder victim, more particularly when he is a President, and that everything in a medico-legal document is "precise", not about 100 percent wrong in distance or in a different part of the body, as this mark is.

Boswell told Levine he thought there had been reference to a vertebra. Humes made no such pretense, and in his description to CBS was careful to avoid the only meaningful point from which measurement is made.

During his conversation with Rather, no little voice whispered in Humes' ear, "That was a whopper," or "Better tell the truth," or "What will history say?" or even "Better late than never." Instead, when Rather asked, "Your re-examination of the photographs verify ..."

"Yes, sir," Humes again said.

These were wonderful "shows". It was as though Ananias sat on the CBS shoulder, Munchausen on the witnesses', and Barnum was in the prompter's pit.

There is more to the magic of this "inaccurate" chart that was never intended to be anything else. (It was, after all, only part of a President's autopsy and its "notes".) This time it is about the fatal head wounds.

"... the measurements which are noted here in the margin of the drawing are precise measurements," Humes said.

Going along with it is the "new dictionary" and special meanings to special words. In passing, it is worth noting how "precisely" and "incontrovertibly" the rear, non-fatal wound is located. This is the beginning point of the interview and the crux of it. The "precision" in locating the wound from side to side comes from its orientation with the shoulder joint instead of the spine. Unless the width of the body is given - and "precision" in this case eliminated that dimension, too (no note in the margin) - there is no horizontal location. In the vertical dimension, orienting the wound with the mastoid is the very apotheosis of "incontrovertibility". The mastoid, you see, is in a different part of the body than the wound. It is in the head. This wound, by the Commission's description and the word of the doctors, was in the neck. By the chart it was in the back. Neither is part of the head where, "incontrovertibly", the mastoid is - even in Presidents. Necks come long and necks come short. It is conceivable that if a Presidential neck were short, with "precise measurements" such as those "noted in the margin of the drawing" - and a few centimeters would shorten enough - this wound would be in the air and not in either the neck or the back. Likewise, if the President's head was cocked slightly to the opposite side, his wound would, by these "precise measurements" that are "noted in the margin of the drawing", have been nonexistent. On the other hand, cock it down a bit, and it is either in the back, had it been in the neck, or farther down in the back if it was where all the observers said it was to begin with - in the back (WHITEWASH 185). *

Of course, the observers - mere Secret Service and FBI agents - had no "notes" in their "margins". They had only eyes.

Thus, the advantages of the "new science", especially if buttressed by the "new dictionary", are readily apparent. They are most suitable when invoked in the analysis and report on the murder of a President. How much more "precise" or "incontrovertible" can one be? Or need one, when it is a President's murder and the autopsy is in a military hospital, conducted by military personnel who have expelled all others?

Rather asked about the head wound. There are no other notes printed in the official exhibit, No. 397, none in File 371, supposedly identical with Exhibit 397. But:

RATHER: Your re-examination of the photographs verify that the wounds were as shown here?
HUMES: Yes, sir, they do.
RATHER: About the -- the head wound --
HUMES: Yes, sir.
RATHER: ... there was only one?
HUMES: There was only one entrance wound in the head, yes, sir.
RATHER: And that was where?
HUMES: That was posterior, about two and a half centimeters to the right of the midline, posteriorly.

Where is the source of Humes's "precise" locating of the fatal wound - and it is precise - "two and a half centimeters to the right of the midline"?

There is no such note in the "margin" (WHITEWASH 197), no such mark on an unidentified scheme of a head wound that is part of Exhibit 397 (17H46), which abounds in other marks, seems as though it might be a chart of the President's head injuries, and seems also not to show this "wound of entry" of the bullet said to have entered the back of his head and to have exploded out its right side - and only its right side.

Thus, when asked, "can you be absolutely certain", Humes declared, "very precisely and incontrovertibly".

Can there be any doubt of the "conclusive scientific evidence", Rather's felicitous choice, when the "precise" and "incontrovertible" evidence is a chart that has none of the measurements and is described as "never meant to be accurate or precisely to scale"?

This is the "new science", reserved for the solution of Presidential murders and the glories of electronic journalism.

*See p. 149.

The President's body was removed from Dallas, where the only applicable law obtained, in deference to the widow's wishes, according to undisputed published accounts. For the same reason, according to the same sources, before it reached Washington arrangements were made for the autopsy examination to be at Bethesda Naval Hospital. In 900 pages of its Report and 26 volumes of evidence, the official record made of this autopsy is so deficient that the Commission saw to it there was no public record of those who attended that autopsy.

No such record in 10,000,000 words about a President's murder!

Why?

As we shall see, it is not because the record was not in its files. Later we shall see significance in its incompleteness.

The examination was by Humes as Chief of Laboratories (Rather might have said, "Now, Civilian" instead of "Now, Captain" for at the time this show was recorded, Humes knew he was quietly returning to private practice immediately after this, his first and only public appearance and comment on the autopsy), assisted by Colonel Pierre Finck, of the Army Medical Service, whose experience is in both forensic medicine and wounds ballistics (he was chief of that Army branch), and Boswell, then Humes's Naval Hospital assistant. Not long after his Commission testimony, Boswell returned to private practice.

From the official account, these three doctors were the ones who actually performed the examination and signed the report on it. So slight was Boswell's participation, according to the FBI, that in their report he is listed merely as among those present.

That Humes did not make any public statement or appearance prior to his telecasting by CBS is not because he was not sought. He just ducked unless he had reason to believe in advance that he would not be questioned about what he had done, unless he received assurances that he would be whitewashed. The same also seems to have been true of Boswell. Finck was more fortunate. His work seems to have kept him out of the country for extended periods. In retrospect, Finck may come to regard the horrors of long medical service in Viet Nam as a blessing.

No civilian expert - no one not in government military service - was permitted at the autopsy examination. Had the autopsy been a model of scientific and forensic-medical precision - which it was not - this alone would have been sufficient to assure doubts and misgivings. It should never have happened this way.

Whether or not Mrs. Kennedy wanted the autopsy examination to be done in the naval institution because her husband's military service had been naval, someone not as shocked by the crime as she, not as stunned by its horror and overwhelmed by the immediate and pressing consequences and necessities, should have seen to it that civilian experts of the greatest experience and highest repute were at least observers. There should have been pathologists not in the military service, not on any government payroll, not in any sense under any official obligation or compulsion and with unassailable scientific credentials in medical understanding of crimes of violence, to assure the impartiality and thoroughness of the examination and its accounting and to satisfy the country and the world that there was no question about either the examination or the official report of it.

Someone with the power and the authority to prevent this accomplished the opposite. In these same 10,000,000 official words on the investigation of the Presidential murder, in those same 900 pages of the official Report on it, the fact of this is entirely absent, as is the identity of the person responsible for seeing to it that there was no civilian check on the military, for seeing to it that there was no single civilian expert present at the autopsy.

Those present at the autopsy examination - even those who just entered the room and then left - were duly, if incompletely, recorded by FBI Agents James Sibert and Francis O'Neill, whose report is in the Appendix.*

*See pp.532ff.

Is it an accident that this obvious failing escaped official Commission attention, an accident that the Commission was without comment on it in its Report and testimony and evidence?

Or is it, as I believe the record establishes, deliberate suppression - part of the whitewashing?

So we have these new insights into the autopsy and the men who did it, the autopsy report that was from data "never meant to be accurate" by a doctor who "would have been more careful" had he known his work "would become public record" - by a doctor who expected secrecy to be the grave of his autopsy work on a President of the United States!

And we now know about it what was not included in the official investigation and the official Report on it:

That microscopic tissue slides were made and "there is no mention of these slides" in the autopsy report;

That, despite their contrary statements under oath, the doctors knew before and during their examination that a tracheotomy had been performed in Dallas and "had already been told of the probable extent of the injuries and what had been done by physicians in Dallas" before the body arrived;

That a revised autopsy was prepared when it was known that, with Oswald's murder, there would be no trial, no cross-examination on it;

That not until they could not probe the rear, non-fatal wound did the doctors take "complete X-rays of the entire body";

That the original notes of the autopsy were preserved but do not exist in any of the duplicate places they are required to exist - although without them there can be no support for the autopsy, whose raw material they are;

That the "precise" location of the fatal entry wound is recorded in non-existing marginal notes on an inaccurate chart, the only existing recorded note of its "location";

That the Commission suppressed the identities of those who attended the autopsy (and, as we shall see, did not call most of them as witnesses);

That the military expelled all civilians from the autopsy examination room (about which we shall also have more);

That the chief of the autopsy joined CBS-TV in lying about when he saw the pictures of the autopsy, how many times he saw them, and what he did with them, all to the complete silence of the press and officials who knew the truth.

We can now better understand that it is this official silence in the presence of "error" and of lies - perhaps perjury - and the blind, uncritical support by a servile press that compound the tragedy of the phony inquest.

43

4. "I DON'T KNOW WHAT I AM TALKING ABOUT, BUT ..."

Based firmly in his own ignorance and political necessities, Texas Governor John B. Connally marked the third assassination anniversary with a Life interview, after examination of their clearest copies of the Zapruder film, followed by a press conference in which he found it necessary to label as "scavengers" those who, unlike him, knew what they were talking about and could not derive political profit from what they said.

Precisely the same political necessities kept any of those who could have tipped him off from alerting the Governor to the self-indictment he was about to issue. His appeal for a return to McCarthyism, for tunately, was passed over. Of needless scandal there already had been too much.

As Martin Waldron put it in the New York Times of November 24, 1966, Connally declared that the Report "should be accepted as final". Simultaneously, he insisted there could be no doubt of it, he was struck by a bullet that did not hit the President. And, "he said he had not read any of the books that have criticized the Warren Commission's findings". Moreover, as Life reported in its issue dated November 25 but distributed earlier, "Connally says he has never read any of the Warren Report, not even his own testimony ...". Here we have his authority and the basis on which he was accepted as an authority: total ignorance.

Divorced from the misrepresentation of the propaganda field-day by the press, Governor Connally, like those who followed him in the intensified campaign (including Malcolm Kilduff, the late President's press aide, whose long experience in public relations, if not his integrity, should have told him better), was saying, "I don't know what I am talking about, but ...", and demanding crediting on the basis of self-proclaimed ignorance.

He got it, too, as did Kilduff and the others, all of whom began with similar or identically worded disclaimers of knowledge.

Now, if Connally was struck by a separate bullet, as he steadfastly insisted, this alone ended the single-bullet, single-assassin parallel theories twisted and press-agented into pretended reality. This alone required at least a fourth shot. With that rifle and in the allotted time of five to six seconds, there was no possibility of even the three shots alleged by the Commission to have been fired, let alone a fourth.

To the Governor, it was not "scavenging" for him to exploit the tragedy (that had touched him more than most men) with a politically, if not financially, profitable exposure in Life, or for him to extract political benefit from the crime by his press conference and the tremendous attention given it, all of it rooted in his self-proclaimed ignorance. But it was sinister, somehow dishonorable - and with "subversive" overtones - for others to spend without pay the thousands of hours he had not poring over the evidence and raising the questions he failed to ask, then proving from these studies, as I had, exactly what he had said but giving it the meaning his ignorance denied him.

If Governor Connally had been struck by a separate bullet, that alone proves the Report wrong, not, as he claimed, right.

As with every effort to defend the indefensible Report, this elicited further damning information, unveiling additional suppressions.

In WHITEWASH (160) I point out that the cleansing of the Governor's clothing destroyed evidence and that the Commission was without interest, in its proceedings or its conclusions.

Both Connallys testified before the Commission (4H129-49). Mrs. Connally's three-page testimony (146-9) took about five minutes. As was customary, when there were embarrassing questions, they were not asked. This was invariably true when these questions were about the character and conduct of the FBI and Secret Service investigations and about evidence that jeopardized the pre-determined conclusion of Oswald's solitary guilt.

Why were the Governor's garments cleaned? How was it possible for this to have happened, for the FBI and Secret Service, both of whom knew the great evidentiary value they had, not to have seized them immediately and carefully preserved them? Scientific analysis could have irrefutably established the direction of the shots and the type of missile. Whether it was deliberately intended, as it may fairly be inferred to have been, especially from what followed, it without doubt resulted in the destruction of irreplaceable and incontrovertible evidence.

The Commission and its counsel, Arlen Specter, were not interested There can be no excuse consistent with competence and honesty of purpose that can possibly justify Specter's failure to seek the answer to these unavoidable, obvious questions. It was his obligation to ask:

What happened to Governor Connally's clothing? How did its evidentiary value get destroyed? Who permitted it?

Did I say "unavoidable" questions? Not for Specter. He did avoid them - did not ask them. Specter met every challenge to his single bullet theory with silence. He could - and did - manipulate the evidence and questioning.

All the members of the Commission compounded Specter's transgressions against truth and the solution to the crime, his framing of the dead accused assassin, by their personal silences. Each member of the Commission, too, is a lawyer. His training, if not his common sense and experience, should have demanded he ask what happened to the Governor's clothing. Like Specter - who did it right to their faces, for Mrs. Connally is one of the few witnesses to appear before the Commission - each failed his obvious responsibilities. Each preserved suppressive silence.

Not until, with the best of intentions, Mrs. Connally destroyed what evidentiary value remained, did any official get interested in this clothing. Once this occurred - once that evidence was permanently irretrievable, its threat to the official pre-determined case ended - there was official interest.

This is what Mrs. Connally told Life, part of what she would have told the Commission had it but asked her or allowed her to volunteer it:

As a matter of fact, it was almost two months before any of the investigators showed any interest in examining John's clothing. When he went into surgery they gave me his tie, trousers and socks in a paper bag. We finally located John's shirt and suit coat, which we were concerned about because of the wallet and personal papers in his breast pocket, in Congressman Henry Gonzales' clothes closet in Washington. I told the Secret Service and I guess the FBI that I had the clothes, but nobody seemed interested. After about seven weeks I took John's shirt . . . it was all smeared with his flesh and blood, and dipped it in cold water several times to try and preserve it. Someone finally came to pick up his clothes. I think the Commission said his shirt was useless as evidence because it had been "laundered". But I never laundered it, I just soaked it in cold water.

Remarkable as this is - that neither its experienced, politically ambitious counsel nor the Commission's lawyer-members had any interest in this destruction of vital evidence or how this could possibly have happened with the fabled FBI on the spot and on the job and with the Secret Service backstopping it - no less remarkable is it that the

Commission - to a man, its counsel and Report - are consistent.

There existed a bullet alleged to have caused all these injuries, to have had a career like nothing in science, or science fiction, or mythology.

Arlen Specter took testimony from Hospital Engineer Darrell Tomlinson (WHITEWASH 161-2,171), who found this bullet. Whereas Tomlinson said he'd not be able to sleep if he said what Specter asked of him, to the Commission Specter said they had the required proof. Tomlinson, on finding this bullet, immediately sent for O. P. Wright, chief of hospital security. Specter, whose legal training and district attorney's experience told him he was required to establish a chain of possession of the evidence, did not call Wright as a witness. Nor, for that matter, did he call a single witness to establish that the bullet he said Tomlinson found is, in fact, that same bullet.

Perhaps what Wright told CBS, which aired him at the conclusion of its four-part series, makes sense of Specter's otherwise incredible departure from the requirements of his profession and of his particular employment of it (Eddie Barker, KRLD-TV News Director, questioned Wright)

WRIGHT: I told him to withhold and not let anyone remove the bullet, and I would get a hold of either the Secret Service or the F.B.I and turn it over to them. Thereby, it wouldn't have come through my hands at all. I contacted the F.B.I. and they said they were not interested because it wasn't their responsibility to make investigation So, I got a hold of a Secret Serviceman and they didn't seem to be interested in coming and looking at the bullet in the position it was in then.
So I went back to the area where Mr. Tomlinson was and picked up the bullet and put it in my pocket, and I carried it some 30 or 40 minutes. And I gave it to a Secret Serviceman that was guarding the main door into the emergency room.
BARKER: Mr. Wright, when you gave this bullet to the Secret Service agent, did he mark it in any way?
WRIGHT: No, sir.
BARKER: What did he do with it?
WRIGHT: Put it in his lefthand coat pocket.
BARKER: Well now, did he ask your name or who you were or any question at all about the bullet?
WRIGHT: No, sir.
BARKER: How did the conversation go? Do you remember?
WRIGHT: I just told him this was a bullet that was picked up on a stretcher that had come off the emergency elevator that might be involved in the moving of Governor Connally. And I handed him the bullet, and he took it and looked at it and said, "O.K.," and put it in his pocket.

The CBS comment is a modest understatement:

CRONKITE: There is little to praise in such treatment by the F.B.I. and the Secret Service of perhaps the most important single piece of evidence in the assassination case. Moreover, the Warren Commission seriously compromised itself by allowing the Secret Service, the F.B.I. and the C.I.A. to investigate questions involving their own actions.

It is just as haphazardly that what we are supposed to believe was the same bullet turned up that night in the White House (WHITEWASH II, 125). As the FBI report put it, Gerald A. Behn, Special Agent of the Secret Service in charge of the White House Detail, "stated that on learning of such a bullet being found at the Dallas hospital he inquired of a group of his agents who had returned from the Dallas trip (how dispassionate can you get!) on the night of November 22, 1963, and Secret Service Agent Richard Johnsen produced this bullet which had been handed to him by someone at the hospital ...".

Did Specter call Behn as a witness? Or Johnsen?

He did not. Instead, he told the Commission members they had the "proof". Here he introduced a radical new concept: "proof" without evidence, evidence without testimony. Don't laugh. The Commission of legal and political eminences accepted it. It and his political apostasy - to Republican - made Specter District Attorney of Philadelphia and, in one term, his new party's mayoralty candidate.

Yet it is this bullet, the one I call magical and with a built-in intelligence, of a fineness of control like nothing ever launched from Cape Kennedy, that is central to the fundamental conclusion, that a single missile inflicted all seven non-fatal injuries on both men. The official approach was straightforward: It would not encumber itself or its "evidence" with the requirements of the law or of evidence, not bother with witnesses, just assert what it wanted and ignore what did not fit or pinched a little.

All in all, it was a truly spectacular performance, particularly by Specter. It is all the more spectacular because 100 percent of the credible evidence is 100 percent in refutation of it, as I have already shown in my first two books. One thing all doctors agreed on is that this bullet could not possibly have had the career officially attributed to it. Specter faced this problem squarely: He substituted a hypothesis for irrefutable proof - fiction for reality translated into "evidence". This in the "solution" to the murder of a President!

At the time he interviewed Specter, _Life_ Associate Editor Richard Billings knew much less of the fact of the assassination and its investigation than he soon learned. Otherwise, he'd have known of Specter's single-bullet theory that, in the lawyer's words, it was already an eliminated alternative. Here is that part of the _Life_ story:

"One of our most impressive pieces of evidence," says Specter, "is the FBI report on an examination of the limousine. It concludes that no part of the car's interior was struck by a whole bullet."
The only remaining place the bullet could have logically gone was into Connally. The FBI film shows that he sat directly beyond Kennedy in the assassin's line of fire. As Specter sums up the Commission's case, "Given the trajectory from the Book Depository window, the autopsy, about which I have no doubt, and the FBI report on the limousine: where, if it didn't hit Connally, did that bullet go? This is the single most compelling reason why I concluded that one bullet hit both men."
As Specter describes it, the Commission arrived at its single-bullet theory by the elimination of possible alternatives. This is a risky procedure in any court of law since no one can be sure he knows all the alternatives ...

It is not the "possible" alternatives that Specter "eliminated", for they still exist. It is any alternative that he wanted to forget, for any alternative meant conspiracy, and that the government had determined from the beginning it would not concede.

The most obvious of the "possible alternatives" is the one the Commission staff dedicated itself to pretending did not exist and, quietly, to undermining in every way possible. This is a shot from the front, which is proven by all the credible evidence, even after the federal hatchetmen thought they had safely cut it down. Consistent with this is the testimony of several witnesses, that they saw bullets strike near the President's car. One of these was expertly handled by Wesley Liebeler, without whose equally spectacular defiance of all the norms of evidence, law and accepted procedures, Specter's valorous contributions would have come to naught. It is Liebeler (who now teaches others how to be lawyers at the University of California at Los Angeles) who twisted poor Mrs. Donald Baker and manipulated her testimony (WHITEWASH II,129-31) so the Commissioners and others later reading the record could not possibly determine whether her observations could be confirmed. His was a surgically sharp examination; and it is he who selected those pictures she would be shown. With no opposing lawyer to keep him honest, he chose only those that could not possibly show what Mrs. Baker testified to, taken from positions and at angles that precluded its capture on the negative. His cutest trick was asking her to locate what she testified

47

to on a picture that did not - and could not - show it! This he then impressively entered into "evidence" as "Baker Exhibit No. 1" (19H112).

Until the Commission and its lawyers started pressuring the medical witnesses, twisting and leading them away from it, all the evidence is that the President was shot in the front of the neck. All the evidence is still that way; it is merely misrepresented by the Commission's defenders as it was by that body and its staff.

"One of the most impressive pieces of evidence," as Specter himself put it, is that "no part of the car's interior was struck by a whole bullet". The only "possible" conclusion is not that this bullet lodged in Connally. That, in fact, is the conclusion that is not possible, for all the real evidence disproves it. There is an answer to Specter's question, "where ... did the bullet go?", the alternative that was not only "possible" but probable. It is that the bullet did not hit the car. This is exactly what would have happened to a shot from either grassy knoll. Such a shot could not have struck the windshield and the President because of the obtuse angle of Elm Street. To hit the President, this shot would have had to miss the windshield if fired at any time in the sequence of shots prior to the hitting of the head. The pretense that there could have been no shot from the front because the windshield was not smashed is but another of the many official diversions.

A relatively flat shot through the President's neck from front to rear would have missed the car as it exited the neck and would have struck the street. This is the "possible alternative" that Specter would not face, pretended did not exist.

This is the fact that had to be suppressed where the pertinent evidence could not be misrepresented, twisted nor ignored. And this is precisely what was done, as what I have dug up from the Commission's record and suppressed files shows.

No single federal or local investigation or investigator believed or said what the Report concluded in adopting Specter's creation as its pretended reality. All, particularly the FBI and the Secret Service, said the opposite. The solution to this problem, insurmountable in a court of law, with opposing counsel, in open hearings, was simplicity itself: Everybody else and all the evidence were wrong, Specter was right.

Truth is wrong; illicit desire is right.

This, too, is the way the President's murder was "solved".

There is, in fact, so much of this official investigative evidence disproving the official fabrication - all suppressed or misrepresented, save what I have already published (in WHITEWASH, WHITEWASH II, PHOTO-GRAPHIC WHITEWASH) - that there here is no need to present all of what is in the Commission's files and, until now, remained secret.

This also is why the immediate, original Secret Service December 5, 1963, reconstruction of the crime had to be thrown out, replaced by the more carefully stage-managed FBI charade of Sunday, May 24, a half-year later. The testimony about this FBI "reconstruction" (WHITEWASH II 175ff.,243,248) is that its purpose was to make it seem that the positions of the bodies of the President and Governor could be tortured into the possibility of a single bullet striking them, not to prove that it did. Even then, this reconstruction was wrong in time alone by 30 per cent! However, to Specter, the Commission and the FBI, this presented no problem. They just ignored that, too.

It was suppressed from the Report!

It was undetected until I exposed it (WHITEWASH II,180).

We do have the official Report on the murder of a President from which the fact that its "reconstruction", the "reconstruction" on which the basic conclusions rest, was an acknowledged 30 percent wrong, and the fact of this error is suppressed from that Report. This suppressed the evidence that the assassination could have taken a third less time than officially acknowledged, making its commission by any single man that much more impossible.

This, too, is consistent.

The Secret Service reconstruction was junked. It had to be, because it made impossible the conclusion that Oswald was the lone and unassisted assassin. It proved there was a conspiracy. It also proved that some of the shooting could not have come from that sixth-floor window of the Texas School Book Depository Building, whether or not Oswald was in it.

In WHITEWASH (p.195) I reproduce photographically part of the first FBI report to the Commission. It accounted for all the shooting without mention of the wound in the front of the President's neck or the shot that is known and admitted to have missed the motorcade, something omitted by other books that thereafter used/misused this same report.

Apologists for the FBI, who are numerous and politically powerful, now say, as with the autopsy, that its report was not expected to be accurate and thorough! For what other purpose could the FBI make such a report, or should it? As a placebo, for propaganda? Then why was it kept secret, a secrecy perpetuated by the Commission that had a 900-page Report and 10,000,000 words and 26 large volumes of space for it? Its purpose, to be the definitive statement of fact, is clear in the announcement of it. Under the headline, "U.S. Inquiry Ordered by Johnson" in the Washington Post of November 26, 1963, where it is the "second lead", or, in the opinion of the editors, the second most important story of the preceding day, this appears:

President Johnson last night ordered "a prompt and thorough investigation into all circumstances surrounding the assassination of President Kennedy and the murder of his alleged assassin". He directed the Department of Justice and the Federal Bureau of Investigation to handle the investigation, a White House statement said. The President also said, the statement added, "that he has directed all Federal agencies to cooperate and the people of the nation may be sure that all the facts will be made public". This investigation is already under way at Dallas, officials said, with the hope of putting a Report on the President's desk very soon. (Emphasis added)

This first FBI report says that "medical examination of the President's body revealed that one of the bullets had entered just below his shoulder to the right of the spinal column at an angle of 45 to 60 degrees downward, that there was no point of exit, and that the bullet was not in the body." It is this bullet that was the "found" one, according to the FBI.

The FBI had available the same evidence and sources the Commission had, and it said this bullet came from "a" stretcher, not the Governor's.

Here again the "solution" was simple and possible because of a self-corrupting press. WHITEWASH, which points out other gross failings of the FBI, aside from the fact of this bullet - the FBI did ignore the front neck wound and it did ignore the "missed" shot and it knew of both - also was ignored. The papers were not about to acknowledge that the vaunted FBI and its almost-holy Saint Edgar would fake their investigation of the President's murder, the only certain meaning of its first report, the Commission's first file.

Instead, focus was on "Inquest", which also ignores these and other glaring FBI errors and seeks to use the report of the FBI agents at the autopsy as a second autopsy report, which it is not. This was convenient to the author of that book because he unquestioningly accepted the basic Commission conclusions and had, despite the contrary flackery of his publisher, made no genuine study of the evidence, of which he was blissfully ignorant. Thus he concluded that the autopsy report was altered after this FBI report was made. Had he read - not studied but read - the unburned version of the autopsy protocol prepared November 24, 1963, part of the official Exhibit 397 on the autopsy (17H29ff.), and of File 371, he would have known that, according to the sworn testimony, these changes were made that day, before typing. A sample is in WHITEWASH (p.198), showing that one change that the doctors did not make was inserted after the doctors turned in the draft and before it was typed.

49

ll other changes were made in Dr. Humes's handwriting, exactly those changes Epstein says were made later.

The change not made in Dr. Humes's handwriting, not made in any writing at all, eliminates his words saying that Dr. Perry had told him the President had been struck from the front!

More magic!

(Specter asked Humes a single perfunctory question about these changes, but made no reference to this one, which is also ignored in the Report. Had he and the Commission not done this, there could have been no whitewash, for Oswald could not have fired simultaneously from front and back.)

In any event, the report of FBI Agents O'Neill and Sibert was not dictated until four days after the assassination, two days after the autopsy protocol was turned in. There are indications of an earlier Sibert-O'Neill report (File 5, folio 149), the existence of which is officially denied. And on November 25, the day before the Sibert-O'Neill dictation, Admiral C. B. Galloway, commander of the entire Naval Medical Center, sent the White House physician, Admiral George G. Burkley, the eighth and last original copy of the typed protocol. This cast of characters and these documents will interest us further.*

This is the kind of "scholarship" that won the approval of the eastern intellectual community, favorable mention by reviewers lost in respect for its "moderation" (thus redefined), and delayed a real solution to the crime and exposure of the fakery of the official investigation. In time this "moderate" young "scholar" became an open apologist for the government, to the reiterated praise of no less an authority on moderation and scholarship than Nixon's Attorney General, John Mitchell+ For Epstein, who sold his own humiliation for a reported $5,000 (WHITEWASH II,71ff.), it was a profitable career.

But of the real evidence, unimproved by "moderation" or "scholarship", there is no question. From the outset there was no possibility of a single-bullet theory. That evolved not because of the compulsive power of the evidence, not because it was the only alternative, but because without it there was no possibility of pinning the rap on the dead, accused and defenseless Oswald. Without it there was no avoidance of the certainty, of the painful but inevitable fact that the President was murdered as the consequence of a conspiracy.

Until government went to work on the evidence and the witnesses, this was what all the evidence and the witnesses proved.

In 900 pages, the Report had no space for this evidence.

Had it found the space, there would have been an entirely different Report.

<hr>

*See p. 526.
+ Convicted in Watergate scandals.

5. THE "THREE MONKEYS" THEORY

Neither beginning nor ending with Governor Connally, but drama-
tized by him, is the "single-bullet" theory - Arlen Specter's - that the
Commission, in its Report, tries to suggest is not central to its conclusions, but really is.

With it, the Commission could pretend to account for all the shoot
ing, even though it could not. Without it, no such possibility existed.
The Report accounts for the so-called "fatal" shot, at Zapruder Frame 313
That, according to its evidence, struck no one else and inflicted no other
wounds on the President. Another shot missed. It could not be associated with any bullet or part of a bullet that struck the car and any of
its occupants. For all the wounds to have been inflicted with no more
than three bullets having been fired charges the "single bullet" of that
theory with causing the remaining seven non-fatal injuries to both the
President and the Governor.

These wounds are said to be in the front and back of the President's neck, the back and front of the Governor's chest, through his
wrist, from the upper side to the lower, and into his thigh, where a
fragment lodged in the bone. These are fully discussed in WHITEWASH, in
the related chapters, "The Number of Shots" and "The Doctors and the
Autopsy".

Thus it can be seen that the "single-bullet" theory is not a "theory" (though it is anything but fact) but is a necessity. If a single
bullet did not have this meteoric life, at least one additional bullet
had to have been fired. That required another assassin. Come what may,
this the Commission was determined not to concede, for another assassin,
whether or not Oswald was the first, meant a conspiracy. (Conspiracy is
a combination to do wrong. It requires but two participants.)

Specter is at once the father of the single-bullet theory and the
first to abandon his child (WHITEWASH II, "Magic, Mystery and Myth"). He
maintains the polite pretense of a relationship behind the facade that
it is not obligatory.

Only because during the Commission's life there was no confrontation with opposing counsel and cross-examined evidence was it possible
to dream that a single bullet could have had this past. The disproof is
abundant in the Commission files, where the staff saw to it that it remained.

The most common form is the proof that, without the missed shot,
all three were entirely taken up inflicting the wounds on both victims.
This is not to say that three bullets can account for all the injuries.
But it is to say that until it became too obvious that the "missed" shot
could not be ignored, it was ignored, by the FBI, Secret Service and the
Commission staff.

The "single-bullet" theory is the invention contrived in an effort
to make it seem that all the shooting could be accounted for in three
shots and that Lee Harvey Oswald could have fired all three shots. Without this the Report had to acknowledge the reality no one in government
was prepared to face, that the President was murdered as the consequence
of a conspiracy.

Without doubt, as the Commission's apologists say, the "single-
bullet" theory came into existence gradually. This is not because there

positive evidence, for that never did exist. It is simply because
the reality that the "missed" bullet could not be avoided was not immediately faced. As it became more and more apparent that there was no
escaping that "missed bullet", it also became apparent that, without
something to take up the slack, there would be a conspiracy Report.
Thus, the extra burden placed on the 6.5 mms. of the "single" non-fatal
bullet.

It is not possible to analyze and report on the autopsy and what
relates to it or to the Commission's other central evidence of the assassination without in some way dealing with the "single-bullet" theory, for
it is one of the more important aspects of the case. There will, therefore, be some repetition later.

In what immediately follows, I have not tried to exhaust the material, nor have I used all that is available. More of it will come up
in later chapters. The purpose is to present at a single point a fair
sampling of the information in the Commission's files but suppressed
from what it reported showing that it, the FBI and the Secret Service:

Never conceived a "single-bullet theory" from the evidence;
Required all three shots they admitted were fired to explain the
shooting, as they think they explained it;
That only in time of dire necessity did it emerge in a temporarily successful but fraudulent effort to overcome the liabilities of
the tangible and irrefutable evidence.

Aside from the unofficial accounts, which can be quoted selec-
tively, in support of a number of theories of what happened, all the
immediate official explanations were other than the single-bullet contrivance the Commission finally fixed upon. None coming from those who
had seen the wounds supported any variant of the single-bullet theory.

As soon as the doctors had finished their emergency treatment of
the Governor and had a moment to collect themselves, the Dallas police
interviewed them and obtained the information needed for the "General Offense Report", a requirement. Its language, under "Details of Offense",
leaves no doubt about why there was no space for it, too, in the 900
pages of the Report, or in the interrogations of the appropriate witnesses. This official document, filed the day after the assassination, says

Mr. Connally sustained a gunshot wound with the point of entry
located in the posterior of the right shoulder, ranging downward thru
the chest, exiting on the right chest just below right nipple. The
bullet continued, striking the right wrist, palmside, exiting 2
inches from the wrist joint. A fragment continued, entered the interior portion of the left thigh causing a flesh wound.

This belief, that a fragment broke off, continued, and embedded
itself in the thigh, eliminating an almost-perfect bullet, what Exhibit
399 is, is also that of Dr. Robert R. Shaw, one of the Connally surgeons
(6H91).

The FBI summary reports of December 9 and January 13 are without
comfort to "single-bullet" theoreticians, as we shall see.

By December 18, 1963, when the Secret Service made its official
report (the Commission's third file), it was cagier than the FBI. In its
own name and on its own authority it did not say how many shots were
fired or what damage each did. This may seem like something less than a
Secret Service report on the assassination of the President it was guarding so he would not be murdered, but it is also a report about which the
Secret Service could not have been criticized for saying what was later
to be unwelcome. The Secret Service played it safe: It said nothing,
acknowledging on its 31st page, in its "Narrative of Events", only that,
after the motorcade was on Elm Street, "there was a sharp report".

When the Secret Service can make this kind of "report" on its investigation of the murder of a President, it makes one wonder what the
Secret Service really does and if the charges of neglect made against it
might not have a basis. File 3 is not a report; it is an infantile evasion.

More important than anything else is bureaucratic security. to play it safe, these stalwart guardians of the President said noth[...] The Commission was without complaint over this callous Secret Service indifference to its official responsibilities, or to its gross incompe[...] tence, for such a childishly inadequate "report" is one of these two things - or much worse. Perhaps the Commission was grateful that in this instance the Secret Service did not give it still another hurdle t[...] scale, further proof of the invalidity of the false conclusions it was to issue.

Even in the appended exhibits, Secret Service Chief Rowley took no chances. Here is the account of the actual assassination that, if anything, is even less meaningful:

12:30 p.m. (Approx.) Because of what appeared to be the sound of a firecracker or gunfire, also because of unusual activity in the Presidential and follow-up cars, we immediately accelerated movement of Lead Car. Information was received over the two-way radio that we should proceed to the nearest hospital, and we were escorted speedily to the Parkland Hospital. The President and Governor Connally were placed on stretchers and were immediately taken to the Emergency Room for medical attention. (See my statement and statements from other agents as to activities during this incident.)

How much "safer" could he play it - or how much less could he say in reporting the murder of the President!

Of course, this was not because the Secret Service did not know better, nor was it because their own investigations had not told them what had happened. The Commission, consistent with its determination to conclude that Oswald was the lone assassin and that there had been no conspiracy, simply suppressed from its Report and the appended 10,000,000 words of evidence that which disproved its predetermined conclusions.

Example after example exists throughout the secret files. Here are a few cases:

Secret Service report of November 28, 1963, from Inspector Tom Kelley to Chief Rowley (Commission File 97, Folder 2, folio 235). This reads:

At the foot of Elm Street, at a point approximately 200 feet east of the Houston Street Triple Underpass, on the approach to the Stemmons Freeway, President Kennedy, who was seated on the right rear seat, was shot. Immediately thereafter Governor Connally, seated in the right jump seat, was shot once. The President was then shot the second time.

FBI report of November 29, 1963, by Agents Robert M. Barrett and Ivan M. Lee (Commission File 5, folio 117):

SA HOWLETT advised that it had been ascertained from the movies that President KENNEDY was struck with the first and third shots fired by the assassin, while Gov. CONNALLY was struck with the second shot.

How Secret Service Agent John Joe Howlett established this is also worthy of note, for it is exactly as the FBI, for the Commission, did it over again in May to pretend otherwise. Howlett

advised that with the aid of a surveyor and through the use of 8 millimeter movie films depicting President JOHN F. KENNEDY being struck by assassin's bullets on November 22, 1963, HOWLETT was able to ascertain that the distance from the window ledge of the farthest window to the east in the sixth floor of the Texas School Book Depository Building, 411 Elm Street, to where the President was struck the first time in the neck was approximately 170 feet. He stated this distance would be accurate within two or three feet.

The facts hadn't changed. The Zapruder film certainly did not, save for a few frames being eliminated from several versions (WHITEWASH 45,206-7;WHITEWASH II,3-5,94,138-9,178,195,215,220-2). In fact, Howlett had a better print of it, an original copy. The surveyor and his instru-

were constant, as was their accuracy. Accuracy to "within two or ~~e feet" is as great or greater than ever achieved.

All that changed was the Commission's problem: It did not dare ~~ore the "missed" bullet. Therefore, the evidence and its meaning had ~ be worked around to be consistent with one shot having missed the ~torcade entirely.

Among the other Secret Service records of the fact that three shots hit the car's occupants are several published in WHITEWASH II.

The Secret Service engaged Dallas Surveyor Robert West to prepare a map of the assassination area. On it was then marked the location of the car when each of three shots struck (WHITEWASH II,167,243).

During its reconstruction, the Secret Service placed a "replica" car where it says the President's was when each of the three shots struck then photographed it in each position (WHITEWASH II,248). These are part of Commission File 88.

Arlen Specter, father of the "single-bullet" theory, was familiar with this file. When he was interrogating Secret Service Inspector Tom Kelley (WHITEWASH II,166-8), he alluded to other photographs that are part of it and entered them into evidence. Specter, however, made no reference to these Secret Service pictures showing the President's car where it was when each of three bullets struck. Inspector Kelley was just as delicate. He remained silent about the unwelcome evidence. Specter did not enter them into evidence.

This is not the only such occasion in the Commission's record or when Specter conducted the taking of testimony. With Dr. Humes on the stand, Specter offered into evidence what was identified as Exhibit 397 (WHITEWASH 183). Specter then identified this exhibit as identical with Commission File 371. When Humes was asked to identify it, he said it included "various notes in longhand, or copies, rather, of various notes in longhand made by myself, in part during the performance of the examination of the late President, and in part after ..."

Now, these autopsy notes, not burned by Humes (WHITEWASH 187) and in his hands months later, when he was on the witness stand, are essential in any examination of the assassination or the autopsy report. Notes are the basis of it. They did exist as of the time of Humes's testimony, they were entered into evidence, the evidence Specter was in charge of, and they have been physically removed from that evidence.

Thus, the evidence of the autopsy has been further tampered with, further suppressed, if not illegally, certainly improperly. These notes are not in any copies of File 371, not in the National Archives in any form. It is another coincidence, no doubt, that this also happened in another part of the case over which Arlen Specter had charge.

Naturally, it is also simply a "coincidence" that these Specter "oversights" just happen to coincide with his sponsorship of the "single-bullet" theory, which is disputed by this suppressed evidence.

In May 1966, after I persuaded the Washington Post to read WHITE-WASH, they finally came out with a story, after asking former Commission personnel questions about this evidence to which they got no satisfactory answers. Government defense against the statements in the FBI report (WHITEWASH 192-5) contradictory to the Commission's medical and autopsy conclusions was that the FBI had not seen the autopsy report. Incredible as this is, it was accepted. However, this cannot be claimed for the Secret Service, which immediately received all eight original copies of the autopsy, from which it then Xeroxed additional ones, and all the pictures and X-rays. This evidence was in Secret Service possession before any of the reports and conclusions here cited were prepared.

On January 30, 1964, ten days after the Commission officially had a copy of the autopsy report, Assistant Counsel David W. Belin wrote a memo to General Counsel J. Lee Rankin on the subject of Oswald's possible knowledge of the motorcade route. This, he said, could have been November

19, when the papers announced it.

The third paragraph discloses that the month-old Commission, by this early time in its "investigation", had determined to limit itself to only three shots having been fired. This is how Belin accounted for them:

In determining the accuracy of Oswald, we have three major possibilities: Oswald was shooting at Connally and missed two of the three shots, the two misses striking Kennedy; Oswald was shooting at both Kennedy and Connally and all three shots struck their intended targets; Oswald was shooting only at Kennedy and the second bullet missed its intended target and hit Connally instead. [See p.492]

In an effort to make this legible, I have darkened the file copy. It reads:

> In determining the accuracy of Oswald, we have three major possibilities: Oswald was shooting at Connally and missed two of the three shots, the two misses striking Kennedy; Oswald was shooting at both Kennedy and Connally and all three shots struck their intended targets; Oswald was shooting only at Kennedy and the second bullet missed its intended target and hit Connally instead.

Expediently, Belin ignored the "missed" shot, of which everyone in government knew, for spray from it caused James T. Tague to bleed (WHITEWASH 158). It was immediately reported by the police. However he explained it, Belin had each shot hitting - none missing. He used up three shots without accounting for all the shooting.

Of course, to the government Oswald was already the lone assassin. But with the second shot striking Connally alone, as this memo also has it, that was not possible. The only thing that later "changed" the facts, apparent to the Commission at the very beginning, was its need to account for the "missed" shot without acknowledging an additional shot. To admit a fourth shot was the same as acknowledging an additional assassin, which it would not do for that, in turn, was proof of a conspiracy to kill the President.

Almost three months later, on April 22, the Commission was still satisfied that each of the three shots struck a man. It was still ignoring the "missed" shot. On that day Assistant Counsel Melvin A. Eisenberg drafted a "Memorandum For The Record" on the "Conference of April 21, 1964, to determine which frames of the Zapruder movies show the impact of the first and second bullets".* Each of these shots "impacted". There never was any question of the "impact" of the third or fatal shot. This is unmistakable, unforgettably preserved in Frame 313. All participants are not named. Those who are include five doctors, three FBI agents, five Commission lawyers, including Rankin, the Connallys and Commissioner McCloy.

Specter alone dissented from the conclusion that Connally's chest wound could not have been inflicted after Frame 236.

By this time what was never proved was being assumed, that the whole bullet had been "recovered from Connally's stretcher". Only one doctor (a veterinarian) considered it even remotely conceivable that this bullet could have caused the damage to Connally's wrist. To put it another way, the "single-bullet" theory was eliminated while it was being dreamed up.

This paragraph of the memorandum reads:

> In a discussion after the conference Drs. Light and Dolce expressed themselves as being very strongly of the opinion that Connally had been hit by two different bullets, principally on the ground that the bullet recovered from Connally's stretcher could not have broken his radius without having suffered more distortion. Dr. Olivier withheld a conclusion until he has had the opportunity to make tests on animal tissue and bone with the actual rifle.

The Commission's solution to this problem was simple and direct.

*See pp. 501ff.

. Dolce, consultant to the Biophysics Division at Edgewood Arsenal, was
t called as a witness. Thus, his "very strong" scientific opinion con-
:ary to what the Commission was cooking up is not in the evidence.

An earlier, similar conference for the identical purpose had been
held April 14. Eisenberg also drafted the memorandum on that one, again
underscoring "impact of the first and second bullets". This memo also
is dated April 22.* Present were all three autopsy surgeons, Doctors
Light and Olivier, five FBI and two Secret Service experts and three Commission lawyers, again including Specter, who noted the same dissent.

Two days later, Eisenberg prepared a memorandum on "Determination
of the Trajectories of the Three Shots". It again accounts for all
three shots without acknowledging what was known, that one had missed
the motorcade entirely. He proposed what actually was staged a month
later, a Dallas reconstruction. His purpose was to locate the car at
each of the three "impacts". He also said that, instead of the "replica
car" that was used (WHITEWASH II,164-8), "preferably, the actual car"
should be used.

His paragraph 4 repeats that all "three shots struck" the men.

From the very beginning, as this memo also reflects, no consideration was given to a shot from any other point or any shot that did not
strike the President or the Governor. Not until it was obvious that the
"missed" shot could no longer be ignored was any consideration given to
it. When it had to be accounted for, the Commission grimly refused to
admit more than three shots had been fired. Acknowledging a fourth concedes a conspiracy. All the evidence is that no single man, not Oswald,
not the best shots the Commission could gather, could have fired even
these three shots. By misrepresenting its evidence, the Commission did
get its false claim that Oswald could have fired these three shots believed. However, there was no possibility of achieving acceptability
for a "four-shot" theory.

These Commission staff and Secret Service conclusions, that all
three bullets hit the two men, are amply supported by the investigations
and conclusions by the FBI and the Secret Service. The very first Commission file, No. 1, is the FBI summary report of December 9, 1963, made
by order of the President (see above; WHITEWASH 192-5). It says, "...
three shots rang out. Two bullets struck President Kennedy, and one
wounded Governor Connally".

The FBI amplified this report with another on January 13, 1964
(Commission File 107). If, as government defenders, including J. Edgar
Hoover, argue, the first report was written without benefit of the autopsy report (and there is no reason why it should have been), this can
not be said of the second report, whose second paragraph contains reference to its findings. The FBI did not retract or withdraw what it
said in the first report, that each of the three shots struck home.

Until the official position changed, the FBI's representation and
reporting fact did not change. After the first shock wore off and it
got to work, it prepared elaborate scale models of the entire area, with
care and infinite accuracy. It then prepared, with customary FBI neatness and trim plastic binding, a booklet of explanation. This is File
298. It is not, you may be certain, in the Report or printed evidence,
which carefully culled out all proofs of more than two impacting shots.

Section 12 begins on page 14. It is headed, "What was the aiming
pattern of the assassin's target?" It could not be more explicit than
it is in the first words of each of the first four subdivisions of this
section:

a. SHOT ONE hit the target from a distance of 167 feet...
b. SHOT TWO hit the target from a distance of 262 feet...
c. SHOT THREE hit the target from a distance of 307 feet,
measured downward along a 15-degree angle from the horizontal...

*See pp.503ff.

There are no ifs or buts here. The FBI, like the Secret Service told the Commission that each of the three shots it says were fired hit the target. It placed the target at the time each shot was fired, with precision. It also specified the time that elapsed between each of the shots hitting the target. There is no reference here to the "missed" shot, no reference to it that can be read in. That shot was defined out of this listing by the FBI (WHITEWASH 156-60), which knew of it.

In short, well after the beginning of the investigation, at a time when simple error could not be claimed (and could either the FBI or the Secret Service be of such unequaled incompetence - each separately and both together - that they could make such "errors"?), the FBI told the Commission that each of the three shots hit one of the men.

There is no evasion, no qualification. No conditions are stipulated. This, like the others cited, is a direct, straightforward statement: The President and the Governor were hit by all three bullets said to have been fired.

The problem is not one of fact but of integrity. There never was any doubt of the missed bullet. That James Tague was injured by it and bled from the slight injury was immediately known to the police, who, also, immediately broadcast it (WHITEWASH 158). The Report acknowledges this (R116). The broadcast was by Patrolman L. L. Hill, who told the dispatcher, "I have on: guy that was possibly hit by a ricochet from the bullet off the concrete." Even before this close-to-simultaneous police broadcast, Tague's wounding was known to Deputy Sheriff Eddy R. Walthers, who had gone to that area, several hundred feet from where the assassination was perpetrated, because witnesses reported bullets striking in that area.

Although it was known - publicly known and officially recorded - both the FBI and Secret Service pretended it did not happen and accounted for all three shots they admit were fired by having the men hit by all, thus not conceding or accounting for the bullet both knew "missed and caused Tague's injury. When the Commission wanted examination made of the curbstone struck by this "missed" bullet, the FBI Dallas office pretended it could not be found, even though it had been photographed immediately and the photos were available to it, as were the photographers. As late as July 17, 1964, Dallas FBI was telling the Commission it could not find where the bullet struck. This is consistent with its certain knowledge that, if three bullets only were fired and each struck the President or the Governor several hundred feet from Tague, one of these three could not have looped its way all the way down to about twenty feet from the Triple Underpass and still have had enough energy to damage the curb and spray concrete or fragments with enough force to wound Tague on the cheek.

J. Edgar Hoover, ultimately, assured the Commission that this "missed" bullet could not be associated with the car bullets. This unwelcome intelligence was postponed until quite late in the proceedings - August 12, 1964 - nine months after the assassination - the month before the tremendous printed Report was issued (WHITEWASH 158-9). Should the reader wonder if this is the vaunted FBI derring-do that radio, TV, newspapers, magazines, cereal boxes, bubble-gum wrappers, and everything else accessible to the FBI's publicists dun into our minds, if this is that unsurpassable FBI speed, perfection of science and infallible efficiency constantly touted, I quote Marina Oswald's immortal words, "That is the FBI for you."

Bitter-ending by the Dallas office got it nowhere. The Commission sent FBI Photographic Expert Lyndal L. Shaneyfelt down to Dallas to find that curbstone with the bullet mark. If this is a new kind of FBI bird-dogging, it worked. Shaneyfelt did what any high school student of average intelligence would have done. He got the existing pictures, the photographers, went where they said, looked where they said, and there it was - where it had been without moving from November 22, 1963. That curbstone's first move was when Shaneyfelt dug it up and took it back to Washington with him.

Belatedly, that curbstone also was transferred to the National

57

chives, where I examined it. Some conscientious soul, no doubt a
ickler for perfection, seems to have patched that flaw with concrete
: different shade and texture. But perhaps it is neater to have a
atched curbstone to enrich the national heritage rather than the old,
punctured one. All it hides is evidence.*

If nothing was said about it, this is not because nothing was
known about it. From the very first, this "missed" bullet loomed as a
very big obstacle to be hurdled by the Commission's no-conspiracy predetermination. Had the Commission, in the end, ignored the "missed"
bullet, there would have been a frightful scandal, for it was too well
known.

The single-bullet theory was less hazardous. The Commission,
clearly, felt that this permitted it to stay within the artificial three-
bullet limitation that, it also felt, entitled it to claim there had been
no conspiracy. It persisted in the pretense that, although the best shot
it could get could not duplicate what it attributed to Oswald, that duffer nonetheless <u>had</u> done it.

This might be termed the "Three-Monkeys" Theory.

The only alternative was the admission of conspiracy. Oswald
could not have fired three such shots, as the evidence proved. To attempt to attribute four shots to either him or that junky rifle was to
tempt disaster. It was safer to attribute both magic and intelligence
to that super-Wagnerian Bullet 399.

At this point, with this partial recounting of some of the evidence suppressed from what was published, omitted from the "conclusions",
and quietly avoided by all the official participants, fresh in the reader's mind, I should like to remind him of the felicitous phrase used by
Wesley J. Liebeler, Epstein's legal Horatio defending the Commission
bridge:

"Truth was our only client."

The FBI and the Secret Service served the same client.

*See pp. 460-1;608-9.

6. CLIENT TRUTH

Many bizarre and inexplicable questions remained when the autopsy protocol was completed. There were even more puzzles, less understandable and not justifiable, when the Commission issued its Report and went out of business. One that struck me on my initial study of the testimony and the examination of the medical witnesses by the Commission, meaning, really, by Arlen Specter, is the utter inadequacy of the deposition taken from Dr. Robert N. McClelland.

McClelland is an experienced surgeon. He taught surgery at the University of Texas, Southwestern Medical School, where he was associate professor of surgery. He testified March 21, 1964 (6H30ff.).

On November 22, 1963, he was a busy surgeon. He attended both the President and the Governor. According to Parkland Hospital operative records, he assisted Dr. Tom Shires in the surgery on Governor Connally's thigh until 4:20 p.m. These records to not list all the doctors in attendance. The senior physicians are noted.

Apparently the first thing McClelland did after he scrubbed up following this surgery was to prepare a "Statement Regarding Assassination of President Kennedy". This is dated 25 minutes later, at 4:45 p.m. The first 22 pages of Volume 17 of the exhibits are a series of "Medical reports from doctors at Parkland Hospital ... concerning treatment of President Kennedy ...". McClelland's is on pages 11-12. He wrote it in longhand on the hospital's printed "Admission note" form.

Later, all the doctors were under considerable Commission and public pressure because their observations when they examined and treated the President were not consistent with the subsequent official version of the shooting and injuries. There is, as I noted (WHITEWASH 180), the question of whether there was both perjury and the subornation of perjury in some of it.

During the tracheotomy, McClelland "was standing at the end of the stretcher on which the President was lying, immediately at the head ..." (6H32) where "I was in such a position that I could very closely examine the head wound" (6H33). So, McClelland is one doctor who was in a position to and who did "very closely examine" the front of the President's head. Emphasis is added to the language of his contemporaneous report:

"Cause of death was due to massive head and brain injury from a gunshot wound of the left temple." After close study of his testimony, I commented (WHITEWASH 169), "It is perhaps significant that ... Doctor McClelland was not asked to retract this conclusion, and he reaffirmed his statement."

What struck me immediately and then baffled me is this: Here was a senior surgeon, an experienced and competent man who, after close examination, said "the cause of death" was "a gunshot wound of the left temple", exactly opposite to the Commission's conclusions. Yet in his questioning, Arlen Specter avoided this left-temple wound cause of death that urgently required examination, as though it would cause an explosion. Specter interrogated McClelland about many things, but not this, the most significant thing in his contemporaneous statement.*

Instead, at the end of the brief deposition, Specter showed him the statement, asked him to identify it as his own and the signature as his, and then asked, "Are all the facts set forth true and correct ...",

*See pp. 382-3.

59

to which McClelland swore affirmatively (6H35).

This is an odd mechanism Specter evolved. He has, since issuance of the Report, been glib in his various explanations. Presumably, he will have one concocted to address this. But when he had, under oath and facing him, a second doctor who also had said that the President had been shot from the front - a statement that wrecked the entire case Specter in particular was building, the case against Oswald as a lone and unassisted assassin - Specter, for the second time, elected not to confront this second doctor with the medical evidence destructive of that prosecution case he was putting together. Whether he went into this with McClelland before he began to take the deposition the record does not show and we may never know. The record does show (6H35-6) that they did discuss the testimony off the record - before it began official]

And it does show that McClelland did reaffirm his statement, the essence of which is that President Kennedy's "fatal" wound was from the front, not the back. *

That Specter would dare ignore this essential evidence - the evidence that ruined the pet case he was building - raises questions not about his competence, which is beyond question, but of his integrity and that of the entire Commission and its Report.

It is Specter who, more than anyone else, sold the Commission and through it the world on the single-bullet theory, which alone made possi- ble the invalid conclusion that Oswald was the lone assassin. Without it, there is little doubt Oswald would have been "exonerated", as the evidence compels. When confronted by a direct challenge to it, Specter asked the doctor about everything but that, the one thing above all he should have asked about.

That he did not - did not dare - is enough, particularly when McClelland reaffirmed that the President had been shot from the front - under oath and to Specter's face.

McClelland was not alone (6H48), although Specter, who was in charge of this aspect of the investigation, made it seem that way to anyone studying the record. Specter controlled what he asked the doc- tors, thus leaving out of their testimony what he wanted out and empha- sizing or deemphasizing to suit his own and very clear preconceptions and desires. He also controlled whom he did not ask to testify.

Specter twice had Dr. Malcolm O. Perry, who had performed the tracheotomy on the President in Dallas, under oath and facing him (3H- 366ff.,6H7ff.), the second time before the members of the Commission. Through the most elaborate evasions and pretenses (WHITEWASH 169-70) he avoided also the similar statement by Perry to the autopsy doctors, that the President's non-fatal injury had been inflicted from the front (WHITEWASH 198).

One of the doctors Specter did not call - whose name is not men- tioned in the evidence because it was kept out by Specter - is Dr. David Stewart, who later moved to Gallatin, Tennessee. Dr. Stewart would have sworn to exactly what Dr. McClelland said - that the President was killer by a shot from the front, which, very obviously, Oswald, had he been in the sixth-floor window and some 300 feet behind the President, could not have fired.

Dr. Stewart made a Rotary Club speech that was reported in the New Lebanon, Tennessee, Democrat of March 30, 1967. At 8:15 a.m. April 10, he appeared on the Joe Dolan Show, then on KNEW, Oakland, California.

Stewart "was in attendance at the time" of the treatment rendered all three assassination patients, but "primarily my time was spent with Governor Connally and later with Lee Oswald". Another group of physicia was taking care of the President on his entry to the emergency room, "bu of course I am aware of their findings as such".

Dolan said he was particularly concerned with the "statement abou the shot" that killed the President "coming from the front". Stewart said, "Yes, sir. This was the finding of all the physicians who were in attendance. There was a small wound in the left front of the President' head and there was a quite massive wound of exit at the right backside of the head and it was felt by all of the physicians at the time to be a wound of entry which went in the front. And this was later corroborated, I think, by the films which showed the President with a rather violent lurch backward."

Stewart is quite right. This is the first of the incredible thing I noted in my very first examination of the Zapruder movie when I saw it in early 1966. I reported this in WHITEWASH II. As I record in PHOTO-GRAPHIC WHITEWASH (pp.25,145), the Commission simply reversed the picture in printing them to make it seem that the President's head moved forward. It did not. It snapped sharply backward before the President fell over to his left, onto his wife.

"And there was blood and brain substance found on one of the po-licemen riding behind on a motorcycle," Stewart said, to which Dolan added, "Behind to the left." This, too, is correct. That motorcycle policeman was Billy Hargis. He was, as Dolan pointed out, both to the left and behind the President, making officially inexplicable the gener-ous splashing of the President's blood and brains he and his cycle got. This spewing to the left of matter from an explosion allegedly out of a defect only on the right is inconsistent, officially unexplained and en-tirely avoided. Mrs. Connally (WHITEWASH 3), who was on the President's left, testified, "... it felt like buckshot falling all over us ... it was the matter, brain tissue ...". Governor Connally (WHITEWASH 5), who was in front of the President, testified, "Immediately I could see on my clothes ... on the interior of the car ... brain tissue as big as almost my thumb (sic)." In his interrogation of AP Photographer James W. Altgens (PHOTOGRAPHIC WHITEWASH 70,203), Wesley Liebeler suppressed what Altgens told the FBI, "that pieces of flesh, blood and bones appeared to fly from the right side of the President's head and pass in front of Mrs. Kennedy to the left of the Presidential limousine".

Instead of addressing this inconsistency, a seeming impossibility, rather than confronting unquestioned evidence that could invalidate the case they were building and the Report they planned, the Commission staff pretended the evidence did not exist.

Dr. Stewart interpreted this phenomenon as one that "completely substantiated the finding that this was a left frontal entry wound" and said the other doctors also did. He also declared the obvious, what any layman can also know with certainty, that it would be "impossible for a marksman in the sixth floor" window "to have created that kind of wound, shooting from behind".

These omissions are really suppressions. They are not unique in Specter's record with the Commission and he alone is not responsible for them, as the until-now secret record proves. Other vital evidence en-tirely opposite to the predetermined conclusions with which the Commis-sion began its work were blatantly suppressed. Expert witnesses, examined in advance by Specter, and others who declared themselves and their knowl-edge of science and evidence to be opposed to these official preconcep-tions, were either not called or were carefully questioned to avoid that to which they indicated in advance they would not swear.

Specter is the chief offender. This, too, is consistent with his subsequent record of public dishonesty, a record he converted into po-litical profit during his mayoralty campaign by his late June appearance on the CBS "specials". After the appearance of WHITEWASH, he refused a dozen or more requests to confront me on radio and TV, including several repeated invitations in his own city, Philadelphia. Instead, he preferred and extensively exploited partisan, mass-distribution sources, like UPI, U.S. News and World Report and CBS.

His disgraceful record prompted me, in writing WHITEWASH II, much of Part II of which is devoted to him and this record, to declare, "he lied without restraint, misrepresented without inhibition" (p.103). These I there described as "harsh words" and said, "They are not used by acci-dent. If untrue they are actionable. If Specter thinks they are untrue, let him sue and confront ... for the first time in the entire fake in-quest an opposing lawyer." He was, as he remains, silent, for I also published the proof of these charges with them.

His appearances on the CBS shows were also characterized by lies. By this I mean not accidental errors, such as an uninformed man might innocently make, but false statements the truth of which Specter knew. Here are a few readily apparent samples:

In the second of these shows he "explained" what was described as a "theory besides the single bullet theory, that would support the conclusions in the Report":

SPECTER: The Commission concluded that it was probable that one bullet inflicted the wound on the President's neck, and all of the wounds on Governor Connally. But you could have three separate bullets striking under the sequence as we know them. For example, the President could have been struck at frame 186 of the Zapruder film, which is a number given to the Zapruder film. Then Governor Connally could have been struck some 42 frames later, which would be a little over two and a quarter seconds at about frame 228 or 229; and then the third shot could have hit President Kennedy's head at frame 313, which was pretty clearly established. So that it is not indispensable to have the single bullet conclusion in order to come to the basic finding that Oswald was the sole assassin.

Now that his single-bullet theory was exploded, Specter preferred the cold wreckage of the old "Tague didn't bleed" fiction to its hot fragments. As the preceding chapter shows, there is no possibility that Specter did not know this statement on CBS was completely false. He also knew that at Frame 186 a bullet could not have had the trajectory attributed to Bullet 399 and there is no evidence of a hit at Frames 228 or 229.

In the last of the series, he volunteered this statement:

When it came time to select the individuals to serve as assistant counsel and general counsel, men were chosen from various parts of the United States who had no connection with government.

Again, Specter knew better. These men were his former associates, men with whom he was still in contact. He knew them and their careers very well. But if he "forgot", the Report documents it (Biographical Appendix IV,475ff.). This is not just a lie; it is a whopper. Let us see who these men "chosen from various parts of the United States" were and how they "had no connection with government".

The Commission's boss, its general counsel, J. Lee Rankin, was Solicitor General of the United States. His staff director, Howard Willens, was loaned by and returned to the same Department of Justice for which Rankin had worked. All the Commission members were or had been high government officials, and all but one, Allen Dulles, formerly head of the CIA, then enjoyed government responsibilities. More than half of the fourteen assistant counsel had been government employees!

Twelve "staff members" are listed in the Report (R479-81). Of these, all but one had been government employees or were at the time of their appointments to the Commission.

But Specter told the world-wide audience of CBS, knowing better all the time, that "men were chosen ... who had no connection with government".

So we know why, when I called Arlen Specter, father of the single-bullet theory, one of the two most important assistant counsel, the man most responsible for the corrupted medical and autopsy testimony and a political climber whose career was made possible by his political apostasy (in Oswald they called it "defection"), a man who "lied without restraint" and challenged him to sue me, he did not.

My purpose was not spectacle, not sensation, but to establish a record, a record as the law recognizes it, not as he and his associates corrupted it in their official Commission function, a record before a judge and a jury, a record of fact tested by that machine for the establishment of truth, as lawyers call cross-examination.

Never once did I exploit this challenge to sell my books, not
in his city, where it could have been used by his political opponents
When I made broadcasts in his city on WHITEWASH II, I never once men-
mentioned it. Of course, this made it easier for him to ignore it, bu
it also did not saddle him alone with a responsibility he shared with
so many others equally guilty of pretending lies are facts.

However, in pursuing his ambition and his attempts at self-justification, Specter has paced his lying with an assortment of devices rang
ing from the unbagging of cats to hiding behind the Chief Justice's
judicial robes. This and his false statements and misrepresentations
are important because of the function he had on the Commission and because of his until-now secret record in that function.

He was interviewed by Joseph R. Daughen of the Philadelphia Bulletin. Daughen's long account of it appeared August 28, 1966. In it he
quotes Specter as saying of the autopsy and what derives from it that it
"rests squarely on the integrity of Humes, Boswell and Finck. We are
talking about the integrity of the doctors and the autopsy."

At that point I wrote (WHITEWASH II,100), "We are also talking
about the integrity of Arlen Specter."

In Arlen Specter's integrity, that of the doctors he named, the
members of the Commission, in fact, that of the United States Government
and all of its people, was vested.

After his CBS appearances - after I obtained a transcript of his
remarks - and prior to writing this, I offered him a chance to withdraw
or retract his false statements that I believe cannot be accidental.
Simple acknowledgment of error could not begin to catch up with the enormous audience that saw and heard Arlen Specter, candidate for public office and greater public trust, tell these lies world-wide on CBS. His
reply to my letter was a reiteration that he had been nothing less than
accurate.

"I have full confidence in the accuracy of all the statements
which I have made concerning the work of the President's Commission on
the Assassination of President Kennedy," he wrote.

On the remote chance that this paragon of political virtue did
not recall what he had said, or the even lesser likelihood, that his intent had been distorted in editing, I sent him photocopies and asked
that he read them and reaffirm that he had been only truthful.

To this the man then but two months away from the election to
choose the mayor of one of the world's largest cities replied that his
previous letter required "no amplification". In short, he persisted in
his lies - this time for political benefit.

Any inquiry into the investigation of the assassination inevitably
is into the integrity of those who conducted it. From that vast suppression of what was in the files and known, should have been made public and
wasn't, I dug up a number of other documents that, to the best of my
knowledge, had never before been published if, indeed, seen by anyone
not in official position. They relate very much to this question of integrity, that of Specter and of everyone else involved. We shall examine
them after a backgrounding look into how the client truth was served.

Whether or not they planned in advance the lies they would tell
to lie out of the mess of the Report, government officials had them ready
when first confronted with the first book that proved they lied. Had
personal knowledge not been represented, it might be possible to consider
this misinformation as less than lies, perhaps merely error. A major
newspaper printed them, and fed them to other papers, possibly in good
faith, and launched and helped achieve acceptability for the line Arlen
Specter and others were to follow.

I know, because I am responsible for that newspaper interest.
The book was WHITEWASH: THE REPORT ON THE WARREN REPORT; the newspaper,
the Washington Post.

Prior to writing that book, I offered co-authorship to the _Post_, soon as I finished my analysis of the Report. This was shortly after was issued in the fall of 1964. The _Post_ decided against my offer, ich was that some of its staff write the book while I continued my investigations.

In May 1965, about three months after I completed the book, a Congressman friend who was also a member of the House Judiciary Committee, within whose jurisdiction consideration would fall were Congress to interest itself in the Report, read the book while recuperating from major surgery. After he was again up and around, he conferred with Alfred Friendly, then managing editor of the _Post_. Friendly was unwilling to believe what was reported to him, unwilling to read the manuscript and unwilling to assign it to a member of his staff. He made the compromise offer that the Congressman select several chapters; he would then have several members of the staff examine them simultaneously. The Congressman, on his part, wanted them to read these chapters, which I reluctantly designated (what a way to determine the content of a book!), in his presence. Because this was an awkward arrangement, requiring a number of busy people all to be free at the same and a predictable time, it never was consummated.

Months later I suggested a compromise to my Congressman friend: Would the _Post_ ask a single trusted staff member to read the book, outside of working hours?

This was agreed to and on September 24, 1965, I delivered it to Laurence Stern, national editor and one of the experienced staff men the _Post_ had sent to Dallas to investigate the assassination.

Larry Stern also stayed busy. When a considerable period of time elapsed and I heard nothing from him, needing that copy, I asked for the return of the book. I got it on November 24, 1965. His marker indicated Larry had read but the first three, the shortest, chapters, but Stern said he had skimmed more and when I could again spare a copy and he had the time he would like to read the rest.

On February 17, 1966, the _Post_ ran an editorial sympathetic to the plight of Russian writers, whom it felt were abused and denied the appearance of their writings. That day I wrote Friendly a needling letter, telling him, "It is as easy to cudgel the other fellow as for pigs to find truffles ... You would cast the mote from the Soviet eye - and with this I am in complete accord - but leave it in your own eye." Then I reminded him of the history of WHITEWASH and of that of the Washington _Post_ with it.

In his response of March 25, Friendly regretted that "a multitude of events conspired against" his answering earlier, defended the decisions of the more than 50 publishers who had before then declined the book (which neither he nor any member of his staff had read) and, in attempted justification, used this, to me, fortuitous expression:

Obviously, if you could demonstrate that the circumstances of the murder and the nature of the investigation were different in major degree than those we have been led to believe, you would not merely have an interesting account but the most sensational story since the assassination itself. Any publisher who provided you the vehicle for such a demonstration would be showered with riches and honor.

He concluded, in effect, that the publishers were correct or I was paranoid.

I quoted these two sentences back at him and asked, "Yet, with the value this could have to a newspaper, with syndication rights available, you will not personally make the simple gesture required to see for yourself whether or not I have what I say. You will not, for your own responsibility as a journalist and an editor, for your obligations to the owners of your paper, if not, indeed, to history, let me prove it, and to you?"

That threat, that the "riches and honors" might escape his stockholders, did it. Friendly invited me in to see him and we arranged for my return on April 5. He was then too busy. Five days later I wrote to suggest that if he were going to stay busy perhaps he might have someone else read the book for him.

April 13 Friendly found about five minutes and I showed him photocopies of the first and eighteenth pages of the FBI report of December 9, which I believed would be a graphic way of indicating there might be something wrong with the Report. He recalled the Commission acknowledged that there had been the "missed" bullet and could see that the FBI accounted for three shots without it and without accounting for the wound in the front of the President's neck.

April 18 he wrote me that he was about to go abroad for several months "and whatever the Post is going to do with your manuscript, somebody else has got to do it. I feel sure that Larry Stern will fall to the problem with dispatch, either handling it himself or getting another qualified, high class executive person to do it."

The next day I saw Larry Stern. He continued too busy and assigned the reading to Dan Kurzman, an experienced investigative reporter who had had similar troubles effecting publication of his own book exposing Dominican Dictator Trujillo, support of whom had been official United States policy. Meanwhile, I proceeded with an earlier decision to put the book into general circulation as a private printing. There was no real alternative.

Kurzman, too, is a busy man. It took him some time to get into the book. When he did, it excited him. By mid-May he finished it, with enthusiasm for it. It was about the best "investigative reporting job" he had seen and read "like a non-fiction detective story". He and Stern and I met in the Post's coffeeshop and discussed what to do to test it, which they seemed to feel they had to do, instead of checking it against the cited sources of the entire text, all of which the Post had in its library. We agreed that they would confront Willens, former Commission staff director returned to the Department of Justice, for whom Stern had respect. He or Stern did not want me present.

Instead, I prepared a short series of questions on the autopsy and the single-bullet theory taking up but a single page. We agreed that if Willens disputed me I would be given the opportunity to cite the evidence

They saw Willens. By appointment, I was in the Post's newsroom when they returned. Kurzman told me they had gotten only disturbing evasions and satisfactory answers to nothing. Stern then told me that while there had been no decision on syndication there would be a story and I would be credited with what I had taken to the Post a year earlier.

This was just prior to an election in the Dominican Republic. Dan Kurzman was the Post's Dominican expert. He was sent there. Richard Harwood, also an experienced investigative reporter, was assigned to this story. It turned out that in a week he had to read WHITEWASH, familiarize himself with the Report and the 26 appended volumes, and then with "Inquest", Edward J. Epstein's book due for publication the end of the following month, of which the Post had obtained an advance copy.

This was an impossible assignment for any reporter, regardless of competence. In the time he had, Harwood could not begin to read this great mass of material, let alone understand all of it. His story appeared in a major front-page display on May 29. The net effect of the inadequate handling was to convince those who, like Specter, were responsible for the monstrous and unnecessary second tragedy, the fake inquest, that they could get away with almost anything so far as the press is concerned. Yet it also cast some doubt on the Report.

Harwood acknowledged that:

On December 18, 1963, the Washington Post and other newspapers reported on the basis of rumors from Dallas, that the first bullet to strike the President "was found deep in his shoulder". This report was confirmed prior to publication by the FBI.

The Post's December 18, 1963, story was written by its honored science writer, Nate Haseltine, whose scientific connections are the best. Those of the Post with the FBI are not as good, for it is not friendly to J. Edgar Hoover. Haseltine did not attribute his information to "rumors from Dallas". The headline on it read, "Kennedy Autopsy Report". He attributed the information to the autopsy report, not the FBI. In part, he wrote:

President Kennedy was shot twice, both times from the rear, and would readily have survived the first bullet which was found deep in his shoulder.

The second bullet to hit the President, however, tore off the right rear portion of his head so destructively as to be "completely incompatible with life". A fragment was deflected and passed out the front of the throat, creating an erroneous belief he may have been shot from two angles.

These are the findings of the as yet unofficial report of the pathologists who performed the autopsy ... the first shot hitting him high in the back shoulder (sic) ...

The disclosure that a bullet hit the President in the back shoulder, 5 to 7 inches below the collar line, came as a complete surprise to the Dallas hospital.

If this was inaccurate, it was not corrected. The Post did not retract. More than a month later, on January 26, 1964, The New York Times reported largely the same thing, saying, in part:

The third bullet, according to an autopsy in Bethesda Naval Hospital in Maryland, ripped away a portion of the back of the President's head on the right side. Fragments from the bullets cut a wound in the President's throat and damaged the windshield of the Presidential limousine.

Investigators are now satisfied that the first of three bullets hit the President in the back of his right shoulder, several inches below the collar line. That bullet lodged in his shoulder. The second bullet wounded Governor John B. Connally, of Texas.

If this was in the autopsy, there was an official conspiracy of unimaginable magnitude, for it is not in the official version subsequentl published. Dr. Humes swore he had completed that on Sunday, November 24.

Harwood devoted much space to justification of the error of the two major FBI summary reports, CDs 1 and 107, and an inadequate representation of the medical evidence. In the limited time he had, it would seem he had been forced to depend upon official sources. Of the first FBI report he wrote:

This report, the FBI said last week, was based on the medical evidence at that time. But there is other evidence that it was based on nothing more than hearsay.

The autopsy on the President began at Bethesda Naval Hospital at about 8 p.m. on the night of Nov. 22.

Wound Confused Doctors.

Two FBI agents who were present overheard Dr. Humes, Dr. Finck and Dr. J. T. Boswell speculate about the President's shoulder wound. The doctors were confused by it because an incision made in the front of the President's throat in Dallas obscured the exit wound.

Before the three doctors at Bethesda had completed the autopsy and before they had traced the path of the bullet from the President's shoulder to his throat, the FBI observers left the room and called in a report that the bullet had not passed through the President's body.

Incredibly, this verbal report became the basis of the erroneous statement that appears in the Dec. 9, five-volume summary submitted to the Warren Commission.

The official autopsy report which contradicts the FBI was in the hands of the Secret Service, not the Bureau, and may never have been supplied to the FBI.

In any case, the basic error was repeated in the Jan. 13 report from the FBI which unaccountably acknowledges that there was an exit wound in the President's throat.

There was no other "medical evidence at that time", only that of the doctors and the autopsy. What the FBI agents reported is exactly what the autopsy doctors said and believed, as they testified to before the Commission.

The autopsy doctors never "traced the path" of the non-fatal bullet, and they did not claim to have done so (WHITEWASH 179;2H368). Of this we shall see much more in coming chapters.

If both FBI agents had left the room together for a single phone call, with a telephone in the room, which is highly improbable, they also returned and remained there for the remainder of the autopsy and through the embalming, leaving at about 4 a.m. Their phone call was about 9 p.m. The autopsy examination began about 8 p.m.

To say, as Harwood was told and repeated, that the FBI did not have any of the eight original copies of the autopsy report or any of the countless Xerox copies made is to dispute Hoover himself, for he testified (WHITEWASH II,223) that "when President Johnson returned to Washington he communicated with me within the first 24 hours, and asked the Bureau to pick up the investigation of the assassination because as you are aware, there is no federal jurisdiction for such an investigation ... However, the President has the right to request the Bureau to make special investigations ..."

In his testimony, as the contemporaneous newspapers also did, Hoover made clear that from the first he and the FBI were in charge of the investigation. The Commission's files prove that the Secret Service then turned its evidence over to the FBI. The FBI's was to be the definitive investigation, "prompt and thorough". Hoover testified that "it was the desire of the President to have this report completed by the Bureau just as quickly as possible and as thoroughly as possible ..."

Without the official autopsy this was impossible. It is not possible to believe that this could have been done without access to that autopsy report, or that the FBI could not get it and did not have it. And, as we have already seen from one of the suppressed FBI reports I found buried in the Archives, the results of the autopsy were promptly communicated to the FBI.

Harwood did acknowledge that same error was repeated in its supplementary report, after the FBI officially admitted it had a copy of the autopsy report.

But suppose the facile lies were correct. Can the FBI be trusted with anything at all if it can err so grievously when it investigates and reports to his successor on the murder of an American President? Can its word ever be taken, in or out of court, in any kind of proceeding? Should anyone ever be convicted on FBI testimony if it can make such spectacular, unequaled "mistakes"? Can it - should it - ever again be trusted to make any kind of investigation?

The indignant editorials that could have been expected had this been done by any agency other than St. Edgar's were totally missing.

Of the medical evidence, Harwood wrote:

The second contradiction involves the conflicting medical testimony on the likelihood that one bullet wounded both Mr. Kennedy and Mr. Connally.
The bullet which caused these wounds was found and was virtually intact. It weighed about 158 grains, as against an original weight of about 161 grains.
Commander Humes and Lt. Col. Finck, the presidential autopsists, doubted that this bullet could have caused all of Gov. Connally's wounds because they had read a medical report from Dallas describing the presence of fragments in his wrist wound. Thus, they thought the bullet must have been broken into fragments rather than emerging intact.
They were unaware that these fragments were miniscule and that Connally's principal surgeon, Dr. Robert Shaw, was convinced that the intact bullet did cause the wounds. The "fragments" it left in

the Governor's body were thin shavings, not much larger than dust
particles.

The final problem--Gov. Connally's own recollection of what hap-
pened--cannot be dismissed.

But his surgeon, Dr. Shaw, had an explanation for that, too. It
is not uncommon, he testified, for people to suffer a wound without
knowing it immediately.

This would account for Mr. Connally's belief that he was not hit
by the first bullet and this explanation is consistent /with his7
failure to hear the "second shot" which he believed caused his wound
and his recollection of the final shot which smashed the President's
skull.

The "single-shot" theory developed by Specter and the Commission,
in other words, is not refuted by the apparent inconsistencies in
the record which Weisberg and Epstein recite.

And so long as that theory holds up, assumptions that there was a
second assassin in Dallas on Nov. 22 can only be assumptions.

All of this was, in advance, disproved in WHITEWASH. Printing it
was but an effort to make an unofficial apology for what could not and
cannot be explained by the evidence. It also is not a reflection of the
Commission's own evidence. But the time pressures imposed upon Harwood
made it impossible for him to understand either source.

The problem was not only the presumed slight loss of metal by this
bullet, but its lack of mutilation or deformity. It was almost pristine,
almost entirely unmutilated, which the doctors found impossible with the
history attributed to it. Rather than being "convinced that the intact
bullet did cause the wounds", Dr. Shaw had actually testified (6H91) that
"I have always felt that" the thigh wound was caused by "a fragment of
it" breaking off in the wrist and "going into his left thigh", exactly
what the newspapers had said and what the police report said. He could
not have said - and he did not say - that an "intact" bullet had also
fragmented.

Shaw also testified that as many as three bullets could have
caused Connally's wounds and that, although a maximum of but 2.4 grains
could be missing from this bullet without weight-loss alone ruling out
the official hypothesis, in the wrist alone "there seem to be more than
three grains of metal ..." (WHITEWASH 174). There were, of course, in
addition to the bullet fragments in the wrist, more than enough to end
this speculation, other fragments in the chest and thigh.

Shaw is not accurately described as Connally's "principal surgeon". He was in charge of one of the three operations; he was not in
charge of the case. Dr. Shires, who was - and who alone of the Dallas
doctors testified in a deposition taken by Specter that there was additional fragmentation in the Governor's chest (WHITEWASH 174) - was not
presented to the members of the Commission, although he was in charge of
the case. His testimony that there was metal in the Governor's chest
could account for this "oversight" of not calling the man in charge to
give testimony to the members. If not that alone, then perhaps his testimony that the Secret Service manufactured medical "evidence" (WHITEWAS
177,199) helped.

Shaw did not explain away Connally's testimony or his recollection. Whether or not, in general, people "suffer a wound without knowing it immediately" is not relevant, nor does it explain away the fact
that Connally heard the first shot, an impossibility if it had struck
him, for bullets travel faster than the speed of sound and the shock
would have blocked his nerves. What Shaw actually testified to, as did
the other doctors questioned, is that "in the case of a wound /sic7
which strikes a bony substance, such as a rib, usually the reaction is
quite prompt" (WHITEWASH 174). Connally's bones in three parts of his
body were smashed and struck by whatever bullet or bullets caused his
wounds.

This and other fact for which there now is neither space nor need
hardly validate the conclusion that I did not "refute" the "'single-shot
theory", nor are the errors in the Report merely "inconsistencies". But
with this the first major newspaper treatment of the first documented

refutation of the Report and Specter's part in it, is there any wonder that Specter could be led to believe he could get away with anything? That he could lie with impunity?

The falsity of the Report does not rest on the single-bullet theory alone, either. None of its conclusions are tenable. The _Post_, for example, would not and did not address the evidence showing Oswald fired no shots. It admitted

> very considerable doubt about the principal conclusions of the principal conclusions of the Warren Commission that "the shots which killed President Kennedy and wounded Governor Connally were fired by Lee Harvey Oswald." They have no bearing on Oswald's involvement but, if true, they point unmistakably to the involvement of at least one other assassin.

The Commission handled this crucial problem, in effect, by rendering a highly misleading verdict:

> "Although it is not necessary to any essential findings of the Commission to determine just which shot hit Gov. Connally, there is very persuasive evidence from the experts to indicate that the same bullet which pierced the President's throat also caused Gov. Connally's wounds. However, Gov. Connally's testimony and certain other factors have given rise to some differences of opinion as to this probability but there is no doubt in the mind of any member of the Commission that all the shots which caused the President's and Gov. Connally's wounds were fired from the sixth floor of the Texas School Book Depository."

Harwood did nail this monumental _non sequitur:_

> Contrary to what the Commission reported, it was not only "necessary" but absolutely essential to determine which shot hit the Governor.

He then quoted Assistant Counsel Norman Redlich as saying that if "they were hit by separate bullets ... there were two assassins". Here the _Post_ and Harwood left it, unresolved.

This is not nor is it intended as a personal attack on Harwood, who is one of the better investigative reporters and who was confronted with an impossible situation. It is, however, an indispensable part of the overall story of the assassination, for this was the first major journalistic treatment of any book critical of the Report, the _Post_ is a major opinion-former, and the same story got wide attention, influencing public and editorial attitudes.

The responsibility is not Harwood's but that of the then-editor of the _Post_, James Russell Wiggins. Despite his oft-quoted pontifications about a free press, Wiggins cast himself and the paper he controlled in the role of apologist for government, and there was nothing those subordinate to him could do about it.

Louis Heren, then Washington correspondent of _The Times of London_, asked Wiggins to see me so I could discuss the _Post's_ unfairness with him. Heren had read the limited edition of WHITEWASH, had been impressed, and had attempted to interest the publisher of his own books in it.

Wiggins saw me, asked what I wanted, and I said I asked nothing but fairness of the _Post_. He asked me to write him a column-length critique of what he had published.

I did. It was thoroughly documented.

Some time later, he asked me to shorten it.

I did that, too. But he neither published it nor wrote or spoke to me further about it.

Instead, book-review editor Geoffrey Wolff was directed not to review any of the books critical of the Report on the spurious ground that they required a lawyer for proper assessment. Book reviews _are_ assigned to lawyers where editors deem it necessary. It was not, _in_ this case, necessary in any event. If Harwood, for example, were competent to write this story, he was no less competent to review the book. The effect was to see to it that WHITEWASH alone of these books would not be reviewed in the Post. It, the first, had to be a private printing. Private printings are ignored by the syndicated book-review supplement the Post uses. As I then accurately predicted in writing to Wolff, this meant that all the critical books except WHITEWASH would be reviewed by the Post. All were, in this supplement.

Wiggins did not stop here, however. He later serialized the sycophantic writing favoring the Report.

If it was too late to undo the harm Wiggins did, the Post and Harwood were later commendably honest about the effect he had had on the policies and content of the paper while he controlled it. In an editorial article on "The News Business" printed July 27, 1971, under the title, "Have Newspapers Muffed Job of Informing on Vietnam?" - which is also a remarkably honest mea culpa on that question - Harwood did set the record straight.

After saying about what The New York Times and the Post had reported of Viet Nam that "into the 1960s" they "continued to accept the basic assumptions of the previous decade", which is to say the official government line, he added that "In the case of the Post, it was only after a change in editors in late 1968 that doubts about those assumptions began to be expressed ..."

Or, not until after Wiggins' departure - to represent the United States at the United Nations.

In that euphoric moment when the Post's writers returned from their meeting with Willens, before the Wiggins influence exerted itself, I assured them that in the National Archives, in which I was then already probing for the graves of the numerous official dead cats, we would find more of the proofs required for the recapture of the national honor and the solution of the crime. What Wiggins saw to it that the Post would not want is in this book.

It includes more than the single-bullet theory. It addresses the suppressed and misrepresented medical evidence and the integrity of the investigation and those involved in it, most of all Arlen Specter's and his work.

7. 23 SKIDOO

Finding Specter's - the Commission's - skeletons did not require opening all the official graves. Indeed, the bulk alone makes this impossible. The files are estimated to total 300 cubic feet. In files, where millions of words can be contained in a single cubic foot, the total is enormous, incalculable. The unpleasant truth is that, once one learns to skip around the extensive junk, the trivia and the great volume of the irrelevant, it is almost impossible not to stub an investigative toe on a promising stone.

When there is a murder, the autopsy and the medical evidence are, of course, essential evidence.

Had Harwood merely phoned the District of Columbia morgue, as I did, he would have learned that its officials would not have been satisfied with that kind of inquest when investigating the murder of a skid-row bum, let alone that of a President.

Only because he failed to look into it did Harwood not learn that those present at the actual autopsy were limited to military medical personnel, except for the assigned Secret Service and FBI agents, the former apparently to keep an eye on the corpse and the latter to eye them.

This, in the files, leads inevitably to Specter, what he knew, what he knew and kept out of the record that, as the Commission's lawyer in charge, he was responsible for, and the alleged basis of the FBI's above-quoted reports.

What one finds here is contradictory to what Specter adduced and to the Report, those parts of which Specter presumably drafted for Commission signature.

The reports of FBI Baltimore ᵁffice Agents James W. Sibert and Francis X. O'Neill were not printed when the Commission had 26 very large volumes it devoted to what, lacking any appropriate designation, has been termed "evidence". Not in the estimated 10,000,000 words was there space for these accounts of who was present at the autopsy and what was observed there before and during the examination. The reports are in the Commission's fifth file.

From the official record built by Specter, one would gather that only these agents and Autopsy Surgeons James J. Humes and J. Thornton Boswell of the Navy and Pierre Finck of the Army were present. This is false. Aside from those who entered on various missions, 13 others were there. Sibert and O'Neill, who may be excused their misspelling of names, if not incompleteness of which we shall learn, list these others with the introduction, "The following individuals attended the Autopsy":

Adm. C. B. HOLLOWAY, U.S. Navy, Commanding Officer of the U.S. Naval Medical Center, Bethesda;
Adm. BERKLEY, U.S. Navy, the President's personal physician;
Commander JAMES J. HUMES, Chief Pathologist, Bethesda Naval Hospital, who conducted autopsy;
Capt. JAMES H. STONER, JR., Commanding Officer, U.S. Naval Medical School, Bethesda;
Mr. JOHN T. STRINGER, JR., Medical photographer;
JAMES H. EBERSOLE;

LLOYD E. RAIHS;
J. G. RUDNICKI;
PAUL K. O'CONNOR;
J. C. JENKINS;
JERROL F. CRESTER;
EDWARD F. REED;
JAMES METZLER.

They specify that others "entered the autopsy room" and note "Lt. Cmdr. GREGG CROSS and Captain DAVID OSBORNE, Chief of Surgery"; "Major General WEHLE, Commanding Officer of the U.S. Military District, Washington, D.C."; "AMC CHESTER H. BOYERS, U.S. Navy ... to type receipts given by FBI and Secret Service for items obtained" (and do not look for these receipts or the itemizations, for they are suppressed from the Report and the printed evidence); these four employees of Gawler's funeral home; "JOHN VAN HAESEN, EDWIN STROBLE, THOMAS ROBINSON and Mr. HAGEN"; "Brigadier General GODFREY McHUGH, Air Force Aide to the President, was also present, as was Dr. GEORGE BAKEMAN, U.S. Navy."

From this, once it is dredged from the official swamp of the suppressed documents, we know that there were not fewer than 23 additional witnesses at the autopsy.

There remained, after Specter finished adducing testimony, the most basic questions about the autopsy, unresolved conflicts and a considerable number of them glossed over. There remained unasked questions and unsought answers, both without justification or excuse.

But not one of these 23 military men, almost all with medical backgrounds and competences, was called as a witness.

There remained the official confusion about the location of the non-fatal injury in the rear of the President's body. Here were 23 more experts who could have provided enlightenment and answers.

They were not called, the answers not sought.

This does not encourage belief that they would have testified in consonance with the official account, that this was a neck wound. Nor does it suggest that the omission of the pictures and X-rays of the autopsy is only in deference to the feelings of the survivors. They were expunged from the record, whereas in any tank-town legal proceeding they would have been required. Anyway, this, the "best evidence" of the autopsy, could have been in evidence and examined but not published.

In his testimony, Dr. Humes said that, although it was "redundant" he did not really know that a tracheotomy had been performed in Dallas and that he phoned Dr. Perry the morning of November 23 - not the night of November 22 while he was conducting the autopsy examination - to find out (WHITEWASH 180).

Sibert and O'Neill also were never called as witnesses. If there was no other reason for it - and there were many, all of which could have made the official verdict more difficult, if not impossible, to render - this language, from the third page of their report, had to be suppressed or the question of perjury had to be faced:

Following the removal of the wrapping /of the President's body7, it was ascertained that ... a tracheotomy had been performed, as well as surgery of the head area, namely, in the top of the skull.

The question of this "surgery of the head area", nowhere mentioned in the testimony, may remain a mystery. It is not a mystery that these agents, unable to spell proper names, knew that "a tracheotomy had been performed". That, and the correct spelling of the uncommon medical term they could have learned only from the doctors.

Harwood's sources in the Department of Justice palmed off on him, and he and the Post accepted, a false explanation of the discrepancies between the FBI reports of December 9 and January 13 and the autopsy protocol. They blamed it on the absence of the FBI agents from the autopsy room and called what was accurately reported and observed "hearsay". This is the source of the still-accepted fiction.

72

The "first incision" of the autopsy was made at 8:15. The phone call reporting the finding of the whole bullet was made at 9:00 p.m. But it was not until "the latter stages of the autopsy" that "Dr. HUMES located an opening which appeared to be a bullet hole which was below the shoulders and two inches to the right of the middle line of the spinal column. This opening was probed by Dr. HUMES with the finger, at which time it was determined that the trajectory of the missile entering at this point had entered at a downward position of 45 to 60 degrees. Further probing determined that the distance traveled by this missile was a short distance inasmuch as the end of the opening could be felt with the finger. Inasmuch as no bullet could be located in the back or any other area of the body ... and inspection revealing there was no point of exit, the individuals performing the autopsy were at a loss to explain why they could find no bullets."

After the agents told Humes of the finding of a bullet at the hospital, he "advised" that "since external cardiac massage had been performed at Parkland Hospital, it was entirely possible that through such movement the bullet had worked its way back out of the point of entry ..." From this, "Dr. HUMES stated that the pattern was clear that the one bullet had entered the President's back and had worked its way out of the body during external cardiac massage ...".

Fractured as this FBI syntax is, it does not stand alone. Other documents to be cited and what I have already printed (especially in WHITEWASH, "The Doctors and the Autopsy", particularly p.185; and WHITEWASH II, "Strange Inquest") are corroborative. It is not really addressed by the official explanations the press prefers to accept, and it does disprove the official explanation of the murder. It is abundantly substantiated by the testimony of Secret Service Agents Roy H. Kellerman and William R. Greer (Specter took no sworn testimony from Sibert and O'Neill although he did interview them, very briefly).

It is not hearsay, but is the personal observation of the agents, confirmed in detail by those others present who were called as witnesses. It cannot be dismissed, as the FBI persuaded Harwood, the Washington Post and those who have since retailed it, by the false statement that the agents were out of the room making a telephone call. It is, in fact, the conclusion that followed that phone call. Because the agents were present throughout the proceedings, from before the arrival of the corpse until the body left at almost 4 a.m., there was no part of the autopsy they did not observe and ask questions about.

The angle of the wound was never commented on by those officials seeking to persuade that the agents were wrong. There is, therefore, nothing to dispute this "45 to 60 degrees" angle of entry, which would eliminate the possibility that the same bullet caused any of Connally's wounds as it would make impossible the causing of the President's front neck wound by the same projectile. This alone can explain its strange omission in the FBI report. If this bullet did not account for it, that meant another bullet - and another assassin. If this evidence is wrong, it was Specter's responsibility to bring it up and prove it wrong. It was not his responsibility to ignore and try to bury it, which is what happened.

If the doctors performed any examination that in any way refuted this observation, it is unreported.

Also ignored by the official and unofficial apologists - and abundantly substantiated elsewhere - is the location of this wound - not in the neck but "below the shoulders and two inches to the right of the middle line of the spinal column". This, too, was personal observation, not "hearsay". And this required no medical degrees for competent observation and understanding. Were it true that the agents were out of the autopsy room part of the time and that some of what they reported was "hearsay" (which, in every other case, the Commission found acceptable evidence), it was not hearsay when they saw the wound and its location.

Specter's suppression of this evidence and his failure to call these agents - or any of the other 23 competent witnesses not called - leaves this FBI report intact, its evidence muted but viable, and raises

the obvious questions about the alleged fact of the autopsy that is neither factual nor sensible and about the integrity of everyone involved -
those who participated or those who knew and were silent.

(It is this sort of behavior that makes particularly appropriate
the title of Sylvia Meagher's book, "Accessories After the Fact".)

This suppression, of the witnesses and the report, in itself is
enough to warrant doubt about the official proceedings, of the Commission and of the autopsy.

As we shall see, it need not stand by itself.

This Sibert-O'Neill report also punctures the FBI balloon that the
autopsy data was withheld from it until after it made its December 9 report. After the "complete listing of photographs and X-rays taken", "11
X-rays, 22 4x5 color photographs, 18 4x5 black and white photographs, 1
roll of 120 film containing five exposures", the report states, "Mr.
KELLERMAN stated these items could be made available to the FBI upon
request."

So, if the FBI, which was, at the time of its December 9 summary
report, in charge of the investigation of the President's murder, did not
have the autopsy evidence, it is not an explanation of excusable error
but a self-indictment warranting something other than the official and
journalistic silence of assent.

This FBI report, as well as the too-many other related documents,
indicts everyone involved, the Commission and its staff, the investigative agencies and the complacent, conveniently blind and mute press. Much
more does it indict the FBI, which rendered "definitive" reports in which
the assassination is minor and a tissue-thin, prosecution case against
Oswald is major.

To account for the assassination - its entire description - on the
first of the three brief pages in the December 9 report is this paragraph

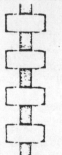

As the motorcade was traveling through downtown Dallas on

Elm Street about fifty yards west of the intersection with Houston

Street (Exhibit 1), three shots rang out. Two bullets struck

President Kennedy, and one wounded Governor Connally. The

President, who slumped forward in the car, was rushed to Parkland

Memorial Hospital, where he was pronounced dead at 1:00 p.m.

From page 18 of this same document, where the evidence against
Oswald is being mustered:

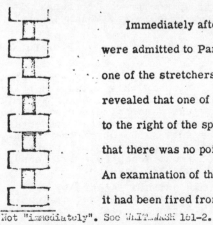

Immediately after President Kennedy and Governor Connally

were admitted to Parkland Memorial Hospital, a bullet was found on

one of the stretchers. Medical examination of the President's body

revealed that one of the bullets had entered just below his shoulder

to the right of the spinal column at an angle of 45 to 60 degrees downward

that there was no point of exit, and that the bullet was not in the body.

An examination of this bullet by the FBI Laboratory determined that

it had been fired from the rifle owned by Oswald. (Exhibit 23)

Not "immediately". See WHITEWASH 161-2.

74

When the flimsy excuse that the FBI had not seen the autopsy evidence - on January 23, 1964, after there was a record of FBI possession of a copy of the autopsy protocol - Hoover included this language in his supplementary report:

> the President's clothing by the FBI Laboratory disclosed that
> there was a small hole in the back of his coat and shirt
> approximately six inches below the top of the collar and two
> inches to the right of the middle seam of the coat. There
> were minute traces of copper on the fabric surrounding the hole.
> Medical examination of the President's body had revealed that
> the bullet which entered his back had penetrated to a distance
> of less than a finger length. (Exhibits 59 and 60)

If there is no solace in the FBI's reporting of the fact of the assassination or its solution, may we not take comfort from the neatness of its packages, the wide margins to the large typing and the beautiful plastic bindings?

Before these reports were drafted, the FBI knew what the Dallas police "general offense report" said of the crime as it related to Governor Connally. It also knew that this was utterly destructive of its own account as it would be of the Commission's. That would seek to make the FBI's unacceptable one more acceptable, to preserve a basis, no matter how tenuous, for calling Oswald the lone assassin. Here are the appropriate sentences of that "general offense report":

Mr. Connally sustained a gunshot wound with the point of entry located in the posterior of the right shoulder, ranging downward thru the chest, exiting on the right chest just below right nipple, The bullet continued, striking the right wrist, palmside, exiting 2 inches from the wrist joint. A fragment continued, entered the interior portion of the left thigh causing a flesh wound.

There can be no doubt of the police source. It had to be the doctors. This, for example, is exactly the medical explanation offered by Dr. Robert R. Shaw when Arlen Specter took his deposition in Dallas on March 3, 1964 (6H83ff.):

Dr. SHAW. I have always felt that the wounds of Governor Connally could be explained by the passage of one missile through his chest, striking his wrist and a fragment of it going on into his left thigh. I had never entertained the idea that he had been struck by a second missile.
Mr. SPECTER. Well, focusing for just a minute on the limited question of the physical characteristics of the wounds on the wrist, if you had that and nothing more in this case to go on, what would your opinion be as to which point was entry and which point was exit?
Dr. SHAW. Ordinarily, we usually find the wound of entrance is smaller than the wound of exit. In the Governor's wound on the wrist, however, if the wound on the dorsum of the wrist is the wound of entrance, and this large missile passed directly through his radius, I'm not clear as to why there was not a larger wound of exit than there was.
Mr. SPECTER. You mean on the volar aspect?
Dr. SHAW. Yes; if a whole bullet hit here -- (6H91)

Specter had little interest in Dr. Shaw's competent medical opinion that there was no "single-bullet theory" (which Specter was then developing), that the Governor's thigh wound was caused by a fragment, not a whole bullet. He had no more interest a month later, when he questioned this same Dr. Shaw about the same evidence before the Commission. (In that strange way of the Commission, this April 21 testimony, taken a

75

month later, is printed two volumes earlier, 4H101ff.) Specter ignored it.

When it was his responsibility to present the medical evidence to the members of the Commission for their consideration and assessment, it was essential for them to know, as Dr. Shaw had already told him under oath, that he believed it had been caused "by a fragment" of the bullet "going into his left thigh". Dr. Shaw, plainly, aborted the single-bullet theory during gestation. By ignoring Dr. Shaw's testimony, Specter willed his stillborn baby into existence and had the birth cer-tificate signed by the members of the Commission.

There can be no doubt that Specter knew of this medical opinion that rendered his theory invalid, as there can be none that he should have known of the police "general offense report" saying exactly the same thing. That was his job, his function and responsibility. Here again the solution was not confronting evidence but suppressing it. That po-lice report is not in the Commission's Report nor, to the best of my recollection, in any of the 10,000,000 words in its 26 printed volumes.

There is more that Specter knew and that he should have known about the autopsy and about the knowledge the FBI and its agents had of the au-topsy and its examination. In the Commission's fifth file, folio 149 is headed "RESULTS OF AUTOPSY ON JOHN F. KENNEDY". Rightly or wrongly, it says not what the FBI agents reported but that the "autopsy revealed one bullet hole located just below shoulders ...".*

We can take comfort from neither the possibility of the FBI's error nor the fact that, right or wrong, it was suppressed from the evi-dence - left to plague the future either way. That the FBI would or could make such a gross error when investigating and reporting the murder of a President - if it is error - is as unacceptable as its perpetuation by Arlen Specter and others on the Commission staff who could and should have raised and answered the question when it was their solemn responsi-bility to do just that.

The concluding sentence presents another and equally inexcusable perplexity: "The above information was received by communication from the Baltimore office, dated November 23, 1963."

Written by the Dallas office, this clearly and unequivocally says that there was a "communication" that was "dated" the day after the as-sassination; a communication, not a verbal message, dated the earliest it could have been, for Sibert and O'Neill were at Naval Hospital until about 4 a.m. that day, November 23.

That, too, is suppressed from the evidence.

More, it is entirely missing from the files. When my own search disclosed no such "communication", I made an official request for it. The official response is that the Archivist could not find it.

That there need have remained no question about the observations of the FBI agents at the autopsy we know from Specter himself. Although he did not call them or any of the other 23 uncalled witnesses of whose existence and competence he knew, he did, personally, interview Sibert and O'Neill. He summoned them to his office on March 12, 1964. His questioning was unduly brief. It lasted from "approximately 10:00 a.m. to 10:45 a.m." He spent the 15 minutes beginning an hour later dictating a memorandum to Commission General Counsel J. Lee Rankin.**

For this memorandum on "Interview of FBI Agents Present at Autop-sy", a mere six paragraphs that could have fitted on a single printed page among those many thousands in the 26 volumes holding the estimated 10,000,000 words that were printed, there was no space. It, too, is sup-pressed from the evidence. This is consistent with Specter's failure to summon these agents or any of the other 23 men he knew were present and take testimony from them.

From it we cannot know what Specter asked them and how they re-sponded. We can know only what he chose to record. That is enough to invalidate the explanation given Harwood and since repeated as the given word by the press: That the FBI agents could have known about the search

*See p.531. **See pp. 537-8.

for the bullet that caused the rear non-fatal wound only from hearsay and that they were both absent from the autopsy at the crucial moments. One can understand Specter's subsequent silence, when this false report was broadcast throughout the world, even if one need not sympathize with or approve this silence when lies were being told about the investigation of a President's murder and he knew they were lies.

SA O'Neill and SA Sibert advised that the autopsy surgeons made substantial efforts to determine if there was a missile in President Kennedy's body to explain what happened to the bullet which apparently entered the back of his body. They stated that the opinion was expressed by both Commander Humes and Lt. Col. Finck that the bullet might have been forced out of the back of the President's body upon application of external heart massage. They stated that this theory was advanced after SA Sibert called the FBI laboratory and talked to SA Killion who advised that a bullet had been found on a stretcher at Parkland Hospital. SA Sibert relayed that information to the doctors.

Thus, as Specter knew, the agents' knowledge was personal, for they gave the doctors the information from which the doctors developed their explanation. This early, as we shall see, Specter was building his case, not really seeking all the fact. Examination of this memo shows Specter was interested in none of the evidence that could have been adduced from the agents, only arguments. For example, could the doctors have advanced the belief that external cardiac massage caused the bullet to have worked its way out? Specter's representation of this is that, while the agents recalled no discussion of it prior to their reporting of the finding of the bullet, "however, neither agent could conclusively rule out the possibility". This and the accepted assurance of the agents that they made few notes and then destroyed those constitute the first half of Specter's memorandum.

This reflects a strange lack of interest in what went on at the autopsy, in the written report of these agents and its sensational information in violent opposition to what Specter himself was later to adduce for the record. That was consistent with his "theory" of the assassination. We can get no help or information from what remains, which is devoted to semantics, the exact words these FBI agents attributed to Secret Service Agents Kellerman and Greer.

There is not a single word in here about who was present at the autopsy; what the agents saw and heard, other than the single reference to cardiac massage; who could corroborate or disprove what the agents reported; what the more important personages were doing - were they just observing, or did the head of the entire Naval Medical installation and the President's personal physician (both a rarity, medical admirals), participate? Did they have knowledge requiring that they be called as witnesses? (Of course they did, but they were not called.) What kinds of pictures were taken when, especially of the non-fatal injuries? At what stage in the autopsy examination? Was the alleged path of this bullet ever actually traced, or was it just guessed at? Were pictures taken that could answer this question? How did the agents know as soon as the body was unwrapped that a tracheotomy had been performed in Dallas when the doctors pretended they really did not know and had to phone Dallas (twice, although the Report acknowledges only one time)?

What about those pictures and X-rays, their number and kind, that, from evidence we shall examine, we know Specter by this time knew would not be presented in evidence, as his own legal training and experience told him they should be?

Silence. Not a single word!

That "surgery of the head area"? Again, total silence. Specter's interest was not in these facts but in the theory he was developing, what became a substitute for fact.

How about the FBI summary and supplementary reports? Specter had the agents from whom their content allegedly came in his office. The question of their possible error? The omission of the "missed" bullet

77

and the front-neck wound, in which he certainly had to have had an interest? What about the minimum of five bullets these two additions accounte
for if they could not be accommodated within the theory Specter was devel
oping? Again, no question, no single mention.

The location of the rear, non-fatal wound is vital to the Commission's and Specter's theory as it is to the autopsy, even though its location where the printed autopsy report and the Commission's Report say
it was cannot in itself validate the Report. Here Specter had in front
of him two men who, in pursuance of their official duties as FBI investigators, had seen this wound and had, to his knowledge, written a report
that totally invalidated his growing "theory" by locating it not in the
neck but below the shoulder.

Rather than abort his gestating "theory" with fact, he asked no
single question about it!

Nothing about its location and nothing about its angle or depth!

Had they been absent for a significant period - both of them -
making a phone call and missed anything important? (Only Sibert left.)

There was a telephone in that room. Why had they left to make a
phone call? Did they want to be unheard by the others? Why? Still
again, silence!

All of these questions demanded asking and required answers. This
was the murder of a President under "investigation". The national integrity was at stake, as was that of the participants. There was the "crime
of the century" to be solved, the honor of the new government and its
head to be protected from the inevitable rumors and questions, such as
"who benefited?", the questions lawyers, properly, always ask.

But these questions, had Specter asked them, would have elicited
the answers we already know, for we now have the suppressed evidence that
holds them. We now know that all of the answers were answers he and the
government did not want. Because there is no question of Specter's competence, nor of his experience, what remains but the deliberate avoidance
and suppression of evidence, the taking of which would record proof that
invalidated the Report not yet written? (As we shall see, the Report
was outlined and its basic conclusions were decided upon although the
"investigation" to be "reported" had not really commenced!)

Unfortunately, bad as this is, it is not all and is not the worst.

This is one way to "investigate" the murder of a President - the
way the murder of John F. Kennedy was "investigated". It is Specter's
way and the Commission's. But let us hope it is not the way the American
people will indefinitely put up with now that the truth, officially suppressed, is at last out.

8. SOWS' EARS, SILKEN PURSES

What is worse and involves more staff members than Specter and his boss, Rankin, to whom the memorandum was sent, is the deliberate suppression of real and credible medical and other evidence. This was tangible, in hand despite the supreme efforts made to avoid it, and ignored or misrepresented in the Report and the testimony. It disproved the official fiction contrived in the Report. We shall see who had knowledge of its existence and its meaning.

What a horrible thing even to think of, how awful it is to say that a Presidential Commission contrived evidence, misrepresented and suppressed the truth about the murder of a President. What I have not yet discovered but suspect exists can make even this Macbethian scandal more calamitous.(See Parts 2 and 3.)

This is not conjecture, not suspicion, hearsay or rumor, not what I expect to find from probing the Commission's records.

It is what I have already found, what follows.

(Some of these documents are in the appendix.)

There are ramifications, but this until now secret and suppressed evidence, known to the staff, including Specter, falls into two broad categories, both essential to the basic conclusions of the Report and to the autopsy. They are on the President's head wound, the so-called "fatal wound", and the single-bullet theory. More than the theory itself, without which the Commission had to have acknowledged at least one additional assassin from the evidence already published, this new evidence bears on when and how many times the President and the Governor were shot.

It is evidence that indicates they were shot earlier and more times than the official speculation alchemized into the pretended gold of the Report says they were. It is evidence that exculpates Oswald, that entirely destroys the Report. Nothing else can account for its suppression, particularly because it was in the files.

First, let us consider two files on that "fatal" head wound. Here it is desirable to refer to the great amount of information on it I have already brought to light in three books. Aside from the foregoing chapters, understanding may be helped especially by reference to "The Number of Shots" and "The Doctors and the Autopsy" in WHITEWASH and "Magic, Mystery and Myth" in WHITEWASH II. Particularly appropriate to what follows are these revelations:

Of an effort at the scene of the crimes to hide or dispose of a piece of the President's skull; and the failure of the Report, even though, unusually, it so promised, to locate precisely and fully discuss this wound (WHITEWASH 36,179);

That the President's head snapped backward in response to the fatal shot, not forward, which it also did, but slightly earlier and in a discontinuous movement (WHITEWASH II,221);

That in printing the individual frames of the Zapruder film the Commission reversed the two following the fatal shot, thus reversing the direction in which the head seemed to snap, from backward, which is inconsistent with a shot from the rear, to forward, which is consistent; and that witnesses saw the President's brains and blood spew in front of Mrs. Kennedy, which would seem to be impossible had the only damage to the President's head been on the side away from her, the conclusion of the Report (PHOTOGRAPHIC WHITEWASH 25,70,145,203).

In the Report and the printed evidence, everything that would ever suggest that the President's head was impelled other than forward by the fatal shot - a requirement if it came from behind and the sixth-floor window in which the Report alleges Oswald was - is suppressed. Thus, it is a remarkable accident, if accident it is, that the frames immediately after the "fatal" shot were reversed in the printed evidence. It is these still pictures alone, made into an album, that the Commission could study and at will. It is these alone that are available to most researching the crime. Consistent with this is the elimination of Frame 284, which also may be innocent. Instead, Frame 283 is repeated (18H55), the second appearance being mislabeled Frame 284. This is about a second and a half prior to the fatal shot and might be the point at which, when seen in action, the head snaps forward.

However, the Commission, whether or not the reversal of Frames 314 and 315 was accidental, knew from the FBI, if not from its own examination of the movies and that of its staff, that the President's head moved, under the force of the fatal shot, as it could not have had that shot been fired from the back. This is disclosed in the FBI's commentary on the motion pictures it had examined. In describing the movies taken by Orville Nix, the FBI declared, "The President's head snaps to the left." (It snaps backward first. Emphasis added.)

Not from a rear shot!

(Parenthetically, I add here what I should have included in PHOTO-GRAPHIC WHITEWASH in connection with the movies taken by Robert Hughes - pp.57-8,86,125-30,132,278-81,283 - that this FBI document additionally confirms my revelation in that book of the fact that the Hughes movie does show the south face of the Texas School Book Depository Building when the President was in front of it. The Hughes film was edited and misrepresented by the FBI, which gave the Commission, as Exhibit 29 to its summary report of December 9, a print that showed only the two easternmost pairs of windows on the fifth and sixth floors. There is no Oswald, no rifle, visible in the sixth-floor window and the three black employees were not in the fifth-floor windows in which they testified they were. The editing and misrepresentation of the Hughes film hid from the Commission and the world the fact that there exists a picture of the motorcade - in front of that building and at the moment of the assassination - with no assassin, Oswald or anyone else, in that window. This, of course, almost certainly exonerates Oswald and destroys the Report. The exact language of this FBI commentary on the Hughes movie, on its eighteenth page, is that the "Presidential car moved out of view after turning left into the Parkway in front of the Texas School Book Depository Building. The Hughes film runs about 17 seconds.")

Consistent with this reported snap of the President's head to the left, which would indicate the shot came from the right, is another suppressed series of documents that I have located. The Nix film here is quite consistent with Zapruder's which, taken from the opposite side, shows the snap to be both backward and then to the left.

Fitting perfectly is Altgens' cited testimony that the spray of brain and other matter was to the left and in front of Mrs. Kennedy - rather than to the right, the only side said to have exploded out of the President's head. Fitting perfectly, also, is the testimony of the motorcycle police that they were behind and further to the left of the car and also were splattered with it.

The Commission suppressed seemingly irrefutable evidence and witnesses bearing on just this point. The documents are in its fifth file, beginning with folio 150. Further investigation is in CD1250:1-3 and CD1269:1-7. What they establish is this:

William Allen Harper, a student at Texas Christian University, Fort Worth, and a Dallas resident, was taking pictures 29 hours after the assassination, in Dealey Plaza, "just south of the spot where President Kennedy was assassinated". He found "a piece of human skull".

The FBI report "located" this spot at "approximately 25 feet south" of where the President was at the moment of the fatal shot. Harper took this "piece of human skull" to his uncle, a doctor, who, with Dr. C. E. Kerns (A. B. Cairns), pathologist at Methodist Hospital, identified it. Twelve pictures were taken. They are suppressed.

Dallas is renowned for its crimes of violence, but even so, there is a limit to how many heads got blown apart at Dealey Plaza! That there is no doubt of the origin of this "piece of human skull" is established by the disposition made of it by the FBI laboratory. It was "delivered to Admiral GEORGE BURKLEY, Physician to the President at the White House"

Any number of members of the Commission staff perforce examined these files carefully. CD5 is a basic one, containing many important early FBI reports. We may now have no way of knowing all who did and did not study it. I believe it is fair to assume that most of the staff at one time or another had to examine this file closely. Each one who did and who has since been silent bears a personal responsibility for this suppression, for each had reason to believe the entire story of the assassination, the entire investigation of which he was part, was false.

That one in particular had this knowledge from another source we know from the printed testimony. Constable Seymour Weitzman immediately found a piece of the President's skull a foot or less from the south curb of Elm Street, where it could not have wound up without assistance were the official story true (WHITEWASH 36;7H107). The eminent California lawyer, Joseph Ball, whose firm is sufficiently prominent to have induced the former governor, Pat Brown, to join it, questioned Weitzman on April 1, 1964. As soon as Weitzman volunteered that he had found a piece of the President's skull well to the left when only the right side of the head is said to have exploded out, Ball interrupted him to say, "Off the record." The printed transcript at this point then reads, "Off record discussion." Thus Ball changed the subject, for his next words were, "What did you do after that?"

So, we have the finding of what seems, without doubt, to be a missing piece of the President's skull, unreported by the Commission in its definitive 900 pages of its Report or 10,000,000 words of "evidence" in 26 large volumes. We also have ample evidence that there was no real search of the crime area. Otherwise, with pieces of the President's skull known to be missing, this one certainly would have been found. Does this not describe the "investigation" at the primary point, the scene of the crime? Should not the Commission, in discharge of its responsibilities, have placed this interpretation upon the startling evidence it suppressed?

But suppose the Commission had elected to fulfill the obligation with which it was charged and disclosed to the world that the Dallas Police Department, the FBI and Secret Service all had failed to find a piece of the President's skull when it was only 25 feet from the exact point of the murder? What then?

Simply this: The Commission would also have had to disclose that this skull fragment had exploded south of the murder site.

This it dared not do without risking destruction and discrediting of its entire work and Report, for the evidence it presented is that only the right or north side of the President's head exploded out. With the pictures suppressed, this is presented graphically in Exhibit 386 (WHITE-WASH 196). How could an explosion out of only the right side of the upright President's head have thrown a piece of it 25 feet in the wrong direction?

Suppressing the evidence was safer than risking the destruction of the Report, the end of the single-assassin-no-conspiracy built-in conclusion with which the Commission's functioning began, whether or not its members were aware of it. With the beginning of the asking of the questions this would have required, there is little likelihood the evidence exculpatory of Oswald could longer have been suppressed and misrepresented. Thus, no pat Report, no placid and safe "solution" of the crime.

The can would have been unlidded, the worms crawling about for all to see.

But it must now be asked: How was the assassination investigated, on all levels? What kind of Commission did we have, what kind of staff served it and us, what kind of FBI could and did file reports like this and preserve silence about them when they were suppressed, and what kind of Report suppresses such evidence, with what kind of "solution" to the Presidential murder?

May it not also be asked what kind of servile, lickspittle press, with this documentation available to it for the asking and looking, and it has been silent about it? Many reporters examined CD5. I saw them. One is Bernard Gavzer, whose later work on the assassination of Dr. Martin Luther King was different, excellent. He was then allegedly working on the intellectual and journalistic finkery to which the Associated Press devoted 20,000 words in its designedly dishonest assault on those of us who dared analyze the Report and show it was wrong, who dared seek the truth about a Presidential murder and its official investigation.

The Washington Post published it in a single, large typographical bellyache, devoting almost all of the Sunday editorial section to it. Others dribbled it out in economical fractions over a longer period of time, up to three weeks. Although the AP exulted in the seven months of its two-man "investigation", Gavzer's working at the Archives was plain flackery. That was not a source of material used in the stories. Those stories were barren save for invective, insult, and twisted quotations. They served and were designed to serve only as a defense of the government. They just happened to coincide with the simultaneous presentation of bias and prejudice - and factual error - by the CBS and NBC TV and radio networks.

This is how such documentary evidence of a fake investigation of a real Presidential assassination can be suppressed and remain suppressed although freely available to the richest, most powerful press in the world. This is how the Report came to be accepted, too.

A few sheets later in CD5 is another series of suppressed FBI reports that once and for all end what never existed except in the Specter fiction that was as warmly received as though it were the true given word, that single-bullet theory. Had these documents not been suppressed - had they not been within the power of the Commission to suppress, with the silent acquiescence of the FBI - Specter could and would not have dared advance the spurious single-bullet theory.

As we have seen, that was a prerequisite in the pre-determined "conviction" of Oswald. While it was beyond the capacity of the best shots the Commission could muster to come even close, under better conditions, to duplicating the three-shot shooting attributed to him - the Report merely misrepresented this, saying it was possible - there was no remote possibility anyone could have fired more than three accurate shots with that junky, bolt-action rifle.

Had these FBI reports, beginning with folio 157, been exposed to public examination, no one would have dared try to pull of a "single-bullet" fraud.

Surprisingly enough, these documents deal with the most essential of the evidence, yet the Commission did suppress them. They are the FBI reports on the X-rays of the Connally thigh wound, that same wound that was simply misrepresented to prevent the demolition of the Report by what was already in evidence about it.

On November 29, 1963, a week after the assassination, FBI Agent Vincent E. Drain received a copy of the X-ray negatives and a covering letter from Parkland Hospital Administrator Jack Reynolds. *

Although the Commission did have the Connally X-rays, it played a strange game and six months later pretended it didn't! Under date of April 15, Arlen Specter prepared a number of letters for Rankin's signature. These were sent to witnesses-to-be in the testimony about the Connally injuries. Two of these suffice to illustrate my point. They were addressed to Drs. Charles Gregory and Robert Shaw, Parkland Hospi-

*See pp. 505-6.

tal. There was none to Dr. George Shires, who was the doctor in charge
of the Connally case.

The third paragraph of each is identical. It reads:

Would you please arrange to bring with you all x-rays showing
Governor Connally's wounds, including the wounds of the rib, wrist
and thigh. We are interested in ascertaining, from the x-rays,
what metallic fragments, if any, remained in the Governor's wrist
and femur.

Obviously, each of the two doctors could not bring the X-rays.
Was it necessary for each to have a separate set? More important, why
did Specter specifically eliminate Commission interest in metal fragments in the Governor's chest? The answer is obvious: It wanted to ignore the metal it - Specter in particular - knew was there. It is to
Specter that Dr. Shires had testified to this on March 23 (6H111).
Specter wanted no additional disqualifications of his single-bullet theory. But Shires should have been called before the members of the Commission, to tell them that metal remained in the Governor's chest. What
better reason could Specter have had not to call him or to recommend
against calling him?

It is Specter who on June 5 wrote the "thank you" letter to C. J.
Price, also identified as administrator of the hospital. In his own name
Specter said, "Thank you for sending us the x-rays on Governor Connally
with your letter of May 29, 1964. We very much appreciate your many
courtesies."

What kind of macabre game Specter indulged in here we can only
guess. One obvious possibility is in the Reynolds letter. Reynolds made
it easier for the FBI but harder for the Commission to ignore. His letter "read" the X-rays and provided specific information that should have
been in the Report and was not; the exact size and location of this
wound, oriented with immovable points so that its location is inflexibly
fixed. Measurements are so fine they are in fractions of millimeters.
A millimeter itself is quite small, measuring but 0.04 of an inch.

Without here repeating these reports in full, they can be summarized in perhaps their most important aspect by saying they give the precise size of the fragment of bullet remaining imbedded in the Governor's thigh bone. When no scale is given, the presumption is measurements are actual size.

They describe it as "irregular" but "roughly oval", "about 3.5
mms" long, and 1.3 mms wide "in the AP projection", 2 mms by 1.5 in the
"lateral projection". It is positioned in a way that would seem to
eliminate the conjectured means by which Bullet 399 is alleged to have
imbedded it:

The long axis of the metallic object is oriented generally along
the axis of the femur.

In other words, side by side, parallel.

The official Commission conjecture press-agented into the pretense
of reality says this fragment came from only the wrong or rear end of the
bullet, which then was flying backward. Nothing else could be considered
because on every other surface the bullet was perfect - unscathed - with
no metal missing. This bullet, like nothing in mythology or science fiction, could have deposited that fragment in the Governor's thigh - or in
effect nailed it to his bone - only by plunging in backward and then, in
the thin layer of flesh above the bone and faster than the eye can see,
turning at right angles to its path and in some mysterious manner slicing
off a piece of its back end - then its forward end - and sticking it to
that bone!

Not very simple? It cannot be any other way. Every other surface
of that bullet (WHITEWASH 208) is so close to perfect none of the bones
in three parts of the Governor's body even scratched the rifling marks!
With this fragment from that bullet - and if it is from any other bullet,
good-bye Report! - the only way it could, from all the evidence, have
been imbedded is by a right-angle turn and a magical slice plus mysteri-

ous bone-glue - all without additional damage to the Governor's thigh. His leg was, of course, closely examined by the doctors. They mentioned no harm from this required maneuvering, no pockets reamed out by a side-turning missile.

Still another reason why these reports on the thigh X-rays had to be suppressed is that they so measurably describe the fragment.

Admittedly, the description, "roughly oval", is vague. To the Commission which had the X-rays and report, and to the FBI, of which this is also true, there need have been and there was no vagueness. Given the will (and nothing else was required of official bodies), this bullet fragment could have been exactly reconstructed from the X-rays. It could have been weighed.

However, the government dared not do this. By stretching everything the way it wanted, the maximum metal it could allege could have been missing from Bullet 399 is only two and a half grains. There was more than this in the wrist alone, as Dr. Shaw testified. There was the fragment Dr. Shires saw in the postoperative chest X-ray (which I think accounts for his never having been called to testify before the members of the Commission although he was the physician in charge of the Governor's case). Small as this chest fragment could have been - and again there need have been no mystery about it - with wrist metal already in excess of the maximum allowable, any addition, no matter how minute, was redundant disqualification of the entire single-bullet theory, hence of the Report that depends upon it.

Slight as may be the weight of this thigh fragment, like that in the chest, it also is repetitious, total destruction of the Report. Hence the trickery with the evidence and its suppression from the Report.

This cannot be just another of those so-convenient "accidents", like the reversal of the crucial frames of the Zapruder film to make them tell just the opposite of truth in their representation of the President's response to the "fatal" bullet. No reasonable man can consider its suppression from the Report, the evidence and the interrogations of the doctors as only an accident.

Here we have, first, the Commission ignoring its own evidence that more than three grains of metal were in the wrist when the doctors saw it (more may have been there before medical examination). Then, we have the suppression of Dr. Shires' testimony that there was a bullet fragment still in the chest after surgery, after it was cleansed and treated. Now we have an additional suppressed bullet fragment, one that in itself could weigh enough to end the single-bullet theory and the Report all over again. And all of this assumes what it is not reasonable to assume, that this was the heaviest possible bullet to begin with, not a bullet of average weight, or one that was less than average weight. We do not even know if there were other fragments that worked their way out, in the context of the official account, when the bullet itself did. No matter how little it weighs, this thigh fragment is redundant disproof of the Report.

It is suppression, exactly the suppression required to eliminate one of the already too-many total disproofs of the Report.

And too many of these are in Specter's department. He was the man in charge of the medical-autopsy testimony and evidence and what related

But alas, we are not finished with the suppresions in Specter's department.

There are others, in those "housekeeping files" that for some strange, really unfathomable, reason Assistant Counsel Wesley Liebeler - when they were safely unavailable - said would exonerate the Commission.

Now, they are not entirely unavailable. I have been in some. They will not make Liebeler happy. Nor Specter.

Five of those available at the time of this writing suffice at this point.

The first in time and logic is the attachment to a memorandum by Specter and his then better-known colleague, Francis W. H. Adams. It is dated January 23, within a few days of Specter's employment by the Commission. It is entitled, "MEMORANDUM OF THINGS TO BE DONE AND SOME OF THE PROBLEMS INVOLVED". This title may be cumbersome, but it, at least, is accurate.

Because so little - almost nothing - is ever heard of Adams, because he was so close to entirely inactive in the Commission staff, and because his qualifications were so close to perfect for this employment, it is worth quoting them, in part, from the biographical appendix of the Report (R476-7):

...LL.B. degree from Fordham Law School in 1928 ... chief assistant U.S. attorney in New York, special assistant to the U.S. Attorney General ... In 1954 and 1955 he served as police commissioner of New York City ...

Had Adams spent his life prepping for this assignment, he could not more admirably have prepared himself. Perhaps this, considered with the suppressed evidence that follows, explains his inactivity.

There are 13 items specified in this memo. All are reasonable. What seems unreasonable is that there should ever have been any question about them.

The last, for example, "Consideration should be given to obtaining the camera," meaning Zapruder's. Consideration should be given? Although it was a minimum prerequisite for the proper admission of the film into evidence, this camera was never more than borrowed until almost three years later, more than two years after the Commission reported and quit, when, as I believe the available evidence shows, I embarrassed the government into an immodestly hasty acquisition of it (PHOTOGRAPHIC WHITEWASH 26,146-54).

The part of this memo of immediate interest here is (g):

There would seem to be a considerable amount of confusion as to the actual path of the bullets which hit President Kennedy, particularly the one which entered the right side of his back.*

Here, shortly after his employment by the Commission, we have the factual determination, over Specter's signature, of what the Commission was supposed to be investigating to learn, not concluding in advance of investigation. He took hold rapidly! He began knowing the answers. That bullet "entered the right side of his back".

Here also, from the man who publicly insists this bullet entered the neck, we have the secret acknowledgment that it was in "the right side of the back". That this is not an accident, a careless phrasing, will become clear. Before this date Specter had seen the autopsy report (WHITEWASH II,97). The fact is that, from time to time in his interrogations, Specter made the same acknowledgment, as did some of the others. When he questioned Roy Kellerman, who had remained with the body and examined this wound (WHITEWASH 186), Specter referred not to a "neck" wound but to one in the "shoulder", a difference small in distance but vast in significance. With Dr. Humes he also admitted "back".

The day before he questioned FBI Agents Sibert and O'Neill, Specter, accompanied by Joseph A. Ball, his fellow assistant counsel, went out to the Bethesda Naval Hospital and interviewed Admiral C. B. Galloway and Doctors Humes and Boswell. In his memorandum on it, dated March 13, 1964, Specter says he dictated it in the 15 minutes before he dictated his Sibert-O'Neill memo and that the questioning lasted two hours, beginning at 3:30 p.m.**

The entire document is worth the closest study by those who want to learn how this investigation worked, how the murder of the President was "investigated", how the staff performed and to what end. Here I shall concentrate on half of it.

The last word in the first line of the third paragraph is the only one to show sign of erasure and correction. There is no obvious reason for this change, and it may be presumed to have been the result of a typographical error. If there is no other reason, this one is sufficient

*See pp. 490-1. **See pp. 539-40.

to focus attention on it. Whatever the word that was there before, even if it was the same word, in the final, corrected form, after attention was directed to it and correction made, that word is "back". That line reads, referring to these three interviewed medical authorities:

All three described the bullet wound on President Kennedy's back

Not in the neck, in Specter's own, independent words, before he was deep into his single-bullet salvation of the lone-Oswald fiction of the assassination, but "on President Kennedy's back".

Without dictation from anyone else, with the correction, for whatever reason it was required, already made, in the privacy of his own office and the secrecy of the suppressed files (at least some of the credit for which is his, for he was in charge of this part of the inquiry), Arlen Specter himself said the President was wounded on the back rather than in the neck and right after and in reporting on his conference with the autopsy personnel!

With any other investigation in our history, total discredit would here be accomplished. With this one, however, the cowardly politicians and the dishonest press insist the sow's ear is a silken purse, so we continue with Specter's personal report on his interview with the autopsy medical personnel.

The remainder of that sentence reads, "as being a point of entrance." How was this established, when all the credible evidence was to the contrary? Remember the Commission's favorite word and that of its apologists, "traced", as what was done with the alleged path of this bullet.

Admiral Holloway /his name is C. B. Galloway7 then illustrated the angle of the shot by placing one finger on my back /again, Specter avoided the word "neck"7 and the second finger on the front part of my chest which indicated that the bullet traveled in a consistent downward path, on the assumption that it emerged in the opening on the President's throat which had been enlarged by the performance of the tracheotomy in Dallas.

I avoid emphasis purposely, so that the reader can get the Admiral's words and science without influence. What the Admiral really told Specter, and what, despite the rewriting of the autopsy report when Oswald was murdered and there was no likelihood of cross-examination on it, it still makes clear, is that the path of the bullet was never traced. The word I used in wHITEWASH is "projected". On the authority of a medical admiral, a medical and a military rarity, a man of high station and presumed highest competence and responsibility, we now know that pinnacle of precision, that epitome of science with which the murder of an American President is "investigated" and "solved", the country saved, its integrity preserved and its future assured.

"Assumption".

Here is the man utmost in competence, exalted of the Naval Medical Corps, the boss of its largest and most important medical installation, and he has solved the assassination with a spectacular breakthrough in forensic medicine!

He guessed it!

How much more precision can one expect of the Navy's top medical brass, of its top pathologists under him, of the most advanced medical science in history!

"Assumption"! Guesswork!

How simple it is to solve the "crime of the century" with such amenable scientists and incorruptible lawyers!

Sherlock Holmes lived and died in vain, for there were Admiral Galloway and Arlen Specter to follow him.

The method of Presidential murder investigation and post-mortem thus firmly fixed in the texts of the future, Specter continued his memo. Its fourth paragraph says,

Commander Humes explained that they had spent considerable time at the autopsy trying to determine what happened to the bullet because they found no missile in the President's body. ... hypothesized that the bullet might have been forced out of the back of the President on the application of external heart massage after they were advised that a bullet had been found ...

Does one wonder why Specter grilled the FBI agents about this almost exclusively, apparently, when the day before the doctors had said the same thing?

And what does this do to the lie told the Washington Post, reported in the earlier chapter, that the FBI agents did not know what happened because they were not in the autopsy room? Here we have confirmation of what they told Specter, that it is they who, following that phone call, told the doctors of the finding of the bullet. It is after this, after the one agent who left returned to the autopsy room, that the doctors developed their theory.

But do not let this distract us from the third description in two short paragraphs of the rear, non-fatal injury as that of the back, not the neck. "Neck" is a word Specter has yet to learn. Even in the front it is not "neck" but "chest" where the admiral placed his finger and "throat" for the location of the tracheotomy.

There is no indication that the doctors ever "traced" the path of this bullet. They dismembered the President's body, as their task required. They could and should have seen where the bullet went. There is no indication, even slight suggestion, that Mr. District Attorney Specter asked this question. *

In the next paragraph the as-yet-not-wary Specter loosed a few more cats from his bag. This he accomplished in quoting Drs. Humes and Boswell on "their current opinions", that is, their opinions on March 11, 1964, five days before they testified, as distinguished from their opinions at the time of the autopsy.

What were their "current opinions", those that evolved after the autopsy was done and over, their reports filed?

...that the bullet passed in between two major muscle strands in the President's back (again, not neck) and continued on a downward flight and exited through his throat. They noted, at the time of the autopsy, some bruising of the internal parts of the President's body in that area but tended to attribute that to the tracheotomy at that time.

Here we have clear and specified distinction between the opinions of the autopsy doctors as of the time of the autopsy and as of the time of their conference with Specter three and a half months later.

How precise is this science, this evidence, if at the time of their autopsy examination the doctors attributed the bruising of the top of the lung to the tracheotomy and later, when primed by questions and needs, their then "current opinion" was that the bullet went between the strap musvles of the back? How dependable is such an autopsy?

What is clear here is that the doctors did not see where the bullet went. Or, as Admiral Galloway put it, they "assumed" its path. This truth is lacking in the Report, which asserts (WHITEWASH 179) that "the doctors traced the course of the bullet through the body ...".

There never was any real question about this, and now there can be none. Unbecoming and unpleasant as it is, inappropriate as it is with anything connected with government and most of all with the Report on the assassination of a President, this, in plain English, is a lie.

As stated in my first book and as these until-now suppressed documents show, the doctors never said that, never did that, and changed thei opinion after their function as prosecutors was over - their protocol done

Here, perhaps, we get the doctrine of some of the autopsy testimony. For example, having told Specter that, at the time of the autopsy, they "at that time" attributed internal bruising to the tracheotomy, in the interpretation of the Report cited above and in testimony (2H363) we get different meanings. Of the bruise of the lung, Humes swore,

It, therefore, was our opinion that the missile while not penetrating physically the pleural cavity, as it passed that point bruise either the missile itself /sic7, or the force of its passage through the tissues, bruised both the parietal and the visceral pleura.

This is not what they told Specter five days earlier. Apparently, though, it was more to his liking for he asked no questions to make this sworn testimony consistent with rather than contradictory to what they had just told him in secret.

Further along (2H367) Specter, in asking about the unsuccessful efforts to probe the rear non-fatal wound, asked if learning of the finding of the bullet at the Dallas hospital called to their minds any tentative theory about entry or exit as related to this wound. Humes' respons (especially in the light of the until-now suppressed Specter memorandum, which distinguishes between current opinion, i.e., as of the time of thei testimony and private interview, and their opinions "at the time of the autopsy") was positive. He swore, "We were able to ascertain with absolute certainty that the bullet had passed by the apical portion of the right lung producing the injury which we mentioned."

Still later Senator John Sherman Cooper, a Commission member, asked Humes (2H369), "... was there any other factor which you could think of that might have caused that bruise ..." and Humes swore,"... I truthfully, sir, can't think of any other way." *

In the printed version of the final, typed copy of the autopsy report discussion of this wound, on its fourth and fifth pages (R541-2), makes no reference to what Dr. Humes told Specter, that they then believed this bruising was caused by the tracheotomy. Nor is there reference to the certainty Humes gave Senator Cooper - that it was caused by and he considered it was caused in no other way than by this bullet. In the conclusions (R543), the last typed page, "based on the above observations", Humes wrote and the others agreed and countersigned that "this missile produced the contusions".

There is no testimony or any proof that the path of this missile was ever traced. The autopsy does not say so; the testimony does not. The word of Admiral Galloway is that it was "assumed". Kinder is my own designation, "projected". The authors of the Report took the liberties required to present it as substantiated, proved, in a way it never was when they represented it as "traced". We shall come to the truth.

Five days before the doctors testified, they told Arlen Specter they then believed that "at the time of the autopsy" they "tended to attribute" the bruising of the lung "to the tracheotomy". In their subsequent testimony, they said, under oath, that at the time of the autopsy they attributed this same bruising to the missile. The distinction would seem to be clear and worth further exploration. So also might be their identification as "current opinion", or opinion of the time of the Specter interview, of their belief that the bullet "passed in between two major muscle strands in the President's back".

And all of this should be considered in relation to the means specified by Admiral Galloway as those used to determine the path of this bullet, "assumption".

The conclusion of Specter's memo is that he asked the doctors to have "drawings" prepared, indication he and they then knew they would be denied what lawyers and the law regard as the "best evidence", the actual photographs of the autopsy.

During this same general period of the Commission's very early life, Specter's colleagues were also writing memoranda of conferences in which he was a participant, along with others on the staff and an assortment of FBI and Secret Service agents and doctors of various kinds.

Melvin A. Eisenberg's April 23, 1964, memo says that conferences

*See p. 594.

"in an attempt to determine the frames in the Nix, Zapruder and Mary Muchmore films which portray the impact at which the third shot struck the President" had been held "over the past several months". Unless one considers the possibility of more than three shots, there is ground for wondering about this, spectacular, unmistakable and completely unforgettable as is the display in Zapruder Frame 313 and those identical with it in other films. (Other references to these films: WHITEWASH 5,43-50, 159-60,167,174-5,206-7;WHITEWASH II,2-5,93-5,128,130-44,146-9,151-2,156, 158-61,164,166,171-80,182-4,195-8,200-1,203,205-6,208,210-23,227,234,238, 245-7,249;PHOTOGRAPHIC WHITEWASH 15-27,30,36,38,42,45-6,50,53-4,61-4,71, 81-2,104,109,119,123-4,138-46,148-9,151-2,154,176,178,182,277,280-1.)

On April 22, Eisenberg drafted memos on each of two conferences * "to determine which frames of the Zapruder movies show the impact of the first and second bullets". Note that here also is an official account of the shooting that has each of three shots hitting the President or the Governor and at the same time, without embarrassment, making no reference to the known "missed" shot. These were held April 14 and 21. Specter is among those attending both conferences. In each case he recorded but a single dissent - the only one registered by anyone. Each time it was to the consensus that Governor Connally could not have been wounded after Zapruder Frame 236, and to nothing else.

These hitherto suppressed staff memoranda reveal what was carefully screened out of the testimony of those participants who also were witnesses and from the Report:

The consensus that the President could have had and probably did have a delayed reaction to being wounded, with him the delayed reaction being more likely than with the Governor (the Report assumes there was no delayed reaction by the President and there was one by the Governor, both assumptions being essential to its conclusion as both are opposed to the suppressed evidence);

That the President could have been struck by the first bullet as early as Zapruder Frame 163!

When it is understood that the Report is also based on the presumption that it was completely impossible for the President to have been struck before Frame 210 - had he been the Report could not have attributed the assassination to Oswald - the significance of this suppression is staggering. So is the steadfast refusal of the Commission to have individual slides for individual and careful study made of any frame prior to 171!

From the supercilious language of the Report, it is possible to infer that the Commission found that a shot from that Texas School Book Depository sixth-floor window could have struck at Zapruder Frame 186. This, however, is false and is one of the careful evasions or escape hatches fabricated in advance. The concept that shot was possible at Frame 186 on November 22, 1963, is based on the presumption that six months later, during a "reconstruction", when there was no wind blowing, for 1/18.3 of a second, there was a clear spot in the live-oak tree between that window on that day and the presumed position of the car six months earlier.

That grown men would even try to palm off such fantasy is a measur of the desperation with which the Report was conceived and drafted. One and eighteen hundredths seconds, so small a fragment of time that the individual cannot measure it, is insufficient for a conscious decision to be made and then followed by the act of sighting and firing a rifle, whic requires a careful, steady squeeze of the trigger. On November 22, 1963, the condition of the foliage of that live-oak tree could not have been identical with what it was on May 24, 1964. The change in position of a twig or leaf - a single one of either - would invalidate this foolishness. More, on November 22, a strong wind had been blowing. It was estimated at 10 miles per hour, almost blew off Mrs. Kennedy's hat (the first Altgens picture captured this), almost unseated Motorcycle Policeman Marrion L. Baker. And were these things not true, a shot at the angle of Frame 186 is eliminated by the trajectories basic to the Report, for at that point the bullet could not have inflicted on the Governor

* See pp. 501ff.

the injuries attributed to it.

There could never have been any legitimate doubt that the President had been struck prior to Frame 210 - not just that a bullet had been fired, but also that the President had been hit - as I show in WHITEWASH II. The chapter, "Willis In His Own Name," proves that Phil Willis took a picture *after* the President had been hit, and that the Zapruder film, which shows Willis, also shows that Willis had taken the picture and lowered his camera before Frame 202. The government's problem is that any shot prior to Frame 210 could not have been fired by Oswald or any lone sixth-floor-window assassin, for it required a fourth bullet.

Here also we find an explanation for the editing of the Zapruder film (WHITEWASH 45,206), for it is in the margins of this film that Phil Willis is seen to disappear from Zapruder's camera's view at just the frames missing in the Commission's evidence! Although they are said to have been reproduced seriatim, beginning with Frame 171, Frames 208-11 are missing and Frames 207 and 212 altered. How remarkably this coincides with the essentiality of having Frame 210 in evidence! That, it should be recalled, is the frame in which for the first time the Commission claims the President could have been hit by a shot from the sixth-floor window.

The consensus of the April 14 meeting was that "the reaction shown in frames 224-25 may have been started ... as early as frame 199 ... or, with a higher degree of possibility at frames 204-6 ...". It was also that "the President may have been struck by the first bullet as much as two seconds before any visible reaction began", although it would probably have been "under one second". Thus, he may have been struck as early as 163, with the delayed reaction of two seconds, or 36 frames, if the first visible reaction is, in fact, in Frame 199. (However, in WHITE WASH II, p.198, I establish a visible reaction at about Frame 192, or with a delay of the possible two seconds, a shot that struck the President as early as about Zapruder Frame 155. Confirming this is my analysis, first reported in WHITEWASH, beginning on page 47, that at Frame 190 Zapruder's camera began to shake in reaction to what he had seen a little earlier. Even CBS, in its video whitewash, agreed that the assassination began before Frame 210, although it supported the Report, unblushingly not acknowledging the incompatibility. CBS also claimed this as its own discovery of "new evidence" in the Zapruder film, although the executive producer of the series had read it more than a year earlier in WHITEWASH, where it had been published exclusively.)

That this, even if only a possibility - and it without doubt was more - could have been expunged from the Report while the memorandum was suppressed from the evidence, is incredible. It casts suspicion on all the participants and the conclusions. This means that all were silent at a false Report which suppressed their own conclusions, that the President could have been and probably was struck at a time when Oswald could not have shot him and must have been killed as the result of a conspiracy, for with the earlier first shot, no one man could have inflicted all these wounds from the alleged sixth-floor Texas School Book Depository window.

The ramifications of the fact of this suppression and of what was suppressed are like nothing in our history, for here is the first credible record of a conspiracy within the government. That this intelligence is in the files and stifled, not in the Report, is really beyond immediate comprehension. It is a sickening fact, one that stuns the mind.

What shocks even more is another and previously undisclosed alteration in the original of the Zapruder film, *Life*'s private property, that exactly coincides with the point at which an earlier bullet could have hit the President! It also accords with Zapruder's emotional description of what he saw through the telephoto lens, a bullet hitting the President before Frame 190. I did not know this when I wrote PHOTO-GRAPHIC WHITEWASH and deal with the spurious account of how the above-described frames came to disappear from the original (pp.19ff.). In its "explanation", *Life* acknowledged the destruction of only those frames I exposed in WHITEWASH.

Since then, however, I have obtained proof of the disappearance from the original of two more frames, at precisely the point this suppressed Eisenberg memo says the experts agreed the President could have been struck! I have the proof in my possession but must protect my source.

The splice is more professional than that which eliminated the frames beginning at 207. It is so close to the horizontal edge of the frames and so neatly done that it long escaped detection. Once perceived, it is quite obvious.

This memorandum repeats twice in a single paragraph (e) that the so-called single bullet to which all the non-fatal wounds were attributed in the Report, according to the consensus, "does not appear to have penetrated a wrist". It also says of Governor Connally's wounds the opposite of the foundation of the Report, that "It is not possible to say whether prior to 236 Governor Connally was ever in a position such that one bullet could have caused the five wounds he sustained" and that "the likelihood of an instantaneous reaction is particularly great in regard to a wrist wound ... since pain is usually felt more quickly in a limb than in the torso".

The expectant reader will not find this most essential intelligence in the Report, which, to the contrary, assumes without proof that: The Governor was struck by one bullet only, prior to Frame 224 and at or after 210; he was also lined up with the President; this same bullet had also gone through the President's neck; and, contrary to the evidence, the President did not have a delayed reaction while the Governor did.

This, of course, has nothing to do with the additional evidence that makes the single-bullet theory a scientific impossibility, some of it in this very same suppressed memo.

Dr. F. W. Light, Deputy Chief of the Biophysics Division of Edgewood Arsenal, is listed as a participant in both conferences. Dr. Joseph Dolce, consultant to that division of the Arsenal, is listed as participating in the April 22 conference only. This memorandum seems like a carefully expurgated version of the earlier one, some of the information in which it duplicates. It is half as long and, predictably, eliminates what we have just quoted.

However, it has this concluding paragraph:

In a discussion after the conference Drs. Light and Dolce expressed themselves as being very strongly of the opinion that Connally had been hit by two different bullets, principally on the ground that the bullet recovered from Connally's stretcher could not have broken his radius without having suffered more distortion. Dr. Olivier withheld a conclusion until he has had the opportunity to make tests on animal tissue and bone with the actual rifle.

It is an unusually naive reader who now will be startled to learn that Dr. Dolce was not called as a witness before the Commission and that there was no duplication of the history attributed to the heroic bullet of Specter's saga, hence nothing upon which Drs. Light and Olivier could base altered testimony. Dr. Dolce's name, in fact, is not mentioned a single time in all the volumes of testimony.

Dr. Light testified May 13 (5H94ff.). His testimony is fairly invoked in the Report:

... testified that the anatomical findings were insufficient for him to formulate a firm opinion as to whether the same bullet did or did not pass through the President's neck first before inflicting all the wounds on Governor Connally (R109);

and,

Based on the other circumstances, such as the relative positions in the automobile of the President and the Governor, Dr. Light concluded that it was probable that the same bullet traversed the President's neck and inflicted all the wounds on Governor Connally (R585).

How Dr. Light knew "the relative positions" at the time of this alleged shot, when no one else does and when no one else knows when the

91

impossible shot was fired, must remain a mystery. What is not mysterious is that he is a career government employee and that all the other physicians agreed with his initial opinion, that a bullet in the nigh-to-perfect condition of 399 could not have smashed its way through a wrist.

The thought of recapitulating the sickening evidence detailed abov from the Commission files and suppressed from its testimony and worse, from the Report, paralyzes the mind as it turns the stomach. Here we hav more than enough suppressed from the Report to destroy it, the integrity of those involved with it, and that of the government that issued and demands belief in it - the same government that the Report, in effect, legitimizes.

Until acknowledgment of its existence was unavoidable, the staff persistently pretended the "missed" bullet did not exist, even though it wounded James T. Tague, who bled from the wound. All of this was instantaneously on the police radio. It was public knowledge. But the Commission staff was prepared to "solve" the murder of the President by making no mention at all of this shot. It could not account for the injuries to the President and Governor and for it with only three bullets (any more meaning a conspiracy and no Oswald-single assassin Report) until Arlen Specter invented the single-bullet theory.

The President could have been and probably was struck much earlie1 than the Report acknowledges as even possible.

His photographed reaction to the so-called fatal shot is inconsistent with the official description of that shot. It is consistent wi1 the suppressed finding of a piece of skull 29 hours later and to the lef1 of where the assassination occurred. Finding the piece of skull to the south, or left, of the scene of the assassination is not consistent with a rear shot and a right explosion of the head, the official account.

The size and weight of the bullet fragment in Governor Connally's leg, in themselves enough to invalidate the Report and all the investigation, were known and suppressed. Experts who told the Commission prior to hearings that this theory was impossible either were not called or, on the basis of no new evidence, testified to the Commission other than as they informed it in private.

The staff papers relating to the President's rear non-fatal wound refer to it as a back rather than a neck wound. If it were a back wound, this alone wrecks the Report and the Commission. The basis for saying its alleged but never traced or proven path through the body was "traced" is an "assumption" and nothing more. This is the word of the admiral in charge of the entire Naval Medical Center. He was present at the autopsy along with not less than 22 others, not one of whom was called by the Commission! And he knew, as I later helped establish. that the path was not traced (as we shall see in Part 3).

The autopsy doctors had earlier told Arlen Specter other than what they testified to, and he, in conducting that testimony, let it pass.

Here, in these hitherto suppressed documents, we have the opposite of what is in the Report - disproof of that Report - and self-administered impugning of character and integrity unequaled in history.

If this is what one lone-and-unassisted man with limited time and facilities can find when a large proportion of the files are still withheld, what might remain to be discovered about:

The fact;
The integrity of the staff, of the Commission, of the Report and of the government; and
The real reason for the assassination and those responsible for it?

9. "KP: J.F.K. 4-1; J.B.C. 1,2,3,4"

In any murder the autopsy is essential to a solution of the crime and its punishment. No less is this true when a President is murdered. Throughout my writing I have referred to this autopsy as a dubious inquest. The dictionary definition of "dubious" is "doubtful", "uncertain", "of questionable character". No autopsy serves its intended purpose, that of a post-mortem examination to determine the cause of death, if it leaves in doubt what it need not, if it does not seek the cause or causes and examines them, if it is uncertain where there need be no uncertainty.

Aside from determining the cause of death, it is expected that the autopsy report will be a definitive, medico-legal statement of what happened to the degree possible to man and science. This autopsy and the report on it are not helpful and not dependable because they lack the essential character of official, criminal, legal inquiry and are not positive. Rather than defining what really happened, as dissection of the President's body disclosed it, this autopsy and its report put questions where there should have been answers. There is nothing in it that really adds to knowledge. Instead, it raises additional doubts and creates confusion. The essence of available fact is not in the report.

Searching for clues to the questions the Report substitutes for answers, I went to the appropriate Commission files. There was no alternative. With 26 large volumes for evidence (and even this enormity was not a limitation externally imposed upon the Commission), the essential evidence of the autopsy and what relates to it are not included in the estimated 10,000,000 words in these volumes, as it also is not in the literary vastness of 900 pages, the verbal expanse of the Report.

It is not in the files, either. Had the Commission published every word in its appropriate files, there would be no essential, affirmative knowledge added to the deficient, inadequate and incomplete material it did publish. Negative evidence is there in abundance. To that we shall return.

This statement is based upon a belief that should be warranted but is not: That the files were not gutted. They were.

Those whose writing careers have been advanced by their joyous escapes from reality, and who pretend to have told the truth about the assassination or to have assessed dispassionately the writings critical of the investigation of the assassination, have not sought the essence in the files or are of contemptible, unspeakable dishonesty - or both. They need only have thumbed through File J.F.K. 4-1 to learn the real truth of the assassination investigation, that it was a whitewash, a put-up job. Had they added to this less than an hour of reading a little more and examined the four categories under "Connolly, John B.", requiring less than an additional hour - and had they been looking for truth, not propaganda - they would have learned that these files are but tinseled window-dressing for the overanxious-to-believe yokels of high station.

File J.F.K. 4-1 is "Autopsy". It is on the second sheet of the "file classification" discussed earlier. First is that on the Texas Governor. Typically, as though cunning gremlins with a deft touch were setting the stage for what was to ensue, each of the three spellings of the Governor's name is incorrect. His name has an "a" in it, but not in the "file classification" where it is replaced by another "o".

It is symptomatic that when, after almost four years, I got a copy of this classification, no one had corrected the only-wrong spellings of his name. That is the way it is with the evidence, as it was with the investigation: Nobody corrected the obvious, original errors.

Each of the four categories under wrong-spelled "Connolly" is vital in study of "J.F.K. 4-1". The doctrine under which the Commission labored, the predetermination it imposed upon itself, that Lee Harvey Oswald was a lone and unassisted assassin, permits no alternative. That single-bullet nightmare holds us all captive, as it did the Commission. The only escape is probing and prodding all the available evidence.

For the government there now is no repair. It has done what it has done. For all its might, power and influence - unequaled in history - it has rendered itself impotent as all the king's horses and all the king's men. Its investigation and its Report are like Humpty Dumpty.

For others, for national integrity, for a free and honorable future, there is the possible escape of truth - truth about the investigation, about the fact of the assassination.

Search for this truth in the files begins with futility of the Report, in which it is absent, and ends with the emptiness of the gutted files.

The answers to the questions that were not answered and too often were never asked are not in the autopsy file nor in the Connally files. Each of the Connally categories is pertinent because the single-bullet conclusion of the Report cannot be separated from the autopsy examination and its report. These divisions are "Shooting", "Injuries--Wounds", "Treatment at Parkland Memorial Hospital", and "Interviews".

But the incompleteness of the Connally files and the gutting of the autopsy file are not the fault of the prosector and his assistants. These are independent of and separate from the autopsy deficiencies. They are staff responsibilities and official actions and, I fear, had this been a competent, thorough autopsy and report, the same thing would have happened, perhaps more of it. By accident or design, there was a conspiracy against evidence. Whether or not the manifestation of the invisible but omnipresent hand of a guiding genius, something always happened to the evidence and the Commission never did anything about it.

In some cases the Commission itself is responsible for what happened to the best of the available and conceivable evidence - did to it what was done. In other cases it tolerated what should never have been done and never should have been tolerated. It happened, because of the nature and function of the autopsy, that much of this is part of or related to the autopsy.

For example, there is the so-called "found" bullet, whose public record is consistent only with a design for it to be "found", with its having been planted. It bears the unmistakable marks of the rifle said to have been Oswald's; that we cannot question. That these marks are as distinctive as fingerprints we also must accept. This, however, is neither legal nor logical evidence that this particular bullet was used in the crime. That it was is an assumption without proof or even the effort at developing proof. All the pertinent evidence, such as its almost pristine condition, is that this bullet could not conceivably have had the history officially bestowed upon it, not if its biographers had been Grimm, Andersen, Mother Goose and Jules Verne, all collaborating and at the pinnacle of their powers.

Misused, as it was, this Bullet 399 became important as a link to Oswald, which it could have been and was not, and from him to the assassination which, if it might have been proven, was not attempted. Failure to seek proofs of this connection is fairly interpreted as indicating that those making the decision knew it would turn out otherwise, that it would prove Oswald was being framed.

When Robert A. Frazier, experienced FBI firearms expert, testified about this bullet to some of the most competent and experienced lawyers who could be assembled, his testimony was significantly evasive, in keeping with the character of the questioning, which was designed for this type of response. Beginning on page 161 of WHITEWASH, I discuss the evidence of the "finding" of this bullet and the science applied to it.

Everything went wrong with the evidence about this bullet as it never should have and never, normally, could have. Examples are the destruction of the evidence mutely borne by Governor Connally's unwanted clothing, or the immediate and continuing suppression of the spectrographic analysis. These two capers would have been disasters for the government in court, where opposing counsel would have adduced the pertinent and painfully obvious evidence that the abnormalities were so suspicious they are indicative of collusion and conspiracy to frame. Had this been a case in court, not before a one-sided Commission, neither the destruction nor the suppression of evidence would have been dared.

When Frazier was on the stand he testified that this bullet had been wiped clean. Not entirely, 100 percent clean, for there remained residues. But clean enough so that he had no additional cleansing to perform prior to making a study of whatever it is that he studied. His testimony does not inform us. It is merely that bullets are of lead, as a child not blessed with FBI training and long experience knows.

From his testimony, what Frazier did not on his own do, and what the Commission did not order him or the FBI to do, was the obvious requirement: Make a study, at even that too-late date, to determine the nature of the residues. It is quite obvious that the FBI knew the hand-to-hand, pocket-to-pocket history of this bullet, as reported in the fantasy presented as evidence. Someone in the FBI or on the Commission, either of its staff or membership, should have ordered tests to determine whether these were human residues. This bullet is said to have gone through the President once, the Governor twice and partly a third time. Was there corroborating evidence?

Frazier certainly knew, as did others in the FBI whose job it was to know, how this bullet got to the FBI in Washington, as an earlier chapter reveals. Knowing this seemingly haphazard journey in detail that is denied most of us, Frazier nonetheless avoided saying in his testimony that, by accident, the residues had been wiped from the bullet during transit. His words are, "The bullet was clean." Asked by Assistant Counsel Melvin Eisenberg, "There was no blood or similar material on the bullet when you received it?" (WHITEWASH 163), Frazier avoided direct answer, saying instead, "Not that would interfere with the examination, no, sir."

Those of us equipped with less science than the FBI's firearms expert might, naively, consider that the purpose of "examination" would include determination of whether there was "blood or similar material" on a bullet said to have inflicted seven injuries on two different men (whose blood types were not state secrets) and to have smashed, splintered and adhered to bones in three parts of the body of one of these men.

Shortly after this testimony, Eisenberg returned to Frazier's less than fully informative remark with less than a Perry Mason zeal. He asked, "You also mentioned there was blood or some other substance on the bullet marked 399. Is that an offhand determination, or was there a test to determine what the substance was?"

"No," Frazier replied, "there was no test made of the materials."

(This is not callousness, calling a President's blood and tissue "material"; it is science. The FBI is very scientific. Its science is impersonal, particularly impersonal where President John F. Kennedy was concerned.)

Those whose concept of the diligence of American lawyers in their tireless quest for truth and justice comes from television and not the hearings of the President's Commission on the Assassination of President Kennedy may be surprised that this, so far as Counsel Eisenberg is concerned, is the full discharge of his responsibilities. He is not without reason to so regard it for the attendance at that hearing on Tuesday, March 31, 1964 (3H390ff.), included:

95

The Chief Justice-Chairman and Commission Members, Representative Hale Boggs and John J. McCloy, his employers on our behalf;

The former Solicitor General of the United States, J. Lee Rankin, then Commission general counsel;

Leon Jaworski, billed as special counsel to the attorney general of Texas, but also director of a CIA foundation/front;

Other staff members, including Norman Redlich; and

Two gentlemen whose booking is ambiguous: "Charles Murray and Lewis Powell, observers", who, in the non-fairy-tale, real-life function they had, were to "represent" Oswald, to look out for his rights and those of his guiltless infant daughters (and for those of all Americans in the absence of opposing counsel), as the representatives of the American Bar Association, a function whose concept and practice was an unofficial Commission adjunct.

Now, if it is suspected that all of these eminences, among the nation's leading legal and political luminaries, were either dozing or with their minds on other weighty problems, one certainly was not. That great international lawyer whose services to several administrations are of long duration and good press, whose special competence is banking, Commissioner John J. McCloy, was wide awake. He immediately asked a relevant question.

But not about these residues, "blood or similar material" in one phrasing, "substance" in another. About this he, too, was silent. He heard the testimony and was undisturbed.

Oh, well, is it not enough to know that the diligent FBI, ever alert, always with at least one eye open, with all that science the unstinting taxpayers provide, was fully aware of the presence of "substance" or of the somewhat less comprehensible "material" that is "similar" to "blood"?

Here it is necessary to caution those whose knowledge of the skill and dedication, the unflagging and undeflected devotion to duty, the relentless, bulldog determined FBI comes from TV that, in real life, when an American President was murdered while it was their job to keep him alive, the FBI is not at all like it is on TV.

And only because in real life the finest lawyers in the land and the most scientific police in our history somehow fell short of what every script-writer, without benefit of Harvard Law or G-man school, knows to write into grade B melodramas, we do not know what was on the bullet.

We do not know because the Commission did not want to know. Because the Commission did not know, it had no difficulty concluding that this bullet had defied all the laws of physics, ballistics and mythology and had, indeed, inflicted all seven non-fatal injuries on both men and, exultantly, emerged from this challenge unscarred.

Not having ordered the FBI to go back to its labs and scratch from the bullet a few microscopic remnants of that or those "substances" or "materials" - or to take a quick check at that then-suppressed and still-suppressed spectrographic analysis and come back with the nitty gritty - the Commission had less to interfere with its reaching this determination that center-stage in its investigation of the assassination was a veritable 20th century Puck of a bullet, Bullet 399.

More suited, perhaps, to the deliberations of the Space Committees of the Congress than the President's Commission is the career thus officially that of Bullet 399. To meet the requirements imposed upon it by this truly august body, these are some of the things that bullet had to have done:

Penetrated the President's neck without striking a bone, and in the course of this beginning of its swift but short active life, to have thumbed its nose at forensic medicine by making a hole about twice as large in entering as when it departed - which nice, true-flying bullets just do not do.

In the span of perhaps a foot or so, having flown with undeviating fidelity to and through the President, it began to wobble a bit when it

plunged into the Governor's chest, under the right armpit. It then settled down to the most spectacular demonstration of self-control since
John the Baptist spurned Salome. Going at about 2,000 feet per second
and with a fineness of control not yet dreamed of at Cape Kennedy, it
flipped around so that only its back end made contact with the Governor's
fifth rib. Perhaps "made contact" is a slight understatement, when what
399 did to four inches of that rib is recalled, but such a career must
be approached with an absolutely uncluttered mind. It is easier to try
to conceive of what, until that moment in all of history, had never been
conceived if we bear in mind that contact with coarse cloth or leather
can mark a bullet, and this No. 399 chap was almost entirely unscratched.
The unaided eye finds no blemish.

Now, what happened inside the Governor's chest, at 2,000 feet per
second, is that four inches of his fifth rib got so smashed up that
pieces of it, in turn, became miniature, individual projectiles.

Commissioner McCloy, possibly reluctant to concede the incredible
melding of might and magic to 399, wondered aloud if perhaps "the actual
bullet could not have hit the rib at all but it might have been the ex-
panding flesh that would cause the wound, or the proper contusion, I gues
you would call it on the rib itself?" His application of the elegant sub
tleties of international finance to the medical description is an expression of fine sensitivity. "The wound or the proper contusion" was the
rib smashing; the "you" of the "I guess you would call it" was Dr. Robert
R. Shaw who, despite the delicate understating and quiet passion - should
we say "desperation"? - of the Commissioner's appeal, would call it no
such thing. Politely but firmly he replied, "I think we would have to
postulate that the bullet hit the rib itself..." (WHITEWASH 175).

There is a way out of McCloy's dilemma (which is, how could an unscratched bullet smash up a tough human rib?). By battering with its
butt end only, of course. And to do this, all that 399 had to add to
those already incredible powers was that of following the graceful, curve
contour of the human rib with its rear-end radar that kept it at the correct, undeviating backside 90-degree angle. For the approximately one-
six-thousandth of a second it required for those four rib-inches to be
shattered, 399 had also to be anticipating the disengagement that would
leave no trace upon his smooth surfaces that bone, even more than coarse
cloth or leather, could trademark. Whether it braked itself or executed
a fancy dance step, with the bullet mute, we cannot really know; but what
we do know is that it succeeded. Whatever the maneuver, it was accomplished with a sideways fillip, for when 399, for a slight fraction of a
second, saw daylight again, it was when making an inch-and-a-half hole
under the Governor's right nipple, a not inconsiderable achievement for
a quarter-inch-thick bullet, especially because in the act it successfully evaded the adjacent rib.

For full appreciation of this fantastic performance, all officiall
certified (for it is essential to the conclusion of a body no less august
than a Presidential Commission, which, in effect, so concluded), the
reader is urged to consider the thinness of the flesh encasing the human
chest. If this is a half-inch, then in approximately one-forty-eight-
thousandth of a second, 399 disengaged the rib he was splintering with
just his rear end and turned sideways, without scraping against any surface of the trademarking rib as he did it. Marvelous, no?

Fresh challenges lay ahead, but with the exuberance of success,
399 improvised at 2,000 feet per second - exactly what was needed to bat-
ter its way through the Governor's right wrist, again without detectably
marking itself. The shattered ruin of the rib is naught to the shambles
of the wrist. Here, carried away with success, 399 indulged in a side
game, sneaking clues into the wound while keeping clues off itself.
Traces of mohair, the doctors correctly told themselves. And they told
the Commission they could not conceive of how 399 accomplished the wrecking of that wrist without leaving a trace on itself.

(Specter temporarily eased past this crisis by asking the doctors
to offer opinions about ordinary, other bullets, not this spectacular
one - could "a" bullet have gone through that wrist and been unmarked.

By going backward, and only backward, the doctors suggested, because the back of a bullet is not encased in a hardened jacket.)

Nowhere in the evidence is there any explanation of how this or any other bullet could have plunged through the solid wrist-bones without getting a little scratched, at least on the sides. In order to proceed, possibly we can imagine that in some mysterious way 399 encased itself in a sheltering remnant of perhaps a Niebelungen past or invoked a fitting necromancy and thus accomplished what was required to fulfill its obligations to the as-yet-unappointed Commission.

Here, with the bullet unmarked and the wrist in shattered ruin, still new and undisclosed magical powers went into play - and how fast! - for in the course of the two inches (what split-split of a split second is two inches when flight is at 2,000 feet in a single second?) of wrist smashing, computer-fast it also planned ahead.

The greatest cunning was still to be summoned, for in whatever short space remained between that right wrist and left thigh, this flip-flopping bullet that had stopped wobbling only to dance, stopped dancing to wobble again, ceased wobbling to guide right and fly backward, curt-sied sideways briefly, then suddenly flew no way but backward and in this fashion latched itself so firmly to the Governor's tibia that months late a fragment was still glued to it, side by side, so attached by a last-minute, right-angle turn inside the thigh.

With all of this, the most spectacular demonstrations were still to be demanded of this little bullet, whose brief life had, without doubt already exhausted it. While traveling through Dallas at a mere mile-a-minute clip from the Texas School Book Depository Building to Parkland Hospital, it had to lie in wait and store up a sort of reverse kinetic energy, then it had to be patient while the Governor in whose thigh it was hidden was rushed to the operating room. After he was undressed - in total silence and when no one was looking - it discharged that reverse kinetic energy with what bowlers call "inside English" - in just the righ arc that would enable it to speed invisibly from the Governor's leg to under the mattress on which he and it had been, not too far under, for it had to drop out when that stretcher was given a jar; not too little under for it had to ride up and down the elevator until Hospital Engineer Darrell Tomlinson (WHITEWASH 161-2) came along to put the stretcher off and then, when jarred a bit, to fall out and go public.

When it is understood that bullets have no fathers to teach them, no seeing eyes to guide them, knowing precisely the arc and exactly the speed is quite an accomplishment for a bullet like this, only a quarter of an inch thick. More so when we consider that it had been officially ruled over-age and declared surplus. Too small an arc and it would have hit the mat and made a hole in it; too large and it would have missed entirely or, horrors! have struck the steel frame which would, at the very least, have marked it. Too little energy would not have put it under the mat far enough to await Tomlinson's jarring; too much would have put it so far under he could not have jogged it out. It calculated perfectly!

All of these things this bullet did, and more with which I have not burdened the reader, for I fear he may be unwilling to concede there ever had been such a bullet as this. Of course, there was, and it was 399, and it is certified - should I say sanctified? - by the Report of the President's Commission on the Assassination of President Kennedy - and how much more official can you get?

It seems it was easier for this Commission to satisfy itself that Puckish, magical 399 did all these wondrous things without complicating and confusing matters with prosaic considerations like residues.

Is it possible that the FBI's science could add to this story, improve on this science? Not likely.

But all of the magnificent performance would have been in vain had it been presented in a court of law. In fact, had it been adduced before a Marine Corps court martial (Oswald, too, had been a Marine), Oswald would have been acquitted. Something remarkably similar - in charge, not victim and conclusion - actually happened in Viet Nam.

It seems that a Vietnamese civilian was shot to death, that a Marine was seen to have fired a rifle from a truck in which he and others were riding, seemingly drunk and in high spirits. He acknowledged firing a shot but recalled it as having been into the air.

The Associated Press reported this, and the Los Angeles *Times* of June 29, 1967, prepared its own story from that of the Associated Press. Here begins a startling parallel to Bullet 399, which, recall, bore the rifling marks of the rifle said to have been bought by Oswald:

The prosecution presented an expended bullet that matched the rifle allegedly held by Collard /the accused/ at the time. The bullet was found on the floor inside the dead man's house. The prosecution contended that this was the bullet that killed the man.

This trial, too, had technical experts:

Leland Jones, retired head of the Los Angeles Police Department's crime laboratory, testified that the bullet could not possibly have entered a human body. /Although/ fired from the rifle ... blood or tissue would have remained on the bullet for years if it had hit the man and he could find no trace of either ..."

The verdict: Acquittal!

"Blood or tissue would have remained on the bullet for years!"

Consider this impartial evidence, accepted by a military court and unrefuted by a military prosecution, which could call on the FBI in addition to its own experts: Although proved to have been fired from the rifle connected with the accused, because of the absence of blood or tissue, which would have been detectable and identifiable for years, "the bullet could not possibly have entered a human body"!

Is it possible to find a more exact parallel? The case against Oswald was weaker, for that rifle was not shown to have been in his possession at the time of the assassination. Bullet 399 is claimed to have passed through two human bodies, not one. and three and a half times, not just once.

The bullet may have been magical, but Presidents and Governors are not. They are men, humans, as are poor Vietnamese; their blood is mortal blood, their tissue mortal tissue.

Here we find explanation for the FBI expert's expert evasiveness when asked about the residues, as we find explanation for the contentment of the Commission of legal and political eminences and their legal staff at the absence of answers about the residues on Bullet 399, as we find explanation for the lack of questions about these residues, about the absence of tests to identify them!

Oswald was "defended" by the great of the American Bar Association, the past, incumbent and coming presidents, including the founder of that noble (and properly anti-Soviet) concept, "Law Day".

How?

By total silence about the suppression of the spectrographic analysis and the complete absence of any questions about that "material" or "substance" that was "blood" or "similar" to it that was on Bullet 399!

That was not in the way of the FBI, so they didn't bother it, didn't test it or analyze it. The Commission and Oswald's "defenders" were satisfied, even though "blood or tissue would have remained on the bullet for years" - had it ever been there!

It all ties together. This has not been an extraneous excursion. The fiction of the defense of Oswald's rights (and it is well not to lose sight of the purpose of the hearing, to find out who killed the President and perhaps why); the real function of the American Bar Association and its honored, honorable representatives (Oswald's counsel, that is); the kinds of hearings held; how evidence was gathered and presented, accepted and evaluated; how the truth was sought and certified; how the autopsy is part of all of it, together with the single-bullet theory, "The Ballad of Bullet 399", "J.F.K. 4-1" and "J.B.C. 1,2,3,4" - all are of the same whole: Threads and fibers woven through the woof and warp of the assassination and its investigation.

If it does not surprise the reader, it did surprise me to find there was nothing of any consequence in the "J.F.K. 4-1" file. If anywhere, I did believe, certainly here there would be some information of significance, some knowledge about the murder, how it was accomplished, what was learned at the autopsy, some of the missing evidence and records

The staff of the archive was going over this tremendous accumulation and preparing more of it to be released. I delayed requesting copie of every paper in the autopsy file until the last minute. Just stop and think of the situation at the end of 1967, four years after the murder, three after its "solution". The world was rampant with dissatisfaction about the inadequate and insufficient Report on the assassination (and this is certainly an understatement of the reality), but the federal government was still keeping vast stores of files secret! In this case, apparently, secrecy was maintained by assigning less than a corporal's guard to do the actual work of making it available. With all the millior of federal employees, a single man of the two assigned to the archive to go over these files and prepare them for "release"! This was not his only responsibility - it is one added to an already full schedule of work In between the other, full-time duties, he did this. The wonder is not that it took so long but that he was able to accomplish anything. In practice, this amounts to a different kind of suppression.

In reality, what it actually means is that, aside from what has been denied under the "guidelines" - which gives each agency that was the source of the defunct Commission's documents the right to suppress what it wants suppressed - great gobs of files were suppressed by the designed malfunction of bureaucracy - by simply not putting the manpower on it. On a subject like this, with the national honor and integrity involved, with Macbethian scandals openly bruited, the government quietly and effec tively gave validity to these hasty beliefs by delaying what it dared not forcibly suppress. It hoped, with each passing day, that somehow that awful pile of dirt swept under the too-small rug would just go away, just be forgotten. Its clear wish was that, with the popular President secure ly buried, with the passing of time, people would forget how he got burie lose interest in his murder and the phony, official explanation of it in that contrived Report.

Simply slowing down what was accessible to the steadily decreasing number of researchers, distressingly small at the peak of interest, was an effective mechanism of suppression, as effective as total suppression, as long as the files could be denied by simple bureaucratic delay. Bungling, crude force, were unnecessary. The government just sat tight and let nothing happen, guaranteeing that nothing would or could happen by not assigning a single special employee to the task of arranging the Commission files for access. The maximum assigned staff was two men who had other continuing assignments!

Meanwhile, naturally, the closing of ranks behind the official fic tion, whether or not of official inspiration, was effectuated by all the mass agencies of news and opinion.

So, delay was as effective as it was simple, and it gave the time required for the greatest campaign of public indoctrination since the Report itself to befuddle the popular mind.

First I was promised this autopsy file, then I was denied it, ther I was promised all but two documents. This was a total of four pages, or a minute of Xeroxing. Of course, I was assured there was no suppression, no violation of regulations. Finally, I got what I was told was all but those special four pages that had to be denied so there could be "orderly processing". These were then promised by September 15 and were not then available.

I completed the writing of this book while I waited for two withheld documents from the "J.F.K. 4-1" file, for four sheets of paper from the file on the Presidential autopsy of four years earlier.

Save for a single sheet, the few pages of what is filed under "J.F.K. 4-1" add nothing to what was already available and known to me and in my own files. There are the same mistakes I found in other files. What was missing, what should be there and is not - what is required to be there - had been gutted. Here is everything in that file:

The brief covering letter of December 20, 1963, with which James ; Rowley, chief of the Secret Service, sent Rankin a copy of the autopsy protocol. This is not an original copy, of which there were eight. An original copy was too good for the archive, too good for the Commission. This, at the very best, is a third generation copy. Some of it is completely illegible. In addition, it has, at some step in the repeated photocopying of photocopies, been reduced in size. But it is supposed to be one of the original eight copies and it should be marked as from the 77th file, "Clinical Records of Autopsy". It is not. Every copy made from what Rowley sent the Commission on December 20 should also show this number if, properly, they come from this source.

An even more remote copy of allegedly the same document, the Presidential autopsy protocol, contains notations not on any of the more than half-dozen copies of this allegedly single version, and an attachment I had not seen elsewhere. It has a source indicated, and that source cannot possibly be the right one, else the list of files is wrong. It is marked as coming from "CR362a", or part "a" of File 362. Now, on page 28 of the list of these files there appears this description of File 362, which is identified as "three envelopes" coming from "AG Texas": "Travis Kirk's letter 437".

In its infinite wisdom, the Report spares us the identification of "Travis Kirk's letter 437", in quotation marks in the listing, and the blessing of revelation is denied us. However, it is not likely that, wit whatever significance can be read into the mystery we must here abandon, "Travis Kirk's letter 437" could have included a copy of the autopsy, nor could "AG Texas" have originated it, estimable as the services of the Hon. Waggoner Carr were.

This authorization is in CD362a, from which I had obtained a copy. For years the Archives had insisted it had no copy of the requisite authorization. The most reasonable explanation appears to have been its withholding from all the autopsy files or its destruction at some later date, with a copy having by some accident been in papers from the Texas investigation under Carr.

But the authorization is not with any of the federal autopsy papers or files in the Archives. Several years later I saw the original.

This set of the autopsy report is the only one of the many I have seen that has a copy of what, in the original or an original copy, should be in this file and, in photocopy, attached to every copy. It is of a generation so remote, so illegible - so indistinct where it is not illegible - that I cannot make out the identification of the government form or be certain of some of the printing on it.

The heading is "AUTHORIZATION FOR POST-MORTEM EXAMINATION".* Wheth or not it is even a copy of an original document is uncertain, for two of the three lines specifically calling for "signature" are typed in. These are the names of the Commanding Officer, Captain R. O. CANADA; and "authority to consent", where the word "wife" is typed in, and the name of "Mrs. JOhn F. Kennedy" (with the error "JOhn" in the typing), the address "White House". The one signature appears to be that of Robert Kennedy.

Two other entries on this form dispel any basis for suppression of the autopsy or any parts thereof, such as the pictures and X-rays, and end forever the question of ownership of the documents of the autopsy, which never, legally, really existed, anyway.

Above the "signatures", with generous blank space separating them from the printed words, is this agreement: "Authority is also granted for the preservation and study of all tissue which may be removed. This authority shall be limited only by the conditions expressly stated below." "Below" is blank paper, not "conditions" or any other reservations Thereby any conditions or reservations are waived.

*See p. 507.

If there ever had been any doubt of whose property the autopsy and everything related to it is (and in my mind there never was), the last words of the first printed sentence end that. They refer to the form and any other papers, to be "attached to this form for permanent file". Permanent file! Exactly what I had reported to the government in protest against the illegal handling of the pictures and X-rays - and let us not forget what is more important - the gutted files, those quintessential autopsy notes!

The Navy's "permanent files"? On November 25, as I have already reported, Admiral Galloway sent the White House the last of the eight original copies of the autopsy and the other records of it not then already turned over. Legally, rightly, these should be a permanent Navy file. According to the available evidence, which must be dug out for the Commission suppressed it, there is no Navy file on the autopsy.

Admiral Galloway also, separately, sent the "Authorization for post mortem examination signed by Attorney General and dated Nov. 22, 1963". This is the last of 11 items in a receipt to Admiral George G. Burkley, executed November 26, 1963, by Robert I. Bouck, head of the Secret Service "Protective Research Service" at the White House. *

Among the interesting, important and suppressed items in this receipt which will again attract our attention are:

One letter - Certificate of Death of John F. Kennedy - State of Texas - dated Nov. 22, 1963;
One carbon copy of letter dated November 26 from Commanding Officer, U.S. Medical School, concerning law and regulations regarding confidential nature of the events;
One receipt dated Nov. 22, 1963, regarding a carton of photographic film, undeveloped except for X-rays, delivered to PRS for safekeeping
An original and six pink copies of Certificate of Death (Nav.Med.N
One copy of autopsy report and notes of the examining doctor which is described in letter of transmittal Nov. 25, 1963 by Dr. Gallaway (sic).

In this case the suppression is much worse, for this PRS receipt was officially entered into evidence as Exhibit 397 (WHITEWASH 183). In offering the file of which it is part into evidence, Specter said (2H373) "May the record show that Exhibit No. 397 is identical with the document which has been previously identified as Commission No. 371 for our internal purposes."

Exhibit 397 allegedly is printed (17H29-48). Part of it is. But only part. Not one of the items listed above! Nor is this PRS receipt, which I got from File 371 and which in the upper right-hand corner has the identification of "Commission No. 371".

Does the reader believe that in the investigation of the murder of his President such items of evidence as the certificate of death, a letter on the applicable law and regulations, what appears to be an additional Navy certificate of death (it is nowhere described, not mentioned in Humes testimony), and the heart of the autopsy report, the "notes of the examining doctor", should be included in the evidence? His Commission to investigate this murder deemed otherwise and suppressed each and every one of these most elemental items of evidence that would have been required had the investigation been not that of a President but of an unwanted, friendless derelict. It then went further and suppressed the receipt that itemized them. (This is developed further in Part 3.)

Once the decision was made to suppress, everything indicating what had been suppressed also had to be expunged. So the innocent receipt, too, was kept out of Exhibit 397. I have made repeated searches of duplicate Files 371 and none of this, except the receipt and the letter of transmittal, is in any of them. I asked that an official search be made by the Archives. Their search confirmed mine. The suppression is total. These items, the beginning point of any serious murder investigation, have been denied even the archive, such is the archive to the murder of this President!

There is no doubt that the "notes of the examining doctor" existed

*See p. 527.

after Bouck signed the receipt. Nor is there any doubt about the nature of these notes. They are the entire basis of the autopsy. It is not in those incomplete marginal notes Dr. Boswell kidded the "star" reporter of the Baltimore Sun into believing that Humes used in writing his report, but these notes, made for that purpose. Others have ignored what I immediately concluded was Humes' vital testimony (WHITEWASH 183):

> These are various notes in long-hand, or copies, rather, of various notes in long-hand made by myself, in part, during the performance of the examination of the late President, and in part after the examination when I was preparing to have a typewritten report made.

The key words here are "during the performance of the examination". These are the missing autopsy notes. Those Humes made thereafter are in the file and the exhibit, because it served Commission purposes to print them. Thus, what Humes burned - imagine burning anything historically and legally important in the investigation of the murder of a President! and imagine a Commission that, hearing of this, was silent! - could not have been in his hand when he testified four months after the burning. This is no reference to the first draft of the autopsy, burned after Oswald was murdered, when there would be no cross-examination of the autopsy surgeons. These are the vital basis of the entire autopsy report that were in Humes' hand, did exist, at least in a Xeroxed copy, are required to have been printed in Exhibit 397 and are not, are required to be in File 371 and are not, that the government suppresses.

This is the way the murder of John F. Kennedy was investigated - by the suppression and destruction of the most fundamental evidence. And this by the government that succeeded his, by the government that came into power by his murder, the murder it allegedly was investigating!

This is not an isolated suppression. Throughout this book there are numerous similar cases relating to other autopsy evidence.

But to return to this particular copy of the autopsy report, handwritten numbers added to the third page of this set of the autopsy report seem to translate 7x4 mm into 7/25 by 4/25 inch, 14 cm into 5.6 inch. (Here I note that another copy of the allegedly identical document, also from File J.F..K. 1, has two notations handwritten on page 6, adjacent to the descriptions of the fatal and non-fatal wounds. These are "#3 Shot" and "#1 Shot".

The Sibert-O'Neill so-called FBI "autopsy" report is in this file, in a version photographically reduced in size from the original and Xeroxed from File 7, where it is folios 280-8 of the first part. File 7 is one of the larger collections of individual reports into book-size documents. It requires about four inches of thickness when bound into two separate volumes.

There is special interest: File 7 warrants a short digression. The last very large hunk of it was entirely suppressed. Although most of the individual reports are but a page or two in length, by "request" - read "order" - of the FBI, pages 494 through 777 are "withheld" - read "suppressed".

Now, with File 7 we are a bit better situated than with most cases of suppression. Here there is a name index. I have made a listing of the names on the almost 300 consecutive suppressed pages. There is one detectable consistent pattern to these names: radical right. Here there is a prima facie case of the FBI ordering suppression for the protection of those whose political bed is warm to Hoover, those from whom he derives his political support, those with whose ideas he is most comfortable and whose ideas he expresses, in sometimes moderate language.

Without something that Hoover has made impossible, close examination of what he has suppressed, it is not possible to tell the whole story of File 7 and its contents. On one score, however, there is no doubt whatsoever: The recurrent, identifiable names are radical right names. But is it conceivable that in a file of almost 800 pages, more than a third - in one big, unbroken mouthful - can by pure accident be suppressed by the FBI? Is it also accidental that these have the strain of radical right woven through them?

In File 7, the Sibert-O'Neill report has a cover page added. It reads, "A. AUTOPSY OF BODY OF PRESIDENT JOHN FITZGERALD KENNEDY." Aside from those copies made by other means or other varieties of copying machines, this bears the printed identification of two different Xerox machines. Attached are an additional Sibert-O'Neill report of November 27. Its four paragraphs cover their interview with Gerald A. Behn, Secret Service Special Agent in Charge of the White House detail.* It describes the chancey manner in which Bullet 399 showed up in Washington, how haphazardly and belatedly a piece of the President's skull and bullet fragments also were found in the car. Its concluding paragraph repeats Kellerman's promise, that "the undeveloped photographs and x-rays made during the course of the autopsy ... could be made available to the Federal Bureau of Investigation on request", further establishing that there is no reason for the FBI to have been uninformed about the autopsy report, if, indeed, it was.

Next are the receipts to the Navy Hospital for what the Secret Service took or got, including these undeveloped pictures and X-rays and "notes of the examining doctor which is described in letter of transmittal of Nov. 25, 1963 by Dr. Gallaway". These notes are part of File 371, which also includes much less legible copies than exist of the handwritten autopsy, etc. Missing are what is required to be in this file (WHITE WASH 183), those identical autopsy notes covered by Admiral Galloway's epistle of November 25. Oddly, however, File 371 was not received until February 7, 1964.

Also in "J.F.K. 4-1" is a Xerox of a "certified copy" of what is politely called the "inquest" held in Dallas. In it Justice of the Peace Theran Ward "certified" that particular proceeding was consummated almost two weeks prior to the assassination! It contains this language:

Witness my hand, officially, this 10th day of November A.D. 1963.

How careful everyone was to be precise, to assure accuracy and completeness when this President was murdered!

There is a copy of Secret Service Agent Elmer Moore's report of December 12 in which that Service found other than the Commission, that from the autopsy report, the Zapruder movie and other evidence later misinterpreted by the Commission, all that could be concluded about the trajectory was that it was "to the rear and above the level of the President" hardly indicating a trajectory to the 66-foot-high sixth-floor window. This report contains a number of other things not supporting the official account.

A single page - the fifth - of the FBI supplemental report of January 9 is Xeroxed and filed here (as it is in "J.B.C. 2"). It is originally File 107.

Illegible, remote-generation copies of Specter's two March 12, 1964, reports of his interviews with the autopsy doctors and Sibert and O'Neill are included. They are so pale and close to illegible that their purpose cannot be serious. Because the remainder of the document is so much paler, the correction of the single word previously referred to, that says the President's rear non-fatal wound was in the "back", is more visible here.

An equally illegible, equally pale copy of an uninformative press release dated March 16 says only that four members of the Commission, listed, heard the three autopsy doctors testify.

Finally, there is a letter from J. Edgar Hoover to Rankin, dated March 18, answering negatively an inquiry by Melvin Eisenberg about several possible scientific tests.

And that (save for the four withheld pages) is the entire content of the entire "autopsy file" of the President's Commission on the Assassination of President Kennedy!

It is not a file, it is a frivolity.

It does not contain what is essential. It contains not a single

*See p. 548.

reference to any effort to obtain what was not spoon-fed the Commission by the federal police. More, it contains no single clue that the Commission of eminences, on their own or under prodding, ever, in any way, did anything to get the missing data that it should have had - could not have discharged its responsibilities without having. One example is the autopsy notes, which were not burned and are officially in its evidence, from which they have been secretly removed.

This, too, is one way to "investigate" the murder of a President!

The Connally files are, similarly, replicas of pieces of other files. They contain repetitive reporting of federal police conclusions, that a separate shot hit Connally. Because these are destructive of the Report, their suppression from that Report and the appended volumes is comprehensible. They contain FBI interviews with close witnesses of the assassination who were not called as witnesses. Several documents reflec poorly on the Dallas police. These include an "arrest report on investigative prisoner" that, with fine judicial impartiality, says Oswald was arrested because "This man shot and killed President John F. Kennedy and Police Officer J. D. Tippit. He also shot and wounded Governor John Connally." No ifs or buts. The police wrapped it up to begin with. No fooling with investigations for them!

The second file (on the "wounds") is carefully gutted to remove the documents I analyze earlier that show the size of the fragment remaining in the Governor's thigh. No reason to spread the disproof of the Report too widely, was there? It also has the proof that the Secret Service phonied its "charts" on the Governor's wounds (WHITEWASH 177,199). The Commission was discreet: It suppressed this from its Report. No nee to embarrass the Secret Service, either. After all, they were only "investigating" the murder of a President! Need they have bothered doctors when they could draw lines and hen-scratches on blank charts themselves, and very neatly, too. The fact is, the Secret Service markings were closer to what the Commission wanted than the reality. That was thoughtful, wasn't it! That this proof of fakery is not in the Report is no accident. The boss, personally, knew about it. The handwritten acknowledgment of J. Lee Rankin, dated February 19, is included. When the Secret Service tried so hard to make the evidence fit the crime, like shots from the sixth-floor window, "moving" the Governor around - in charts - so his wounds would seem to line up, etc., the Commission owed it a slight consideration for its "assistance"!

In short, there is nothing I had not already located elsewhere in these Connally files. There is no need to delay the reader with what would by now be but redundant exposition of their flimsiness and lack of support for the official version of the assassination. They reflect well on no officials and do not help the Report.

There is nothing in them that fosters confidence in the integrity of any persons or agencies involved in the investigation or in the Report itself.

During the course of my protracted efforts to shake loose some of the "withheld" autopsy evidence, I sought information from the Archivist. On September 14, 1967, he confirmed that what is not in this autopsy file also is not elsewhere in the "relevant files". After years of effort, as Part 3 shows, I did recapture and there print much of it.

In short, what this part of my investigation proves is that the essential original evidence of the murder and the investigation of it is lacking. The files do not show who got what of the evidence, what any of them did or did not do with it. In fact, it is not possible to account in any way for any of the original copies of the autopsy report, which is as novel a concept of evidence as it is an original method of "investigating" the murder of a President!

To those who may wonder if it is, indeed, the way the murder of a President should be officially inquired into, I can say only that this is the way the murder of John F. Kennedy was "investigated" and "solved"!

10. FOR THEM NO JUDAS

Before leaving what is - and is not - in these files, perhaps there should be a word on what an autopsy is and should be. It is, of course, a post-mortem examination, with dissection. It is not standard throughout the country. Within any one state, practices can vary, legally. Within Maryland, where the President's body was taken, as elsewhere, state autopsy regulations do not apply to those performed on federal property. Private studies evaluated autopsy practices in some states as entirely inadequate.

Dr. John M. Nichols, University of Kansas Medical Center pathologist, informs me that "In a few states the laws are quite loose and the coroner himself can legally do the autopsy even if he is a truck driver in complete ignorance of things medical." On the other hand, in Connecticut, "it is a legal requirement that the pathologist be 'certified'," meaning by the American Board of Pathology. As I also learned, a pathologist experienced in determination of the cause of death from natural causes may be without the required competence when he probes for the actual cause of death in crimes of violence.

When I learned from my own local officials that getting a definitive statement of the State of Maryland minimum autopsy requirements would be impossible or meaningless, on May 24, 1966, I tried the District of Columbia, which is under federal control. A phone call to the coroner's office there was quite informative until it was clear my interest was in what the autopsy protocol would have contained had it been that of a President. Until that moment the requirements were explained with care

Suppose a man had been shot to death, I was told, and there were two bullets in his body, or two bullet holes. The autopsy examination would include taking his body apart to actually trace the paths of both bullets. If the bullets were fired from different weapons or by different people, the autopsy would be required to show which had been fatal. When a derelict is shot to death in the District of Columbia, this is what happens. " Just the other day," I was told, there had been a case like this. And, I was assured, there is no body glue to patch flesh rent by bullets.

With a bum in the District of Columbia, where the President lives, this is what happens. With the President, examined just across the boundary line, in a federal hospital in Maryland, with autopsy surgeons on the federal payroll, it is what didn't happen but should - and could - have.

Dr. Nichols is making a study of the Kennedy autopsy. He has already published a "Special Contribution" in the July 10, 1967, Journal of the American Medical Association. His earlier researches indicate that the President did have Addison's disease, an adrenal deficiency. His medical sleuthing was careful and detailed, extending backward through medical annals and newspapers for a period of 10 years. While he found it "noteworthy" there was no evidence this ailment ever handicapped the President, that despite it he "was continuously engaged in strenuous mental and physical activity", Dr. Nichols also felt impelled to comment that "the autopsy protocol is curiously silent" on the Addison's disease "as well as on details of the pituitary, of his vertebral column and sacro-iliac joints".

The reader will recall that the President had survived almost fata:

spinal surgery.

There is no stigma attached to Addison's disease and control over it can be maintained more perfectly than, for example, over diabetes. It need never have interfered with his activity as President.

The public should be entitled to know the state of health of the President and all candidates for that office. Addison's disease had been an issue in the campaign. The silence of the autopsy on this point may be explained by the intrusion of relatives or federal officials. Regardless of inspiration, the answer belonged in the autopsy and it is not there.

Because not only writers but scientists and scientific groups had commented unfavorably about the deficiencies in and inadequacies of the autopsy, I asked Dr. Nichols' comments on the essential requirement of autopsies. Here are a few excerpts from his answer:

... The prosector must approach his legal problem somewhat differently than the usual hospital autopsy ... defense counsel may request their own observer ... The body must be absolutely identified. The protocol on the late President does not indicate that he was identified! The body must be weighed, measured and inspected all over; all orifices must be examined ... Sketches with measurements must be made of any unusual findings together with color and black-white pictures ... x-ray the body completely. The films must be developed and inspected prior to starting the autopsy; this may require 15 minutes but knowing the number and position of bullets is important as well as broken bones, tips of knife blades, etc. The pathologist keeps the film negatives himself to use at trial.

In carefully pointing out that the autopsy protocol is used by coroners and prosecutors "to apprehend and convict the guilty", Dr. Nichols also expresses the corollary purpose, "or acquit the innocent". Among those "cases on record" where autopsies acquitted the innocent, he cites one "where the deceased was shot in the head and chest six times while" presumably asleep in bed. The accused confessed. However, microscopic examination of the heart revealed death occurred four hours prior to shooting. The accused was released because "you cannot kill a dead man".

Nothing like this was involved in the President's murder, but the same principles are, the same scientific and legal requirements - which were not met. When the examination was conducted, there was a live Oswald to be defended in court. After he, in turn, was murdered, a "revised" autopsy report, which would not be subject to cross-examination - for there was then nothing to take to court - was filed. It was suppressed for ten months and then only partly released, with the mass and sensation of the Report, which submerged it and denied it the close scrutiny it required and thus escaped.

There is nothing right about this autopsy, nothing final, nothing that satisfies the need for definitive, irrefutable fact. It is inadequate, incomplete, incompetent, lacking honesty and objectivity in its report and in every single official use and misuse that was made of it, beginning with suppression and continuing with gutting.

We have as a national record, a final memento of a President, an eviscerated autopsy report in eviscerated files - eviscerated evidence, eviscerated history.

This, unfortunately, is not untypical. It is the total picture, of all the evidence, all the investigation, all files and records.

For this President the archive is adequately served with nothing closer to original than carbon copies and Xeroxes of them of uncertain generation; altered and incomplete documents; doctored pictures never original, never properly introduced into evidence (none of the vital ones - not a single one - in accordance with the minimum requirements of law), and only those that could not be avoided - then only when they could no longer be avoided; and unstinted, uninhibited suppression, with each of those agencies having a vested interest in suppression exclusively empowered to decide upon and effectuate it.

This archival monument to the President is like the investigation of his murder, for that, too, was of conspicuous incompleteness, designed dishonesty and calculated indefiniteness. Essential witnesses were neither sought nor called, their evidence denied to the solution of the crime and history. Evidence was destroyed. Its destruction was virtually assured by official inaction and action - in the case of the pictures, as PHOTOGRAPHIC WHITEWASH records and documents with the Commission's own until-then suppressed files - and in the case of the landmarks vital to photo intelligence.

Paul Hoch calls my attention to a simple but painfully comprehensible illustration of this point that I first raised in WHITEWASH (p.45). In the Texas State Archives he found a February 24, 1964, letter from General Counsel Rankin to Texas Attorney General Waggoner Carr. A few days longer than three months after the assassination, the federal government found a roundabout way of seeming to ask what it did not and then almost asking for what it said it did not want.

Essential in any photographic analysis is background. With the Zapruder film, for example, any single branch of hedge along the concrete work at the eastern edge of Dealey Plaza could be an orientation point, with Zapruder's known position and that object making the end points of a line that would locate what was between them. For serious inquiry, as in locating the President at any specific frame of that movie, such point are vital. Another is in locating Phil Willis, the essentiality of whose fifth picture is that it was taken not where Wesley Liebeler and the Commission wrongly allege, but just before that and just after the President was shot (discussed at length in WHITEWASH, 44-6, and in two chapter of WHITEWASH II, "Willis By Another Name" and "Willis in His Own Name"). Cropping, or cutting off its sides, destroyed background orientation points in the Willis pictures. Analysis of this fifth Willis picture and the Zapruder frames establishes beyond doubt that the President had been shot before Frame 202, whereas the Commission falsely claims he could not have been until Frame 210, at the earliest. It is not evidence that controlled the Commission's "conclusion", but the distress of its "Oswald-lone assassin" theory, for prior to Frame 210 the President could not have been struck by a shot from that sixth-floor window.

In discussing this in WHITEWASH (p.45), after explaining that any alteration of the landscaping or furnishings of Dealey Plaza amounted to the destruction and mutilation of evidence, I there said, "If the Commission did not know it sooner, it learned it not later than the testimony of Emmett J. Hudson, groundskeeper of Dealey Plaza (7H564). Hudson said, '...Now they have moved some of those signs...' Assistant Counsel Wesley J. Liebeler asked, 'They have? They have moved it?' After Hudson reaffirmed his statement, Liebeler contented himself with explaining, 'That might explain it, because this picture ... was taken after the assassination and this one was taken at the time ...'."

The sign about which Hudson testified is the one over which Zapruder took his pictures. Moving that sign, no matter how slightly, distorted or destroyed its relationship to everything on the film, hence mislocated anything oriented with it. This is exactly the end served, as the government knew. There is no doubt this was wanted. It also was accomplished. This was a minimum necessity in any phony reconstruction of the crime. Without a phony reconstruction it was not possible to begin to pin a bum rap on the dead accused Oswald.

The file copy of Rankin's February 24 letter is dated with a stamp and is close to illegible. This is distressingly typical, especially of Rankin's letters. In the upper left-hand corner is the date "2/17/64" and initials indicating the letter was drafted for Rankin's signature by Charles N. Shaffer, Jr., whose involvement in the misuse of the Altgens picture is in WHITEWASH II (p.187).

Other initials written in the margin indicate the letter was approved by Howard Willens and Rankin 2/20/64.

With the importance of the contents of this letter, delay of a week is an odd circumstance. But lack of mention of its contents - their very real suppression - is more so. In 10,000,000 printed words the Commission found no space for them. Further delay was achieved by the invocation of bureaucracy. Rankin's message was for Dallas, so he wrote Texas State Attorney General Waggoner Carr, in Austin. Four days later Carr wrote the mayor of Dallas who, on March 3, acknowledged receipt of the message drafted three months too late by the federal investigators.

By the time he got to the middle of his letter, Rankin said, "... the Commission has asked me to request through you that the Dallas authorities make no change or alteration in the physical surroundings of the assassination scene without first advising the Commission of its intentio to do so."

The time of the assassination was the time to assure no changes would be made. It should not have been necessary to tell any honest and competent police department to preserve its evidence, but it is proper that the possibility of accidental alteration in Dealey Plaza be prevented. Rankin's belated letter, however, could have been interpreted as meaning changes would not be unwelcome, for it does not say "under no circumstances may changes be made", but only "advise us when you do it". Until after the investigation was completed, no change should have been considered or permitted. That the FBI did not assure this as soon as it took charge of the investigation, or the Secret Service before it, means they were derelict and permits belief that they were parties to improper acts and destruction of evidence.

Rankin then did what to any reasonable man should have been entirely unnecessary. He defined and described Dealey Plaza: "In the Commission's view, this would include the area north of Main Street, Sout of Elm Street, West of Houston, and East of the first viaduct ..."

This description is of less than half of Dealey Plaza!

It eliminates the entire assassination scene!

It eliminates the alleged source of the shooting!

It eliminates the grassy knoll!

And it was made too late - after what it pretended to avoid had been accomplished.

The assassination was not "south of Elm Street", but on and north of it. The government alleges the shooting came from the Texas School Book Depository building, which is also north of Elm. The President was on Elm Street, not "south of Elm Street". The "grassy knoll" is 100 per cent north of Elm Street, thus also was defined out of the area to be preserved. Yet, from the very first moment, there was evidence that shots came from there. This is one possible reason for the illegibility of the file copy of the historic hand-lettered memo with which the Zapruder film was flown to Washington assassination night (PHOTOGRAPHIC WHITEWASH 15, 138-9). It reports this is what Zapruder told the Secret Service - shooting from the knoll. It is in contradiction to what he was brainwashed into testifying when Wesley Liebeler carefully controlled and led his testimony (WHITEWASH II."Can Pictures Lie?" and "Pictures Do Lie").

How can one regard all of these things, none of which should ever have happened, with less than warranted suspicion? How can one regard this official language, drafted by staff members - lawyers of the highest competence - with anything other than the deepest misgivings? Can we assume nothing but the grossest incompetence by the man selected to conduct this investigation, perhaps the most significant one in our history? Aside from his other legal experience, J. Lee Rankin had been Solicitor General of the United States, the government's top lawyer.

And what was J. Edgar Hoover doing besides reveling in the publicity glorifying his FBI and himself? He was, as he told the Commission (WHITEWASH II,223), the man in charge, from the first day!

It is all part of a pattern. Whether or not so designed, deliberate design could no better have misrepresented what really happened when the President was killed and how he was killed - and by whom - and why. No monster conspiracy, such as those who pretend to defend the government say would have been indispensable in whitewashing the assassination, could have succeeded more admirably.

And we cannot be content with the assurance the work was "sloppy", that everybody involved was incompetent. But if the best the government could employ were incompetent when they investigated and analyzed and reported on the murder of a President, is there any ground for believing government competence is of higher order when it tells us why it is fighting an undeclared war in Viet Nam (which the murdered President carefully avoided and sought to prevent); or what is at stake in that war; or how we got into it ("blundered"); or how it can end; or how each repetition of a previously unsuccessful policy is the one that will succeed; or when it addresses the problems of the cities and the poor and the denied of our society?

Is our federal government of selective incompetence, wrong, stupid "sloppy", only when the exalted of our political life and the best men and brains they could assemble "investigate" the murder of the President whose murder made possible these changes in his policies?

If government can be so monstrously wrong and blindly insist it is right when it investigates the murder of a President, can it ever be trusted? On what can it be right if, on the "crime of the century", it can be so wrong? If it lies when its own legitimacy is at stake, about what will it not lie?

If it cannot be trusted to - if it will not - reexamine its own, let us call it, "error" when its and the national honor are so deeply committed and when it is so overwhelmingly and publicly established in "error", is it capable of rectifying or even considering rectification of its error on anything else, especially those policies that can bankrupt us or, worse, incinerate the world?

Had any official on any level ever at any time suggested there might be the slightest chance of any mistake in the assassination investigation or the Report on it, there might be occasion for faith and trust. The monolithic insistence the naked emperor is in fine raiment is a horrifying atavism in the age of nuclear rocketry.

Examination of the official record is no ground for reassurance. There is nothing in the government's record to show that it ever intended to tell the truth about the assassination, or even to try to learn it. As I said in the first words of my first book on this subject, it sought only, to the degree possible, to achieve acceptability for the fiction of Oswald's singular guilt that, thanks to the parallel - shall we again call it "error"? - of the press, had been widely publicized.

If we are to look for motive, where better to seek than in the record? In this and the earlier sections of my own report on the Warren Report and the extensive documentation cited and printed with them, so much of it previously suppressed, the reader can find his own evidence and attribute motive and intent as he will. There are now close to a million words of my own documented analysis for him to consider and analyze on his own.

There are two quite comprehensible additional measures of purpose and direction in the investigation and Report that here and in this context, I believe, are significant and bear heavily on intent.

If the Commission intended to conduct a serious investigation, to determine all the fact it could, to establish truth, follow leads, question witnesses for the open purpose of learning, it required as an absolute minimum the most intimate knowledge of its own evidence and files. Because witnesses are people and people are the source of information and also are those involved in the assassination and observation and knowledg of it, this meant that every scrap of information about every person was required to be immediately available to the whole staff. In turn, this required not less than a complete name index to the files. These files are estimated to total several hundred cubic feet of space, each one of

which can store a million words. No photographic mind can retain and
spontaneously recall and locate every name in this vast store of data.

The Commission appears to have recognized this and to have begun with a proper name index. It immediately abandoned it, before its
hearings were really underway, before even a decent pretense of any investigation had been or could have been made. I found this proof in a
February 28, 1964, memorandum from Howard Willens. His recommendation
found a tuned ear in General Counsel Rankin, who launched his own personal economy wave when the President's murder was investigated. He
pinched pennies to the end that there now is and forever more can be
no complete photographic record of the assassination and so that the
Commission could not have these vital pictures (PHOTOGRAPHIC WHITEWASH,
"'Video' Means 'Unseen'";260ff.) when it so urgently required them for
knowledge of the fact of the assassination and for evidence.

Once Willens learned that the National Archives would be doing
something that could be considered a partial replacement for some of the
use of a name index, he recommended dropping it. Not to do this, he
said, would be a "waste of our limited manpower".

Perhaps it was not realized before, but when the murder of this
President was "investigated", there was a manpower shortage! And penny-
pinching! That assassination economy wave! Not enough people to do the
minimum, essential work, as there was not enough money to buy the pictures - that did not have to be bought, anyway, for they were available,
free, under subpena!

This is another and a pertinent indication of how the Commission
investigated - how it intended to investigate. Paralleling it is a series of documents I resurrected from the oblivion of that tremendous
cubage of suppression in the files. They disclose there never was any
intent to do anything other than charge Oswald with the crime - which
means framing him - because it was recorded, even if secretly, before
the Commission's investigation was under way!

Here I would like to have it understood that the list of the
Commission's files (WHITEWASH II,"Epilogue") that is regarded as a
bibliography is not, is largely meaningless, chiefly in the political
shibboleths of the FBI (and then with no revelation of content), and
is entirely inadequate for any serious work. More, the secret staff
memoranda and letters are not included in that. Researchers can find
not even such a halt and blind seeing-eye dog to lead their painful
step-by-step path through the files of the Commission itself rather
than of its sources. Once he learns about it, he has only the close-
to-meaningless "file classification" described earlier. So there is
no way of searching for the things I have rescued from oblivion except
by plodding work, instinct and good fortune. These are not enough to
insure completeness or success.

Prior to Monday, March 9, 1964, when no real investigation had
been conducted and only the federal and local police had done any real
work, no testimony about the assassination had been taken. There had
been the window-dressing questioning of the Oswald family and what related (like that of James Martin, Marina's business agent), and of Mark
Lane, which had as its intent clobbering the man who had sought to defend his profession, the law, and the murdered accused assassin.

Beginning 9:10 a.m., March 9, four of the Secret Service agents
in the Presidential escort were questioned by the Commission. Roy H.
Kellerman was first (2H61ff.). This examination was not the beginning
of the investigation. It was, rather, the beginning of the establishment of the background to the assassination and the seeking of the recollections of those who were with the President and, while in the motorcade,
were unaware of the assassination until it was over. They had not observed it, although they were present.

However, before this, the Report and its basic conclusions had
been decided upon!

At the very latest, six days before Kellerman took the stand, the
Report had been discussed in detail and an outline of it ordered. If not

earlier, at the very latest on Tuesday, March 3, Commission Editor Alfred Goldberg was directed to draft the outline of the Report on the hearings not yet held! His subsequent memorandum to Rankin on this, accompanying the outline of the Report, is in the eleventh part of the Commission's personal "PC" file. *

This memo is undated. A handwritten notation, "approx. 3/14", has been added.

By the time he got to the seventh and last paragraph, Goldberg said "it is possible to begin drafting" the first four parts! His last sentence is, "I am prepared to begin work on these four sections at your direction."

Assistant Counsel W. David Slawson prepared a commentary on "Dr. Goldberg's Proposed Outline of the Report of the Commission", dated March 23. Here we find further proof of two of the things I have charged from my first written word, that the "investigation" and its Report were a pre-mixed whitewash, and that dominating and controlling all of it was the overriding concern for the protection of St. Edgar's stoolpigeons, more important than establishing truth and the fact of the truth of the President's murder. In his first paragraph, for example, Slawson told Rankin that in some "situations the (FBI) report may have to be 'sterilized'", i.e., "references to the office or the name of the special agent or a few other sensitive words deleted. A more difficult problem will be the use of those reports which involve statements by informants." Immediately after this, Slawson reveals that, in the face of a "strong stand", the Commission would back down. **

But imagine that when, above all else, the government should have wanted, next to the solution of the time, acceptance of its Report and no doubt about its authenticity, the Commission of eminences and their topflight lawyers began with the plan to substitute untested FBI and Secret Service reports for sworn evidence; on top of this, were prepared to delete from the record not only the names of the agents (whose reports at best could have been hearsay), but even the offices out of which the agents worked; and then, even before St. Edgar blew his horn, collapsed their own wall in submission!

What a way to plan to "investigate" the murder of a President!

If there was any doubt about the given word before Slawson's memo - and in my mind and files there is not - there can remain none as of Monday, March 23. By that time there was no need to investigate. Slawson, at least, knew the truth, all the answers. Only Oswald was the assassin, anything else was a "misconception" requiring refutation. One cited example is one of the most flagrant abuses of public trust of the Commission's many, that of the Altgens-Lovelady picture (WHITEWASH II, inside back cover; PHOTOGRAPHIC WHITEWASH 27,31,33,38,44,48,56,65-9,72, 74-76-7,97,109,120,161,169,191-6,198-201,294). Here the Commission dealt with only tainted evidence, delayed attempting to accredit it until late July - FOUR MONTHS AFTER THE SLAWSON MEMO! - and in addition to all of its other misfeasances, malfeasances and nonfeasances, atop all its other dishonesties, misrepresentations and suppressions, failed to call as a witness the woman who saw Oswald on the first floor at a time that precluded his having fired a shot from the sixth! It suppressed from its Report and appendices any reference to it, including the corrupted FBI report on it (PHOTOGRAPHIC WHITEWASH 74-6;210-1)!

Here, as in all cases, the Commission knew the "fact" before investigating and holding hearings - without investigating and taking testimony! How much more authoritative can you be? How much more "right", worthy of trust? Slawson was very worried that Goldberg's outline did not sufficiently emphasize these "factual misconceptions" that "must be set straight in the public's mind" so that it will "not be misled by wild theories"!

With the benefit of the Slawsons and their Harvard Law Review backgrounds, naturally the Commission knew all the answers before it asked a single question! What is unfortunate is that these geniuses were so modest - that they did not set this forth in the Report they drafted for the

*See p. 494. **See p. 500.

signatures of the members of the Commission. Then the "public" would know exactly how the murder of the popular President was "solved" and could be confident its "mind" had been "set straight" and freed from the imprisonment of "factual misconceptions".

So, the outline of the Report that was outlined before the hearings on which it "reported" were held, before the evidence these hearings were to develop was gathered, before the Commission began its work, was revised. With that dedication to precision that pervades the Commission's every labor, this revision is undated. I got it from the same series of suppressed files. It is of that approximate date. Of it, what is here most relevant comes from a January 23, 1964, memo to Rankin from Specter and Francis W. H. Adams (who soon quit the Commission). At that early date, it is titled, "REVISED OUTLINE OF SUBJECT MATTER OF PHASE I". I present merely that part we should be able to accept as the essence: "THE ASSASSINATION: PRESIDENT KENNEDY'S ACTIVITIES FROM DEPARTURE TO DALLAS THROUGH AUTOPSY." This is broken down into five major divisions, each of which is further subdivided in the five pages of this part of the outline.

Without going into all of it in detail - by now that should be unnecessary - I here note but two parts: "B. The Assassination" has five subsections, the last four of which are on the shots. "Part 2. The first shot" has, under "e. impact on victim", six different categories, including "point of entry", "path", "damage", etc. Under "3. The second shot" and "4. The third shot", we find these words in parentheses, "analysis of all topics set forth under 'first shot'". In short, here in the Report outline prepared not later than March, four months after the assassination, before the single-bullet myth had been adopted, the Commission was still acknowledging what everyone else knew, that each of the three shots it admitted had been fired struck a victim. There was still a total dishonesty, the pretense that there had been no "missed" shot.

The last part is "F. President Kennedy's autopsy at Bethesda". Of its six sections, almost none can fairly be stated to be in the printed Report. Here is that section:

F. President Kennedy's autopsy at Bethesda

1. Times of commencement and termination of autopsy

2. Personnel in attendance
   a. educational background
   b. experience
   c. specialization, if any

3. Visual findings of medical personnel

4. Details of xrays or tests, if any

5. Details of analytical operative procedures

6. Conclusion on cause of death

Although at the beginning, before the autopsy itself was looked into, it was clear that there should have been at the least a list of "personnel in attendance", that is not in the Report. This is understandable, for the Commission could not print the names of not fewer than 23 competent military witnesses plus those of the two FBI agents in attendance without raising eyebrows, if not headlines, for not calling them to resolve the existing, if suppressed, conflicts. Moreover, it is even suppressed from the so-called evidence and the hearings. Even Admiral Galloway's name is not mentioned once in all the hearings! "Visual findings of medical personnel"? That we do not have, only a careful surgery, excising the essentials and leaving the propaganda. "Details of xrays or tests, if any"? No such details, really. No X-rays at all. They are still suppressed. And note the "if any". What kind of investigation had been going on the previous four months if the staff of the Commission did not in March know the answer to "if any", whether relating to X-rays or tests? The truth, however, is that neither is in the Report or the printed evidence - even the suppressed files! "Details of analytical operative procedures"? It may be alleged that there were such details. I believe it is fair to declare the opposite.

There is nothing that can be called an autopsy and nothing that can be said, from the evidence, to be either "analytical" or a competent description or reporting of "operative procedures".

Need there have been? Didn't the Commission know all the answers in advance - before its investigation and hearings? Of course! Else how could it have outlined its Report before investigation?

Are they not honorable men, eminent, trustworthy, incorruptible? Then why not just take their word for it - even if their word is that of their staff, even after what we have seen of some of the staff and its performance?

We do have a choice.

We can believe that honorable, eminent, trustworthy, incorruptible men are incapable of error; that their staff, even if of incompetents, sloppy workers, liars and geniuses, also blundered through and in the Report was not sloppy, was not incompetent, did not lie, displaying only genius. We can believe that because of the genuine eminence of these eminences and all that jazz there need have been no real investigation; that a little angel or a divine spirit would see to it that, whether or not determined in advance, whether or not the result of avoidance, misrepresentation, mutilation, destruction and manufacture of evidence, whether or not witnesses, pictures and other evidence was suppressed, the eminences and their staff were infallible; that the Report is a statement of divine truth, the real given word.

We can believe that all of this is right and proper; that when a President is murdered, in the last half of the 20th century, not the 10th this is the normal and acceptable functioning of honorable government. Nothing is wrong.

We have been taught to believe that Jesus could err, that he could, mistakenly, trust Judas. Now we are to believe that these political eminences are wiser than Jesus, that, unlike Jesus, they are incapable of error, that for them there was no Judas.

On no other basis can the Report of the President's Commission on the Assassination of President John F. Kennedy and its "solution" of the crime be accepted.

We do have a choice!

11. "BACK AWAY...CONSISTENT WITH OSWALD'S INNOCENCE"

Investigating the investigation of the murder of President Kennedy, with an estimated 10,000,000 published words of what, for lack of an accurate designation, has come to be known by the official euphemism of "evidence", and an estimated 300 cubic feet of files of incalculable wordage and all that is available that the government shunned, confronts him who essays it with an endless job that cannot possibly be completed in an adult lifetime devoted to nothing else.

In my own "Report on the Warren Report" I have sought to analyze each of the more important aspects, as I could, from the documentation I could find. What I could and did find depended upon the time I had available, for I was simultaneously an author, one full-time function, a publisher, which entails more numerous specialties, and my own investigator/researcher. To a large degree, what my probing the files yielded was controlled by instinct and luck, for they are arranged in a manner designed to frustrate logic and waste enormous amounts of time. It was also controlled by what was available.

Initially, 100 percent of the staff papers were denied. It is no distortion or exaggeration to say they were suppressed. Beginning about the first of 1967, a few were allowed to peek from behind oblivion. Meager as is the medical-autopsy data the Commission permitted itself to possess and dubious, evasive and woefully incomplete as that tiny percentage of those 300 cubic feet is, I postponed that part of my inquiry and writing in the hope that I would be able to draw upon these still-secret working papers.

When this could no longer be delayed, still seeking what had been suppressed, I had to begin writing this part of this book.

I requested and paid for the Xeroxing of every paper in the essential files. Here I ran into the obstacles already described. Finally, I did get all but what I was told had been withheld, two memos, unidentified, four short pages. They and a then-undisclosed number of additional documents would be available simultaneously. The promised date of by September 15 was delayed only five days. The official reasons for this delay do not make sense to me.

In any event, on September 20, 1967, researchers, of whom I seem to have been the only one with manifested interest, were permitted to examine these two documents that until then were withheld from the J.F.K. 4-1 or "autopsy" file, plus 12 additional boxes, each holding about four inches of documents. It should be apparent that a two-foot stack of documents requires a considerable amount of time for the briefest scanning. An inquiry of this sort should, properly, proceed more slowly. Were I to do that, however, I would never complete this task. This is a subject that goes to the heart of the democratic society, one from which every national act and policy subsequent to November 22, 1963, stems. There was a change in administration and there were changes in policies brought about by this murder and by it alone. The murder and the analysis of its official investigation, already established as at best entirely inadequate and dishonest and at worst a deliberate fraud, possibly conspiratorial, therefore cannot await the slow workings of history and the as yet unmanifested interest of professional historians, the official "scholars". Nor can it await the belated assumption of their responsibilities by the lawyers who were the first to abdicate their responsibil-

ities; that of the press, which has concerned itself only with sycophancy
and slander; or an official investigation, of which there is no sign.

So, I have to make spot decisions on what I will read and how carefully I will examine or not examine each paper within a folder, each
folder within a file, each file in each box. This I had to do without
benefit of any really meaningful guide to the contents of the considerable stack of materials. Our government can burn millions in Viet Nam
every day of the year, but it cannot afford to spend more than the part-
time work of two men in going over the monumental chaos dumped on the
National Archives by the Commission. No matter how competently or with
what dedication these two men perform their functions, they are immersed
in a vast verbal accumulation and can do only so much each day, especially because they are also the ones who make what has been released available to those who seek it and because of the necessary additional time
consumed in working with materials that are, properly, kept under lock
and key and may be examined only under guard.

They cannot make an index to the clutter, nor can they make a
meaningful table of its contents. They can compose only the most rudimentary guides. For these two feet of documents, here that is:

```
        Alphabetical Files of Outgoing Letters and Internal Memoranda
            (1) General
General         Box 1  A - R  (Letters to witnesses and the general public)
             "     2  S-- Z; General Circulars
Rankin    (2) Internal                    Green              Memo
              Box 3  Rankin; Commissioners (by name); Staff (by name)
(in general)  Box 4  Commission (in general); Staff (in general); Memo-
                     randa for the Record; Internal Circulars
            (3) Government
              Box 5  Agriculture - White House
```

        Government Agencies Involved
            Seven boxes of correspondence, memoranda, and all or parts
            of Commission documents relating to Federal and other gov-
            ernmental bodies

With so much of this book written, other work begun and no meaningful guide to that imposing stack of papers, there was no time to begin to make a real study, without abandoning all other work, of what is
hidden in those essentially undescribed two feet of largely illegible
carbon copies made less legible by repeated Xeroxing. When any single
sheet of paper may have the most vital significance, this is a considerable defect and a liability. It is unavoidable, but the reader
should be aware of it.

By the time a single man could study two feet of documents with
the requisite care, there would be another two feet demanding the same
or more attention, and there would be no writing, no book, nothing publicly available. I see no alternative but unending silence to this undesirable and unfortunately incomplete approach. However, because I print
the entire document wherever possible, the reader can see for himself
that I have taken nothing out of context and have restricted myself to
data whose essential meaning cannot be altered by the availability of
documents still suppressed. Further information might strengthen the
case against the Commission and its staff but cannot change what these
documents say and mean.

From the brief description above, it is apparent these 12 boxes
of Commission papers do not focus on the medical and autopsy facets of
the case. Here I include a few of the items buried in those secret
files that may illuminate some of the points I make. The medical-
autopsy content is a tiny fraction of them.

In what I have gone over, there is not a single page that in any
way disputes this book, not one that even indicates I have made any unfair or unwarranted representation either in this book or the earlier-
completed four. Everything I have seen substantiates my analysis and
conclusions.

While it would have been better, from a literary perspective, in any event, had this material been worked into the appropriate chapters, that is not feasible. It may, too, serve a value to isolate a few samples of what was suppressed and show how contrary it is to the official story lustily propagandized throughout the world. It may give an additional insight into how the Commission worked and thought and into the minds, if not the hearts, of several of the more prominent staff members.

Staff Director Howard P. Willens, a Department of Justice man, was an important Commission official. He also wrote many memos, most of which, without doubt, I have not seen. Whatever gentler word the Commission's apologists would prefer, one in reality suppressed until September 20, 1967, when most of the interest in the Report had slacked off in response to the tremendous propaganda campaign in support of the Report and attacking its critics, is among those then made available. Under date of August 8, 1964, Willens sent General Counsel Rankin a critique of "Chapter IV - Draft dated 7/21/64".

Without exception, every copy made for me of those reports suppressed until that day is exceedingly pale, more so than necessary, even if all come from indistinct carbon copies. This one is especially poor. The date seems to be "7/21". It may, if one ever saw an original, be a day or so later. My copy came from the internal staff memoranda file. There is another in File "Rep 2" and, presumably, other copies are in other files. Many copies were made before the one Xeroxed for me.

In the Report as issued, Chapter IV is "The Assassin". From internal evidence Willens' memo discusses what, in essence, was in this chapter. Comparison of this illegible critique and the final, printed Report indicates much of what Willens demanded he got.

On the second page he has this intriguing paragraph:

3. I still have a question about the validity of including as a minor finding Oswald's capability with a rifle. I think our case remains the same even if Oswald had limited or negligible capability with a rifle. In a way, we are emphasizing an argument we don't particularly need, which prompts controversy and may tend to weaken the stronger elements of our proof. I believe that this material should be discussed somewhere, and probably in this chapter, but I question whether it should be elevated to one of our eight major conclusions on which the Commission relies. An alternative to consider might be to place the question of Oswald's capability as a subheading to one of the first two major conclusions.

Here he says "why weaken our case by considering whether Oswald was mechanically capable of the crime? What difference does it make if it was impossible for him to have done that shooting?" The really truthful statement was not intended to be interpreted as I do:

I think our case remains the same even if Oswald had limited or negligible capability with a rifle.

This is exactly true. The case remained the same - no case at all. It was a frame-up. The best shots the Commission could get, under improved conditions, could not duplicate the shooting attributed to Oswald (WHITEWASH 26), and Oswald was a truly lousy shot who, when last tested, on an easy course, scored but a single point more than the absolute minimum demanded of every serviceman (WHITEWASH,"The Marksman"). In the appraisal of the Commandant of the Marine Corps, he was "a rather poor 'shot'" (WHITEWASH 30).

5. On page 4 I do not see the significance of the first full paragraph, with the exception of the first sentence. We know that Oswald lived in Dallas at the relevant time and I do not believe it is significant that Oswald did not receive mail from the box after he left Dallas for New Orleans on April 23.

That Willens is a lawyer trained in the adversary system, in which he has an opponent to present the other side, is here clear. This nine-page critique has 41 numbered items. They seek to reenforce in the Report not that meager bit of the other side of the evidence that, unwanted crept in, but a partisan presentation of what the Commission wanted believed. This is what permeates his demands and suggestions. Nor is he unaware of it. In the seventh item he argues the presence of an old, hidden palmprint on the rifle that could not have been made during the assassination is sufficient (there being no other prints on the rifle allegedly used and hidden in great haste). By item 14, he recognizes the weakness of attempting to use the discovery of Oswald's fingerprints on cartons it was his job to handle as a means of placing him at the sixth-floor window at the time of the assassination. In an effort to strengthen the prosecution case, not get the truth out, Willens forthrightly states:

The basic question is when he was at the window and when we come near to that question we back away from it. Furthermore, we never do make an effort to refute the many other possibilities for these fingerprints which are consistent with Oswald's innocence.

Recognizing the great weakness of using the incredible Howard Leslie Brennan as an "eyewitness" to identify Oswald at that window (WHITEWASH 39-42), Willens argues in his 18th item, "I would eliminate this comparison here and perhaps make a reference to it later on when the Tippit shooting is discussed." This exactly confirms what I said in WHITEWASH ("The Tippit Murder"), that if the Tippit murder hadn't happened, it would have had to have been invented, to affix the stigma of "cop-killer" on Oswald, thus making seem credible the very weak evidence of him as the assassin. The incredible Brennan is, to Willens (item 19), "a good witness", and the Commission "should reaffirm" his testimony "as to the source of the shots".

The reader will recall that the Report argues that Oswald took the alleged assassination rifle to work the morning of the assassination only because he was seen to carry a bag. The testimony was given by Buell Wesley Frazier and his sister, Mrs. Linnie May Randle (WHITEWASH 12-23). Oswald is said to have claimed he had curtain rods in this bag. All the testimony about the bag and its contents is 100 percent against the Commission's conclusions. The Commission got around this by simply asserting that this bag could not have contained curtain rods. The Commission, in the absence of any testimony whatsoever, simply said the rifle was disassembled. Had this been true, the bag of this, the only testimony, still could not have held it. Like the FBI before it, the Commission conducted no investigation to see whether Oswald had carried curtain rods with him. So, Willens wants the Commission to conclude (as it did) that "He lied about the curtain rod story and the paper bag" (item 23). It is not inconsistent for him then (item 24) to argue that "The discussion ... regarding disassembling seems to have limited relevance". His concept of the use of the "Frazier-Randle testimony", under a reorganization he proposed (item 27), is "so as to prove that Oswald carried the paper bag to work, and then turn to the question whether the bag contained the assassination weapon". What this means, simply, in the absence of proof that the bag held the rifle, is that the Report would be reorganized to poison the case against Oswald. Prove that he carried a bag and then pretend that the bag held the rifle, therefore, he took the rifle to work. This is what the Commission and the Report did. It is contrary to the evidence. It would not have been dared in open court.

The entire memorandum is of this nature.

Here again, ample reason for keeping these files away from those researching the assassination and its investigation. For whatever reason, this is exactly what happened. For whatever reason, when the question of the integrity of the Commission's work and conclusions was under sharp attack toward the end of 1966 and early in 1967, this and the ample similar evidence was suppressed. They are pertinent to the character of the Commission and that of its work.

If it was too difficult for the Commission to undertake such simple pertinent tasks as asking Mrs. Connally to mail it the Governor's clothing before the evidence it bore was destroyed, or to ask such readily available "celebrities" as Cliff Carter what he did with this clothing, which we will soon examine, there was nothing too difficult or too expensive when it came to spying on those who were critical of the Commission and the government's pretended investigation of the assassination.

Willens wrote several memos relating to this. I had long had one dated February 29, 1964. But one he had written three days earlier was suppressed until September 20, 1967. This does not lend credence to the Archives' explanation that it was required to make orderly and "chronological" release of the files. The real reason is more likely the gross impropriety of the Commission consideration of having the FBI put a full-time tail on Mark Lane, then lawyer for Oswald's mother. For this there was no shortage of FBI manpower or money. Only for sending for Governor Connally's clothing before its evidentiary value was destroyed, or getting the irreplaceable pictures of the assassination before they disappeared, was there penny-pinching.

Here is every word of the two paragraphs of Willens' memo, which is deliberately made so illegible it is unsuitable for reproduction:

During the course of my discussion this morning with Mr. Malley of the FBI he brought up the matter of your interest in having coverage at the lectures given by Mark Lane before various meetings. Mr. Malley pointed out that the FBI is not currently covering Mr. Lane on a day-to-day basis. The FBI does know however that Mark Lane does attend small meetings of approximately 30 or 35 people which are not publicly announced. If these meetings are not publicly announced the FBI cannot get actual recordings of the presentation made by Mr. Lane.

After our discussion Mr. Malley agreed that he would write a letter to you setting forth what coverage the FBI can provide of Mark Lane's activities under their current procedures. At that point if the Commission desires fuller coverage we will have to make some specific request to that effect to the FBI. I think that we will want to consider very carefully the problem inherent in requesting fuller coverage of Mr. Lane which might require placing him under full surveillance by the FBI. Such a procedure would inform us as to his location, give us some indication of all meetings which he attended, but would still not enable us to obtain recordings or knowledge of the substance of his presentations at the meetings which are not open to the general public.

The FBI had taped Lane's appearances, as the CIA at least did mine. The tapes became national secrets and were so classified.

What impelled the withholding of this Willens memo is clear. There is nothing in it to make the government proud; nothing to make citizens feel free or that they dare even dream of exercising those "inalienable" rights, those "God-given" in the political addresses; nothing that helps solve the assassination. Only repression is in them and fine self-portraits by the Commission and the FBI.

Howard Willens, who, despite Arlen Specter's contrary account, is a Department of Justice lawyer, wrote a memo to the former Solicitor General of the United States, then the general counsel of the Commission headed by the Chief Justice of the United States, bragging that it was having its secret police eavesdrop on the lawyer representing the mother of the murdered accused assassin and telling them how they could further rape American freedom and justice if this were not enough, by having the secret police penetrate small, private gatherings. His lament was that in such small groups it would not be possible to tape-record.

He didn't consult the right part of the FBI. One of my speeches was visibly bugged by radio. This was in mid-December 1966, when I had just published a book saying the FBI had engaged in a cover-up.

He didn't get any reprimand, either, so far as I can learn. He continued in his position of trust and authority throughout the life of the then-young Commission. His thoughts were the Commission's thoughts, his lusts theirs, too.

When Rankin became New York City's lawyer, he took with him as his Assistant Corporation Counsel Norman Redlich, who had been a professor of law before he became an assistant counsel for the Commission. He alone had been the target of a radical-right red-baiting attack, for he alone they found too "liberal".

We have already seen that the Commission was preparing its Report before it held its hearings. Willens and Redlich teamed up and on March 31, 1964, sent Rankin their "Proposed Outline of Final Report". They suggested a Chapter 4 titled "Lee Harvey Oswald as the Assassin". So, before March 31, here is still another evidence the Commission reached its conclusions prior to its investigation to determine what they would be. Oswald was "guilty" to begin with - without any investigation.

What this outline calls for that the Commission did not print is on the last page, "Reports of Federal Bureau of Investigation and Secret Service on location of President's Car at Time of Shots". The Commission was lemming-like, but not that lemming-like! When there is no one to keep tabs, it is easier to suppress. The Commission did this, ad lib.

Among those documents suppressed until September 20, 1967, is an April 27, 1964, memorandum the former Solicitor General of the United States apparently considered a fine recommendation, for he did hire Redlich as his assistant corporation counsel in New York City. This document is so unclear it is not only entirely unsuitable for reproduction, but some of it cannot be read at all. I therefore quote only parts of it and comment on them, indicating where illegibility makes words uncertain.

The first sentence puts him and others of the staff in that ample majority who knew three shots had struck the car's occupants and who ignored what all must have known, that there had been a "missed" bullet by which Tague had been hurt. "The purpose of this memorandum," Redlich said, "is to explain the reasons why certain members of the staff feel that it is important to take certain photographs in connection with the approximate points at which the three bullets struck the occupants of the Presidential limousine."

"We have expert testimony to the effect that a skilled marksman would require a minimum of 2¼ seconds between shots with this rifle."

This is false. That testimony was entirely different, that a really skilled man (and it must be kept in mind that Oswald was only a duffer) could reload the rifle in 2-1/3 seconds. Thereafter, he would have to re-sight and fire, both operations requiring additional time.

But even in Redlich's terms, "It is apparent, therefore, that if Governor Connally was hit as late as frame 24? (the third number is indecipherable), the President would have to have been hit not later than frame 190 and probably even earlier."

The last half of the sentence is undoubtedly true. It is the midwife of the single-bullet baby.

In his next sentence, Redlich states the consensus, that the Commission and everyone on it had already decided that Oswald was the lone assassin, what they had been assigned to investigate, not, presumably, what they had been expected to frame up: "We have not yet examined the assassination scene(?) to determine whether the assassin in fact could have shot the President prior to frame 190." Thus, he clearly states that before its investigation had really begun the Commission had decided where all the shots had come from and who fired them.

What was the honorable purpose, the dedication that led to this staff appeal?

Our intention is not to establish the point with complete accuracy, but merely to substantiate the hypothesis which underlies the conclusion that Oswald was the sole assassin.

How well he put it in papers never intended to be published. The Commission began with the conclusion "that Oswald was the sole assassin" and did not reach this "conclusion" after a long and painstaking investigation. This is exactly what I first declared in WHITEWASH.

Redlich expanded on his demand for an on-the-site "reconstruction"

I have always assumed that our final report would be accompanied by a surveyor's diagram which would indicate the approximate locations of the three shots. We certainly cannot prepare such a diagram without establishing that we are describing an occurrence which is physically possible. Our failure to do this will, in my opinion, place this report in jeopardy since it is a certainty that others will examine(?) the Zapruder film and raise the same questions which have been raised by our examination of the films. If we do not attempt to answer these questions with observable facts, others may answer them with facts which challenge our most basic assumptions, or with fanciful theories, based on our unwillingness to test our assumptions by the investigatory methods available to us.

Here we have an honest statement of the purpose of the so-called "reconstruction": To keep the Commission from pursuing its pre-determine conclusion without satisfying itself of the physical possibility. Not to establish how the President was murdered, just to keep from falling flat on their eminent faces. It was a physical impossibility for Oswald or anyone else in that sixth-floor window and with that rifle to have committed the assassination if each of the three acknowledged shots, in Redlich's words, "struck the occupants of the Presidential limousine".

How strange it is that this had to be a demand from the staff! Imagine a Presidential Commission rolling unconcernedly to its pre-determined conclusions without knowing that it was within the realm of physical possibility!

Unfortunately, the Commission did not answer the facts in its own files "with facts". Its answers are the "fanciful theories" Redlich predicted, including the single-bullet fraud.

Note that Redlich has described the "conclusion" the Commission then had already reached as a "hypothesis" or "assumption".

His penultimate paragraph is less than generous to the federal police:

I should add that the facts which we now have in our possession, submitted to us in separate reports from the FBI and Secret Service, are totally incorrect and, if left uncorrected, will present a completely misleading picture.

Redlich did not see fit to delineate what he meant by "totally incorrect" investigative reports. Perhaps this was well enough known among the staff and to its head to require no exposition. However, from his own first sentence it cannot be the general agreement that each of the three shots "struck the occupants of the Presidential limousine".

Those who seek to defend the Commission and its Report claim it is honest and impartial because it is critical of the federal police. What little it did say of them is ridiculously scanty, in view of the record. However, it did not at any point or in any way tell the people that their FBI and Secret Service investigated the murder of their President and filed reports that "are totally incorrect" and "will present a completely misleading picture".

Redlich's words are an adequate representation of the doctrine and methods of this Commission. Oswald is guilty, we know that before we begin, and it is our responsibility to prove it, doing whatever it takes, or we'll soon catch hell from our own evidence. No further elaboration is necessary.

However, respects are due Redlich's foresight. His devils did find the scripture he and his associates left, and just where he predicted.

It is Arlen Specter who interests me most in this book and who is also of most interest to me in these documents that were suppressed until September 20. Those two withheld of the until-then suppressed Commission staff files on the President's autopsy were both Specter memoranda to Rankin. The earlier one, dated April 30, 1964,* is headed "Autopsy Photographs and X-Rays of President John F. Kennedy". That of May 12 precedes this title with "examination of". It reads, "Examination of Photographs

*See p. 549

121

and X-Rays of President Kennedy.⁴

Specter is less well represented in the other until-then suppresse
Commission files than others of the staff. In his file there are copies
of pro forma memoranda only, and very few of them. However, some of the
memos he addressed Rankin, in the Rankin files, are not of the kind he
could use in his political campaigns. They do not give Specter a good
character.

Although it is chronologically out of order to do so, I think the
first that should be noted is the shortest. It is two sentences long,
requiring only five short lines of typing. It is dated June 11. It
reads:

If additional depositions are taken in Dallas, I suggest that
Jim Tague, 2424 Inwood, Apartment 253, and Virgie Rachley, 405 Wood
Street be deposed to determine the knowledge of each on where the
missing bullet struck. These two witnesses were mentioned in the
early FBI reports, but they have never been deposed.

Brief as this is, it admits much.

The staff knew about Tague from the beginning, for he was in news
stories and on the police radio. The government had a number of transcripts of the police broadcasts, all contradictory, but Tague is an earl
feature. Although it is a secret withheld from the Report and the 26
volumes, it also, very early, obtained sound transcripts and had the actual voices in the actual police broadcasts. The FBI reports are enough
to establish the fact, and these Specter acknowledges. He thus acknowledges both personal and Commission knowledge of the fact of Tague's wound
ing and, as he put it, of "the missing bullet".

The Commission had originally planned to end its work by June. On
June 11, Specter recommended only that "if" the Commission was to examine
additional Dallas witnesses, Tague be one of the two he believed should
be examined. (He thus had no interest in some of the most important witnesses, like Mrs. Sylvia Odio, who had been told by anti-Castro agents
escorting The False Oswald that Kennedy should be murdered and The False
Oswald had told them how; or in any of those who had taken the vital,
actual assassination film, like Zapruder, Altgens and Willis, none of
whom had then been examined by the Commission and none of whose film had
been authenticated.)

Thus, we have a picture of the Commission that was willing to come
to the end of its "investigation" of the murder of the President without
accounting for another bullet it knew had been fired during the assassination, the bullet that it had not accounted for while accounting for
all it acknowledged had been fired during the assassination. Thus, too,
we have the Specter of the single-bullet theory who was part of this with
personal knowledge of it. All he could bring himself to do was suggest
that perhaps Tague might be questioned. So mild and understated is Specter's brief memo that it does not record the wounding of Tague by this
"missing" bullet. Or that Virgie Rachley saw an entirely different one.

Imagine! A man was wounded during the assassination and he had
been ignored until months after the Commission had outlined its Report
and had planned to finish its work and at that late date, more than six
months after the assassination, Arlen Specter was only suggesting that
if it wasn't too much trouble, maybe someone ought to speak to him.

What uncompromising integrity! For six months the government's
investigators and lawyers had been contentedly accounting for all of the
shooting during the assassination, blandly pretending "Jim Tague" didn't
get hurt by the bullet it pretended hadn't been fired!

One of Specter's earlier assignments had been the preparation of
the questions to be asked of a number of prominent witnesses. There are
a series of these in the once-suppressed files. All are incorporated
into memoranda addressed to Rankin on March 31, 1967.

When Mrs. Kennedy was a witness (5H178ff.), the Commission heard
from the only close eyewitness of her husband's murder in the entire

world. There were quite a number of others who were not far away who
were not called. Phil Willis told me he now understands the real reason
his wife was not called as a witness when she was so much closer to the
actual murder and had such a clear recollection. Mrs. Willis also saw
the President's head snap sharply backward when the "fatal" shot hit.
The Commission took testimony from not a single person who would have so
testified, for this would have made clear what it also suppressed and
misrepresented about the Zapruder and other films: That the "fatal"
wound was from the front. When the FBI reported its belated June 17 interview with Mrs. Marilyn Willis (PHOTOGRAPHIC WHITEWASH 179-80), it managed to exclude this intelligence also. Specter was like the FBI, only
more so. Mrs. Kennedy was less than half an arm's length from her husband and looking directly at him during that most awful moment through
which a woman could live. She alone of those close to him was looking
at him. What better reason did Specter need for leaving out of the questions to be asked her what she from her own observation knew of this
wound and his reaction to it? Of course, all the schmalz that is not
useful in an investigation of the murder he did include, and questions
about all the chitchat.

The closest Specter came to planning a question of genuine significance about the President's wounds was in Question No. 62. There,
unbagging cats again, he wrote, "What wound, if any, did you observe on
the President's back?" Here again, as without variation in the secrecy
of the unseen documents he always did, he referred to the rear, non-fatal
injury as "on the President's <u>back</u>". <u>Not the neck!</u>

When Mrs. Kennedy's testimony was taken, Rankin asked the questions. At the point where she got to the wounds, her only possible significant testimony, the printed transcript (5H190) reads, in brackets,
"Reference to wounds deleted." From this transcript it appears that Mrs.
Kennedy volunteered this testimony about the wounds. It is not in response to a question about them, for there was none. *

When Governor Connally was a witness (4H129ff.), it is Specter who
conducted the questioning. In the list of questions he prepared in advance, Specter got to the shooting with No. 19. He planned to ask Connally to mark a photograph to "state where" he believed the car was when
the first shot of which he was aware was fired, to state the time, things
like that.

What could have been meaningful with the photographs Specter
avoided, in his prepared questions and during the examination. He should
have shown Connally the Zapruder movie and asked this. He dared not,
however, for as he well knew, as we already have noted, Connally would
have testified that the first shot came earlier than the Commission would
concede, at a time it could not have been fired by a solitary, sixth-floor
window assassin. The staff knew this if the members did not. Failure to
ask Connally this while he was looking at the Zapruder movie is deliberate
suppression.

Consistent with this is the failure to plan to ask him to identify
the frame of the Zapruder film in which he was struck. <u>There is no projected question about the Zapruder film</u> and what it shows or Connally
sees in it. <u>Not one!</u>

With the "best evidence" of Connally's wound Connally's body,
Specter had no plan for him to display his wounds to the Commission.
This was especially important so they could decide not whether a single
bullet had inflicted all the non-fatal injuries on both men but whether
it was at all possible.

Before the Commission, Connally did display his wounds. And he
did testify to the frame of the Zapruder movie in which he believed he
had been struck. His testimony was no comfort to single-bullet theoreticians or the authors of the Report. If it is correct, the Report is
wrong. Specter's preparation was to plan to omit this vital part of
Connally's testimony.

Earlier, I recounted the profound disinterest of all officials
of all levels in the Connally clothing and the quintessential evidence

*See pp. 386-7.

it could have held; for example, the direction of the bullet and, by spectrographic analysis, the type. Such analysis would have made it possible to identify with Bullet 399 the infinitesimally small traces of the bullet remaining on the cloth had 399 been the one to rend the garments as it tore and battered the Governor. Neither the local nor the federal police had any interest in the Governor's clothing until Mrs. Connally felt she just had to do something. She dipped them in water. Not being a criminologist, Mrs. Connally had no way of knowing that, as soon as this happened, the evidentiary value of the clothing was forever lost.

Then the federal police suddenly became interested.

The Commission, until then, also was without interest. Then it, too, became interested. Once it was too late, it was also safe.

The first person into whose hands the Governor's clothing passed is Clifton C. Carter, then an assistant to Vice President Johnson. Nurse Ruth J. Standridge gave him the Governor's clothing. She identified Carter as an assistant to the Governor. The Commission's mishandling of these simple events can be interpreted to mean that Carter misrepresented himself as a Secret Service agent. I tell the story in WHITEWASH (p.160) There I also point out that

He never appeared before the Commission. There is a two-page affidavit from him (7H474-5) executed six months after the assassination. In it, Carter makes no mention of this clothing.

In the light of what I then knew, this was a considerable understatement. For example, this "affidavit" as printed in the Commission's "evidence" has no notarial seal, no notary's name or identification of any sort - no indication that it was ever sworn to in any way - in fact, is so utterly and unspeakably incompetent it does not bear the designation of the jurisdiction in which it was allegedly executed.

In the light of Mrs. Connally's revelations, as readily available to the Commission and its staff as to Life - the difference being Life was interested and the eminences and their legal eagles were not - what is in these staff papers held secret until the end of September 1967 is particularly interesting and, I think, significant.

On April 16, 1964, Arlen Specter addressed another memorandum to Rankin. It is entitled "Remaining Work in Area X". It is broken into six sections. The first is headed "Obtain statements of the assassination from the eyewitness celebrities." This section has seven parts. In the first four, Specter recommends the calling before the Commission of President and Mrs. Johnson, Mrs. Kennedy, Governor and Mrs. Connally, and Senator Ralph Yarborough of Texas.

The first person against whose appearance before the Commission Specter recommends is Carter. In section (e) he says, "Clifford /sic/ Carter - He has been interviewed and a statement has been prepared for him to sign based on that interview. I recommend that he not be called before the Commission."

To those who may say that calling Carter before the Commission would have accomplished nothing because the Commission members were incompetent in their brief and infrequent questionings and the Commission staff asked only what they wanted, I can say only that he should have bee called before the Commission and asked about Governor Connally's clothing - to whom had he given it and why. Then the Commission might, as it should, have traced what happened to this evidence and history would not have to depend on a magazine when there was a Presidential Commission assigned to learn and report fully on the crime. The Commission followed its standard formula: It ignored what was unpleasant, what really reflected on the federal police, and whatever it dared that might tend to exculpate Oswald.

From Specter's memo we do learn that Carter's statement was not one that he drafted himself. It was "prepared for him to sign". In short, the statement of what Carter allegedly swore to was prepared for him by the Commission staff. It is they who suppressed the entire story of the culpable design for the destruction of evidence. Indeed, it is the staff that is responsible for that destruction of evidence, for it was their responsibility to obtain and safeguard it.

We do not know who on the staff prepared the statement for Carter's signature and carefully suppressed all reference to this. We do not know whether Specter was just modest and did not brag that he had done this, too.

But what we do know, without question, is that Specter had knowledge of it and recommended against calling Carter to give testimony.

We also know that spectrographic analysis of the Connally clothing could have ruined Specter's single-bullet hoax before he had it fully shaped.

And we know this knowledge was suppressed until September 1967. By then most interest in the Commission had abated. At the very time I got access to this document, Specter was busy running for mayor of Philadelphia aided by plots he claimed to exist in which blacks were going to poison him. The source of the story - an obvious boost to Specter's chances, particularly because it associated him with the magical names, FBI and J. Edgar Hoover - was a man already in jail and therefore more subject to pressures.

One wonders if he, too, signed an "affidavit".

As I said, once the evidence was safely lost forever, Specter and the Commission moved fast. On April 9, he drafted a letter to Hoover, for Rankin's signature. First, the FBI was telephoned (very few of the letters indicated that this happened, although in most cases it must have Then, for the yokels and those who followed, this polite record was left. Modestly disowning parentage, Specter wrote, "The theory has been advance that the bullet entered Governor Connally's back, exited from his lower chest, entered the dorsal aspect of his wrist, and then entered his thigh What the Commission wanted to know is, could it have happened? It was safe to ask the question because one disproof had been destroyed. This the government had already guaranteed.

Now, in this case the Commission was in a great hurry. There is a handwritten note at the bottom of the page reading, "Original signed by Arlen Specter". Suddenly, this couldn't wait for Rankin to sign his own mail. Then there is a typed note, also indicative of the great speed that didn't begin until it was too late to do any good. It reads, "Original and courtesy copy given to SA Robert E. Neill, FBI, 4/9/64, by Mr. Specter."

They had an FBI agent drop everything and rush over to pick up the destroyed evidence. Neill dutifully signed a receipt for Connally's jacket, trousers, shirt and tie.

Two months later Hoover sent this brief letter to Rankin, "By Courier Service" (the unvarying use of "Courier Service" is hardly an indication the mail service to the FBI and Commission was like mine, as set forth in OSWALD IN NEW ORLEANS!). The paleness of the photocopy, which bears no file identification but was in the "J.B.C. 2" file, indicates it is not very close to the original. The notations were added by the Commission staff. It appears in facsimile on the next page.

The Commission was almost as anxious to get rid of Governor Connally's clothing whose evidentiary value had been destroyed as it had been not to get it until after this destruction. Hoover's letter was dated June 17. Arlen Specter wrote a brief letter to Connally, for Rankin's signature. The date typed after his initials says he did this June 18, about the earliest he could have. Oddly, though, the part of the letter that went to Connally was dated June 23. In the lower left-hand margin of the pale copy, Rankin initialed it June 19. Oh, well ... The letter covered the delivery to Connally of the jacket, trousers, shirt and tie and thanked him for his "fine cooperation".

Because there was no evidence left on the garments, it might be injudicious to wonder about the anxiety of the federal government to hurry essential evidence out of its possession. However, with the great

UNITED STATES DEPARTMENT OF JUSTICE

FEDERAL BUREAU OF INVESTIGATION

WASHINGTON 25, D.C.

June 17, 1964

By Courier Service

Honorable J. Lee Rankin
General Counsel
The President's Commission
200 Maryland Avenue, Northeast
Washington, D. C.

Dear Mr. Rankin:

Mr. Arlen Specter of the Commission's staff provided this Bureau with four photographs and the clothing worn by Governor John Connally on November 22, 1963, for use in connection with the re-enactment of certain aspects of the assassination of President Kennedy at Dallas, Texas.

The photographs and the clothing, consisting of Governor Connally's coat, trousers, shirt and tie (FBI ... C311 through C314) were returned to Miss Mary No..... at Commission on June 16, 1964.

Sincerely yours,

J. Edgar Hoover

care it took to preserve Marina Oswald's nail file for the national heritage, to preserve imperishably in history a blank subscription form to Life and newspaper clipppings on cooking, crocheting and child care, and with its determination to memorialize in perpetuity Ruth Paine's Minox camera, which is relevant to nothing, might it not be asked if the National Archives, in its archive on the murder of President Kennedy, might not also have enshrined as the equal of countless files of empty envelopes, the clothing worn by the Governor and damaged in the assassination?

It does, at least, show where his garments were damaged.

Or is it that, in its determination of what "the national interest requires", the Commission could not abide anything relating to its single-bullet adoption from Specter?

126

Any evidence about any of the shooting is closely related to what here is most important, the autopsy. Even if too late, the Commission did examine the Connally clothing. However, with the autopsy it never examined the "best evidence" and, with existing major conflicts safely, if temporarily, suppressed in its files, it failed to call any of the at least 23 witnesses who might have helped resolve the suppressed conflict. Why did it call not one of these observers, among whom were men of the highest medical competence?

Is it possible that in some mysterious manner Specter did not know of the others at the autopsy? Could that page, for example, have been missing from the copy of the Sibert-O'Neill report, or had he shuffled his notes of what he wanted to ask them and mislaid that sheet? Is it an accident that he did not call any of these other 23 qualified witnesses to the autopsy, most of them to all of it?

It is not. Seemingly, Specter had a literary-legal guilt feeling about that Sibert-O'Neill report, too.

He quoted it - but privately, very privately.*

On February 19, 1964, he addressed a lengthy memorandum to General Counsel Rankin. He titled it, "Comprehensive Memorandum of Phase I."

Throughout this quite lengthy opus, he had abundant footnotes to his sources. In the 16 lines of typing prior to what I here refer to, he has six such citations. Then, on page 80, he has a category, "Autopsy". The first subsection is "Persons Present". And lo! there are the names from the Sibert-O'Neill report! Complete with all the errors. Admiral Galloway comes out "Holloway", Admiral Burkley is "Admiral Berkeley", and on the lower levels, there is "J. T. Bozwell".

Except where Specter shortened it, the Sibert-O'Neill report is there, names in the same sequence, word for word.

And without a single footnote of reference on either of the two pages, 80 and 81, until the end where Specter identifies the signatures on the autopsy itself. Here he has a citation, to the official file on the autopsy, No. 77. His citation was an unnecessary one. There was no need to cite a source for the signatures on the autopsy report. However, in doing this, he makes it seem that File 77, not the Sibert-O'Neill report, is the source of all of the foregoing, unattributed, information.

That "neck" wound? Specter has a subhead for his technical reference to that. Nowhere does he mention what the Report calls a "neck" wound. Here on page 84, it is "Upper Trunk Wound". In February, before he really went to work on it, what proof did Specter find that the doctors had "traced" the path of this bullet? Such words are lacking. The one he found apt is "postulated". "The autopsy report further postulated," he wrote, that the front wound was of exit. According to Webster, "postulate" means anything but proved. It is something that is taken for granted, or a hypothesis, or an essential prerequisite. So, on page 85, about the same autopsy report by the doctors said to have "traced" the path of this bullet, which they never said and never did, the strongest statement Specter would make is that it must be taken for granted, must be assumed. Not that it was ever proved. Taking something for granted is a kind of proof fortunately not recognized in courts of law.

Nor is there any doubt Specter uses exactly the word he meant. On the same page he describes these as "the presumptive points of entry and exit". If there should be in the mind of the reader any doubt about whether the rear, non-fatal injury was in the neck, let me quote Specter's language from page 86:

During the latter stages of the autopsy, Dr. Humes located an opening which appeared to be a bullet hole below the shoulders and two inches to the right of the middle line of the spinal column.

He quotes the angle of the shot as "45 to 60 degrees" and says that it penetrated less than a finger's depth.

His source is the Sibert-O'Neill report. Here there cannot be the lie given the Washington Post as an "explanation". There is no doubt Specter did have the official autopsy report, which he cites here fre-

*See p. 86

quently. Where there was need to "correct" some of it, he did. An example is the belief that the bullet found at Parkland Hospital had come from the President's stretcher. "Later investigation," he says, "indicated" it "most probably came from Governor Connally" (sic).

So, when he was in possession of all the fact - only not yet aware of all the requirements of a single-assassin theory - Specter had no misgivings about the FBI report on what the autopsy disclosed.

And he did tell the Commission the President had been shot in the back, not the neck!

There is some mystery about the statement given by Darrell Tomlinson, hospital engineer who took manual control of the automatic elevator about 1 p.m. Specter's reference to it establishes its existence. Of the foyer in which Tomlinson placed the stretcher, Specter quotes him (a month later, 6H128ff.), in paraphrase, "...had been secured by the Secret Service, with only hospital personnel and officers allowed inside. Here we have proof of two unwelcome things: The existence of a statement from Tomlinson for which there was no space in 10,000,000 words of evidence; and proof that if, as is most likely, that bullet was planted, only "hospital personnel and officers" could have done it.

It was an hour after Tomlinson took over the elevator before the bullet was "found".

The truth of what happened - not in the Report or the 10,000,000 words of testimony and exhibits - is that Tomlinson then immediately called O. P. Wright, hospital chief of security. Wright had the greatest trouble getting either the FBI or the Secret Service to take any interest in this bullet. (After all, why should they have? It was only a President they were protecting who had just been murdered by bullets!) Finally, Wright persuaded Secret Service Agent Johnsen to take it.

In Specter's report (p.98), this comes out thus: Tomlinson "then turned the bullet over to Mr. O. P. Wright who gave it to SA Johnson(sic

He certainly has a terse style, that Specter!

What a fortunate accident for the shattered official account of the assassination that this was not one of the documents available at the time the government was in such distress over the Report, when the mass media had not yet launched its tremendous, coordinated defense of the Report. How fortuitous that it could not be made available until September 20, 1967, three years after the Report was issued!

This is just as true of much of the other numerous boxes of staff papers suppressed until then. They are destructive of the Report and of the integrity of so many involved - of the Commission as a body, and of the government.

Maybe, in part, they also explain Specter's silence when I called him a repetitive liar and dared him to sue me for libel, his reluctance, as I challenged, to make this a question of fact before a judge and a jury - and with opposing counsel.

Currently, those autopsy pictures and X-rays concern everyone. During the secret life of the secret Commission, this particular secret, if it disturbed no one else, did worry Arlen Specter. This we know from at least three of his memoranda, three I have in my possession. There may be more. Of course, everyone on the Commission - its members and its staff - should have been disturbed. The suppression of these pictures and X-rays, regardless of reason, has become a national calamity.

For some strange reason, Specter's previously quoted April 16 memo on "Remaining Work in Area X" bears no file designations other than "Internal". It should have been in a number. For example, under part 2, "Obtain further medical evidence", Specter has this subdivision that certainly should have been in the Kennedy and Connally files:

(e) Depending on the testimony of Governor Connally and Drs. Gregory and Shaw, we may wish to call expert medical witnesses to testify about reaction time of an individual who has been struck by a bullet if the evidence indicates that President Kennedy and Governor Connally were struck by the same bullet.

What this says is that the single-bullet theory requires competent testimony on delayed reactions to gunshot wounds. The Commission found out that delayed reaction was more likely with the President, where it says no bone was hit, than with the Governor, where bones were shattered. Once the Commission got this scientific evidence destructive of the Report, which is based upon the opposite, it did not call these expert witnesses. Instead, it suppressed the whole thing, as we have seen.

Perhaps we here have an explanation for the filing "oversight".

In any event, the very first thing Specter says under "Obtain further medical evidence" is,

(a) Photographs and X-rays of the autopsy should be examined to make certain of the accuracy of the artist's drawings of President Kennedy's wounds.

Much more than this was involved. The accuracy of all the autopsy testimony is cast in doubt by the suppression of this "best evidence" of the autopsy. There can be no legal justification for it.

Perhaps Specter's perturbation derives from the fact that it is he who conducted the examinations of the autopsy doctors and failed to enter this requisite evidence into the record. Perhaps his certain knowledge that this was legally indefensible, whether or not he was under orders, is what nagged at him. If this is the case, the ancient, honorable and respected remedy of public servants was open to him and required by good conscience: resignation. When it was time to be heard, he elected silence instead. Later, after the Commission was ended, he engaged in public justification of the unjustifiable thing he had done. His reward was a successful political career. He selected his appearances and restricted them to those he had reason to expect would be friendly (WHITEWASH II, "Magic, Mystery and Myth").

Arlen Specter went so far as to say that it was okay that the pictures and X-rays had not been produced before the Commission because they would only "confirm" the autopsy testimony. Without seeing them, he could not know this, but he got away with it. This, however, is not the burden of those two reports of his that were suppressed from the autopsy file until September 20, 1967.

The first of these, dated April 30, 1964, enlarges on his worries embodied in the memorandum of two weeks earlier. It is entitled "Autopsy Photographs and X-Rays of President Kennedy". It consists of four paragraphs explaining why "it is indispensable that we obtain the photographs and x-rays".

In this memo Specter makes two references to the rear, non-fatal wound. Now, this was six weeks after he, personally, had taken the testimony of the autopsy doctors. It is he who made the detailed study required for the taking of that testimony. In the first case he refers to "the hole in the President's back" and in the second to "the bullet hole on the President's back". In no case does he refer to a neck wound, the official designation that is without substantiation.

Arlen Specter, worried and safely encapsulated in the inner Commission secrecy, is anything but like Arlen Specter, ambitious politician in public. These are the three paragraphs of argument. The copy in this file is so indistinct it cannot be legibly reproduced in facsimile:

1. The Commission should determine with certainty whether the shots came from the rear. Someone from the Commission should review the films to corroborate the autopsy surgeons' testimony that the holes on the President's back and head had the characteristics of points of entry. None of the doctors at Parkland Hospital in Dallas observed the hole in the President's back or the small hole in the lower portion of his head. With all of the outstanding controversy about the direction of the shots, there must be independent viewings of the films to verify testimony which has come only from Government doctors.

2. The Commission should determine with certainty whether the shots came from above. It is essential for the Commission to know precisely the location of the bullet wound on the President's back so that the angle may be calculated. The artist's drawing prepared at Bethesda (Commission Exhibit #385) shows a slight angle of declination. It is hard, if not impossible, to explain such a slight angle of decline unless the President was farther down Elm Street than we have heretofore believed. Before coming to any conclusion on this, the angles will have to be calculated at the scene; and for this, the exact point of entry should be known.

3. The Commission should determine with certainty that there are no major variations between the films and the artist's drawings. Commission Exhibits Nos. 385, 386 and 388 were made from the recollections of the autopsy surgeons as told to the artist. Some day someone may compare the films with the artist's drawings and find a significant error which might substantially affect the essential testimony and the Commission's conclusions. In any event, the Commission should not rely on hazy recollections, especially in view of the statement in the autopsy report (Commission Exhibit #387) that:

> "The complexity of these fractures and the fragments thus produced tax satisfactory verbal description and are better appreciated in photographs and roentgenograms which are prepared."

Understated, aiming at self-justification and possible self-defense Specter put the minimum case well. It was, indeed, "indispensable" that the Commission "obtain the photographs and x-rays". (He later got a consolation prize, a sort of "feelthy-peectures" peek at one he described as "not technically authenticated" /WHITEWASH II,109/ when, according to my information, Tom Kelley, then Secret Service Inspector, flashed it before him during the May "reconstruction" in Dallas.)

No less sensational is Specter's concluding paragraph, which reads:

> When Inspector Kelly talked to Attorney General Kennedy, he most probably did not fully understand all the reasons for viewing the films. According to Inspector Kelly, the Attorney General did not categorically decline to make them available, but only wanted to be satisfied that they were really necessary. I suggest that the Commission transmit to the Attorney General its reasons for wanting the films and the assurance that they will be viewed only by the absolute minimum number of people from the Commission for the sole purpose of corroborating (or correcting) the artist's drawings, with the films not to become a part of the Commission's records.

Aside from what is obvious and needs no amplification, there is a potential major explosion buried here.

The official explanation of the suppression of the pictures and X-rays of the autopsy is that the Kennedy family blindly insisted upon it. That is anything but what Specter says here. First, he establishes that the Commission did not discuss this with Robert Kennedy but used the intermediary of the Secret Service inspector, at best a questionable procedure. Second, he records that Kennedy did not refuse to make them available. Here we ignore the fact that it was illegal to give this evidence to anyone, including the family of the murdered President, that the government should not have done it, and that copies of some of the pictures existed. How unlike the official posture is Specter's phrase, Kennedy "only wanted to be satisfied that they were really necessary".

Specter established the essentiality of the pictures and X-rays. He says that under these conditions, they could be available. The Commission did not have them. This raises doubt about the honesty of the official explanation, that the Kennedy family denied the investigation access to the pictures and X-rays.

In less than another two weeks, Specter sent another memorandum to Rankin, this one indicating he expected the autopsy pictures and X-rays to be examined by the Commission. Under date of May 12, with the title, "Examination of Autopsy Pictures and X-rays of President Kennedy", he wrote:

When the autopsy photographs and x-rays are examined, we should be certain to determine the following:

1. The photographs and x-rays confirm the precise location of the entrance wound in the back of the head depicted in Commission Exhibits 386 and 388.

2. The photographs and x-rays confirm the precise location of the wound of entrance on the upper back of the President as depicted in Commission Exhibits 385 and 386.

3. The photographs and x-rays confirm the precise area of the President's skull which was disrupted by the bullet when it exited as depicted in Commission Exhibit 388.

4. The characteristics of the wounds on the President's back and on the back of his head should be examined closely in the photographs and x-rays to determine for certain whether they are characteristic of entrance wounds under the criteria advanced by Doctors Finck, Humes, Boswell, Gregory, Shaw, Perry and Carrico.

5. The films and x-rays should be viewed in conjunction with Commission Exhibit 389 (a photograph of the frame of the Zapruder film immediately before the frame showing the head wound) and Commission Exhibit 390 (the frame of the Zapruder film showing the head wound) to determine for certain whether the angle of declination is accurately depicted in Commission Exhibit 388.

I suggest that we have a court reporter present so that we may examine Dr. Humes after the x-rays and photographs are reviewed to put on the record:

1. Any changes in his testimony or theories required by a review of the x-rays and films, and

2. Corroboration of the portions or all of his prior testimony which may be confirmed by viewing the photographs and x-rays.

Here again there are two references to the rear, non-fatal wound, neither as a neck wound, both as of the back: "on the upper back" and "on the President's back".

In all the many hours I have spent over Commission files, if Arlen Specter ever once referred to the rear, non-fatal injury as of the neck, I have not seen it. On not one occasion did this man, in charge of that part of the Commission's work, say it was anywhere but in the back, on the back, of the upper torso, below the shoulder - anywhere but in the neck! However, unless this wound was of entry and in the neck, not a single word in those 900 pages of the Report can even begin to have any meaning. The entire Report, the entire "solution" to the assassination, hangs on what Specter never once would say, that the President had an entry wound in the back of the neck.

In these suppressed memoranda Specter felt compelled to write and file, we have a clear expression of his apprehension about the validity of the autopsy testimony. Specter bespeaks the deepest doubts about it. If anyone on the staff could and should have, it is he. His desire for a re-examination of Humes is barrelhead stuff. Above all, it is designed for the protection of Arlen Specter who, having made inexcusable mistakes, wanted protection from the consequences.

The autopsy is essential evidence in a murder. It is the post-mortem examination intended to reveal all the possible medico-legal fact about that murder. It is supposed to be the most precise and scientific statement possible. That, certainly, was not true of the post-mortem of President Kennedy. It was, as I said in WHITEWASH II (p.110), "an autopsy unworthy of a Bowery bum".

There was then no reasonable doubt. There now can be even less question of it.

Why these documents were so long withheld I cannot pretend to know. I cannot refute the official explanation and I cannot accept it.

If the purpose was suppression, to delay as long as possible revelation of wrong-doing in the so-called "investigation" of the assassination, the character and content of the documents that I here for the first time reveal, removed from sheltering official secrecy, are consistent with an official desire to suppress. Because what I here publicly disclose was expunged from the Report, which pretended all of it did not exist, and because, regardless of any more polite official designation, it was officially denied for three years after the publication of the Report, there is no exaggeration in the use of the word "suppression". That is exactly what it is.

Again I ask, "Is this the way to investigate the murder of a President?"

And again I repeat, it is the way the government "investigated" the murder of John F. Kennedy.

Can there now be any doubt in the minds of reasonable men that the kindest thing that can be said for the Report of the President's Commission on the Assassination of President Kennedy is that it was a whitewash

Can there be any doubt that the government set out to make acceptable, to the degree possible, its predetermined official decision, that the crime would be laid to a solitary, friendless and safely murdered accused assassin, that it never really investigated and never really intended to investigate the murder of John Kennedy?

Can there be any doubt that the Commission knew more than is in its evidence, better than is in its Report, and simply suppressed what did not comfort its predetermined, built-in conclusions?

Each time new, suppressed files are released from suppression, they cast doubt on the Commission's intent and its conclusions. They more than challenge official integrity - they destroy it.

The foregoing are but samples of some of the disclosures of one end of some suppressions. By much effort I resurrected the most probative and sensational medical evidence. During the several years required to carry this investigation forward, I also engaged in other investigations.

12. THE MINISTER OF JUSTICE AS THE MINISTER OF TRUTH

New Orleans District Attorney Jim Garrison had charged a prominent local patron of the arts, Clay L. Shaw, was part of a conspiracy to kill President Kennedy. The indictment did not claim Shaw was part of the successful conspiracy, only that he was in a conspiracy. The case had been long delayed, in each and every instance because of legal maneuvers by the defense. As many of us had, Garrison said the President had been killed as the result of a conspiracy. Ultimately, Shaw was acquitted.

Because the charge was conspiracy - meaning merely a combination to do wrong and requiring two or more participants - Garrison subpenaed a number of items of Warren Commission evidence he deemed bear on conspiracy or indicating or proving that more than one person fired at the President. May 9, 1968, he obtained a subpena from Judge Edward A. Haggerty for the pictures and X-rays of the autopsy from the National Archives. Consistent with its record of the past, the district attorney's office in Washington, there part of the federal Department of Justice, refused to serve the subpena.

After the Supreme Court denied a number of legal actions on behalf of Shaw and the case was again set for trial on January 21, 1969 - the day after the Nixon administration took office - Garrison again sought the pictures and X-rays and Judge Haggerty again signed the order. Because of the federal opposition to the move, as the federal government opposed every move to look at the Report, Garrison asked Bernard ("Bud") J. Fensterwald, Jr., to act as his Washington counsel. "Bud" agreed to do the legal work, but he opposed the move. He feared, as I had for so long, that what might be produced might not be genuine. He declined to make the court appearance. I had been scheduled to go to New Orleans for the Shaw trial. Bud insisted that, because of my investigations of the autopsy and what relates to it, I be in court to help. I agreed. Garrison's office sent Numa Bertel, an assistant district attorney who had not been working on this inquiry because all those who had been were occupied with the impending prosecution. The case was set for hearing Friday morning, January 17, 1969. I met the assistant DA at the Baltimore airport 60 miles away and drove him to my Frederick home for dinner.

We were half-way through the meal when Bud phoned to let us know he was available and to confirm the date for us to meet at 9 in the morning, an hour before court opened. Within ten minutes he was again on the phone.

"Pack your toothbrushes and come down," he directed, in feigned flippancy. "The Department of Justice has some kind of big publicity play in the works. I'll have the story by the time you get here."

The trip from Frederick, Maryland, to Arlington, Virginia, took a little over an hour. When we reached his home, he had been to Washington and back and had a sheaf of papers filed with the judge by the Attorney General. It was, indeed, a major publicity play, by then blaring from radio and TV.

Ramsey Clark had secretly impaneled an "expert" junior-grade Warren Commission of his own. As it turned out, the competents among them were incompetent, had undertaken an impossible task and performed in a legally incompetent manner, but with the fanfare the Attorney General of the United States can trumpet, the chorus played "Warren Commission supported". No such thing.

While Numa and Bud examined the legal papers, I went over what was alleged to be fact. It was not.

We worked until 3 in the morning, then went to court, bright and anxious, for while there might have been a legal question or two, there certainly was none of fact. What the Attorney General, in his frightened desperation, said and probably believed supported the Warren Report, in actuality, destroyed it and the integrity of everyone involved. We had decided that at a certain point Numa would put me on as a witness. The issue was the autopsy, what parts of it were sought and the government's handling. Under these circumstances, where otherwise experts on the subject might not qualify as witnesses, the lawyers felt I would. I primed Numa with the first question he would ask me.

It was, "Have you studied the autopsy report?"

Now, in their report, this panel of forensic experts claimed to have read the "original Autopsy Report". My response to Numa's question was to be, "Which one? The one the doctor burned, the one he turned in or the one the government turned out, none of which agrees with the others?"

We felt that would capture the judge's interest. I then planned to hand him the two contradictory existing documents, the handwritten one and the typed one, and to trace the history of the burning of the original, the destruction of which had official approval from Humes' immediate superiors to the Commission. Then, systematically, all that had been suppressed on the autopsy that I had dug out. With the issue on which the judge later fixed, that posed by the subpena, had the President been shot from two or more directions, what I had from cursory examination of the panel report was in point and our way.

Charles W. Halleck, Jr., was the judge. He is the son of the former Republican leader in the House of Representatives whose successor, Gerald Ford, was a leading member of the Warren Commission.

Halleck seemed put out by the highly unusual moves - stunts really - by the Justice Department. Subtle, polite and proper as he was in court, it showed. At least, we so interpreted some of the things he said It is usual, necessary if the legal proceeding is to have meaning and reach an end with the possibility of justice, for opposing counsel to provide each other with copies of papers filed in court and in sufficient time for each side to make intelligent response. In this case, Clark did the opposite, carefully rigged what he had done to make it impossible, hardly the lofty impersonal behavior one expects from the nation's highest law officer, the administrator of justice.

Eleven months earlier, he had convoked this panel, the second of two secret ones, in an attempt to infuse life into the skeleton of the Warren Report, the autopsy. He did this by stealth, then sat for 11 months on their report before handling it like a commercial product promoted on TV. He filed the papers after the end of the working day the night before the hearing. Neither then nor since did he provide us a copy. In fact, when I detected a misrepresentation in the courtroom and asked one of the eight Department of Justice lawyers for a copy to check, he claimed to have no extra one with him(!) and promised one for after the lunch period. Neither then nor since has he provided it. Through a friend, Bud had obtained a copy, getting it and knowledge of it by accident. The Department of Justice was so determined we would not know what they were alleging, they gave up the possibility of making the morning papers and the prime evening TV news programs, withheld the work from its pressroom until after the working day (the pressroom told me they turned it out at night) and, when they felt we could not get it, pulled the public-relations plugs.

In court, the judge made casual allusion to this. The Justice lawyers assured him, as we had so often before heard about so many unaccountable things, that it was pure coincidence that the Attorney General released his ex parte "study" on the eve of the first challenge in court!

The hearing went as we had anticipated. The judge, who had

134

prepared himself on the law and previous decisions (so well that he spotted the miscitation by which the Justice Department pretended that a decision in a foreign jurisdiction was local! - another "coincidence"), had also studied the panel report. Knowing none of the fact of the case, which was also true of opposing counsel, he was impressed by the touted nothingness he had. Our moment came to respond. I awaited Numa's call.

At that dramatic moment, the clerk reached over from his bench between the judge's podium and counsel table, handing the surprised Numa the telephone. "It's for you," he said. Numa said, "Hello?" and then listened for a short period. "I can't talk now," he said in a hoarse whisper. The person on the other end of the line kept talking. In various ways on three or four occasions, Numa explained that he was in the courtroom and could not talk. Finally he said, impatiently, "Look, we are in the middle of arguments. Call you during the lunch recess." He hung up, handed the phone back to the clerk, and, instead of calling me to the stand, started a futility, asking permission to present affidavits to the court.

Now the law, properly, prefers the production of live witnesses, subject to cross-examination by the other side. You cannot cross-examine an affidavit. When Numa stopped talking, I whispered, "How about putting me on?" At first, he did not respond.

Bud came up and urged him to do this immediately. "The time is now!" he pressed Numa. "Put Hal on!"

"Can't," Numa said.

"It was all agreed," Bud and I responded.

Numa then, hurriedly, explained that he had been ordered not to put on any witnesses.

Bud and I, separated by ten feet, sank into gloom together. Here was the opportunity so rich, so perfect in every way, we had never dreamed we would find so rare a combination, an honest judge intent upon truth and justice, not intimidated by federal power and a little up tight over its abuses, with the unusual courtroom situation that made my accreditation to the National Archives my qualification as a witness, and I had all the requisite documents with me.

There was an interruption during which Joseph M. Hannon, chief of the Justice task force - so many lawyers for so simple a case! - came over to Numa and asked his permission to request an early recess. Numa, unknown to his opponent, was more than willing. When the judge returned, Hannon told him, falsely, that counsel joined in the request for the recess, making it seem as though our side had also requested it. Hannon is an experienced courtroom operator. He did the courtroom work, although the names signed to the brief included that of Assistant Attorney General Edwin L. Weisl, Jr., and United States Attorney for the District of Columbia David G. Bress, above his.

The opportunities we then had that had little chance of again offering themselves! Dr. James B. Rhoads, Archivist of the United States, to whom the subpena was addressed, was in the courtroom. In an effort to frustrate the legal action, which was the request that he deliver the pictures and X-rays to the New Orleans courtroom, he had filed a lengthy affidavit saying how busy he is, how it would be a hardship on him, and how this action would endanger future collections of historic papers. He had invoked a law for the preservation of presidential records. This had the effect of pleading that, were an effort made to kill a president with a knife, if that knife were presented to the government or a President's library, the fingerprints on it could never get before a jury. It was pretty weird to us, and the judge seemed to feel the same way.

Of course, Rhoads is loaded with assistants, including those in direct control of the Warren Commission materials, any one of whom could have been a competent courier and certifier that these were the original evidence under his immediate control. The pretense of the Archivist's affidavit was that he ran the whole works and could not take off part of a day for attendance on a court. In his literary effort to establish this fiction as the reality, he had enumerated all of the functions that are, bureaucratically, under this office. On page 4 I had spotted this of his functions:

"Administration of Federal Records Centers for storage of noncurrent federal records."

Those ordinary words to describe a dull function lit the lights brightly. In an effort to make him appear mentally ill, the government had "leaked" to the press what it alleged were Jim Garrison's Army medical records. The Pentagon had assured it would investigate itself, for what was done was illegal, and punishable by a jail sentence. It had then fallen silent, not even responding to indignant Congressional inquiry. The federal government can get away with anything, any illegality, if it is so determined. However, here were the prosaic words that seemed to say the head of the National Archives, the man seeking to frustrate appearance in a Louisiana court, with the evidence and subject to cross-examination, was the man in charge of those identical records that had so mysteriously been "leaked" to the press in an effort to poison the public mind against Garrison in this same case.

On the way to Bud's office, Numa explained that he had been called by Charles Ward, whose position was next to Garrison in that office. Garrison was then just out of the hospital and recuperating in a dry climate Ward had ordered Bertel not to put on any witnesses, to argue that this would have the effect of trying a Louisiana case in a Washington court, and that his dedication to the rights of the states and to the security of the case he would himself present in New Orleans precluded his offering live witnesses in Washington.

This was worse than nonsense and had the effect of preventing the instantaneous and total destruction of the most awful lie in American history, the false federal accounting of the murder of John Kennedy. Numa called Ward from Bud's office phone. He did not put me on the line as I had asked so I could give Ward the factual information so entirely lost upon Numa. I then phoned Charlie, whom I knew well. He did not take the call. The switchboard operator replied to my insistence that I knew he was there, having sat next to Numa while they spoke, with the message, "He does not answer the page." She might more accurately have said "He told me to tell you he doesn't answer the page."

I made three efforts to get through and failed in all. I then left messages for two assistant district attorneys working on the case and my friends, Jim Alcock and Andrew Sciambra. Each I asked be marked "urgent". It was so frustrating! Here was the first chance we had ever had for the destruction, the total, beyond-repair, courtroom demolition of the Warren Report, and it was, so mysteriously, being frustrated in New Orleans, where what was sought was said to be essential for the prosecution.

I was again in New Orleans two days later. The messages never reached either Alcock or Sciambra. These are the only messages I have ever left with the competent switchboard operators that never got to the intended person. None has ever been left for me that I did not receive.

After this I told Numa to be prepared for what I would do when we returned to court. I asked that he tell New Orleans, for in the judge's, as in the public, mind, we were associated. After recess, I asked the judge to recognize me as "amicus curiae", or "friend of the court", so I could show him how he had been imposed upon and lied to and how the evidence had been misrepresented, probably with neither counsel being aware of it. Halleck was so surprised that before he could eject me he asked me to repeat what I had said. This, at least, permitted the establishment in the official record of the charge against the government.

From the corner of my eye, I could see the silent approach of the United States marshals. Until they were abreast of me, I continued to talk. When the judge ruled I had no standing as "friend of the court", I expressed my deep regrets, turned and took a seat on the other side of the bar. For whatever purpose, whatever use, if any should ever be possible, there was, at least, a court record.

Needless to say, neither the Attorney General nor any of his assistants had any interest in the fraud he had perpetrated in open court, nor in answering the charge that he had filed lies in court, had misrepresented evidence. His purpose was served by these things, and his only interest was serving his selfish interest. The means disturbed him as little as the consequences.

Numa was adamant but polite. He repeated the same refrain, that he could not try a New Orleans case in a Washington court. The judge was patient as a loving father with an erring son, preserving Garrison's rights despite Garrison's assistant's best efforts. He had ruled against every one of the Justice Department's pleadings save one, that a showing of materiality of the pictures and X-rays in the New Orleans case be made. Had the judge not agreed with this and had he ruled against the government, there is every prospect he would have been reversed on appeal. Despite Numa's failure to seek an extension, the judge gave two weeks to reconsider and produce what the subpena said Garrison had, proof that the pictures and X-rays would or could show the President had been shot from two directions.

When the hearing ended, we walked to the parking lot a block away. We had left the press, there in large numbers because of the attention to the hearing the Attorney General himself had generated, still in and around the courtroom. As my ignition key turned, the 3 p.m. news came on. It began with a bulletin. The Garrison office had announced that the refusal of the federal government to produce the pictures and X-rays of the autopsy made prosecution of Clay Shaw impossible!

This was utter foolishness, complete nonsense. Similar evidence could have been introduced by other means. This had been the plan. I had personally arranged for some of the technical experts. It immediately dawned on me that the announcement had been made before the end of the hearing. And then, regardless of what New Orleans said, the judge had not ruled against it.

As I drove home, additional bulletins spelled out the rest of the story. The Garrison office had asked for a continuance in the Shaw case, the first it had sought in almost two years, until the federal government produced this evidence. The move made it possible for the federal government to block the prosecution.

That night friends in the Garrison office told me this had been done without consultation with him, something I have trouble believing.

In any event, on Sunday, two days later, I was in New Orleans, working on other evidence with two assistant District Attorneys. The next day, Monday, to everyone's surprise, Alcock appeared in court to withdraw the motion and the following day, Tuesday, January 21, the case really did start, with the great tedium of selecting jurors. During the five days I remained there, I studied and completed most of an analysis of the papers Clark had filed. I concluded he must have been terrified at the impending (to him) doom of having the secrets of the autopsy made available, panicked and, without consultation with the White House, made his highly improper but, to me, extremely gratifying move. We perhaps will never know whether, in desperation, he did this on his own or whether he was so ordered or was persuaded by subordinates.

Most surprising of all was the absence of a press release. It is the usual custom for the government to supply prepared statements saying what it wants said, directing attention where it prefers attention to be focused and, in effect, writing the story it wants written. All of this was verbal, and not for the first time in Clark's intrusions into the Shaw case and Garrison's trial. This is set forth at length in OSWALD IN NEW ORLEANS, my book on that case.

Clark traded heavily on the Kennedy name, suggesting the family backed his statement.

Cagey political maneuverer that every cabinet officer is, Clark omitted from what he gave the court a "statement" by Burke Marshall that went to the press.* Marshall, a former assistant Attorney General of the

*See p. 574.

United States, represents the executors of the murdered President's estate. I had long sought an opportunity to give him an understanding of the invidious role he filled, to let him know what it seemed he could not know about how he was being used and, through him, the name of the President's family, its prestige and influence, in a successful effort to block the truth of his murder. Marshall is all-knowing. Until then, he never responded to a single letter and besmirched himself and the family as none other could have done for him and them.

His January 16 (the day of Clark's propaganda field-day) statement prepared not on the government machines and xeroxed rather than mimeographed, contains considerable material for analysis.

I had earlier concluded from the internal evidence that, although on behalf of these executors he had signed the fake contract by which the government suppressed the filmed evidence of the autopsy, he had not drafted it and he was not their representative at the time it was drafted I had deduced it was prepared by the government and he had later assented This film was returned to the government the end of October 1966. I was therefore pleasantly surprised to read the careful language of his statement:

> Since October 1966 I have acted on behalf of the Kennedy family as their representative in dealing with all matters and inquiries regarding the Letter Agreement of October 29, 1966 and the X-ray and photograph material relating to the autopsy of the late President Kennedy.

Among the things Marshall here says and does not say, he does not say he negotiated the return of this material, does not say he represented the family during the negotiations or the drafting of the Letter of Agreement contract. In saying "since October 1966", he just might have been saying "since October 29, 1966".

Next he said, "Last year the Attorney General informed me that he had ordered the 1968 Panel Review ... He described the contents of the panel report."

Here, in the subtleties of lawyers, Marshall really says he was not consulted on the appointment of the panel or by it and that all he knows of their report is what Clark told him. On this basis, Marshall says, "I concluded that the report simply confirmed the autopsy report and saw no reason to concern the members of the Kennedy family, and did not do so."

Clark asked him if he objected to the release of the report and Marshall said only, "I see no basis to object." After being informed by Clark, Marshall spoke to the widow and the surviving brother, who "will have no comment to make".

On the basis of this, Clark led the world to believe his act had the imprint of Kennedy approval. That is anything but what Marshall said. However, in associating himself with this unscrupulous maneuvering and high-level operating against truth and the national interest, Marshall should have known and, without doubt, could and did anticipate what misuse would be made of his name and connection. In Washington, this was predictable.

The record, however, is a fascinating one. Here, for the first time, Marshall, and perhaps, through him, the family, shows the first signs of retreat, what can be taken as the beginning of the realization of what happened and what it has become enmeshed in. Perhaps this interpretation is not entirely accurate, but Marshall's guarded use of carefully picked words does permit this translation from lawyer's lingo.

Clark cited his authority for having examinations made of the pictures and X-rays in the brief filed in Judge Halleck's court (p.12). It is "pursuant to paragraph II(2) of the letter agreement". That paragraph permits access only to "any person authorized to act for a Committee of Congress, for a Presidential committee or commission, or for any other official agency of the United States Government, having authority to investigate matters relating to the death of the late President ..."

The Department of Justice has such authority, but it would seem only if it is investigating "matters relating to the death of the late President". If the Department is and has been conducting such an investigation, it has kept that fact a real secret. Most of the rest of us have the impression the government considers the case closed. If the Department does consider the case closed, wherein is its authority? Has it not, in fact, violated the agreement? If it does not consider the case closed, it can hardly have faith in its own Warren Report.

The agreement, whether or not valid, does make this limitation. It would seem that the Attorney General was required to file with the court evidence that he had not violated the agreement he insists is valid. That he did not do. Instead, in his brief, he cited (p.13) what he said was the reason for these examinations:

> To further assure the preservation of a record concerning the nature and contents of the X-rays and photographs ... and at the written suggestion of Dr. Boswell ...*

The Attorney General is so accustomed to taking the law into his own hands, he forgot himself. There is no provision for Dr. Boswell's suggestion in the agreement. And, Boswell is not and cannot be an "official agency of the United States Government". Moreover, a "record" is strictly outside the provision of the agreement permitting any examination of the film at all. It seems pretty clear that the Attorney General was so indifferent to the agreement, so confident of his own raw power, so determined to do what political exigencies impelled him to do, he personally violated the agreement he then went into court to pretend to keep inviolate.

Clark also released this letter to him from J. Thornton Boswell, one of the original autopsy surgeons.* Strangely, for a man with an office and a profession, it is typed and signed but on no letterhead, with no return address and, even more intriguing, on government-size paper, which is a half-inch smaller than standard. The use of Xeroxing to achieve the effect Clark wanted discloses this intelligence. I am suggesting that Boswell's letter was both inspired and prepared by the federal government. It is self-serving less than it is government-serving.

Under date of January 26, 1968, Boswell, saying he was speaking also for Dr. James J. Humes, Jr., his former associate and superior in the Bethesda Naval Hospital and at the autopsy but not mentioning the name of the third participant, asked for the impaneling of "an impartial board of experts". With the integrity of his work the issue, it seems just a bit peculiar that he focuses in his very first sentence on only the "x-rays and photographs". What is even stranger is Boswell's consistent, undeviating refusal to discuss his work with anyone having knowledge of it or the context of its use and misuse by the government. When I mailed him my first book, which is severely critical of that work and that misuse and sought an interview, he was afraid to respond, afraid even to complain. When a news reporter who had spoken with me before seeing Boswell did speak with him, Boswell then complained that I had written without speaking to him. Again I challenged him and again he was silent, as he has remained, save when he is in the company of those who are ignorant of his performance and know nothing of the subject.

What Boswell really did in writing (or should I say "signing") a letter to the Attorney General was to give Clark the excuse for convening such a panel. Whether or not they were "impartial" or qualified "experts" time, if not what follows, will establish.

Some of the lemmings that lived with the Warren Commission crept into "Boswell's" letter. He asked that such a board "examine the available material". A man seeking truth, a man of science, a medical man, an expert, certainly might have been expected to insist the truth requires all "available material". How closely Clark and his "impartial" panel took Boswell's hint will not long be denied the reader.

Never has there been an Attorney General so subservient to the slightest whim of private citizens, never so prompt in performing duties asked of him (if this is what Clark was and did). One month to the day

*See p. 574.

after the date on "Boswell's" letter, his "impartial" panel met and began its dirty work (oops!) - that is, its two-day scholarly and scientific deliberations and investigation.

The lemmings were omnipresent. I have written of the so-called Kennedy family-General Services Administration "contract" elsewhere. Here I note that the compelling needs of the Attorney General required it to be attached to the Rhoads affidavit. Two of the gnawings of those federal lemmings entirely escaped the so-called inquiring eye of the press. In that (and I use and repeat the phrase not without intent) so-called contract, under IV on page 4, paragraph (2) reads:

> **(2)** The Kennedy family representative for the purposes of this agreement shall be BURKE MARSHALL. A successor representative of the Kennedy family may be designated in writing to the Administrator from time to

[Fuzziness and gray in facsimiles from government rexeroxing of xerox copies.]

Only by looking at the original is the cat out of the bag. Marshall's name was hand-lettered in. From this, two obvious deductions follow: Either he had had nothing to do with the negotiating and/or drafting of the contract or, if he had, had hoped to avoid further association. Under other circumstances, would his name not have appeared in the typed copy? I think it would. I suggest this really means the contract was drafted by the government, trusted by the family and their representative, included what the government wanted included and nothing else, was prepared without any representative of the family involved in that preparation, and was signed and agreed to because the family trusted the government of which the former head had been its most prominent membe and another the Attorney General himself.

It is not a contract to the family interest, as I wrote Marshall after, under the most dubious circumstances and in open violation of regu lations, it was given to the New York Times on what amounts to an exclusive basis. As Boswell would not talk to me because I am expert on his work and its inadequacies, deficiencies and errors, so the government persistently denied me this contract and then, in effect, leaked it to this newspaper whose reporter, Fred Graham, is preeminent among those who regard ignorance as qualification for pretended expertise. Predictably, Graham treated the contract as a sensation, which in those days was true of almost anything unpublished and bearing the Kennedy name. He made virtuoso display of his ignorance in the doing.

Attached to the contract is a sheet of two appendices, identified as Appendix A and Appendix B. The seven items in the second are a listing of the photographic items "given" the government. I use the quotation marks because this was in no sense a gift. By that time, "possessic of" the pictures and X-rays, which may or may not have actually been in Kennedy possession, had become a considerable liability to the then-living Senator Robert Kennedy. Much worse, in plain English, they were government property that had been, in effect, stolen. They were given away by those without the legal right to do so and accepted by those who knew it was not legally possible for this property to be given away.

For an inventory, this is a carefully imprecise tabulation. At no point does it say how many pictures and X-rays of what types and sizes were taken or included. In fact, it is so carefully prepared that there is no way of gleaning this information, which is one way to keep the most precious of the records of the murder of a President, by his government or by his family. It cannot be added up, nor can it be reconciled with the publicity about them. Neither the types nor the numbers tally. We shall return to this. For the moment, let us ignore all but two items:

3. 5 envelopes containing 4 x 5 exposed film containing no image

4. 1 roll of exposed film from a color camera entirely black with no image apparent

Identification of a non-existent "color camera" is the least incredible part of this listing.

Medical photography is a high specialty in the military service. Those practicing it are skilled. Photographers, by their calling, are men attuned to crisis, less disturbed by it than others. Here we had the most important of all the evidence of the President's murder, and it is now non-existent. More, it is not mentioned - not by the Warren Commission, not by the family and not, as we shall see, by the "impartial" eminences. Can this be?

The pictures were given, exposed but undeveloped, to the Secret Service. They are never mentioned in the testimony. There is no explanation of them in 26 enormous volumes of so-called "evidence" which never deals with this, the quintessential. That is enough of a self-characterization of the "investigation". This, and I emphasize not to suggest they were the murderers, is the same Secret Service whose responsibility it wa to prevent the murder of the President who was murdered while under its protection.

And every voice is mute.

Consultation with professional photographers reveals that what is here described is as close as anything can be to a photographic impossibility. Modern cameras are such that, with film exposed at all - that is, with the shutter snapped, any picture taken at all - some image would be on the film. There might be an improper exposure, not expectable from such professionals. The setting might permit too much or too little exposure. Nonetheless, some image would be captured. To say that there was "no image" - and with two different cameras - is to say that there was dirty work.

Poor Attorney General! He and his predecessors and the rest of the government had so restricted his options it was no longer possible for him to draw a string without unbagging cats. He could not do anything without revealing something hitherto suppressed. Given the choice between calling him stupid or ignorant (other possibilities are obvious but more unpleasant), I believe that he, like all the others, was the captive of his advisers, depended upon them for his knowledge as Marshall, in turn, trusted and depended upon the Attorney General.

Nonetheless, in order to argue the legal fiction that he would not make the pictures and X-rays available because they were "privileged" by a contract, that contract had to be before the court. So did the great photographic scandal that could not be eliminated from the contract, despite the rather successful efforts to minimize what could be learned.

It is not remarkable that the self-important Fred Graham, who, besides being a reporter for a great paper,* is a lawyer and its Supreme Court reporter, did not catch this. With him, indifference contests with ignorance in his reporting about anything connected with the assassination, and he is untroubled as long as he can lick the official spittle.

In order to array all his cannonry, Clark unostentatiously disclosed still another "autopsy report" by the autopsy doctors. It is so unworthy of serious consideration, he did not deem it worth a title. Neither he nor they, or whoever drafted it, bothered to date it. We know of this only that it should be possible to assume the report was written after the examination. That was on January 26, 1967.**

If anything these doctors do has any meaning at all, is worthy of any thought or belief, there still was no serious purpose served by this examination, said on the first page to have been "requested by the Department of Justice". Yet these are the same doctors the same Department of Justice had asked to do exactly the same thing on November 1, 1966, for the same purpose, of telling the lie that was told in order to get the headlines that, by it alone, were gotten. On that day Boswell and Humes had re-examined the X-rays and, for the first time, seen the pictures. They swore to the Commission that they had never seen the pictures, they took receipts for "undeveloped" film, and they, on the same page of the report here considered, repeat that they had not seen the

*Later with CBS. **See pp. 575-9.

pictures at the autopsy. Therefore, when propaganda was the federal intent, they announced that they had "re-examined" and "confirmed" the pictures. This was a lie that is conspiratorial, that cannot have been inadvertent. They were capable of it. In that, aside from the character of their work and their testimony about it, we find measure of the dependability of this new report.

There could be only one reason for Clark's obtaining a new report from them: Propaganda. Of course, he might not have been satisfied with their earlier work. In this event, if he asked for more, it was not because of his certainty of their dependability or his satisfaction about their competence. It would then have been because they were malleable and available. The conclusion is the same. His purpose, in any event, was the use he made of this new prostitution of science and medicine: Propaganda.

It is not often that a single member of a President's cabinet so neatly displays the combined qualifications of a Minister of Justice and a Minister of Truth (only the fascists were honest enough to call it "propaganda").

When Judge Halleck's hearing was held less than four days remained of Clark's ministration of "justice", no full working day.

UNITED STATES GOVER........ENT   D..ARTMENT OF JUSTICE

Memorandum

TO : Mr. Marion Johnson   DATE: JAN 21 ??
      National Archives

FROM : Frank M. Wozencraft   by: Martin F. Richman
       Assistant Attorney General   First Assistant
       Office of Legal Counsel

SUBJECT: Authentication of Kennedy Autopsy Pictures

We believe that the press inquiries on the above subject should be answered by a statement along the following lines:

"On the day after the Kennedy family deposited the autopsy X-rays and photographs in the Archives, the deposited items were examined by four members of the Naval Medical Staff who had participated in the autopsy of the late President (including two of the three autopsy surgeons, the third being on duty in Viet Nam). They stated to the Department of Justice that the deposited items include all the X-rays and photographs that were taken by them during the autopsy, and that they have no reason to believe that any others were made during the autopsy."

In addition, requests to see any documents which contain descriptions of the autopsy pictures should be denied on the ground that we agreed with Burke Marshall not to disclose such descriptions, for much the same reasons that the pictures themselves are not available for non-official access at this time.

142

13. THE SUB-MINISTERS OF TRUTH AND THEIR MINISTRATIONS

If anyone in the United States should know the law, it should be
the Attorney General. A lie under oath is a crime, if it is about a material point. He who solicits that lie under oath, who forces, persuades,
cajoles, or is in any way its sponsor, is also a criminal. That crime is
known as the subornation of perjury.

In my first book on this subject, but not for the last time by far,
I raised the question of perjury and its subornation (WHITEWASH:180), and
with regard to the autopsy and the autopsy surgeons. I then sent a copy
of the book with a letter of challenge to each of the autopsy doctors.
Each was silent, then and since. It is not alone Boswell who said nothing. He is alone only in having uttered a childish complaint that
reached me.

Thereafter, in my second book, WHITEWASH II: THE FBI-SECRET SERVICE
COVER-UP, where I devoted all of the second part to the autopsy and who
and what relate to it, I called Arlen Specter, the Commission lawyer who
handled this testimony and the pertinent exhibits, a liar. I embellished
this to say he was a willful, deliberate liar. Then I noted that if this
were false it was actionable and said I awaited word from the man then
District Attorney of Philadelphia and aspiring to be its mayor.

Specter was less vocal than the doctors.

During his mayoralty campaign, I was invited to make a public
speech in Philadelphia. Preparatory to it, I phoned the papers, told
them what I had written and reported my intention of repeating it. I
did, in public, and without the presence of any reporter from the major
papers. Later, on the largest radio station in his city, I dwelt at some
length on Specter's record. It was a four-hour broadcast that elicited
no response from him.

In this speech during his campaign, I added chapter and verse to
the challenge that he sue me for libel and dared him further by saying
the only reason he could not and had not sued me was because he knew the
truth and knew that I knew the truth and would not dare a judicial determination of the fact, even in the city in which he had the great legal
muscle of being District Attorney.

Specter is a man of such unlimited personal courage he has to
save himself - for those appearances where he is unopposed or - and then
rarely - where he faces pushovers. He had only once, after several dozen
invitations, agreed to face me. Then we were to have been far apart, in
TV studios, he in Boston and I in Washington. I showed up. Specter did
not, perhaps fearing that even distance was not enough protection. He
was asked to face me in New York, but found it more expedient to go to
England instead, where he was flanked by British and American legal eminences and still did not account himself well.

He is at his best on protected video whitewashes such as the four-
hour, four-night CBS spectacular of 1967. There, facing no one but semi-
official apologists, he repeated some of the same lies, thus becoming -
and knowing he was becoming - one of history's best-exposed liars.

Immediately after this demonstration of his bravery, personal and
professional, his jealous regard for his reputation and integrity, his
unlimited confidence in his righteousness and that of his cause, and his

143

command of the fact about which he was the world's greatest expert, having been its manufacturer, I wrote him in similar vein.

I will say this for Arlen Specter: He did reply, even if his tail was tightly legged and even if he did not accept the challenge to sue me - or even to debate me or defend himself.

And I will add this: With all the United States Government to defend him and all the United States press to suppress his record and the charges against him, he is not very lonely.

So, consideration of the ministrations of the doctors in the cause of truth is presented in the form of a new challenge to them. If they find harsh what I will here say of them, if they feel it is actionable - and if they are men with the convictions and guts of men - they can do what Specter did not and will not.

In saying this, I realize I am betting a sure thing, and I want the reader to know I am not hiding it. I say it straight out. Neither Specter in the city where he has great influence and power and I have none, nor the doctors, in Washington, where we all know who has and exercises the muscle, literally and figuratively, will sue me. Neither will face a judicial determination of fact. There is no court that can be so fixed or stacked, no jury that can be influenced enough, no weakness I have (and as a man without influence or means, I will have to depend on court-supplied or volunteer counsel), that can tempt them even to look from behind the federal skirts.

In addition, they know the truth and they know that I know it. They will do whatever they can to keep it out of any open court as they must to keep themselves safe and secure in the hands of such champions as the Attorney General. They prefer ex parte proceedings, where they face no opposition, will not be cross-examined and know that if there is any examination at all, it will be friendly.

There are few men who will avoid such challenges, but we are dealing with those who have and will continue to.

To avoid the remote possibility that, in haste and passion, I might not make direct challenge to the autopsy doctors on their integrity, I begin with it.

At the very beginning of their unheaded, undated and, I emphasize, unworthy report, used by the Attorney General as one uses the contemptible, are these statements:

> The autopsy began at approximately 8:00 P. M. on Friday, November 22, 1963, and was concluded approximately at 11:00 P. M. The autopsy report, written by Dr. Humes with the assistance of Dr. Boswell and Dr. Finck, was written on November 23 and the morning of November 24, and delivered by Dr. Humes to Admiral Burkley, the President's physician, on November 24 at about 6:30 P. M.

It is a minor complaint that the examination, in a very real sense began about 25 minutes earlier, when the first of the pictures and X-rays were taken. They are part of the autopsy, suddenly a very real part to Boswell, Clark, Garrison and the court.

In every respect other than time, this statement is in conflict with Humes' testimony (2H373). For example, his testimony on when he wrote the autopsy (and Boswell and Finck had no part of the writing):

> Commander Humes. In the privacy of my own home, early in the morning of Sunday, November 24, I made a draft of the report which I later revised and of which represents the revision. That draft I personally burned in the fireplace of my recreation room.

The Commission and all the government and press, then and since, have apparently seen nothing ghoulish, nothing at all wrong in the burning of a President's autopsy in a recreation room. Some "recreation"!

The difficulty here is determining whether Humes is a simple liar

144

in his services for Clark or a perjurer in his Commission testimony. Perhaps, as one could be certain with an honest government and a dedicated judicial system, we will know. That, however, is not as important as the deliberate deception and this part of the rewriting of history and recasting of the assassination.

The difference in when Humes burned his evidence - and his observations in the draft of the autopsy he burned was evidence, for he was the chief expert witness - is material. It is highly significant. Note that he says the draft that he wrote November 24 - and he specifies it was a Sunday morning - is what he burned. There exists a draft that was the revision. It is this he held in his hand. It is part of the Commission's 371st file and of Exhibit 397.

So there can be no doubt of the materiality, I quote his answer to a question by Commissioner John J. McCloy on the next page.

... I was working in an office, and someone had a television on and came in and told me that Mr. Oswald had been shot, and that was around noon on Sunday, November 24th.

The Commission that accepted this false statement is the one that accepted many others it also knew were false. It had to have been later than he said for Oswald was shot later. With Oswald dead, he knew there would be no cross-examination on the autopsy report. The changes he made are not editorial, not with "low" becoming "high", "left" changing to "right", "puncture" - meaning entrance - being eliminated, and many, many other such things. These changes might anywhere else be regarded as culpable, but with Arlen Specter, this Commission, this Attorney General and Department of Justice, when a President is murdered, they are normal, essential, natural as breathing. I emphasize he said he was still working on the autopsy after Oswald was shot, and after he knew it.

Unless he casts himself in the role of an errand boy and the Navy as employer of the world's fastest typists and those of rarer skill that will earn our attention in coming passages, all signatories of the Clark special autopsy report lied in saying that the autopsy was "delivered by Dr. Humes to Admiral Burkley, the President's physician, on November 24 at about 6:30 P.M." The alternative to calling him other than a liar is to make a more serious charge, for he certified the other version. It is his November 24, 1963, "Certificate", countersigned by his superior officer, Captain J. H. Stover:

I, James J. Humes, certify that all working papers

associated with Naval Medical School Autopsy Report A63-272

have remained in my personal custody at all times. Autopsy

notes and the holograph draft of the final report were handed

to Commanding Officer, U. S. Naval Medical School, at 1700,

24 November 1963. No papers relating to this case remain in

my possession.

[Burkley approved.See p. 525.]   J. J. HUMES

Thus, it is clear that Humes gave the autopsy he had written to Captain Stover at 5 p.m. the day he said he gave it to Burkley an hour and a half later. He also said he had not a scrap of paper in any way relating to the autopsy in his possession beginning at 5 p.m. So, what had he to give the admiral at 6:30? What he was also saying, and this has to be read between the lines, is that he worked it over until well after morning, well after he knew of Oswald's murder, until about dark the day he said he cleaned it all up in the morning.

The Navy put up with and was part of an awful lot. There is no

145

reason to believe it will be chagrined by such a "certificate". Nor the Attorney General, past or present.

So, there is no doubt about what I say and charge, and I can present the rest of the analysis and commentary without having to concern myself with its repetition.

In the very first paragraph, where the doctors present their credentials for a forensic-medical purpose, two omit any at all, which is not an oversight because they have none. "None" are exactly the credentials most compatible with the interests of the Attorney General, stalwart upholder of the law and its requirements, standards and niceties that he is. The third, Finck, says only that he had earlier been accredited. If he had any experience in it, he felt it unworthy of mention. There is nothing in his testimony before the Warren Commission, which strained at the same gnat, to indicate that he had, in fact, any valid experience of the kind required for the honest discharge of its responsibilities. Again, this made him and Boswell and Humes the best, the most acceptable kind of experts for its real purposes.

Dr. Humes was chosen to perform the autopsy because of the decision to bring the body of the late President to the Naval Medical Center ...

This makes as much sense as saying he would rather go to New York than by bus. There is no relationship between his being on the staff at that hospital and his being in charge of the autopsy simply because he was. What that autopsy required was two things, and it had neither: Civilians and genuine experts in forensic medicine. It was grossly unjust to Humes and the others, who were under military discipline, to require them to attempt a task for which they were so perfectly unsuited.

Had the government wanted real experts, had it wanted any civilians - and it wanted neither - it could have had them there before the body arrived. Almost all of the country's real experts are very close to Washington. The three best known are and were less than an hour away. One is the Dr. Russell Fisher of Clark's panel who was that close by car. Not only did the government want no civilians at the autopsy, it posted guards and kept them out of all the autopsy proceedings. The only exceptions were the Secret Service men, Roy Kellerman and William Robert Greer, who kept an eye on the corpse, and the two FBI agents, James W. Sibert and Francis X. O'Neill, who eyed the Secret Service.

When the doctors say that "x-rays and photographs of the President's body were taken during the autopsy", they say too little and help complicate the problem of learning what should hardly be a tightly-guarded state secret: How many and what kind of each were taken. What they do not say is that, after the autopsy examination, there were no pictures or X-rays of the laboratory examinations. Specimens were, as they had to have been, taken for such purposes. The brain was removed. Were pictures or X-rays taken of it? If any were, they are not in the tabulations. They remain unaccounted. Can there be any excuse for this in the investigation of a President's murder?

This reference to "x-rays" presents a welcome clue to the suspicious writer and analyst who finds such a letter as Boswell signed strange and out of keeping in such affairs. In all the papers Clark made available, there are only two places where the word is misspelled. They are this report and the Boswell letter. If I am not lost in admiration of Boswell as an expert in forensic medicine, which he is not, I am confident that, as an experienced lab man, as a pathologist, he knows the word is not "x-ray", as do the others who, with him, signed the report, but is "X-ray". This is a reasonable indication that the place where the report was typed has a typist who is not accustomed to typing medical documents and who seems to have been the one who typed both documents. Could it have been the Department of Justice, for which it was made, which kept it secret for so long, and which ultimately released it as part of the propaganda barrage? An alternative is that the same person prepared the draft. I do really believe that Boswell, Humes and Finck can spell "X-ray".

The record already being what it is, perhaps it is just as well to make no real issue of the fact that many of the pictures and X-rays were taken before 8 p.m. and he says they were all taken during the autopsy that began at 8 p.m. It does help confuse the already too-confused - the inexcusably confused - records of the pictures and X-rays, to which we return later.

Phrasing of the Department of Justice "request" is quaint: "to examine the x-rays and photographs for the purpose of determining whether they are consistent with the autopsy report." If not, are we to assume the pictures and X-rays in error? Of course, there was no reason for the Justice Department to be interested in learning whether or not the autopsy report and the Warren Report were correct. Those in it who counted knew. They are the ones who helped guarantee error, who made some and helped arrange others. There is no suggestion there could be anything wrong; there was no request to determine accuracy. After all, it was only a President, and he was dead anyway, wasn't he? So, that great, imaginative soul, the Attorney General, asked a new investigation, by the doctors investigating themselves, to see if there was anything wrong with the pictures and X-rays, or the pictures and X-rays that still existed, or the pictures and X-rays that were shown the doctors. We are not told which, not told the number and description, which is a new zenith in forensic medicine, a new high standard of evidence, a new search for the most perfect and faithful reporting.

He was a ground-breaker, that Attorney General Ramsey Clark, good ol' Dallas boy that he is. Even if he had asked exactly the same thing of exactly the same doctors only a few months earlier, on November 1, 1966, and had received the most absolute assurances. Perhaps he wanted to satisfy himself that the pictures and X-rays had not changed themselves in a couple of months, or multiplied themselves? Or that a few had not died and been buried. Of course, if he had the numbers made public, he would never know, for there would have been no time at which he would have known the number that could have increased or decreased.

The one thing he would know is that he would be assured that the pictures and X-rays were "consistent with the autopsy". That was as certain as day following night. And he was right. He was so assured.

Of course, it is possible Clark really gave the doctors a different directive. Their representation seems outside the provisions of the already-quoted agreement. If he did, when he had his chance, indeed, the responsibility, to specify in his brief (p.13), he avoided it. Because he there sets forth no purpose at all and it is the only record, then it would seem he had the pictures and X-rays examined for no purpose at all. Which makes at least as much sense as what the doctors say - but that, too, is against the contract - even for the Attorney General.

The doctors were willing to work overtime. It was "after our regular work day", which means after the longest-working of the three had finished, "on January 27, 1967," they met "at the office of Dr. Robert H. Bahmer, Archivist of the United States, where the x-rays and photographs were made available to us". Bahmer worked overtime, too. He has since retired, his retirement not delayed by what he had to do and what he did do with and about the pictures and X-rays.

What they learned, what they determined, how they established "consistency" with the autopsy for that large number of pictures that showed "no image", with their very special kind of science, the doctors do not report. They confirmed. Is that not enough?

(How hard these doctors worked is emphasized again in the last paragraph of their report. There they stipulate "our examination of the photographs and x-rays lasted approximately five hours". Now, they began "after our regular work day" and they worked for five hours on their examination alone! They make it look easy, but it sure seems like some kind of hard work.)

At this point the doctors are ready to get down to their case, and they do. First, they quote their autopsy report as saying the "neck wound ("back wound" to the panel) was "presumably of entry". This is precisely what they do say in their edited and rewritten version. It is on page 9 of their holograph. The difference is that, until they made their last revision, the word "presumably" was not there to weaken it. "Consistent with" this is their page 4 comment that in the holograph, after correctic describes this as "7 x 4 mm oval wound". Until they got to working the facts around, they had the word "puncture" as a description of the wound. "Puncture" and "entrance" are synonymous.

The question arises, if they are now so positive and were when they first revised the autopsy no less unequivocal, why did they have to eliminate direction entirely from the first mention and qualify it in the second? Is it their confidence thus expressed, their skill and competence?

Next, they twice assure (in the same paragraph) that "Photographs Nos. 11, 12, 38 and 39 verify the location of the wound" in the back "and confirm the accuracy" of their measurements. Those are really magical photographs. If it is not too much to assume that the autopsy and panel doctors had the same pictures (there is no other way of keeping the autopsy doctors honest, for their "report" has no listings of any kind), the description of the panel doctors of photographs 11 and 12 lead to the wonder if they were some new hybrid. They are described as "Head viewed from right and above to include part of the face, neck, shoulder and upper chest". All this and the back, too?

No accident, no mistake. These wonders of the medical world are talking about pictures that show the wound they describe as "in the right posterior thorax", "low in the back of the neck", and they go so far as to explain when they give the measurement "that it was 14 cm. (5½ inches) from the tip of the mastoid process". They add in parentheses "(behind the right ear)".

That is indeed marvelous photography, showing both the front and the back at the same time when they were of the "head viewed from right and above".

The possibility of confusion cannot be ignored. Perhaps these, for example, are not as described by the panel. Or did the autopsy doctors have different pictures? What then? Would it not have been nice if the autopsy doctors had specified what they were consulting, at least have listed the pictures they claim support their interpretation and representation of what they say they saw? If, faced with the questionable description of the panel doctors and the non-existent descriptions on the non-existent list of the autopsy doctors, there is a lack of clarity, the Attorney General was confused, he was silent and did not complain. With this kind of "verification", he was happy. He even presented it in court.

There was a body chart made by Boswell during the autopsy examination. It is, much to his regret, in evidence as part of Exhibit 397 (17H45). He has, under his embarrassment, for it shows this same wound five to six inches down on the President's back, claimed that if he had had the slightest notion anybody would see his work, he would have been more careful. This is a new and exalted concept of the forensic-medical science, you are careless if you think you will not get caught and you do work you expect no one to see. Or, perhaps it is just the prevalent concept when a President is murdered. Anyway, having already been quoted in the papers on this, Boswell seemed content for a different account still to be in this report. The report says it "purports to show the approximate location of the wound, and specifically states that it was 14 cm (5¼ inches) from the tip of the mastoid process". After a few other choice words, without appetite, the report acknowledges, in a modest under statement of the reality if it is at all correct, that "the drawing itself may be somewhat misleading as to the location of the wound, making it appear at a point lower than it actually was." That it did, if the wound was in the neck. Six inches down on the back is certainly not in the neck.

But what does this reveal of the dependability of Boswell, who could make so gross an error when he was occupied in attempting to establish the cause of death and then give such "explanations"? Or of

Humes, who was without correction when he examined the papers when he was a witness? Or of Boswell and Finck who then and there remained mum and, when asked, had no change to make in what Humes said? If he could be that wrong on that when he had the body before him, how dependable is anything he said then or now says? How reassuring is the plea of such an "expert" that no attention be paid to his basic work? And how much credence can today be placed in what he has since said?

This report is correct in saying that the chart also includes the notation that this wound was "14 cm" from the mastoid. It is not, however, correct in saying that this measurement puts the wound in the neck. With the great care exercised in the pursuit of detail and precision in the autopsy examination, and with the crucial measurements involving the length of the President's neck, entirely unnecessarily, that dimension is entirely lacking in all the records. If I measure this out on myself, it comes well down on my back, not in the neck, where each of the non-doctor witnesses placed it.

And no less a person, no less an expert than Dr. Malcolm Perry, the Parkland Hospital surgeon in Dallas who performed the tracheotomy operation on the neck, told me that his plotting of these measurements makes it a back wound.

Having been so helpful with their description of the "location" of this wound, the doctors next address themselves to "Entrance". Here they forgot that they edited their autopsy report, which is another measure of their dependability, another good reason for the Attorney General's confidence in them. The very first line in the preceding paragraph, in dire quotes, repeats the autopsy report's final statement that at most this wa "presumably of entry". Their first statement under "Entrance" is, "Our finding, as stated in the autopsy report, that the wound low in the back of the neck was an entrance wound ..." That is not what they said. They only said maybe.

These same photographs, the doctors next report, "show the edges of the wound to be inverted, regular and smooth". These are "the principal characteristics of an entrance wound". There is but one necessity not present. The doctors probed that wound with the finger. Pushing the finger in also pushed all the edges in. If they were extruding before the probing, they need not have been afterward. What is here lacking is the statement that the pictures were taken before the probing and only before the probing. Can it be that such experts in the art of legal medicine and its requirements, men so deeply involved in the integrity of their evidence, were unaware of this simple fact?

Indeed, this may have been the appearance of the wound if no one had ever touched it. But would it not be nice to know? Especially when the panel doctors, looking at exactly the same evidence, have either no confidence in this description as of a wound of entrance, for they use none of it, or did not see any of it. Making the same determination based on identically the same evidence (or at least it is so said), they find that what marks this "as having the characteristics of an entrance wound of a bullet" is "a well defined zone of discoloration of the edge of the back wound", and absolutely nothing else.

"Science" is a remarkably flexible and adaptable thing, as are "scientists".

But the really important thing is here. That they did not forget. The government got what it wanted and, with it, didn't give two hoots about the "science" by which it got it. It did not get it from the doctors' examination of the pictures. Those pictures do not exist. The tactful doctors avoided all-around embarrassment by not saying so. Instead, they invoked sketches they had made by an artist, some months later and from their verbal descriptions of what remained in their minds. The artwork, they say, shows it was all okay. Just the way the autopsy report says. Of course, no one asked how much after the autopsy report the art was made.

These doctors did not trouble the Attorney General, the Director of the Archives - or themselves - to make an examination of the President's clothing. They were thoughtful and farsighted that way. Now there is no need to worry, from their report, about the holes in the back of the clothing being five inches down. Or that all observer testimony is "consistent" with the clothing and describes a back wound.

What is under "exit" is worth word-for-word, careful reading:

> The autopsy report states that the "wound presumably of exit" was that described by Dr. Malcolm O. Perry of Dallas. This wound was used as the site of a tracheotomy incision, and its character thus distorted. Photographs Nos. 1-6 inclusive, 13, 14, 26-28 inclusive, 40 and 41 show the wound as being below the Adams apple.

> It should be noted that the morning after the autopsy, Saturday, November 23, 1963, Dr. Humes telephoned Dr. Perry at the Parkland Hospital in Dallas. Dr. Perry was the physician who attended the President immediately after the shooting. Dr. Perry advised Dr. Humes that he had observed a missile wound below the Adams apple, and that the site of this wound had been used as the site of the tracheotomy incision. This information made it clear to us that the missile which had entered the back of the neck had exited at the site of the tracheotomy incision.

These paragraphs are an excellent demonstration of the great desire of the autopsy doctors to have things neat and clean. If we compare this account with their sworn testimony and that of others, it is not nearly this neat. And not clean at all.

From the top:

The autopsy report states that the "wound presumably of exit" was that described by Dr. Malcolm O. Perry ...

They skipped a couple of autopsy reports here and ignored any version written by themselves. The oldest extant holograph, to the contrary, says of this that Perry "noted" a "puncture wound in the low anterior neck in approximately the midline".* But in skipping the drafts, they did get the benefit of editing. Only they did not wind up with what Perry "described". They did, on the other hand, wind up with what they wanted.

The characteristics were "distorted" by the tracheotomy. But not so far as identification of the wound is concerned. That was merely sliced in half. Both halves could have been put together again by competent prosectors, as undoubtedly they were by the morticians. Together or not, unless the surgery pressed the edges outward, which is not likely, the characteristics were unchanged and determinable.

How the 12 photographs "show" the wound might very well have been explained, especially from what will become clear in the sections on the panel. These are photographs of unending marvel, showing what they do not show. There are none of the front of the body.

That single telephone call alluded to here? Well, it was two calls. Perry told me about both of them. Humes testified about one, pretended there was but one, characterized it as "somewhat redundant", and in that understated. Perry's description of what Humes asked is of foolishness. He asked only about what he already knew, what was medically obvious. The real purpose of those calls was to shut Perry's mouth.

Describing Perry as "the physician who attended the President"? That makes Perry about a dozen people, for he was not alone. What he did is not adequately covered by saying he "attended" the President. Perry did the surgery. It is not that he just casually "had observed a missile wound below the Adam's apple". He is the one who looked at it closely - as he made an incision through it. He was hardly so standoffish as to imply to the autopsy doctors, who knew the truth and for that reason called him, that this site had been used by others for the tracheotomy.

*See p.570.

Those not knowing the fact and reading this section would be led to believe this.

The concluding sentence is a lulu. It says the information they
got from Perry "made it clear to us that the missile which had entered
the back of the neck had exited at the site of the tracheotomy incision". Considering that the holograph quotes Perry as having said the
front-neck wound was of entrance, it is not at all clear how things became "clear" to the autopsy doctors.

At this point, as in the same point in the Warren Commission testimony, Humes must have been seized by a fit of pique, or perhaps professional jealousy. Neither he nor the others describe the tracheotomy
incision. Mostly, it is assumed to be a vertical incision. However,
Perry is one of those who prefer a transverse or crosswise incision. He
likes this, as he explained it to me, because when it heals the folds of
the skin hide the scar. His reasons are cosmetic. Perhaps on that day
he had no reasons, acted automatically.

With this in mind, we can perhaps reexamine a preceding sentence
about the 12 pictures that "show the wound as being below the Adam's apple" and wonder why the doctors did not say "bullet wound". To a doctor
a surgical incision is also a "wound". These reports contain such references. But if the dozen pictures show the tracheotomy wound, what have
these doctors really done? Have they not pretended the dozen pictures
show the bullet wound? That seems impossible, as we will learn.

What is presented under "Head Wound", first breakdown, "Entry",
is good enough to keep until we get to the panel section of our analysis.
The reader should fix these things in his mind for that moment: The entry wound "is situated in the posterior scalp ... slightly above the external occipital protuberance (a bony protuberance at the back of the
head)". The doctors explain, "In non-technical language this indicates
that a small wound was found in the back of the head ..." They cite four
photographs that "establish that the above autopsy data were accurate".
If they were, Clark should have done something about his panel.*

Still sticking to the photographs, the doctors say of the head
wound, allegedly of entrance, "this is not recognizable as a penetrating
wound". Here they argue that in their autopsy they cite other evidence
leading them to the conclusion it was an entrance wound. Assuming they
are correct, their argument does not find support in the pictures they
are to say authenticate their autopsy report. In fact, examination of
the existing autopsy reports shows that, while the holograph did call
this a "puncture" wound, which is one of entrance, in the revision this
word was changed to "lacerated". That means "torn", "mangled", or "irregularly cut". These are the opposite of the characteristics of wounds
of entrance. Eliminating the description of an entrance wound in the
holograph and substituting a description of an exiting wound is a pic-
turesque way of saying that the autopsy report discloses a wound of entrance. It hardly promotes confidence the doctors are firm and convinced
on this point.

Although the doctors refer to having gotten some of the missing
scalp and skull during their autopsy examination, they carefully do not
say they got all of it. This was wise, because they did not. However,
long before the time of this junior autopsy report, in fact, just a day
or so after it was exploded out, another missing piece of skull was in
Washington. What it disclosed is no more in this report, or that of the
autopsy, than it is in the Warren Report. In fact, the proof was totally
unknown until I discovered it in the suppressed files in the Archives.
It still would be good to know what, if any, evidentiary intelligence it
contains. If the Attorney General isn't curious, I am certain most Americans are.

In their autopsy report, the doctors do what they avoid here. They
say "see skull roentgenograms".

Strange the doctors do not invoke the X-rays at this point. But
perhaps in later chapters the reader will find this other than strange.
Stranger still, they avoid all the X-rays all the time. But, to para-

_____
*See p. 590.

phrase Lincoln, they will not be able to avoid all of the X-rays all of the time.

Until that time, we may as well skip their self-serving verbiage.

What I like best of all in this jewel of a "report" is the last and shortest section, "No Other Wounds", they call it. A rather inadequate title. Better might be "Shooting Down Doctors" or "Professional Suicide", things like that. There are but two sentences in this section. The first suddenly becomes interested in the neglected X-rays:

> The x-ray films established that there were small metallic fragments in the head. However, careful examination at the autopsy, and the photographs and x-rays taken during the autopsy, revealed no evidence of a bullet or of a major portion of a bullet in the body of the President and revealed no evidence of any missile wounds other than those described above.

This takes the cake. The doctors said they took X-rays of the entire body, but the panel report shows this is not the case and that there are no X-rays of the extremities. Therefore, if there were a bullet wound, for example, in one of the hands, or if a fragment had struck or lodged there, without the X-rays of that area, how could the doctors say that no matter how "careful" their "examination", what they did not see showed nothing? This is three-monkeys medicine, Presidential-murder style. It is not science or legally-sound investigation.

In making this point, I regret diverting the reader from one of the smoother cases of semantics in forensics. It is the cute little bit that there was no evidence of "a bullet or major portion of a bullet in the body". Okay, let's believe them. There is no bullet and no major portion of a bullet. Now let us get to how many minor portions of a bullet (or bullets) there were in this "careful examination" of the X-rays. What the doctors do not say here is that there was no portion or portions of bullet or bullets of any size. Not only should they have been explicit, but if at any point in the body there is the slightest trace of bullet, their entire autopsy report is false, false as only the Warren Commission Report can thereafter be.

Now, it happens the doctors did testify about this under oath. Humes was the witness, but the other two subsequently, also under oath, agreed with him. Specter asked Humes (2H364), "Did you search the body to determine if there was any bullet in the body?" Odd how Specter managed to specify a whole bullet only, isn't it? Humes gave his reply in two instalments. In the first, he said that, before Finck's arrival, "we had made X-rays of the head, neck and torso of the President, and the upper portions of the major extremities ... At Colonel Finck's suggestion, we then completed the X-ray examination by X-raying the President's body in toto and those X-rays are available."

They may have been then, but they are not now. In fact, one of the soft criticisms by the panel, presented not as criticisms but as detached comment, is that those of the extremities were not before them. Let us not anticipate this further at this point.

Humes then became really specific. "They showed no evidence of a missile in the President's body at any point. And these were examined by ourselves and by the radiologist who assisted us in this endeavor."

Here Humes is saying there was no trace of even a fragment of a bullet.* The smallest part of a bullet - or of a broken-off bone fragment, too - is a "missile". In their testimony about Governor Connally's wounds, those doctors referred to the pieces of bone becoming "missiles".

So much of this "science", this official reporting on the autopsy of a murdered American President, is already in the class of soap opera, at this point we will enter into that spirit and allow the denouement to await the revelation of what the panel found and said on this point.

---

*He is even more specific at 2H361.

152

As with all good things, this, too, must come to an end. That comes with "Summary". It has three short paragraphs. We have quoted the final one, which brags that their examination lasted five hours, after which they returned the photographs and X-rays to the Archivist. The other two read:

> The photographs and x-rays corroborate our visual observations during the autopsy and conclusively support our medical opinion as set forth in the summary of our autopsy report.

> It was then and is now our opinion that the two missiles which struck the President causing the neck wound and the head wound were fired from a point behind and somewhat above the level of the deceased.

With these doctors and their semantics and reports, when they use odd phrasings, the mind tends to pounce on them. Why, for example, need they specify that the films "corroborate" only their "summary"? Is there a difference between that and the entire body of the work? If not, why limit it, why not say what they were expected to say, that the films corroborate all of the autopsy report?

The doctors' insistence in the second quoted paragraph that at the time they prepared their autopsy report and at the time they prepared the Clark variation they believed the President had been struck by two bullets can, today, be interpreted to believe they have no confidence in the Warren Report, that they believe it wrong, that there had to have been at least two assassins. Prior to their testimony, it may be they were unaware of the other facts of the assassination. After they finished testifying, whether or not they read any of the critical writing (and Boswell, at least, indicates he has), they knew that for there to be any chance at all for all the shooting to have been by one man, the bullet said to have caused the "neck" or "back" wound must also have been responsible for the five wounds in Governor Connally. Each and every one swore that this was impossible. For them to insist that two different bullets had hit the President knowing that one missed the motorcade, which the Warren Report concedes, and that there remained those five Connally wounds to be accounted for, these doctors also are saying they know the Warren Report is fiction, that there was a conspiracy to kill the President.

Which is certainly one, if original, way of "supporting" the Warren Report. It may also account for the unusual formulation of their assigned task, as they understood it. This was cited earlier. It was, as they put it, "to determine whether (the pictures and X-rays) are consistent with the autopsy report". (Not just its summary, please note.)

Clark got what he wanted, He interpreted it the way he wanted, without regard for the contents. So, it really did not make too much difference what the doctors said.

Clark said they all supported the official story.

By the time this analysis is completed, the reader will have a better understanding of the dictionary used by the Minister of Truth.

14. CRY "NAKED"

It was not the overwhelming confidence he felt in the dependability of the autopsy doctors and their reassessment of their own work that impelled the Attorney General to go out and get himself another panel of doctors. Nor can it have been the persuasiveness of their report. With the government in acute distress over public disapproval of and disagreement with the Warren Report, he was not about to sit on the newer and junior-grade autopsy report if he felt it would have helped to release it. When the Attorney General has a release to make, he usually gets pretty good attention from the press.

Needing the support, needing something to change public opinion, knowing the press would be for him and this report, especially when he said it supported the Warren Commission, the Attorney General had to have persuasive, compelling reason for not using this ammunition. The most obvious is his lack of confidence in it. There was always the chance some reporter or editor might be like the little boy in the fable of the emperor's clothes and cry "Naked!" A perceptive mind, without the technical, detailed knowledge necessary for a good analysis, might spot what it is the doctors said they were confirming and understand that, even if this were so, it was not enough and that, with it not enough, there had to be a reason the doctors did not say more.

Standing by itself, the autopsy doctors' report on their report is a new nothingness. If it did everything it claimed for itself, it did far too little and that not at all well. So, the Attorney General tossed it in the Department of Truth files to await the proper moment, if any, for its use. His failure to title or date it does not indicate he placed great store in or held high hopes for it.

If he had felt he dared subject the work of the autopsy experts to impartial analysis, that he would have done. People are not often persuaded by the argument, "I am right because I say I'm right and my saying so proves it." To ask why the Attorney General did not go out right away, once the autopsy was under attack, and get a panel of solid forensic pathologists to review that document, compare it with all the available evidence and give him an opinion of its solidity, is to ask a self-answering question.

How the government then could have used the support of recognized authorities! It did not seek it only because it dared not risk exposing the autopsy report to any kind of honest, competent study. The Attorney General knows the law" He cannot impeach his own witness. He would have been stuck with his own endorsement of those he had every reason to believe would find the autopsy report no good at all. In advance, he would have been vouching for what such experts might have said.

No, that he dared not risk.

Nor did he risk giving out this triviality by the autopsy doctors themselves, their self-serving nothingness in which they did not dare say even that their work was full and correct - in which, carefully disguised, they _actually_ say their report and their work were _wrong_.

If perjury, its possible or probable subornation, frequent and effective lying and a servile press could not succor the government on this issue, it was in bad shape.

154

One of the few wise things Clark did on this subject was not to make use of the self-glorification by the inglorious autopsy doctors. Instead, he waited.

By the beginning of 1968, there was the new official worry that the oft-delayed Clay Shaw trial in New Orleans might come off and, regardless of what the admitted evidence proved, there is always the possibility of an unpredictable jury. Airing this evidence with the press competitively present was sufficient hazard. The government was in trouble and it knew it.

It had to go around its own doctors' certification they had done the job in the autopsy. Their report*is notoriously indefinite on its origin. It says so close to nothing that it really says nothing about why it was brought into being. Although the panel report never so states, indicates or even in the most subtle manner hints at it, the purpose, as provided Judge Halleck by the Department of Justice, was "To further assure the preservation of a record concerning the nature and contents of the X-rays and photographs ..." "Further"? "Assure"? The Department has a special dictionary. It will soon be seen this is not what the panel undertook or said it did. In fact, this is one of the few cases where it disputed the official accounting, saying all the X-rays were not presented to it. So, if the Department of Justice told the judge the truth, its own panel refutes it. If it did not tell the judge the truth, its own panel proves it deceived the judge, the people and history. Either way, the panel does the opposite of "support" any-thing.

By accident, we know now it was never impartial, knew it was never intended to be, knew it was supposed to keep its collective mouth closed - and did.

One of the authentic forensic-medical experts is Dr. Cyril Wecht. He has the additional qualification of being an honest man, a man dedicated to truth as he is to his professions. Unlike the unfortunates ordered into the autopsy room, he is both a doctor and a lawyer. In each of these professions, he has specialized in the areas required for forensic pathology. His professional standing and his personal reputation are such that, when the government finally decided to risk another examination of the most dubious autopsy, it dared not ask him to serve.

Only after he got a copy of the panel report did Wecht make sense out of a chance meeting three days before the panel sat and deliberated. He was at a professional meeting in Chicago and had a chance meeting with Dr. Russell S. Fisher, who is professor of forensic pathology at the University of Maryland and that state's chief medical examiner. Fisher has enjoyed one of the best reputations in his field. During this meeting, he kept pumping Wecht about his knowledge of the Kennedy assassination of which, clearly, he knew nothing. He never disclosed he had a purpose, that he was about to be part of a panel meeting on the subject. Instead, he sought to learn all the arguments of those experts who considered the Warren Report and that on the autopsy wrong. Fisher wanted to learn what he had been appointed to refute. The most casual reading of the report he and his colleagues ultimately produced establishes its lack of impartiality, its open partisanship, its conceptual intent of supporting the government at whatever cost, to the degree the panelists dared risk, to the degree the clever use and misuse of words and evidence made possible.

Fisher's appointment was quite a coup, for his is an established reputation in the proper field. Dr. Alan R. Moritz, Professor of Pathology at Case Western Reserve University, Cleveland, Ohio, formerly was Professor of Forensic Medicine at Harvard University. He, too, should be recognized as having the correct credentials. But if Dr. William H. Carnes, Professor of Pathology at the University of Utah and a member of the State's Medical Examiner's Commission, or Dr. Russell H. Morgan, Professor of Radiological Science, School of Hygiene and Public Health, at Johns Hopkins University, are experienced in forensic medicine, Clark failed to exploit it in the report and publicity on it.

Clark got his recommendations from university presidents. These

*See pp. 580-96.

are just the men who depend heavily on government grants. One, Dr. John A. Hannah, President of Michigan State University, then headed a college deeply involved in covert CIA operations and scandals. He soon became head of a government agency frequently used as a cover by the CIA.

In most disciplines, university presidents might make a suitable nominating board. However, when the special needs of this study and qualities of the panel are given thought, it would seem that the proper place to go for recommendations would have been the Academy of Forensic Sciences. That Clark avoided as though his life depended on it. It can be argued that his political life did. The Academy was already on record (in its Journal of July 1966) with the deepest misgivings about the Warren Report, its manner of collecting and using evidence, and about the autopsy in particular. Rather than allow a determination to be made by authentic experts recommended by the genuinely qualified, he took the safer course of avoiding those not prejudiced in his favor.

With Wecht an official of the forensic-experts organization and having questions about the autopsy, Clark's reluctance to have the dubious document examined by a man who began with misgiving, or by those recommended by doubters, can be appreciated. If the government had begun with any confidence in its evidence, it would have subjected it to the toughest examination, for from that it would have achieved a higher degree of acceptability.

Nonetheless, the Clark panel was of men with well-established reputations. It was not a bad idea to have a radiologist on the panel, though it would have been much better had he had experience in the kind of work and analysis demanded of him. There is a vast difference between inquiries into public health and hygiene and into murders. The others are, with or without forensic experience, well-known pathologists.

So the glitter of the panel lit Clark's and their way. Only those who knew the field, a tiny and uninfluential fraction of society, would have noted the possible lack of best qualification by some of the members. From these alone would come those who might suspect Clark's motives as reflected in his panel choices and the manner in which they were selected.

The panel's report begins auspiciously, with the addition of a new qualification for each of the members - ignorance. "No one of the undersigned," it says, has had "any previous connection" with any previous investigations, thus "each has acted with complete and unbiased independence free of preconceived views ..." It is not only by connection with previous investigations that the panel could be less than independent. One of the more obvious pressure points need never have been squeezed. There is no one connected with a major university today who can make a completely free and unbiased decision not consistent with what the federal government wants without worrying about the effect on federal purse strings, hence on his school and thereby on himself.

The panel's unacceptable boast of independence is just about all it says of itself. This should not be permitted to hide those additional assurances required and missing, that additional basic information not provided in the report. For example, who was the chairman or directing head and how was he selected? With the legal member not signatory to the report, what part, if any, did he play in the deliberations, conclusions, the means by which they were arrived at and the manner and phrasing of what is reported and concluded?

Where did the panel meet? Alone or with observers and, perhaps, assistants of various categories? If there were others, who were they, by whom employed and paid? Was the panel paid? There would be nothing wrong if it was, but hiding it could be misconstrued.

What facilities did they have? By whom provided? Were they adequate? Were they able to illuminate the X-rays properly, enlarge and project the pictures properly? Did they try, and if they did, were they able to compare and match each photographic print with the proper negative, and to satisfy themselves beyond question that no one of the print was a reduced version of any of the negatives? Did they assure them-

156

selves that none of the pictures or X-rays had been altered in any way, by cropping or by adding or replacement of parts? In fact, did they satisfy themselves that these _were_, in fact, the pictures and X-rays of the John Kennedy autopsy, _all of_ them, untainted in any way? If they did, they are silent on it. If they did not, has their report any standing at all? Can they vouch for what the pictures and X-rays say without vouching for their authenticity and totality? From the evidence of their report, they neither did this nor were they able to. Throughout the ensuing analysis, on occasion after occasion, the reader will understand why this is the prerequisite of legal proceedings and why the law requires proof of authenticity and completeness. If there is but a single picture or X-ray missing, it might contain evidence radically altering what can be deduced from the other film.

With this beginning requirement not met, with no hint, no matter how slight, that it had been, and with the ample indication to which we will in due course come that it was impossible, is there significance in the absence from the signatures of that of the counsel? With or without his signature, how could he serve any but a public-relations function if he did not provide proper counsel to the medical members? If he gave them this advice and they didn't follow it and failed to acknowledge it in their report, can their report be considered at all? Has it any standing?

It would seem that these, too, are self-answering questions, as they are complete disqualification of the report. They are the required basis for the consideration of anything that follows. Without these and similar questions being raised and answered, no matter how valid all ensuing reporting is, it would have no standing in a court of law and is not worthy of consideration in any other forum of legal or quasi- or pseudo-legal form.

No one in the United States knew this better than the Attorney General, the man who appointed and charged the panel, accepted its report and, after long delay and when it seemed to him to best suit his other purposes, only then used it. In the light of this, it must be considered that the Attorney General knew his use was an improper one and that he elected an improper use.

Did the panel have enough time for its work? Could it possibly have considered the necessary evidence in the two days it took?

This is another self-answering question. It is obvious that comparing the pictures and X-rays with all of the autopsy testimony and exhibits cannot be done in so restricted a period of time - and that is but a small part of what was required for even the less-than-minimum undertaken by the panel.

Like little boys who silently tell themselves they are not lying when they say they do not have their hands in the cookie jar, having removed them full, this eminent panel began with one formulation of its responsibilities and what it studied and wound up with another. Its very last words, its conclusions, are:

The photographs and X-rays discussed herein support the

above-quoted portions of the original Autopsy Report and the

above-quoted medical conclusions of the Warren Commission Report.

Obfuscated at the beginning and not quoted at the end, by persevering through the verbiage we can determine, without question, that what the report concluded is not what it was asked to do. Their purposes, as they themselves state in the first paragraph, are entirely different:

to examine various photographs, X-ray films, documents and

other evidence pertaining to the death of President Kennedy, and to evaluate their significance in relation to the medical conclusions

recorded in the Autopsy Report on the body of President Kennedy

signed by Commander J. J. Humes, Medical Corps, United States Navy,

Commander J. Thornton Boswell, Medical Corps, United States Navy and

Lieutenant Colonel Pierre A. Finck, Medical Corps, United States

Army and in the Supplemental Report signed by Commander Humes.

When the panel was investigating a murder, and that murder was of a President, and allude to it with the understated description of a "death", they raise questions about their attitudes and beliefs as well as their partiality or impartiality. The President was murdered. He did not die a natural death.

Here the panel says its purpose was to compare and evaluate pictures and X-rays with "the Supplemental Report signed by Commander Humes" If it did this, it performed miracles because

a) it had no pictures and X-rays identified or identifiable with that supplemental report;
b) it has no reference to the supplemental report in its text; and
c) it makes no reference to the supplemental report in its conclusions, which are presented in full above.

In stating its purposes, the panel was careful to avoid saying it was going to compare the X-rays and photographic evidence with the other evidence. Only by the closest scrutiny of the full text of their report can it be gleaned that this panel set such limited and evasive purposes for itself or had them set for it. In all that has been written and said of the panel, the impression taken is that it proved the Warren Commission and the autopsy right. It did no such thing, it attempted no such thing, and it engaged in deception by not making this explicit and clear. It had to know this is the interpretation that would be placed on everything and anything it said.

The stated purpose is so evasive it does not in any way say the inquiry was to determine the accuracy of the medical conclusions of the autopsy report. It was allegedly limited to an "evaluation" of "their significance in relation to the medical conclusions" of the autopsy report. This is a real fingers-crossed business, for in their evaluation they could justify to themselves finding the evidence entirely other than the conclusions warrant and still not be or feel bound to so declare A reading of their "conclusions" shows this is what really happened. This panel knew the evidence was contrary to the autopsy report and made no sound, uttered not even a weak peep of protest.

In fact, it wrote entirely different conclusions, and of the most limited kind. It said only that it found the medical conclusions of the Warren Report consistent with those of the autopsy. Perhaps it would be more exact to say it implied this. It also said these were "supported" by the film. By "support" they do not say "prove", what the court and press construed. They do not mean "prove" - they really mean the opposite. By extension, the best their flippancy with the turning point of modern history can be tortured into meaning is that, under duress, they might find remote and slight justification for the language of the autopsy report in a narrow area in what they can interpret some of the pictures and X-rays to show.

And that is a far cry from any legitimate purpose or any use they could have anticipated their work would be put to. It is, in fact, the kind of use they could and should have anticipated and refused to associate with. As the analysis unfolds, this will become pinpoint sharp.

In their "conclusions", they dragged in something not in their stated "purposes", what they call the "medical conclusions" of the Warren Report. We shall see that, even in so simple a thing as reading the

Report and finding and understanding - and correctly quoting and referring to the "medical conclusions" - this panel failed. It did none of
these things. In saying it did, as in other of the above-enumerated
statements, it lied. Each and every one of the members who signed the
report lied. There can be no excuse, no plea of innocent error, none of
ignorance. They lied repeatedly. They had the intent of lying. And
they lied about a matter of the greatest national urgency, one in which
the entire national honor and integrity is inextricably involved. As
evil as themselves lying, they protected the lies of others, lies that
had the same importance and effect.

These are serious, harsh charges. The panel can do as Specter
has not, as the autopsy doctors have not and all will not - and as I
predict no single member of the panel will. They can sue and get this
aired in open court if they feel such condemnation is in any way wrong
or even unfair. They cannot and will not stand scrutiny.

There will be no doubt as we proceed with the analysis, for this
report was a contrivance, not a serious study. It was, and was designed
to be, a vehicle of government propaganda, not a search for fact. One
need read only the statement of purpose and conclusions to understand
this. It was, in no sense, a serious study. It was never intended to
be. It did not reach - could not and would not have reached - meaningful conclusions.

With serious purposes, the panel would have examined all the evidence. In its own left-handed way, this panel specified it did not and
never intended to. This we will come to in their limited tabulation of
what they saw, which begins on page 5 of their report. This is actually
a list of the materials available. It does not mean and does not say
the panel studied even that woeful insufficiency. It is painfully obvious it did not.

There is no seriously adverse comment, only bland, often unspecified agreement with what cannot be agreed to. If the panel found parts
of the autopsy report not warranted by what they saw, it was their obligation to say so, out loud, specifically and forcefully. One would never
know that the panel found the basic information in complete error - and
was silent.

Here I note the obligation and responsibilities of the legal member, Bruce Bromley, a lawyer of first-class connections, the nominee of
the American Bar association, which acted as an arm of the Commission
during its days and for this alone permanently disqualified itself as
partisan. He was to serve a legal rather than a public-relations or
propaganda end. As the minimum, then, he should have convinced himself
that the panel served and fulfilled all the responsibilities it assumed,
that it assumed the right ones, that it had done its work in a manner
and to a degree that satisfied the law, and that, as the legal member,
he had inquired to the degree necessary and had so assured himself. If
he did not, he was an adornment for ulterior government purposes.

The above-cited language leaves ambiguities that must not be ignored and cannot be in an honest report. Are there any "medical conclusions" or evidence not "recorded in the Autopsy Report" or in the text
but not the "conclusions"? Here the panel must address at least these
possibilities: What exists in the evidence and what it might anticipate
exists but might not be in the evidence or the presence of which in the
evidence might, in such an awesomely voluminous body of data, be present
and unknown to them. In assuming this task, the panel also assumed the
obligation to satisfy itself there was no void in the autopsy report and
its evidentiary backstopping. If it did not do this, it could not have
had honest purposes.

Nor could the panel report on any limited responsibility it might
have been assigned or undertaken without specifying it had these imposed
limitations and why it had accepted them. The most obvious of these is
a comparison between the autopsy and its conclusions and the rest of the
evidence. They begin their report with a subtle limitation entirely ignored in the use made of their report by the federal government, that

they evaluated the autopsy report "in relation to the medical <u>conclu-</u><u>sions</u> alone. They cannot rightly ignore, although they specify they did, an evaluation of the so-called "medical conclusions" against all the relevant conclusions of the Report. Their evasion here is under "Previous Reports".

I cite two semantic evasions in this sentence, one partly alluded to above. They limited themselves to the conclusions that are "medical", whereas the autopsy report did not. They refer to the autopsy report having been "signed by" rather than prepared by the enumerated doctors. Was it not the responsibility of the panel to satisfy itself that the signatories were, each and every one, without question about the accuracy of each and every word in the autopsy report and each and every addendum or each version? Was it not also the responsibility of a forensic panel to satisfy itself that there was not any contradiction between the various versions or even simple stenographic error in the typing of the final copy? Was it not the responsibility of the panel to ascertain that the final report was amply substantiated by its raw material, of which the film could have been but part? For example, had any of the doctors made a simple error in transferring a figure from notes to draft? This it could not do because it did not have the suppressed notes. They were denied it.

In this connection, its citation of the two autopsy reports to the Warren Report is not without significance, for there are parts of Commission autopsy exhibits that are not included in the Report itself. The exhibits include contradictory attachments to the reports that are omitted from the Commission Report. Indeed, the failure of the panel to note the sharp and destructive contrast between the official exhibits of the autopsy reports and the shortened version included in the Report is, in itself, in my opinion, sufficient to establish that the real purposes of the panel were to buttress the Warren Report and in no sense to evaluate the evidence or conclusions, medical or any other. There can be no comparison or "evaluation" of the final version of the autopsy report that ignores the extant holograph, does not appraise the nature of the changes made and that disregards the burning of the initial holograph.

Half of the panel was without any qualification in forensic medicine. To none was attributed any qualification in photography. The absence of a qualified photo-analyst should, in itself, be considered a potential disqualification of the panel, for basic questions remaining about the autopsy report and the Warren Report are susceptible of photographic answer where they are not from the published evidence and conclusions, susceptible of answer by X-rays.

The panel report specifies that the legal member, Bruce Bromley, was "nominated" by the president of the American Bar Association. It is lamentable that this happened and that, after it happened, the involvement of former presidents of the Bar Association, hence the association, as Commission partisans is not set forth. There is an inherent pretense of impartiality that is totally lacking in reality and is, in fact, directly contrary to that reality.

There is no doubt that if, as he should have been, the legal member was present throughout the deliberations of the medical members (this is the word used in the panel report), he was either not qualified for his task, did not do his job, or was present and aware of all the defects in the deliberations, available and examined evidence (or its lack), and the piecemeal and total conclusions.

None of the panelists "had any previous connection with prior investigations of, or reports on the matter, and each has acted with complete independence free of preconceived views ...", the report states. This can hardly be said of a man with Bromley's auspices, as explained above. Nor can it be said that any American who lives outside a cocoon has not been subjected to one of the most enormous exposures in history to one side of the controversy, that of the government. To cite no official and direct connection with previous investigation and writing is not to cite enough and is to brag about ignorance, inappropriate in

160

such a panel and report and, in itself, a kind of propaganda. It is not to cite proper credentials, in any event, for a critical panel should have had an awareness of existing and unanswered criticism.

Without getting into the report proper, questions exist about the purpose or purposes of the panel, its own interpretation of its function or functions, its performance, and the integrity of everyone involved, in the government and on the panel. Unless these questions are answered in the report - and they are not - the report must be examined with unfeigned suspicion. It cannot be a dedication to science or truth when its purposes and design are as they appear and when everyone involved had to know it.

Although the pretense is otherwise and care has been exercised to gain acceptance for that pretense, the careful analysis it has until now escaped establishes the report is a work of official propaganda. However, propaganda can still be truth, if angled and accented. If propaganda is repugnant on such a subject, the possibility remains that, regardless of its lack of initial integrity, the panel may have come up with the truth or a reasonably close approximation. Analysis of the report can disclose that.

15. "PRESERVATION OF A RECORD"

How the judge and the press could have gotten past the first two
sentences of the body of the report (p.2) without going up the wall is
a mystery. For the judge there may be justification. Garrison did not
claim the pictures and X-rays were fakes or in any way impure. The essence of his petition is that they were usable to him as solid evidence.
The job of the judge at that point was not to determine whether or not
the film was genuine, but whether or not the New Orleans jury could be
shown them. Only a stupid or corrupt press, however, could ignore the
first two sentences, their content, the skill with which they were
drafted to hide what the panel sought to hide while keeping itself in
the clear, and their disqualification of all three reports, those of
the autopsy, the Commission and the panel.

Disarmingly, these read:

The Autopsy Report stated that X-rays had been made of the

entire body of the deceased. The Panel's inventory disclosed X-ray

films of the entire body except for the lower arms, wrists and

hands and the lower legs, ankles and feet.

An honest panel writing an honest report for and capable of passing the scrutiny of an honest Attorney General would never have put it
this way. Instead, it would have had a different second sentence reading, "However, the panel did not have access to complete body X-rays.
If they were taken, and the evidence shows they were, they either do not
exist today or were withheld from us." It also should then have itemized the parts of the body not adequately covered in the X-rays it had.

But this was a tricky panel, writing a tricky report for a tricky
Attorney General. There was no device too shabby for it. Its intention
to dissemble is clear. Its devices were the cheapest. For example,
whereas it knew and in this undetected evasiveness did record that X-rays
of a President's autopsy were missing, it was so intent on the shadiest
kind of record, it did not even say what its examination showed. It contented itself with saying "the panel's inventory" did not contain such
views. The fact is that, regardless of the inventory, if the panel was
competent and made an examination, it was its own examination that proved
the essence of these vital films. Did it not examine the X-rays?

However, whether or not important evidence is in the missing X-
rays is immaterial in an examination of the honesty of the autopsy and
what was written about it. If there were any pictures or X-rays missing,
especially with their most dubious history, doubt is cast upon everything. Can any part of the entire suspect business be credited when
basic evidence is missing? Can anything said by a secret panel be trusted
when it is making a secret examination of the secret evidence and it is
silent after it discovers some of the most vital evidence is missing?

Even this casual passing of the buck to the inventory when the
panel was supposedly making the closest possible study of the X-rays
themselves is a considerable understating of the fact. Not alone does
the autopsy report say that full body X-rays were taken; there was sworn
testimony about it. In the light of the suppressed and misrepresented

162

panel discovery, Humes' testimony assumes additional significance, engenders greater suspicion.

Specter had asked (2H364) a question not designed to elicit the answer it fathered: "Did you search the body to determine if there was any bullet in the body?"

Eventually, Humes did answer the question. His reponse will interest in another context. Here, for immediate purposes, his evasion inspires gratitude:

Before the arrival of Colonel Finck we had made X-rays of the head, neck and torso of the President, and the upper portions of his major extremities, or both his upper and lower extremities. At Colonel Finck's suggestion, we then completed the X-ray examination by X-raying the President's body in toto, and those X-rays are available.

Translation: "We didn't bother to X-ray his forearms or hands, legs or feet, but when Colonel Finck got there, he screamed and we had to. We turned the X-rays over to the Secret Service. They then included the entire body." Or, "But the Navy held some back."

How remarkably unsuspicious the panel was when just those X-rays it knows to be missing are exactly those the Navy autopsy doctors tried to avoid or did avoid taking until the arrival of the Army member compelled them to. Of course, this can be another "coincidence", a testimonial not to the corruption of the Navy autopsy doctors as much as to their incompetence. One of the two it must be. Either is total disqualification.

So, we do have X-rays missing, they are those originally avoided for whatever reason, and the panel is silent. The government, too, is silent on the missing evidence but is loud in proclaiming its purity and that of the Commission, the autopsy and all the evidence.

This one sugar-coated but exceedingly bitter pill is enough to destroy every report of whatever origin and with each the integrity of those responsible for it. Most of all does it require doubt about the purposes of the panel and the Attorney General and about the competence, if not the integrity, of those performing the autopsy. This is without regard to the content of the X-rays, for that they were not before the panel is more than enough to justify this doubt.

However, there remains the question of what the missing X-rays could show. With the security imposed upon them, it cannot be regarded as accidental that they are missing. Nor can the lack of a proper inventory on their return to the government be considered an unfortunate carelessness. What they could disclose might explain why they are missing.

A small metal fragment in any of the missing X-rays means the entire explanation of the assassination and the Warren Report are wrong. Metal in any part of the body means more than one assassin. This means a conspiracy, something the government has clamored against blindly, from before there was any investigation of any kind or calibre. There is nothing in the autopsy report or any other to indicate whether there was or might have been any injury to any of the parts of the body of which X-rays were not before the panel.

Consistent with this suspicion is the total absence of any pictures that might have covered the same areas. Here the panel, like every official body before it, found silence expedient. It does not say what pictures it did not see, what parts of the body it could not examine. However, its inventory discloses this. There were no pictures of any part of the body other than the head and back.

Can anything warrant or require more suspicion?

In all that remains of this section of the report of the panel, there is no meaning whatsoever. In fact, this section contains but four sentences of the panel's own language, the two above that should have been one and each of those introducing quotations. The first, a brief excerpt from the protocol, says only, "The Autopsy Report also described the decedent's wounds as follows." The use of the word "also" here, when it refers to nothing, is dubious. It cannot be regarded as an accidental transgression against pure science and complete honesty. The excerpt quoted is not sufficient. It is only part of the summary (p.6). It is as though carefully selected from the autopsy report to parallel and exonerate the language especially selected to be cited from the Warren Report. This will interest us further. That excerpt is introduced by the sole remaining sentence written by the panel. As will be seen, it says absolutely nothing: "The medical conclusions of the Warren Commission (p.19) concerning President Kennedy's wounds are as follows:"

This even briefer excerpt is as disqualified and inadequate as that from the autopsy report which seems, as said, to have been chosen to present the seeming justification of the language of the Report. I note the failure to cite the edition or version of the Warren Report to which reference is made. There were a number of not-identically paged versions, official, authorized, unauthorized and condensed. However, in any edition, this is a reference to what in the official edition is the first chapter, entitled "Summary and Conclusions" but to the wrong page. Now, that chapter of the Report was intended as and was accepted and used as its press release on the Report. To cite but one example, it was used as its story by the Associated Press. That chapter, further, can in no way be described as containing or having had the purpose of containing "the medical conclusions of the Warren Commission Report." We go into this elsewhere. To the degree that the Commission's medical evidence and conclusions are at all embodied in its Report, they are readily discovered by use of the table of contents. If the table of contents of the Report is not cited in the inventory of what the panel examined, it should be a safe presumption it was available to the panel; if not to its medical and forensic experts, then to its legal counsel.

So the reader will not misunderstand the employment of this language, I point out that nowhere in the entire 900-page Report is there an adequate or meaningful description of what the Commission says is the fatal wound. I encourage the reader to ask himself whether, in the absence of such a description, promised one place and presented nowhere, either the Commission or the panel could say there was but one head wound and not more than one.

If it is the inadequacy of the Report that compelled the panel to cite the press release or, if less forthright language is used, the condensation for popular consumption, was it not also incumbent upon the panel "evaluating" the "medical conclusions" of the Warren Report to note the inadequacy? If, on the other hand, in its opinion there was no such deficiency in the Report, how could a competent medico-legal panel cite as the "medical conclusions" of the Warren Report what is not?

To return to the title of this meaningless section, "Previous Reports", there are other reports not included, both official and unofficial, medical and otherwise. They are neither quoted nor in any way referred to. They are pertinent and they are ignored. The heading is as deceptive, therefore, as the section itself and no less inadequate. For example, there are the medical reports from Parkland Hospital in Dallas. In Dallas, what was not seen and reported in Washington was seen and recorded and was in evidence before the Commission. If the Commission ignored and misrepresented these reports, that is bad enough. But for the panel "evaluating" the work of the autopsy doctors and the Commission to pretend to have considered these reports without having done so is indeed culpable and a more than adequate reflection of the hidden real purpose of the panel, to validate the medical conclusions, regardless of evidence or its lack.

There are but six breakdowns under the heading, "Inventory of Material Examined". There is no discussion of any or under any. Perhaps it is worthwhile citing the words of the heading as a subtle concession by the panelists that they did not examine or have all the

evidence and that they were aware of it, whether or not they reported
their failure to study the other, readily available evidence. Their employment of the word "examined" is limiting. Any proper panel would
have an "Inventory of Material", without the finger-crossing or the
cemetery-whistling of the reservation, "examined". The panel had to
know the entire world would assume it had examined and evaluated all
the evidence. Its own minimal function required no less of it.

First in the inventory is "Black and white and colored prints
and transparencies". Here I note that:

The number of each and the total are not given. This is hardly
consistent with precision but is consistent with the fact I had
earlier brought to light, that the officially released numbers used
on various occasions are not the same. This is consistent with the
panel's awareness of the liability, destruction of official integrity, and sought to avoid the required censoring.
The prints and transparencies are not isolated. From this tabulation, which is a print, which a transparency, and whether one is
a duplication of the other, further compounding the culpability of
not specifying the number existing and examined, cannot be determined. Neither the size nor the variety of film is given in a
single case.
The meaning, if any, of the numbering is not given. The inconsistency of the panel numbering system with that used by the autopsy
doctors in their report to the Attorney General is neither acknowledged nor explained.
Under their scheme, the numbering has no meaning. It would seem
that the pictures should have been taken in some meaningful sequence
and that they should have been numbered in some kind of relationship to their sequence and content.

In the eight terse breakdowns, I note the absence of any pictures
or any breakdown indicating pictures of the head, neck or body taken
from the front. This cannot be regarded as an accident without assuming the total incompetence and dishonesty of the autopsy surgeons and of
the panel. It is, however, subject to other explanation. That would
justify no more moderate language. The front views might, by the most
remarkable of "coincidences", have all been included in what is masked
in this panel report but cannot be and was not in Appendix B to the
Kennedy family-General Services Administration "contract" (attached to
the Rhoads affidavit). There, quietly and without detection and reporting by the press, it is disclosed that two batches of film contained "no
image"!

As though aware of the lack of proper specification of numbers,
the panel report concludes this first itemization with a paragraph that,
rather than eliminating the confusion, adds to it. With a truly amazing
lack of embarrassment, it acknowledges "there were seven black and white
negatives of the brain without any corresponding prints". This can mean
only that they were never studied or that the prints suffered an unreported fate. It also means that the panel would seem to have been in no
position to have made a study of the brain damage or the evidence of the
brain damage and hence was not in a position to make any comment of any
nature on it or the autopsy report discussion (or lack of discussion)
of or related to it. (Of course, it could have had prints made. Its
failure to do this is eloquent.)

When the panel report next says of these same negatives that they
"appeared to represent the same views as #46 through 52", it evades.
These are itemized as views of the brain from above and below. There
are no other pictures of the brain from any other perspective in the inventory. This is the same as saying there were no pictures of the brain
taken from any of the sides and that no study was at any time ever made
by anyone in any capacity to determine whether the damage to it was in
any way either consistent or inconsistent with either the conjectures
or the statements presented as fact about the performance of any missile or missiles, ballistic or other, or of the presumed damage or the
source, direction or number of shots.

Can it be regarded with less than suspicion that these are the precise deficiencies that cannot exist if there have been or if there are ever to be answers to the questions that have existed from the moment anyone had the first look at the corpse? For example, whether there was front entrance of any projectile, in either the neck or the head, and in each case there exists unanswered affirmative evidence, scientific and of contemporaneous observation as well as photographic? The identical deficiencies of this character that exist in the Commission's medical evidence and reporting and in the autopsy report itself are faithfully duplicated in the panel report.

Also passing strange is the last sentence of this brief, six-line paragraph at the end of the film listing. It is vague, in reference to the seven unprinted negatives, or to all the pictures. We can not know which. It reads, in full, "All of the above were listed in a memorandum of transfer, located in the National Archives." * However, such a memorandum does not exist in the inventory, nor is there any item that could conceivably contain or allude to it. Interesting, also, is the peculiar choice of words, "located in the National Archives". By whom, when, under what circumstances, in the pursuit of what purpose, in what connection or file, with or without what else, is not indicated. If a layman can properly draw upon a legal phrase, the panel here is considering what was not in evidence before it and considering it either in no context or out of any context.

When I asked the Archives for a copy, they suppressed it, giving no reason and persisting in giving no reason in response to repeated and proper requests. We shall explore this in a separate chapter.

For there to have been a chain of possession, something that should have concerned both the medical and the legal members of the panel, this and every other memorandum of transfer, record of handling or possession, are vital to establishing authenticity. There is no other reference to any possession or transfers and in this case the panel avoided any reference to the parties of the transfer. When it is further considered that there is no indication of whether these were official or other than official hands and these were federal property, the enormous significance of the avoidances by the panel come into their own kind of perspective. This, again, beshadows the panel, its report, its integrity and its alleged purity of purpose.

Such holy men, so pious in purpose! Let us review this purpose of their sacred study as set forth in the Department of Justice brief of January 17, 1968:

"To further assure the preservation of a record concerning the nature and contents of the X-rays and photographs ..."

Ah, that holy brother, the Attorney General! He takes his vows with his fingers crossed behind his back. Not once does he say anything about the number of pictures and X-rays, does he? Nor does his panel. That, however, is the greasiest kind of kid stuff, the childish non-reasoning of the troubled adult mind looking for the non-existent out and finding only a thin evasion, a fiction.

There is no list, no statement of how many pictures and X-rays were taken, before, during or after the examination of the body on the autopsy bench!

"Preservation of a record"!

So, we do not know - after the Attorney General's panel made its "study" for the "preservation of a record".

No loss; there was no better earlier record, either.

So, if any pictures were taken and no longer exist, no loss. We didn't know and in now not knowing we are no worse off.

Instead, let us bow to the east and give thanks for the Attorney General of the United States, who "preserved" the record - and indeed he did.

For we do have a record, the kind he didn't anticipate, the kind

*See Ch. 26; pp. 558-9.

the panel could not have expected to be winnowed from its report:

No pictures of the front of the body, and from the first there has been the question of shots from the front;

No pictures of any of the extremities - which just happens to coincide with those X-rays known to have disappeared - those X-rays originally not ordered taken, then specifically ordered taken and, under oath, certified to have been;

Negatives without prints, including after panel "examination";

No means of determining what size or variety of photographs were taken;

No means of knowing whether any photographs were taken after the main examination, during the lab work; or, if any were, which they are;

No photograph of any side of the brain - and that is where the Commission and all other officials say he received the fatal shot - and no examination at all of the left half;

No photographs of the separate piece of skull and scalp retrieved before the autopsy was completed, or the piece later recovered and suppressed from the evidence;

No explanation of any numbering system;

No explanation of contradictory numbering;

No statement of whether the panel numbered the unprinted brain negatives or whether they had numbers but no prints;

No explanation of different numbering systems;

And no statement of how many pictures there were, the varieties of each kind, those printed and how many prints of each there were.

Indeed, the Attorney General did "preserve" a record, aided by his panel!

The record that is here set forth in what should be sufficient detail is his numbers game-shell game "preservation".

There were, we are told, 45 pictures taken. If we take the pictures numbered 1 through 18 and ignore the letters with each, in parentheses, and take the pictures numbered 26 through 52, their total is, indeed, 45. But what about those seven negatives? Prior to the panel or by it they were numbered, "19 through 25(JTB)". Now, there are no pictures numbered with the letters "JTB" appended. These just happen to be the initials of one of the autopsy doctors, J. Thornton Boswell. Eighteen pictures numbered 1-18 happen to coincide in this inventory with 18 others numbered in the same range but with the initials "JB", also those of the same doctor. However, the numbers run in roughly the opposite order. Picture 1, if they are identical, is also Picture 18JB. Picture 1JB, then, is also Picture 18. Picture 2(JB) is 17; Picture 17 is 2(JB); 3 is 14(JB); 14 is 15(JB). Confusing? Yes; but "preserved".

Without this mysterious seven, there are already the recorded 45 pictures, hence, we must have as a minimum 52 - unless, in saying these "appeared to represent the same views as 46 through 52", the panel, whose imprecision we must recognize and learn to cope with if we want the truth it helped us escape, really meant "identical with".

If the pictures with the letters "JB" are not identical with those differently numbered in the same range but without letters, then we have 45 plus 18, or 63, or 45 plus 7 plus 18, or 70.

This leaves mysteries - too many - any one is too many - but there remains no mystery on one score - the official but suppressed number of 45 is false.

Was there a reason for using the initials "JTB" on the extra seven and not in any other case?

Of course, we also know two unidentified batches show "no image". They are not included. Were there any other "defectives" of any kind?

167

Is it possible the United States Government performed an autopsy on the corpse of a murdered President and took no pictures of his front, the front of his torso, neck, face or head; no pictures of his arms, legs, hands or feet, front or back; no pictures of the parts of his martyred body blasted off? Unless it is more than possible that this inconceivable thing did happen - <u>unless it is absolutely certain</u> - then there were more pictures than disclosed in the Clarkian arithmetic.

More than 45, or 52, or 63, or 70. Or, if the panel assigned numbers to those seven, more than whatever number plus the seven once numbered 19-25.

It is no help to consult the press. There we find still a different number, also official - one no arithmetic with the panel's figures can add up to or subtract down to.

In his November 1, 1966, story reporting the restoration to the government of the pictures and X-rays, <u>New York Times</u> reporter Fred Graham said this:

The Justice Department said there were 14 X-rays, 25 black-and-white negatives and 26 four-by-five inch color transparencies. The spokesman gave as one reason for the department's request for the data the desire to complete the historical record of the assassination.

This comes to 51 pictures.

Clark sure worked a long time on his "preservation" and "completion" of the record! What delayed him?

In this story, Graham found it necessary to report the Department was so proud of its "completion" of the record its spokesman would not permit the use of his name:

A Justice Department spokesman, who asked not to be identified, said tonight that the action was prompted in part by a number of recent books that expressed doubt about The /sic/ Warren Commission's conclusions concerning the assassination.

Is it that there was no need for a "complete" record until doubt was publicly raised, first by me, then by others?

Only because this was a panel of experts in forensic medicine, those skilled in pathology as the law assigns it importance in criminal investigations, men of boundless integrity, limitless dedication, undeviating and total devotion to their professions - men so far above and beyond the ability of any mortal to in any way influence - even an Attorney General of the United States - have we the "preservation of a record".

And such a record! Has there ever been one to exceed it in the annals of science, the pages of the law, the histories of government?

On TV the former Attorney General came through like a modest man. In saying he sought the "preservation of a record", he was too modest, for he is responsible for the preservation of more than one record:

That of the autopsy and those associated with it;
That of the Warren Commission, especially Arlen Specter;
That of his panel of the great of pathology and radiology, the forensic-medical experts, mark the word;
That, in fact, of the entire government, most particularly, that of Ramsey Clark.

And he preserved the record of how a President was murdered, of how the government that became the government through that murder explained the murder, and with that its own legitimacy.

Second itemization in the inventory is "<u>X-ray films</u>". There are nine categories. An introductory sentence reads:

(The films bore the number 21296 and an inscription indicating that they have been made at the U.S. Naval Hospital, Bethesda,

Maryland on 11/22/63.) /sic7

Whether or not it is or might be significant to know who made
the inscription and when it was made, the affixed date limits the character of the X-rays that are included in the inventory. That is, it
raises the question whether any were made of any lab specimens or to
see whether there was metal in any of the specimens. It also makes one
wonder whether brain X-rays, for example, were made later. None are on
the list. They certainly should have been made. Is it possible the
unprinted seven photographic negatives, which are of the brain, were
made after specimen material was removed? Might not X-rays then have
been made, and for the same reason pictures were? And also hidden for
the same reason? It would not seem inappropriate to wonder whether, in
the removal of the brain or other parts for laboratory examination, it
was possible to dislodge and lose particles of metal. The presence of
the most minute in any location could have been of utmost significance.

Six X-rays of the skull are listed. "#1" is "A-P view". This
means "Anterior to Posterior" or front to back. It is the only one in
this projection. There is none from the back, as there should have
been. "#2, 3" are "left lateral". Perhaps there is good reason for
taking two X-rays of the same side, and perhaps even more might have
served a purpose. However, with the official account of the head damage and the autopsy report specifying there was no damage to the left
side and massive damage to the right, is the layman's concern over the
absence of any X-ray or X-rays labeled "Skull, right lateral", without
scientific, medical and legal warrant? Would not right-side X-rays have
less density to penetrate, been clearer?

"#4, 5, 6" are "Skull, fragments of". Here, especially with the
limitation of the quoted introductory sentence, the panel encountered
and ignored a major problem. All of the fragments of the skull were
not available for X-raying the night of 11/22/63. The medical evidence
here ignored is that all of it was not recovered. The investigative
evidence is that a major missing portion was discovered more than 24
hours after the murder (a word not once used in the panel report).

"#7, 11" are "Thoraco-lumber region, A-P view". No other X-rays
of this region are listed. The question arises, does the existence of
two X-rays of this single perspective eliminate the need for others from
other perspectives, particularly laterally? With a rear wound, there
was no rear X-ray. It is this wound the doctors acknowledged baffled
them. This makes more puzzling their failure to X-ray it from the rear.
Would front to rear X-raying fully record what might show in lateral X-
rays, for example, how deeply a possible fragment might have penetrated?

"#9" is "Chest, A-P view". It seems that the same questions and
concerns apply, for there is, in these regions, the greatest interest
in the presence of bullet fragments, bullets or other evidence, such as
fragmented bones.

A total of 14 X-rays are listed. The others are of the right and
left hemi-thorax, in each case with "shoulder and upper arm, A-P view";
"Pelvis, A-P view" (13), and lower femur and knees (12) and upper legs
(14), both A-P views.

This number is inconsistent with the suppressed record made by
the Department of Justice agents at the autopsy (File JFK-1). In the
course of their "preservation of a record", the panel found it expedient
to eliminate this conflict by paying no attention at all to it. Let us
here, in our own way, preserve our own kind of a record by recording
these quotations from the observations of Agents James W. Sibert and
Francis X. O'Neill, Jr.:

The following is a complete listing of photographs and X-Rays
taken by the medical authorities of the President's body ... X-Rays
were developed by the hospital .....11 X-Rays ... (p.5)

Upon completion of the X-Rays and photographs, the first incision was made at 8:15 p.m. X-Rays of the brain area which were
developed and returned to the autopsy room disclosed a path of a
missile ... (p.3)

There is no doubt the FBI agents, not medical men, might have been wrong. Would it not be nice to know! Especially with the possibility that both figures for total X-rays, 11 and 14, are wrong. One possible difference between these total figures may be explained by the language of the agents, "of the President's body". If they meant this literally and for some special FBI or Department of Justice reason considered the skull fragments not part of the body, then these three listed in the inventory, Nos. 4-6, could account for the discrepancy.

Nor can it be said that "X-Rays of the brain area" means only those taken after the brain was removed. It would, however, be so good to know, particularly when we are "preserving" a record, when a panel of the eminent has been convoked for this purpose and it alone - according to the Attorney General, that is.

Not according to the Attorney General, not according to his learned panel engaged in this sacred "preservation of a record", but according to our piecing together, the number of 14 X-rays just happens to coincide with those listed by the FBI agents at the autopsy. These views add up to 14.

At the autopsy, a serious error had been committed and was rectified when Finck requested it. On his late arrival, he discovered the entire body had not been X-rayed. Thereupon, according to the sworn testimony (2H364), X-rays of the entire body were made. This is also stipulated in the autopsy report (p.6). What, by the most remarkable magic of all, is here not listed exactly coincides with the X-rays not taken until Finck had them taken. Just those he asked for are just those not tabulated here.

Yet the number is exactly that "returned" to the government with the pictures.

The rectification seems to have been rectified.

Perhaps it was not an "omission" that caused some not to be taken?

Would it not be nice to know!

And would it not be nice for the record "preserved" to include what it does not - the missing X-rays of the President's autopsy!

It is in this report that 45 pictures are accounted for: "22 4 x 5 color photographs; 18 4 x 5 black and white photographs; 1 roll of 120 film containing five exposures." This is the balance of the tabulation that begins with "11 X-Rays". Thus, we know that not fewer than two different cameras were used and that "no image" pictures came from at least two different cameras, for the film sizes are different. This, however, raises new questions about the listing in Appendix B to the "letter agreement". Of the roll film it says only, "1 roll of exposed from a color camera entirely black with no image apparent". And of the other it says merely, "5 envelopes containing 4 x 5 exposed film containing no image".

There are some problems here. With part of a roll only exposed - and no camera in current use gets fewer than six exposures from a roll of 120 film - all of it would not be black after processing. Normally, only the unexposed part would be different. That would be entirely clear. For the exposed and the unexposed portions of the film both to be "entirely black", the entire roll of undeveloped film had to be exposed to light. The chances of this happening by accident are so small as to be unworthy of consideration. This is particularly true of color film, where processing involves critical temperatures and is done only in the best equipped darkrooms by the most experienced technicians.

The 4 x 5 film is this size in inches and is taken by what is commonly called a "press camera". Each film is separate, like a plate. In developing, each is separately inserted into a tank. The smallest known tank for home processing holds a dozen individual 4 x 5 films. There were a total of 40 of this size, 22 in color and 18 black and white. The chances of five only being accidentally exposed to light in processing and thus ruined is even more remote than with the roll film, for the same "accident" would have to be repeated on a selective basis. Normally, this film would have been processed in two batches, separated by type. While the listings are vague, not specifying whether what had "no image" was black and white or color or both, if we ease the great burden on the government and assume all were of one type, there is no likelihood at all that, of one batch, five of 18 or five of 22 would be light-ruined.

The care with which the government handled this precious film and recorded what happened to it permits nothing but conjecture. The Warren Commission conducted no investigation. Its Report was without concern for the film or the tragedies that befell it, as it was without criticism of those who made it possible or who did it on purpose. No investigations by other agencies, especially those responsible because they did it or because it happened while the film was in their care, are included in the Warren Commission files. The totality of lack of official concern is beyond belief. However, if, on the basis of what little is officially acknowledged (though it was entirely suppressed) and what is known about photography, we were to make the best possible guess, it would be this: Light-exposed film of the same characteristics was substituted for that exposed at the hospital. Assuming nobody lied.

In other words, someone in official capacity or acting for someone in official capacity deliberately replaced part of the good film made at the autopsy with ruined film. The chances of any other explanation of the facts we have are so fractionally small they amount to impossibility.

If no other single thing connected with the assassination and its investigation should have galvanized all officials aware of it, most of all the government's chief law officer, the Attorney General, and his table-of-organization right-hand, the indispensable-man director of the FBI, this inexplicable and unnatural destruction of the best possible evidence of the murder they had the responsibility of solving should have. That complete silence was preserved and still is, that no investigation was made and reported, and that even when these documents are presented in court there is no comment or explanation, is culpable as nothing else in American history is culpable.

But - it does "preserve" a record!

Next in the tabulation is "Bullets". Listed are four exhibits only: 399, "a whole bullet"; 567, "Portion of nose of a bullet"; 569, "Portion of base segment of a bullet"; and 840, "3 fragments of lead".

These do not exhaust the "portions" of bullets. There are, if the "three fragments of lead" are those recovered from the Presidential car, still the fragments recovered from the bodies of the President and Governor Connally. More, in giving the heading "bullets" to "fragments of lead", the panel is making a determination without evidence. It is specifying a conclusion that these three lead fragments are, in fact, parts of a bullet or of bullets, of which it cites no evidence.

What is entirely missing is fundamental to any evaluation of the autopsy report and of the Warren Report as well. That is the spectrographic analysis of all of this lead. If that does not establish beyond reasonable doubt that all of these fragments as well as what is not cited - the metallic residues on the windshield and its trim - can be from the same original bullet, the entire autopsy report and the entire Warren Report are without validity. Spectrographic analysis could prove or disprove this. This spectrographic analysis was made for the Commission by the FBI. It was suppressed from the Commission's record and was ignored by the panel.

The best shots the Commission could muster were unable to fire three such accurate shots as those credited to Oswald within the allowable time. Oswald was a "rather poor shot", so he could not have done nearly as well. The Commission stretched everything to allege that Oswald had done the impossible. It dared not consider more than three shots were fired, for it strained credibility to allege Oswald had fired three. The "missed" bullet accounted for one. The nearly perfect 399 accounted for the second, and all seven non-fatal injuries to both men. Fragments were recovered from Governor Connally. The last of the bullets is alleged to be one that exploded in the President's head and did all the rest of the damage - killing him, cracking the windshield, denting the trim, and shedding all the fragments recovered from the Presidential limousine.

It cannot be because the spectrographic analysis proved what nobody believed - that all the fragments from the car and the corpse and all the traces from the windshield came from a single bullet - that it was suppressed. If it proved this, it could have proved a major part of the Commission's unproven case. The Commission was not about to suppress what rescued it.

On the other hand, if any fragment from Connally could be tied to this or any other bullet, on that proof the Report also disintegrated. That, too, would ruin the contrived reconstruction and would prove conspiracy. It cannot be because the spectrographic analysis saved the Commission on this score that it suppressed it.

If the whole bullet could be traced to a Connally fragment, that tended to support the Commission's case. If it did not, the case was ruined.

Why the government had to suppress this spectrographic analysis is now obvious. The panel could not make any dependable assessment of the accuracy of any medical Commission conclusion without examining the spectrographic analysis. So, it, too, ignored this evidence and, instead, made a determination of "fact" in its inventory, alleging that the three "fragments of lead" were of bullet. That the panel made this determination on the cheap, without access or reference to the available proofs (or disproofs), casts doubt on the panel and its report. That it was willing to make any sort of determination without access to the available and vital evidence raises questions of its integrity as well as that of its purposes and its report.

"Motion picture films" is the next category. Of the number available, three only are cited, those of Zapruder, Nix and Muchmore, none in their original form and the Zapruder, in particular, in incomplete form. It is, in fact, synonymous to say "copy" (which the panel report does not) and to say "incomplete", for in copying 8-mm. motion-picture film, which all of these are, about 20 percent, that exposed film between the sprocket holes that advance it, is eliminated automatically.

For no apparent reason, the panel limited itself even more severely than the Commission in its examination of the individual frames of the Zapruder film or, what may be worse, allowed itself to be so restricted. Without citing the version, origin or source, which presumably but not certainly is a selection of 35-mm. frames made for the Commission by Life magazine, it says it considered only Frames 215 through 334. In itself, this is redundant disqualification. The Commission acknowledges that the President could have been struck beginning at Frame 210. The exhibit from which these frames come extends through Frame 343. There is evidence in those frames before and after the cited ones. In the case of those following 334, they include views of the President's exploded head, the nature, location and extent of his injuries, and things of that sort. Essential as is this medical information, it fails to exhaust the intelligence that can be extracted from a thorough, impartial analysis. Among these is the direction from which the shot recorded in Frame 313 came. That, without doubt, is from the front and disproves the Report the panel says it "supports". Not by careful examination or understanding of these movies.

With these observations perhaps the more important, it is also important that the panel refers to "single frames", which is less than a precise, therefore less than appropriate and accurate, medico-legal description, for the Commission's "single frames" made for it in 35-mm. size (size here is not specified) actually include a part of the preceding frame in each case and, in all the crucial ones, include also the entire view of the President on the preceding and otherwise incomplete frame.

Now, the FBI, for unspecified purpose and without exposition of any reason, made a series of black and white copies of the 35-mm. color slides provided by Life. If it is these the panel examined, it either imposed the limitation on itself or Exhibit 885 was edited before it was presented to the panel. It is a bound portfolio, including Frames 171-334. The Commission had and withheld Frames 335-343 until I exposed this suppression. It is conspicuous that, with the three movies identified with an exhibit number, these "slides" are not. If the album of black and white FBI photographic prints were used instead of the color slides, the panel lost the benefits of color, clarity and motion, to enumerate some only.

It also is obvious that the panel did not examine - indeed, seems to have been entirely unaware of - still pictures of the actual murder, of which it should be necessary to enumerate only those of Altgens, Moorman and Willis.

Next to the last item in the inventory is "Clothing". By this time, it should be apparent that deficiencies can be expected. Without the assurance that the clothing was in pristine condition, that is, as it was at the moment of the murder, it was without evidence of the direction of the shot or shots. The fibres, unmolested, would point the way the bullet went. This assurance was lacking because it was impossible. Examination of the clothing without this specific reservation and observation - even listing it as evidence - become willful deceptions. Moreover, here again the missing spectrographic analysis becomes absolutely essential for without knowing the limits it imposes no competent examination of the clothing could be made. Even more of a transgression against honest and uncomplicated purposes is the mention of the tie without access to this analysis, for the existing testimony about it specifies the tie was without the traces necessary to consider that the damage to it was caused by Exhibit 399, the "whole" bullet. If this was not, in fact, the case, neither the autopsy report nor that of the Commission can be considered accurate or honest.

Last of the categories of "material" examined by the panel is called "Documents". It is fully consistent with everything else in the panel report that the panel lists and examined nothing at all that could be called "documents" or even a single "document". Interestingly, the Commission did not call its files "files"; it called them "documents". This is known to many people, certainly to all engaged in any kind of work in the field. Thus, if the word was read by those not having access to the original report, which covers almost 100 percent of the people and the media, a confusion, if not, indeed, a deception, was inevitable. With the utter inappropriateness of the designation selected of all the accurate ones available, the question of intent cannot be ignored. Why did this panel of medical, medico-legal and legal experts select for this category so deceptive and misleading, so inaccurate, a designation? Is there - can there be - any other immediately apparent reason other than deception?

What the panel lists under "Documents" is a single item, "The Warren Commission Report and the accompanying volumes of Exhibits and Hearings". This it immediately limits, without any description of the limitation, with the parenthetical sentence, "(Study of these Documents was limited to those portions deemed pertinent by The Panel)".

When we have a panel that boasts of its ignorance, of its lack of connection with or knowledge of any previous investigation or report, can one do less than wonder how it decided what "portions it deemed pertinent" of those 27 large volumes? Is there less cause for - let us term it merely "perplexity" - when it then fails to itemize what it "deemed pertinent"?

We are left with no knowledge of what the panel says it considered, that too-little it claims to have selected as the base of its further deliberations.

Did it, for example, consider any of the testimony about Governor
Connally's wounds? All five of them must have been caused by the same
"whole bullet", Exhibit 399, that also caused the wounds in the front
and back of the President's "neck" and emerged from all of this almost
perfect. Did it study the testimony of the autopsy doctors and the more
important of the Texas doctors about this possibility? Without exception, these competent authorities described the career attributed to
this single bullet as impossible. Yet that same career is the foundation rock of the autopsy report as it is of the Warren Report. If the
panel did not consider the unanimous competent opinion of these medical
authorities, which includes all who had this competence and saw the non-
fatal injuries on the President before and during the autopsy, how could
it have, offer or reach any valid opinion or judgment? How could it
pass on the autopsy and Warren reports based upon a misrepresentation
of all the competent testimony?

Did it consider the questioning of Commission Counsel Arlen Specter and the citations of the Report? When faced with the unanimity of
competent opinion against this very basis of the Report, Specter substituted an incompetent hypothesis for the reality and asked each of
the doctors the same question about the hypothesis. In the Report, the
affirmative answer to the hypothetical question is substituted for the
negative responses about the reality.

This might be carried to great length with almost all the medical evidence. There would seem to be no need, so entirely crippling is
what is set forth immediately above.

There is, however, almost no reasonable limit to what is relevant
in this single voluminous source and quite obviously ignored by the
panel. One example that comes to mind without urging is the bullets
fired in pretended duplication of the assassination and the wounding of
Governor Connally. They disprove the presumptions of both the autopsy
and Warren Reports. Was there any examination of the appearance and
expert testimony about these pretended duplications? There could not
have been without the panel reporting these were unfaithful experiments
that, in every way possible, avoided faithfulness in duplication and
still disproved the Report. So, the panel "deemed" those "portions"
not pertinent and ignored them.

Do we here have a possible explanation of some of the earlier-
cited and self-imposed limitations and proscriptions, the unique selection of words and titles, even such things as the quotation of a press-
oriented summary from the Report to compare with an inadequate selection
from the autopsy report, with the open misidentification of the selection from the Report, mislabeled as the "medical summary" when it was
not?

Continuing this analysis of the "material" is as intolerable for
the writer as it must be for the reader, so it is carried no further.
What appears in the panel report is consistent with its refusal to examine any of the evidence about Governor Connally's wounds. Trying to
assess either the autopsy or the Warren Report without it is like teaching shrimps to whistle. It cannot be done. No panel could honestly
undertake such an assessment without this evidence. If the panel considered any of the Connally medical evidence in any form, from any
source or in any direct or indirect manner, the proof, indeed, even the
suggestion, is totally absent. The opposite is the case.

Without having done this, the panel forfeited its right to serious consideration, destroyed its own report and with it its own integrity. It could not have considered this essential evidence in the time
it had and, when it was as impossible medically as it was legally to
reach any honest conclusion without it, did just that.

This "Inventory of Material Examined" is, for the panel, what a
barker is for a girlie show. It is a come-on, no more. The panel had
no more chance of "examining" the "material" in that "inventory" in two
days than stones have of swimming. It shilled its dubious work with
tawdry.

174

Only cheapness restricted their "examination" to two days - its stinginess with its time or the government's with its money. Or, perhaps, the government imposed this needless restriction to prevent the panel's learning the truth. In a reputable study, the time limitation and the reason for it would have been explained. In this one, it could not be.

There is no point in trying to examine the stated purposes of the study, for they are meaningless and contradictory. The panel and the Attorney General give different and inconsistent versions. The real intent was to hoke up a support for the Warren Report and to lay a basis for resisting court action designed to force the pictures and X-rays of the autopsy out of secrecy long enough and far enough for them to be examined. If the government did not fear Garrison's case, it knew from the day its repossession of the film was announced that I would file suit when I could get a lawyer willing to take the case. It had reason to assume, if not certain knowledge, that others had the same intention. This was the design. Dishonest as it was, it is further dishonored by the transparent deceptions by both the government and its sycophant panel.

No single item in this inventory could be properly "examined" in two days. The pictures had to be compared with the X-rays and the X-rays with the pictures, and both had to be compared with the expert and eyewitness testimony, with that of the autopsy doctors and with the exhibits. With someone to guide the panel through the organized chaos in those 27 very large books, the Report and its appendages, the words could not be read in this limited time. And who was there to show the panel where to look? How would it know? The Commission was foresighted and did not have any subject index of any kind and had no name or any other kind of index for its exhibits. Not even the geniuses of this panel could pick a path through that tortured verbal wilderness in the time it had if it did nothing else.

The slightest "examination" of the pictures and X-rays raises questions we shall raise. The panel should have answered them - or an honest panel would have felt impelled to. One simply put and basic, did they have all the film? There is reason to believe they did not. If the panel answered the simple question in its two allotted days, could it also learn what was missing in that time? Could it then, within two days - if it did nothing else - locate and study what was missing? It could not begin to, even if it had not been destroyed or stolen.

Any proper "examination" of the four exhibits under "bullets", any warranting the uses to which the panel knew its conclusion would be put, was a long-time job, with detailed testimony and reports to be found and mastered.

If the panel did nothing else for two long days, it could well spend that much time studying the Zapruder film, noting and learning something new with each viewing. The slides made from it - rather, from parts of it - cannot be understood in a two-day study, particularly without knowledge of the enormous volume of relevant testimony and other evidence. Instead, the panel repeated what it had been told the film shows, what is contrary to what it actually shows. Only to slightly lesser degree is this true of the other movies.

As we shall see, the panel did nothing with the clothing, learned nothing from it, said nothing about it. Its inclusion here is to prevent criticism sponsored by its omission and to lend a fraudulent air of authenticity to its potboiler.

When we get to the "documents", we really have the intellectual depravity laid out bare. There are an estimated 10,000,000 words in those bulky 27 books. What is necessary for and relevant to any medical study at all is still an enormous volume. Aware of this, the panel qualified its listing with a complicating dishonesty, the proviso that its study "was limited to those portions deemed pertinent by the panel". What a fraud! Knowing nothing at all about the evidence, it had no means of determining, no way of learning, what it could possibly "deem" pertinent. Incorporation of this item was perhaps because it dared not omit it, perhaps because it looks impressive. It is not and could not have been for honest reasons, because, with all the other things required of it in even two long days, it could not have begun to find, let alone read and understand, all the "pertinent" evidence.

In any event, for the Attorney General's declared purposes, all the volumes were not essential. Only a small part of one was. Knowing its real rather than its pretended purposes, the panel wisely lied and deceived, compounding the dishonesty with the depravity of pretending it did make a serious study of these volumes.

Of course, in any press treatment of the report, this is the neatest kind of trickery. Reporters and editors would immediately assume that the panel really did get to the nitty-gritty, really had a basis for decision and thereby earned the right to have its conclusions considered seriously. That is what all this window-dressing is for, public acceptability, which means kidding the public - tricking history.

The contempt held by the panel for the public and the press and its own disregard for the reputations and self-respect of the members is reflected in its unabashed representation of the impossible, that it seriously "examined" this "material" in two days (after which it deliberated and agreed, then drafted, revised and polished a technical report 16 pages long)!

It certainly is a rare, if not entirely unique, official report or medico-legal study that cannot survive examination of its source materials alone. The report of this panel is such a precedent.

16. IF PICTURES DON'T LIE -

Finally the panel gets to its task with "Examination of photographs of head", a section introduced with the identification of Photographs 7, 14, 42 and 43, which, it says, show the back of the head. Then, in the very next sentence, it locates "an elliptical penetrating wound of the scalp situated near the midline and high above the hairline". Thus, they begin their "confirmation" with a location of this wound other than it is located in what it "confirms". The autopsy doctors and the Warren Report locate it near the hairline, as did the official Secret Service observers.

Rather than measure the wound, the panelists preferred to estimate its size. "The wound," they say, "was judged to be approximately 6 millimeters wide and 15 millimeters long." It is not remarkable that their estimate, substituted for what should have been a very precise measurement, just happens exactly to coincide, save for the reversed sequence, with the measurements of the protocol, "measuring 15 x 6 mm." The suggestion here is more of a rubber stamp than of science.

Where the protocol locates this wound is to the right of the head, the panel report places it "near the midline". This need not be inconsistent, but the failure of the panel to seek and report precision - in other cases, it measured, as it should have - does not build confidence in it.

What it does not at this point say is that the wound is precisely as the protocol says it is.

When the panel examined "the frontal region of the skull", using Photographs 1, 22, 44 and 45, they found a "lack of contrast". "Due to lack of contrast and ... lack of clarity of detail in these photographs" it concluded "only" that "there was no exiting bullet defect in the supra-orbital region of the skull". How much more comforting it would have been if they had also specified no entrance wound in the front of the skull, for other evidence, like the Zapruder film, indicates the fatal wound was from the front.

Finding the pictures did not show an exiting wound and that they are not definitive, there were the X-rays, considered later and without regard to the pictures, as the pictures here are with no reference to the X-rays. It is more than interesting that the panel did not conclude there was no bullet wound in the right frontal region, nor that there was no entering wound, but merely that there was no wound of exit.

The evasiveness here is as remarkable as it is transparent on analysis. The almost meaninglessness of the "conclusion" is further limited by an evasion that, although of childish simplicity, also escaped detection. The panel says that its "only conclusion", that "there was no exiting bullet defect in the supra-orbital region of the skull", was "reached" only "from study of this series" of photographs. Now, there is no reason why the panel had to reach any conclusion from this series of pictures, or from them alone. It examined the clothing without hint of a "conclusion". More, it did not have to consider these photographs in any sequence or separation. That distinction it imposed upon itself, as though for a purpose. It certainly did not have to examine this limited series of four pictures in isolation. Of the acknowledged pictures, 41 are of the head, skull and brain - 41 out of 45!

177

Yet it here alludes to merely four of these! It did not have to consider only those that it says lack contrast and clarity of detail. From their own description, these pictures show the forehead. It is not possible that these pictures came out at all without showing whether or not there was a hole in the forehead. Nor did the Commission have to ignore the other evidence. For example, the only Dallas doctor to have stood at the President's head and looked down on it during the emergency procedures, Dr. Robert N. McClelland, in his report on "cause of death", attributed it to "gunshot wound to the left temple".

Now, it happens that, in its own and artificial breakdown of the photographs, the panel consigned a minimum of seven to "head and neck viewed from left side". At no point in its "examination of photographs of head" does it even acknowledge the existence of these pictures. It never at any point or in any context discusses the left side of the front of the head. Thus, in its "preservation of a record", its alleged only purpose, the panel guaranteed there would be no record. Here, where it evades any meaningful comment on the right front of the head, it makes none at all on the left. And, aside from pretending there was no other evidence, like the medical reports, of which Dr. McClelland's is but one of many, it considers only its own artificial selection of pictures, those that "lack" both "contrast" and "clarity" - and it considers them in a vacuum. It does not, as it should have, relate them to the X-rays. It is almost as though the panel arranged the pictures in groups so it could say this area was clouded. It does not fault any of the other pictures for "lack of contrast and lack of clarity of detail".

This is in sharp contrast to its treatment of the photographs of the back of the head. There it says, "(See description of X-ray films)". Here it makes no citation of the X-rays. In the first case, it is without complaint about the quality of the pictures. Yet where it does find the pictures lacking, it also fails to refer to the existing X-rays, which it also examined.

Adding it all up, what this amounts to is the careful contrivance by the panel of a means of saying nothing at all about the photographs of the front of the head, one of the most crucial examinations it was called upon to make, and doing this in a studied evasion that is just as carefully contrived to appear as a genuine scientific analysis - which it is not. To say that no bullet exited the front of the head is to say nothing. There was no reason to believe a bullet had exited the front of the head and every reason to believe none did or, under any circumstances, could have.

When it later addresses the representation of this area in the X-rays, the language is such as to defy the lay reader. It is so technical there is little prospect a harried newspaper reporter, had the press been handed copies of the document, could have understood what was said. Here I suggest there may be no accidental correlation between the release of this information so late that the Department of Justice press room worked at night to get it out, as it confirmed to me personally on January 17, 1969, the day of its use in court. The release was so unusual, after almost a year of delay, so hasty, that it was too late for that prime target of government public relations, the early editions of the morning papers and the prime evening TV newscasts.

In the discussion of this wound as seen in the X-rays, the panel says it went from back to front "to explosively fracture the right frontal and parietal bones as it emerged from the head". It is noteworthy that the panel cites no proof of the direction of this bullet and does not exclude others. It does not say anything that suggests it precludes this was not a rear-entry wound. What it says relating to the recapturing of the head damage by the X-rays, is that some of the damage and resultant "changes are consistent with an entrance wound of the skull produced by a bullet similar to that of exhibit 399".

Skipping for the moment the highly prejudicial language, for it was dragging Bullet 399 in by press release, not science, that bullet being like most other bullets in every meaningful way, the panel fails to say that this reported change is in any way inconsistent with exactly the opposite of what it says it is consistent with. Therefore, despite the overwriting not usual in a medico-legal document, it in no way rules out the possibility of the reverse path of the bullet and by its failure in any way to raise or address the question, justifies the belief what it saw is also consistent with a front-to-back direction, the opposite of the one it seems to have merely conjectured.

In the study of this panel report, as with everything connected with the Warren Report, we are never far removed from magic, mystery, conjuration and coincidence. Here, with the quintessential importance of proper and unequivocal evaluation of the medical evidence on the head wound, ("preservation of a record"), we have only "a lack of contrast" and a "lack of clarity", not at all the normal performance of skilled medical photographers under the direct supervision of high-ranking and experienced medical officers. But suppose we do consider this just a "coincidence"; and suppose also that we regard the total absence of any pictures of the front of the neck as also no more than another coincidence; and then, when we consider that two entire batches of film are said to have no image at all, and in the face of this, the panel and the Warren Commission and its Report are silent on the point, let us stretch all the too-many points and say that, unlikely as is this concatenation of deficiencies, all are coincidences. With the charity no medico-legal document could anticipate in a court of law, where its signatories would be cross-examined, let us assume there is nothing sinister here, nothing wrong, nothing in any way out of the ordinary. Let us tell ourselves that the government can photograph from remote space with such perfection that it can make out the thin painted stripes in parking lots; that, from a distance equivalent to that between New York and Washington, it can perform such photographic marvels with no trouble and that it is only when a President is murdered that its photography becomes incompetent, less than amateurish - and all of this should inspire no suspicion or mistrust. Assure yourself that it is the regular course of events for the entire medical and photographic governmental establishments to fall entirely apart for no reason at all.

For the knowledge here denied, let us turn to the separated, unrelated and uncross-referenced discussion of the X-rays, treated as though they are of a different world, in no way integrated with the analysis of the photographs. That on the skull, by far the largest single portion of the entire panel report, begins above the middle of page 10. It is an argument against the unseen, unrecognized critics, a pseudo-medical polemic rather than a medical fact-finding. It ends with a frank argument, a strange formulation we shall concern ourselves with. The non-sequitur conclusion that, because there is no metal in the left side of the head, the bullet had to have gone from back to front, is followed by the declaration that, hence, "it is not reasonable ... to postulate that a projectile passed through the head in a direction other than" from back to front. Irrational, illogical, this, nonetheless, is what this learned panel does actually say.

Then there is this quiet comment:

"Of further note, when the X-ray films of the skull were presented to The Panel, film #1 had been damaged in two small regions by what appears to have been the heat from a spot light." Be assured, for it is the assurance of this eminent panel, that this did not "interfere with the interpretation of the films".

Before those by this time possessed of the notion that nothing would have interfered with precisely this interpretation, regardless of what was or was not examined, indulge the panel and restrain suspicion while we consult the list of X-rays. What is #1? That can be found in the inventory on page 5. It is "Skull, A-P view".

It is also the only front, back, or front to back, or back to front, X-ray! The only other X-raying of the skull was from a single side, the left. This would seem to mean there was no X-ray of the top of the head, the right side of which was blasted out, or of the right side, which was said to have been exploded above the ear and toward the front, and none of the back, where a bullet hole, damage and fragmentation are specified.

And this fragile single X-ray, required to bear all the evidence, including that part beyond its physical capacity, was burned "in two small regions"! Without question by any official medical or legal inquirer? Without explanation of any kind! Without note in the Warren Report or by the Commission, without reference even in its suppressed files? With no official record of how it happened - or _that_ it happened at all! Without location of the "regions", description or hint of description or location!

So the reader can understand the meaning of "small", as the panel here uses it, the diameter of the bullet, to which this panel semantically attributed the responsibility it cannot and does not by evidence, is but a quarter of an inch. Need it be said how much more minute a fragment might be? How much less than even a quarter of an inch?

Can it be assumed, when this panel of eminences fails to specify it, that on this single _existing_, this single _taken_ X-ray, the burned places are in the margins, where none of the _content_ would be destroyed with the burning? Can it be assumed, when they suggest the damage was by a spotlight, that there was not a purpose in using the spotlight? It is employed for greater light penetration. That is done - a spotlight is used - when there is something to examine and to examine more closely. Yet with the precious and only X-ray once burned, we have skilled experts repeating the same rare blunder, burning a second hole! It would seem the burns served but one purpose: to destroy evidence. And on the _only_ X-ray that _could_ contain this evidence.

Is it not surprising that a forensic panel "preserving" a record is without question of _how_ the X-ray was burned, by _whom_ and _under what_ conditions? The only known examiners of the X-rays were official. If the doctors who performed the autopsy burned the film, they were in a position to duplicate the X-rays. There seems no excuse for their not having done so. The official story is that nobody ever saw them until they were "confirmed" by the same doctors and their radiologist who exposed the original plates. It is a false story, but if we do not accept it, we have to conclude that those allegedly investigating the murder irreparably damaged the evidence they pretended never to have examined. There remains another alternative, that the responsibility is that of the family of the murdered President. To eliminate this scandalous inference, now and in history, would seem to have been the obligation of the representative of the family, the attorney, Burke Marshall, who concurred in everything, including excessive and inappropriate publicity.

The panel, it should be recalled, had a legal member who could not have been unaware of the foregoing and could not properly have been unaware of what will appear in the analysis of the commentary on the X-rays. It had a famous radiologist and three professors of the forensic and medical sciences. They were engaged in a forensic pursuit as close to sacred as any ever performed by their peers in history.

They do _not_ ask the necessary and obvious questions. They do _not_ give any explanation or answer of any kind, any suggestion of inquiry, or even of suspicion. Were all of this innocent, susceptible of innocent explanation, is it at all possible that men so acutely aware of their legal obligations, their historic functions, of the minimal requirements of their professions and their oaths in their professions, could by accident have avoided establishing the record of innocence?

Had this panel report after 11 months not been smoked out by official distress over the lawsuit - after the end of the court day and without notification to the other side, in a manner guaranteed to prevent critical examination prior to the proceeding on the docket of the coming morning - none of this would or could be known. There would be still another ghost, to arise in the future and haunt the nation and its history, to dog the family, to plague everyone.

Now let us add this to what we have burdened charity with:

None of the requisite front pictures exist;

Two entire batches show "no image";
Those artifically segregated as relevant lack "clarity";
The single overburdened X-ray is burned;
And all this is accepted as though it were as natural and neces-
sary as breathing.

Can we still be without suspicion?

Can we be _less_ than suspicious when this is the report of such a
panel, with such purposes - and with the highly publicized and equally
improper use that was made of it?

Or can it be doubted that the government might have special reasons for suppressing the film and fighting to prevent its proper use in
a proper legal proceeding when that is ordered by the presiding judge?

Untroubled by the unclear, unquestioned, unsought, unasked and
missing, the panel nonetheless reached a "conclusion". It labeled this
as "the only conclusion reached by The Panel from study of this series"
thus strongly hinting that other conclusions should have been expected
and flowing from this "study". That "only conclusion" from examination
of all X-rays of the cranial cavity is "that there was no exiting bullet
defect in the supra-orbital region of the skull" - no front exit - which
was never an issue or a possibility.

Were any reason given, the "only conclusion" might be uncomforta-
ble in a paragraph saying the informational materials were nonexistent,
destroyed or incompetent. Of course, the panel eschews these words.
But not the facts. It merely hides what it dares and gilds the rest.

The panel describes four photographs of the "inferior aspect" of
the brain, 46-49, and the three of "the superior aspect", 50-2, specifying no conclusions in the paragraph about each but presenting "findings" in a third paragraph that is also the final one of the section on
photographs. It is therefore unclear whether its "findings" relate to
the entire section, to the part dealing with the skull photographs or
to the parts about both sets of brain film.

The best guess seems to be that there are neither conclusions nor
"findings" about the brain and that the "findings" are imputed to the entire section. One might, therefore, wonder why it reached only an "only
conclusion" about the study of the frontal region of the skull, where it
was forced to make entirely insufficient and deceptively unconcerned
concession that it really had very poor information to work with, and
none about the brain photographs, which seem not to suffer this deficiency. Perhaps the answer lies in the nature of the "only conclusion",
which is a vapid argument against a shot from the front.

Here was an appropriate point for reference to those previously
referred to, mysteriously found, mysteriously receipted, mysteriously
unprinted seven brain negatives so mysteriously numbered. There is none.
They might as well not exist. In this they are not alone. In all, despite the official record that only 45 pictures were taken and that, of
these, two uncounted batches (consisting of five pictures on a roll and
whatever number was in envelopes) showed no image, we can now, as an absolute minimum, enumerate not fewer than 48 pictures showing the head or
brain. In its exhaustive study and analysis, its "preservation of a
record", this section alludes, most often to say nothing at all, to but
25 of them. In almost all cases, it says only that it looked at them.
Thus, it does not claim to have even looked for data about the head and
brain in 23 pictures, almost half.

This is one way to "further assure the preservation of a record",
to "support" the autopsy and Warren Reports!

By this point in the panel report, it is apparent that it has the
same preconception as the Commission, to insist that only two good shots
were fired and both came from above and behind. Not faced with this compulsion, the panel need not have reached an argumentative "only conclusion" with incompetent and insufficient evidence. Were its motivation
strict impartiality and detached scientific study of the autopsy of the

President, at this point it should have had no difficulty reaching a series of rather obvious conclusions about the quality of that autopsy and the evidence upon which that was based.

Here the panel is consistent. Faced throughout its work with inadequacy, incompetence, incompleteness and destructions, in the autopsy and in the evidence it was "studying", it manages to say no single critical word and to so phrase the one slight critical comment it did not dare avoid, to which we will come, that none save the most expert could sense it. That one comment entirely escaped public attention, yet attention to the panel report, in all media, was extensive.

Perhaps the fact already reported by the Commission about the "right cerebral hemisphere" persuaded the panel to resist even an "only conclusion" about it. It found, "in the central portion" of the base of this half of the brain, "a gray brown /sic/ rectangular structure measuring approximately 13 x 20 mm. Its identity cannot be established by The Panel" (p.8). There the matter rests, save for the endorsement of the autopsy that ignores it by the panel that could not identify the seeming foreign body in the brain, if this is what a "grey brown rectangular structure" about a half by seven-eighths of an inch is.

This panel made invisible, unspecified conclusions. It had its own technique, a rather clever and effective one. In this paragraph is a lucid example. "The right cerebral hemisphere," it said, "is transected by a broad canal running generally in a posterior-anterior direction and to the right of the midline."

Why this canal runs from back to front and not from front to back is neither stated nor apparent nor factual. It runs no less from front to back than it does from back to front. The difference is this: This panel, like every other element of government, insists blindly - and despite the solid contrary evidence - that the President was shot only from the back. There is no device it, like everyone else connected with official investigations, found available and failed to use when it could propagandize this false presumption. Nothing was too thin, too tenuous, too cheap, too ridiculous - even too false. Therefore, a canal that runs in two directions, neither more nor less one way than the other, is said to run in only one, a subtle suggestion that the bullet, by the "evidence" of this canal, entered the back. The panel report does not so state, but could it be more explicit if it did?

The "findings" are, in dictionary meaning, quite indefinite. In the manner in which presented, they are made to seem positive. They are also in error. Here is the exact language:

These findings indicate that the back of the head was struck by a single bullet travelling at high velocity, the major portion of which passed forward through the right cerebral hemisphere, and which produced an explosive type of fragmentation of the skull ...

If these findings could be depended upon, then there would be little doubt of Oswald's innocence. There is evidence on the velocity of the bullet of the kind allegedly fired and on the rifle. There is also the earlier counterpart of the writing of this panel, that of the Warren Report. It willed the so-called Oswald rifle into firing a high-velocity bullet. It persistently used this phrase, when corrected, when disputed, and in the face of the entire body of evidence on the subject. The medical people said this was not a high-velocity bullet. The FBI ballistic expert specified it was of but a nominal medium velocity. But the phrase "high velocity" connotes greater killing power, a more ruthless and determined killer. Therefore, it is used by those with other than unbiased purposes. The panel had and sought no evidence; it was content to parrot the deliberate error of the Commission.

There is no enumeration of "these findings" which merely "indicate" the bullet entered in the back of the head. The reason is simple: There are none. Not a single one in the entire section. There is the "lack of contrast", there is the "lack of clarity", there is the canal, and there is reference to damage to the skull, but not a single solitary thing proving or in any way, no matter how remote, even suggesting a

scientific proof the bullet entered in the back. There is but the careful selection of misleading words, those like "high velocity" in this
case, or those pretending that a canal running <u>between</u> front and back
runs only from back to front.

The next argument - it cannot be dignified by a legal or medical
designation - is that "the appearance of the entrance wound in the scalp
is consistent with its having been produced by a bullet similar to that
of /sic/ exhibit CE 399". This we have to take apart for analysis.

The "entrance wound" has not here been established as an entrance
wound. The panel could, of course, have described it as the rear wound,
but that would not have indicted Oswald or exculpated the autopsy doctors and the Warren Commission. It is willed into "evidence" by this
unwarranted description, not established there by the medico-legal realities presented. They are lacking. Only the propaganda is not.

Even more blatantly, nothing but propaganda is that jewel of a
return to Goebbels, "consistent with ... exhibit 399". The beauty of
this deception is that, like his "strategic withdrawals" after major
defeats, quite literally it is not a lie. That is what makes it so
enormous a lie. It <u>is</u> "consistent with its having been produced by a
bullet similar to" the one allegedly fired from this rifle. It is no
less consistent with <u>all the other similar bullets fired from all the</u>
<u>other rifles in the entire world with similar characteristics.</u> So ut-
terly barren is this part of the panel report where such unwarranted and
unscientific conclusions are drawn - in some cases manufactured - that
the evidence available to it was not used. For example, it had the fragments of the bullet allegedly used in this shooting. There was a spectrographic analysis made by the Department of Justice - the same Department of Justice that created the panel. This analysis would prove beyond
any doubt if it were possible that the imputed murder projectiles were
from the same or more than one bullet and whether they were "consistent
with" that infamous 399. The panel's failure to cite this evidence is
no more persuasive than its presumptions over-written into pretended
fact. This analysis was also suppressed by the Commission, which even
refused to take competent testimony about it. The spectrographic analysis is not in the evidence and is still, persistently, denied those researching the assassination. I am suing to get a copy.

The effect of its words intoxicated the panel. So swept away
with emotion was it over the two-way canal that goes only its way, the
"consistent with" contrivances and the like, that in the very paragraph
in which it emphasizes that the bullet exploded and fragmented, it also
restores it to virginal purity in still further effort to have the writing say what the cited evidence does not, that the bullet was from the
rear.

"The photographs," it says, "do not disclose where this bullet
emerged from the head." A bullet having already fractioned into countless pieces and particles - 40 were counted in X-rays - leaving the head
as an entity, at a single point? Of course, to those with fewer degrees
and less exalted station in non-professional life, this is an impossibility. Not to Attorney General Clark's panel, however. To it anything
is possible. (This is not the only place the exploded bullet is restored
to pristine singleness.)

Is the panel merely foolish here, careless, or "sloppy", to use
the defense once invoked for the Commission? No, it is not. It has a
point in this exemplary utilization of the native tongue. In saying that
the photographs do not prove where the exit(s) was (were), it hides the
fact they also do not prove where the entrance(s) was (were), either.
The photographs prove nothing about either, from the citations made.
The panel report was careful not to say that the "entrance wound in the
head is consistent with", etc. It used an inapplicable word instead of
"head". It said "scalp". Now, when that bullet transited the scalp,
it also transited the bones and other matter of the head. The appearance of a wound of entrance is that of a hole in which the tissues seem
to go inward. However, if they go outward, the human touch can also
make them go inward. If the tissue extends outward, a finger can reverse

its direction. This was made explicit in FBI Agent Robert Frazier's scientific testimony about the holes in the clothing. Entrance wounds are also smoother in appearance than those of exit. With the autopsy report before it, or rather, I should say, two of the three contradictory versions of the same autopsy report before it, the panel did not deem it wise to quote the evidence on this point. The doctors signatory to that autopsy are the ones who examined this wound in human rather than photographic form. That paragraph of the existing holograph is one of the most heavily edited in the entire heavily-edited autopsy report. This is perhaps as good a point as any to repeat that the first autopsy report was burned by the doctor in charge, without any question by any legal or medical government officials, without the lifting of the eyebrow of a single one of his superiors, without concern to the Commission that investigated his report as part of the assassination investigation. He rewrote it, with many, many changes of fact - substantive, not just editorial changes. His altered protocol was further changed, and not in his writing, before or while it was being typed. The change is fundamental. It was suppressed by the panel as it was by the Commission. In the form in which he turned in his draft, the front neck wound is described as a "puncture wound", meaning a wound of entrance. In the form in which the government turned it out, "puncture", without any notation on the holograph of any kind, was mysteriously eliminated, replaced by two other words, "much smaller". This the panel, like the Commission before it, found unworthy of note. Had each not, each might have been inhibited in the similar tasks each undertook. (Interestingly enough, a "much smaller wound" is usually an entrance wound. With proper official determination, this, too, was ignored.)

This "entrance" wound, in that autopsy report, is described as a "lacerated wound" after correction. Now, a lacerated wound, from the Commission's evidence, is more like a wound of exit than one of entrance, for the skin is lacerated as the bullet leaves it. Before this change was made in the autopsy, this identical wound of which the panel speaks was described as a "puncture wound".

Perhaps the doctor made a mistake in calling this an entrance wound. Perhaps he did not make a mistake and really intended to. We can conjecture about that endlessly. What we cannot conjecture about is the fact that the man who saw the real thing, not the pictures, changed his mind after drafting the second version of his protocol and wound up not using the word "puncture", which meant entrance, and using "lacerated", which suggests and usually means the opposite.

We need not conjecture about the panel. It had the two existing versions of the autopsy report before it and it was silent on this point. It did not trouble the Attorney General, the press, the Kennedy family or the people generally, true to the Warren Commission tradition it so closely followed in so many ways.

The panel's science was its skill with and its use of words.

Thus, with no "finding" in any way establishing direction, it "found" that this head bullet entered from the back. That is where Oswald was said to have been. Had it said anything else, Oswald could not have been the lone assassin.

As I said earlier, this was a consistent panel. It had before it no evidence at all bearing on the velocity of the bullet that rated it at more than medium velocity. It had no evidence of any kind on the velocity of the bullet except that of the Warren Commission. That Warren Commission evidence, without exception, says the velocity of which this imputed bullet was capable was at most medium velocity and is explicit in proving it could not have been of "high velocity". Therefore, this panel calls it "high velocity". There was no evidence to orient with or link to any bullet in the world to the exclusion of others, therefore this panel says the wound was like that from "Oswald's" rifle and no other.

The concluding words of this section are a promise: "Additional information regarding the course of the bullet is presented in the discussion of the X-ray film." Here the panel keeps its promise. We may anticipate that section to this extent: The panel does not content itself with mere repetition of the canard about exhibit 399. That it does, in the same words, verbatim, "consistent with" and "produced by a bullet similar to that of exhibit 399" (p.11). It does not repeat the canal business, although it duplicates it in talking about the scattering of minute metal fragments. It introduces a new concept of science, evidence and physics in the X-ray "discussion". It says that, because these metal fragments were not on the left side of the head but were all on the right, the bullet had to have gone from the back to the front and that it therefore "is not reasonable to postulate" that it went in any other direction (p.12).

The wonders of modern science, scientists, scientific panels and their use by the Department of Justice!

Such wonders are easier to achieve in the evaluation (read "authentication") of a Presidential autopsy when the required pictures do not exist, when large numbers of those taken show "no image", and there are no straight-on pictures from the front at all. It obviously is much easier to persuade there were no holes in the front when there are no pictures to show them - especially when the only X-ray that might is both unclear and twice burned. This fortuitous combination of circumstances considerably lightens the burden on science - and scientists.

The next section heading was drafted without consultation with such mundane sources as dictionaries. It reads:

Examination of photographs of anterior and posterior views of thorax, anterior, posterior and lateral views of neck (Photographs 3, 4, 6, 9, 10, 11, 12, 15, 17, 18, 26, 27, 28, 29, 30, 31, 38, 39, 40, 41) (All emphasis added.)

This is quite an impressive listing of photographs and numbers, and here the panel needs seem impressive. Thus, it did not deign to save space as by citing photos 9-12 or 26-31, etc. No, sir; it reeled them all off. All 20 of them, by far the largest, hence most impressive, listing of photographs on any single point. Impressive as it is, however, it in no way overcomes the liability of impossibility for, many pictures or few, there exists, from its own inventory, no single "anterior" picture. There is not a single picture from the front. It makes one wonder how the panel could, as it says it did, examine the pictures of the front. Of course, its language (also making it seem more impressive) is a little technical, taking the mind away from the fatal defect. But even technical language cannot eliminate the total absence of front pictures, any more than ignoring it - which this panel does - eliminates the questions that remain to be answered about how there were two batches of film that allegedly show "no image" and others do not exist.

For the benefit of those backward-looking irreconcilables who firmly believe all concepts of fairies and needles disappeared from science in the middle ages; those philosophic reactionaries who consider "anterior" means only "front"; those without imagination holding that only that which exists can be seen; those nit-pickers and sticklers fixed in the odd notion that scientists cannot project themselves and their eyes past the barrier of invisibility; those literal-minded with both feet securely and immovably planted in the dictionary; and those intellectual Neanderthals so narrow in vision they cannot conceive that back and front are the same, perhaps it is obligatory to show how the panel could honestly say it examined front views when they, in my old-fashioned interpretations, say there are none, especially when the panel itemizes 20 different pictures.

The panel proves its point in two ways. The less original manner is to bracket each use of "anterior" with another word meaning another direction. Thus, of the thorax, they specify "anterior and posterior", and of the neck, "anterior, posterior and lateral". If in any way any one of the pictures in either grouping, neither of which is identified with any specific number, shows the tiniest peek of the front of the neck, cannot the panel say it studied front views?

The other way is by the impressive use of numbers. Here its method is the logic of the dim, remote, long-forgotten past, as estimable and reputable in science as compurgation and trial by fire and by champion are in the law, as firmly fixed in genuineness as in their own discipline is the witches' cauldron. A rough but handy paraphrase of the logic seems to be one part of the body is the same as other parts of the body. Perhaps, if we break down that imposing tabulation of 20 cited photographs, this will become clear.

All 20 fall into three groupings. We should be able to accept the honesty and integrity of these categories because they are those of the panel. There was no _diktat_ from the Attorney General or the Warren Commission.

First is "head viewed from right and above". Here, on page 5, the panel itself classified 3, 4, 11, 12, 26, 27, 28, 40, 41 (one less than half of its 20).

Next is "head and neck from left", including 6, 15, 17, 18, 29, 30, 31.

The remaining four, 9, 10, 38, 39, are "back of body".

Ergo, in the "head viewed from the right and above", "head and neck from the left" and "back of body", we have all the front views in that impressive, one-by-one listing of all numbers. Q.E.D.

We should not make hasty judgment. There has already been too much of that. The panel and its science are not _sui generes_. They take their solid doctrine and method from Urban VIII, the Inquisition and its science.

However, dazzled as we must be by this brilliance, we must not be blinded by that which, with no less validity, follows. However, it is but to pay the panel its just due to concede that its examination of these "front" photographs is "consistent with" much else of its report.

The section opens with reference to "an elliptical _penetrating_ wound of the _skin_ of the back" (p.8). It does not take much of a wound to "penetrate" the skin, on the back or anywhere else. What the panel here does is begin by inferring that the wound goes _through_ the body. It has and cites no such proof, here or anywhere else. It makes this conjecture and ultimately, though in language to be cited at that point not seeming like speculation, concedes it is conjecturing. But it is better to have a solid foundation for speculation, so here it is contrived, right at the outset.

In passing, in the report that ostensibly supports the autopsy and Warren Reports, it is worthy of note that the panel does not call this a neck wound. It is specific in using the word "back" - a "wound of the back", not, as did the Commission, a wound of the "neck".

Although supposedly evaluating rather than parroting the autopsy doctors, it orients this wound in precisely those unusual and something less than scientific and precise means employed by the autopsy doctors. With the rigid immovable spine the usual fixed point of lateral body measurement, and with the numbered vertebrae an inflexible reference point, the imaginative doctors, autopsy _and_ panel, elected instead to measure from the shoulder joint. Thus, they conveniently introduced a flexibility, the width of the President's body - which is, with great care, nowhere stated. Each, with no less originality, located the wound vertically by the President's mastoid. This rather exotic concept introduced as an indispensible the length of the President's neck. It therefore is neither given in measurement nor hinted in characteristic. If these two needless variables did not sufficiently defy any effort to locate the wound exactly ("back" to the "confirming" panel, "neck" to the Commission), there remained the mobility of that neck and position of the head. The measurement from the mastoid downward could be lengthened by cocking that side of the head up, shortened by tipping it down.

There are two slight problems here, both addressed with the infallible method of the Commission. As Wesley Liebeler, Commission counsel, put it when he was confronted with a perplexity indicating conspiracy that he could not resolve while deposing Postal Inspector Harry Holmes, "We'll add that to the stack" of similar remaining and ignored problems. The autopsy measurements are 14 cm. from either point. However, with exactly the same evidence, allegedly, before it, the panel located this wound 15 cm. from the shoulder joint. The difference is not great, not quite a half inch. In three considerations, however, it could loom enormously:

Are these the actual X-rays of the President's body?

Is the autopsy accurate?

Could a shift in the alleged entry point have caused the bullet to hit or miss a bone?

Immediately upon reading this report, I consulted a local radiologist, previously unknown to me. He knew nothing of the Warren or autopsy reports, although one of the participants was favorably known to him. I reached him by the random method of calling the local hospital and asking for the X-ray department, then asking the technician in charge the name of a radiologist I could phone.

It is his opinion that there is no problem in marking evidence of this sort and measuring it precisely. The point of beginning measurement can, if necessary to distinguish between the vertebrae, be marked on the X-ray or in the pictures. He also describes the scapula, the shoulder bone so often referred to by only its medical designation in the various documents, as the most floating, the most mobile, in the torso. It moves with use and the position of the body.

To make his point on the scapula plain, this radiologist told me that, subject to variations in individual anatomy and exact positioning, the difference in where a wound seemed to be if inflicted while the victim was sitting but viewed when the body was prone could easily be two inches. I asked him if the converse were true and he said it is.

Is it not strange that a country doctor would know this simple fact about the human anatomy and all those beribboned and epauletted military doctors did not? Or that the author of a standard text on forensic pathology was unaware of and all his eminent associates did not remember what immediately suggested itself to this ordinary country doctor as soon as I posed the question to him?

And so we have the apotheosis of 20th-century medico-legal science when a President is murdered, in its exemplification by the Presidential Commission, the autopsy doctors and the blue-ribbon Attorney General panel.

However, the autopsy's notable contribution to forensic medicine so pleased those on the panel who teach it they developed their own variant of "fixed" reference points, "a transverse fold in the skin of the neck". Can there be a reference point in the neck, which has rigid, countable bones, or anywhere in the spinal column, with its numbered vertebrae, that allows for such convenient flexibility? Of course not! Therefore, these forensic-medical scientists and their legal member seized upon that rippling cross-wise fold in the skin and from it they measured. It was 5.5 cm. to the wound by this new "panel positioner".

Picture the haste in which the medical texts will now be written, especially Fisher's famous one, so forensic-medical experts of the future will all be skilled in solving crimes and giving testimony about fixed points located by flexible orientations only. Ah, the joy to the jurors, each of whom will escape the boredom of prosaic evidence and become his own Perry Mason! Oh, the opportunities for crusty judges who will refuse to consider the inflexible, hard-and-fast, now-outdated rigidities by which wounds are positively and inflexibly located, enjoying their castigations of those recidivists who persist in harking back to the pre-panel concepts of wound location. And thus the spine will be cast into a deserved legal limbo, forever its vertebrae expunged from the court records, police portfolios and detective stories. Before us lies a new era, an age of forensic flexibility, a romantic period in which every medico-legal witness will become a cross between Jake Ehrlich and Baron Munchausen.

If we understand the President was sitting erect in his limousine when murdered and measured prone on the autopsy table at Bethesda Naval Hospital, new vistas glow ahead. Almost any panel constituted like this one can prove almost anything about how any President might be killed.

This must have been a pretty heady experience for the Clark panel.

Exhilarated, it eliminated the problem created by the total absence of pictures of the front of this wound with a combination of discreet silence and clever improvisation. It took a side view and measured downward from that transverse tracheotomy, the ends of which were visible, to the intersecting line of the folded skin. The distance was 9 cm. In the panel report, these measurements are not so close together, a paragraph of argument being intruded, in keeping with the established spirit.

With all these delightful, pseudo-scientific games with the corpse of a President, with science, the law, and the national and individual honors, the panel lost sight of the possibility of eliminating one of the signal deficiencies of the autopsy protocol. It could have measured the <u>angle</u> downward, to establish whether or not, if this wound were in all other respects precisely as the Commission stated, the bullet could have originated in that sixth-floor window in which Oswald, allegedly but never provedly, lurked in his "sniper's nest". This downward angle was simplicity itself, and the layman can come pretty close for himself. However, had the panel elected to compute one angle, that up and down, it could hardly have avoided the other angle, from side to side. With the probability this would have resulted in a total wrecking of the Warren Report, that was uncongenial to the panel's overt purposes. With Governor Connally sitting directly in front of the President, and with the Commission saying the one bullet, going to the left through the President, inflicted two wounds on him and five on the governor (the first on the governor being further to the right than either on the President), it is not likely that any supporter of government theory would establish a lateral trajectory of something like 45 degrees to the left through the President's neck. The greater the angle, the more ridiculous the whole thing became. Like the Commission, the panel preferred pretending there is no such thing as an angle in evidence or in forensic medicine.

As I said and repeat, this was a consistent panel.

That intervening paragraph identifies the edges of the back wound as discolored. This, "most pronounced on its upper and outer margins", is what "identifies it as having the characteristics of the entrance wound of a bullet". This is tantamount to saying that all bullet wounds do not discolor, that only those of entrance do, an arcane expression of this twentieth-century science of Presidential murder investigations.

Still in the mood for flexibility, the panel describes the measurement of this wound as approximately 7x10 mm. by the simple expedient of including its "marginal abrasion". There was inconceivably little abrasion, if the autopsy doctors are correct, for their measurement of the wound itself was 4x7 mm. Thus the area of abrasion around the wound was about a sixteenth of an inch along the edges.

At this point, the panel repeats its refrain about "Bullet 399", saying, "the dimensions of this cutaneous wound are consistent with those of a wound produced by a bullet similar to that which constitutes exhibit CE 399". Here the panel comes in conflict with the Commission's evidence, reality and what it prefers to ignore, the wound it says this bullet caused in exiting. That bullet is approximately 25 caliber, or a quarter of an inch in diameter. All the Commission's testimony is that its greater consistency is with the dimension of the wound in the front of the neck before surgery. That wound was approximately 3x5 mm., not 7x10 or 4x7. It is usual for a pristine bullet to make a smaller hole on entering than on leaving. The exception is a tumbling bullet.

As the panel here ignores the front wound's size, it also entirely ignores the rest of the requirement imposed on the bullet for any of the Warren Report to be considered possible. The bullet must have inflicted five additional wounds on Governor Connally, and from that tremendous additional burden to have emerged in close to original condition. Had it been a tumbling bullet, according to the evidence, it could not have made as small a wound in the front of the neck as it did. But, were it not tumbling, how could it have made so elliptical a hole in the back? In the testimony, it is indicated that an oval hole can be made by a pristine bullet in true flight only if the entry is tangential. This would mean that if the back wound were of entrance, the bullet had to have come downward at a rather steep angle, one precluding its emergence at the Adam's apple. And that is consistent with evidence as totally ignored by this panel as it was by the Commission, the personal observations and reportings by the FBI agents of what they were told by the autopsy surgeons. These FBI agents were present throughout the autopsy examination and its preliminaries. What they record in their official report is confirmed by the testimony of the two Secret Service agents, also in constant attendance. The doctors explained as they proceeded and were questioned by the agents. The Commission dared not call the FBI agents to testify, and it dared not publish their report. So, it did neither. That report places the downward angle of this wound at 45-60 degrees. If that angle is consistent with an oval back wound being of entry, it also makes entirely impossible this panel report and that of the Warren Commission, both of which permit a trajectory of about 15 degrees, possibly less.

This is one possible explanation of the omission in the panel's report of any comparison between the wounds it says are of entry and exit. It certainly can explain their avoidance of the seeming medical and legal requirements that the angles of the wounds be given. Had the panel, like the Commission before it, not ignored these angles, all five of Governor Connally's wounds would have to have been attributed to a non-existent bullet or bullets or the presence of more than one assassin - the central point of the suit in Judge Halleck's court - had to be acknowledged.

To borrow from the panel report, this is more "consistent with" whitewashing than with a medico-legal purpose. The report continues in the same vein to say of the front wound that it "has the appearance which is characteristic of that of the exit wound of a bullet". The evidence of this, it would seem, is simply that it is a hole. And a bullet hole is made as much on entering as on leaving. The panel is understandably vague at this point, a minimum necessity imposed by the evidence, which contradicts it.

First of all, it is describing a bullet hole invisible in the pictures it says it is examining. There is no picture of the wound. Period. There are lateral pictures in which, perhaps, some part or parts of the tiny, quarter-inch defect might show. The panel cites no evidence at all to warrant its assertion that this defect is even a bullet wound. That is its presumption. If it is permissible for the panel to make this presumption, is it less than mandatory that it identify the supposition as what it is? Rather, it pretends it had examined such a bullet wound. But the pictures showing it do not exist. As indicated earlier, the panel is following the line of a relatively long surgical incision, the line of which must be visible in lateral pictures.

The panel does not burden its report with any meaningful description of this incision. However, it had the measurement before it in the autopsy report. For the neck, a 6.5 cm., or more than 2½-inch incision, is a rather long one. More, as the doctors failed to say, instead of the customary vertical incision, Perry made a transverse cut, at right angles to the neck. Its ends could show in views from either side. The doctors, seeing any irregularity in the surface of the skin in lateral pictures, can assume, as these apparently did, that the irregularity is that of the bullet wound. What they cannot assume and what all the evidence before them assures beyond reasonable doubt that they cannot assume, is that the representation of this wound captured on film can be that of the wound at the moment it was caused.

As earlier stated, the tissues at a wound of entrance tend to turn inward in following the force of the projectile. As the missile emerges, it tends to tear the tissue more and the tissue, again, tends to follow it. This results in a little more tissue extruding at the point of exit. However, as the panel says and as all the evidence agrees, this wound was transected by the surgical incision of the tracheotomy. That was enough to deform the wound, alter its original characteristics. Moreover, the surgery was performed for a purpose and that purpose was served. Tubes were inserted into the President's body to remove fluids. When those tubes were withdrawn, the tissues, as with bullets (likely even more so), followed them, causing the edges to extrude.

More, although this is enough to disqualify these panel observations, it was hours before the pictures were taken. The tracheotomy was completed before 2 p.m. Washington time. We do know that the picture-taking could not have begun until after the arrival of the President's body. That was after 7:30 p.m. Washington time, or more than five and a half hours later. We do not know that the pictures were not taken before the autopsy doctors began their examinations and probings. From their testimony, which is general and relates to no specific pictures, we do know that film was exposed both before and after their examination began. Therefore, any comment, any observation or interpretation of the appearance of this wound in the front of the President's neck, as this panel knew better than most Americans, required the certain knowledge that it had not been in any way defaced or altered. This panel had the unquestioned assurance that precisely this alteration had occurred. It also knew that others are possible, almost certain. It therefore had no way, "consistent with" dedication to science and legal and scientific fact, of describing the "appearance" of the wound or of estimating its appearance at the only relevant time, that of injury.

The last words of the panel discussion of the pictures are sufficiently indefinite to cast doubt on its purposes. As explained above, the angles of this wound, both vertical and horizontal, are essential to any and every basic conclusion of the Warren Commission. This panel, with the evidence available to it - even with that limited portion before it - could have and should have measured and presented both angles. It did not. It didn't even estimate them, It failed to give the slightest hint of the angles. Knowing as it did that a steep angle downward destroys the Warren Report and that of the autopsy; knowing without question that any but the narrowest deviation from a right-angle trajectory through the neck from back to front was also totally destructive (for only an almost straight path made even hitting Governor Connally's body possible); and knowing more, that only the widest possible angle could permit the bullet to transit the neck without touching bone, the panel ends its "discussion" of the pictures and of this wound with the indefiniteness that abundantly discloses its guilty realization. It says the bullet "followed a course downward and to the left in its passage through the body".

With the purposes for which it was convened, the responsibility with which it was charged and had assumed, this panel had the obligation of informing the Attorney General and the people whether or not the conclusions of the Warren Report were even possible. Here, at a crucial point, it abdicated and evaded, lending itself to further obfuscation and national deception.

The panel's study of the autopsy pictures disclosed or developed no proof of the validity of either the autopsy or the Warren Report. That study brought to the panel abundant, overwhelming disproof of the official conclusions. Indeed, from what the panel itself reports, the most serious doubt is cast upon the competence of the autopsy examination and the autopsy and Warren Reports are shattered beyond repair. The method of the panel in saying otherwise is a mixture of avoidance of evidence and misuse of language.

17. DO X-RAYS LIE?

Four pages of the most technical writing are introduced by the heading, "Examination of X-rays". The writing is unnecessarily involved and unvarying in the use of medical terms where those comprehensible to ordinary people, including Attorney Generals and reporters, would have served as well, if not better. However, without this - had the panel presented its report in the simple English that was possible - it would not have pretended to "support" the autopsy or Warren Reports.

It does not.

It wrecks both - completely.

The opening of the section is a disarming listing of the X-rays. In number, they equal that of the appendix to the contract, 14.

First in the discussion is an account of what damage is visible in the skull, the fractures, pieces missing, etc., and the presence of numerous minute bullet fragments. No fragments are visible in the left side, none below the floor of the front of the brain cavity ("anterior fossa of the skull").

Second is a description of what is seen in X-ray #2. With X-ray #3 identically described, "Skull, left lateral" (and here I repeat that it seems unusual that there is no right lateral X-ray, when the damage was said to have been restricted to the right side of the head and a right view would be clearer, there being less density to penetrate), it does seem odd there is no reference to X-ray #3 at all. We do not know whether it "shows no image", whether it entirely supports the interpretation of X-ray #2, whether, what cannot be ruled out, it shows what is not consistent with the interpretation of X-ray #2. For purposes of the panel report and its discussion of the head injuries, there just is no X-ray #3, just as there is no X-ray on the Towne projection, that is, at an angle - the normal X-ray in this kind of examination.

"On one of the lateral films of the skull (#2)," this paragraph begins, "a hole measuring approximately 8 mm on the outer surface of the skull and as much as 20 mm on the internal surface can be seen in profile approximately 100 mm above the external occipital protuberance."

The report returns to this on the next page, to conclude what this "indicates". In order to properly understand what is "indicated", we must first, in layman's language, understand what is presented as the basic fact.

First, the location of the hole. The "external occipital protuberance" is the knob on the back of the head. The distance, 100 mm., is approximately four inches. The hole, then, is approximately four inches above the knob on the back of the head. It will help to understand this if the reader will look at himself in a mirror, holding his head erect and with a straight-edge parallel with the ground under this knob. He will see that the bottom of this knob is only slightly below the top of his ear. In my case, it is about an inch below. Four inches above the bottom of the occipital protuberance is approximately the top of the head!

Months after this autopsy examination, the prosector, Dr. James J. Humes, presented a visual representation of this wound to the Commission. He knew he would have neither the X-rays nor the pictures to use as the basis of his testimony, although they are the legally required "best evidence". So, he gave a verbal description to a medical artist who then prepared drawings on which, conveniently, no dimensions are indicated and much of the visible damage is eliminated, thereby simplifying and alleviating the problem. These are Exhibits 385 and 386. There will be wider access to them in my WHITEWASH (p.196) than in the Commission's 26 volumes of appended material (16H977).

There is an additional drawing, Exhibit 388 (16H984). It is separated in the evidence by seven pages. It also lacks scale. It is a representation of the President's head at the moment of impact of this bullet. That could have been reproduced with complete fidelity by examination of Frame 312 of the Zapruder motion picture. Individual frames, on a selective and incomplete basis, are printed at the beginning of Volume 18. Frame 312 is on page 69. If one studies the position of the President, it is certain that he is in an upright position, his body turned slightly to his left, with his head bowed forward and a little to the left. If precision is desired, a simple plastic triangle or the triangular protractor used by school children will show that the forward angle of his head can be established in this way: The occipital protuberance is approximately on a vertical line through his body. This can be measured in two ways, either against the bottom of the picture or against the body of the car. The street at this point has a maximum decline of about 4 degrees, negligible for our immediate purposes.

Examination of the preceding frames shows no signficant alteration in the position or angles of the President's body. The first significant change is in Frame 313, where the explosion in the head is vivid and unforgettable. In Frame 313, the head is more erect, more to the right than in the preceding frames.

The panel experts had before them the motion-picture version of the Zapruder movie, the 35-mm. color transparencies that include these frames, and the printed volumes in which they appear in black and white.

Exhibit 385 is a right lateral representation of the President's head and upper torso. Its ostensible purpose is to show an estimate of the path of the non-fatal bullet through his neck. It shows none of the head injury. It will soon become clear that the probable reason for this omission has nothing to do with confusing what is shown of the ostensibly separate neck wound or wounds.

Exhibit 386 is a rear view in which it is alleged the points of these two alleged wounds of entry are indicated. Both are shown as almost on a line with the right vertical line of the President's neck, the back wound in the muscular curve as the neck joins the back, that in the head on the horizontal line of the top of the right ear.

But if we turn the seven pages to Exhibit 388, we learn that its physical separation in the evidence may not be happenstance or, if it is, that happenstance serves a practical purpose. In Exhibit 388, the entire upper torso is bent forward. Were it side by side with the two exhibits of the body in the upright position, this would be obvious. Over and above this, the head is then bent even more forward, to the degree that the artist was required to draw in the folds of the flesh under the chin that results from such downward and forward pressure on it.

The angle of the occipital protuberance measured against vertical is thus manipulated to about 50 degrees!

This, too, was before the panel. It was without comment in its appraisal of the autopsy evidence it was convoked to examine.

Returning to the description of the evidence in X-ray #2 on page 11 of the panel report, we find part of a description of the wound as inflicted on the bone. It says, "a hole measuring 8 mm. on the outer surface of the skull and as much as 20 mm on the internal surface". It further says this can be seen "in profile". This is both incomplete and inadequate, knowingly so. It lacks the required description of the shape of the hole and all of its dimensions. It also lacks any meaning-ful explanation of the real significance. Let us analyze it and compare it with the autopsy report content on the same wound. Remember, it is this autopsy report the panel report is said to substantiate and support.

First of all, there should have been, in any competent radiologi-cal examination, X-rays that disclose all the essential information of all wounds, both of entrance and exit. Here we have, if not an expla-nation of the absence of reference to X-ray #3, at least a proof of the need for those X-rays not taken or not existing, which we cannot know, thanks to the Commission and both panels. (Nor is there any discussion of X-rays 4-6, "Skull, fragments of", which we do know show metal frag-ments that can disprove the official account of the assassination.)

Next, we have the unhedged statement that the outer wound is "8 mm in diameter". This, without using the words, says the wound was approximately round in shape. Next, we have a different description of the internal wound, "as much as 20 mm on the internal surface". There here is no reasonable suggestion of a round wound. If we consider the words that follow, "seen in profile", it is reasonable to conclude that this was not a round wound, that the panel doctors knew it was not a round wound, and that for undisclosed reasons they felt it expedient to disguise this fact.

However, if we here invoke the testimony of all of the autopsy doctors, particularly that of Army Lt.-Col. Pierre A. Finck (who, among his medical and other qualifications, had the experience required to be head of the Army's wounds-ballistics branch), especially a scheme he presented that is included in the evidence in Exhibit 400 (17H50), we learn that this greater damage on the inner surface of the skull than the outer is known as the "coning effect". It is comparable to the dam-age caused by a pebble or other missile striking glass, where the defect at the point of impact is considerably less than that on the opposite side.

The panel ignored this essential interpretation of the coning ef-fect, as it avoided complete description of the hole. It preferred the refrain, "These changes are consistent with an entrance wound of the skull produced by a bullet similar to that of exhibit CD 399". It here is not necessary to add comment on the injudicious and unscientific pur-poses for which such language is misapplied in a pretendedly medico-legal document of the strictest impartiality. What should be added is that the fallacious and deceptive conclusion is a diversionary avoidance of the astounding meaning of the evidence of the X-ray considered.

There is no doubt this was a wound of entrance. There also is no doubt it was "consistent with" almost any rifle bullet having caused it. But this non-conclusion or propaganda must not divert us from the shocking hidden meaning of the section of the panel report on the skull damage.

The autopsy report (Exhibit 387) has a section on "Missile Wounds" (16H980). There is no way, in comparing that description with this panel reading of X-ray #2, of knowing both medical teams are speaking of the same wound!

The autopsy language begins with a description of the large fault of the head resulting from the shot. It is relatively precise (unchar-acteristically so for this autopsy report), with a general description of its appearance ("large, irregular defect of the scalp and skull on the right"), extent ("involving chiefly the parietal bone but extending somewhat into the temporal and occipital regions", or, in non-medical terms, from the front to the back of the head), its size ("approximately 13 cm. in greatest diameter", or more than five inches long), and meas-urements from it to four other fixed points in the head.

This, however, is a description of the exiting damage, as the testimony establishes. It is entirely lacking in the panel report, which almost entirely ignores it. To all practical intents, it does not exist in the panel report, such is its dedication to the establishment of the medical and legal fact, to "preservation of a record".

The autopsy report does contain a description of that which the panel read from X-ray #2. It begins, "Situated in the posterior scalp approximately 2.5 cm. laterally to the right and slightly above the occipital protuberance is a lacerated wound measuring 15 x 6 mm." Here the autopsy does what the panel does not but should have; it gives the side-to-side location of the wound of entry, about an inch ("2.5 cm.") to the right of center. It is in this sentence that, for a reason never sought nor offered, the previously quoted change appears, where the autopsy doctors originally described the wound as one of entrance ("Puncture"), then substituted the word "lacerated", which has not the same meaning at all.

However, we also find that the two medical-legal teams give radically different measurements. Where the panel says there is a round hole ("measuring approximately 8 mm in diameter"), the autopsy gives what must be taken as actual measurements made on the actual corpse while it was on the autopsy bench, "15 x 6 mm". The autopsy language leaves no doubt it is not in reference to the inner damage, for it continues, with nothing omitted from the above quotation, to describe that in these words, "In the underlying bone is a corresponding wound through the skull which exhibits beveling on the margins of the bone when viewed from the inner aspect of the skull."

From these violently different "measurements" certain conclusions are inevitable:

Given the opportunity, the autopsy doctors failed to measure the consequences of the "beveling effect" when they "viewed" it. Thus, the only description is that of the panel, which is of one dimension only, the longer ("as much as 20 mm"). There is thus, in all official sources, only inadequate delineation of the inner aspect of the wound of entrance.

However, on the descriptions of the outer aspect, the point at which the bullet first hit the skull, there is that of the panel, of a round hole of 8 mm, versus that of the autopsy, of an oval wound twice this size in maximum dimension.

If for no other reason, this alone precluded panel authentication of the autopsy report. However, without expressed reluctance, the panel did precisely that.

Now, if we assume what we should be justified in being able to assume without hesitation, that both medical teams were competent, honest, and without ulterior purposes, we face the possibility that what the panel saw were X-rays other than those of the autopsy of President John F. Kennedy.

If the panel accurately measured its X-ray evidence, as men with less than their established proficiency and exalted station could have done, and if they accurately reflect their measuring in their report, as men of their established scientific and legal competences and high stations in law and medicine certainly would, they describe a different although similar wound. The difference of a measurable 100 percent on the same X-ray is not an acceptable possibility - if all the conditions enumerated above pertain. These include honesty of intent.

An 8-mm. wound is not a 20-mm. wound.

Therefore, the panel doctors did not have before them X-ray #2 of the autopsy of President John F. Kennedy.

The alternative gives it no more comfort, lends no more credibility or support to its "conclusions", for if it could make an error of 100 percent in simple measurement of the most important evidence of all that under consideration, the fatal wound, can its word be taken for anything?

Nor is it reassuring to realize that this panel knew it was appraising the autopsy of a President of the United States, and in the special context of the distress of the federal government over those critical, really destructive, criticisms of that and the Warren Report. If it were confident that the autopsy doctors had made a 100 percent error in their "measurement" of the point of entry of the fatal wound, still the quintessence of the autopsy as it was of the panel report, how could it fail to so state and how could it possibly endorse anything at all in that autopsy report?

One way, it would seem, the panel is incredibly incompetent, the other inconceivably corrupt. Neither alternative permits it to emerge with the slightest credibility.

Worse, even, than this is the dispute between the autopsy and panel doctors in the location of this wound of entry on the President's head. The eminences of the medico-legal world on the panel neglected to locate the wound laterally. The autopsy places it to the right of center by an inch. It is possible to believe this was no oversight on the part of the panel, for this entry point and the location of the major parts of the head exploded out pose certain problems in considering whether the bullet had the possibility of originating in the sixth-floor window of the Texas School Book Depository Building.

As we also have seen, the panel is specific in its location of the wound of entry in the vertical plane. The variation it allows is less than a centimeter, for it says that the 8-mm. (8/10ths of a centimeter) hole is "approximately 100 mm above the external occipital protuberance". This, we have seen, is about four inches above the head knob. The autopsy, on the other hand, for all its precision in demarking the borders of the enormous wound of exit, is silent on the vertical point on the head at which the bullet entered. It avoided the problem of the point of origin of the bullet with this studied indefiniteness, despite the precision that was possible:

... slightly above the external occipital protuberance ...

Now, four inches, on the head, is anything but a slight measurement. It cannot be considered merely an accident that the autopsy doctors failed to give the precise location of the point of entry. With the body before them, with the X-rays available to them, they simply left it out.

So what do we have?

The autopsy doctors say that the fatal wound was in the back of the head and the panel, which proclaims its agreement with the autopsy report, says this same wound was in the top of the head. Both cannot be right. Further, there no longer is any possibility that, regardless of who is right here, the panel can be trusted on anything. If it is not wrong in this crucial measurement, it is culpably wrong in its silence over this gross error in the autopsy report.

By indefiniteness, by misleading description of "slightly above the external occipital protuberance" to describe a wound the X-ray places at the top of the head, and by deliberate distortion in the artist's conception substituted for the irrefutable pictures when presented to the Commission, the autopsy doctors contrived a false representation of the fatal wound of a President of the United States. Had they not distorted the sketch, they could not have conjectured a trajectory from the sixth-floor window. Had they not then distorted their locating of the wound, it would have been obviously inconsistent with any possibility of a single assassin and no less inconsistent with any chance a shot originating that high in the air could have gone as this is said to have in the President's head.

Here, not in carelessness, we also have an explanation of the omission from the panel report of any meaningful measurement or description of that enormous flaw in the President's head from which the bullet is said to have exploded. How could a bullet have originated from so high above and hit so high in the head, going toward the front, without going down deeply into the head or going out the front? No matter how the representation of the position of the President's head was falsified, this could not be represented in any conception, artist's or other.

How could the rest of the head damage be explained? Or the omission from the artwork given the Commission of any top view of the fatal injury? Can it be believed that the expert prosecutors on the Commission staff were unaware of this defect, any more than the autopsy or panel experts? Or of what the panel uses to misinform, the fact that all fragments of the bullet were to the right of the midline of the head? We are asked to believe that this bullet entered near the midline, at most an inch from it, and made a conical injury, almost an inch in diameter, on the inside of the thin skull; then, magically, while maintaining the power to blast out much of the right side of the President's head, including the bone there, to have been impotent to the left and unable to deposit a single fragment so small as to be invisible save to the X-ray, where it would appear as a tiny star - and none did, they say. Has such a bullet yet been invented?

The doctors of both groups record many things about the damage and the fragments, sometimes in fine detail, sometimes in what approximates legal frivolity. For example, at the bottom of page 10, the panel, with seeming authority and meaningfulness, says, "Distributed through the right cerebral hemisphere are numerous small, irregular metallic fragments, most of which are less than 1 mm. in maximum dimension." If the mind stops to compute that one millimeter is about a twenty-fifth of an inch, indeed small, it is diverted. This device is a plagiarism from the autopsy doctors and their "no major portion" of a bullet technique. The reverse question is left unanswered by the panel: How many, if fewer in number, are fragments larger than 1 mm., and what do they and do all total in size or estimated weight or bulk of a bullet or bullets? We know of these only that they are not as numerous as those dust-sized.

The essence only escapes the doctors and through them their audiences. Of course, that which the panel regarded as expected of it is present. Thus, we find that toward the bottom of page 11 they resort to their technique with the brain canal that ran two ways but whose existence, to them, meant but a single direction. They refer to fragments "distributed in a posterior-anterior direction" without in any way indicating there is any reason to preclude the possibility that the fragments are "distributed" in the opposite direction, from front to back. The absence of any suggestion of evidence on direction does not sponsor the acceptance of this prejudicial formulation as more than medico-legal mumbo-jumbo - propaganda.

The possibility that, in either case, the measurements given are accidental carelessness is eliminated because, in each case, they are repeated, and in precisely the same formulations. They disagree violently with each other but not with themselves. In Dr. J. Thornton Boswell's autopsy body chart (Exhibit 397) made at the bench, this wound is placed in almost the midline and roughly on a horizontal line with the top of the ear. It is marked, in what he has identified as his handwriting, as "15 x 6 mm." The artwork, Exhibit 396, the view directly from the rear, also locates this wound directly opposite the top of the right ear and, with proper regard for the seeming magic of the controlled explosion of that remarkable bullet, directly under the most leftward fault it created in exploding inside the head. So there will be no doubt, what this drawing says is what the panel report presents in words, that there was no explosion to the left of the point of entry and an enormous one to the right side and above the point of entry. They disagree on the point of entry (which somehow prompted the panel to say it "supports" the autopsy report!).

Gratitude is due the panel if for no other reason for their dedication to the literary alchemization of fiction into nonfiction. This led them to the arguing of their non-conclusions presented as "indications" (on page 12). Here they repeat the entry point, forget that they had omitted the lateral measurement and include it in this orientation:

"... the decedent's head was struck from behind by a single projectile /no evidence on this was suggested or in any way considered; there is no previous mention of either a single missile or any reason to eliminate more than one7. It entered the occipital region 25 mm. to the right of the midline and 100 mm. above the external occipital protuberance."

In neither case, then, is there any but the intended representation of the point of entry of this so-called fatal bullet that, in each case, is termed the only one. The autopsy doctors reduce by about three-quarters the distance above the fixed point, the external occipital protuberance, or the knob on the back of the head, as measured by the panel on the X-ray.

From this, it unavoidably follows that, on the most fundamental element of their inquiries, the cause of death, one panel of doctors proves the other wrong and wrong in such a way and to such a degree that willful deception is the kindest possible representation that can be made. No competent doctor could possibly make so enormous a mistake, certainly less than other doctors a pathologist, and of pathologists none less than experts in forensic medicine. The government gives us this accreditation of both of its medical task forces. Both groups, it says, are of forensic medical qualification. Nor can it be considered that when the Attorney General himself selected a lawyer as prominent politically and socially as Bruce Bromley, he chose on this basis alone and picked, of all the lawyers in the United States, a man without qualification. If the panel is right, the autopsy doctors perpetrated a monstrous fraud. If the panel is wrong, the magnitude of their guilt is the greater for they did not work under stress, under the crisis pressure of one of the horrible turning-points in history, under the frightful emotional impact of a Presidential assassination - and theirs is indubitably the higher professional qualification. Their purpose was the "preservation of a record", authentication of the autopsy. How could they say they "support" it? After this disproof? How could they?

Again, there is an alternative that, with the history of these pictures and X-rays, cannot be lightly dismissed. This is the possibility presented above, that the panel did not see the X-rays of the autopsy of President Kennedy. I am not saying they did not. But the difference in the crucial measurement given by each group of doctors makes this a possible alternative. The Archivist did write me that there is no chain of possession on the film. The panel does not refer to any "no image" pictures.

Only government can supply the answer. There is, with this incredible but authenticated history like nothing since the councils of kings - nothing like it in American history - no reason to assume it will be any more honest than it has been. The Attorney General is the government. The Warren Commission was the government. The autopsy surgeons and everyone connected with them and the autopsy were government employees, all in military service and under military discipline. The panel of experts were government-appointed, served a government function, gave the government the right to suppress their report. They were silent prior to its release and without complaint about the unusual, unseemly, really improper, circumstances and uses of its release. All the lies have been government lies, all deceptions official deceptions.

When Marina Oswald was caught in endless lies by the Warren Commission and it was disturbed about her total lack of credibility, she told them not to worry because henceforth she would be the soul of probity. Her words are more pointed. She said she would lie no more. The Warren Commission was anxious to accept and did accept this spurious guarantee. The rest of us, knowing what befell the Warren Commission, ought not be prepared to welcome such facile assurances - if and when they are made.

What remains of the panel report on the examination of this single skull X-ray has been analyzed in earlier passages. It can here be repeated with the guarantee that it is not treated in that report as a fairy tale: "... it is noteworthy that there is no evidence of projectile fragments in the left cerebral tissues or in the right cerebral hemisphere" below the floor of the cranial cavity; it is "not reasonable to postulate that a projectile passed through the head in a direction other than "from back to front". If this panel was not given pause by the enormous difference between its location of the large hole in the head and that of the autopsy, so coolly noted in its preceding para-

197

graph, we can get an independent reading of what it considers "not reasonable" from its lack of comment on the absence of any X-ray of the damaged right side of the skull, its own total lack of comment on the second X-ray of the left side, and its failure to note the incredible, that after removal of the left half of the brain, no examination was made of it!

There is little point in a detailed analysis of this studiously evasive language designed to say what to this panel is "not reasonable" Two things should be noted, however. What is or is not, may or may not be reasonable is not in the charge to this panel. That sort of comment is outside their responsibilities (to say nothing of their competence). Also, this passage has an excellent example of the panel's mastery of propaganda devices. They refer to merely a single projectile, giving the idea it was impossible for the President to have been struck in the head by more than one. However, at no point do they really consider this and at no point do they say it was not possible. The possibility of another bullet is real. The panel's phrasing is imprecise. Fragments of bone are also "projectiles". When the left half of the brain was never examined, can it be known whether a bone fragment damaged it, for example? It notes this unidentified, mysterious "gray brown structure" that does not exist in the autopsy and still says it supports the autopsy? And how does or can the alleged absence of fragments in the left side relate to the direction of the bullet? Without explanation, the panel gives this as proof.

The subsection on "neck region" is a brief two paragraphs (p.13). The first is 67 words in which all the intelligence gleaned from X-rays #9-11, all taken from the front, is incorporated in the first two-thirds and what is not seen is in the last third. Most important of what the X-rays do not show is not hinted at. The second paragraph is of conclusions again characterized as "indications", which is something less than an affirmative declaration. "Indications" are not "conclusions".

The first statement of what these three X-rays show is "subcutaneous emphysema". This means a swelling under the skin. What skin is not stated. A layman might seem justified in wondering if it were the front or the back of the body. This swelling is "just to the right if the cervical spine and immediately above the apex of the right lung". But it is connected with nothing, except by inference. There is no statement that it was caused by a bullet, likely to have been, anything like that. (Remember, there had been surgery there.) As expressed here, the words have no more real meaning than the observation the President had freckles on his back.

This kind of writing, as a substitute for evidence, is the standard device. Bracketed with this is a sentence saying "the foregoing observations indicate that the pathway of the projectile involving the neck was confined to a region", etc. We should take this apart. The panel did not know what "the pathway of the projectile" was. It assumes a single bullet, assumes it went from back to front. But there is - and it has - no proof. The X-rays, as it fails to say, cannot and do not show the bullet holes. They cannot and do not show the "pathway". Three pages later, elliptically, it concedes the pathway was never traced. But here it pretends there is no question. The shrewd panel does not say there is proof. It merely refers to "indications", knowing full well this word would be misconstrued to be a statement the panel did have the proof.

It should be noted that the language "the projectile involving the neck" is imprecise. This panel consistently refers to that injury as a back injury. The Warren Report called it of the neck. Now, if the bullet causing the hole in the back was "involved" with the neck, the proof is totally lacking. This, too, is a standard panel device, dared only because it presumed no cross-examination. This kind of liberty with words is designed to do exactly what it does, misinform and mislead. Stripped of its verbiage, imprecise and intendedly deceptive language, this section entitled "neck region" contains not a single bit of proof substantiating anything. It is all in the flashy writing.

Failure of the panel to state that the X-rays showing the back injury show no confirmation at all does not inspire confidence. Only an intention to deceive can explain this gross omission. It is almost as though the panel developed a guilt complex because it is beyond the capacity of X-rays to record what it wants believed. Had it been less intent upon presenting a contrived, partisan case, preconceived to succor the government, it might have realized that honesty and forthrightness at this point cost it little and might have gained it much, in the future if not when composed.

To alleviate this minor panel discomfort so unscientifically translated into its report, I assure the reader the limited capacity of the X-ray is in no way the fault or responsibility of the panel. Only its dissembling can be held against it.

So, the X-rays fail in any way to affirm that there was a bullet in the neck or that it went from back to front and in no other direction. This I repeat because unless both are true and true beyond question, there is no life left in the Warren Report and it, too, is in for an overdue autopsy. It should be recalled that this pair of wounds is attributed to Bullet 399, said also to have smashed or damaged bones in three parts of Governor Connally's body while inflicting five wounds on him alone. Like nothing in science fiction or the recorded history of bullets, it emerged from this unparalleled and unprecedented career in almost perfect condition. It should also be recalled that, when the doctors who examined the President in Dallas and Washington were asked if this was possible, they agreed it was not, the word "inconceivable" being employed. This bullet was so close to perfect, the only metal presumed to be missing from it, postulated by the most dubious evidentiary flimflammery to be of minuscule weight, was already exceeded by what was lost in Connally. It could not be attributed to any other bullet without wrecking the Report.

And so, aside from the awesome power of the government to compel belief in falsehood, there was, from the first, no reason to believe the single-bullet theory invented by the lawyer handling that part of the case. (He is Arlen Specter, referred to earlier.) Without the single-bullet theory, even that limited amount of shooting acknowledged to have taken place cannot be explained as within the capacity of a single marksman of the greatest proficiency and speed. And there is nothing in the X-rays to in any way buttress this impossible preconception that was in no way ever substantiated.

What the panel doctors could not avoid is their own unintended contribution to the autopsy of the Warren Report. It is in the third sentence of the first paragraph. They say it quietly, understating and avoiding any "conclusions", "indications", "consistent withs" or even "inconsistent withs". They connect it with nothing, leave it, hopefully, in a vacuum. Here we can find more than enough cause for its failure to examine any of the medical evidence relating to Governor Connally without which there can be no honest consideration of the neck-back wound. That sentence entirely escaped attention until I spotted it. This is what it says:

"Also, several metallic fragments are present in this region."

By this point, the reader of the panel report is inured to the reporting and description of bullet fragments. And only those with the most intimate understanding of the complicated evidence out of which the Warren Report was fabricated can detect its significance. However, we can be direct and unequivocal: If there is any metal at all connected in any way with this wound, the Warren Report is so far past the condition for an autopsy, it is fit for only an ignominious funeral. There can be no metal in the area of the body, with all the injuries having been caused by an almost perfect bullet that had already shed more of its weight than could be accounted as missing from it, and any tiny remnant of that Report remain accepted. And there are grounds for a perjury charge.

The tiniest fragment of bullet in this area of the body is enough,

immobile as it now is, to kill the reputations of everyone in any remote
way connected with the Report or the medical or medical-legal work. Most
particularly is it fatal to the reputations of Specter and the autopsy
and panel doctors.

Because of the Attorney General's desperation, there is also the
until-now suppressed and undated second report of the autopsy doctors on
their second examination of the pictures and X-rays. In it is their belated acknowledgment of what they suppressed from their autopsy report
and their Commission testimony. Carefully included in the wrong place,
in the two-sentence brevity headed with fine editorial inapplicability,
"NO OTHER WOUNDS", is this intelligence:

> However, careful examination at the autopsy, and the photographs
> and X-rays taken during the autopsy, revealed no evidence of a bul-
> let or of a major portion of a bullet in the body of the President
> ..

This is not a statement that there were no fragments of bullet
anywhere in the vicinity of or associated with these wounds. It is not
even a statement that there were only minute traces of metal (although
there may have been very little; we do not know because we are not told).
By the obfuscation "major portion", the autopsy doctors do not even say
that in added minor portions there is less than the equivalent of one
or more bullets in accumulated weight. Translated, they do say there
was, to their suppressed knowledge, metal where their report and their
testimony says there was none. They limit the amount of metal only to
the extent that no single fragment was as much as half a total bullet
in weight or size. Knowing as they by the time of their suppressed report had to know, that any bullet fragment or fragments in the President's neck-back area was the ruin of the entire official fiction, they
still hid their guilty knowledge, still disguised it to the degree possible. Unless we assume the corruption of the Attorney General and all
of those under him, we must acknowledge the degree of their success.
It was perfect. Therefore, their confession presented as the contrary,
in which they fail to acknowledge exactly what fragment or fragments
were in the body, remains culpable, and their conduct is that of men
continuing to hide guilty knowledge and perpetuating perjury.

Indeed, this carefully imprecise formulation carries an additional self-stigmatization. These doctors said that their knowledge of
the presence of a fragment of less than half the size of a bullet, which
is a very large fragment, or others of the same limitation, dates to the
"careful examination at the autopsy". Perhaps they didn't mean this,
but it is what they said. On the other hand, if they did not mean it,
they do endorse their lack of professional qualification, for that knowledge is preserved in the X-rays they had made and studied at the time
of their autopsy examination. Unlike the pictures, which were taken
from them exposed but undeveloped, the X-rays were immediately developed
and remained with the doctors for their use until after they completed
their examination. It was, in fact, more than four hours after the
completion of the examination that the X-rays left the hospital in the
possession of Secret Service Agent Roy Kellerman.

The doctors did read the X-rays. They swore to it (2H362). They
also perjured themselves. I repeat Humes' answer to Specter's question,
"What did those X-rays disclose with respect to the possible presence of
a missile in the President's body?"

Humes testified, "They showed no evidence of a missile in the
President's body at any point. And those were examined by ourselves and
by the radiologist who assisted us in this endeavor."

There was no finger-crossing, no cemetery-whistling here. At no
point was the question about a bullet or a whole bullet, nor was the
answer. The words "projectile" and "missile" mean anything moving and
acting as a projectile, of which a bone fragment is an example.

If this is not perjury, then the X-rays of the President's autopsy have been substituted or faked.

These cannot be accidental concessions in the Clark reports, as they were not accidental suppressions. The panel even repeats its hidden admission under "Other Regions Studied" (p.13). Here it fails to identify what might easily be identified and should and would have been in any competent and thorough study that had scientific and legal purposes and none other. It says that "on film #13"(which is of the President's lower back area), "a small round opaque structure a little more than 1 mm in diameter is visible just to the right of the midline of the first sacral segment of the spine. Its smooth characteristics are not similar to those of the projectile fragments seen in the X-rays of the skull and neck." The inventory lists <u>no X-ray of the neck</u>. The doctors are playing tricks with words again. There is no X-ray <u>showing</u> the neck that is not of a part of the body. Here again, acknowledgment of bullet fragments - and not necessarily in the neck itself, but in the entire X-rays that show the neck as well.

With his history of near-fatal back surgery, the President's pin at the base of the spine should not have been so difficult for these eminent specialists to identify. Their failure to do this is consistent with combining two problems: Covering themselves and hiding the evidence

Their final comment on the "indications" of the "neck region" X-rays is a jewel of scholarly evasiveness. They say the pathway of the bullet, which they conjectured without saying so because the X-rays did not show it (as they also failed to state), was merely "confined to a region to the right of the spine" because any other "would have almost certainly fractured one or more of the bones of the right shoulder girdle and thorax".

Here they were addressing those same lateral and vertical angles they avoided, that they here still avoid. And they were assuming what they did not prove, that the only possibility was that the bullet entered in the back. Now, with the deviation from a path directly through the body, there was no problem in presenting the angle that would avoid the very thick bones of the neck that are so large a part of it. The problem was not technical; it was political. That angle is so wide it cannot be believed that the same bullet could have struck and inflicted those five wounds in three parts of Governor Connally's body, and unless it did, goodbye Warren Report. Likewise, if the rear non-fatal wound were where 100 percent of the other evidence placed it, down on the back, a bullet from the front would have been able to avoid all the bones save that of the spine, for it would have been below them when it exited in the back.

There is no reference to any fragment of bullet in any association with the non-fatal Presidential injuries in the Warren Report or its evidence, including the autopsy report and the testimony about it. Any such evidence is fatal to the Warren Report and to the reputations of those who presented and adduced the testimony and who composed those parts of the Report. All the doctors knew of the presence of just this destructive evidence. All were then and have since been silent, stifling their guilty knowledge. Here no further comment is necessary on the medico-legal evidence of either the autopsy or panel reports or those who prepared them.

18. ENDURING SHAME

With three short and unquestioning paragraphs devoted to avoiding the mute evidence of the clothing, the heading, "Examination of Clothing", seems like a headline euphemism. Each paragraph has a subhead, the first being on "Suit Coat". Here the panel acknowledges a hole other than that caused by the bullet and dismisses it as of no consequence with no explanation. That it may have been of innocent origin is not important. What is significant is the cavalier attitude of this blue-ribbon panel of legal and forensic luminaries who are so unconcerned with the evidence before them they ignore what they please, contemptuous of their responsibilities of the present and in history. Using the metric scale (5 cm. and 12 cm.), they locate the bullet hole four and three-quarter inches from the top of the collar - a different measurement than any in the Commission's evidence - and two inches to the right of the midline of the jacket. The measurements of the Report, which was before them, part of the panel's evidence, are "5-3/8 inches below the top of the collar and 1-3/4 inches to the right of the center back seam" (R92). Did the panel have a different coat or a different ruler? And here they abandon the jacket. The purpose for which the panel deigned to look at it appears to have been so they could not be charged with not having done so. They draw no conclusions, though conclusions there were and are to be drawn. And they sneak the hole in the back up a little closer to the neck.

Roughly coinciding with this hole in the back of the jacket is one in the shirt. Of the two tears in the front of the shirt, the panel says only they would coincide with where one might expect the knot of the tie to be. That the forward edges of a shirt collar is where one normally finds a tie is less than an earth-shaking observation, but there is nothing else - save innuendo.

The tie gets a single sentence saying that it had a 5-mm. flaw in it, an inch below the top of the knot and to the left of the midline. This sentence is worthy of careful analysis as a sample of the method of this panel and its willingness to disagree with the other evidence and the Warren Report while maintaining a discreet if unmedico-legal silence.

Tie (CE 395) In the front component of the knot of the tie in the outer layer of fabric a ragged tear about 5 mm. in maximum diameter is located 2.5 cm. below the upper edge of the knot and to the left of the midline.

The Commission was like the panel in seeking to avert interest in the prime evidence of the President's garments. It has an elaborate, 8-page table of contents, well larded with propaganda headings. A few samples are, "Scientific Evidence Linking Oswald and Rifle to Paper Bag" (the Commission's way of saying there was no such evidence); "Eyewitness Identification of Assassin" (meaning there was no "eyewitness identification" of the alleged assassin); "The Richard M. Nixon Incident" under "Prior Attempts to Kill" (there was no "Richard M. Nixon Incident" and no proof whatsoever of any "Prior attempts to kill"). However, the interested reader cannot locate what too-little the Commission says about the President's clothing from either the table of contents or the index of the Report for there is no listing. (It is on pp.91-2, under the President's wounds!) The Report has this two-sentence description of the damage to the tie:

The tie had a nick on the left side of the knot. The nick was elongated horizontally, indicating that the tear was made by some object moving horizontally, but the fibres were not affected in a manner which would shed light on the direction or the nature of the missile.

The Commission gives no measurements but drops a few other nuggets. The panel gives no meaningful information and a meaningless measurement that, though without meaning, is not consistent with the Commission description. Both dishonestly mislocate the damage.

When the panel says "5 mm. in maximum diameter" it suggests a hole and describes a flaw that should be other than what the Commission calls it, a "nick" and a "tear". The Commission, unable at this point to avoid some honesty, describes the direction of the "nick" or "tear" (neither word is descriptive of bullet damage) as "horizontal", opposite the imputed direction of the alleged bullet. The panel, less honest or more dishonest, makes no reference to the direction of the damage, content to give the impression that it was caused by the bullet that it says entered the President's back and exited the front of the neck. It carried out the same plan in the last sentence of its preceding paragraph on the shirt, where it says, "Two linear holes 15 mm. long are found in the overlapping hems of the front of the shirt in a position corresponding to the place where the knot of the neck tie would normally be". However, the Report, whose authors knew it would be made public, acknowledges there was no proof the holes in the shirt were bullet holes (R92). And the FBI expert witness, Robert A. Frazier, testified "the hole in the front of the shirt does not have the round characteristic shape caused by a round bullet entering cloth" (5H61). We shall carry this further in the last part of this book.

Both intend deception, intend giving the idea the tie had a hole in it that is "consistent with" the holes in the front of the shirt and that both are "consistent with" a bullet having entered the President's back and come out at that point in the front.

What the quoted words really mean is the exact opposite. Neither the Commission nor the panel says what caused the damage to the tie. There is not even evidence to warrant the Commission's use of the word "missile", selected to suggest a bullet. Both, however, knew that it was not a hole and did not go all the way through the tie. Especially because this damage coincides with that to the shirt, this actually constitutes proof that no bullet had exited there at all and destroys the entire learned, scientific and very official verbal house of cards.

Still again, the substitute for evidence is words, wrong words, wrongly used. Neither the panel nor the Commission uses honest, direct language. According to the panel report, if read closely, the "tear" is in the "front" of the knot only, in the "outer layer of fabric" only. According to the Warren Report, the "nick" is "elongated horizontally", made "by some object moving horizontally", but is at no point a "hole". It is only a "nick" or a "tear". And the tie was not unknotted when removed at the Dallas hospital. It was cut off to the "left of the knot, leaving the knot in its original condition" (R92).

With no hole in the parts of the garments coinciding with the location said to be that of the back wound and with coinciding holes considerably below that point, one might not have expected such a panel to dignify probative, material, tangible evidence of this character, it is that destructive of the case the panel built. One cannot believe the panel ignored this mute pointing finger because it was confident the evidence was without significance. Nor can it be because the collateral evidence argues with the silence of the clothing. Three Secret Service agents gave testimony consistent with it. Two of them were present at the autopsy. A fourth saw the impact of the bullet in the back four inches below the neck. This evidence is in what was before the panel, in the Commission's volumes. Two FBI agents said essentially the same thing in a suppressed report the Commission did not publish. It was available to the panel. The panel preferred not to have it. It had enough trouble with what it could not avoid.

More, there was a spectrographic analysis of the residues left on the garments, as there was of the whole bullet and fragments of a bullet or bullets said but never proven to have been used in the assassination. Had this panel asked for the spectrographic analysis, incompetent testimony about which was before the panel in the Commission's volumes, does anyone think the panel would have been denied? The spectrographic analysis, vital and basic in any assessment of the assassination and the ballistics and medical evidence, is not in the Commission's evidence as it was not in that considered by this panel. The mere absence of so essential an item of evidence from the consideration of any body is enough to disqualify that body. (I am suing for it.)

Again, there is an easily understood explanation. The spectrographic analysis establishes that there are no bullet traces on the parts of the tie and front of the shirt that are damaged (5H62). Therefore, there is no proof that a bullet damaged the tie or the front of the shirt and, conversely, evidence that the damage was not caused by a bullet.

Further, this panel had every reason to expect it had an unquestioning audience, captive and receptive, an audience that would say nothing. Therefore, it could take chances and congenial liberties. That was much safer than unplugging the spectrographic analysis, less hazardous than facing the proof the tie and shirt were not damaged by a bullet. This is an experienced, sophisticated panel. It did not have to be told that a spectrographic analysis supporting the official account of the murder would hardly be suppressed. It without doubt assumed the analysis did the opposite and, like the Commission, it cast a jaundiced eye at the sleeping dog.

We thus find that the panel so willing to conjecture and equate conjecture with fact, as with the "pathway"; so unabashed in its overt propaganda, as in its repeated prejudicial and wrong allusions to Bullet 399 in a manner to suggest its companions are the source of the other wounds, entirely unwilling to bring out and ponder the evidence that could, beyond cavil, say whether its snide, unscientific wisecracks were within the realm of possibility, put an end to conjecture retailed as science, and show whether one bullet could have caused all the non-fatal injuries and whether another could have caused all the others (both being prerequisite to the Warren Report and the autopsy report).

Its device is to pay lip-service, making meaningless remarks and drawing no conclusions from the tangible, credible - irrefutable - evidence of the clothing. It apparently decided that if it could not live without this evidence so contradictory to everything it pretends is reality, it had better devise a means of living with it. That means was to pretend to examine the evidence while ignoring it. This is what the panel did.

In the doing, it ended the report of its "study". This is followed by two pages intended to be described with the heading "Discussion". The panel appears to have devised its own dictionary. Its "discussion" is its conclusions. They begin by saying that "the foregoing exhibits", or what we have just analyzed, hardly the required or the complete evidence, did nothing but "support" its conclusions. In another sense, this can be taken as admission that the evidence does no more than "support" - does not prove these conclusions. Its statement on the cause of death is likewise equivocal. The President was "wounded by two bullets both of which entered his body from behind". It does not, here or elsewhere, say he was not struck by more than two bullets. It does not say which bullet was fatal! Indeed, save for describing the wounded man as the "decedent", it does not even wind up its report by saying the President is dead!

It is here, in its conclusions, not its "evidence", that the panel finds it expedient to refer to an unspecified "observation" by an unknown person or persons of unknown integrity or competence, that "he was leaning forward with his head turned obliquely to the left" when struck in the head. As we have already seen, this is hardly a representation of the existing photographs, of reality, known and established fact - truth.

Then it says, again with a lighthearted lack of specification, that "the photographs and X-rays indicate that it came from a site above and slightly to his right." Were this the case, and we have seen it is not, there still would be a very large part of the northeast end of Dealey Plaza, with a minimum of four relatively large buildings, that would fit this description. In fact, the extreme vagueness of the "turned obliquely to his left" bit compared with the suppressed and misrepresented evidence about the head wound, here for the first time exposed to public attention, might extend one possible source of the shooting to include still other buildings on Houston, the street to the east of the President when he was killed.

On page 15, the evidence in the style of Gilbert and Sullivan is resurrected and the panel again says that, because there was no injury to the left side of the head (well, it implies this but falls short of actually saying it), it could "eliminate with reasonable certainty the possibility of a projectile having passed through the head in any direction other than from back to front". It really does say this (p.15), just as though it makes sense or had a scientific founding. The lack of injury to one side of the head and the direction of the bullet enjoy the scientific relationship of the moon and green cheese.

With gay abandon, the panel addresses itself to the "back" injury. It makes no pretense of calling it a "neck" injury, even specifies it is "at the base of the neck". That, in the back, is not part of the neck and the injury, therefore, is not described as the Commission did. This is a new way of supporting the Commission, by saying it is wrong. The panel says it "considered" whether this bullet could have followed a different "pathway". That "consideration" is not contained in its report. It does not say there was no other "pathway". Instead, it evades, saying "no evidence for this was found". The panel achieved this happy condition, as we have seen, by refusing to have that evidence or to look at what it did have. With this as the criterion, there could have been neither a Warren Report nor that of this panel, for neither bases its conclusions on "evidence". Both, favored by the absence of opposition or examination of any kind, content themselves with guesses, estimates and conjectures, secure in the knowledge they had no one to confront, that none could gainsay them.

At this point in its report, the panel again refers to the presence of "small metallic fragments" associated with this wound. And once again the mention is casual, for all the world as though it were well-known fact instead of a major revelation destructive of the Warren Report. It lacks the courage to tell the truth, that the presence of bullet particles here was suppressed in the Warren Report. Living still in government-assured security against real examination and within the scheme of its preconception that this wound was of rear entry, the panel pontificates that "any other path" than the one it nominated "would almost surely have been intercepted by bone and X-ray films show no bony damage in the thorax and neck".

Of course, the failure of the panel, like that of the autopsy surgeons and the Warren Commission before it, to locate the rear back wound with any kind of dependable description or measurement makes it easier for the panel to say whatever it began by wanting to say. Having proved neither that the hole was where the autopsy report says it was nor that there was a shot from back to front and never addressing the very real questions, was there evidence of a front-to-back shot or of more than one hitting below the head, the panel presents its speculation as fact, saying that if "the" bullet followed any other "pathway", there would have been bone damage. This is true only if one ordains the conjectures into certainty and if one abandons all the credible evidence. It would not be true if the bullet came from the opposite direction, as it would not if the hole in the back were lower. No more comforting to the panel, if what it says were true, it still destroys the Warren Report because that requires so broad an angle through the neck, the bullet could not have inflicted the five wounds on the governor. The assassination, in this event, still requires at least one additional assassin and that still destroys the Warren Commission and its Report, beyond repair.

Immediately, the panel pretends to address itself to this nonfatal injury in another fashion. Here it seeks self-support by seeking to eliminate other possibilities. If the conclusions seem to be a strange place for the introduction of commentary and the examination of evidence, it is no more strange than the citing of conclusions not based on evidence as though this constitutes evidence, which is the manner and style of this panel:

The possibility that the path of the bullet through the neck

might have been more satisfactorily explored by the insertion of a

finger or probe was considered. Obviously the cutaneous wound in

the back was too small to permit the insertion of a finger.

Those who ignore the fact and reality, those with blind dedication to officialdom as infallible, those unwilling to concede that a President can be murdered and his murder be lied about by the government that became the government by his murder alone, those who just will not confront the overwhelming and unassailable evidence, here must take pause. That thing the panel said was "obviously" impossible was done, was testified to, was questioned by the Commission and established as having been done!

The most accidental contact with the most basic evidence would have told this panel of world-famous experts that "with the finger" Humes had probed that very wound - and more than once. Here is the account from the O'Neill-Sibert report, page 4:

This opening was probed by Dr. HUMES with the finger, at which time it was determined that the trajectory of the missile entering at this point had entered at a downward position of 45 to 60 degrees. Further probing determined that the distance travelled by this missile was a short distance inasmuch as the end of the opening could be felt with the finger.

Humes confirmed to the Commission he had "probed" the wound with a finger (2H367).

In his excited testimony, Secret Service Agent Roy Kellerman told how, in addition, Finck probed the wound "with a probe". He repeated, saying, "he is probing inside the shoulder with his instrument" (2H93). Secret Service Agent William Greer also testified that the doctors had probed the wound (2H127).

If this does not exhaust the evidence before the panel and available to it, is it not enough to provide a basis of judging the value and dependability of its collective medical opinion? If it says that it was "obviously" not possible for a finger to probe the wound and the finger was used and was known to have been used, does it not appear that it does not know its business or did not know what it was talking about? Yet it was willing to say and did say what it thought the government wanted, what it knew would help the government, regardless of factual basis or its absence?

Can the members of this panel be regarded as anything less repugnant when self-animating, whether or not self-motivating, rubber stamps, as indiscriminate as the inanimate?

It is simply incredible! All the autopsy participants and observers affirm that this hole was probed, and repeatedly, by the prosector.

The unmistakable import is that he did this persistently, trying to reach the bullet believed still in the body. So the panel offers its considered, scientific and legal opinion that it was impossible!

By the time the government finishes its endless investigations and investigations of investigations of the murder of the President, only the observation that the airplanes stay in the air will permit belief that science in the United States is real.

However, even this captive, sycophant panel knew it could not ordain acceptability for the incompetent examination of the back wound. It therefore waited until the very end (p.16) to pretend to address itself to this. It dared only in an effort to exonerate the incompetent:

Although the precise path of the bullet

could undoubtedly have been demonstrated by complete dissection of

the soft tissue between the two cutaneous wounds, there is no reason

to believe that the information disclosed thereby would alter

significantly the conclusions expressed in this report.

Here I would not dare argue with their eminences, for I am absolutely satisfied there is nothing that would or could have persuaded them to conclude other than they began with the intention of concluding, exactly what the government said and wanted them to say. This is what they did, and their here-quoted attempt to justify the unjustifiable is a concluding reaffirmation. If there is but one thing analysis of the panel report proves, it is that nothing could or would have altered their predetermined conclusions.

Let us seek to analyze this perfection of forensic medical science as produced by such renowned practitioners, especially as they employ their even greater skill with words.

They say "although the precise path of the bullet could undoubtedly have been demonstrated ..." They should have begun with criticism that no effort was made to do this. No effort was made, and it was requisite. Instead of the required criticism, they have their semantics. There is only a single path of a bullet, precise or otherwise, and that is the one it took. It is not the path conjectured, not the one later decided upon. There is but a single path of a bullet in an autopsy and that is the one established as fact. If it is not so established, it is not established at all. If dissection is required, there is dissection or there is no competent autopsy.

Then there is the direction of the bullet. That, too, is never established, yet that, too, could have been, without peradventure of a doubt, had the desire not been so completely lacking and the fear of proof so contrary to the officially-desired been so great.

The panel argument about the path diverts attention from the lack of proof of direction. Both are essential in any solution to the crime. Neither is established as fact by any official investigation or investigation of any investigation.

In saying the path "could have been demonstrated", the panel is guilty of an unintended honesty, a slip for which we can perhaps forgive it. This is an acknowledgment that the path never was "demonstrated", by the autopsy, the panel, or any of the many reports. This is another diversion, for the panel, sitting in judgment, fails to say what was required of it, that it was the minimum responsibility of the autopsy to establish both path and direction to the degree humanly possible - and that this autopsy neither did nor tried to. All that was needed was what is normal in every autopsy following a crime of violence. That is a birthright of every American - save the murdered President.

If the panel suggests by the use of the word "complete" that any kind of "dissection" of the soft tissue was part of the autopsy, it cites no proof and none exists. In fact, the opposite is true. The Navy's finest did nothing but guess the path, and that they did not less than twice, in two contradictory ways, as abundantly established elsewhere. If it intends to suggest that there is anything extraordinary or repugnant in any kind of necessary dissection in an autopsy, it is below contempt, for these men above all know dissection when and where required is the purpose of an autopsy - every autopsy - save when a President is murdered. And how far from it were they when they removed and weighed such organs as the heart, lungs, spleen, liver and kidneys?

What, then, has the panel said and disclosed in the conclusion to its conclusions?

That it has no faith in and does not practice its own science.

That it insists the standards and minimums not be abided by and certifies the accuracy and competence of those who so widely and consistently abandon these standards, requirements and minimums - when a President is murdered.

That in a secret report its members are willing to and do do what they would never dare get caught doing and saying in public - when a President is murdered - and they without hesitation espouse and approve - certify - what their own professions will not and do not.

That they can and have examined the apotheosis of incompetence in an autopsy and without shame or qualm endorse it - secretly when a President is murdered.

That with all of this - even in secret - they would not and did not make complaint or protest, would not even in darkest secrecy utter a polite verbal wrist-slap - when the President was murdered and his murder left unsolved by an autopsy that was in no sense what an autopsy must be, yet these are among the country's conspicuous experts on the requirements of autopsies.

And that nothing would, could - or did - change their minds!

When these men accept what their professions require not be accepted, and when they say that what their professions require is without meaning and would not change their conclusions, they are the leaders of the medical equivalent of the flat-world society, not of a medico-legal system in a free society and a society of laws and order.

They uphold and practice the medical and legal standards and concepts of other recent societies thought to have ended with World War II.

To all this the panel appends a "Summary" (p.16). That is still another repetition of the repetitious and unestablished, that the President was struck from the back by two bullets. Again it fails to specify only two bullets, without which nothing it says has any meaning. It here adds "examination of the clothing" as a prefix to the well-cracked record and substitutes "reveal" for the hackneyed "indicate". Otherwise, it is the same conjecture presented as though it had been proven. But its examination of the clothing could "reveal" nothing about the direction of the bullet that exploded in the head and it did reveal nothing about the direction of the bullet that made holes in the back of the garments. By the time it saw the clothing, that was no longer possible. It could learn direction only from knowing which way the torn fibres pointed immediately after penetration, before the garments were subjected to repeated handling and long storage. Its section on the clothing holds no such comment or conclusion.

Even in the final gasp, this panel of the great of the medico-legal world fails to mention the absence of a single photograph of the front of the President's head, neck or torso; or to note - even in the secrecy it anticipated - that two batches of pictures showed "no image"; or to evaluate this in terms of how "accidental" it could be. It nowhere asks if the pictures that "didn't come out" could by happenstance include all the vital pictures from the front and only those. Without asking and answering this question, there can be no integrity in a review of the autopsy, whatever it discloses or does not disclose, regardless of whether it is otherwise credible or not. No less is this true of the missing X-rays, of which there is no mention here.

Instead, again with that fingers-crossed language already cited from its earlier use, it concludes in a non sequitur, that "the photographs and X-rays discussed herein support the above-quoted portions of the original Autopsy Report and the above-quoted medical conclusions of the Warren Commission Report".

A book could be written analyzing this perfection in evasions. Let us isolate just a few, so that the "conclusions" may be understood for what they are, verbiage and nothingness, glib "outs" for the signatories and the unsigning legal member of the panel - and what the Attorney General wanted.

"The photographs and X-rays discussed herein" certainly exempts the doctors from those not discussed. Those not discussed are those that they elected to ignore, those that do not exist or those that exist and are said not to. This, not the proper criticism for the destruction or suppression, is the "out" chosen by the doctors for their ignoring what they could not honorably or professionally ignore. In fact, there is nowhere a suggestion that they sought to learn how many photographs and X-rays were taken so they could know whether all were before them. As professionals of high standing, they should have noted the absence of all photographs from the front and the absence of those X-rays that are normal in a murder inquiry (save when it is the murder of a popular American President). They did not require that the missing films be presented them - and their own inventory proves they were not. Here all over again they forfeit honor and integrity and any consideration of themselves as other than official apologists hiding behind a false pretense of science and impartiality.

What does the panel do, aside from lie, when it says it supports "the above-quoted portions of the original Autopsy Report"? It engages in propaganda, for the reality is that its report, despite its very good and valorous efforts, utterly wreck that autopsy report. Whether the falsification is from ignorance or venality is of little consequence save to those who uttered it, for the result is the same. There here is no point in repeating what in the foregoing is so abundantly and repetitiously demonstrated, that the panel report ends any possibility of crediting the autopsy or the Warren Report.

Now let us address that noble and high-sounding fairy tale, "the original Autopsy Report". There was not but a single autopsy report, as it was the obligation of this panel to know. There were three and all three were contradictory. The first was burned, an inconceivable raping of all medical, legal and historical requirements that should have sent this panel up the wall. If its silence is from ignorance, that is, perhaps, less easily pardoned than if from corruption. There is no doubt the first autopsy was burned, and there is no doubt the panel had the proof before it. It cites the source in its single item under "documents", for if it had in this category only the published Warren Commission material, that is all it needed. It is contained in Exhibit 397, the autopsy, and the testimony of the chief prosecutor, Dr. James J. Humes. This is a most important part of that material in its study.

The second autopsy is that turned in by Humes. The changes he made in it after drafting it and before it was typed should have raised the hackles of any hep forensic cats. This panel was silent. Did it have the proof before it? Indeed it did, in the same Exhibit 397. These are substantive, not editorial, changes in which "front" becomes "back" and the word "puncture", meaning "entrance" wound, is eliminated every time he used it save once. It is this version of the autopsy that said the front neck wound was a "puncture wound", one of entrance. Did the panel examine that? If it did, it is without voice. How could it - how dared it be? The third known version (were there more?) is the one turned out by the government. What of that? That one eliminates the statement that the President had been shot from the front. This is done without comment, authority or apparent explanation, for that version of the autopsy is said to be identical with the one turned in by the pro-

209

sector. His version, visibly, does say the President was shot from the front; the typed one does not. Magic. Gremlins? Convenient ones, then, and outside the notice or comment of the great of the forensic-medicine world, or the legal profession, the nominee of the American Bar Association, those whose duty it was to detect just this kind of carrying on with the evidence.

"Original" autopsy? Only if Humes had not cleaned the ashes from his fireplace and those who now tenant the home he has long since departed preserved them so four years later the panel could reconstitute and read ashes!

But might we not ask if there is an unconscious reflection of guilty knowledge in the use of the word "original"? Had this panel of medical and legal ferrets reason to assume there is any other kind? Or, can there be an "unoriginal" autopsy? What, indeed, could have inspired this, if anything more than the techniques of propaganda was in their minds?

The panel restricts what it is endorsing to what it calls the "above-quoted portion" of the autopsy report and "the above-quoted medical conclusions of the Warren Report". We have already shown that it was careful to select from the autopsy what it could readily duplicate in the Warren Report. That the photographs and X-rays - whether or not they are genuine, whether or not complete - do not support either set of conclusions need not again be repeated.

How much more than absolutely nothing does it say when it claims to "support" the few selected words of both the autopsy report and the Warren Report? Is it conceivable that the Warren Report misquotes the autopsy, which was the basis of its medical "evidence"? Or that, if these few isolated words are correct, there can be error in the remainder of either document and the work of this panel have meaning?

The quotation from the mislabeled "medical conclusions" of the Warren Report is its own kind of illumination of the panel and its report. First of all, and "consistent with" the record already delineated, it cites the wrong page. Rather than page 19, the given source, its excerpt begins on page 18 - and it is not labeled and cannot be described as the "medical conclusions".

What to the Commission are its medical conclusions are in Chapter III. Had this scholarly and learned panel the perspicacity of a normal, not unusually gifted, grade-school student, it would have consulted the table of contents and learned this for itself. Finding it requires no advanced degrees, none of those skills this panel teaches the "experts" of the future. This is the chapter on the assassination. It has a separate section on the wounds, with three subsections, all neatly itemized in the table of contents. It also has conclusions, cited to page 117 where, indeed, they do appear.

There is also a section of the Report entitled "The Autopsy" (pp.59-60). That the panel preferred the press-release part of the Report to its substance and conclusions can be better appreciated if one examines what was thereby avoided.

That section says two things directly refuted by the panel report. The panel report could not quote them and still say its study confirms "quoted" parts of the Warren Report, could it? Both statements are on page 60. There it is falsely stated that "the doctors traced the course of the bullet through the body". This the Commission knew was a lie. Because the lie was essential to the credibility of the Report, credibility was extorted by a conscious, deliberate lie. The panel, in fact, in its own strange way pointed out above, does note that the path had not been traced at all. The second quotation contradicted by the evidence has been treated at length above. It is the assertion by the autopsy doctors that the rear occipital wound the panel locates at four inches above that point, or at the top of the head, was only "slightly" above it and in the back of the head. Not even this panel dares quote what the Report really says when it is, on such absolutely vital issues, so diametrically opposite the truth and so completely at variance to what the panel could not avoid reporting, even though its reporting was so thoroughly obfuscated its real meaning until now escaped comprehension and exposition.

Had these falsehoods not embarrassed the panel (and despite its now-clear record, there is no reason to presume it is entirely immune to embarrassment), might not this unfulfilled promise on page 60 of the Report have been enough? "The nature and characteristics of this neck wound /a back wound to the panel7 and the two head wounds are discussed fully in the next chapter." This is a reference to pages 85 following of the Report. There, under the discussion of the "neck" wounds, we find what might have inspired fear in the panel. The Report says, falsely, that "the front portion of the President's neck" had "been cut away by the tracheotomy" (R60) and that "the tracheotomy incision had completely eliminated that evidence" (R88). Nothing of the sort ever happened, as I learned from Dr. Perry who performed that surgery. A tracheotomy is but a slit incision in which no tissue is removed. Also at variance with the false statement of the panel report are two adjacent references to the autopsy doctors' "exploration" of the rear, non-fatal wound, the self-same exploration the panel ordained impossible (R88).

"The President's Head Wounds" (R86-7) is so devoid of fact it does not specifically locate the fatal injury. This panel was not so casual it would direct even secret attention to that glaring omission in this so-definitive Report! So, the panel, not daring cite the correct references to the Report, solved its dilemma by simply citing the wrong ones and was merely consistent in citing the wrong page - unless it also sought to divert attention from what follows.

If it cannot and should not be presumed that its ignorance of the case that Attorney General Clark cited as prime qualification for the study by this panel, selected for possession of these arcane prerequisites, it also cannot be assumed that its ignorance extended to not reading the appropriate passages of the Report during its "deliberations". Of course, sticklers and nit-pickers may argue that two days was little time. True! There was no possibility this panel could glance at the evidence it says it considered, incomplete as it was, let alone study it. It could not even begin to. But it would seem that, before quoting the "medical conclusions" of the Report, it gleaned a sufficient consciousness of the limited medical contents of only a few pages to know what it wanted to quote. It then also learned what it had to avoid if it were not to declare the Report and the autopsy false. This the panel did avoid, by mislabeling the press-release part into the "medical conclusions". By this adroit misrepresentation, it found an adequate solution to a hairy problem and stayed away from those sticky pages.

However, in doing this, the panel made a separate problem for itself. That is handled with admirable directness. It edited out what it didn't want to acknowledge. There is no perfect solution to every problem. Quoting the wrong part of the Report had the substantial defect of introducing a name the panel was determined never to mention - and it never did.

At two points in its quotation from page 18 (could this be the reason for the "error" citing page 19?), three asterisks appear, indicating omissions. Now, both omissions total but six words. They are not left out because of urgent space requirements, for that page of the panel report (p.4) has three full inches of blank white space at the bottom and wider margins by far than any save one other of the remaining 15 pages.

Nor can the omissions be attributed to public indecencies, vilifications, libels or anything else of an offensive nature. In this case - for both are identical - it is not even a gross Commission error the panel could not stomach.

What the panel could not abide may astound the reader until he considers it carefully.

It is the name of Texas Governor John Connally. That is all.

211

Why? It is not a bad name. Political considerations do not apply. There is no ground for assuming a personal animosity.

But he was cast out by the panel. His name is the only part of the Warren Report it found so anathematic. It is but a single sentence that so moved the panel.

The first omission is of the words "and Governor Connally". The sentence begins, "The nature of the bullet wounds suffered by President Kennedy and Governor Connally." The second reference is in a clause that, without expurgation, reads, "striking the President and the Governor". Is there any evil here? Nothing nasty.

Why, then, did the panel pretend the Governor did not exist, was not wounded - expunge him from this single innocent sentence so otherwise entirely consistent with its own report? Look at it. Does it annoy you?

> (e) The nature of the bullet wounds suffered by President Kennedy and Governor Connally and the location of the car at the time of the shots establish that the bullets were fired from above and behind the Presidential limousine, striking the President and the Governor as follows:

18

Think back to the single-bullet theory, that invalidity Arlen Specter contrived into the rootrock of the Report. The non-fatal bullet is said, without proof, to have entered the back of the President's neck and exited the front and then to have preserved its original purity while smashing its way through and into bones in three parts of the Governor's body while inflicting an additional five wounds on him. So, the panel absolutely had to pretend he did not exist. It could go only so far in jeopardizing its reputations and professional standings even for the Attorney General of the United States. It did not dare take the "single-bullet" contraption under its protection. That was no more welcome to it than a bastard in an aristocratic home. The panel did, as shown above, ignore this foundation of the Report it pretends to have validated. The panel members are quite cagey on this point, too. They are careful not to actually say they validated the Report. They whistle past that cemetery by insertion of the otherwise meaningless qualification, "above-quoted", as though this in any way restricted the use that was, without their protest, made of their prostitution of their professions, or in any way denied the certainty of the purpose and use for which they were assigned and accepted their task.

It was a sophistry for the panel to "examine" the non-fatal Presidential wounds in the context of the Report without examining the rest of what was and had to be attributed to that single bullet for the Report to begin to be believed in this or any other way.

The panel did not consider any of the evidence, medical or other, relating to Governor Connally. It could not have and still have drafted its report as ultimately released. On the other hand, it has no basis for honest and scientific consideration of the non-fatal Presidential wounds without simultaneous consideration of all the gubernatorial wounds. Unless it began with the assumption the Warren Report was wrong. But how could it "support" an erroneous Report on the murder of a President? Therefore, knowing full well what it was doing and with no possibility of doubt about the inherent and pervading dishonesty of what it was doing, it suppressed and avoided all reference to him and his wounds.

For no other reason were the innocent words "and" and "the" and the previously unblemished name of the Governor like bitter poison in the pens of the panel. Here it is the panel's rather than the Commission's crookedness that is hidden. But is it not truly remarkable and poetically appropriate that, in the very simple and beginning necessity, in quoting from the Report that which it sought to authenticate, the panel could not do so honestly, could not do so without destroying its integrity, that of the Commission and its Report, that of the government whose handmaiden it became?

It fared little better with the autopsy doctors.

Here it quotes, not from the discussion of the wounds in the main body of the autopsy report, but the center three paragraphs only from its "summary".

It dared not quote the entire page. The first words on it are false - and this panel proved their falsity - or it proved that some of the X-rays are missing and denied it! Neither choice is pleasant to consider, not for the Attorney General, the government, any of the doctors, any of the staff or members of the Commission - any American.

"Roentgenograms are made of the entire body" are the words of the first line of the quoted page.

The panel was adept in fielding this one. Before the reader of its report comes to anything other than the few introductory remarks, including its membership and their qualifications, there is the introduction part of the report itself. Under "Previous Reports", as earlier noted, the panel has but four sentences of its own writing. The rest is quotations from the Report and the autopsy report. So, the reader knows nothing, has no preparation for the first two sentences. The panel just could not risk saying nothing. It elected instead to say next to nothing and that in the least meaningful way. It just slipped in enough so that it could later point back and say it did not entirely ignore this. By proceeding with its "study" in the face of it, not making the strongest possible representations to the Attorney General and, above all, by its silence and lack of the required and very important minimum comment, that the film had, in fact, been made impure or stolen or destroyed, it nonetheless clothes itself in the government's guilt.

Here again is the way it sneaked that one in:

The Autopsy Report stated that X-rays had been made of the entire body of the deceased. The Panel's inventory disclosed X-ray films of the entire body except for the lower arms, wrists and hands and the lower legs, ankles and feet.

Or, these are not X-ray films of the "entire body", which is not said.

The panel was making this study for the Attorney General of the United States. It knew him to be a busy man. It knew also he is not a medical man and might, in his haste in scanning it (unless he assigned that chore to a subordinate who might be more handicapped), not grasp the significance of the inadequate representation of this national scandal that would hardly be credited in a work of fiction. Unless it knew he was privy to this frightful, unbelievable thing that had happened, like nothing ever in our national history, it had the obligation of telling him forthrightly that the evidence was tainted, that photographs and X-rays of a President's autopsy had been stolen or destroyed. On the other hand, if the panel knew the Attorney General shared its guilty knowledge, it became part of a conspiracy with him. Either way, it has no excuse, cannot escape its own permeating dishonesty and enduring shame.

Never dreaming that a devil loving scripture would ever scan its report, or possibly the converse, being more fearful that one would, the panel did not excise the parenthetical words in the first paragraph it does quote. These are "(see lateral skull roentgenograms)". These, too, superficially, are innocent words. But in their innocence, they destroy that of all the doctors. They establish not only that the autopsy doctors had lateral skull X-rays taken, but that they had studied them and were familiar with their content, knew or could have known, as their assignment required of them, the exact measurement from that rear head bump to the point of claimed entrance of the rear headwound. From these innocent words, we know it cannot be a simple accident that impelled the autopsy doctors to hide the fact that the entrance wound was so close to the top of the head that it rendered the official explanation of the assassination impossible. We now know that, aside from the fact that they had the cadaver before them and could have (and, of course, should have) measured all factors precisely, they could at any time have rectified this inexcusable transgression against the minimal requirements of an autopsy and the national honor and security by consultation with the X-rays.

They also disclose that, had anyone in authority in the government at any time had the slightest interest in learning the basic fact of the assassination, it was available to them in the X-rays, and they so knew.

Those seemingly innocent words in parentheses rip away the fig-leaf. There is no doubt that the autopsy doctors studied the X-rays, at least of the fatal wound. There is likewise no doubt that the panel doctors and their legal member either knew this or they knew nothing and were disqualified, for this autopsy protocol is what they set out to authenticate. This is the very part they quote. They knew the awful thing the autopsy doctors had done, and they were silent, as they knew and were culpably silent about the presence of bullet fragments where they could not be and the Warren and autopsy reports survive, adjacent to the non-fatal injury, yet never once mentioned anywhere.

How poetic the justice of the innocent, or seemingly innocent, words behind which the panel seeks to hide its guilt and its knowledge of its own guilt, with the amateurish evasions of its very last sentence. It is so transparent to one who, for many years, has lived with the official Aesopian lingo of legal and political luminaries. It rends forever any possibility of ever thinking or believing anyone involved in this most monstrous and intended miscarriage of justice in American history could escape the fouling of his own nest.

There remains yet to be addressed the Commission and its staff. They have to this point not been mentioned because they wrote neither the panel nor the autopsy reports. But they did write that of the Commission, they did procure the testimony on which they pretend to base that Report. How clean are they?

It is their and the official pretense that no one ever saw the pictures and X-rays of the autopsy. In other writing, I have and will again address this self-serving canard in the most intimate detail. Here, so they cannot escape the opprobrium they have more than earned, I cite one secret about the X-rays (more will follow):

In the awful and deliberate falsification of the account of how, why and by whom the President was murdered, everyone had a petard, hoisting on which he feared. The Secret Service was no exception. It had had possession - original and continuing possession - of both the pictures and X-rays.

My first book has lengthy explanations contrary to the official ones of the autopsy. It points out the deficiencies and the perjury and subornation of perjury that are an inescapable probability from even cursory examination of the testimony. It attracted considerable public attention in Washington in May of 1966. It was featured on radio and across the top of the front page of the Washington Post, together with Inquest. And it completely destroys the autopsy report and the reputations of everyone connected with it. In it, I also raise the still-unanswered questions about these pictures and X-rays.

The Secret Service felt the heat.

It prepared a simple statement in an effort to cool itself, hide its guilty face. Paul Hoch, a graduate student at the University of California at Berkeley, then in Washington conducting his own excellent researches, obtained a copy toward the end of June.*

Of the many things in it that are excitingly interesting, for our

*See p. 555.

immediate purposes, one sentence suffices:

The X-ray films were used for the briefing of the Warren Commission's staff on the autopsy procedures and results.

So, the Warren Commission knew that the autopsy was false. Preeminently, the sanctimonious District Attorney of Philadelphia, Arlen Specter, who proclaims the purity of Caesar's wife, was "briefed", for it is he who conducted this part of the Commission's inquiry, was responsible for this part of its Report.

Holy, indeed, are Specter and his breast-beating former colleagues!

How pure, how holy, how honest can you be when you have - are "briefed" on - the very evidence that proves what you are doing is false and you then do it?

Specter is not just an ordinary lawyer, familiar as all are with the requirements of evidence. He is and then was an experienced prosecutor who knew even better than most lawyers what is "best evidence" - and how to fake or beat it.

So, the Commission does not escape the contamination of the panel report. Who is there among those responsible for the promulgation and dissemination, for the believing of the false account of the President's murder, not contaminated by this pseudo-science, by this overt falsification proclaimed the given word by the Attorney General? (In so doing, he was careful to leave no record of his own contaminating involvement. Uncharacteristically, he saw to it there was no press release. And how he traded on the names of the survivors of the martyred President! To defend the successor, the first beneficiary of the assassination, his fellow-Texan?)

One element, indispensable in this rewriting of history, this reassignment of guilt, remains to be considered. That is the press.

If a dogcatcher of the opposite political faith incurs the wrath of the owner or editor of a paper, he may assign a reporter to hound the object of his displeasure endlessly, for day after investigating day. Some major papers assign key men to steep themselves in the every act of important politicians to the end these politicians may be exposed. An editor of one nationally-famous paper told me long after Lyndon Johnson became President that he kept a man full-time in a search for "dirt" on the President. Yet no studies of any part of the assassination story have been made by the press except as sycophant. The spittle dribbles and is licked. Those of us who have dared question the official fiction crammed down the national throat (by this same press) have been defamed and vilified, lied about and, when all else failed, suppressed.

The use - misuse - to which, in the final gasps of his Attorney Generalship, that good ol' Dallas boy, Ramsey Clark, put this panel report he had been sitting on for almost a year was an undisguised abuse of power, authority and public trust. He saw to it there was no possibility of its analysis by the reporters who would be writing about it and knowingly precluded cross-examination, the keystone of the American judicial system and justice. He waited through the long days before the January 17, 1969, proceeding, then, with the enormous publicity the Attorney General can command, released it to the press. He said what is not true, that this report supports that of the Commission and the autopsy doctors. It is this lie that Americans got with no possibility of learning it _is_ a lie.

Headlines from diverse papers reflect this. The Washington _Evening Star_ headed its story, from United Press International, "Kennedy Autopsy Study Supports Warren Report". The _Medical Tribune_'s own report is similar: "4 Physicians Back Warren Report on 2 Bullets". It had a four-column-wide continuation. The heading there differed only slightly, as the panel emphasis led: "4 Physicians Back Warren Report on _Direction of_ 2 Bullets".

So intent was Clark upon making it impossible for the other side, of which I was part, to examine these papers before court convened the next morning, that he delayed even reproducing them until after the end of the working day. To assure we could not examine his lies dignified by big reputations, he gave up his first-edition morning-paper press and the mass-audience evening TV news programs by delaying release. He filed the papers with the sitting judge without the normality of giving a set, even too late, to opposing counsel. The purpose, aside from dishonest courtroom advantage, was to preclude any possibility of public exposure of the falsity of the claims.

Knowing these papers were false, his Department then sought to withdraw them, having with them and the abuse of the practices of law and lawyers achieved the capturing of the judicial mind and the proceeding. The judge denied this, as he denied the hollow claim of the Department lawyers that the release after 11 months, just at the moment of the litigation and only after it was impossible for the other side to consider them, was mere coincidence.

There is no single issue over which the American press would have remained silent at this abuse by federal power and wealth, aside from this one. There were no ringing editorials denouncing the Attorney General as a legal charlatan, as a scoundrel, as a practitioner of dirty tricks, as a disgrace to the justice he was appointed to uphold - by the President who, by the murder of his predecessor alone, became President.

Nor did a single paper make the slightest effort to learn what the panel report really says. I am well known to many editors and reporters of all the media. Not one sought my analysis or opinion.

The autopsy report was a falsification. The Warren Report was the anointment of that falsification, a further falsification, a deception sanctifying the deception of the autopsy report and those counted and proclaimed thousands of the federal investigative agencies. Statistics, too, become part of the propaganda campaign to sustain the Report.

It was hailed as the gospel, not lies, by the press, by all concerned and involved government agencies and their heads, and by the President himself (as though he knew what he was talking about).

One fillip, perhaps significantly, is missing. That is the name of the then not-yet-murdered former Attorney General, Robert Kennedy. His name is not associated with the panel report. Can it be that Clark had no authority to use it?

Crooked in concept as it was in performance, the panel's work could not bear examination. He therefore prevented its examination. He had the heft, and he used it.

This is justice in the United States of America?

This is how truth is established?

How crimes are solved?

Is it a wonder crime is rampant when there is no criminal more evil than the government evil, when the crimes of the government are greater, more far-reaching, no longer even hidden?

With this record of the Department of Justice, what can one expect of the poor, the humble, or the greedy and bad?

When such real criminality is the practice of government, how can it ask better of the ordinary people, how can it inspire confidence in the law or compliance with it? When it is so crooked, how can it expect others to be and do better, to have faith in it?

With open crookedness the unhidden way of government, what is the standard set for youth, for all under the dominion of that government? Can it expect better than it does, than it gives?

In truth, the watchman waketh in vain.

19. MORE PYROMANIA

With true nobility of spirit and purity of purpose the government - regardless of which party is in power - proclaims it has nothing to hide. Should it, when a president or this President is killed and the government "investigates" that killing? When this "investigation" establishes legitimacy, the sanctity of the succession?

Of course not!

Therefore, it suppresses evidence, law or no law - and there is a law - until faced with suit or the threat of suit, secure in the knowledge that the press, which has its own invidious record to live with, will not expose official wrongdoing.

Over a period of years, by filing actions in federal court and in some cases by taking the required preliminary steps with the agencies involved, I have forced the official disgorging of what officially was alleged to be nonexistent. The final part of this book contains numerous instances of this. It includes many of these suppressed official records.

As explained earlier, the middle part, to which this is an epilogue, was written in haste, partially so the information would be organized and in hand for the hearing in Judge Halleck's court. Its sensational content was not enough to destroy my innocence. I actually believed that the government would learn from its mistakes and not repeat them.

I was wrong.

Its mistakes are not accidents. They are purposeful and premeditated, the end product of considered, official judgment. These things that are wrong are deliberated, decided policy, not the consequence of haste, pressures, hysteria or incompetence.

Naively, I did believe that, with all that should not have happened at and after the autopsy on the President's corpse and with the extensive and embarrassing publicity on it beginning with my first book and continuing into 1967, the government would avoid repeating the same "mistakes". If I had little hope that the first of the two panels would do better, the prosectors having their particular pasts to live with, I did expect more from the second, the eminences, particularly from Fisher, who is not excessively modest about his reputation in forensic medicine, teaches it and authored a basic text used in teaching it.

Thus I spent more than two years in a futile effort to obtain what the law describes as "public information" about the work of these panels.

It took one year for the Mitchellisti Department of Justice to acknowledge that former Attorney General Clark was talking through his hat when he referred to the "sworn statements" of experts other than these panels, including "neurosurgeons", and alleged they corroborated what the Warren Commission reported. When, after more than a half-year, Deputy Attorney General Richard G. Kleindienst* did deign to acknowledge my request for these statements, it was with such evasiveness and nonresponsiveness that even Mitchell could not support it. Thus, a year and a day after that request for what Clark referred to, Mitchell himself ruled that "I have ... to treat the Deputy Attorney General's

*Convicted in Watergate scandals.

letter to you as though it were a denial of your request to him." Under date of December 8, 1971, Mitchell told me that "a thorough search of the Department's files has failed to reveal any information indicating" the existence of what Clark cited.

And the panels' notes, working papers, rough drafts, internal correspondence, deliberations - any record of their work or existence other than their final statements?

Nothing!

The National Archives is the ultimate official repository of all official papers dealing with the assassination. It also runs the Kennedy Library. It insisted it had nothing at all about the panels save their reports. The Department of Justice, which had convoked both panels (the operating people, who persist from administration to administration, being careful to do it in Clark's name), also claimed to have no single paper dealing with either panel, aside from the same reports. The Department suggested I ask the panels. I did.

Under the so-called "Freedom of Information" law all except carefully-defined government information is public information, information to which all citizens are, theoretically, entitled to free access. What I asked for is not encompassed by any of the law's nine exemptions. Moreover, under a precedent decision (American Mail Lines, Ltd., v. Gulick), if the government makes any use, no matter how indirect, of what is exempt, it thereby nullifies the exemption and legally cannot withhold that information. For this reason, I made my requests in terms of the published work of the panels. Thus, because after long suppression the reports were used by the government, all the papers of both panels were not subject to withholding, from me or from anyone else. In this way, also, the government waived any right to withhold any of the raw materials of both panels, including all autopsy film, which both "reviewed".

I wrote both panels in my own name. I asked friends to write them. Others, in their own interest, also wrote and in some cases received replies.

A number of interesting and relevant facts came to light in this long inquiry. In some cases it is necessary for sources to be hidden. One, for example, is a member of the family of one official who was involved. That official talked, in the privacy of his family. Then a family member also talked.

The weekend before the first hearing in Judge Halleck's court, Department of Justice lawyers, including one not directly involved in that litigation, drove to Baltimore to see Fisher. They were uncertain about the medical evidence. Fisher whipped them into line by presenting a strong case for support of the Warren Report's so-called "medical conclusions", which are not its medical conclusions, and with a personal attack on Wecht, the fellow forensic pathologist who had criticized the autopsy report. Aside from their doubts about the medical evidence, there had been rumors inside the Department to the effect that the FBI had covered up evidence about the assassination to hide its own failures.

Not long after the final hearing, Fisher disclosed, in private correspondence, that he also had some misgivings and "quite some time after the panel report had been submitted" had made tests with cadavers. Because it was "purely to satisfy my own interest I made no report to anyone," he said.

Fisher also laid to rest a subsequent allegation, that the panel's measurements were not precise because the scale of the pictures and X-rays is unknown. Of this he said, "The measurements ... can be assumed to be accurate. They were measured by scale. We had photographs which showed a scale. We were able, therefore, to confirm the measurements ..."

Moritz told a secret, that at the time the report was made public, "it was agreed that the release to the press or others of any information other than that contained in the report would be made by Dr. Russel Fisher as spokesman for the panel" (sic).

Carnes said, "The distribution of metal fragments shown by X-rays was carefully described by Dr. Russell Morgan ... if the Attorney General has not made it available to the public, I would not feel free to release it ..."

But Fisher's purpose in conducting his later clandestine tests with frozen human bodies was to establish the possibility that a bullet could fly the conjectured course through the President's neck without hitting bone and not fragmenting at all. He said, "... we were convinced it was possible for a bullet tract to connect the entrance and exit wounds without being deflected by, or hitting the bony vertebrae."

As we have seen, unless this had happened, the Warren Report is a fraud. This fragmentation proves it a fraud, thus the Fisher panel's avoidance of the Connally wounds.

Dealing with the alleged proof that the holes in the front of the President's shirt were caused by this same unfragmented bullet, still another requirement for the survival of the Warren Report, Fisher achieved a new pinnacle in forensic science. He just dismissed the evidence that these holes were not caused by that alleged bullet. His "proof" consisted entirely of "Surely there is no question that a bullet made the holes in the shirt." And of the proof to the contrary, he pontificated, "it seems somewhat futile to debate the issue."

Morgan, privately, said exactly the opposite of Fisher. Having in the panel's report supported the so-called "medical conclusions" of the Warren Report, in private he conceded their invalidity by admitting that this alleged bullet "grazed the transverse process" and that this "bony structure broke away a few metal fragments from the bullet."

On another occasion, Morgan indicated these fragments were more numerous. He then said that some were quite small and "others overlapped each other on the film." This means there were more fragments than could be isolated in studying the film.

At one point Fisher developed a liking for the phrase "nitpickers" and so designated those who disagree with the Warren Report. He then went much further and said "it was not our charge to nit pick with the details of the original pathologists' report." At the same time he conceded "information we found contrary to the autopsy report" but claimed this was not "a serious deception". He attempted to characterize as "minor" the "differences in our findings and the original report". And of all the incredible defenses he could have made to allege "the variations are of not real significance" (sic), he cited the gross error in locating the fatal head wound. While describing it with a considerable understatement, as "higher in the photographs than was recorded in the original report", he protested this made no difference because "the bullet did come from behind and above and that is the key observation."

The puerility of this pretense by the master of forensic science, the purpose of which is to establish guilt as well as innocence in crimes, becomes obvious when it is understood that all of the buildings in Dealey Plaza, the scene of the crime, are "behind and above" where the President was when he was shot. Almost all of the people at the scene of the crime likewise were "behind and above" the President. And if one limits consideration to the Depository Building alone, more than 50 of its windows were "behind and above" the President, not just one in which Oswald was alleged to have been when it was known that he was not and could not have been.

The real "key observation", I suggest, is the total invalidation of the autopsy report and with it the no less total destruction of the Warren Report and, to Fisher's expert knowledge, the "solution" to this terrible crime.

Ultimately, Fisher lost his cool completely. He declared "the only commitment I consider I had was to present our report to the Attorney General." One might have expected he felt an obligation or a "commitment" to the truth, to history, to the country, or to his calling.

Despite all of this, Fisher later was candid enough when he

219

moderated a medicolegal discussion sponsored jointly by the American Medical Association and the American Bar Association. It was held at Cesar's Palace, Las Vegas, Nevada. He opened the second session, on Friday afternoon, March 14, 1969, by saying, "Obviously, the conviction or acquittal of the accused is going to hinge on the kind of medical evidence that's put in and how thoroughly it was collected and interpreted." From his own experience he asserted "nothing takes the place of expertise."

When Fisher says that evidence disproving the Warren Report validates it, and when he admits that there was error, serious error, but claims it is without significance because the alleged general direction from which the fatal shot came is consistent with what the autopsy report says, he seems to have put it well in saying that conviction "is going to hinge on the kind of medical evidence that's put in" and "nothing takes the place of expertise."

These are not the only areas of Fisher's "expertise".

He also ran the panel show, from controlling the other members and their report to whipping the Department of Justice lawyers into line. He made no effort to hide his arrogance in his correspondence. It was inconceivable to him that anyone could consider questioning him about anything. If he said black was white, then black had to be white.

I sent all of my letters to each member of both panels. Fisher's replies make it clear he was the boss. Until he became incensed at being questioned over the semantics of which he is a master, he pretended responsiveness when he was unresponsive. In so doing he spotlighted one Department of Justice lawyer and his role. Fisher told me that his panel "submitted only one report", the "same report that was ultimately released by the Justice Department." What the panel "submitted" and what it drafted are not necessarily identical, just as the first, burned draft of the autopsy report is not identical with the final version and that final version is not identical with the intermediate version, the one that escaped the fire in Humes' recreation room. This "submitted" report "was transmitted by Mr. Bruce Bromley to Mr. Carl Eardley of the Justice Department."

(Eardley, it will be remembered, was the man in charge of that battery of Departmental legal eagles at the Halleck hearings. He appears to be the Department's expert on all assassination questions under civil law. His role in the Department's effort to deny me copies of the evidence used to get James Earl Ray, the accused killer of Dr. Martin Luther King, Jr., extradited from England, is set forth in the final chapter of FRAME-UP, my book on that assassination. In that case, which began with the Department denying it had the public records I sought - the records it originated and submitted to the British court and thereafter confiscated from that court with the collaboration of the British government, something unprecedented in Anglo-Saxon jurisprudence and "justice" - Eardley had a unique record of never once telling the truth. It ended when I won a summary judgment against the Department in federal court, something of a rarity.)

Fisher conceded too little in this paragraph, as I was able to get him to admit:

We drafted a report while still meeting as a Committee in the whole /sic7 in Washington. It was subsequently edited and rewritten, but the intermediate drafts were not preserved.

He also reported that "we agreed at the outset not to maintain individual, private files, notes or other information," leading to wonder about how any questions of fact in the editing and revision could be resolved. He blames this "restriction" on "the Kennedy family". Not, mind you, because they did or said anything, but only because "it was felt" this way.

However, what was in question was not what he represented, "individual private files", but the essential working papers without which this report could not have been prepared. He threw in these meaningless words to tell a lie while seeming not to lie. I had not asked for any-

220

thing "individual" or "private".

Had the panel members maintained private papers, they might indeed have violated the right of privacy of the Kennedy family. However, no such question existed. Fisher created it as a diversion. There was every reason to prepare and preserve necessary working papers. They could and should have been submitted with the report. Among the more obvious reasons is to protect against simple typographical errors, or the accidental error that is possible in transcribing numbers. The preservation of such papers is necessary to the support of the final report. The panel's charge was to "preserve" a "record".

I had requested only the "working papers" of this panel. To that Fisher did not respond. He pretended to answer an unasked question instead.

I chided him about this, saying, "Your panel report is a brilliant exercise in the specialized use of words to make them appear to say what they do not", said this was also true of his letter, and then specified his evasions and contradictions. He did not like it, but he did, if with petulance, add some of the missing detail. This includes an explicit disclosure of his role as boss:

> Once and for all, I have no working papers, drafts, etc. concerning the Panel review of the Kennedy autopsy report in my possession. The Panel met in Washington February 26 and 27, 1968 and drafted its report on Feb. 27, 1968. I pulled this together in the next few days and submitted copies to each member of the Panel, who edited them and returned them to me. I correlated the edited reports and once again submitted them to the Panel for final editing. Again the copies were returned to me and final copies typed and submitted sequentially to each member of the Panel for his signature. When all signatures were obtained I personally delivered the original and 5 signed copies to Mr Bruce Bromley and he subsequently sent one copy to Drs Carnes, Morgan, Moritz and myself and the original was submitted to the Justice Dept. I have not seen it since, but am informed the copy released by the Justice Dept was a photocopy of our report without changes of any kind from our submitted copy.
> In line with the agreement mentioned in the last paragraph of my letter of Feb 19 1970 Mr Bromley and I, or I, independently, destroyed all intermediate copies of the report. *

If the panel "drafted its report on February 27" and had met for only two days, it spent remarkably little time in study and deliberation.

But if it drafted its report, what Fisher "pulled together" remains a mystery. Either it did not draft its report or Fisher did something other than merely "pull" it "together".

There exists a question about what happened to the "working papers". Fisher avoided that. He did not account for them. No report of this length, complexity and detail can be prepared without careful and specific notes. None exist, according to every possible official source. The Archives, the Justice Department and the panel all claim not to have any - not a single scrap of paper other than the final version of the report - all earlier copies of which were destroyed, for no apparent need or reason.

How this could be permitted to happen after the scandal of the destruction of the autopsy draft and the disappearance of the notes supporting it one can only conjecture. It cannot be because the government and its panel did not know better; cannot be because the panel was without legal counsel; cannot be because Fisher was lacking in knowledge of the requirements of forensic medicine.

Nor can it be the proper way to "preserve" a record, the panel's responsibility.

But there is no question about what happened to all the "inter-

*See p. 596.

mediate" copies of the panel's report. Fisher, with or without Bromley's participation, personally "destroyed" all copies.

He falls short of saying it was in his recreation room.

Fisher sent copies of his letter to all the other panel members, including Bromley, and to the Department of Justice. None has disputed any word in it.

His concluding sentence said "this is the last correspondence of yours that I intend to answer with regard to this matter."

What more - what else - can he or anyone else say?

What else need be said once it is established that every scrap of paper was destroyed?

To "preserve a record" of how this President was killed, of how this government investigated his assassination, how it came into dominion?

Fisher said it all.

The words are his. He did not originate the idea. Orwell called it the "memory hole".

It is, as it has been, the way of evil governments from the beginning of governments.

There was, is and can be no innocence.

The panel knew its records were destroyed. Each member preserves a self-describing silence.

Each member knew the autopsy report was in serious error. Acknowledgment is in private. Each signed the public report saying the opposite, saying he supported what he knowingly and falsely described as the "medical conclusions" of the Warren Report.

How safer - or better - "solve" the assassination of the President who had begun to change national policy to liquidate the shameful foreign adventure that led to horrible official crimes, but also meant opportunities for promotion for the professional military and countless billions in profits for those who make the materials of modern war?

This, then, is the official "validation" of the "solution" to that crime and of the suzerainty of the Johnson regime and its entirely different national policy, a policy of undeclared war and the enrichment of the few therefrom.

It is not the whole story.

There remains that of the suppressed evidence and how I got what I did get, what had been withheld from the Commission and this panel, neither of which was anxious to get it and both of which could have. That follows.

20. SHANEYFELT, FRAZIER AND ORWELL IN THE FBI,

or HOW THEY GOT THEIR MAN

To date there have been but two legal assessments of two things involved in this book: the government's interpretation of the medical evidence it had and had not suppressed and my work with and investigation, recovery and analysis of that evidence. The government's interpretation did not survive either.

The first of these legal testings of fact in the traditional way, by the adversary system of justice, is presented in the preceding part of this book. The second was in the trial of Clay Shaw in New Orleans. Shaw had been charged by Jim Garrison, New Orleans District Attorney, with being part of a conspiracy to kill the President. Shaw's last attempt to avoid trial was rejected by the Supreme Court toward the end of 1968. The day of that decision, apparently motivated by his concept of the dramatic, Garrison set as the trial date the first full day of the Nixon administration, January 21, 1969.

My own investigations in New Orleans did not relate to Shaw as such. They were concerned chiefly with aspects of Oswald's career mishandled or entirely suppressed in the official investigations.

In the Shaw case, one element of the prosecution addressed the question, had there been a conspiracy to kill the President. In this area I agreed to help the prosecution in advance of and during the trial, but I was not there for the trial. I left to work on the Washington case and Part II of this book while the jury was being empaneled. My help consisted, in part, of suggesting witnesses from whom certain evidence could be adduced and in making parts of my own research, investigations and writings available. Part I of this book and my earlier writings about the medical evidence and what related to it was included. Xerox copies of Part I were given to Louis Ivon, the chief investigator, Alvin Oser and William Alford, the assistant district attorneys who were to handle this evidence in the trial. In addition, I spent hours with Oser, now a judge of New Orleans Criminal Court, and Alford, who quit the office in a great burst of publicity in mid-June 1971. The Sunday after the Friday of the first hearing in Judge Halleck's court in Washington, they met me at the New Orleans airport. I had taken the first plane out of Baltimore. We spent the rest of that day working in Oser's home, largely on this medical evidence I had mustered. I suggested what should be asked of those government witnesses who had been witnesses before the Warren Commission and provided the documentation I had rescued from the buried files, plus parts of this book for their use.

The January 21 trial date presented a much greater problem to the prosecution than it did to the defense. Garrison believed he would never be permitted to take the case to a jury, that federal power would in some way block him. Thus, there appears to have been no real Shaw investigation. The work in which I was engaged in my own interest was not duplicated by the Garrison office. The net effect is that the defense was admirably prepared, the more so because Tom Bethell, a trusted employee, had stolen Garrison's files and delivered them to Shaw's lawyers. But nobody in Garrison's office was working on the Shaw case. The assistant district attorneys, who expressed to me their dismay and bewilderment at the selection of so close a trial date (I was there when Garrison made the announcement before the TV cameras in the reception room of his suite of offices), had all been working on the regular office business. Alford had never had any connection with the assassination investigation. He had not even read a single book about it as of our Sunday conference. Others, like Oser, had done no work on it for more than a year. They were not only not prepared but had no time for adequate preparation.

This made such knowledge as I could impart more important.

Considering the diffuse evidence he had to handle in other areas of the prosecution, under the circumstances, Oser's use of my work is perhaps as good as could have been made and better than could reasonably be expected. His examination of Dr. Pierre Finck, then a full colonel, elicited complete confirmation of this work and my interpretation of the meaning of the medical fact.

Lyndal L. Shaneyfelt, the FBI's and the Commission's photographic expert, was called as witness by the prosecution; Robert A. Frazier, his ballistics counterpart, by the defense. Any unprejudiced appraisal of the testimony of these expert FBI agents leaves the official accounting of the assassination a shambles. Both show that the FBI "investigation" was never more than an effort to pretend that the predetermined conclusion was tenable. Their opinions about possibilities, no matter how remote, were translated by the Commission into expert opinions on the actualities.

In his February 14 questioning of Shaneyfelt about the single-bullet impossibility already fully explored, Oser asked,

"Am I correct in stating that you used the skin hole for Kennedy and the coat hole for Connally?"

Shaneyfelt replied, "Yes." He was then asked, "Why didn't you use Kennedy's coat?" He replied merely, "I don't know."

Obviously, these were neither identical nor comparable. With equal obviousness, Shaneyfelt, an experienced technician, knew that what he had done was wrong. He did know why he did it, whether or not it was wrong. The clothing, in the most comprehensible formulation, is movable. Connally's, at the moment of wounding, was not skin-tight and, therefore, could not represent the point of impact on his body. Only the point of impact on the body can be used in reconstructing a trajectory. Connally's coat could have been raised, twisted to either side, or both raised and twisted, which is the known fact captured on film and in evidence. It is intended as and is deceit.

Frazier's testimony extended for two days, February 21 and 22. Throughout it he swore that, when the point of impact on the President of the so-called nonfatal bullet was marked on the reconstruction pictures, it was placed in accord with the autopsy measurements. Two convenient citations of the New Orleans transcript (p.107) read:

I lined up the telescopic sight on that point. This point was determined from the medical testimony. They placed a mark on the coat -

That is, on the coat worn by the stand-in for the President in that reconstruction, made in Dallas May 24, 1964.

On the next page, "Therefore, they placed a mark to represent the actual bullet impact point ..."

Those who may prefer to doubt me will find Frazier's Warren Commission testimony more readily available for checking. In it he was asked by Arlen Specter (5H166) about exactly this, with Commission Exhibit 889, one of the reconstruction photos, in his hand. Asked to explain it, Frazier replied:

They had marked on the back of the President's coat the location of the wound, according to the distance from the top of his head down to the hole in his back as shown in the autopsy figures.

For the FBI, it is a minor complaint that there was no such measurement "from the top of his head." The measurement was from the mastoid. It also is the fact that the point of impact marked on the reconstruction picture by the FBI is not where the Commission said it was and in and of itself destroys the credibility of the entire official account of the assassination.

As reproduced by the Commission (18H87), this photo is not quite an inch and a half in diameter. However, it is clear enough. It shows the point of impact is about six inches down from the top of the collar. This Commission evidence contradicts and refutes the Commission's "solution" - makes it impossible.

Even the Sibert-O'Neill report (CD7:284 and JFK4-1) is FBI reporting contrary to the official claim. They locate this bullet wound at "below the shoulders and two inches to the right of the middle line of the spinal column." It is at this point where they say it "had entered at a downward position of 45 to 60 degrees" (sic). Here also they report what we have already established by other sources, the taking of "total body X-rays". This is, in fact, one of the more interesting parts of that report the Commission considered it unwise to publish. Here also is it disclosed that, at the time of the examination of the corpse, Humes already had knowledge of what had been done in Dallas, his explanation of the absence of a bullet in this hole being "since external cardiac massage had been performed at Parkland Hospital ..." the bullet had been forced out and lost.

Frazier was asked by Oser on cross-examination (p.76), "Did you consider all the evidence?" His answer was, "No, sir." Among the amplifications of what makes the FBI tick, what makes a competent, expert witness (p.87), "I don't consider my study of the Zapruder film a thorough study."

As the questioning proceeded, Frazier acknowledged a Gilbert-and-Sullivan FBI and an ignorance of the scene of the crime beyond belief in an "expert". He was asked if there could have been a shot fired from the Records Building (p.113). Now, that building is at the east end of Dealey Plaza, an official building and one of the more prominent landmarks. His answer is, "I don't know what the Records Building is." Oser showed it to him in a picture and Frazier replied, of this building diagonally across the street from the Texas School Book Depository Building, "I couldn't tell you. I was never there."

"There" is where the reconstruction of which he was part was made, Dealey Plaza!

None of the test-firings of the rifle he personally made accords in any way with those imputed to Oswald. Asked about the distances from the target in his testing and if those distances were even <u>approximations</u> of any during the actual assassination, in each case he swore, "I don't know" (p.130).

In his tests he used "a still target, not a moving target" to duplicate alleged shooting at a target going downhill and away on an S-shaped street (p.131), his "out" being quite the opposite of the official representation, he was "conducting accuracy and speed tests" only, and those in a vacuum. Or, providing inaccurate raw material to be wrongly used. Oser pinned him on this:

You were not interested in ascertaining whether or not someone on the sixth floor of the Texas School Book Depository could have gotten off three shots with the alleged accuracy you talked about at a moving target at the respective distance?

Frazier answered,

That was not the purpose of our test, otherwise we would have fired at moving targets.

That was <u>never</u> done, although these phony contrivances were then used by the Commission as exact and meaningful duplications. Asked if <u>any</u> moving-target tests were ever made, Frazier said, "No, sir, we didn't do that." (p.131)

When Oser returned to this (pp.138-9) to ask, "At any time, Mr. Frazier, did you conduct any of these firing tests with this particular rifle in any close proximity to what is alleged to have happened on November 22, 1963?" Frazier's apparently unembarrassed reply was simple: "No, sir."

Even the conditions of Frazier's own "accuracy" testing were fraudulent. "They did not" take into account "how long it took to draw the first bead" (p.140). Thus, all the otherwise unfaithfully-computed times attributed to Oswald, plus skills nobody in the entire world possessed, were also fraudulent because, in Frazier's own words (p.141),

It would take somewhat more time to aim the first shot, yes, sir. How much I have no idea of knowing (sic). You could take an hour to aim the first shot.

What a sense of humor! And how perfectly appropriate!

That Frazier knew his were fraudulent tests and did not reveal "an approximation of the time as to how long it took" him in his own "testing" to "get off three shots" he admitted in claiming duplication of reality "was no part of our test." His feeble defense-explanation befits the title, "Orwell in the FBI". It is,

We paid no attention to the time required, since we were instructed to time the shots from the sound of the first shot ... There was no point in recording an unknown aiming time before the test began (pp.141-2; emphasis added).

This merely repeats the unquestionable fact that the phony figures manufactured by fraudulent "testing" are even more fraudulent because they do not include the time to aim the first shot - and this deliberate fraud is what he was "instructed" to perform.

Naturally, none of this is in either the Commission evidence or its Report, for any of it would have made it impossible to get the members to sign the Report and would have totally discredited it to even the complacent press that uncritically accepted the issued fiction.

No less Gilbert and Sullivan is the weapon allegedly selected for "the crime of the century." Asked, "Can you tell us whether or not in rebolting the gun you had to move your eye away from the scope," Frazier answered that it was, indeed, "necessary." Why? "To prevent the bolt of the rifle from striking me in the face as it came to the rear" (p.148).

How is that for planning "the crime of the century": select a weapon not designed for a scope and so undependable it was called Mussolini's contribution to humanitarian warfare; and of all of these readily available, one of the most rickety, one a danger to use - a weapon that had to be taken away from the eye after each shot before it could be reloaded in order for the alleged assassin to keep from putting out his own eye!

Frazier demolished the official computations based on the weight of Bullet 399 by admitting what the Commission did not. The Commission talked about the removal of but a single sample for spectrographic testing, a sample of the jacket taken from the nose of the bullet. However, Frazier admitted he also "removed" samples from the "lead base" for testing. The significance of this is that the Commission pretends all the lead core missing can be accounted for in Governor Connally's wounds alone, something entirely false and fully denied by all the medical experts. But without this lie, the Commission could not begin to write a single-assassin, no-conspiracy Report. Frazier's acknowledgment that he removed some of the lead, a fact hidden with such care in everything of the Commission's, makes the impossible history credited to this bullet even more impossible. Some of the missing lead Frazier removed. It was not shed in Bullet 399's alleged criminal career. *

Now, the Commission's basic conclusions (R19) are "that there were three shots fired," and all "were fired by Lee Harvey Oswald."

Every official involved had to have known this was completely

*See p. 602.

impossible, not alone for the certified duffer Oswald, but for the world's best shots. Oser concluded this questioning, the results of which were so widely ignored by the press, by asking (p.194):

Can you name anybody in the Federal Bureau of Investigation or any expert rifleman under the Bureau's direction who can accomplish the same feat that is alleged to have been accomplished by the Warren Commission, namely that the rifleman was in the sixth floor some 60 feet off the ground level at a distance of 265 feet away at frame 313, and with a moving target?

The syntax was jumbled, as is not uncommon in extemporaneous speaking, especially under stress, but Frazier understood the question. Himself one of the very best and fastest of riflemen, he replied: "I know of no such tests or individuals."

In plain English, none of the required, proper tests were ever made and there is nobody, not the world's very best rifleman, who could duplicate the feat attributed to the incompetent, inexperienced Oswald.

It may seem incredible, for the integrity and conclusions of the entire investigation have been totally destroyed countless times, but the major media simply will not pay attention. It does not report these facts, this news.

Frazier even admitted that no effort was made to solve the crime, the sole official purpose being to see if the government could hope to get away with claiming that the preordained "solution" was possible. Neither he nor anyone else ever tried to find out if any of the shots could have been fired from any other point, what everyone assumed any investigation would have to begin with:

Q. Did you test any other originating point from where the rifle may have been shot?
A. I didn't test any and I don't know of anyone else who did.
Q. Why didn't you test any other originating point other than the Texas School Book Depository Building?
A. I was not asked to.

This arrogance is the Nuremberg pleading, the Eichmann defense.

It is, unfortunately, not an exception to the FBI rule. It and Frazier did exactly the same thing in the "investigation" of the assassination of Dr. Martin Luther King, Jr., thus framing James Earl Ray as another lone assassin after perfecting an illegal extradition from Great Britain (FRAME-UP,441-2,505) with the same kind of corruption and deception.

Frazier swore in an affidavit filed in the British court that was - with the connivance of the British court and the British government - later confiscated by the American government:

Because of distortion due to mutilation and insufficient marks of value, I could draw no conclusions as to whether or not the submitted bullet was fired from the submitted rifle.

To complain that there ought to be a law against this is to protest too little. There are laws, but Frazier's employer, the Department of Justice, enforces them, giving them and him immunity. This amounts to a perjurious oath and much more.

First of all, there was no "submitted bullet". There was only a fragment removed from the King corpse. The bullet exploded, a fact that was hidden with great care in Frazier's and all other evidence but is unquestionable. To hide the truth, the medical evidence was suppressed and distorted. Sound familiar?

To say merely that there was "distortion and mutilation" when to his knowledge the bullet exploded and he had but a part of it and no more; and to say it is this, not the absence of the rest of the bullet, that kept him from drawing conclusions, is at best a planned deception disguised in cunning language.

227

Under the law, there is no identification in Frazier's affidavit. In the absence of proof that the fatal missile was fired from the alleged rifle, to the exclusion of all other rifles ever made, the legal presumption is that it was not fired from that weapon. So, Frazier got around this with the gratuity that the sample he had was "consistent" in its characteristics with the characteristics of the so-called Ray rifle, which is to say no more than that it was similar to the characteristics of a fair percentage of all the rifles ever made.

In the absence of cross-examination - and the Department of Justice conveniently arranged for that, too, to be impossible - he and it got away with this gross deception and false swearing.

This misrepresentation of evidence is a perfect parallel of the false ballistics "evidence" so vital to the earlier framing of Sacco and Vanzetti. In that case, another Frazier swore with the same word, "consistent", that the fatal bullet could have been fired from the alleged murder weapon when he was certain it had not been.

The FBI learns its lessons well.

With his Shaneyfelts and Fraziers, the unending, indispensable J. Edgar Hoover and the sacrosanct FBI can "solve" any crime.

Especially the assassination of a President Hoover hated.

In murder cases, the autopsy is a medical and a legal necessity. Among its functions is to establish the cause of death. Supposedly, it is not an argument but a statement of medical fact. It is supposed to help solve the crime. The autopsy performed on the President was not even a rational argument. When what is irrelevant and outside the personal knowledge of the doctors and what they omitted and what they hedged on, what they were untruthful about and what they did not do that they were required to do, are all added together, the autopsy remained, in the strongest defense of it that can be made, a very doubtful document. It could not stand alone. It had to be buttressed.

The first and comparatively honest reconstruction by the Secret Service, made December 5, 1963, before the last part of the autopsy, the supplement, had been forwarded by the Navy, established the impossibility of any single assassin, as I brought to light in WHITEWASH II. That reconstruction says three different shots hit the car's occupants, the first and third hitting the President only and the second the governor alone. Pictures were posed showing the position of the limousine at the time each of the shots impacted. These I published in that book (p.248). The Commission hid them in its files, from whence I resurrected them.

In an earlier account dated November 28, 1963, the Secret Service reported that "President Kennedy ... was shot. Immediately thereafter Governor Connally ... was shot once. The President was then shot the second time." Again this is not in that 26-volume literary monstrosity, not in that definitive Report. This also I published in facsimile in the same book (p.168).

That there since has been only complete silence about this evidence from all officials and all their unofficial spokesmen and apologists is a legitimate and effective point, but not the one that here needs emphasis. In and of itself, the Secret Service reconstruction of the crime destroys the subsequent official one. It does this thoroughly and completely while it still does not account for all the shots known to have been fired. Therefore, it had to be hidden; and for the official, predetermined "solution" to be made to appear credible, the arcane sciences of the FBI were enlisted. Frazier and Shaneyfelt are two of the more important recruits, practitioners of this "science". They were willing recruits in the campaign to build a false "solution". Their work, especially their May 1964 "reconstruction", was intended to lend credibility to the incredible, predetermined official conclusions and most of all to the incompetent, inadequate, unacceptable and untenable autopsy report.

These brief selections from the New Orleans testimony, of truth so carefully hidden in Washington and in the Report - if not also from the Commissioners - establish the true and phony character of the Shaneyfelt-Frazier-FBI-Commission staff attempt to validate the false by means of "expert" testimony dealing with photographic and ballistics "proofs".

What this really shows is that no effort was made to solve the crime, that all effort was directed at framing Oswald as the lone assassin, and that only by lies and misrepresentations could there have been the slightest pretense that this modern FBI "science" in any way supported the unsupportable post-mortem.

21. FLATULENT FINCK AND HIS IN-COURT SPELLING BEE

Arrogance, self-importance, a determination to be judge, prosecution and defense lawyers and witness - to ask the questions he wanted to answer or to answer not the questions asked of him but those he wanted asked - a scarcely hidden and fierce partisanship highly improper in a man of science and an expert witness in forensic medicine in a criminal proceeding - permeate all 269 pages of Colonel Pierre Finck's New Orleans testimony of February 24 and 25, 1969.

Finck was cocky. He had been expected to be a prosecution witness. The prosecution, not satisfied with what it had gotten from Shaneyfelt, changed signals and decided not to call those other government witnesses who had testified before the Warren Commission. The defense then called Finck as its witness.

Tom Bethell had stolen the prosecution plans and witness list and given them to the defense. Members of the detached, objective press had been visiting these witnesses before the trial began, intimidating them in the guise of interviewing them. During the trial, this same delegation of the press, which violated a noble tradition by becoming part of one side of a case it reported, augmented with new recruits, some from out of town, held nightly strategy meetings, the better to fulfill its concept of the tradition of "dispassionate" reporting.

And so Finck, perhaps, felt he had reason to be cocky.

He soon faced a problem: Bethell had not been able to steal the plans for the Finck questioning because they did not exist at the time he delivered the prosecution's case to the defense lawyers. Nor did Bethell have copies of the part of this book which provided the basis for Finck's questioning.

His testimony should have created a national scandal. It was so inadequately and incompletely reported it went almost unnoticed then and is unknown today.

It entirely confirms the serious charges of this book. "Scandal" is hardly a sufficient description, but there is no word for that which has no precedent in American if not modern civilized history.

With major reporters involved in the defense and so many others of them and newspaper management so strongly opposed to Garrison on the one hand and any responsible airing of any fact of the assassination on the other, the shortcomings of the reporting are understandable and explained.

Of the autopsy surgeons, Finck is the one with claim to extensive experience with gunshot wounds. He was head of the army's Wound Ballistics Branch. Accredited in forensic pathology, of the trio performing the autopsy, he had experience in that specialty. Once Oser began to question him with vigor, Finck pretended his was a minor role. He almost did not belong there, one would think. But precisely because he was schooled and accredited in the legal aspects of medicine is his courtroom behavior hardly that of the dispassionate man of science serving the law, truth and justice.

He even argued with the judge!

Fully analyzing his testimony could make an overly-long book. There here is no space for that. Nor is there the need. Therefore, unparalleled as are the reluctant confessions and admissions wrung from him, verbally kicking and scratching all the way, excerpting on a few of the points should suffice.

But if one wanted to weave a real, honest-to-goodness military conspiracy out of the assassination of President Kennedy - to write an "Eighth Day of May", so to speak - Colonel Finck is a real help.

And he has real, very real, and higher-ranking military help.

For the military did move in at Bethesda, did take over, did put all civilians out and keep them out until the corpse was ready for the embalmers, did see to it that there was no real autopsy - and did threaten all the military who were there with court-martial if they so much as breathed aloud about anything that happened.*

Reading is not believing with much of Finck's testimony. It is difficult to believe such a man possible and the uninformed may find it impossible to believe some of his testimony can be true.

He appears pedantic, impatient with those hardly-tolerated ig- noramuses so much beneath him - judge and lawyers - so little worth the time they are taking from him, so far below understanding which he alone can have. Whether a subconscious compulsion or some other pecu- liar psychological quirk, a remnant of some hidden elementary-grade relic far in his past, or a deliberate way of showing the contempt his words and manner so clearly indicate he felt for the mere mortals of a system of justice or God alone knows what, Finck spelled out almost everything.

Literally.

Not that he was asked to. He just did it. Including the sim- plest words. This begins with the first thing asked of him (p.2) by defense counsel Irving Dymond, that he "state" his name. In the next few pages alone, the words unsolicitedly spelled out for those stupid ones who had merely completed college and law school, opposing counsel and the judge, or, possibly, for the unerudite of the press, include Frankfurt and forensic (p.4), forum and wound (p.5), Edgewood (p.7), riots (p.8), Humes and Boswell (p.9). And this was only the beginning. It goes on and on, diminishing somewhat when he was pressed on cross- examination, but persists as a compulsion I have never encountered in the examination of thousands of witnesses, some with accents which make their English almost incomprehensible. It does not characterize his Warren Commission testimony.

For whatever reason, Finck conducted an in-court spelling bee for those he regarded as so clearly inferior to him in every way. And this accords with his permeating contempt for the proceeding and its participants that is often specific, is rarely hidden, and is particu- larly inappropriate in an allegedly impartial and dispassionate expert witness, most of all in one with his training in the legal aspects of medicine. This includes the requirements of evidence and the restraints and obligations imposed upon expert witnesses. He may, perhaps, have intended masking the legal and scientific inadequacies of his previous testimony and record that he knew he would have to face.

Finck is undisguised in his open, deliberate evading of ques- tions when those questions called for answers he, from his lofty and superior position and understanding, just did not want to answer. Much of his deliberate evasion of response and the clear meaning of the ques- tion asked is undisguised. Often he is skilled, so smooth that neither judge nor prosecutor caught him. But, when caught and ordered to re- spond, he out-and-out refused to do as directed. He undertook to give everyone else legal advice from the witness chair until finally told by patient Judge Edward Haggerty to suspend his legal lectures, that he, Finck, was not running the show.

Finck's testimony grew increasingly reluctant as Oser questioned him. Finck was a veritable verbal, medical snake, impossible to believe, most of all because of his experience, training, background and former use by the Warren Commission as an expert to authenticate what he had

* See p. 303.

to know was a fake; because he consciously sought to hide evidence that decency and honor compelled of him almost as much as did his function as an expert witness in a criminal proceeding; and because, instead of answering the questions asked of him, he pretended more congenial questions were asked and to the unasked questions he volunteered unasked and self-serving answers. His appearance was an unending argument in which usually he was not responsive. Whenever he could get away with it, it was also volunteered and voluble propaganda.

One example is his response to a very simple direction, that he mark on the back of the shirt of one of defense counsel the spot the rear, non-fatal wound entered the President. Not content with doing as told, as he knew, all he was supposed to do, Finck then launched into an entire page (p.12) of propaganda, for all the world as though he had been asked a question, which he had not been, beginning with an orientation of the wound by what his training told him is wrong, only moving parts of the body. This means the wound is not and cannot thus be located, for there is no way of knowing the position of each of the movable parts at the time of measurement.

The verbal torrent gushed out, all improper, all non-responsive, all propaganda I think compelled by a guilty conscience, a compulsion for self-justification. One of the gross examples is, "When examining this wound, I saw the regular edges pushed inward, what we call inverted." He then repeated this same thing, the second time spelling "inverted".

This was deliberate deception.

There was, to Finck's knowledge, an explanation for the condition of the tissues at the edge of this wound and the fact that they were "pushed inward". They had, in actuality, been pushed inward at that hospital before his arrival but to his subsequent knowledge. This most unscientific probing was by his naval colleague, Doctor Humes, who had, unnecessarily, having already taken X-rays, in which lead glows like fluorescent light, pushed that tissue in with his little fingers!

So, Finck's outpouring of the unasked, unsought and false is not without purpose. It is propaganda, not fact or testimony. It was not in response to the very simple direction, not even a question, that he "point out on his (Shaw's lawyer's) anatomy the approximate location of the wound," a request made a page and a half earlier. It is typical of Finck.

Even Dymond thought he had better bring this to an end before the judge did and tried to stop Finck when he interrupted his propagandizing to spell "inverted" for the blighted judge, lawyers, court stenographer and world press. Dymond spoke only four words before he, too, was interrupted by his witness, Finck, who was determined to control both defense and prosecution proffers of evidence. The omniscient Finck cut him off after "Doctor, did you make - " to insist on adding further propaganda, his reiteration in different words of the alleged appearance of the edges of this wound.

This is just openers (pp.11-3). It never stopped. It gives the feel of the enormous ego, the man who alone could put it all together, the man who dominated and sought to dominate what evidence could be sought and obtained as it relates to the autopsy and its procedures.

And when the defense lawyer whose witness he was finally turned him off before there was an eruption from the judge or opposing counsel, Finck returned to his spelling fetish, with words so difficult for lawyers, the judge and the press to understand, "abrasion", "entry" and "entrance" all spelled out on page 13.

But, even in the presentation of the defense side of the case, it was not long before the sneaky Finck, who might better have accomplished his illicit purposes by saying much less and letting the skilled lawyer Dymond run the show, started making the most serious errors in judgment and volunteering what would, in any decent society, be the basis of criminal charges against him and his associates.

232

For example, he was asked a simple question to which he should - and knew he should - have answered merely "yes" or "no": "Now, Doctor, did you examine on the remains of the late President Kennedy a wound in the frontal neck region?" Finck launched into a combination of futile self-justification and a mumbo-jumbo of meaningless pontification, complete with another needless spelling, this time inaccurately, adding a characterization of that wound as one of exit, while also admitting he did not then see it. After a half-page of this rambling, he went into a double hearsay, what he knew was improper and incompetent, that on the day after the autopsy, "Dr. Humes called the surgeons of Dallas." This is hearsay, for Finck was not there, and error, for Humes phoned only one doctor. Finck added, "and he was told that they" - hearsay twice removed, for Finck did not hear what, if anything, was said - before Oser interrupted, "I object to the hearsay." (p.14)

Then Dymond pretended to caution Finck - a caution entirely unnecessary to a man certified in forensic science - "You may not say what the surgeons of Dallas told Dr. Humes. That would be hearsay." Finck argued with him, beginning with, "I have to base my interpretation on all the facts available and not on one fact only ..." Patently, this is false. The proper and possible answers are "yes", "no", or "I am not certain." If necessary, Finck could then ask permission to amplify his answer. Here it was not necessary except for propaganda, which is not the purpose of a legal proceeding. Dymond, of course, was quite anxious for Finck to load the record with all the propaganda and irrelevancies he could get in and to complicate Oser's alseady serious problems as much as he could. So, he let Finck carry on without interruption for most of a page (15) until the judge, for the first but not the last time, called Finck to book.

Knowing full well it was entirely improper, Finck had gotten to where he argued, "I insist on that point, and that telephone call to Dallas from Dr. Humes - " when Judge Haggerty chided him, "You may insist on the point, Doctor, but we are going to do it according to the law. If it is legally objectionable, even if you insist, I am going to have to sustain the objection."

(As a measure of Finck's knowledge, even of hearsay, I note that Humes made not "that telephone call" but two of them.)

Dymond took the cue, brought Finck back to what he had volunteered and thus gotten into the record, "when the X-rays I requested showed no bullets in the cadaver of the President," to broaden the interpretation to what may well have made it perjurious in fact as it was in intent, "you say the X-rays showed no bullet or projectile in that area of the President or in any other area?"

Finck still would not give a simple "yes" or "no" response. He first said that "I requested whole-body X-rays" and then added that the only "fragments" they saw in the X-rays were in those of the head and "due to another bullet wound."

The line crossed, this is perjury. But nothing will happen, unless Finck gets another promotion. He got one after similar perjurious testimony before the Warren Commission.

Prior to this New Orleans testimony, as we have seen, Finck had given Attorney General Clark, who had become one of the needless victims of all this official dishonesty, a statement in which all three autopsy doctors acknowledge the presence of fragments of bullet in precisely this area, making their earlier Warren Commission testimony as criminal in character as Finck's here is.

There were fragments there. These fragments alone destroy the official "solution" to the crime. Therein lies sufficient official motive for both the perjury and its protection, in the case of the Warren Commission, its subornation also. This is not the only such testimony, but it is clear enough so the repetitions (as on pp.47,125,127 and especially 137) are not needed to establish criminality and gross and deliberate deception.

Finck made other errors, engaged in further deceptions, but to

233

rehash all of them at this point, significant as any one is in court and in an investigation of the murder of a President, would be to coal Newcastle. The next one worthy of special attention begins on page 48. By that time Finck had found it necessary to help the local yokels of the legal, judicial and journalistic fraternities by spelling out such difficult and unusual words as "entered", "cratering", "crater", "perforating", "missile", "scheme", "cranial", "inner", "shattering", "in", "out" - and "path" two different times.

In no case was he asked to, never was he not understood, not once did he have to repeat anything. How depressing it must have been for this towering intellect, this one man in whom the providential deity had deposited the sum total of legal and medical knowledge and understanding, to have to associate with such an ignorant rabble as those New Orleanian lawyers and judge, those backwoods court reporters and the illiterate representatives of the press of the entire world.

By page 48, however, Finck was running backward fast, as in insisting, when asked merely if he had not been "a co-author" of the autopsy report, which he had signed and had affirmed under oath before the Commission, "Wait, I was called in as a consultant to look at the wounds; that doesn't mean I am running the show."

This was the break for which I had carefully prepared Oser that long Sunday in his Metairie home, for which he had documentation, including the first part of this book.

Before long Finck had admitted that the autopsy doctors were mere figureheads, that "an Army General, I don't remember his name," was "running the show" (p.48). But, Finck was "one of the three qualified pathologists standing at the autopsy table."

"Was this Army General a qualified pathologist?"

"No."

"Was he a doctor?"

"No."

Could Finck remember the name? Again, "No, I can't. I don't remember."

After all, why should a mere expert in forensic pathology remember anything about an Army General who could ruin his career? Or bring charges against him (a reality to be considered in the proper context)? Or who could not, in an autopsy room of another branch of the service, really be the man "running the show".

If for some reason not immediately clear, a reason Finck was careful to avoid exploring, with all the "insisting" and volunteering that characterizes his testimony, the buck had to be passed upward, the Army does not control Naval installations. This was the Navy Hospital, part of the Naval Medical Center, and the upward chain of command goes from the commander of the hospital, whom we shall not forget, to the commander of the entire installation, who has attracted our attention and will again, to the Surgeon General of the Navy, who - to now - has succeeded in avoiding any attention.

But no general of any army rank controls any naval installation - not normally, anyway. So, the next day he changed his testimony about the man in charge being a general, saying he was an admiral.

Oser eased off a bit for several pages and then came back to this strange and seemingly unnecessary factor in an open and above-board autopsy of a President, the domination of it by the top brass who had no business interfering and no competence to make decisions.

While claiming that, in addition to this unnamed general, "there were law enforcement officers, military people with various ranks, and you have to co-ordinate the operation according to directions," a rather Nazi-like concept of the performance of an autopsy under any conditions (pp.48-9), Finck resisted efforts to get him to identify these others (p.51), resorting to generalities, pretending he had been too busy to

234

note the names of the top brass, conspicuous because they served no medico-legal function.

Even for high military muckty-mucks, hardened as they may be to the consequences of war, there would seem to be no joy in watching the dissecting of a human body, not ordinarily, anyway, not for normal people. Nor does it seem that medical personnel would find pleasure in watching the taking apart of a President. Surely most normal people would prefer to avoid so gruesome an examination, especially because it was made on the corpse of a murdered President.

Nor were these high-ranking military personages required as official observers. The Secret Service served that function.

Finck departed from strict truth (p.52) in claiming that "The room was crowded with military and civilian personnel and Federal agents, Secret Service agents, FBI agents ..." The only "civilians" permitted in the autopsy room were the "Federal agents". Other than these agents, despite Finck's claim, there were no civilians there during the autopsy, the military having seen to that. They posted a military guard and excluded civilians.

Finck did acknowledge he did not have "to take orders from this army general that was there directing the autopsy ... because there were others, there were admirals."

"Admirals?" asked Oser, to whom I had given the names of two.

"Oh, yes," Finck expanded, "there were admirals," adding in attempted self-defense the Eichmann/Nuremberg concept utterly irrelevant in the United States and in a medico-legal function, "and when you are a lieutenant-colonel in the Army you just follow orders ..."

Now, it happens that the all-anticipating military establishment did anticipate medico-legal needs. The specific and written orders and directions, special regulations and an entire Armed Forces Institute of Pathology manual on "The Autopsy", do not include being told what to do and not to do for political purposes, real or fancied.

Finck continued (with no omission in quotation), "and at the end of the autopsy we were told - as I recall it, it was by Admiral Kenney, the Surgeon General of the Navy - this is subject to verification - we were specifically told not to discuss the case," to which he added "without coordination with the Attorney General."

That never-ending effort to blame the Kennedys!

(Although the Navy declined to be helpful when the admiral's name first appeared in news accounts of the New Orleans testimony as "Kiney" and thereafter was variously spelled, Paul Hoch checked three standard sources. The 1968-9 edition of Who's Who in America reads: "born 2/19/04; M.D. U.Cin. 1929; advanced through grades to rear adm., 1957; surgeon general of the Navy, 1961-5; rear admiral, ret., presently Dir. Med. Edn., N. Broward Hosp Dist. Office address: 1600 S. Andrews Av., Fort Lauderdale, Fla." The Fort Lauderdale telephone-book listing of Edward C. Kinney is Middle River Drive. The New York Times for January 28, 1965, announced his plans to retire on page 11, column 5.)

Throughout his testimony, reluctant as he was to admit it and hard as Shaw's lawyers tried to testify for him, to come to his rescue when he was pressed and did not want to admit what was damaging to the official account of the Presidential assassination, Finck nonetheless was forced to acknowledge that the nature of the examination made and not made was not determined by the requirements of the law or regulation but by direct orders given on the spot by top brass.

Important as was the tracing of the path of that magical Bullet 399 through the President's body to learn if, in fact, there was any bullet that did or could have taken this guessed-at path, Finck finally admitted the doctors were ordered not to do this obviously necessary thing (2/24,pp.115-9,148-9;2/25,pp.4,8,32-6). First he tried to blame Robert Kennedy (p.115). In the end, after what amounts to repeated evading and lying, he admitted the orders were military orders and had nothing to do with the family. Not until the second day of his testimony was the deliberateness of his intended deception and the viciousness of this military effort to blame the family for the gross and shameful deficiencies of the autopsy fully laid bare.

Toward the end of the first day, he acknowledged that this was not "a complete autopsy under the definition used by the American Board of Pathology" (p.199). This seemingly full admission is far from it. The military autopsy manual requires examination of the thorax and neck organs. It has special sections describing the incisions, exposure and inspections to be made.

What is required for everyone else, including the unwanted, the abandoned, the dregs, apparently is too good for the President of the United States when the ever-loving, dedicated military takes over.

Yet even into the second day he tried to pretend the required examination, the tracing of the alleged track of the alleged non-fatal bullet through the cadaver, was not done "not to create unnecessary mutilation of the cadaver" (p.17). Of course, this was entirely false, the cadaver having been laid open pretty completely, much as he tried to weasel (pp.32-6).

"The chest cavity of the President" was laid open (p.33).

"The usual Y-cut incision" was made (p.34).

This lays open "the rib cage - so you can get the vital organs of the body" (p.34).

And this means all the organs. Reproducing such a picture is unpleasant. It is impossible with the President. It was not impossible with Oswald, who had no rights to privacy. Nor were the rights of his survivors considered, there being nothing that needed hiding for which this could have provided a convenient excuse as there was with the President.

So, those who do not have access to medical texts can see just how completely the necessary "Y" cut does mutilate a body by consulting page 119 of Dallas Police Chief Jesse Curry's futile attempt at justifying his own and the Dallas police record, his JFK Assassination File. Oswald's genitals are hidden by a sheet. From below the upper edge of this sheet to several ribs below the nipples there is a single, straight cut upward. At this point the arms of the "Y" begin, two angular lines to the armpits, where there are smaller "Ys", back to the chest and up to the shoulder.

As illustrated in the military autopsy manual, the "Y" cut begins above both armpits, into the shoulder joints, is semicircular to below the nipples, and from the center extends downward to the genitals.

This is not "mutilation" enough? It was done.

With this much mutilation acknowledged, is it credible that a slightly upward probing would cause objectionable "mutilation"?

It is a lie. The purpose of the lie is to suppress evidence.

But, regardless, it was an examination required to be made. And it was not made.

The reason had nothing to do with the alleged wish of the family, that unending and shameful effort to blame the bereaved family for the deficiencies of the autopsy.

Finck admitted that Admiral Galloway personally ordered changes in the autopsy report after it was drafted (second day, p.4-5).

The autopsy surgeons were threatened by high authority (p.5) if they said a word. The man in charge was not this unnamed general but "the Adjutant General" (he meant the Surgeon General) of the Navy, "Admiral Kinney" (p.6).

Skilled and resourceful as he was in misrepresenting, evading and deceiving, in not answering questions, in arguing with everybody, in refusing to behave as a witness, requiring repeated, patient admonition by the judge, Finck, for all his gall and verbosity, also made other sensational disclosures, besides these.

Those autopsy notes I had traced, the existence of which was repeatedly and in writing denied by the Archives, although my "chain of possession" was from the autopsy table to the Commission witness stand? They did exist, made by all three surgeons, Finck included. He is the one who devised the meaningless means of measuring, flexible measurement, from the mastoid. He also did some of the measuring, and he made notes he turned in. In his presence and to his observations, the others also made handwritten notes that seem to have found their way into the official memory hole for they no longer have official existence. Can there be a better way of assuring the integrity of the investigation, preserving the reputation of the military, than by the destruction of the evidence? Of course not! Therefore, it was destroyed.

References to the making of measurements and taking of notes abound in Finck's testimony, including pages 69-70,76,80-5,92-6,123, 129-31,149-50,159-60.

Despite his evasiveness, Finck is specific enough on this point. Of his own note-taking:

When I walked out of that autopsy room I didn't have notes with me, to the best of my recollection. I remember taking measurements and giving them to Dr. Humes and Dr. Boswell. (p.96)

What immediately precedes this identifies these as written notes he personally made during the autopsy. They used small pieces of paper besides the autopsy descriptive sheet. Twice on this one page alone Finck admits that both the others also took notes:

"I saw both Dr. Humes and Dr. Boswell taking notes at the time of the autopsy" and "both of them made notes during the autopsy."

Among the many impermissible, intolerable facts established beyond doubt by Finck's New Orleans testimony is that, although all the medical men knew that the alleged path of the allegedly nonfatal bullet through the President's body had to be traced, it was not done; all made written notes required to be preserved, and they no longer exist; what he participated in cannot and does not qualify as a full autopsy; top military brass immediately took over the autopsy, severely limiting what the surgeons could do and ordering them not to do what they had to do, what had to be done; the commanding officer of the Navy Medical Center ordered changes in the written autopsy after it was prepared, the most substantive changes; and the autopsy surgeons were threatened with retaliation if they opened their mouths.

This much the reluctant Finck did admit. There was much more he did not. For example, all medical personnel present at the autopsy or who merely passed through the room while it was being conducted received the same threat, in writing.

Aside from the grossest improprieties in taking over a medico-legal function required to be completely independent, especially when that is an inquest into how a President was assassinated, can this threatening, this ordering of what must be left out or altered, do other than feed conspiratorial belief about the involvement of the military in some kind of plot?

Why should any general, any admiral, any officer of any rank, want to interfere in any way with what the autopsy report would say about how the President was killed? Why should anybody order that required examinations not be made and reported?

Is there any reasonable non-conspiratorial explanation that can be made?

Why should anyone in the whole world, assuming there had been no conspiracy of any kind, have wanted anything but the most complete, the most dependable, the most unfettered autopsy examination and report, made with total and complete independence?

One that would permit the existence of no unasked or unanswered questions.

Inevitably, this record requires better answers from the military than silence, lies, destructions and evasions. Something more than the self-serving falsehoods of the TV tube, the evasions and lies of the unpublicized testimony, performances that I believe involve criminal conduct requiring criminal action.

During the autopsy, news correspondent Benjamin Bradlee, a close friend of the slaughtered President and his bereaved wife, was comforting her in the 17th-floor tower suite at the Naval Hospital. Kenneth O'Donnell, the appointments secretary, invited Bradlee to attend the autopsy. Bradlee later became managing editor of The Washington Post. He remembered O'Donnell's openness in offering to have him present at the autopsy and, naturally enough, assumed there could not possibly have been anything wrong with it, else would he have been invited to the cutting-up? This, also naturally, had much to do with the subsequent editorial policy of The Washington Post, where Bradlee's influence was and remains great, if not with the beliefs of the media in general.

Whether or not one is a close friend, watching an autopsy is a gruesome prospect for the most steel-nerved and iron-stomached. For a close friend, it must be more unbearable, even to consider. This is anything but a criticism of Bradlee for not attending the autopsy, for remaining in the tower suite to attempt to comfort the newly-widowed friend. I doubt I could have brought myself to observe such an examination.

But what Bradlee does not know and then did not have any reason to suspect is that Kenny O'Donnell had no more to do with who could or could not be in that autopsy room than he had over who could pass through the gates of Heaven.

But had Bradlee been made of tougher stuff than I, the whole needless national trauma, all those unnecessary tragedies in the wake of the greatest one, might have been avoided.

And the truth might have been forced out.

Had he or any other competent reporter sought access and been refused it, he would have noticed that not the Secret Service but the military had taken control. Had the press asked for the customary "pool report", the truth might have come out. Had anyone any way of learning and reporting that all civilians were expelled from the autopsy room and kept out by military force; had anyone had any way of reporting the complete military takeover of this civilian, nonmilitary function; or had any had any way of reporting the completely unacceptable character of the incomplete and inadequate examination of the corpse and that this, too, had been ordered and required by the military, this fake inquest could not have been suppressed for those eleven months during which the unacceptable Report was being made more acceptable by controlled leaks to the essentially unquestioning press.

Much if not all of subsequent history might have been different.

22. BACK FROM THE MEMORY HOLE

To quote William Manchester (<u>The Death of a President</u>) in a work like this is to cast swine before pearls. His is a work of unrivaled inaccuracy. Were Pulitzer or Nobel prizes to be awarded for conspicuous inaccuracy, Manchester would be without peer. Only were bad taste to enter into the weighing could he have a rival, Jim Bishop (<u>The Day Kennedy Was Shot</u>).

In an era of commissioned and rewritten and simplified history, there is, unfortunately, no other choice, the assassinated President's physician not having been a witness before the successor President's Commission that brought us this definitive study, this Report to ask and answer all questions, this last word on how the President was cut down and all that is relevant to it, including how his corpse fell into the hands and under the scalpels of the military.

Perhaps the best explanation of the omission of George G. Burkley as a witness is that he is the <u>one</u> medical man who <u>was</u> in the motorcade when the crime was committed, <u>was</u> in the plane on the way back, <u>was</u> in the Navy autopsy room, and <u>was</u> the recipient of all the official evidence.

It is to Admiral George B. Burkley that <u>all</u> that is missing was delivered, <u>all</u> that was withheld from the Warren Commission <u>was</u> funneled.

Some of that is still missing. Some I have recaptured. And some makes no sense.

Burkley was a ranking military man and a ranking medical man.

Could there be better reasons for <u>not</u> calling him as a witness?

Or a better one for giving him all that did not reach the Commission?

Or, one might ask, a better reason for wondering about the military and the autopsy, the military and a possible conspiracy?

It is my resurrection of the first of those suppressed Burkley papers that I removed from the first part of this book for further effort. It and the results are here for the first time reported.

<u>Not</u>, I emphasize, found <u>anywhere or in any form in the Commission's files, Report or interests</u>. Not even in its "TOP SECRET" executive sessions, which I do have, from which even its staff was banned and denied access to the transcripts.

Thus it is that we are bankrupted into dependence upon Bishop and Manchester. So the reader can, after four years, better estimate that literary nightmare in which Washington became a rewritten Camelot, Manchester's two preceding paragraphs are included:

The clutch of men standing around her emptied glass after glass, and in the staff cabin Kilduff was setting something of a record. Mac was drinking gin and tonic as though it were going out of style. He later calculated that between Dallas and Washington he consumed nearly two-thirds of a bottle of gin. Like the Abbe Sieyes, who regarded the Reign of Terror as something to live through, each of them was trying to survive the hideous ride, and if liquor would help they wanted it.

239

Liquor didn't help. It didn't do anything. Nothing tes-
tifies more persuasively to the passengers' trauma than their
astonishing immunity to alcohol. O'Donnell's instinct had
been correct; in time of stress, when emotions have been rav-
aged and shredded, spirits are usually medicinal. Up in the
control cabin Colonel Swindal, who couldn't touch anything
now, was promising himself a tall jigger when he reached his
MATS office at Andrews. He would keep that promise--and discover that it was like drinking tap water. Kilduff, having
downed more than enough to anesthetize him, gave up in despair. He was still cold sober. And when Ben Bradlee met
Mrs. Kennedy and her escorts at Bethesda Naval Hospital, he
was outraged; from their conduct he assumed that no one had
had sense enough to give them something to drink.
     The decision to move to Bethesda was made by her. Dr.
Burkley, kneeling in the aisle, explained that because the
President had been murdered there would have to be an autopsy. "Security reasons," he said, required that the hospital be military. The option lay between Bethesda and
Walter Reed.
     "Of course, the President was in the Navy," he said
softly.
     "Of course," said Jacqueline Kennedy. "Bethesda." It
was then that Godfrey left to place his exasperating call
stipulating an ambulance.
     "I'll stay with the President until he is back at the
White House," Burkley promised, and he, too, left. (pp.349-
50)

     As befits Camelot, these are the one-name characters incom-
pletely identified (and not Manchester's closest buddies):

     Malcolm Kilduff was assistant press secretary.

     Kenneth O'Donnell was appointments secretary.

     Colonel James Swindal was pilot of the President's 707, then
called Air Force One.

     Brigadier General Godfrey McHugh was then the President's Air
Force aide.

     Andrews refers to the military airfield at Washington, Andrews
Air Force Base.

     In Bishop's also-rancid rendering, here is how the same goose-
fat comes out (pp.274-5):

     General Clifton asked Andrews to have a forklift ready
to carry the casket down the rear exit ... He also phoned
the Army's Walter Reed Hospital and said that the autopsy
would be performed there.
                         * * * * * *
     Dr. Burkley, standing alone, noticed that Mrs. Kennedy
was alone. He approached and, rather than bend down to
speak to her, dropped to his knees. It was a comical attitude for the dignified admiral. He was at eye level with
her and said: "It's going to be necessary to take the President to a hospital before he goes to the White House." She
was in a trance-like state, but the young lady came out of
it quickly. "Why?" she said. The tone was sharp because
she had had her fill of hospitals and their cast-iron rules.
     Burkley looked like a supplicant at prayer. "The doc-
tors must remove the bullet," he said. "The authorities must
know the type. It becomes evidence." Mrs. Kennedy could
understand the situation. The admiral did not use the word
autopsy, which entails evisceration and the removal of the
brain and other organs. She asked where the bullet could be
removed. Burkley said he had no preference although he had.
He was a United States Navy admiral, and Kennedy had been a
Navy lieutenant. "For security reasons it should be a military hospital," he said.

Mrs. Kennedy was prompted to say the right word. "Bethesda," she said. The admiral was satisfied. He got off his knees and went forward to the communications shack to alert the naval hospital ...

By all available versions, there was no doubt that, after the corpse was removed illegally and with Washington's raw power alone, none but some military establishment was ever considered for the performance of the autopsy.

From these accounts we have agreement on two things that are significant and may account for the inability of the Commission to reach an acceptable conclusion (or at least provided it with a phony basis for telling itself it could conclude only as it did). There was never any question but that, for no reason whatsoever, no need of any kind, the autopsy would be at a military hospital. It seems that Admiral Burkley was responsible for the choice of Bethesda, where only what could not and should not ever have happened anywhere is exactly what did.

There is another and potentially perhaps more significant consistency. To avoid the possibility of misleading the reader and making what may not be an accurate record, it is necessary to return to the opening thought of this chapter, the undependability of the sources. Manchester, in particular, has accomplished the close to impossible, the absolute perfection in inaccuracy under conditions that make this accomplishment the very apotheosis of egregiousness. He was permitted, through Kennedy influence, to sit in on the Commission's secret sessions - and all but one were completely secret, one, when it was meaningless, partly open. He also had a private office, taxpayer-provided, in the National Archives, complete with cot. From the evidence of his book, he used it for no more than a pad and a base for the sleaziest plagiarism. Of what he reports, the one thing that can be accepted without qualm is that the President was dead. That conclusion did not require access to the secret, a taxpayer-provided private office in the Archives, and Kennedy sponsorship. Bishop's concept of history and reporting is the ultimate in contempt for the reader and his intelligence. His work is the most commercially acceptable of literary scrimshaw.

Saying this is not to say that nothing they report can be truthful. If their accord in some things is close enough to suggest they had identical sources or that there was copying, where there is accord it also can betoken that one confirms the other. Thus, without assuming it to be dependable, but recognizing the meaning if it is, there should be consideration of their consistency.

Burkley said the purpose of the autopsy was to remove and identify a bullet. Burkley was in the Dallas emergency room, saw, knew what had been observed, understood and believed probable there. The nature and magnitude of the damage to the head eliminated all possibilities but one, that whatever caused it had exploded. There thus could be no expectation of recovering a bullet from the head.

Officialdom thus is hoist on its own evidentiary petard. Its explanation of the lack of mention of any wound in the back is that the body was not turned over in Dallas. Thus, the sole point from which a bullet could be recovered, from all official knowledge as of the time of the flight back to Washington, had to be of the wound in the front of the neck, meaning that this was a wound of entry.

With Oswald allegedly behind the President shooting at him, he could not, simultaneously, have been in the front. All contemporaneous accounts of this front-neck wound attribute it to a shot from the front. Officials did contort themselves to try and explain how Oswald could have hit the one target simultaneously from two opposite sides.

Long after completion of the autopsy, at the time of the December 5 official "reconstruction" of the crime in Dallas, we have this explanation given to Joseph A. Loftus, whose story appears in The New York Times of the next day:

One question was how the President could have received a

241

bullet in the front ... after his car had passed the building ... One explanation from a competent source was that the
President had turned to his right to wave and was struck at
that moment.

"Competent source" here is one of the traditional euphemisms for
an official who would not permit the use of his name. There were no
others with any knowledge of the official reconstruction.

Doctor Humes is then quoted as saying "he had been forbidden to
talk", which is understatement of the truth.

What follows is partial explanation of how the knowledge could
be controlled, how the press could have been foreclosed from any independent investigation.

Most private citizens who had cooperated with newsmen reporting the crime have refused to give further help after being interviewed by agents of the Federal Bureau of Investigation.

So did all local officials:

One high officer said he wished he could answer questions
"because it would save us a lot of work."

So thoroughly did the FBI close every mouth that even the Secret
Service was immediately frozen out, as I reported in WHITEWASH II.

This front-neck wound, never described as anything other than an
unmistakable wound of entry until Arlen Specter went to work on it and
the experts, is the rock on which the official "solution" must founder,
hence attention is called to these agreeing sources, that the purpose
of the autopsy as explained to the distraught widow was to recover a
bullet for identification, when the only possible point from which a
bullet could be recovered was the front of the neck.

If we assume what it may not be safe to assume, that these literary schmalz-men are accurate, that Burkley swung the deal for Bethesda; and if we assume what without any question is true, that once the
President was murdered, there was no question of "security", what grist
for the conspiracy mill! An admiral talked the widow into the naval
establishment in which everything wrong did happen and nothing right
was possible - where the solution to this monstrous crime was immediately made close to an impossibility!

Need one know more to fret about the possibility of a military
conspiracy?

Especially when the military then and there prevented the most
essential examinations from being made?

Even more, when all those present were threatened with retaliation if they ever said a word?

Here, perhaps, there is a concept of "security" but what a monstrous conspiracy that would have to conjure! Can this be possible -
can this be conceived - in the United States of America in 1963?

On the point of "security", one of the knee-jerk irrationalities
that have dominated American life for so many years, Burkley himself
supports Manchester and Bishop. There is, dear reader, a Burkley file,
and there is a Burkley report on these tragic events, written five days
after Dallas. The original of his report is not in that file. Nor is
a copy of it, with all those Xeroxes working overtime. What is filed
is a retyped copy, seemingly edited, and that by a person not familiar
with the White House, its personnel or operations. One clue is that
"Air Force One" appears as "Air Force '1'".

As retyped, Burkley's is a nine-page statement. The rest of
the Commission's once-secret Burkley file consists of 34 pages in which
there is casual mention of his name, most often as riding in the ambulance to the hospital. There is no report of any interrogation of the
President's physician by the Commission, Secret Service or FBI. Only
in retrospect, with an understanding that the purpose of the entire
"investigation" was to avoid fact and knowledge, can there be sense in

the avoidance of questioning of the one medical man who had been in the Dallas emergency room and the Navy autopsy room - the one medical man present at all medical examinations of the corpse.

And thus it is that the nine-page statement by the President's own physician is the one source that reports least of a medical nature. From it one can assume that the real cause of death was complications following the ingrowing of a toenail. Those of a more conspiratorial bent might from it assume that the real cause of death was a tainted oyster, a la Harding.

Of what Burkley saw at the Dallas hospital? This is all save for a few words on the fruitless treatment:

I immediately entered the room, went to the head of the table and viewed the President. It was evident that death was imminent and that he was in a hopeless condition. (p.2)

Hence the basis for wondering whether oysters or toenails was the immediate cause of death. There is no mention of the visible wounds, the exploded head.

Here is the medical man most directly responsible for the President's health; he was there, at the crucial place, at "the head of the table", and he "viewed the President". What better reason for saying nothing about what he saw when, by the time he prepared this statement, that was already a swirling controversy? Of course, as the reader should also remember from Part I, by the time Burkley wrote this, the only man accused of the crime was safely dead, so why louse up this nice clean "solution" with fact and detailed medical observation?

Now, this is not to suggest that the dashing admiral did not do his duty as he saw it, through Rudolph Friml's eyes.

On Mrs. Kennedy's "desire to be in the room" where the Dallas doctors were working over the corpse. Burkley felt it was "so right" for her to be in it rather than at the door to it that

I overrode the protests of some of the people in the room and brought Mrs. Kennedy inside the door where she stood and with my arms protecting her, she momentarily rested her head on my shoulder. (p.3)

Loyal servant, "protecting" the poor widow from the great danger to her person from all those doctors, Secret Service and FBI agents? From whom else could he have been "protecting" her?

The admiral, from his own statement, was not without regard for his medico-legal responsibilities for he describes what happened after the casket had been taken out of the emergency room:

At this point I again examined the room and they had cleaned the room. The roses which had been in the car with the President were in the wastebasket, however, and two roses which had broken off were lying on the floor. I picked them up and put them in my pocket ... (p.5)

Thus, from two examinations of the room, the evidence rescued for the solution of the crime of the century, the character of which is completely undescribed by the man who "viewed the head", is, with the sensitivity of the poetic soul, not the roses from the wastebasket but two that had broken off. Concluding this paragraph, the admiral says that on the way to the plane

I then reached into my pocket and took out the roses I had gotten from the floor and gave them to Mrs. Kennedy stating what they were. She took them, put them in her jacket pocket, smiled and thanked me. (p.5)

Entirely consistent is the admiral's contributions to understanding of the crime from his observations at the Navy Hospital and in its autopsy room:

The body was taken to the mortuary where I met it and observed the transfer to the table. The examination was per-

243

formed by Commander Humes and members of his staff. Also present were Admiral Kenny, Admiral Galloway, and Captain Canada. General McHugh had remained in the vicinity of the President constantly throughout this time. (p.7)

If the admiral provides no help in resolving possible conflict between tainted oysters, a possible complication from an ingrown toenail and perhaps a black curse as the cause of death, it is not because he was unaware of the true nature of the real responsibilities of the physician to the President:

I made numerous trips to the 17th floor for reassurance to those in that area -

("Reassurance"? Was some magical power about to restore life?)

- and to supply them with some idea of the contemplated departure time. On one of these occasions, Mrs. Kennedy spoke to me in the bedroom of the suite expressing her appreciation which was greatly valued by me and which I will long remember. The body of the President was fully clothed in a blue suit, white shirt, tie, socks and shoes. His hair was combed in the usual fashion and his appearance in the casket gave no evidence of the injury he had received. (pp.7-8)

This is one of the places in Burkley's statement that leads to the belief it was edited. I have omitted nothing from this direct quotation, beginning with "the body was taken to the mortuary." The President goes, in this account, right from autopsy-table dissection to restoration of the body to "usual fashion and appearance", from medical nakedness to beautiful, funereal garb, with nothing in between save the visits to Mrs. Kennedy's tower room.

It would be a deception to lead the reader to believe Admiral Burkley was incompetent in either career, medicine or military, much as this, the only statement from him in the Warren Commission's file on him, indicates that he filled no more than a handle-polishing, musical-comedy role in real life. There is every reason to hold the contrary view, that as admiral and as doctor George B. Burkley knew his business. That this is the only statement from him in the Commission's file can hardly be blamed on him. He did not conduct the investigation, did not run the FBI or Secret Service.

Unfortunately, because the President's physician was also a military man, it does tend to fuel conspiratorial suspicions. On how the corpse got to the Naval Hospital, where the impossible did happen, Burkley is not inconsistent with Manchester and Bishop, both of whom can always use shoring up on what they present as fact. He is just missing some of the details:

... During the course of the flight, determination of the immediate action on arrival in Washington was made to assure complete compliance with Mrs. Kennedy's wishes. I spoke to her while kneeling on the floor so I would be on the level of her face rather than leaning forward, and expressed complete desire of all of us and especially of myself to comply with her wishes, stating that it was necessary that the President be taken to a hospital prior to going to the White House. She questioned why and I stated it must be determined, if possible, the type of bullet used and compare this with future material found. I stated frankly that I had no preference, that it could be any hospital, but that I did feel, if possible, it should be a military hospital for security reasons. The question was answered by her stating that she wanted the President taken to Bethesda Naval Hospital ...

Viewed in the light of history, this limited representation of the many medico-legal purposes of an autopsy to identifying of a bullet is not without interest, nor is this senseless preoccupation with "security" for a President already assassinated. What is interesting is the total absence of any fact about the evidence of the crime so well known to the President's own physician long before he wrote this "report" which, assuredly, is without serious purposes. Unless one considers schmalz and mythology, sticky goo and that Camelot jazz, serious and of purpose when a President is murdered.

What Burkley knew - what was until now suppressed - is hardly encompassed by any designation as modest as "national scandal". It is in one of a series of items of evidence denied the Warren Commission itself that, after long effort, I was able to get.

Yes, dear reader and doubting Thomases, there is evidence that was denied the Presidential Commission itself. Every one of the numerous items of this suppressed evidence that, after so many years, I have been able to obtain is exactly what every investigator, every lawyer, knows he must have. So, the withholding from the Commission could not have been pulled off by the executive agencies without the complicity of the Commission and its staff. There is no reason not to wonder whether, in fact, someone on that body did not let it be known that it would be better for such unequivocal evidence not to reach the Commission.

There is no doubt about the Commission's duties and responsibilities, and there is unanimity in description of them and its power and authority. The language of Executive Order No. 11130 creating it directs and authorizes it "to evaluate all the facts and circumstances" (R471). The White House release is almost identical, "to study and report upon all facts and circumstances" (R472). The opening paragraph of the Foreword of the Report (ix) concludes, "The President directed the Commission to evaluate all the facts and circumstances surrounding the assassination ..." And in Public Law 88-202 (R473-4), the Congress gave it all necessary powers. The first, that of subpoena, was given to the Commission or any authorized member "requiring the attendance and testimony of witnesses and the production of any evidence that relates to any matter under investigation by the Commission."

The Commission and its staff could not have been prevented from having this suppressed evidence had they desired it. But had this Commission had what will follow, it could never have issued the Report it was so clearly understood it would write before it began its work, before it made any investigation, as the preinvestigation outline in Part I so abundantly illustrates. *

There is no reason not to pinpoint the primary responsibility. For the medical evidence, it is that of a man who is no stranger, that former and present prosecutor, Arlen Specter, an ambitious man well-schooled in the evidentiary requirements of murder investigations and prosecutions.

What I am about to disclose was not in the Commission's files. I have every still-existing paper of every one of all the appropriate files from which I shall quote, the product of what was, for me, great effort and cost. I also have written assurances that here the official files are more like Mother Hubbard's than Earl Warren's - bare.

In the face of this suppression, there were many difficulties to be overcome in making it possible to persuade the production of the missing evidence. I could not steal from hidden, locked safes, nor could I club recalcitrant public officials into proper behavior. Persuasion was my only possible means.

One problem was the law. Until July 4, 1967, under then-existing law, the government could invoke any kind of fancied excuse, with no requirement to disclose it, allege what was then called "good cause" or "the national interest", and send citizens packing. Then a new law, Public Law 89-487, was enacted.** It was signed by President Johnson a year to the day before its effective date. Even that President could not have been more glowing in his rhetorical exultation over the freedoms to be bestowed by this law which his and the successor administration began flaunting at the moment of self-glorification and have without end thereafter.

"No one should be able to pull curtains of secrecy," Johnson declaimed. "I have always believed that freedom of information is so

*See Ch.1; pp. 111-2; pp 467-72.

** Freedom of Information Act, 5 U.S.C.552.

vital that only the national security, not the desire of public officials, should determine when it must be restricted."

That liberal Attorney General who convoked his panel in complete
secrecy, held its fake report in total secrecy, then suppressed all the
relevant papers and evidence in open violation of the law, was not to
be outdone by his fellow Texan on so ennobling and inspiring an occasion:

Nothing so diminishes democracy as secrecy ... Self-government ... is meaningful only with an informed public ... this
statute imposes on the executive branch an affirmative obligation to adopt new standards and practices for publication and
availability of information ... disclosure is a transcendant
goal ... be the general rule, not the exception ...

Those with a stomach for more of this verbal political ginger-
bread can get all of it plus the text of the law, plus the official
interpretation, all for 25 cents, sent to the Government Printing Office
in Washington. Ask for the Attorney General's Memorandum on the Public
Information Section of the Administrative Procedures Act.

Quite properly, Congress said that "good cause" is a bad excuse,
that "national interest" is whatever any politician thinks serves his
selfish interest, and these and similar dodges henceforth are illegal.
So, theoretically, these can no longer be used as excuses for denying
the people their own information.

The law does have nine exemptions, each a proper one. Each has
since been officially twisted into another excuse for suppression. Almost anything the Department of Justice has in its files it defines as
"an investigatory file for law-enforcement purposes". When, in one of
the suits I subsequently filed to break this dam of official suppression, the federal attorney was asked what law was being enforced, there
being none, he claimed there had to be a "natural law" and the rubber-
stamp judge agreed with him.

Who needs a Constitution when one has so imaginative a Department
of Justice with such creative federal attorneys able to conjure up instant law where there is no federal law to be enforced? Who need fear
for his freedoms with such a government, such judges? Or, as also happened in this case, with FBI agents immediately available to swear
falsely in matters where even their qualifications to swear at all were
not established and did not exist.

As of this writing, that case is under appeal. John Sirica,
the judge who presided, was then Chief Judge of Federal District Court
for the District of Columbia. That suit, Civil Action 2301-70, is for
the suppressed spectrographic analyses of the alleged ballistics evidence in this assassination. It will interest us further in its proper
context. The Warren Commission never had it, never wanted it, never
saw it. [See further developments in the last part of this book.]

If these analyses confirmed what is imputed to them - there was
no competent testimony from anyone about them - the government would be
doing everything to draw public attention to them short of spending
Richard Nixon's campaign funds for TV commercials to advertise them.

It is no less obvious that no concept of "national defense" is
involved and that none of the exemptions apply. The assassination of
a President was not then a federal crime.

Despite these seemingly insuperable obstacles, the law does have
possibilities. By winning the first suit under it (Civil Action No.
718-70 in the same court, before a different judge), I did establish
the possibility. This is the suit reported in the final chapter of
FRAME-UP. In order to use the law, a tedious series of administrative
remedies must be exhausted. And they can be exhausting. I began while
the law was being considered by the Congress.

That was in the days when I really believed the National Archives
was the repository of the most sacred objects in our national heritage
and that it was run by scholars with nonpolitical, scholarly purposes
and interests and for the benefit of the people. I was trusting - and

246

foolish - enough to say so on coast-to-coast TV.

Following earlier verbal efforts, on May 23, 1966, when only WHITEWASH and a little-known other book (Sylvan Fox's Unanswered Questions) had been published, I began a systematic written effort to gain access to all the "autopsy or medical papers of any kind or description." The file of subsequent correspondence is thicker by far than the manuscript of a large book.

And this is exclusive of court papers. In one suit, Civil Action No. 2569-70, the lower-court papers alone also are much longer than a long book.

Even letters do make a kind of record for history, as some officials came to realize. Court records can and do document, and in this case it is of government falsification of the most incredible kind.

At first I believed the policy of the National Archives was to be helpful, genuinely helpful, and that what its staff could not provide just did not exist. It was a short honeymoon.

There is no longer room for doubt about the intended dishonesty of the Commission's Report as well as of its record. The Report is internally inconsistent. It is in violent disagreement with the testimony upon which it is based. That testimony also contradicts itself, as it does its alleged documentary substantiation. And the most vital documentation, as I soon learned, was missing.

This may seem strong talk to the reader, even at this point, so I refresh his mind on the glaring and irreconcilable conflicts that hit me immediately, as set forth in considerable detail in "The Doctors and The Autopsy", the last chapter of WHITEWASH:

The Report promises to pinpoint and describe the fatal headwound at various places but at no point does.
The Report says that all the doctors swore that its alleged single-bullet basis is possible, but in fact, all swore it was impossible - every single doctor questioned did. Caged, ambitious Arlen Specter, about to make a new career for himself by abandoning Americans for Democratic Action and the Democrats to run (successfully) for Philadelphia District Attorney as a Republican, after adducing this monolithic refutation of his contrived "solution", pulled a pair of quick switches;
   a) he asked each doctor to ignore the reality - "not this bullet, any bullet" - and then asked no more than could one bullet wound two men;
   b) he substituted this hypothesis and the meaningless testimony about it for the reality and then had the Report quote all the doctors as agreeing to his theory which all denied and refuted.

The chief prosecutor, Doctor Humes, swore in identifying the papers constituting Exhibit 397 that it included two pages of his own notes, some made during the examination of the President's body in the autopsy room itself, and they are not in that exhibit, in its printed version or any of the numerous others, each, later, with some care and effort, recaptured from the official oblivion so Orwellian in character. Here (2H272-3) are the exact words:

Mr. Specter. Now, Doctor Humes, I hand you a group of documents which have been marked as Commission Exhibit No. 397 and ask you if you can identify what they are?
Commander Humes. Yes, sir; these are various notes in longhand, or copies rather, of various notes in long-hand made by myself, in part, during the performance of the examination of the late President, and in part after the examination when I was preparing to have a typewritten report made.
* * * *
Mr. Specter. May the record show that the Exhibit No. 397 is the identical document which has been previously identified as Commission No. 371 for our internal purposes.

There was no legal authorization for the autopsy, the initial requirement. Regulations specify "next of kin", which Robert Kennedy was not. The widow was.

And there was no certificate of death, the final requirement.

Or, as I was soon to write in WHITEWASH II, the accused assassin got an autopsy worthy of a President of the United States, while the President got an autopsy unworthy of a Bowery bum.

Any one of these deficiencies in the evidence was more than enough to set any legal or criminal investigator off on an evidentiary search. There were these and many more, so in the spring of 1966 I started.

This brief recapitulation is intended to show the reader that before any book on the Warren Commission was published - including my first, which was the first - I knew the most important evidence, by any standard, from legal to literary, was suppressed and that, as soon as the material in the Archives was accessible, I had superabundant confirmation.

Or, I knew from the first this was not a wild-goose chase. The only questions were, had it all been destroyed and could I get any or all of it?

There were many conferences, including with the Archivists and their top assistants, as well as Marion Johnson, the man in immediate charge of this archive. They produced what can be expected from such conferences when suppression is the official policy, nothing but polite stalling and outright lies. Before long it was taking months to get answers to simple requests. Today some remain unanswered after more than four years.

Then, as I began to ferret through the unpublished files, interesting, important unpublished evidence came to light. Initially, it had been expected that none of the Commission's files would be public. The political intolerability of this decision was apparent to the pros where it was not to the eminences, and the pros saw to it that under careful control some of the files would be available. This was not the most publicized fact in government. It was, in fact, little known.

Two of the first discoveries were among the most exciting. One is the Sibert-O'Neill report analyzed earlier. By accident, it reached another writer, Edward Epstein, who, not understanding it and not realizing it refuted the basic tenets of his over-advertised Inquest, added it, out of context, to the paperback reprint. The other is the receipt in CD 371.

If what Sibert and O'Neill reported of the medical evidence is true, the Report had to be a fake. And, the main FBI summary report, CD 1, medically based on Sibert and O'Neill, failed to account for all the shooting or all the wounds. Hoover at his legal, scientific, investigative best.

The receipt accounts for the existence of some of this missing medical evidence as of the time it reached the White House. Added to the sworn attestation to its subsequent existence as of the time of the Commission's hearings, it had to be obvious that evidence was suppressed, destroyed or both.

To this day, the existence of these autopsy notes is denied, although every source stipulates their existence, from Doctor Humes' Commission testimony to that of Doctor Finck in New Orleans - he expanded knowledge in admitting that all the autopsy doctors had made notes and he had turned his in before leaving - to Admiral Galloway's covering letter with which he sent them to the White House and Doctor Burkley's receipt for them to the Secret Service.

But after years of trying, and I mean "years" literally, I have finally obtained some of this missing evidence. After July 6, 1966, certification by the Archivist, then Dr. Robert H. Bahmer, that it was not in the Commission's files - not one item of it.

My first direct effort with the Secret Service also was on May

23, 1966. It drew no response from Director James J. Rowley. After a little more than a year, I renewed the correspondence, this time invoking the Attorney General's executive order. Rowley insisted that "the Secret Service never did withhold any evidence" from the Commission, subsequently amplified in a manner that can explain the absence from the Commission's files of what the Secret Service did have and the Commission should have: "...all the information available to the Secret Service relating to the assassination of President Kennedy was made available to the Warren Commission and its staff." Based on those items of suppressed evidence where I can make an evaluation, I am prepared to believe that the Commission, or, more likely, some of the staff, declined to have what it did not use and was not in its files, not that Rowley hid it from them.

It was at this point that Thomas J. Kelley, by then promoted to Assistant Director in Charge of Protective Service, took over the correspondence that grew to an extensive file.

Inherently, writers make judgments, whether or not so realizing or intending. I prefer to make mine explicit. The Secret Service was part of a cover-up, the specific charge of my second book. It was silent when it should not have been, and it remains silent when the course of honor and really dedicated public service requires that it and its personnel speak out. However, when the pressures of the unprecedented situation, which would have required that a relatively minor agency set itself publicly against a clear federal policy determination as a substitute for fact and truth, and the adverse effects on employment and careers that would have been inevitable are considered, the silences can be understood, whether or not one agrees with the fact or the motivation. In various ways I did receive expressions of the deepest misgivings held by some of the agents through their relatives and friends.

The first thing I went after really made no great difference, but it had the advantage of letting the Secret Service know the act of coughing up need not be painful. A missing one of the original copies of the autopsy protocol thus was added to those estimated 300 cubic feet. It was a redundancy, but it was also a precedent.

The first thing of real substance I was able to get, that which I first added to Part I and then removed for further investigation, is Admiral Burkley's copies of the still-existing autopsy papers. These are the originals. The terrible blots on them include the President's body fluids. They are here reproduced from Xeroxes, not the color photographs I have. That the President bled once is too much. It is not necessary to show his blood. *

However, when, finally, the Secret Service produced these papers, it did not come up with all of them. It, the Commission and Specter all managed the same omission, the first two pages of the file, CD 371. One is the November 26, 1963, receipt the Secret Service gave Admiral Burkley for 11 itemized pieces of evidence. The second is a November 25 letter from Admiral Galloway to Admiral Burkley. Reason for the remarkable consistency in what is missing is not hard to find: Almost without exception, the items covered had disappeared, were not in the Commission's files, in some cases are still missing, and all raised substantial doubts about both the autopsy and the integrity with which it was performed and reported.

Of all these things, despite his contrary assurance that Exhibit 397 "is the identical document which has been previously identified as Commission No. 371", in the evidence Specter included only a copy of the holograph of the autopsy, one of the typed copies of it, the two November 24 certifications by Doctor Humes, the body chart, and what with typical vagueness is made to appear as something separate, the head sketch previously referred to. This is all, as Volume 17 shows.

The rest, memory-holed.

I can now clear up a perhaps minor mystery. Regardless of when he did it, and I emphasize that this is one of the many points at which

*See pp. 509ff.

one must question Finck's evasiveness, that head sketch is on the reverse side of the original of the body chart. These forms are one long sheet of paper. It would thus seem to be a sketch he made at the autopsy bench. And bearing on the number of sheets of notes, this is but a single sheet. The only one ever produced.

Two of the articles still missing need not greatly concern those whose interest is establishing the truth about what happened and exploring the nature of the investigation in its various forms. They do, however, limn the thoughtful care with which everything was preserved for investigation, for posterity. I have verbal and written assurances that they have disappeared. They are the first items, "One piece of bronze colored material inadvertently broken in transit from casket in which body was brought from Dallas," and the fourth, "One receipt dated Nov. 22, for bed sheet, surgical drapes, and shroud used to cover body in transit."

Why these things were permitted to disappear, why the name of the maker of this November 22 receipt was avoided by Robert Inman Bouck in preparing the receipt he gave Burkley, may remain among the minor continuing mysteries, none of which, I hope all can agree, can be regarded as acceptable when the assassination of a President is "investigated".

At that time in 1967, other of the receipted evidence also was missing, I was likewise assured. In time, I have been able to inspire sufficient official diligence to retrieve them from the memory-hole file that in this case did not bottom in an incinerator. We shall address them after considering this first resurrection.

It is the official White House copy of what the Commission designated as its File 371. The first thing in it, this Burkley receipt to Bouck, was omitted - meaning suppressed. Regardless of who did it, and that we have no way of knowing, the responsibility is Specter's. If, as is customary in such cases, the file the members were given is identical with what was published in the hearings, then the members did not know of this itemization of evidence in the Burkley receipt, although a copy was in the Commission's files, where I found it in early 1966. It is not in Exhibit 397, was not published by the Commission.

Examination of the listing provides immediate and obvious explanation for this omission, which must be regarded as not accidental but deliberate. The first seven items were not in the Commission's files. Of the others, parts of three only are and the fourth was hidden.

Item 2 is described as "One letter - Certificate of Death of John F. Kennedy - State of Texas - dated Nov. 22, 1963." We have already examined a Texas certificate of death, part of an "inquest" dated ten days before the assassination. But there is no such letter. And, should it not be asked, how can an official inquiry into this death have published that verbal monstrosity of all those volumes without including any certificate of death?

There were at least two. The other, also missing, is the sixth item, "An original and six pink copies of Certificate of Death (Nav. Med.N)" (sic).

In each case we shall come to a good reason, if "good" is the word, for each omission.

Item 3 does not begin to describe what it covers, for in the end I also fished it out. The description reads, "One carbon of letter dated November 26 from Commanding Officer, U.S. Medical School, concerning law and regulations regarding confidential nature of the events." Aside from the date, no part of this description is accurate, not even the name of the institution, that "U.S. Medical School".

The fifth item covers and will be part of a scandal that will not rest in perpetuity. Phrased with inept bureaucratic evasiveness, it reads, "One receipt dated Nov. 22, 1963, regarding a carton of photographic film undeveloped except for X-rays, delivered to PRS for safekeeping." This is the receipt Roy Kellerman gave for what was represented as but was not all the film. Ultimately, I got this receipt, too. It is sufficient to prove that the missing X-rays were not given to the Secret Service. "PRS" is the "Protective Research Service" of the Secret Service, the Presidential-protection section.

How reminiscent that "safekeeping" is of the biblical maiden's lament in the Song of Solomon: "My mother's children made me the keeper of the vineyards, but mine own vineyard have I not kept."

Seventh is, "One receipt from FBI for missle recovered during the examination of the body." There is no evidence of or testimony about the recovery of a "missle".

The Commission did have an edited version of the eighth item, described as "One letter from University of Texas South West Medical School including report from Dr. Clark and summary of their findings of treatment and examination of the President in the Dallas County Hospital. Said letter of transmittal states that three carbon copies have been retained in that area." (sic)

That edited version is in CD 392. It is in the Report as the first thing in Appendix VIII, the so-called medical appendix (pp.516-46). Because it is reproduced in facsimile, it is surprising that the diligent press did not note as I immediately did (WHITEWASH 168) that the "covering letter" is no such thing as published but is, rather, two paragraphs, entirely unidentified and unsigned, and without subtlety cut out of something also not identified. Even the size of the typing is different from that of the following two pages headed "SUMMARY".

Next is "One copy of autopsy report and notes of the examining doctor which is described in letter of transmittal Nov. 25, 1963 by Dr. Galloway."

That letter by Admiral Galloway is the second page of CD 371. It is not as described and, naturally, was also not published or included in that "identical" Exhibit 397.

For some reason, an unknown somebody marked both margins at this item on the original. Perhaps because it includes what is missing still, "notes of the examining doctor".

"Transmittal letter and seven copies of the above item (autopsy report)", the next listing, also is missing, although at least some of the copies had to have reached somebody.

And the last is that suppressed authorization for the autopsy signed by Robert Kennedy that I had earlier obtained. All but a single misfiled copy, the one I did find, had been destroyed or removed or suppressed from every one of the many "autopsy" files, although the initial requirement of any autopsy.

Of the many existing self-descriptions of the official investigation as at best a fraud and at worst a conspiracy, this is one of the most damning, the first itemization of the best official evidence of the crime, most of it withheld from the Commission, which did know of its existence and made no effort to obtain and consider it, permitting it - knowingly permitting it - to be suppressed. And what of that evidence? Not one item in the list without taint and almost all missing - suppressed until after I spent years of the most disagreeable labor, persisting, arguing and, ultimately, threatening legal action, some of it was finally given to me.

Can there be a more frightening self-description of that of which officialdom is capable? And of all the stifled voices, muted for undisturbed employment or, perhaps, from fear - is not this silence an awful crime in itself?

With this the official record when a President is murdered, of what is officialdom not capable? Who can expect to enjoy any rights, can consider he can live without any fear of what officials can do to him?

23. MORE FROM THE MEMORY HOLE

As delivered to the Archives with a covering letter by Rowley, what I had decided to investigate further is described as:

Handwritten notes by Dr. J. J. Humes which include the holographic draft of the autopsy report; the autopsy description sheet; two certificates dated November 24 by Dr. Humes (Commission Exhibit 397); and the official autopsy report (Commission Exhibit 387).

The self-serving comment that follows is both accurate and deceptive:

Copies of these documents, as you know, were furnished to the President's Commission on the Assassination of President Kennedy and are Commission exhibits which have been widely reproduced.

Had it been Rowley's intention to persuade scholars of the future that it would be a waste of time even to look at these seeming duplications of the published, he could not have phrased it better. But, the very opening sentence of his letter makes all of this false and dishonest. It refers to "the following original documents ..." (emphasis added), and the Commission never had copies of these "original documents", which are different from the copies the Commission did have, those made from copies, not the originals.

I had no trouble getting a Xerox of what Rowley then gave the Archives under my persistent prodding. But it was some time before, by accident, I located the actual originals. Had I not been lulled by Rowley's clever phrasing, this would not have been the case, for what was added to his attached receipt should have led me to it.

For some reason not immediately apparent, this required two different receipts. And, again without explanation, the receipts for this imperishable national treasure are not signed by the Archivist or his numerous top assistants who do act in his name, nor are they signed by the man in immediate charge of this archive, Marion Johnson. For this purpose, the lowest man on the bureaucratic totem pole, John F. Simmons, known as "Mike", Johnson's friendly and conscientious assistant, was used. No title is included. Neither receipt even says "National Archives".

The first is on a Secret Service letterhead form used for communications to be filed by their file identification - not Rowley's letterhead. The second is a carbon copy of another receipt.

The first reads, "Received from the United States Secret Service the following material - Commission Exhibit # 387:", followed by this, indented:

(A) Original Autopsy Proctocol dated 22 November 1963 signed by Cmdr. J. J. Humes - standard Form 503, six (6) pages. Countersigned by Cmdr. J. Thornton Boswell and Lt. Col. Pierre A. Finck. (sic)

(The supplemental autopsy report, forwarded by the Navy December 6, was not included.)

The second, a two-page work of propaganda and rather carefully drawn, not an objective receipt, was copied for me with 1-5/8 inches of the top of each page missing. (The same amount of copying was eliminated from Rowley's letter and the first receipt.) The bottom of what seems to be the seven capital letters possibly spelling "RECEIPT" barely show at the top of the first. This is the copy supplied me:

Received from the United States Secret Service the following material - Commission Exhibit 8397: Story 24

(A) Original copy of sixteen (16) pages of handwritten notes. The first page comprises notes made by Dr. J. J. Humes when he talked with Dr. Malcolm Perry on the telephone. The next fifteen (15) pages comprise the original holographic draft of the Autopsy Protocol described on Pages 372 and 373, Volume 2, *Hearings Before the President's Commission on the Assassination of President Kennedy*. (These sixteen (16) pages are portrayed on Pages 29 through 44, Volume XVII, *Hearings Before the President's Commission on the Assassination of President Kennedy*.)

(B) Original Autopsy Descriptive Sheet. Form NMS Path 8, (1-63). - NMS # A 63 #272. - (1 Sheet) dated November 22, 1963 (1 Sheet written on both sides). Described by Dr. Humes as notes actually made in the room when the examination was taking place. (Page 373, Volume 2, *Hearings Before the President's Commission on the Assassination of President Kennedy*.) This sheet is portrayed on Pages 45 and 46, Volume XVII, *Hearings Before the President's Commission on the Assassination of President Kennedy*.

(C) Original certificate dated 24 November 1963 by Cmdr. J. J. Humes certifying that all working papers associated with NMS Autopsy Report # A 63 #272 were in his custody at all times. Autopsy notes and holographic draft of the final report were handed to the Commanding Officer, U. S. Naval Medical School, also certifying that no papers relating to this case remained in his possession. Certificate countersigned by Cpt. J. H. Stover, Jr. This certificate is portrayed on Page 47, Volume XVII, *Hearings Before the President's Commission on the Assassination of President Kennedy*.

(D) Original certificate dated 24 November 1963 by Cmdr. J. J. Humes certifying that he destroyed by burning certain preliminary draft notes relating to NMS Autopsy Report # A 63 #272 and had transmitted all other papers related to this report to higher authority. This certificate portrayed on Page 48, Volume XVII, *Hearings Before the President's Commission on the Assassination of President Kennedy*.

(Signed) *John J. Sommers* NND

(Date) 10-3-67

With regard to "(A)", that is not "the original holographic draft of the Autopsy Protocol" for, as consultation with the cited source shows, it is the original of the revision of the "draft" (2H373). This misrepresentation may give even more point to the totally unnecessary fate of the original, the sworn word of then-Commander Humes from the same paragraph: "That draft I personally burned in the fireplace of my recreation room."

From Specter's and the Commission members' total lack of interest or reaction, no question being asked, no eyebrow raised - no consternation or concern - the proper place for the autopsy protocol of an assassinated President is a "recreation room", not a hospital, and the proper disposition is Orwell's, to be "personally burned" by the prosector. Sure as hell, that burned draft, the original that was not destroyed until it was known that there would be no trial, Oswald also having been put away, is not going to be quoted now by some devil like me loving scripture!

The reader might want to consider why some unnamed bureaucrat had to lie. Why any lie is necessary or acceptable about anything connected with the assassination of a President or its investigation.

(In this, Simmons is innocent, for the nature of his multitudinous duties precludes his having made the study of this verbal enormity that I have. That cannot be true of the writer of this false, propagandizing "receipt".)

This is not the only lie - should one mince words on such a subject? - in this paragraph. The parenthetical conclusion is deliberately false. It is not "these sixteen (16) pages" that are on "Pages 29 through 44, Volume XVII" of the Hearings. Had they been, the international uproar would still be echoing after seven years. Shortly the difference will become apparent.

Nor is "(B)" not similarly false. This is not the same "Original Autopsy Descriptive Sheet" that is "on Pages 45 and 46, Volume XVII" of the Hearings. The words "autopsy descriptive sheet" are not on page 373 or anywhere else in Humes' testimony. Nor can these possibly be that for which I had for so long made repeated requests, all of the "notes actually made in the room where the examination was taking place". We have not only Colonel Finck's sworn word that he, personally, made notes and handed them in before he left and that all three doctors made notes on pieces of paper. Moreover, on the page prior to that cited in deceptive argument, hardly appropriate in what is guised as no more than a "receipt", Humes had sworn, in describing what he held in his hand, not an "autopsy descriptive sheet" nor "Form NMS Path", both being headings on that required Navy Medical Service form, nor did he cite the identification of the autopsy by the number that appears on it, "A 63 #272". He could not identify it by the name of the President, for this autopsy was performed with such tender care, with such regard for precision, history and the legal aspects of medicine, that the blanks required to be filled in for a number of entries, including name, date and hour expired, diagnosis and physical description, are all blank.

Humes' under-oath description of what he held, what was then and there placed into evidence, is "these are various notes in long-hand, or copies, rather, of various notes in long-hand made by myself, in part during the performance of the examination of the late President and in part after the examination when I was preparing to have a type-written report made."

However his cited testimony from page 373 is interpreted - and it is hardly the function of a simple receipt to make interpretations - it cannot be limited to this autopsy descriptive sheet, for in the testimony he describes handwriting that "in some instances is not my own." Humes is blessed (as I see it) with a distinctive, backhand style, and none of the entries - these are not notes but entries on a form - is in his handwriting.

Besides, Boswell told Reporter Richard Levine that he had filled out this form. From the original I now have, it is easily discernible that two different implements were used, one by Finck and one by Boswell. In neither case is it by Humes, so any notes he made "during the

performance of the examination of the late President" <u>are not here -</u>
<u>or anywhere else.</u>

The Archivist of the United States, the custodian of the most precious documents in our national heritage, kept busy writing lies to me and arguing. Instead, he should have been searching the files and demanding those he did not have from those who did, which is his official responsibility. I decided to do what had not been done: compare this lie, earlier written to me, that these are all the notes and those to the holding of which Humes swore, with the finished report itself, to see if it has descriptions or measurements not in this autopsy descriptive sheet. To assure true impartiality, I asked Howard Roffman, a brilliant young student, then in high school and then writing his own book on this assassination, to make this comparison for me. He found, as I was confident had to be the case, what is required for even a lousy pretense of medico-legal science such as this, much more than is noted on this single sheet. (The second side holds only four brief notations and five measurements, all related to the head only.)

From my own checking in 1964, I knew the autopsy report held facts not contained <u>anywhere</u> in any of the published evidence. As soon as the 26 volumes became available, my wife and I had made a word-by-word comparison of the 15 pages of holograph with the typed autopsy report and had found substantive changes, <u>some to diametric opposites.</u> So, I knew in advance what Howard's study would show. What surprised me is the extent, much greater even than I had expected.

What I asked of Howard was much work. He compared everything available: the two versions of the autopsy report; the notes printed in CE397, said to be all the notes, whereas none are properly described as notes and none meet Finck's New Orleans descriptions of those all the doctors made; and the reports of the two panels made public by the Department of Justice so long after they were completed and when the government was in distress. These two panels, of course, conducted their studies long after the Report was issued and from the existing evidence only. The 1968 panel report includes an inventory of what it examined. Both panels are silent on the contradictions and omissions. This silence is a remarkable self-exposure and a self-condemnation, an attack on the integrity of both panels and of the Department of Justice no writer, no passionate language, can approximate.

Howard's factual listing is 15 single-spaced typewritten pages. To make this study and comparison, he isolated every single statement of fact in the typed autopsy report. He then sought for each fact or even an approximation of it in each of the other sources, the so-called notes. This leaning-over-backwards is an effort to be as fair as possible by including all that any carping critic might later complain should have been. However, it is obvious, with only these so-called notes as sources, unless some notes had been destroyed at some point, there could have been no other sources for the holograph than there were for its typed version and no other sources for the two much-later panels to draw upon.

Howard's study shows a statement of a total of 88 facts. Of these, <u>only 24 are in the "notes". Sixty-four statements of facts in</u> <u>the autopsy report are not in any of these "notes"!</u>

Because this is the autopsy of a President, because the credibility of the official Report on his assassination, that of all the Commission and its staff, the Department of Justice, all those medico-legal eminences and, indeed, of the military, too, hangs on this alone, let me express these shocking figures in two other ways.

Of the "facts" stated in the autopsy report, <u>almost three out of</u> <u>four have no existing source.</u> The percentage is just under 73 - 72.7 percent.

Or, putting it the other way, of what is represented as fact in this autopsy report, only <u>one in four exists in any existing written</u> <u>source!</u>

It can, of course, be argued that some of the doctors might have remembered, such as the color of the President's eyes and hair. This cannot be true in most cases, for of these unrecorded 64 facts, 59 include or are solely of physical characteristics. Most of these are of parts of the body and their condition. Often they relate to the bullet wounds.

And of these, the startling number of 15 involve numbers and figures. These are essentials it just cannot be believed the doctors carried in their heads. Many of these are of measurements referring directly to the wounds - their size, their distances from other parts of the body.

This is complex data, often of minute measurements, and those had to have been the most emotional days in the lives of all the doctors. They simply could not have carried all this in their heads.

And more incredible still, a third of this number is of cases where figures are used that conflict with the final autopsy report! These range from what Howard, more tolerant than I, regards as possible "minor misquoting" - I regard no error in this autopsy as tolerable - to the size of the missing piece of scalp. The figure of the report, 13 cm, exists nowhere in any notes and actually appears to be in contradiction to what is recorded in them.

This is but a brief summary of the great labor Howard undertook for me, countless hours of detailed work.

No matter how generously one regards it, no matter how much apologists may prefer to discount, I do not believe that reasonable men can conceive that three-quarters of the fact of anything as complicated as the autopsy performed on a human body, especially that of a President, can possibly have been reported except from written notes.

They no longer exist.

The destruction of such records of any murder, particularly the assassination of a President, and false swearing about it or them, are criminal. When the government that has to be the prosecutor and alone can make the charges is itself criminally responsible, neither charging nor prosecution is likely. However, I have repeatedly invited those I accuse to file charges against me and seek a judicial determination of fact. None has - or will.

"(C)" is relatively innocuous - that is, compared with the foregoing only. It is sufficiently serious to deceive in this affair. It is undoubtedly true that, as Humes certified, he had turned in to Captain J. H. Stover everything he had not already destroyed. Stover's countersigning means no more than that Humes had done this. It does not mean that neither he nor his command nor the Navy then had no other records. Somebody had the missing X-rays. Again, this is not identical with what is "on Page 47, Volume XVII" of the Hearings. There is no deviation. "(D)" is identically misrepresented as exactly what is "on Page 48".

Whoever cooked up this deliberate deceit sought to hide behind the use of "portrayed". That is a semantic "Emperor's clothes" for there is a vital difference, a difference not simply that Humes and the Commission had Xeroxes, whereas what I had finally forced out of suppression in secret files are the originals.

The difference is what was added, by Admiral Burkley, by hand, to each. *

The Warren Report and Burkley's notations cannot coexist. It is impossible.

Thus, this Commission, all of whose members were lawyers, including the Chief Justice, and its competent, large legal staff, dominated and headed by the former Solicitor General of the United States, the government's lawyer, went out of their way to accept what should not be accepted in the most blighted backland jerkwater court: secondhand evidence when the originals were available, were known to be available, and could have been obtained for a phone call.

*See p. 262.

There is no other reason for avoiding the originals, no other reason for their being hidden, none for its taking so much dogged effort to obtain them.

Now that I do have them - color pictures and Xeroxes, both made from originals - let us consider them in the sequence of the longer receipt. Let us see what they say, understand what this means.

First is the original of Humes' rewritten draft of the autopsy report, the closest thing to the original, that having been burned, not in innocence but after it was known that, with the only accused himself assassinated, there would be no court in which any evidence had to be produced and subjected to cross-examination.

Admiral Burkley countersigned and approved the handwritten autopsy report, as he also approved the retyped version. To be certain that there was no question, he initialed the first page, "GGB", as he did the last. Humes, it will be remembered, personally delivered everything to Burkley and Burkley had been with the body when it was being treated and examined in Dallas and during the autopsy in Bethesda, the one medical man in the world and, except for a few Secret Service men, the only man in the world of whom this is true.

What distinguishes this and what follows from all other copies of all versions in all files and published - what was so carefully suppressed - is Burkley's personal, handwritten approval.

The substantive changes, changes of fact, not opinion - not all of those made after Oswald was killed but only those made in what was not removed from the draft that was burned - are incredible and all, we now for the first time know, are approved by the President's own physician! The unknown, the conjectured and invented, none of which belong in a medico-legal document, least of all in the autopsy report on a President, they also are approved. To cite what in context is minor but in fact is major, the first page is typical. Where in his version Humes had the car "moving at approximately twenty miles per hour", something neither he nor anyone else knew or could know and twice as fast as it was, that was crossed out and changed to "moving at a slow rate of speed", something none of the signatories had any way of knowing and certainly not their own observation. Also unknown to the signatories, the last sentence began with an argument, not fact, "Three shots were heard and the President fell face down to the floor of the vehicle." This was completely false, a fabrication. The "correction" was no less an invention, an invention entirely consistent with every argument and change in the autopsy, to make it seem that all the shots had come from the back and that the accused Oswald was the lone assassin. After this change, the autopsy report reads, "Three shots were heard and the President fell forward." (Emphasis added.)

He did not.

"Puncture" in describing the nonfatal bullet wound means entrance. It had been used repeatedly in what survived the recreation-room burning. In every case but one, it was removed, including those cases where, without doubt, it was meant. One example is on page 4, a point on which the entire autopsy, the entire "solution" to the crime and the Warren Report itself all hang. The last full sentence, in describing what has come to be known as the rear, nonfatal wound, said to have been in the neck, the description of "a 7x4 mm oval puncture wound", with the elimination of "puncture", became "a 7x4 mm wound".

On page 7, in a single sentence where there are seven changes of fact about the head wound, the description "puncture" is twice eliminated, although in later testimony it was, with Specter's deftness in the absence of any adversary, reintroduced. In one of these cases, nothing replaced it; in the other, a word that is anything but synonymous, "lacerated". And, on pages 8 and 9, "puncture" is stricken through, replaced by nothing on 8 and by "occipital", which is entirely different, on 9.

On the other side of the same coin, where the wound that it was later decided, contrary to the existing evidence, had to be an exit

257

wound or there could be no single-assassin, no-conspiracy Report, the qualification "presumably" was inserted on pages 8, 9 and 10.

Other factual changes are to opposites. One of the most readily comprehended is on page 5, where "left" was changed to "right". On page 14, where the rear wound was related to the plane of the body and thus not dependent upon what was unknown, the position of the body, the change was to what amounts to a deliberate, unscientific and unwarranted attempt to frame the accused and the solution. As altered, this reads, "The projectiles were fired from a point behind and somewhat above the level of the deceased." Without knowing the position of the body in three different ways, this could not be said. Was the President at the time of each shot vertical, bolt erect? Was he turned in either direction from at right angles to the length of the car? Or was he, while erect in a vertical plane as compared with the car or the seat, leaning to either side?

At best, these changes reflect such uncertainty as to disqualify the autopsy report in its entirety. At worst, they are, because agreed to by so many, a deliberate conspiracy to frame the then-dead accused, to corrupt history, and to vindicate any assassin or assassins.

But what is most incredible of all in this rewriting of fact to ordain falsehood as truth is a failure by all. Neither Admiral Galloway, who dominated and ordered changes made, nor Admiral Burkley, who was everywhere and approved, nor any of the three surgeons themselves caught the one slip-up. Five medical military officers are involved in this, each culpably.

In a single place they neglected to murder truth. In a single place an accurate description of a wound remained. And say what they now may or will, it is an uncontested fact that all five did agree on it. It is the one vital fact to escape that recreation-room assassination of the medical truth.

The fourth paragraph of the holographic autopsy report begins,

Dr. Perry noted the massive wound of the head and a second puncture wound of the low anterior neck in approximately the midline. (Emphasis added.)

This is entirely in accord with everything, fact and all the initial medical statements, all of which had the President shot in the front of the neck.

There is no change here in the holograph. Nobody, at any time - Humes or anyone else - noted any alteration here in what he wrote on his blue-lined, white, letter-paper-sized pad.

But somebody in the military's butcher shop of history at Bethesda did eliminate this truth before the report was typed. In the typed version, the word "puncture" was eliminated. In its stead there appears "much smaller". The dramatic representation, that the Dallas doctors said the President had been shot from the front, fell victim to those in the military determined to rewrite what happened when the President was gunned down in cold blood in broad daylight on the streets of a major American city.

If we today cannot pinpoint what person did this, absent confession, there is no possibility of doubt about where it was done. All the evidence is that Humes turned in his draft to his superiors at Bethesda, and that all of this was supervised by the commander of that military installation, Admiral Galloway.

And this, too, was verified by another admiral, the President's personal physician. Burkley approved the original truth saying that the President's wound in the front of the neck was caused by a shot from the front, and he approved the mysterious change which attempts to hide this fact.

I have no doubt that Humes intended to change this. I do not know if he was ordered to and, if so, by whom. But my first accusation of perjury, in WHITEWASH, is on this point and to this day remains undisputed.

The day _after_ the autopsy examination, Humes called Perry twice. The Report acknowledges but a single call. Perry personally confirmed to me when I interviewed him that he had received two calls from Humes, both the same day. He had, prior to these calls, scheduled a press conference.

Perry is a man deserving of both pity and sympathy. He is friendly, personable, conscientious, and, without doubt, dedicated to his calling and justifiably proud of his skill in it. A bizarre touch in what he told me is that, although he knew the President to be irreversibly dead the moment he saw him, when he performed the surgical process then called a "tracheotomy" and since retitled "tracheostomy", he made it in the most cosmetic manner. Instead of the usual vertical incision, he made a transverse one, a cut from side to side. His purpose - and he had, he told me, done this several hundred times - was so that, upon healing, the incision would be made invisible by the natural folds of the skin.

But he was forced into perjurious testimony by national policy, his personal situation, and, above all, by Arlen Specter, the man whose personal assassination of truth and his political apostasy he parlayed into the office of District Attorney of Philadelphia and almost into the office of mayor. (He is reported to have higher political ambition.)

As I have repeatedly charged, including in public appearances in Philadelphia announced to and covered by the press, Specter suborned perjury, a crime.

Knowing full well that Perry and the other quoted Dallas doctors had said immediately that the President had been shot from the front - and that Oswald could not possibly have fired that shot, proving there had been a conspiracy - Specter pretended to the Commission that the TV tapes and radio recordings were not available (3H377ff.). And he pretended there was no printed press at all in the United States! In an embarrassed, bumbling and hesitant effort to circumvent this obstacle to the writing of the Report of the predetermined conclusions, he said, for all the world as though he, not Perry, were the witness,

> ...we have been trying diligently to get the tape recordings of the television interviews and we were unsuccessful ... our efforts at CBS, and NBC, ABC and everywhere including New York, Dallas and other cities were to no avail ... The problem is they have not yet catalogued all the footage they have ...

Picture of the American electronic media come apart, unable to operate!

It is Specter's picture, not the reality, as I discovered later in ransacking the files on this point, too. One inventory of one Dallas station alone is more than 100 pages long. And restricting this solely to Dallas and TV, only one station, located outside of Dallas, KTVT-TV, had no video tape. Three others in that area, WFAA, WBAP and KRLD, _all_ offered to duplicate for the Commission _all_ of their tapes. This is set forth in elaborate detail in one of a number of Commission files on this subject, No. 962, which also suggests that the Commission had delayed its inquiries for inventories and so late that some were about to be erased for reuse.

Specter was not under oath, so he did not commit perjury. But he lied in telling the members of the Commission that "the problem is they have not yet catalogued all the footage". (And suppose, were cataloguing the real question, that all but one of the stations had catalogued, or 99 percent of the footage had been catalogued, "all the footage" still would not have been, would it?) But the Commission's needs and purposes did not require "catalogues"; they required Perry's words, and they _then_ were readily available, including in the Commission's own files.

This is the way Specter gandy-danced his way past the disaster Perry presented.

Before the Commission he led Humes into testifying to making but a single "redundant" phone call to Perry (2H371). Questioned twice and separately (6H16 and 3H380, the earlier testimony in the later volume), Perry told Specter of two. He said of the second of these two calls Humes placed to him that "he told me, of course, that he could not talk to me about any of it and asked that I keep it in confidence, which I did" and "he advised me that he could not discuss with me the findings of the necropsy." On all counts, according to other and probative testimony and what Perry told me, this is false.

There was no legal need for secrecy and an urgent need for public information that was truthful. The entire world was in turmoil. Humes did "discuss" with Perry "the findings", based on which, as Perry later told me, he knew the wound officially described as in the back of the President's neck was actually in his back. And, although he said he did not tell anyone, Perry had to and he did.

He did have an announced and scheduled press conference on the medical evidence for that very day, undoubtedly the real purpose of Humes' call. Had it been for information, he would have telephoned Perry the night before, while he was examining the body and could check it, not after the body had been surrendered and long after the embalming and reconstruction had been completed and the corpse was in the White House.

It is Dr. Kemp Clark who first pulled the plug on this perjury (6H23):

Dr. Perry stated that he had talked to the Bethesda Naval Hospital on two occasions that morning and that he knew what the autopsy findings had shown and that he did not wish to be questioned by the press as he had been advised by Bethesda to confine his remarks to what he knew from having examined the President, and suggested that the major part of this press conference be conducted by me.

Having already told the world that the President had been shot from the front, could Perry the next day say the opposite? Or can anyone blame him for going on an unannounced vacation - translation: into attempted hiding?

Clark, also under oath, named two other witnesses to this conversation. Need it be added that Specter and the Commission had no interest and questioned neither these two nor any others about it? These were the hospital administrator and Dr. George T. Shires, both of whom Specter interviewed on other matters.

So, especially with the reports that only one bullet was expected to be recovered from the body, and that possible only from the wound in the front of the neck, there is great point in Burkley's affirmation of Humes' quotation of Perry's statement that the anterior neck wound, which he did see clearly and through which he made the tracheostomy incision, was caused by a shot from the front.

It is doubtful if there ever has been any proceeding of the importance of this assassination investigation in which there was as much perjury, except for the Reichstag fire trial. And there the falsely accused was acquitted, not killed.

The difference between the original autopsy descriptive sheet that had been suppressed until I forced it out - that had never been seen by the Commission - and the copy used in the hearings and in the Commission's files is a difference that, were the official conclusions at all tenable, would in itself entirely destroy them.

The reader will recall that when I first published a copy of the Commission's copy, this exposure and Reporter Richard Levine's needling led to the fantasy-land "explanation" that Boswell had merely been a bit careless in marking the back wound, never for a moment dreaming that in the autopsy of a President there is any need for care or accuracy. (What better qualification for a Navy Chief of Pathology?)

The wound was in the back, not the neck, as all official observers testified. Only when Specter went to work to rescript the assassination into a fake solution consistent with the official predetermination of what would be called truth and fact was there ever any question. Until then all the evidence was of a back wound. This includes Specter's own suppressed notes of his own interviews with the autopsy witnesses before their testimony.

Now, we know that Admiral Burkley placed it there, too. And Burkley certainly knew. For the moment we shall restrict ourselves to this first rescue from oblivion. In the lower left-hand corner of the front of the form he wrote, "Verified GGBurkley," all run together.

He did not just initial it. He did not just sign his name. He used a word that cannot be fudged as Boswell fooled the press. The meaning of "verified" is not subject to argument. Webster could not be more precise and limiting:

1. To prove to be true; to conform; substantiate. 2. To check or test the accuracy or exactness of. 3. To authenticate; specif., Law, to confirm or substantiate by oath or proof; also to add a verification ...

Those who instinctively grasp at evidentiary straws to support the official mythology would do well to restrain themselves, for there will be more on this point in what follows. I here make this comment so that those who think they see invisible straws and grab at them do not imagine that a medical man who rises to be an admiral in the Navy and physician to the President does not know the meaning of simple words and here, for no reason at all, just got "careless" and threw in an extra and a wrong word.

Burkley's additions to both the originals of the certifications are word for word identical.

The one that says Humes turned in "all working papers associated with" the autopsy, including the "autopsy notes", at 5 p.m., Burkley endorsed with "Accepted and approved this date", signing it with his full name, "George G. Burkley", and as "Rear Adm M C U S N Physician to the President". *

This constitutes Burkley's certification that those now-missing autopsy notes at that moment did exist and, when added to the receipt and letter so carefully omitted by Specter in publishing File 371 as Exhibit 397, were in his possession. That receipt, the item marked in both margins and the only item in it marked in any way, reads, "One copy of autopsy report and notes of the examining doctor which is described in letter of transmittal Nov. 25, 1963 by Dr. Galloway." And Galloway's words are, "Transmitted herewith by hand is the sole remaining copy (number eight) of the completed protocol in the case of John F. Kennedy. Attached are the work papers used by the Prosecutor and his assistant." (sic)

The next day Burkley gave all these items to the Secret Service, which gave him the receipt from which I have quoted.

When Burkley noted "accepted and approved" to Humes' other certification, what he actually did is mind-boggling. This admiral "accepted and approved" what Humes admitted, "that I have destroyed by burning" his first draft of the autopsy report on the President! **

Aside from what I have already established beyond peradventure, that this revision and conflagration was not until after Humes and everyone else knew that nobody would have to face examination of his records and cross-examination by defense counsel in a trial of Oswald, by then safely murdered, can anyone conceive of any good reason for the destruction of any record in a crime of this nature? Or its acceptance and approval by the President's physician - an admiral?

When the nature of the changes now known to have been made are considered, and with the until-now suppressed confirmation that the Commission's medical evidence in its entirety is dubious and in all essential elements false, can even the most tolerant put any but the most disturbing interpretation on, first, the unpunished destruction of

*See p.525. ** See p. 524.
261

imperishable, irreplaceable evidence by a man qualified in forensic pathology and, second, the unhesitating acceptance and approval by the physician to the President himself?

When all the experts were military men, when all civilians were kept out of the autopsy room by military guard, when the military destroyed the evidence and the military approved the destruction of the evidence, and when this new evidence proves the testimony about the wounds was perjurious, criminal, and all of this criminality, this false swearing, was also by the military, is not a question of some kind of military conspiracy unavoidable?

And must I not again ask, is there anything like this in our history or that of any other land considering itself free and civilized?

On the left is an excerpt from the Xerox copy of the "Autopsy Descriptive Sheet" printed by the Commission in CE 397. On the right is the identical section of the "Descriptive Sheet" excerpted from the original, which the Commission never had. Missing from the Commission's copy is the handwritten verification of Admiral Burkley, the President's physician. For the full original "Descriptive Sheet" see p. 310.

24. RECEIPT OR RECIPE?

There are too many major problems for the writer working with this kind of material. One is the number of specialized roles in each of which he requires some proficiency. He must be a researcher with instincts equipping him to cope with official dishonesty and an unlimited official willingness to suppress information, regardless of any considerations, moral, ethical or legal. On most subjects, preparation for adequate research is one of the by-products of the typical education. Not on this. He must also be an investigator, for what he needs is hidden. He first has to locate the material, prove that it exists, for he is deceived and lied to. He must be prepared to prove that he has been deceived, and that to the satisfaction of those who deceive him. He must find people with the information and get them to talk to him. In the end, he must be prepared to litigate.

In some aspects of my personal investigations into the political assassinations, this was not difficult, the chief prerequisites being finding and spending the time, having the cash to travel, always a problem, and speaking to the people in a way that can earn their confidence and their willingness to talk. Although there is no way of really knowing and although my lack of finances severely limited my ability to travel, I think it is probable that I have interviewed more people in my investigations than all others working on the assassinations. One of the surprising things is that almost nobody declined to see or speak with me.

In Memphis, for example, on the King case, of all the witnesses I sought to interview, none refused and only one declined to permit me to tape-record what he knew relevant to the assassination and its official investigation. And the only opposition, the only unpleasantness, the only improper and, in fact, illegal behavior was by the office of the prosecutor.

No single person elsewhere, including Dallas and New Orleans, refused to see me on the JFK case. Of these many, it was rare when any of them objected to taping. Those who had been offered bribes confessed it, those who had violated laws spoke of their illegalities without inhibition. In some cases, these are people who find joy in notoriety. But for the most part, they are just ordinary people, deeply disturbed that their President can be assassinated and kissed off into history without their being told by their government what did happen, how it happened, who did it and why. For some of them there was an element of risk in their willingness to help establish truth, let it be known what did - and did not - happen when the President was assassinated and that, in turn, was investigated by those whose job it was to keep him alive and by the government that came into suzerainty through that murder alone.

The experiences of Orestes Pena are not typical but they do illuminate what can happen. The only official interest in him was dual: Oswald is supposed to have had a supercolossal drunk in Pena's Habana Bar and Lounge, on the tough Decatur Street waterfront in New Orleans, at one edge of the French Quarter; and officials tried to frame him with something never made quite clear and what may have been only an extensive effort to discredit him.

On the occasion of our first contact, when Pena made a date to telephone me at a certain hour on a certain date and left his own noisy bar to do it, he was lead-piped. He called me hours later, from the hospital, while X-rays of his head were being read. If attacks are not uncommon in that part of New Orleans, it is the only one on him, and he had been willing to contend with the FBI, as few ever dare. While Orestes is not cowardly, and, in fact, is a brave man who loves his adopted country and was much attracted to the murdered President, this did not encourage completeness in telling me what he knew or in leading me to others who, to his knowledge, had information I should have. The first step in overcoming this came later, when Orestes went to see his own lawyer, having made an appointment in advance. This lawyer, then also a local judge, opened the meeting with a caution that Orestes was into a bad and dangerous business. He then removed an FBI file on Jim Garrison and showed it to Orestes. This gross impropriety, the more so because Garrison was the elected district attorney and was conducting an investigation into the assassination, turned Orestes on again.

On my next trip to New Orleans, when he could, Orestes drove me around until far into the early morning, seeking and interviewing witnesses. Someone made this expensive and distasteful to him. One after-midnight, when he returned me to my motel, there was a message that a source of information had agreed to meet me back in the French Quarter. Orestes drome me to that apartment and waited while I conducted the interview. When we returned to his brand-new Cadillac, parked under a streetlight, it was the only car in the block whose tires had been slashed and ruined. Inherent in this pinpoint vandalism is that worse could follow.

The major problems of my investigation have been of official origin. Ordinary people want the truth known and want to help make it known. Impropriety and suppression are an official monopoly.

The only people declining to be seen are Kennedys and of the Commission. The unfortunate truth seems to be that the Kennedys, having spent their lives doing everything with money and the power it can buy and, without so intending, having bought their man, bought a whore who didn't know how to do it. Manchester's sole qualification seems to have been sycophancy, having written an uncritical book about the President. Hidden in the remote recesses of his psyche was a literary and political time-bomb, an enormous ego and a contempt for what he did not know and did not understand. He thus wrought another and shameful national scandal by simply writing what he wanted to have been the truth for what was truth, the result being what it is no exaggeration to describe as a work of such overwhelming inaccuracy that a writer knowing nothing and preparing a work of fiction would have been closer to reality.

This resulted in a kind of Kennedy self-blackmail, undoubtedly inspired a new fear of the entire subject that, when added to the official blackmail, terrified all Kennedys and all their employees and hangers-on, made them all distrustful of the only ones who could help them avoid still-new scandals and denied them knowledge they could not get on their own or from officials.

It is in this way, I believe, that the Kennedys became an essential if unwitting part of the official suppressions.

Government was not unwilling to exploit this, for government did have the desire to suppress. When it could not suppress in any other way, it suppressed in the name of the Kennedys, openly blaming the family for it.

Under the law, none of the suppressions with which I have had to contend and only some of which I have overcome can be justified. But overcoming them requires lawyers and extensive expenses and fees few writers can meet and I cannot. This led to my being my own lawyer, a function for which I am not prepared, there being no other way in which I could get the evidence we here consider. And all of this denied evidence was suppressed for one of two reasons: The false claim that it was lost or in the name of the Kennedys.

I asked for evidence only, nothing personal.

This preface to what I have, up to the moment of writing, been able to rescue from official oblivion, is intended for perspective and dimension, so that there may be understanding and meaning. The mere fact that what I here for the first time bring to light was suppressed, was lied about, officially and repeatedly - was withheld from the Commission or, in any event, was not in its files and did not get its consideration - has such obvious and frightening implications they need not be expounded upon to be comprehended. They provide a special context for this new evidence which, had it not also been suppressed, would all over again have prevented the writing and the accepting of the false official account of how the President was killed and by whom.

If the reasons why officialdom saw to it that only falsehood about the assassination was permitted to become official truth may still have to be conjectured, the fact of it can no longer be questioned.

None of the remaining items covered in the Bouck-to-Burkley receipt came to me voluntarily or without some effort and trouble on my part. Inherent was my willingness to sue to get it. For one item, no immediate explanation for suppression suggests itself. Nor is any urgent reason apparent for its corruption by the Commission. Dishonesty simply became the norm.

This is the eighth item in the receipt, the description already quoted. As finally provided, it was accompanied by an entirely different description:

Copy of a letter dated November 22, 1963, from Dr. M. T. Jenkins, Department of Anesthesiology of the University of Texas Southwestern Medical School, subject: Statement concerning resuscitative efforts for President John F. Kennedy together with the letter of November 23, 1963, from Dr. Kemp Clark and the summary of treatment and examination of the President in the Dallas County Hospital.

"Copy" the provided Jenkins statement is, and a very poor, remote-generation copy at that. The original was used as part of Exhibit 392 and was published (R529-30). However, as used by the Commission (R516), the Clark letter was replaced by the unidentified paper, the first thing in this exhibit, from which half of the sheet was physically removed. It is followed in the exhibit and in the Report by a different copy of Clark's summary (R517-8).

In tracing this suppression, ten months before I finally got the Clark letter, I had obtained two identically-worded but not identical copies of the substitute for it, each bearing the Secret Service control number for this file (No. 561, part of Commission File 87), both reduced-size copies of another paper and each of different size. Both bear the identical printing instructions. But they are not Clark's letter, not part of it, do not say what it says and do say what it does not. It includes what is not true and is obviously untrue. Neither the "summary of treatment" nor "examination of the President" are mentioned. Nor does it include such diverting items as "the President's wife refused to take off her bloody gloves, clothing. She did take a towel and wipe her face."

This is the pointless substitute for the real covering letter, replaced without explanation, by those who claim they withhold evidence of the crime itself to protect the privacy and shelter the feelings of the survivors!

Among its other false and irrelevant statements is that the President "was in the back seat, Gov. Connally was in the front seat of the same car." Why this false statement I simply cannot understand for immediately the entire civilized world knew the truth through the most widely published pictures in photographic history; both were in back of the car, Connally on the "jump" seat in front of Kennedy. Moreover, the Commission did publish the real Clark letter (21H150).

Clark used the regular letterhead. No need to excise that. His opening was certainly innocent enough: "As you requested, I enclose an abstract of the admission of the late President John F. Kennedy to

Parkland Memorial Hospital, Dallas, Texas."

The next paragraph says no more than that the summary was "prepared from the statements of several physicians". These statements were given to the Commission and published by it. The third paragraph explains why three copies were kept locally. And the conclusion is an expression of condolences.

That this was eliminated in favor of an inaccurate statement that has been snipped up first, was irrelevant and its antecedents hidden, is a simplistic example of the kind of investigation this was, with hiding so much the norm that it was done without sense or reason, even when there was nothing to be hidden.

If this is innocence, here innocence ends. That "lost" FBI receipt withheld from me for more than three years during which its existence was repeatedly denied, that receipt missing from the Commission's files and not mentioned or addressed in all its work, is a receipt for the non-existent. It also leaves without a receipt what does exist. The poor Xerox copy of unknown generation reads, in full:

22 November 1963

From: Francis X. O'NEILL, Jr., Agent FBI
       James W. SIBERT, Agent FBI

To: Captain J. H. STOVER, Jr., Commanding Officer, U. S. Naval Medical
       School, National Naval Medical Center, Bethesda, Maryland

1. We hereby acknowledge receipt of a missle removed by Commander James
    J. HUMES, MC, USN on this date.

[signature] Francis X. O'NEILL, Jr.

[signature] James W. SIBERT

Now, it happens that the official version is built around the claim that no "missle" was recovered from the body.

I got this receipt from the Secret Service. I asked the Archivist to see the "missle" it covered, he being the official custodian of all the records and his agency the legal inheritor of the Warren Commission's records. He suggested "CE843 consists of bullet fragments recovered during the autopsy, and there is information concerning a receipt given for these fragments by the FBI on page 284 of CD 7 and page 4 of CE387. We can show you this exhibit in the National Archives. We have no other information relating to a missile recovered during the autopsy."

His first reference is to the Sibert-O'Neill report, which has fascinated me since I discovered it in the spring of 1966. The reader is already familiar with this report and the various FBI interpretations of it. CE387 is the typed version of the autopsy report (16H978-83).

"Fragments" is accurate, but misleading. In CE843 supposedly two tiny particles of metal are stored on cotton in a small plastic container. The Commission published a picture, with the container lid removed (17H841). The published exhibit list (17HXXIII) also says two. But the picture seems to show three.

266

The disposition of the Archivist may have been to be helpful, but he added confusion where there is already more of it than can be coped with or adequately explained. He did not say how many of these metallic specks are in CE843, only "bullet fragments".

Had he really intended to be helpful to me, to attempt to assist accurate reporting and record-making, he would have told me as his assistant, Herbert Angel, acting in his name, confirmed to Howard Roffman, that this container does hold three particles.

However, the autopsy report at the point to which he referred, well-known to me from much study, says "two small, irregularly-shaped fragments ... measure 7 x 2 mm. and 3 x 1 mm." (16H981). The larger is about as thick at its thickest as a toothpick. Its maximum length is about a quarter-inch. The smaller is less than half this minute size. And the protocol says the receipt for these two specks is attached, but it is not, not in any of the many copies in many files. I have checked them all. This leaves open the questions why this receipt disappeared, whether it was these virtual fly-spots of metal or that for "a missle", or whether there is more we do not know.

But neither of the fragments shown in CE843 (17H841), assuming that exhibit contains and the picture shows only two fragments, can possibly be either described by the FBI or the autopsy report. While neither is square, both are roughly rectangular. The smaller seems to be of a fairly regular pentagonal shape, the larger has a proportion of two to three, not seven to two.

It would seem that all of the fragments removed from the body remain to have an official accounting and none of this contained in CE843 is acceptably accounted for.

The FBI's second summary report, CD107 (p.5) is not helpful, not drafted with the explicitness TV viewers expect of their FBI. It says only that "several fragments of lead were recovered" and includes in "several" the five pieces said to have been recovered from the limousine in two different searches (both after it was washed). Thus, although CD107 and CD1 were to have been the two really definitive reports by the FBI, they tell us nothing about "a missle recovered" from the President's head.

With these fragments from the car, there is not, as with the head, an extra one not accounted for. Now, with that diligence with which this historic evidence is preserved by the government, with its deep concern that everything vital in the evidence be kept secure, carefully and tenderly, as is appropriate to the memory of a President and evidence of his assassination, it has managed, somehow, to dispose of one of these car fragments. It no longer exists. Again it is Howard Roffman who detected its absence in a picture taken for his study, and again it is Angel who confirmed the fact but offered no explanation. It is typical of this Commission and this evidence that whatever could be was scattered. Thus, these five fragments were introduced into evidence at two different points and with three different exhibit numbers. The two larger ones are CE567 and CE569 (17H256 and 257). The three smaller ones, of which one has disappeared - without Hoover's complaint, explanation or investigation - are all CE840, of which the picture is published on the page facing that of magically expanded CE843 which cannot be CE843 (17H840).

Oh, that unsung Song of Solomon!

Rhoads' kindness in directing me to page 4 of the Sibert-O'Neill report, which is also page 284 of CD 7, leads to language similar to Rhoads': "During the autopsy inspection of the area of the brain, two fragments of metal were removed by Dr. Humes, namely, one fragment measuring 7 x 2 millimeters, which was removed from the right side of the brain. An additional fragment of metal measuring 1 x 3 millimeters was also removed from this area," placed in a container and "following the signing of a proper (sic) receipt were transported by Bureau agents to the FBI laboratory." (CD7:284)

This does not mean the FBI had teams of agents standing by for messenger service and other duties at the autopsy. It was not immediately after the receipt was signed that unnamed agents rushed the specimens to the laboratory. Sibert and O'Neill remained at the hospital until everything was done, not leaving until the next day. It was not until then that they, personally, made this delivery. In their own words,

The two metal fragments removed from the brain area were hand carried by SAs Sibert and O'Neill to the FBI Laboratory immediately following the autopsy and were turned over to SA KURT FRAZIER. (CD7:285)

There is a permeating inaccuracy in FBI reports, a looseness of language that may be one of Hoover's real reasons for never wanting them seen, for to see them is to catch them chronically wrong. After careful examination of thousands of these FBI reports, I am astounded that they can so often be so wrong, that they are never full and complete, and wonder how many innocent have been victimized by them, whether or not this is the intent of the agents. These reports first influence the Bureau, then the Department's lawyers, and then judges and juries. No wonder Hoover is so secretive about them.

Where the reader may in his own mind assess blame or make other judgments based on quotations from FBI reports, this persistent infidelity to strict fact and a customary incompleteness in them should not be forgotten.

Official help is of selective kindness, as is official help in research. Rhoads ought not have overlooked page 283 of CD 7. Perhaps another quotation from the typed protocol may explain his oversight:

From the surface of the disrupted right cerebral cortex two small irregularly shaped fragments of metal are recovered,

the sizes following.

Or, both these two 7x2 and 3x1 mm, came from the same part of the brain, in the Sibert-O'Neill language from page 283, "behind the right frontal sinus". This was disclosed by the reading of the X-rays or, if Sibert and O'Neill are correct, not too long after 8:15 p.m. at the latest, that being the time "the first incision was made", and the X-rays were read first.

The next sentence of this report was so completely ignored I also forgot it and thereby missed a significant part of the Clark panel's report that Howard Roffman did not miss. These are the words of the Sibert-O'Neill report that immediately follow those quoted above: "The next largest fragment appeared to be at the rear of the skull at the juncture of the skull bone."

"Largest" need refer to no more than length or the larger dimension in a single plane. There is no reference to any X-ray in more than one projection.

Now, the "rear of the skull" is not "the right frontal sinus". This is, without doubt, a fourth fragment, the second with which the good doctors did not burden what remained of their effort after the recreation-room conflagration as they did not disturb history or the solution to the crime. It would, indeed, have been a burden to the solution. Or to the Commission, which does not have this fragment as an exhibit; or to Clark's panel, which noted it as showing on the X-rays but failed to report it missing to the trusting Attorney General.

One magical bullet was already too much. All the damage to the head and more had to have been from this single exploded bullet. The impossible already required of it without these oversights is to have exploded God knows how many fragments into Dealey Plaza with the side of the head, left five fragments in two parts of the car, cracked the windshield, dented the windshield trim, left two recovered fragments in the head where it also shed some 40 smaller particles, then, somehow, in a manner J. Edgar Hoover himself said was not possible, to have looped several hundred feet and struck a concrete curbing with sufficient force for the spray from it to have cut the face of James T. Tague.

Now, in addition to all this spectacular and, save for Bullet 399, entirely unequaled virtuosity, it had to have deposited still another fragment at the other end of the head?

I suppose when out-of-date, war-surplus bullets are used in one of the world's poorest and least dependable rifles, allegedly by one of the world's worst duffers, we must expect the bullets and the rifle to become magical and the duffer a veritable William Tell, if the assassination of a President has to be accounted for.

Roffman spotted the size of this unaccounted head fragment, not given by Sibert and O'Neill, in that panel's report. It is 6.5 millimeters and may well be the largest of all in volume.

With all of this, however, we still do not have "a missle recovered" from the corpse.

We finally do have the receipt for it.

We have four fragments large enough to be recovered, of which we are to believe only three (accounted as two) were and the fourth just disappeared. Of course, we may believe, if we want to be really mean, that the FBI has that, too, and just is not saying. If true, this would not encourage belief that analysis of it shows it to be from the same bullet.

And it wouldn't be the first time the FBI was not saying. After all, the President <u>was</u> dead, was he not, and not even Hoover could bring him back to life.

I am sorry I could not do as well with the "lost" fragment as I did with the "lost" receipt for "a missle". I inquired but got no response.

This should be enough for one official skulduggery when there are so many. Especially when a President like John F. Kennedy is assassinated.

Especially with military bullets designed, in compliance with the Geneva Convention on humanitarian warfare, to make this kind of almost infinite fragmentation an impossibility.

25. FILM-FLAM

There is mystery and crookedness with the film of all kinds. Another of those "lost" receipts deals with the disappearance of evidence, disinterest in it, and still more official lying.

Although for years I had been told that "the" receipt which Roy Kellerman signed for the film had just disappeared, and the Secret Service, too, said they could not find it, Tom Kelley, by then promoted to Assistant Director in charge of Presidential protection, did get it for me finally. Not the original, but a copy with some signatures, far enough removed from the original to be almost illegible. Kelley had also said "we do not have a copy" of it. In fact, he eventually produced two copies of two different receipts.

One pair is of poor, unclear carbon copies; the other, a clear retyping. The retyped copies are certified by Admiral Galloway as commanding officer of the entire National Naval Medical Center and Captain J. H. Stover, Jr., as commander of the Naval Medical School of that center. Plain paper, not letterheads, were used for all. *

One pair deals with X-rays, the other with "photographic material". Only the retyped copy of the receipt for this "photographic material" is "accepted and approved" by Admiral Burkley, his handwritten notation and signature. The other three do not bear his name.

Each is in the form of a memorandum, those on the X-rays from Commander John H. Ebersole, Acting Chief of Radiology of the United States Naval Medical School, part of the Naval Medical Center; those on the photographic film from Stover as school commander. Both are addressed to Kellerman, who wrote "Rec. by: Roy H. Kellerman, U. S. Secret Service, 11-22-63" on each.

The original receipts were typed by Chester H. Bowers of the Navy "who visited the autopsy room during the final stages of such to type receipts given by FBI and Secret Service for items obtained" (CD7:283).

The photographer was John T. Stringer, Jr., who countersigned that original receipt, appending "photographer" after his name. Under it appears the writing, "Floyd A. Rabe, HM2, USN". The name "Rabe" does not appear in the Sibert-O'Neill report.

The Sibert-O'Neill account of the transfer of the film (CD7:285) is:

The following is a complete listing of photographs and X-Rays taken by the medical authorities of the President's body. They were turned over to Mr. ROY H. KELLERMAN of the Secret Service. X-Rays were developed by the hospital, however, the photographs were delivered to Secret Service undeveloped.

They list "11 X-Rays, 22 4 x 5 color photographs, 18 4 x 5 black and white photographs, 1 roll of 120 film containing five exposures."

Lack of precision here creates a major problem.

In their secret 1967 review of their own work for Attorney General Clark, these three autopsy surgeons, rivaling their report in imprecision, if not in medico-legal deficiency, do not list the X-rays they had had taken and subsequently examined, nor do they give any

---
*See pp. 546-7.

totals. Sibert and O'Neill say there were 11. But the 1968 panel
lists, gives rudimentary descriptions of and numbers a total of 14.
As we have seen, none of these include the full-body X-rays all that
all sources, including these FBI agents, agree were then taken at
Finck's request. Nor does the 1968 panel list any X-rays not described
as taken the night of November 22, 1963.

But the FBI says there were only 11 X-rays when 14 does not account for all known to have been taken.

The Ebersole receipt reads, "Eight (8) 14 x 17 inch X-Ray film"
and "six (6) 10 x 12 inch X-Ray film", which is essentially the language and precisely the accounting of the Appendix B listing on page
seven of the GSA-Kennedy family contract.

By examining the original receipt, before it was retyped, it may
be possible to account for part of the error, that by the FBI. In its
initial form, the second entry read "Three (3) 10 x 12 inch X-Ray film."
This was corrected by hand in what appears to be Ebersole's writing and
with his initials, "JHE," to read "six", the numeral also being changed.

For the moment, there is nothing further that can be done to
reconcile the discrepancies or to account for the missing X-ray film,
including those of the full body and the extremities, already discussed.

The Navy insists it turned over everything "to the White House".
When I first made inquiry, Captain K. W. Wade, Deputy Chief of Information, told me, "The entire record of the autopsy was delivered to the
White House immediately afterward." This left open the possibility
that, to comply with its own regulations, the Navy kept copies for itself. On subsequent inquiry, Wade said, "The complete record was delivered to the White House and no records remain with the Navy."

Tom Kelley tells me that, on April 26, 1965, he turned over all
of this to the President's former secretary, Mrs. Evelyn Lincoln, who
was then working in the National Archives, presumably on behalf of the
Kennedy library. And this most essential evidence was and is missing,
with there never having been any but contradictory accountings of what
has not disappeared.

It would seem that from the FBI, Secret Service and federal forensic pathologists, when they report on their own work, we should be able
to expect precision, most of all when they are investigating how a
President was killed. This surely is a prime example of one hell of a
way to investigate a President's murder.

This absolutely incredible record is even worse with the photographs. Aside from what we have already gone into in earlier parts of
this book, we have new inconsistencies, new disagreements that are not
reconciled. They are consistent in hinting at chicanery from the outset.

Not until the 1968 panel review was there anything that could be
called a listing of what pictures were taken. This is not because there
are not standards for proper procedures. The Navy has a separate manual
on them. The panel's listing is inadequate and does not account for
pictures that had to have been taken. The Stringer list does not say
what pictures he took, but it does specify that "on this occasion" he
took no others. Aside from laboratory samples, there were at least two
occasions on which pictures were taken, prior to the examination of the
body and during it. However, he may have meant the entire autopsy procedure by "on this occasion". Here is the body of his retyped receipt:

The following items of photographic material were placed in the custody

of Mr. Roy H. Kellerman, Assistant Special Agent in Charge, United

States Secret Service, 22 November 1963 at the Morgue, U. S. Naval

Hospital, Bethesda, Maryland:

271

(a) 11 graphic film holders (4 x 5) containing 16 sheets of exposed

Ektachrome E3 film

(b) 9 graphic film holders (4 x 5) containing 12 sheets exposed

Portrait Pan film

(c) 1 roll 120 Ektachrome E3 exposed film.

To my personal knowledge this is the total amount of film exposed on

this occasion.

It is requested the film holders be returned or replaced.

It is an insignificant point that the miserly Navy requested
return or replacement of the inexpensive film holders, return costing
more than not returning them. It does, however, indicate what was of
major interest, what occupied official minds. And that is not an exact autopsy or solving the crime, but pennies. How cheap can the military be when a President is assassinated?

Prior to retyping and certification by the top brass, the
Stringer receipt, too, had been altered or corrected, one hopes the
latter, the number of holders being changed, in what seems to be his
handwriting and with his initials opposite each. Item "(a)" first appeared as "8", then was changed to "11". Item "(b)" was changed from
"6" to "9".

With such film holders, it is customary to use two small sheets
of film, the two-sided holder being reversed in the back of the camera
after one exposure. So, in the original listing, counting two pieces
of film in each holder, there is, in each case, twice the number of
sheets there are holders.

No accounting of this film was ever sought by anyone before me.
None was volunteered by anyone. It was a subject of total official
disinterest. There was no official interest in the ruin of so much of
the film. It was totally ignored and completely hidden until I brought
it to light. Nobody on the Commission, apparently, knew about it. Or
cared. Or insisted on seeing all the photographs, the best possible
evidence of the crime, the legally defined "best evidence". From the
false official published record, nobody on the Commission saw any of
these pictures. Or even knew how many were taken, what they show or do
not show, which was only the center of the alleged investigation, the
crux of its alleged work and charge to it by the President who has, in
a sense, become one of the victims.

So, we are left with considerable confusion, the undeviating evidentiary condition when a President is killed and his killing officially
investigated.

The until-now suppressed official records I have been able to obtain seem to be contradictory. This leaves me with no alternative but
to present them as records and suggest what they can mean.

The Stringer receipt was changed by three with each of the kinds
of 4x5 film. I suggest this does not mean that three sheets were shifted
to separate holders in each case. I think it more likely this represents pictures taken after the original receipt was first typed. Such
things as whether these are black-and-white and color shots of the same
views we cannot know. There are the same number of extra holders with
each variety of film, Portrait Pan, which is a fine-grained black-and-
white film, and Ektachrome, or color film. In each case, the additions
can mean from three to six more exposures.

If the supposedly unerring FBI is right about the pictures as it
was wrong about the X-rays, there were 18 black-and-white 4x5 negatives

and 22 4x5 color. With the corrected number of 11 color-film holders each holding two sheets of exposed film, there would be 22 color shots, which is what the FBI says. With each of the nine Portrait Pan holders containing two exposed films, there would be 18, again what Sibert and O'Neill list. The FBI list shows that only five of the film in the roll of 120 color were exposed, permitting a total of 45 as the maximum number of autopsy pictures taken in all, aside from laboratory shots that may and should have been taken later and of which there is no accounting, the norm when a President is murdered and autopsied with the military in complete charge, with guards posted to keep all civilians out.

It is now necessary to consult the accounting of the GSA-family contract, where the film is inventoried as "Appendix B Materials":

APPENDIX B

1. Envelopes numbered 1 to 18 containing black and white negatives of photographs taken at time of autopsy

2. 7 envelopes containing 4 x 5 negatives of autopsy material

3. 5 envelopes containing 4 x 5 exposed film containing no image

4. 1 roll of exposed film from a color camera entirely black with no image apparent

5. Envelope containing 8 X-ray negatives 14" x 17"; 6 X-ray negatives 10" x 12"; 12 black and white prints 11" x 14"; 17 black and white prints 14" x 17"; all negatives and prints pertaining to X-rays that were taken at the autopsy

6. 36 8" x 10" black and white prints - autopsy photos
   37 3 1/2" x 4 1/2" black and white prints - autopsy photos
   27 color positive transparencies 4" x 5"
   1 unexposed piece of color film

7. 27 4" x 5" color negatives of autopsy photographs
   55 8" x 10" color prints of autopsy photographs

Not one of these seven categories or inventories is, in itself, meaningful or definitive. Not one is unequivocal, tells us, for example, how many different pictures survived the military photography or what I will soon expose, the military processing. For the moment, since we are trying, among other things, to learn a very simple fact, how many different pictures exist of the wounds to the President, let us restrict ourselves to two items, one of which is positive in a negative meaning. Item 4 says that not one of the five exposures made on that roll of 120 Ektachrome survived. It is "entirely black with no image apparent". Item 3, which is in terms of "envelopes", saying nothing about what is in each envelope, lists "5 envelopes containing 4 x 5 exposed film containing no image". The government was so careful in its simplest recordkeeping it does not specify whether this was color film, black-and-white or some of each that, with all the skills of official medical photography (a classification with exacting requirements in the military - a classification limited to skilled photographers who also have medical training) did not come out.

May I suggest, parenthetically, that when I had immediately asked for a copy of this contract, which could not be denied me under the law, and was denied it, the foregoing explains why it was denied to me? May I also suggest that the failure of Fred Graham to note the sad fate of the film in his New York Times story when it was leaked to him explains why he was given an also-illegal "exclusive" on it?

With some difficulty, I did obtain from Tom Kelley a partial explanation of what happened to the film. Because it is an inadequate and incomplete explanation, I feel it is necessary to say what I can for him: that, under the law, if there are no existing records, there is no requirement for the government to report what is in employees' minds and not on paper. Therefore, what he did tell me, if inadequate, remains more than what it was legally incumbent upon him to tell me. Kelley is a lawyer. If he did not know the law, the Secret Service has its own general counsel and the extensive legal staff of the Treasury, of which it is part, to draw upon. Therefore, although the following report is unsatisfactory, it does represent a step toward public disclosure of suppressed evidence, a plus that in my experience is almost entirely limited to the Secret Service. It took four years of trying to get this much, Kelley's May 19, 1970, response to my last previous inquiry of six days earlier:

To our knowledge the X-rays for which Mr. Kellerman signed a receipt were all of the X-rays which were taken during the autopsy. All of the X-rays for which Mr. Kellerman signed a receipt were in the possession of the U. S. Secret Service from the time of their receipt to the execution of the Memorandum of Transfer. The Secret Service has no knowledge of any X-rays taken which were not included in those for which Mr. Kellerman signed the receipt.

The Secret Service has no record of the development and processing of each of the films which were turned over to us, but relying on the recollection of our employees who handled the film, the following information may be of use to you.

From the night of November 22, 1963, until April 1965, the photographic films were in the custody of the U. S. Secret Service. Mr. Kellerman delivered the films to Robert I. Bouck, U. S. Secret Service at the Executive Offices Building, Washington, D. C. On or about November 27, 1963, Bouck gave the photographic film to Secret Service employee, James K. Fox, who took the film to the U. S. Navy Photographic Laboratory. The black and white film was processed, black and white negatives were developed, and colored positives were made from the colored film. The processing and development was done by Lieut. V. Madonia, U. S. Navy, at the laboratory. Fox remained with the film at the laboratory and all the photographic film was returned to Mr. Bouck the same day. The processed film was placed in a combination lock-safe file; the combination was known only to two persons. A few days later, black and white prints were made by Mr. Fox in the Secret Service photographic laboratory. On or about December 9, 1963, Mr. Fox took the colored positives back to the U. S. Navy Photographic Laboratory and observed while enlarged color prints were made. All the color positives and prints were returned by Fox at 6 p.m., the same evening and returned to the locked safe.

All of the photographic material received by Mr. Kellerman on the night of November 22, 1963, all the processed and developed material, and all the prints made from the film were included in the Memorandum of Transfer mentioned in your letter.

Very truly yours,

Thomas J. Kelley
Assistant Director

The one thing on which there is complete accord is that the photographic film was undeveloped when given to Kellerman. Sibert and O'Neill also note this (CD7:285).

In dealing with so many contradictory accountings, all equally official, there seems to be no means of eliminating all confusion, no certain order of presentation that can, in fact, minimize it. Therefore, let me record two beliefs at the outset:

I believe Kelley's paragraph on the X-rays. I do not think anybody outside the military ever saw those missing X-rays, in one description, "full-body"; in another, the extremities. I do believe that what was given Kellerman, a package the contents of which were unknown to him, is what he did deliver to the White House. I believe the Secret Service also preserved them until, illicitly, it unloaded them on the Kennedys.

I also believe that the Secret Service was not responsible for the destruction of any film, however that was accomplished, whether accidental or deliberate. The suppression of this fact could be the normal workings of an uptight bureaucracy had the destruction really been an accident, hard as that may be to believe when even the corner drugstore does better.

On the other side, Kelley confirmed to me verbally the accuracy of the previously quoted and almost entirely ignored Secret Service statement that it had shown the Commission staff the X-rays, which gives a special perspective to Specter's belated effort to overcome his own transgressions against the requirements and obligation imposed upon him by his job and destroys his innocence. Kelley said of this three things, all of which I do believe:

a) that he, personally, had done this, had shown the staff the X-rays;
b) that it was prior to the taking of the medical testimony and included the medical witnesses (if in seeming contradiction of the Commission's record, personally, I believe Kelley);
c) that, as of that time and to the best of his knowledge, the mechanical damage to X-rays reported by the 1968 panel did not exist.

Where Kelley's explanation falls short, among other places, is in his accounting of what pictures he showed to whom. He confirmed that he had shown a picture of the rear nonfatal wound to Specter in Dallas. He did not report any other showing of any pictures to anyone.

This is not in his written account. Nor did he acknowledge what the "TOP SECRET" Commission executive sessions show, that the Commission did have autopsy pictures, described only as "the".*

In one of the earliest of these secret gatherings, that beginning at 2 p.m. December 16, 1963 (p.12), after a discussion of carefully hidden but rather thorough dissatisfaction with the FBI be-all, end-all summary report, CD 1, extending even to the grammar, Commissioner John J. McCloy complained, "It does leave you some loopholes," one of the larger understatements. To this he added, "This bullet business leaves me confused." Warren agreed "it's totally inconclusive".

The late Senator Russell commented, "They couldn't find where one bullet came out that struck the President and yet they found a bullet in the stretcher."

Fortified a bit by the support of Warren, Russell and Senator Cooper, McCloy declared, "I think you ought to have the autopsy documents."

Warren first said, "By all means ... they might play a very important part in it," then added (p.13), "So if there is no objection we'll settle for whatever medical reports there are ..."

"The autopsy documents" and all the "medical reports" should have included all the film, which is an integral part of "the autopsy documents" and basic to the "medical reports".

*See WHITEWASH IV, p. 102.

This meeting was held in the National Archives, with a government-supplied court reporter. By the time of their January 21 meeting, the Commission had its own offices and had just obtained the thoroughly dependable services of the court-reporting firm of Ward & Paul, official reporters to a number of government bodies, including the Congress. Ward & Paul had had special covers for the transcripts printed to the Commission's satisfaction. Aside from full identification of the proceeding, they contain this small-type parenthetical notation: "Stenotype tape, Master Sheets, Carbons and Waste turned over to the Commission for destruction."

Another sign they expected no devils-loving-scripture like me ever to see them.

This January 21 meeting, which began at 2:10 p.m., was the day after delivery of the typed autopsy report to the Commission.

The agenda had been covered by page 35 of the transcript. Cooper was about to discuss "questions raised" when McCloy interjected, "About direction." Cooper got in that in his mind he had "one or two" of these questions "it might be well to discuss", and McCloy continued with this:

Let me ask you about this raw material business that is here. /They had just finished discussing the second unsatisfactory FBI supplemental summary report, CD107./ Does it consist of the raw material of the autopsy? They talk about the colored photographs of the President's body -- do we have those?

Rankin's answer was unequivocal, no "ifs" or "buts": "Yes, it is part of it, a small part of it."

McCloy, an experienced lawyer, was not satisfied with this seeming deprecation of what lawyers call "best evidence" of an autopsy, even if it came from the former Solicitor General of the United States. He pressed Rankin, "Are they here?"

After again giving unequivocal response, "Yes," Rankin did that in which he was most adept, switched, ever so gently, away from the pictures and the Commission's having them to their not having something nonexistent for which they had asked, "the minutes of the autopsy", from which he again digressed further, to whether what some doctor said in those "minutes" "is supported by the conclusions in the autopsy and so forth".

Before long, he had the old biddies away out in left field. But they did have, at the very least, "the colored photographs of the President's body".

Unless, of course, Rankin is the most unconscionable liar, a man who would run the investigation of the killing of an American President and deliberately lie about the most essential evidence.

This need not be inconsistent with the precise wording of Kelley's May 19, 1970, report to me. In it he limits what was kept "in the custody of the U. S. Secret Service" and "in a combination lock-safe file; the combination was known only to two persons," to but a single thing, "the photographic films". Now, films are not prints. Perhaps Rankin was not this big liar and Kelley merely sloppy in his phrasing. But Kelley does distinguish between "films" and "prints", and he does not say that all prints were never out of Secret Service "custody".

Kelley may seem to be in conflict with another Sibert-O'Neill report (CD7:286-7), that of their November 27, 1963, interview with Gerald A. Behn, then "Special Agent in Charge, White House Detail, United States Secret Service". It concludes:

Mr. BEHN advised that the undeveloped photographs and x-rays made during the course of the autopsy conducted at the National Naval Medical Center, Bethesda, Maryland, are in the custody of Mr. BOB BOUCK, Protective Research Section, United States Secret Service and could be made available to the Federal Bureau of Investigation on request. *

*See p. 548.

There are a number of possibilities that can credit Kelley's version. One of the more obvious is that this interview suggested that the film should be processed and that, after the reminder, it was. Another is his care in specifying he is not absolutely certain of the exact date, his words being "on or about November 27".

My purpose here is not to defend Kelley but to try and cleanse a dirty record. The precise moment of the processing is not the major conflict, it is not in question. If, at some later time, the precise moment is an urgent need, unless the Navy has destroyed or otherwise divested itself of all its records, those of its laboratory will show when this work was done.

Aside from the developing of the exposed film, while Kelley does not account for any use or showing in his report, he does specify what else happened to it. If there is error, it is omission that will soon be specific.

James K. Fox, of the Secret Service, made "black and white prints" himself, "in the Secret Service photographic laboratory". Kelley does not specify their number. This was a few days after November 27 and presumably before December 9, when he returned to the Navy laboratory, this time with "the colored positives", or still film, where, under his observation, "enlarged color prints were made".

Thus, prints had been made of all good, receipted film almost two weeks before Rankin told the members of the Commission in their sanctum sanctorum, with no single member of the staff present, that he had the autopsy picture prints.

Returning now to the Appendix B itemization of the contract, we get into real confusion that, like all the rest about the film, is possible only because of uncharacteristic military departure from military regulations and regular medical custom, practice and law, all of which required autopsy film to remain with the Navy.

Contract Item 5 is the only one dealing with X-rays. Its accounting of negatives, or film, by size and number, is exactly that of the 1968 panel report. This is less than a major surprise because this is what was given to that panel. But it also specifies what was never, including by that panel, ever mentioned: that prints were made of these X-rays.

There is no way of knowing how many prints were made of what negatives or for what purpose or purposes. Of these prints, 12 are of a size not that of any negative (11 x 14). There are no prints coinciding with the six 10 x 12 negatives. There are 17 14 x 17 prints. There are eight negatives of this size. There is no way of knowing which were repeated or why, whether all were printed, whether the 14 x 17 prints are of 14 x 17 negatives, or anything else at all except maybe this one thing, depending on the interpretation of the word "autopsy": If as used in this receipt "autopsy" refers to the examination of the body made before embalming, then this item means there are no X-rays of any specimens removed, as, for example, of the brain, made after the completion of the body examination.

Should one want to conjecture, what may be part of a pattern is possible. There are 12 11 x 14 prints, or twice the number of 10 x 12 X-rays. And there are 17 14 x 17 prints, or twice the number of X-rays of that size plus one. If it actually was this way, that would provide one complete set of prints for the Secret Service and one for either the FBI or the Commission, plus one extra copy of one X-ray in which there could have been special interest.

The only specific accounting of black-and-white negatives is in the first item. It is simultaneously as unspecific as it can be, identifying these negatives only by the number of envelopes in which they are held. The most this can be taken to mean is that there are 18 good black-and-white negatives.

Item 2 is unspecific, "7 envelopes containing 4 x 5 negatives of autopsy material". Because Item 1 does say "black and white", perhaps

Item 2, the only remaining possibility, is all color film. If true, the number of good film remains clouded and can range from seven upward if only one, the proper method, was in each envelope.

The third and fourth items are on "no image" film, the fourth with the word "apparent" added, for all the world as though some invisible photography were used permitting the not apparent to be preserved unnoticed on the film. The fourth is certainly the 120 color and, unless deceit is practiced, the use of the word "roll" should indicate that none of those five shots came out or survived processing. However, when the same listing, made by supposedly proficient lawyers, refers to the nonexistent, "a color camera", can we safely assume that any of these words mean anything. On the other hand, when the fourth listing in Item 6 is "1 unexposed piece of color film" perhaps it can be taken that Item 4, although described as "1 roll", is not, is but part of a roll, the exposed part only.

In Item 3 there are "5 envelopes". These contain "exposed film", a description specified in the Sibert-O'Neill report.

We are left to make assumptions and then without certainty of their reasonableness. One that seems fairly safe, if official words ever have any meaning and can ever be trusted when a popular President is slain, is that all the black-and-white 4 x 5 negatives did come out. The number exposed and the number of envelopes holding them coincide, 18.

Of the 22 4 x 5 color negatives, all are stored in 12 envelopes. With proper regard for safety, it would seem that only seven are good. There is no clue in the remaining items to clarify this.

Of the four things covered in Item 6, the first, "36 8" x 10" black and white prints - autopsy photos", seems to indicate two each of 18 good ones. The second is subject to what would seem to be reasonable interpretation, that contact prints were made of these black-and-white negatives. This means actual size, not enlarging. The language used is "37 3½" x 4½" black and white prints - autopsy photos". The holder of this kind of film generally masks part on each side of it. With special handling, contact prints can be 3-3/4" by 4-3/4". However, in normal commercial practice, without special care (and nothing but hiding and destruction seems to have received special care) the resultant contact print from a 4 x 5 negative has 1/4" margins, making prints of the listed size, 3-1/2 x 4-1/2. If we do not know how many of which were printed, one guess could be two contact prints of each plus an extra print of one, making a total of 37.

The third is the only remaining listing in this item, "27 color positive transparencies 4" x 5". In this case, the words "autopsy material" used in Item 2 or other formulations, such as "autopsy photos", are missing. One possible interpretation is that, as should have been done, pictures were taken of specimens removed for laboratory examination. If only seven of the autopsy color pictures came out, this could indicate 20 such specimen photos.

Now, the total number of these "transparencies", meaning positive film, exactly equals the first listing in Item 7, "27 4" x 5" color negatives of autopsy photographs". In order to make prints, negatives were made from the transparencies. If what seems possible with the black-and-whites is also possible here, then the remaining listing, "55 8" x 10" color prints of autopsy photographs", can be two prints of each plus a third of one.

This seems to parallel the possible practice in printing the X-rays.

When the official records are so deliberately beclouded, when there is so much secrecy, hidden destruction, there is no choice but to conjecture. In this case, we have to conjecture with numbers. So, let us terminate this disgusting business with a bit of simple arithmetic that may represent no more than an improbable coincidence:

The total number of exposed color film listed in the Sibert-

278

O'Neill report is 27, 22 4 x 5s and 5 120s. This number of exposed film, forgetting for a moment the film that "shows no image", a fact first recorded October 29, 1966, almost three years after the assassination and exposure of the film, exactly equals the number of transparencies listed in Item 6 and negatives in Item 7.

They may or may not be the same film, but this arithmetic is fact, not conjecture. What we have to conjecture is what film shows "no image", why and what the image should have been.

It may be other film, not that exposed by Stringer the night of November 22, 1963.

This is conjecture.

About the purpose I would no more like to conjecture than about all the secrecy; or the seeming destruction when none but the most proficient technicians were involved; or the reason for complete military control of the autopsy that has to be forensic-medicine's more thoroughly unacceptable; or the need for "security" specified by Admiral Burkley when the President was already dead; or the urgency of keeping all civilians out of the autopsy room; or the failure to bring in the most highly-accredited civilian experts in forensic medicine, a goodly number of whom could have been at the hospital before the corpse arrived there; or the refusal of such lawyers as comprised the Commission's membership and staff to use this "best evidence" of the crime, what all knew was required in any genuine investigation or acceptable solution; or the steadfast refusal of survivors and friends of the deceased to evince any interest at all in how he really was killed, by whom and why - or any of the other ghastly lingering and troubling questions of military or other federal conspiracies of various kinds.

For those not troubled by these lingering doubts, questions and disturbing facts, for those not easily frightened, I have saved a comparison with another official record said, albeit falsely, if in court and by the Department of Justice, to have been

To further assure the preservation of a record concerning
the nature and contents of the X-rays and photographs ...

These are the government's words, in State of Louisiana v. Clay L. Shaw, in Washington, in response to Garrison's subpoena for evidence, including this film, to describe the report of the 1968 Clark panel. We have already taken a hard look at it. Now let us take a short look backward, at its "Inventory of Material Examined".

The first material listed is "Black and white and colored prints and transparencies". They are broken down into eight categories, by what these pictures show. Neither here nor anywhere else does this panel report a single film that shows no image!

All the pictures it examined were good, showed a described and identified image!

The minimum number of good pictures is 52, and one of the two sets of numberings goes seriatim to 52.

Two categories of brain pictures are numbered consecutively beginning with 46 and include 52.

This division of the inventory is the only one to have an appended explanation. That begins, seemingly innocuously enough, "The black and white negatives corresponding to the above were present and there were also seven black and white negatives of the brain without corresponding prints."

This only seems innocuous. What this and the listing really say is that this official panel found 45 film with corresponding prints, exactly the total of the receipt for so long "lost", exactly the number of the contract's Appendix B list - and all were good - all show an image.

The extra seven pictures are of the brain, which was removed during the autopsy and of which there is no reason to believe that the pictures were not taken later, after required fixing of the soft tissue in formalin, the procedure testified to and normal.

Now, it cannot be that on October 29, 1966, half the categories of the pictures taken during the autopsy show no image and by the second January following all do. The government is possessed of great magic, witness the bullets! but it has no cockamehmeh science with which it can spit on and rub bad film for 14 months and suddenly have it show an image not preserved on it.

If those pictures showed no image October 29, 1966, they could never show an image.

If the pictures the panel examined in January 1968 did show an image, there never was a time they did not.

It cannot be both ways.

Or, two different sets of pictures are involved. *

There simply are no other alternatives.

Crookedness beyond description!

There is something rotten in the City of Washington. Its name is "Government".

One further comment should be absolutely safe: This should never, ever happen when a President is killed; when the military takes over a medico-legal civilian function and orders what can and cannot be done, regardless of all law, regulations and requirements; and when there is an investigation of that assassination by the government that killing puts into power.

---

* 2H363; p. 594.

26. MEMORANDUM OF TRANSFER

The "Equal Justice Under Law" proclaimed on the face of the
Supreme Court Building in Washington has never been a reality. It is
rarely "equal", too often not "justice", and the law itself is not
uncommonly a means of illegality.

During the Great Depression, when hunger strode the land, children starved and there was neither work nor relief for the unemployed
and their families, there were not infrequent cases of men being shot
and killed stealing a loaf of bread or a bottle of milk for their children, and of long prison sentences meted out to those whose crimes were
measured in pennies, bread then costing less than 10 cents a loaf. At
the same time, it was not uncommon for cashiers to unload the safes of
their banks and, when caught, to be sentenced to but two or three years,
after which they emerged from jail to take their places among the
wealthier and respected men in their communities.

Major crimes sometimes are not regarded as crimes at all. Our
multitudinous murders in Southeast Asia, so vast in number they are
beyond calculation or even reliable estimate, the burnings and maimings
of humans by napalm, barbarities like few in history, are never compared with Hitler's gas chambers, for example. And because the agents
of the crime, those who flew the planes that dropped the jellied gaso-
line and superbombs, had no personal contact with their unseen victims,
.they do not regard themselves as subhuman. When, finally, public exposure forced government acknowledgment that soldiers had shot a few
civilians, there were show charges, show trials, and effort by the
government to cleanse its own soiled skirts. In the very few admitted
cases, the men involved were only those who had direct contact with
their victims. Those who killed and seared the larger numbers of victims but who had no contact with them are never mentioned as war criminals. And the legal basis for all of this, our invasion of another
land, was sanctified with the explanation that we had to "keep our
word". This has as much legal and moral standing as justifying the
taking of another's wife because the lusting one promised himself he
would.

On the one hand, petty crime has come to be regarded as not crime
at all, and on the other, the governments that administer the law have
come to believe and achieve an acceptability for the belief that anything government does is legal because government does it.

If a government employee steals government property, he can be
charged with a crime and punished. It is a crime to steal the property
of the government, which is the property of all the people. But whether
anything happens depends on who steals what property.

There is also law against the giving away of the property of all
the people. Were this not the case, there would be fewer typewriters
and chairs in government offices. The means by which government property can legally pass into private hands are quite limited.

All the film exposed at the Bethesda Naval Hospital was government property. If Stringer had taken those few packs of 4 x 5 film and
that roll of 120 and put them in his pocket, he would have been a crook.
Admiral Galloway had no authority to give this film away, not to
Stringer, not to anyone else. In the case of the film, it is not merely
the fact that it was government property. As we have already seen,

281

medical film is in a special category, and Galloway did not have the legal authority to give it to another agency of government.

I learned of the special status of medical film from personal experience, when my wife fell and broke a bone 50 miles from our own doctors. I took her to the closest hospital, where she was X-rayed and received emergency treatment. But when I asked for the film to take to our doctors, having paid the hospital for the film and its services, I learned that under the law, even though I had paid for it, the film was not my property.

Nobody, not even the President, had or has the right to give the film of that autopsy to anyone. It was done for special reasons, to prevent embarrassment to the government because the government had lied about the evidence. Even the means by which it was accomplished discloses this. In Kelley's previously-cited letter, he used the phrase always used. The 1968 panel used the same phrase, "Memorandum of Transfer". Had what was given to the Kennedys been their property, it would not have been a "transfer". Any record of the return of Kennedy property to the Kennedys would have been no more than a receipt.

Nor was there any legal way of suppressing the evidence of this film if it remained in government possession. So, those who worry about these things contrived to shift the onus to the distraught Kennedys, exploiting their real concern over undignified or sensational use of that which could in such use scorch the souls of those who had suffered so much more because their suffering had been so very public.

In their "TOP SECRET" executive sessions, the members of the Commission were always told by Rankin of the sensitivity of the Kennedys on this point. They believed it and, naturally, were anxious to avoid further pain to the survivors. But the truth is in that secret memorandum of Arlen Specter's that I dug up, that April 30, 1964, memo in which he tried to make a record that could justify his own transgressions against the requirements imposed upon him by the law he practiced and the nature of his assignment. The reader will recall this from Part I:*

> According to Inspector Kelly /sic7 the Attorney General did not categorically decline to make them available, but wanted to be satisfied that they were really necessary.

This is Specter's self-serving version. I suggest the reality is that Robert Kennedy did not have possession of the film during the Commission's life and objected to publication only. Need it be asked why a Presidential Commission had to deal with the Attorney General of the United States through a relatively minor employee of the Secret Service? Kelley and the Secret Service were used - abused. The film should never have remained in the possession of the Secret Service. If it was proper for that agency to have the film for investigative purposes, once it was no longer in charge of the investigation, it did not have that right or obligation. But if the Commission really wanted the film and Robert Kennedy declined to make it available, the Commission needed only to write out a simple subpoena for it.

The truth is the government wanted the film suppressed. Because it was in the possession of the Secret Service it remained there, becoming, in time, a source of embarrassment to it. The military did not want this evidence of its own guilt in its own files, where law and regulation required it to be.

My own knowledge of this transfer did not begin with the release of the 1968 panel report while I was preparing for the court hearing in an effort to force production of this film in the then-pending New Orleans trial. That panel use provided two new things, the designation of the transaction and the legal means by which a private citizen could get access to what had been suppressed. Under the Freedom of Information law (5 U.S.C. 552) what may properly be withheld under its exemptions can no longer be withheld once any use is made of it. Under the American Mail Lines, Ltd. v. Gulick decision, mere reference is a full waiver of any previously existing legal right to withhold. So, it was

* See pp. 129-30.

not until after the panel inventory of its materials was released that I could hope to gain access to this Memorandum of Transfer by means of the law.

It was in the early winter of 1966 that I first heard of how the government had divested itself of this evidence and who had, until then, held it. Another writer with powerful connections to the government, including the military, was my source. Richard Whalen, an accomplished investigative reporter who had written a book (The Founding Father) not favorable to Joseph P. Kennedy, was told to seek my help by an editor of The Saturday Evening Post, which had assigned him to do a story on the assassination. Another editor of the Post had wanted to serialize WHITEWASH (his employment did not long survive that desire). My work was known there.

Whalen spoke several times to a high Treasury official, David C. Acheson, got varying accounts and shifting positions. At one time he expected to get to see the suppressed film on a confidential basis. Then came the family contract and that was all over.

Whalen had three telephone conversations with Acheson on November 1, 1966 - the day the existence of the contract was made public. In the third Acheson said, among other things, that "everything" was turned over to the Kennedy Library depository in the National Archives on April 26, 1965. He described "everything" as involving "a great mass of materials".

As soon as I could after the panel report was released, I started trying to get a copy of this Memorandum from the Archives, Secret Service, Department of Justice and Burke Marshall, the attorney for the executors of the estate. The full story of this effort to get public information, a supposedly public document, would make a book-length study of the workings of government and of official trickery deemed fitting on this subject and proper under the law by those whose sole purpose was to hide official misconduct and evidence.

Here there is neither space nor need for the full story, so I summarize that which is necessary to an understanding of how and why the autopsy evidence was suppressed and what was suppressed.

My first request was on January 22, 1969, by telephone. This was a few days after release of the panel report, by then actually suppressed for a year. When there was no response, I wrote letters, on February 28 and March 23. Three weeks prior to my first letter, I met Rhoads in the courtroom the day Judge Charles Halleck ruled these materials had to be made available to Dr. Cyril Wecht to study as a basis for his scheduled testimony in Louisiana v. Shaw. By filing an appeal, the government was able to frustrate this, for the appeal could not be heard until after that trial and, were the government to lose that appeal, it would then appeal to the Supreme Court. On this occasion Rhoads assured me of a prompt response he never made.

Finally, under date of April 4, Rhoads sent me the Rube Goldberg-type pseudo legalism they had cooked up to circumvent the law. He did not invoke any of the exemptions of the law, which are not applicable, saying, instead:

> Although left at the Archives for safekeeping, that memo-
> randum is a private paper which is not the property of the
> United States. It belongs to the Kennedy family, and requests
> for permission to see it should be addressed to /Burke Marshall7.

In my return-mail response I told Rhoads that I knew some of the content of this memo, that it included the film, and ridiculed the notion that the wealthy and powerful Kennedy family could not store private papers safely except in government vaults. Did it take 82 days to learn this was a "private" paper, I asked? But, assuming that he was refusing me the copy of this memorandum that was given to the family, I asked instead for a copy of the government's copy.

I asked and I asked and I asked, without response, in letters of April 7, May 27, July 14 and August 15. Finally, under date of October

31, he wrote a nonresponse, that they "affirm our previous advice /sic7 to you that the memorandum is not the property of the United States but belongs to the Kennedy family."

Even their numerous and vocal enemies never accused the Kennedys of claiming ownership of government_files. Rhoads made no reference to the government's copy.

In rejecting my request for other factual, public information about the film and its history so that the conflicts in the published accountings might, if possible, be reconciled, this keeper of the national heritage refused absolutely, saying that what was in the panel review (the cause of most of the conflict) and the GSA-family contract (the original of it) is all anyone in this land of freedom will be permitted to have. His reason, since he could find none in the law?

To furnish such information might tend to encourage the morbid curiosity concerning the autopsy materials which the terms of the letter agreement were partly intended to prevent.

Aside from the fact that this is false and but another official effort to make the Kennedys seem responsible for the suppressions, in which he had the collaboration of their lawyer, Marshall, and over and above the fact that the contract provides quite the contrary, as I was later able to force the Archives and General Services Administration to admit in federal court, can it be that an accurate accounting of the number of film would cause "morbid curiosity" where all the contradictory accounts do not, that suppression does not cause "morbid curiosity"?

November 4 I reminded Rhoads that after all those months he had responded to the wrong thing, not an accident, that I had asked for a copy of the government's copy, not for a copy of the Kennedy copy. He never answered this or subsequent letters until August 19, 1970, more than a year and a half after the initial request.

By that time I had used other approaches.

Over the years, and especially after the effective date of the Freedom of Information law, I kept after Rowley for information I could prove the Secret Service had that was not in the Archives. (Kelley later joked that he had been told that if he wanted to know what was in the Archives to ask me. I assured him it was, as it is, an exaggeration.) Time after time Secret Service responses were inaccurate and, unfortunately, sometimes deceptive. They made so many blunders, all of which could be very embarrassing to the Secret Service if used in a wrong context, that finally, under date of February 24, 1970, Kelley invited me to a conference in his office the morning or Wednesday, March 4, "with a list of the material which you claim is being withheld from you". They would then "discuss with you what our file reflects was the disposition of the material which came into our possession."

At that meeting, Kelley was joined by the Secret Service's agent in charge of public relations and their general counsel.

In fairness to the Secret Service, the reader should bear in mind that it was immediately cast by the FBI into a relatively minor role in the investigation despite the FBI's lack of jurisdiction, and then by the Commission, which became so dependent on the FBI it became the Bureau's creature. The Secret Service was in the position of having been told by the FBI what the official line on the assassination was and having to hew that line. Its own early reporting, despite its many deficiencies and despite the bureaucratic falling into position on the framing of the evidence, history and Oswald, was entirely inconsistent with the official explanation as I set forth in some detail throughout WHITEWASH II.

By and large, it was a friendly meeting at which, for the most part, the Secret Service was honest and forthright, admitting some of its errors, showing (and later providing) copies of what it had denied having and discussing the background of some of the events and materials. From my notes as they relate to what is here relevant, this included showing me the original autopsy authorization, of which there is no doubt the Archives copy is authentic and needlessly unclear. The originals of some of the CD 371 receipt items were shown me, including the various receipts. There is no doubt of the authenticity of the copies provided me.

It was on this occasion that Kelley first told me that it is he who showed the X-rays, not the pictures, to certain members of the Commission's staff. Although he did not know the exact date, he is certain it was before the autopsy doctors testified and as a preparation for the taking of that testimony. The Secret Service also provided the viewer in which the X-rays - all those the Secret Service had - were shown.

Among the things they never had is any of the tissue slides, such as that made of a piece removed from the edge of the rear nonfatal wound for examination that could establish through the nature of the damage to the tissue (as burning) whether that was an entrance wound.

On Robert Kennedy's position in the withholding of the evidence, Kelley was more explicit and unequivocal than Specter's representation of it. Robert was never consulted until after the taking of the autopsy testimony and he did not then refuse the Commission and could not have because he did not possess anything. Kelley's account to me on the handling of the film also establishes this as it relates to that film because it was kept in a doubly-locked Secret Service safe to which only two people had the combination.

Although the Appendix B listing shows prints made of the X-rays, the Secret Service did not make any copies of them. All the film was printed.

Incredibly, the limousine was washed in Dallas, Kelley believes under the supervision of agents. He was unaware of a picture I had seen showing no agent at the car when it was still at the hospital.

We spent much time discussing this memorandum of transfer. Although it was all in Robert's name, delivery was made to and receipt was signed by Mrs. Evelyn Lincoln, formerly the President's secretary and then at the Archives in the interest of the Kennedy Library. Our discussion sometimes got fairly pointed. I made it clear that I preferred not to sue but was also prepared to do so if necessary. The lawyer nodded assent when I said that under the law the references to it and the uses already made of it nullified any right to withhold that might have been claimed under the law. On the other hand, I offered to abide by their judgment as to whether there is anything in it subject to scandalous use. If they assured me this was true, I would be satisfied with a copy in which any such material was masked out in copying, so long as it reflected what was transferred in a meaningful way. As an alternative, if they preferred it, I would accept a typed list if they would show me their original copy, which would enable confirmation of the accuracy of the retyped list.

(Except for illegalities, what would be scandalous in a receipt for the transfer of property?)

They did not hide that they had been in constant touch with the Archives, which was just as good, because I had already learned of Archives requests for Secret Service letters to be rewritten to make them more congenial to what the Archives preferred to have recorded in its files, an arcane concept of detached scholarship.

It was apparent to me that there was no Secret Service desire to withhold this and a considerable volume of other material that had been withheld, although even then, at this late date, they claimed not to have what they actually did and later produced. I believe this conference and what was perhaps the first full disclosure of unofficial interests, their nature and the public purposes they could serve, may figure in the relatively high percentage of Secret Service material made available in the regular 1970 review later that year.

It was well into lunchtime when the meeting ended. I had given

Kelley the list of materials I wanted for which he had asked. I was fairly certain when we broke up that the Memorandum of Transfer would be given me. It was and remains one of the essential links in evidence, as part of a chain of possession and as an inventory of the greatest importance.

On the last day of the month, when I was again in Washington, I telephoned Kelley. He was in conference with Rowley, the chief, preparatory to leaving town the next day. His secretary told me that the day after this conference he had written the Archives and sent them a copy of the Secret Service copy of the Memorandum of Transfer for me. Consistent with its scholarly dedication, the Archives neither gave it to me nor informed me about it. Kelley later confirmed that it had been sent to the Archives to be given to me.

After the lapse of more time, I asked Marion Johnson about it. He confirmed receipt of the Memorandum copy intended for the Archives to have and of which it was to have provided me a copy and said that their lawyers were considering whether to do this.

In plain English, what this actually meant is that the Archives was, as they had earlier, taking time to try and figure out a way of denying it to me that could seem to have the countenance of the law. Officially, the Archives pretended none of this had happened, responded to no written inquiry, and did not address it until they had cooked up their scheme. This was their letter of August 19. It took the General Services Administration and Archives five and a half months to work out this scheme of suppression.

By then I had made so many inquiries that their opening sentence says it responds to seven letters going back to March 13.

They finally acknowledged having

an electrostatic copy of the Government copy of the "memorandum of transfer" of the materials relating to the autopsy of President Kennedy. This copy is withheld from research under the terms of 5 U.S.C. 552, subsection (b)(6), as part of "medical files and similar files, the disclosure of which would constitute a clearly unwarranted invasion of personal privacy" of the family of the late President Kennedy.

I appealed. The appeal was denied by the Assistant Administrator for Administration of the General Services Administration, W. L. Johnson, Jr., under date of December 8.

It should be apparent that a list of evidence and the illegal transfer of government property into private hands in no way violates anybody's rights of privacy. There is nothing too despicable for the government to do to suppress the still-hidden evidence of how the President was killed. If this means blaming his survivors for it, that is done, specifically or inherently. And the survivors, who have no way of knowing it as long as they suffer the "honorable men" syndrome, will continue to be hurt still more by that assassination.

After the Archives first intercepted the copy of the Memorandum of Transfer the Secret Service had provided for me, not letting me know about it, and until Johnson's refusal to let me have it, I first waited, then asked and asked and wrote and wrote. Finally, I returned to the Secret Service. Under the official interpretation of the law as changed by the Mitchellisti Department of Justice and communicated to me by Kleindienst's assistant, H. Richards Rolapp, I am required to make any request of what is called the agency of paramount interest. This is diametrically opposite what the Attorney General's own printed 53-page interpretation says (p.24):

Where a record is requested which is of concern to more than one agency, the request should be referred to the agency whose interest in the record is paramount, and that agency should make the decision to disclose or withhold ...

This is a Secret Service receipt, a Secret Service record and of proper concern to that agency only. Yet the Archives, in performance of its new role of official censor, overruled the Secret Service.

I told Kelley the Archives refused me the copy sent me through it and asked for one from the Secret Service, which had retained the original, quite properly. His response was that he would have to consult the Department of Justice. In time, the Department of Justice came up with a solution that seemed to get the Secret Service off the hook and the Secret Service, which was anxious for me not to sue it (as I also was) did as told. The Mitchellisti solution was for the Secret Service to divest itself of all copies of the memo, depositing whatever it had in the Archives. Of course, the Department of Justice was prepared to defend the Archives in court.

Despite all pretenses that the government seeks to avoid needless torment for the President's survivors and preserve their privacy, this might have involved them in an extremely unpleasant litigation if I did sue, so I decided to wait and see if the angel of decency could at some time bring itself to touch one of these corrupt and corrupting government officials, to hope that there might be an official change of heart. It is probably a futility, but I did not want to have the family in court defending a suppression of the "best evidence" of how its most famous member had been murdered. The government, not I, trades on the Kennedy name.

So boldly does the government exploit the Kennedy name that, in his rejection of my appeal, Johnson made clear that, even were I to obtain the approval of the family or its representative, he would not automatically provide this memo that he cannot, legally, deny me or anyone else. All he said was that he would review his decision.

And the Kennedy representative? He is a man made something by the assassinated President. Kennedy appointed Burke Marshall to be Assistant Attorney General in Charge of the Civil Rights Division of the Department of Justice. Marshall has done nothing since leaving the government inconsistent with still being in its employ.

The government never had any interest in protecting anybody's rights to privacy, rights people do have and should be able to enjoy when they are invoked legitimately. But if this is a sincere official concern, how explain the availability of the psychiatric records of Jack Ruby's deceased mother and her fishbone syndrome? Or the release of some 40 pages of FBI reports dealing with Marina Oswald's pregnancy? Or the military records of men with emotional problems that rendered them impotent? Or the large volume of reports on alleged homosexuality where it is not relevant to anything? Not one of these things is in any way remotely connected with the assassination or any proper investigation of it. They are but a few samples of the kinds of irrelevancies with which the ever-lovin' Hoover smothered the Chief Justice for whom he had no affinity. All these and many more violations of genuine rights to privacy have been released and are readily, and improperly, available.

One picture of Lee Harvey Oswald's autopsy has been published, including by former Dallas Police Chief Jesse Curry, but when I wanted to examine merely the wrist pictures to be certain that they show scars consistent with an alleged Oswald suicide attempt in Moscow, a suggestion also made to the Commission by the head of the CIA but not recorded as done in any of those 27 tomes, I was denied access to them by the Archivist. Governor Connally's X-rays were printed by the Commission, which had no concern that it intruded upon his privacy, nor did he allege it, for it is no intrusion, any more than it would be with the President.

The family is entitled to privacy where that is a genuine concern. In every instance where the government gave me that excuse, it was a phony deal, an effort to blame the Kennedys for suppression.

The Archivist's description of what is covered by the memorandum should not be taken at face value, such is the state of official scholarship in the era of political assassinations. It is not "materials relating to the autopsy of President Kennedy". It is no more than a list and a receipt.

Kelley told me it included the President's clothing, for example. Now that, although official evidence, was private property. -In all other cases, the government merely confiscated what it wanted, including such irrelevancies as a camera belonging to Ruth Paine, with whom the Oswalds lived in Irving, Texas. Some of this clothing was not in evidence. The President was also wearing a strong back brace and a large Ace bandage. His shoes, socks and underpants are not in evidence (he was not wearing an undershirt, despite the whispers about one). Everything he had on except his wallet had been given to the Secret Service. They had no right to keep it indefinitely.

No, the government has no concern for anybody's rights, least of all those of the Kennedys. It has, shamelessly but successfully, exploited the Kennedys from the first to cloak the nakedness of its official suppressions.

Nor is it in the personal property that I have any interest. It is in the hidden evidence and that alone, the reason for need of a copy of this memorandum. With the arrogance that comes from raw power and utter and complete contempt for the law and decency, it was and is suppressed. Only by accident was its existence ever acknowledged. And no federal agency then did it. They all hid its existence.*

*See pp.405-6;558-9.

27. HADES - NOT CAMELOT

Throughout I have suggested and made explicit charges of wide-spread and official trading on the Kennedy name, exploitation of the family's grief for political and propaganda purposes, blaming members with suppressions for which they neither had nor could have had responsibility - with every sin beyond their desires or capabilities.

Much more than this is involved - much dirtier politics made possible by their unthinking silence so widely interpreted as unmanly. At some point, for all of these disclosures to be in focus, another dimension must be added or there can be a lack of perspective, a flat image, without depth. This requires an interruption in the narrative account of the disclosures of the suppressed evidence, fault for which was so carefully attributed to the family by those not friendly to it and those the beneficiaries of this vile misrepresentation. Perhaps where the discussion of that "Memorandum of Transfer" is fresh in mind is the point of least intrusion.

Framed, then murdered, Robert Kennedy was assassinated twice.

First came his political assassination, carefully arranged by the Johnson administration, in a successful effort to make it seem that deficiencies in the investigation of President John F. Kennedy's murder were Robert's responsibility. In its secondary intent, silencing criticism, it also succeeded.

Robert's muted mouth may have endorsed his death warrant. I think it did. It and acceptance of the unacceptable Warren Report certainly encouraged assassins to believe they could get away with further assassinations.

Once Robert endorsed that fictitious account of his own brother's assassination, as he did March 25, 1968, the attempt on his own life became more certain, as I hinted to him on March 30 in the last of a series of letters I wrote him. Then I told him that "what you do with your own life ... is entirely your affair ..." but what he did "that affects the honor, integrity and ... security of the nation is a proper concern of all."

One of the things that seemed to lend credibility to the Warren Report is the attitude of the surviving Kennedys. Some of the Senators and Congressmen who had doubts calmed them. In the words of one I approached, "Bobby is one of the toughest-minded men in political life. If he has no questions, I have to be satisfied."

One of the questions most often asked on the hundreds of talk shows on which I appeared was, how could there be anything wrong if Bobby was silent?

Not until severely pressed by discontented students at San Fernando State College, when he was past exhaustion in his successful campaign in the 1968 California primary, did he lose his cool and take a stand. His words of March 25 qualify as among the most famous-last-words in history: "I would not reopen the Warren Commission Report," he asserted, and of what was hidden in secret government files, "I have seen everything that is in there and I stand by the Warren Commission."

Aside from the lie, for neither he nor any other busy man could possibly "have seen everything that's in there", this seems like and certainly was taken as an unequivocal endorsement. Whether or not it would have been had he not also been assassinated may remain a puzzle until the end of time. He could not, in my view, have survived a Presidency in which he persisted in what this seems to mean.

Secretly, he did have doubts, and in the privacy of his official life he did express them. After Robert was killed, Frank Mankiewicz, the lawyer who had been press secretary, admitted this to Thomas B. Congdon, Jr., who quoted him in the July 13, 1968, issue of The Saturday Evening Post. At about the time Robert was telling his "seen everything" lie, Congdon "sat with several press people and" Frank Mankiewicz, who declared that Robert "had never read any of these assassination books" and had never ordered any of his staff to digest or report on their contents. But, "once," according to Mankiewicz, "he said something to me that just barely suggested that one of us ought to be up on those books, just in case he'd need to be briefed. And so I've read them all."

If Mankiewicz did, and whether or not he understood them if he did, can be gathered from Congdon's next line:

"For him," he went on, "his brother is dead. It wouldn't make any difference if it were disclosed that a conspiracy of twelve homosexuals and seven tattooed Cuban refugees had killed him."

Colorful words, but hardly what one would expect from a man dedicated to the law, conspiracies being crimes and unsolved crimes anathema to any system of justice (as is indifference to how a brother was slaughtered as unbrotherly an attitude as can be).

This peculiar Mankiewicz concept of the law and informing the man who depended upon his information was not restricted to Mankiewicz among those upon whom all the Kennedys depended. Because of their wealth they were able to hire the assistance of many brains of high repute. Theirs was a task-force system, where these reputedly big brains were put to work studying various special subjects. What all the Kennedys came to know and believe is what those they trusted reported to them.

It is not only that these were the best brains money could buy, which they were. These were also well-intentioned, principled people. Mankiewicz' writing and his electronic-media commentaries disclose him to be a man with sincere concern for the kind of society we have. Unfortunately, concern and intended decency are not enough, not when a political personality depends upon fact and does not get it. Decency and concern are not a substitute for information.

Had Mankiewicz done what he says Robert asked of him, he could never have told Robert what Congdon attributes to him. And had he given Robert a minimal analysis of what the published material alone indicated was what Robert had to understand for his own security, Mankiewicz would have had to indicate that no Kennedy president could survive as a self-respecting or respected man, if not survive in fact, with a single unasked or unanswered question about John's assassination. No reading of the responsible assassination literature permits any reasonable intelligence to ignore the probability of the existence of a conspiracy in this crime. With surviving conspirators, whether or not Oswald was considered part of it, the hazard to a President who would have had to press a new investigation should be obvious.

It appears not to have been obvious either to Mankiewicz or to any of the others upon whom the remaining Kennedys depended for what they knew. There are several other examples I can cite, but one more should suffice. Several of Robert's former associates and assistants in the Department of Justice rose to high positions in the press. One of these is John Seigenthaler, who became editor of the Nashville Tennesean. In 1971 he brought forth a mistitled book, A Search for Justice, pretendedly dealing with the Shaw, Ray and Sirhan trials but actually a milktoasty pseudo-defense of the press, misdirected criticisms and biased attacks on Jim Garrison and the late Judge Preston Battle.

This book has its antecedents in a large journalistic failure. It is the sweepings of that failure.

On March 13, 1969, which was but three days after Ray was salted away for a crime he did not commit by the big-named Percy Foreman, who served no other purpose in his "defense" of Ray, The New York Times carried an explicit story from Martin Waldron, its correspondent at that trial, written the day before and headlined, "Several Books Planned on Ray Case." One of the five listed is by "James D. Squires, a Nashville newspaperman". Squires, who was Seigenthaler's man at the trial, is quoted as saying his "writing should be completed in the next two weeks". He described his book as a "complete account of the murder of Dr. King, the arrest of Ray, the hiring and firing of Hanes and what went on in Memphis!" What the New American Library, the intended publisher, did not publish is the dregs adequate for Seigenthaler more than two years later.

Squires is one of the three reporters who covered the three trials whom Seigenthaler used to write the three parts of his book, which is in no sense any kind of search, for justice or anything else. A minor example of the care with which this late-coming potboiler was fueled is the introduction, titled "Justice Under Law...And Order." There Seigenthaler identifies himself as no more than "a former official of the U. S. Department of Justice". He does not say that he was one of Robert's close associates there, does not give his title and function.

Seigenthaler is generous with his "Acknowledgments" (ix-x). They disclose that he drew heavily upon the morgues of various newspapers, a legitimate source, but a restrictive one if used injudiciously and by those without understanding. He has special mention of a researcher who, among others, helped these four experienced reporters in this single book, and a rather astounding series of partisans with vested interests, in every case in the government side. These range (x) from the man in charge of the actual prosecution of Ray, to whom special indebtedness is confessed, to Fred Graham of The New York Times, whom we discuss elsewhere.

The essence of Seigenthaler's criticism of the late Judge Battle who presided over the Ray case, is that Battle restricted the press in its diligent quest for fact and truth. This is a false criticism. But Seigenthaler's "search for justice" is silent about Battle's violations of judicial standards, including in presiding over the deal that covered up "what went on in Memphis", as Squires describes it, for which Battle should have been criticized.

Likewise did Seigenthaler's "search for justice" as an editor not include any mention of my suit to obtain what his Department of Justice hid and confiscated of the public evidence in the Ray extradition or the fact of this suppression of evidence. It was not from lack of knowledge for I had telephoned Seigenthaler's Washington correspondent, told him about it, given him the official court copies of the proof, and he had promised me a copy of any story used. I got none. Naturally, when Seigenthaler's book did not appear for more than another year, he had no space for anything of this character in his "search for justice" and "fact" in the Ray case.

If this gives one kind of insight into the dispassion and dependability of the information available to the Kennedys from those upon whom they depended, there is another that addresses its integrity elsewhere in the book (pp.338-9), in Seigenthaler's wrap-up of the three earlier parts, titled "It Won't Be Done".

The major assault in the book is on Jim Garrison. It is so excessive, so selective, that it dulls and ignores the legitimate criticisms that can be made. Here Seigenthaler picks it up again for a new charge, and a very serious one, that Garrison deliberately withheld the most important evidence and that he did, in fact, have possession

of this evidence. It begins with recounting that Judge Halleck held
the hearing we described earlier and

> ruled that a Pittsburgh pathologist, Dr. Cyril H. Wecht ...
> should be allowed to see the autopsy reports. Wecht, ex-
> pected to be called as a witness for the prosecution by Gar-
> rison, never was put on the witness stand in New Orleans.
> Would his testimony have been relevant? Judge Halleck also
> directed the U. S. Archivist, Dr. James Rhodes /sic/ to take
> the rifle the Warren Commission concluded Oswald used, to
> New Orleans along with other physical evidence kept in the
> Archives. Garrison had these items which were surely as
> "relevant" as much of his evidence. These were never in-
> troduced by Garrison as evidence. Garrison's final jury
> argument was that a massive federal conspiracy had covered
> up facts. Interestingly, the jury never knew that Judge
> Halleck had ruled to allow Garrison's subpoenaed patholo-
> gist access to the reports. Here again, the adversary
> system gives to the prosecutor the right to pick and choose
> evidence which agrees with the state's theory in the case,
> regardless of what a search for truth would show ...

As we have seen, Garrison never "had these items". The Department of Justice - Seigenthaler's former friends and associates - had
seen to it that Garrison would not and could not have this evidence
for that trial.

This fact was in all the newspaper morgues Seigenthaler used.
It also was duly and accurately reported by the wire services and most
newspapers, if not, in fact, his own. And if these demon newsmen and
all those they correlated and the competent librarians of all the newspaper morgues failed to provide it, the truth was immediately available
by consultation with the Washington papers. The Evening Star, in reporting the Halleck hearing (February 18, 1969), in its very opening
says Garrison would have no "victory" because "Government attorneys
said they would appeal the Halleck ruling today in the D. C. Court of
Appeals."

Had this seeker for justice, if that is what former Kennedy-
adviser Seigenthaler really is, done the next obvious (assuming all
other efforts failed) and sent his Washington man to the clerk of the
Court of Appeals, he would have learned, as I did, that the government
never had any intention of letting Garrison have this evidence, that
in advance of the Halleck hearing it had prepared that clerk for the
appeal that would prevent access for longer than the Shaw trial could
last.

Error of the kind for which cub reporters are chastised permeates the book. There is gross error in fact, redundantly, and consistent error in names not one of which can be attributed to anyone but the
authors. They did not even know the names of those on whom they reported. Often they did not know complete names. In names alone, error
ranges from several of Seigenthaler's betes noir to hotels and includes
lawyers, a reporter, a political party, a police official, the Archivist, a publishing house, a national figure, an expert witness, and even
the place Oswald worked!

What kind of reporting and editing is this, by Seigenthaler, by
his man in New Orleans, and by all those legal and journalistic luminaries on whom credit is so fulsomely lavished? This is not an example of the kind of simple, honest error to which no writer is immune.
It is a self-characterization of the authors, a self-description of the
book as a work of propaganda.

Wealth and ample resources are no advantage to any political figure who depends upon those like these, the prisoners of whose minds the
Kennedys were and are. For whatever reason, all failed, all are today
compromised by their failures, and there is none of these, the ones to
whom any Kennedy would turn, from whom any could have gotten or can now
get dependable, uncompromised information. Seigenthaler and Mankiewicz

are not alone among the former Kennedy sources who were and remain partisans, not sources of fact or understanding.

The book is the self-composed epitaph of reporters and a big-name editor who went for a big story they did not get, did not see and did not understand. In each case, it was there for the getting. Journalistic failure is cloaked in feigned journalistic indignation. The frustration of failure is written in venom. The tragedy is not alone that of these four failures. It is also tragic that most of those who will read the book have no way of knowing how wrong it is.

Today Robert cannot say what his inner thoughts were. But the surviving brother, Senator Edward M. Kennedy, can and did. What he has said is inconsistent and contradictory. He directed his administrative assistant, David W. Burke, to write me under date of February 27, 1969, "with Senator Kennedy's best wishes," that "this Report was prepared by a body of highly respected men and there is every reason to have confidence in their findings."

On July 31, 1966, when WHITEWASH was attracting considerable attention, Edward Kennedy was quoted by UPI as saying of the Warren Report, whose accuracy he presumed, "I have never read it. And I do not intend to do so."

There are two bases on which this attitude can be justified. Reading that Report would be excruciating pain for any survivor. And it is a kind of survival insurance.

Warren Rogers interviewed the Senator for _Look_. His article "Kennedy's Comeback: Will He Or Won't He?" appeared in the issue dated August 10, 1971. _Look_, which has done and commissioned some of the best investigative reporting, has cast itself in an unquestioning, sycophantic role in writing of the political assassinations. How its money prevented the functioning of the law and justice in the Martin Luther King, Jr., assassination I documented in FRAME-UP without even perfunctory denial.

What _Look_ left out of the published Rogers article it found fit for promoting the magazine, fit for commercial purposes, sensation. As AP reported it on July 26, 1971,

> Sen. Edward M. Kennedy says the possibility of assassination attempt was the "most crushing" consideration in deciding not to seek the 1972 Democratic presidential nomination, Look magazine reports ...

The fear is warranted. No Kennedy president could live with a single question about the assassination of John unasked or unanswered.

This apprehension did not originate with nor was it restricted to Edward Kennedy. In _An American Journey: The Life and Times of Robert Kennedy_, interviews by Jean Stein edited by George Plimpton, Arthur Schlesinger, Jr., the historian who had worked for JFK, is quoted as saying,

> Early in the winter I was having dinner with Jackie, and I told her how important I thought it was for Bobby to run. She listened very quietly. Then she said, "I hope Bobby never becomes President of the United States." I said, "Why?" She said, "If he becomes President, they'll do to him what they did to Jack."

Master politician Lyndon Johnson understood the Kennedy problem well, having created it. Framing Robert was one of his first official acts as President. Robert was then still Attorney General.

With the attention WHITEWASH and the books that followed it attracted, Johnson was asked about the assassination investigation in his November 24, 1966, press conference. His answer was neither responsive nor truthful. It was clever propaganda. He said two things he above all had to know were lies. His verbal Brutus' knife is recorded in the official transcript of that press conference:

... if there is any evidence and it is brought forth, I am sure the Commission ... will take any action that may be justified ... The late, beloved President's brother was Attorney General during the period the Warren Commission was studying this thing. I certainly would think he would have a very thorough interest in seeing that the truth was made evident.

This is the same Johnson who had, on September 24, 1964 - more than two years earlier - accepted his copy of the Report that was released three days later. With the rendering of its Report, the Commission ended its official existence. To Johnson's personal knowledge, there was no Commission to "take any action that may be justified".

Johnson did not want any, Commission or evidence, or any questions asked, for every question inevitably was a potential questioning of the legitimacy of his succession.

Not until years later was there any reporting of what immediately preceded this Johnson press-conference viciousness and it is even more obscene. That reporting went unnoted in the United States press. It is an article by Mikhail Sagatelyan, then an official of the Russian Government press, in the July 1971 issue of the official English language publication Sputnik, condensed from Aurora, of Leningrad. The author had been a Washington correspondent at the time of the assassination and for some years following.

Of White House reaction to WHITEWASH and the books that followed and prior to this press conference, this correspondent reports that

through journalists close to the Administration it spread the following explanation of the demands for a re-examination of the "Kennedy Case": it was all part of Robert Kennedy's political game; he was preparing to fight Johnson for the presidential nomination and was not above exploiting his brother's death for his own ends and had therefore raised the fuss around the Warren Report.

Johnson's anti-Kennedy campaign was also waged through his intellectual-in-residence, John P. Roche, his "cultural adviser", earlier head of Americans for Democratic Action. Roche has since preserved "liberal" pretensions in a regular, syndicated column in which he misses few chances to justify the Johnson record, especially in Southeast Asia.

John Sparrow, warden of All Souls College, Oxford, England, a man with longstanding intelligence connections, was one of the first to assume the role of sycophant. He reassumed this besmirched mantle in the December 12, 1967, issue of the Literary Supplement of The Times of London, in a long article that subsequently appeared as a small book in the United States. It, of course, defended the Report. Anthony Lewis, former Supreme Court reporter for The New York Times and a Warren devotee, apparently thought he was defending his idol in his account of the Sparrow sycophancy. The headline, appropriate to the story, reads, "Scholar Upholds Warren Report. Briton Says Its Critics Are Reckless and Foolish."

Roche and The New York Times took up the cudgels so fast that Roche's letter to the London journal was published by Lewis, from London, in New York before it appeared in London. Scholarly as hell, and just as false, Roche pontificated, as befits a "liberal" and a "scholar" who writes on White House stationery and speaks for the President:

There is one point that Warden Sparrow did not make which seems to me vital to any non-paranoidal assessment of that awful day. Every one of the plot theories must necessarily rely on the inconceivable connivance of one key man: Robert Kennedy, then Attorney General of the United States.
Those of us who have any knowledge of the relationship between President Kennedy and his brother have assumed from the outset that had there been the slightest /emphasis in original7 trace of a conspiracy the Attorney General would

294

not have slept or eaten until he had reached the bottom of the matter.

And any fair analysis of Senator Kennedy's abilities, his character and the resources at his disposal as Attorney General would indicate that if there was a conspiracy, he would have pursued its protagonists to the ends of the earth.

Roche reached that "bottom" Robert Kennedy could not.

Not only because Robert had been Attorney General, but for many reasons, especially that GSA-family contract referred to before and to be discussed again, it is necessary to understand the Kennedy position and role in this entire "matter", as Roche described it, or "thing", in his master's voice.

There is perhaps but this one instance, in which he certainly did not intend it, that J. Edgar Hoover, who hated all Kennedys, laid Robert's defense. The only indispensable man in the history of American government deigned to appear before the Warren Commission. I add emphasis to his testimony of May 11, 1964 (5H98-9):

When President Johnson returned to Washington he communi-cated with me within the first 24 hours ... to initiate the investigation and to get all the details and facts ... then prepared a report which we submitted to the Attorney General for transmission to the President ... I have read all the re-quests that have come to the Bureau from this Commission and I have read and signed all the replies that have come to the Commission /sic7 ... it was the desire of the President to have this report completed by the Bureau just as quickly as possible ... I myself go over these /reports7 to see that we haven't missed anything or haven't any gap in the investiga-tion ...

There it is, from the horse's mouth. Hoover, not Robert, was in charge and that from the very first. Robert's function was limited to forwarding Hoover's first report, the one that was supposed to be definitive and complete, that missed nothing, had no gaps.

Any contrary statement is no better than the political assassi-nation of Robert, the fraudulent attempt to make him seem to be re-sponsible for the deficiencies of the investigation of his own brother's assassination. In itself, without an exhaustive, independent investi-gation, this was enough to clamp Robert's tongue.

Hoover's hatred of Robert is Washington folklore, as is Robert's belief that Hoover had him bugged. Hoover seems particularly to have resented the fact that any Attorney General would want his private "hot line" to his chief investigator on that investigator's desk rather than a secretary's. Robert insisted it be moved to Hoover's desk, saying when he used that line, he wanted to talk to Hoover, not be stalled by a secretary. Hoover's first act after the assassination seems to have been to move the phone back to the secretary's desk. He is quoted as having said he then refused to talk to Robert, theoretically his boss, for the last six months of Robert's Attorney Generalship.

But if Robert had read Hoover's so-called report of reports that told all, had no gaps, what would he have learned? No more than the official Hoover line that immediately boxed in the Warren Commission, the lone-assassin fiction. Knowing what he did, Hoover could not dare tell the Commission what he knew and pretend there had been but a sin-gle assassin, Oswald or any other.

First facsimile reproduction of this Hoover report was in WHITE-WASH (p.195). In order to make it seem that no more than three shots had been fired, Hoover left out the wounding of James Tague by concrete sprayed from the "missed" shot, a wound Hoover was later to acknowledge he could not associate with any of the shots that did hit (WHITEWASH 158-9; 21H475-7).

Although this report was five volumes in size, for the central point Hoover found but 14 words, "... three shots rang out. Two bullets struck President Kennedy, and one wounded Governor Connally." Two bullets hit Kennedy plus one bullet hits Connally, two plus one equals three, three shots were already more than could have been fired in the time of the assassination, so the hell with how Tague got hurt and the case is solved.

It was no less easy for this great investigator to dispose of the best evidence of the crime, the wounds and the cause of death: he just ignored them! How much more definitive and certain "that we haven't missed anything or haven't any gap in the investigation" can the world's greatest investigator be? The outline of his report neither lists nor provides for any discussion or reporting of this, in the lawyer's phrase, "best evidence".

The words quoted above are on the first page. Skipping to the 18th, there is this one other reference:

Medical examination of the President's body revealed that one of the bullets had entered just below his shoulder to the right of the spinal column at an angle of 45 to 60 degrees downward, that there was no point of exit, and that the bullet was not in the body.

And that is all of it!

What about the wound in the front of the neck? Since one man could not have been shooting from the front and the back at the same time and with this back wound "there was no point of exit", Hoover's attitude was why mention it at all and confuse everybody?

The conflict between the Commission's version of the identical evidence, less than a quarter of this alleged downward angle, and in the neck rather than "just below his shoulder"? Mankiewicz put it well: The President was dead anyway, wasn't he? What difference did it make?

The wounds in the head? Well, the head only exploded, scattering the life as it splashed the living blood and tissue all over everybody. It was only the assassination of an American President, only the definitive investigation by the world's greatest investigator, so why ruin with petty details his neatly gotten up report with its pretty plastic binding, its wide margins, and all that wonderful biography of that awful "Marxist" Oswald?

Who needs relevant fact or evidence when he has Hoover?

So suppose what did not happen, that the then Attorney General actually read this report-to-end-all-reports by the greatest, what would he have known about his brother's assassination, what could he have seen in it so "he would not have slept or eaten until he had reached the bottom of the matter", so that "he would have pursued" anyone "to the ends of the earth"?

Nothing. Nothing at all. Why should he have gone without sleep or food, chased to the ends of the earth, inspired by no more than page after dismal page of dreary trash he had no possible means of evaluating, a tawdry pretense of a biography of Oswald all in terms of Hoover's own special kind of right-extreme politics?

Only a Hoover would have had the gall to try and pull this kind of caper. And only THE J. Edgar Hoover could have pulled it off, "accounting" for the assassination of a President of the United States to a President of the United States without accounting for the wounds or the cause of death.

For this Robert Kennedy can hardly be held responsible. Even if he had read Hoover's masterpiece, although all the evidence is that he did not and that he did no more than "transmit" it to Johnson, which did not even require that he touch it or have it in his office.

The effort to trade on the Kennedy name, to involve Robert in some kind of endorsement of the Warren Report, did not begin with Johnson and his lackey for culture. It was an unsuccessful Commission ploy. They also wanted Robert's approval. They were able to get it only so indefinitely phrased it was meaningless (26H573). The Commission converted it into an absolute endorsement and made overtly dishonest use of it in the Report (R374).

Even Hoover's involving of Robert as forwarder is not the strict truth. Hoover's report was forwarded to the Chief Justice on December 9, 1963, not by Robert but by his deputy, Nicholas deB. Katzenbach. Katzenbach dealt with the Commission, and Robert, who had nothing at all to do with the investigation, was dragged in only under threat of being called as a witness when he was a witness to nothing.* It was all done with some cunning. That it required some negotiating is revealed by correspondence for which, naturally, there was no room when there were but 26 volumes.

Whether or not it was his idea, the job was pulled by anti-indexer Howard P. Willens, then still in the pay of the Department of Justice, although assigned to the Commission. After the Commission, he returned to his Department of Justice job. His own memorandum of June 4, 1964, tells enough of the story:

June 4, 1964

MEMORANDUM

TO: Mr. J. Lee Rankin, General Counsel

FROM: Howard P. Willens

SUBJECT: Proposed Exchange of Letters between the Commission
         and the Attorney General

Attached are drafts of a proposed exchange of letters between the Chairman of this Commission and the Attorney General. As I have mentioned to you, this recommended procedure is the result of my recent discussions at the Department with Deputy Attorney General Katzenbach and the Attorney General. The Attorney General would prefer to handle his obligations to the Commission in this way rather than appear as a witness.

The proposed response by the Attorney General has, of course, not been approved by him or on his behalf by the Deputy Attorney General. It represents a revision of an earlier letter which I did show to them during my conference with them today. At that time the Attorney General informed me that he had not received any reports from the Director of the Federal Bureau of Investigation regarding the investigation of the assassination, and that his principal sources of information have been the Chief Justice, the Deputy Attorney General and myself. This accounts for the specific mention of these persons in the second paragraph of his letter to the Chief Justice.

Attachments.

This, also quite naturally, the Commission found no cause to publish, even buried in the last of those tomes. The reason is obvious: Robert knew nothing. "He had not received any reports from the Director of the Federal Bureau of Investigation" and of the little he had heard, which is hearsay, not evidence, "his principal sources of

---

*See WHITEWASH IV, pp. 57, 134-5.

information have been the Chief Justice, the Deputy Attorney General and myself." It thus becomes obvious that the threat to have him "appear as a witness" is crude blackmail, exploiting the great pain that would have caused.

The letter Willens prepared for Warren's signature reads:

DRAFT

Honorable Robert F. Kennedy
Attorney General of the United States
Department of Justice
Washington, D. C.   20530

Dear General:

Throughout the course of the investigation conducted by this

Commission, the Department of Justice has been most helpful in forwarding

information relevant to this Commission's inquiry.

The Commission is now in the process of completing its investiga-

tion. Prior to the publication of its report, the Commission would like

to be advised whether you are aware of any additional information relating

to the assassination of President John F. Kennedy which has not been sent

to the Commission. In view of the widely circulated allegations on this

subject, the Commission would like to be informed in particular whether

you have any information suggesting that the assassination of President

Kennedy was caused by a domestic or foreign conspiracy. Needless to say,

if you have any suggestions to make regarding the investigation of these

allegations or any other phase of the Commission's work, we stand ready

to act upon them.

On behalf of the Commission I wish to thank you and your

representatives for the assistance you have provided to the Commission.

Sincerely,

Chairman

This did not suit Rankin, who wrote on Willens' June 4 memo to him, "Please modify as indicated." Something happened. Were I to guess it is that they tried to take some blood with Robert's flesh and to that he would not agree. Willens annotated his own memorandum returned to him with Rankin's instructions, "Done - HPW 6/8/64." But the letter to Robert was not changed. The undated "DRAFT" in the Commission's files is word for word identical with the copy mailed June 11. The carbon of this letter in the Commission's "GAI Justice" file indicates it was actually written by Willens on June 6, not the 4th, 8th or 11th.

The draft of Robert's reply, also prepared by Willens, is word for word the letter he signed under date of June 12 and later was published, save for a blank in the draft for the date.

The blackmailer gave his receipt. Willens wrote Katzenbach on June 12 enclosing a copy of the letter Warren had signed. He also said:

> In light of our discussion on Thursday, June 4, 1964, I have prepared a proposed response to this letter from the Commission. The letter is completely satisfactory to Mr. Rankin and the Chief Justice, and the Chief Justice feels that such a response will eliminate any need to call the Attorney General as a witness before the Commission.

(This barely-visible initialling appears at the left edge of the page: 〳)

Here it is spelled out a little more clearly, for it was never intended that any outside eyes would see it: Robert's signature "will eliminate any need to call" him "as a witness before the Commission".

A "witness" who knew nothing, to the Commission's own knowledge knew nothing - who depended upon the Commission and the FBI for all the hearsay he heard - but possessed of the magical name.

The letter extracted from him by this blackmail has a greatly modified version of what Willens' June 4 memo discloses of Robert's sources. It makes no reference to his having gotten nothing from Hoover, and does not even say that he knew only what he had been told. Instead, that comes out as "I have, however, received periodic reports about the work of the Commission" from Warren, Katzenbach and Willens.

The endorsement lies in this language (from which, if later quoted, the first four words could easily be omitted): "Based on these reports, I am confident that every effort is being made by the President's Commission to fulfill the objectives of Executive Order No. 11130 by conducting a thorough investigation into all the facts relating to the assassination."

Considering that he had no knowledge at all, it was no problem for him to agree to say "that I know of no credible evidence to support the allegations that the assassination of President Kennedy was caused by a domestic or foreign conspiracy."

The Commission was taking no chances. It started getting that Kennedy imprint early. The Commission was anything but "now in the process of completing its investigations" on June 4. It did not take its last testimony until September 15. The sole purpose of this lie was to lean on Robert more heavily.

And even then, he delayed answering until August 4.

Politics and public relations, it seems, were as important as fact or evidence. The Commission wanted acceptability, not solution. To get this, it was willing to do and did do whatever was necessary. If that meant blackmailing Kennedy, was not its pure purpose nobility itself - "solving" the crime of the century?

With regard to the medical evidence in particular, the government has always traded on the Kennedy name. Despite what necessity compelled of them, the Kennedys tried to and did stay away from any involvement in the investigation. Stripped to essentials, what they did say, except for Robert's last words, was no more than that they had confidence in the government and the eminences.

Did not almost everybody else?

Robert cannot now explain the almost two months it took to sign a letter already written for him, especially when the Commission informed him it was practically under the gun. However, whatever apprehensions he may have had, the language arrived at after negotiation by Katzenbach really commits him to nothing - were he around to read it and give it proper emphasis. It says "I am not personally aware" of the results of the investigations; that his Department has cooperated; that he trusted the Commission to do its appointed job; that he knew of no evidence of any kind of conspiracy; and that he had no suggestions.

It depends on who reads this letter, and then with what emphasis, what it can be claimed to say and mean. It says nothing. It means nothing. It is a self-indictment by a politically oriented Commission. It is a shameless and shameful blackmail, unfortunately, not the last.

It does not in any way change the real Kennedy position, that of detachment. There is nothing in the record to justify the claim that it was a Kennedy investigation or that it had Kennedy approval.

The Commission was not easily deterred. In its own report it did with black ink what it could not do with blackmail. Citing Kennedy's then unpublished refusal as its source, it concluded its mistitled chapter "Investigation of Possible Conspiracy" with this utter misrepresentation: "The conclusion that there was no evidence of a conspiracy was also reached independently by" Kennedy, three cabinet members and the heads of the Secret Service, FBI and CIA (R374).

There is almost nobody who undertook to defend the indefensible Report who did not invoke the Kennedy name. One of the more extreme examples is from Defense Counsel Irving Dymond's summation at the end of the Clay Shaw trial in New Orleans. According to Dymond, for the Warren Report to be wrong, Robert Kennedy had to be wrong about his own brother's murder.

Trading on the Kennedy name was rampant inside the Commission, too. If the members may not be the best possible sources, not even on their secret deliberations, where attendance was spotty and irregular and rather consistent lack of understanding and knowledge was undisguisedly and repeatedly articulated, there are some things others are not in a position to know. Nor were the members only under-informed or uninformed.

The Appendix documents that Warren had ordered an examination of the autopsy film by a member and one of the autopsy doctors. Also, the staff did see the X-rays at the very least and Specter saw at least one picture. Because Warren gave this order (in a secret session) to Rankin, it seems a fair inference that Rankin saw to it that this was not done. That it was not done is confirmed by McCloy, who said this in the fourth and last part of the largest TV apology for government error in history, CBS's videowhitewash, broadcast June 28, 1967:

I think that if there's one thing that I would do over again, I would insist on those photographs and the X-rays having been produced before us. In the one respect, and only one respect there, I think we were perhaps a little over-sensitive to what we understood was the sensitivities of the Kennedy family against the production of colored photographs of the body, and so forth.
But those exist. They're there. We have the best evidence in regard to that - the pathology in respect to the President's wounds. It was our own choice that we didn't subpoena these photographs, which were then in the hands of the Kennedy family. I say, I wish - I don't think we'd have subpoenaed them. We could have gotten - Mr. Justice Warren was talking to the Kennedy family about that at that time. I thought that he was really going to see them, but it turned out that he hadn't.

No subpoena was needed. The Commission was never turned down. It just did not ask for this "best evidence", not because of Kennedy hardnosedness, but because it had to avoid the irrefutable evidence. The panel report is an excellent example of some of the many reasons. All of this book addresses others. To blame the suffering Kennedys is indecent.

For the reader to understand government use and misuse of the Kennedy name in connection with the medical evidence and that relating to it, it should help to have this perhaps incomplete (who can know when so much is hidden and suppressed?) but I hope adequate recounting of the Kennedy positions and the heavy-handed, unnecessary, really obscene, federal conniving to create the pretense of Kennedy approval.

Nothing need be added to what Marc Antony said about honorable men.

Now let us resume our examination of the course of honor traveled by other honorable men.

28. "AN ORIGINAL AND SIX PINK COPIES"

Of those things receipted by the Secret Service to Admiral Burkley that are not still said to be nonexistent, three remain. Two are real shockers, even after what we have been through, and the third has never been suppressed. The Commission did not have space for it in those estimated ten million published words, but it was never suppressed, not literally. A stupidity well below it by the Secret Service is, I believe, one of the embarrassments that led to our face-to-face meetings.

After all, as Mankiewicz had so bluntly put it, the President was dead, was he not? Why bother with such trivialities as certificates of death in the investigation of the murder? Or, if you are a Mankiewicz, a lawyer and the close associate of a to-be-assassinated Kennedy, with any of those thousands of things that should have sent all decent lawyers crawling the walls?

There are two death certificates, neither in evidence or the Report.

We have addressed the Texas certificate, the one prepared with such punctilio that it certifies to the inquest 12 days before the killing that is its subject.

Well, when Kelley wrote me on August 6, 1969, saying that "we have again reviewed our file and find no copy of the post-mortem authorization", the same one of which I had long had a rather indistinct copy and had gotten that only because it had been misfiled, the one of which he was later to show me the original, he also said, "We do have a copy of the death certificate, which is enclosed."

What he really enclosed is one of the three pages of that grim Texas joke saying that one of the wounds was "near the center of the body and just above the right shoulder" when it is the official story that nobody in Texas ever saw that wound.

And, of course, the receipt lists two death certificates, the other the Navy's.

My reaction to this helped persuade the Secret Service to provide what it, without any possibility of doubt, was still withholding.

Beginning with the real "State of Texas Certificate of Death", not that crumbun "inquest" never held.

It is a hand-executed form only partly filled in. The second side is completely blank. Except for the identification of the city, county and hospital, there is little on the face side, most of its blanks also being void. The "date of death" and the name "John F. Kennedy" appear, but not the fact that he was President, not even one of his addresses - certainly not the White House! Too much for Texas, that. Aside from an unclear signature that seems to be that of Dr. Kemp Clark certifying that at 1 p.m. he had seen the deceased and the "immediate cause" of this death was "Gunshot of Brain", it says nothing.

At the bottom of the Xerox of the Xerox of which Kelley gave me this copy is written, "orig. to Insp. Kelley 11-27-63 RIB", the initials of Robert Inman Bouck.

I do not attribute anything to the carelessness with which this

302

required form was executed save disregard for the fact that the victim was the President of the United States. There is nothing the Texas form could have said that could have meant anything once the corpse was kidnapped. Yet there is a strange psychological subtlety here, that in Dallas, the over-wealthy stronghold of those who look so steadfastly backward, there was this perhaps subconscious compulsion to leave the murdered President of the United States completely anonymous, as a matter of official certification of his death. Guilt syndrome?

In the Kelley letter as in the Bouck receipt in CD 371, those looking for psychological quirks may find them in the next item, which is not properly described anywhere. Kelley improved Bouck's language, but it is not a "copy of a letter" but a memorandum, and it is not "concerning laws and regulations regarding the confidential nature of events".

It is, rather, as any close reading of Finck's reluctant admission in New Orleans categorizes it, a threat. It is a threat of military retaliation against any military mouth that is not clamped shut in perpetuity.

It is addressed to nobody. The copy provided the White House is dated "26 November 1963". It is "From: Commanding Officer, U.S. Naval Medical School". But, after "To:" there is nothing. This is a form threat, a copy, apparently, given to every one of the military men listed in the Sibert-O'Neill report and others they did not list.

Finck certainly got the message, loud and clear.

And so, from the record of monolithic silence, did everyone else.

It was not some unnamed general who made the threat, gave the orders. Except for Stover's typed signature, this is all the rest:

1. You are reminded that you are under verbal orders of the Surgeon General, United States Navy, to discuss with no one events connected with your official duties on the evening of 22 November - 23 November 1963.

2. This letter constitutes official notification and reiteration of these verbal orders. You are warned that infraction of these orders makes you liable to Court Martial proceedings under appropriate articles of the Uniform Code of Military Justice.

Thus it would appear that one mystery is solved - why the Surgeon General of the Navy escaped any official attention, is mentioned nowhere in any official record, until the first part of this book opened Finck's lips a bit in New Orleans. He is the one who threatened everybody.

How subtle to describe an overt threat as "law and regulations" dealing with the "confidential nature" of what they observed or were part of - not "events"!

The basis of the threat is not any cited "law" or "regulation" but only the "verbal orders" of the military - the same military whose wings the assassinated President had been attempting to clip for some time - without too much success.

There was need for the threat. Those mouths had to be closed. The military can do this, effectively - which need not be taken as an explanation of why Burkley arranged for a military autopsy that was a gruesome medico-legal farce. No civilians could have been ordered to do what these men under military discipline did. Nor could civilians have held their silence for so long, so many knowing so much about what was so wrong, so very, very wrong.

Should there remain any still doubting, as long and painful experience with the irrationally unseeing, the blinder simply because they refuse to see, persuades me is inevitable, for those capable of opening their eyes and possessed of a high-school vocabulary, the remaining item of the Bouck receipt to Burkley so long suppressed should eliminate all doubts - _any_ possibility of _any_ reasonable doubt.

It is official - could not possibly be more official. It is the solemn word of that most eminent and qualified authority, the President's own personal physician.

It is the federal "Certificate of Death", on Form "NAVMED N" as revised in April 1958.

When Tom Kelley finally disgorged, he really spewed it out. What he gave me is more than he described, "The original and six pink copies of Certificate of Death (NAVMED N)". He also gave me Admiral Burkley's handwritten copy. All _eight_ copies. This suppressed death certificate appears in the Appendix.

Less than a single sentence is all that is required from Burkley's "Summary of Facts".

This, the only medical man in both Dallas and Bethesda, the man most required to know, the "Physician to the President", as he signed himself, described the so-called rear nonfatal wound as "in the posterior back at about the level of the third thoracic vertebra".

In the _back_, not the neck, and _far down_ from the neck, at "the third thoracic vertebra".*

Here, for the first and only time, after years of sequestration in government vaults, orientation of this wound with an _inflexible_ point on the body. This is the requirement in medicine, in law, in fact - in every case, it would seem, except when a President is killed.

Or in a case where government wants to rescript that killing.

Then flexibles, imponderables are wrongly - _knowingly_ wrongly - introduced, as he belatedly confessed in New Orleans, by the Army's contribution to the Navy's frame-up of history, the crime, its solution - and of the safely assassinated, lone accused.

Here there is and can be no question. This is the official, federal certificate of death by the one man most uniquely in a position to know what did happen, the one man most qualified to execute the certificate.

Is it not now time to wonder if others also were not framed by the withholding of the official certificate of death and substituting a fiction for it?

Could not these seven honorable men be victims? Or, in the context of their other lives, their dependence upon their staff and federal agencies for what they knew and could know, can they not, without excess charity, be conceived as hogtied, thoroughly bemused and confused about the conclusions they felt they could agree to or visualize?

Could any of the Kennedy family have had this knowledge and been silent? Are they not also victimized by having all the film evidence they could not bear to see - and never had in their physical possession - dumped upon them in violation of the law as a means of suppressing it while what they might genuinely want, this certificate of death, was hidden from them as it was from the rest of the world until now? Meanwhile, the official mythology has been fixed in the national mind as the actuality, the Kennedys are blamed for the suppression of evidence, and there is no official willingness to seek and reveal truth.

It is with the official falsehood about the assassination as it was with study of the victim's brain, which had to be fixed in the chemical formalin before it could be handled safely.

The reader can find the third thoracic vertebra on his own back by counting the bumps as he fingers down from the most prominent one, where the neck joins the torso.

And before the professional doubters can suspect that Burkley merely plagiarized this from the "erroneous" body chart with which Boswell had been no more than a bit "careless", it should be pointed

*For location see p. 312.

out that Burkley executed this certificate after he left the hospital and the day before he got the hospital records. Blank No. 32, right before "signature", reads, "Date signed". Lettered in and accurately transcribed in the typing is "November 23, 1963".

Here Burkley signed his full name, George Gregory Burkley, and his rank, Rear Admiral.

This makes for a rare unanimity in all official records of the fake inquest.

All - not just some or most - all - 100 percent of the probative evidence.

All of the records of the autopsy.

All of the Dallas doctors and all of the autopsy doctors, too - each and every one of whom, under oath, swore the career attributed to Bullet 399 was impossible.

All of the official observers - Kellerman, Greer and Hill of the Secret Service and Sibert and O'Neill of the FBI.

And, on a lesser level, all of the initial Secret Service and FBI reporting and reconstructions. Plus all of the initial medical statements and all the official "leaks" to the press.

Only Arlen Specter had the gall to father that illegitimacy that Raymond Marcus so aptly termed "The Bastard Bullet" and then to forge a fake birth certificate certifying it legitimate.

Even Henry the Eighth had more concern for popular regard. He had the decency to lop off Anne Boleyn's head.

And all the learned, looking at the naked bastard, vied with each other in proclaiming the beauty of its raiment, taking time out from their praises only to berate those who, like the little boy of the fable, cried "naked" at the bastard who made an emperor.

As Ecclesiastes tells us of time and as that Old Testament philosophy of which the assassinated President was so fond also tells us of place, should we not, here and now, ask a few of the obvious questions springing from this single element of the suppressed medical evidence, this one part of the reassassination of the autopsy? Now, having the official certification and its verification that, knowing this wound was in the thorax, well down on the back:

How, innocently, explain Specter's substitution of those fake charts, Exhibits 385 and 386, for the existing and now "verified" autopsy chart of this same combination of nonfatal wounds?

How, innocently, explain Humes' willingness to instruct an artist in the fabrication of evidence when Humes knew truthful evidence existed - and the fabrication was contrary to the existing evidence? Or his telling the largest TV audience in history on this subject on those CBS videowhitewashes this identical misrepresentation, that the back wound was a neck wound and higher up than it was?

How, innocently, accept the official poppycock that the investigators could not see the actual pictures of the autopsy and did not see the X-rays?

How, innocently, explain Specter's silence in the hearings he conducted and that part of the Report he wrote about having seen a picture of this back wound (WHITEWASH II:109), confirmed to me by Tom Kelley, who showed it to him? Or Specter's failure to correct the fake record he manufactured? Or his pseudo-campaign for access to the X-rays already shown the staff?

How, innocently, explain Boswell's new concept of science, that the pathologist is "sloppy" in the investigation of a President's murder and his explanation that he did not expect anyone to see his work on this wound, the correct positioning of which he designated careless error, first to Richard Levine and then, when it seemed like the kind of ploy that the press would go for, feeding the same guff to the Associated Press?

How, innocently, explain the absence of the admirals from the 553 designated Commission witnesses? Could it have called Burkley, as it should have, and ignored his, the original, set of those autopsy papers that survived the naval-recreational conflagration, with his approvals and verifications added; or his, the official, death certificate; or his sanctioning of the destruction of evidence and his silence at its misrepresentation? Could it have called Kinney and Galloway and not made a record of their domination of a supposedly impartial, detached and precise medico-legal autopsy; their ordering that what had to be done to meet the requirements of the law and to solve the crime not be done; their threats to any under military discipline who might find the manhood, decency and patriotism to protest?

How, innocently, of all the many other questions the concerned will be asking themselves and should ask their government, answer the one other I here pose: How explain the incredible, that this Commission could and did conclude wholly opposite all its credible evidence, which is exactly the same as the evidence denied it or eschewed by it (one doing it no more credit than the other) and say this back wound was in the neck and thus issue a false "explanation" of how the President was killed?

Regardless of all the other complete refutations of the official mythology foisted off on a grieving family and a tormented people, this is one that in and of itself destroys the "solution" to the assassination as the work of any one man, Oswald or any other, for in the most modest representation it means that, beyond any question, there was not and could not possibly have been any single bullet that could have inflicted all seven nonfatal wounds on both men, the President and the governor.

Even more - much worse - should this hole in the back be, as claimed, a wound of entry, then it leaves other unaddressed, unanswered mysteries and requires still another shot, for it could not possibly have caused the acknowledged and misrepresented much higher wound in the front of the neck without coming from inside the rear cushion of the back seat or some similar impossibility.

If there was but a single head shot, which is far from certain, if, indeed, possible; if all of Connally's wounds were caused by a single bullet; then there still had to be a separate bullet to cause each of the following injuries, were this back wound one of entry:

The minor injury to James T. Tague, so far away;
the anterior neck wound; and
this one.

Or, a total of not fewer than five from the official accounting alone - and there is probative but ignored evidence of others.

At least five shots.

Five shots. From at least two different directions!

Not even the magician Oswald with his magical rifle that barely worked and then only inaccurately and his also-magical, out-of-date bullets, none ever really connected with any of the shooting, was capable of such Wagnerian virtuosity.

And all over again there is nothing left of that Warren Report and the "crime of the century" is without solution.

The Chairman. Of course there are so many Spanish-speaking people down in Texas.

Mr. Rankin. In the area.

The Chairman. That she might have gotten it from someone else.

Mr. Rankin. Then there is a great range of material in regard to the wounds, and the autopsy and this point of exit or entrance of the bullet in the front of the neck, and that all has to be developed much more than we have at the present time.

We have an explanation there in the autopsy that probably a fragment came out the front of the neck, but with the elevation the shot must have come from, and the angle, it seems quite apparent now, since we have the picture of where the bullet entered in the back, that the bullet entered below the shoulder blade to the right of the backbone, which is below the place where the picture shows the bullet came out in the neckband of the shirt in front, and the bullet, according to the autopsy didn't strike any bone at all, that particular bullet, and go through.

So that how it could turn and --

Rep. Boggs. I thought I read that bullet just went in a finger's length.

Mr. Rankin. That is what they first said. They reached in and they could feel where it came, it didn't go any further than that, about part of the finger or something, part of the autopsy, and then they proceeded to reconstruct where they thought

TOP SECRET

As of late January, 1964, the Commission knew that JFK had been shot in the back, below the level of the front neck wound. This was spelled out to it in detail by Rankin, as revealed in the above page from the transcript of the 1/27/64 executive session. Rankin also says that the Commission had at least one of the autopsy pictures showing "where the bullet entered in the back." Arlen Specter later admitted that he was shown an autopsy picture depicting the back wound.

COPY

CERTIFICATE OF DEATH
NAVMED N (REV. 9-58) (3061)

The White House, Washington, D.C.

President John Fitzgerald Kennedy

President of the United States

2 years
11 Months

NA   NA   NA   NA   Brookline, Massachusetts

May 29, 1917   46 years 6 months   Catholic

Blue   Auburn   Ruddy   72"   172

20. MARKS AND SCARS (Noted in Health record)

4" scar 2nd, 3rd and 4th lumbar spine
4" scar upper left leg, well healed

22. NEXT OF KIN OR FRIEND (Relation, name and address)

Mrs. John Fitzgerald Kennedy, The White House, Washington, D.C.

The White House, Washington, D.C.

15. PLACE OF DEATH

Parkland Memorial Hospital, Dallas, Texas   November 22, 1963

Gunshot wound, skull

This is the front side of the one-page death certificate executed by the President's
physician, Admiral Burkley. Its existence was known to the Commission, which had
copies of the receipts for its transmittal to the Secret Service. However, the Commission never asked for and never received a copy. The official certificate of death
would seem to be fundamental to any investigation of a murder, but not so far as the
Warren Commission was concerned. Had the Commission put this certificate in its record,
it could not have written the Report, as the next page makes clear.

308

President John Fitzgerald Kennedy, while riding in the motorcade at Dallas, Texas
on November 22, 1963, and at approximately 12:30 p.m., was struck in the head by
an assassin's bullet and a second wound occurred in the posterior back at about the
level of the third thoracic vertebra. The wound was shattering in type causing
fragmentation of the skull and evulsion of three particles of the skull at time of
impact, with resulting maceration of the right hemisphere of the brain. The
President was rushed to Parkland Memorial Hospital, and was immediately placed under
the care of a team of physicians at the hospital under the direction of Dr. Malcolm
Kemp Clark. I arrived at the hospital approximately five minutes after the
President and immediately went to the emergency room. It was evident that the
wound was of such severity that it was bound to be fatal. Breathing was noted at
the time of arrival at the hospital by several members of the Secret Service.
Emergency measures were employed immediately including intravenous fluids and
blood. The President was pronounced dead at 1:00 p.m. by Dr. Clark and was
verified by me.

31. DISPOSITION OF J PAINS

To the White House, Washington, D.C.

32.

DATE SIGNED __November 23, 1963__   SIGNATURE ____George Gregory Burkley____
                                              Physician to the President

- FORMED COURT OF INQUIRY, OR BOARD OF INVESTIGATION _____   33. HELD.
                                              (will or will not)

. SI _____   SIGNATURE _____
                                              (Commanding Officer)

COPY

This is the reverse side of the Certificate of Death wherein Admiral Burkley, present
at the autopsy, reports with assurance and precision that the President had received a
wound "in the posterior back at about the level of the third thoracic vertebra." It
is significant that Burkley provided this description on November 23, for it was not
until the following day, the 24th, that he saw and "verified" Dr. Boswell's similar
locating of the wound on a body chart, reproduced at p. 310. For a depiction of the
exact location of the third thoracic vertebra, see the skeletal diagram at p. 312.

AUTOPSY

NMS # A 6 S # 2 7 2 DATE 11-22-63 HR. STARTED _____ HR. COMPLETED _____

NAME: _____ RANK/RATE _____

DATE/HOUR EXPIRED: _____ WARD _____ DIAGNOSIS _____

PHYSICAL DESCRIPTION: RACE: _____ Obtain following on babies only:

Height _____ in. Weight _____ lb. Hair _____ Color

Color eyes _____ Pupils Rt _____ mm, Lb. _____ mm

WEIGHTS: (Grams, unless otherwise specified)

Crown-rump _____ in.
Crown-heel _____ in.
Circumference:
Head _____ in. Chest _____ in.
Abd. _____ in.

LUNG, RT. 320	KIDNEY, RT. 1305	ADRENALS, RT. _____
LUNG, LT. 290	KIDNEY, LT. 140	ADRENALS, LT. _____
BRAIN _____	LIVER 650	PANCREAS _____
SPLEEN 90	HEART 350	THYROID _____
THYMUS _____	TESTIS _____	OVARY _____

HEART MEASUREMENTS: A 7.5 cm. P 7 cm. T 12 cm. M 10 dm.

LVM 1.5 cm. RVM .4 cm.

NOTES:

Verified
G G Burkley

Pathologist _____

Vomer crushed

glide at eye

Fracture through floor

Falx loose from sagittal sinus from the Coronal Suture back

3 cm

19 cm

10

10

17

missing

The "Autopsy Descriptive Sheet" is a single sheet of paper with notes on both sides. The <u>only</u> "autopsy notes" in the Commission's files are Xerox copies of both sides of this sheet. There <u>were</u> other contemporaneous notes, <u>not</u> destroyed but missing today. Printed here for the first time anywhere are the front and back sides of the <u>original</u> of the "Descriptive Sheet." The Commission used mere Xerox copies lacking Burkley's verification. A comparison of the original and the version printed by the Commission appears at p. 262. The location of the back wound marked on this sheet and verified by Burkley corresponds almost exactly with the level of the third thoracic vertebra.

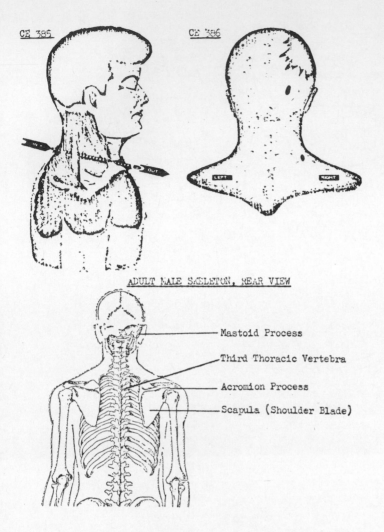

CE 385

CE 386

ADULT MALE SKELETON, REAR VIEW

Mastoid Process

Third Thoracic Vertebra

Acromion Process

Scapula (Shoulder Blade)

Knowing the Commission would not put the autopsy pictures in its record, the doctors had drawings made to depict the President's wounds. CE's 385 and 386 were prepared in March 1964 under Humes' supervision. These illustrations deliberately misrepresent the back wound as a neck wound, a discrepancy of which the doctors and the Commissioners had to be aware. Burkley and Boswell had originally located the back wound at the level of the third thoracic vertebra, depicted on the skeletal chart here. The wound in the neck depicted in CE 386 is markedly higher than the third thoracic vertebra. The immediate significance of this information is that a bullet entering the back at the third thoracic vertebra and traveling at a downward angle could not emerge at the front of the throat, thus proving the autopsy report and the Warren Report wrong.

29. MASTER OF DECEIT

The problem of doing something about the political assassinations has never been one of fact.

The problem has been the unwillingness of every source of real power in the country to consider the facts. From the outset there has never been any question about the dishonesty and unacceptability of the investigations of these assassinations.

Everything the Warren Commission did it did in secrecy. And everything of any consequence to its conclusions was leaked in advance to the complacent news media. The people were conditioned to believe that Lee Harvey Oswald alone killed the President. Thus, before the Report was issued, the essence of what it had been determined in advance would be the official conclusion had been dinned into the national ear. Over and over again, in varying forms, the same central themes.

Whether the major elements of the press are, on this gut issue, this central issue of these days, unwilling to report any doubts about the solution to the assassination, fearing the consequences, as I believe is the case, or whether they conditioned themselves to believe the inherently unbelievable, and that was enough, they have, from the first, given major attention to one side only, the official mythology and its protagonists.

Beginning with the first book, the Warren Report itself was a corpse. In the words the New Republic used in 1966 to describe the effect of WHITEWASH, the Report was in need of an autopsy. A few of the minor elements of the press were, for a short while, a bit troubled. But in time they danced to the same federal piper.

Moving the effort to establish truth and end suppression of evidence into court did not overcome the reluctance of the press to report anything but the most irresponsible "news" about any of the assassinations. As of this writing, I have filed three lawsuits, all unreported. The first ended in a legal rarity, a summary judgment against the Department of Justice, but that also was not news. The net effect of this press boycott was to embolden the government, out of court and before the bar, to refuse more and to lie more openly.

The second suit is for the spectrographic analyses in the John Kennedy assassination. This represents still another way to seek other suppressed evidence fortifying what is now exposed for the first time in this book. What I sought had been widely disseminated in paraphrase and so published by the Commission and Dallas Police Chief Jesse Curry. But the actual FBI laboratory reports are not in the Commission's files and never were. Spectrography can show possibility and impossibility when used in testing and comparing traces left by a bullet with the bullet itself. It cannot show that a damage was caused by one particular bullet, but it can show that this bullet could have caused that damage. Where it is positive and beyond question is in making possible scientific proof that damage could not have been caused by the tested bullet.

My first request for access to these unsecret laboratory tests was made May 25, 1966. Hoover has not gotten around even to saying "no" since then. He responds promptly to letters of praise. Even slips up sometimes when he is flattered enough.

Can it be believed that if the spectrographic studies prove the official version Hoover and the Commission would not have been proclaiming it throughout the land? There is only one reason for suppressing it, and that is because it proves the official story false.

The case finally came to trial before Judge John Sirica, a self-activating rubber stamp for the government. This did not discourage President Nixon from promoting him to chief judge of that court when the position was open.

The government claimed this was an investigatory file for law-enforcement purposes and thus exempt under the law. We showed it was not an investigatory but a laboratory file and that there was no law-enforcement purpose, the assassination of a President not then being a federal crime.

To persuade the willing court that black is white, up is down, the Department of Justice filed an affidavit in support of a motion to dismiss my case. It falsely swore that what I sought is an investigatory file.

So blatant is the government's contempt for the law and so certain its dependence upon the favor of some of the judges that the FBI agent making the affidavit, Marion E. Williams, did not even bother to claim that he was competent to swear to what the affidavit says.* The FBI has specialists, as it must, for all of its technical work. The agent who is an expert on fingerprints may know no more about handwriting analysis or fibre identification or chemical tests or typewriter comparisons or thousands of other needs of law-enforcement science than the average citizen. In this case, Williams identified himself only as an agent assigned to an entirely unidentified laboratory. If he is qualified to do more than sweep floors, it is not specified. Neither on this basic point of competence with spectrography nor on others, such as his interpretations of the law, did Williams or the lawyers who procured his affidavit even suggest, let alone establish, that he was competent to swear to that to which he did swear. Apparently, it is to be believed that an FBI agent is presumed to be the world's best-qualified expert in anything and judges genuflect thrice to the east in awe. Sirica did.

Williams swore that he had "reviewed" these spectrographic examinations and that they "were conducted for law enforcement purposes".

This is perjury, and J. Edgar Hoover himself is proof of the fact.

Perjury is a false swearing to what is material. The main issue here, hence material, is whether this was, as the exemption of the law requires, for "law enforcement purposes", words Williams therefore used.

In opening his May 14, 1964, testimony before the Warren Commission (5H98), Hoover swore:

.... as you are aware, there is no federal jurisdiction for such an investigation. It is not a federal crime to kill or attack the President ... /Emphasis added/

Hoover went further in defining the FBI's investigation as other than for law-enforcement, making specific the fact that it was for an entirely different purpose:

However, the President has a right to request the Bureau to make special investigations, and in this instance he asked that this investigation be made. /Emphasis added/

It is clear that, unless Hoover committed perjury before the Warren Commission, his agent Williams did in Federal District Court in Washington. This is a crime. He should be punished. Instead, he will probably be promoted for it.

Throughout, Hoover's interpretation never changed. And he, not flunky Williams, is the best authority on this within his Bureau.

As the Commission's existence neared its bitter end, on September

_____
*In WHITEWASH IV, pp. 187-8.

23, 1964, the day the Report went to press, the day before a copy was
given to President Johnson, Hoover wrote Rankin leaving no doubt that
the FBI not only had no law-enforcement purposes, but that he did not
even know what to do with "information" that "will continue to be received" where the only responsibilities of the FBI would be "checking
out" what it got. This is that letter, in full:

OFFICE OF THE DIRECTOR

UNITED STATES DEPARTMENT OF JUSTICE

FEDERAL BUREAU OF INVESTIGATION

WASHINGTON, D.C. 20535

September 23, 1964

BY COURIER SERVICE

Honorable J. Lee Rankin
General Counsel
The President's Commission
200 Maryland Avenue, N. E.
Washington, D. C.

Dear Mr. Rankin:

On September 22, 1964, during a discussion by you
with J. R. Malley, the matter of information relating to the
assassination of President Kennedy continuing to be referred to
the FBI and subsequent investigations made as a result of these
referrals was discussed in some detail. Particular reference
was made to the necessity of this Bureau, as the investigating
agency, being able to refer results of its investigation to some
authority designated for such purpose after the termination of
the President's Commission.

It is quite possible that information relating to the
assassination of President Kennedy will continue to be received
for an indefinite period of time and the FBI will continue to fulfil
its responsibilities in checking out to the fullest all information
which is received.

It would be appreciated if you would advise the name
of the appropriate authority to receive such investigation conducted
by this Bureau following termination of the President's Commission.

Sincerely yours,

315

By every test, there was no law-enforcement purpose. Deception of the court, violation of the law, and suppression of what could not be suppressed were the perjurious purposes.

Williams next swore that this file "was compiled solely for the official use of U. S. Government personnel ... not disclosed .... to persons other than U. S. Government employees on a 'need to know' basis."

This, especially so long after the Commission, is similar, knowing, deliberate criminality. The contents were testified to before the Warren Commission, what was represented as a fair summary was given to it and Dallas Police Chief Curry, both of whom published it, and the official intent, from the beginning, was quite to the contrary.

The paraphrase copy printed by the Commission (24H262-4) as part of CE2003 is from its 81st file. It is on the printed FBI form 7-1a (rev. 9-7-60). The printed heading of this form is "REPORT OF THE FBI LABORATORY, FEDERAL BUREAU OF INVESTIGATION, WASHINGTON, D.C." *

Inside the federal government and on a "need to know" basis only? It was addressed to Curry. Five tests are listed, the second "Spectrographic". The summary of the spectrographic analysis that this point was limited to the recovered metal only is without any meaning.

Specimens identified by code numbers are, in order, Q4 and Q5, each "Metal fragment from the President's head"; Q9, "Metal fragment from arm of Governor Connally"; Q14, "Three metal fragments recovered from rear floor board carpet"; and Q2, "Bullet fragment from front seat cushion". Not included is Q3, "Bullet fragment from beside front seat", which in itself, it here lacking explanation, raises some questions.

This "laboratory", not "investigatory", report says of the spectrographic comparisons only that "the lead metal of Q4 and Q5, Q9, Q14 and Q15 is similar to the lead core of the bullet fragment Q2."

Had they all been pieces of discarded lead plumbing, old pieces of newspaper type metal, perhaps fishing-line sinkers, would they, if made of lead, not have been "similar" to the fragment with which they are compared without the specification of metals other than lead and their percentages? Alloys are used in bullet cores. This "scientific" report says no more than that one book is like another book, one woman like another woman.

What about comparison with "Q1 Bullet from stretcher", good ol' magic Bullet 399?

What about comparisons of the alloys in the jackets?

Or the notation that comparisons are to be made with traces remaining on the President's clothing? Or the governor's clothing, never sought by the FBI and not in government possession for months, and then only after insistence by the governor's wife, as she first reported two years later to Life magazine, the FBI and Commission having so carefully avoided it?

Two of the earlier examples showing there was neither intent nor need to so restrict any of the laboratory examinations are a letter Texas Attorney General Waggoner Carr, who headed that state's investigation, wrote to Warren December 5, 1963, and Deputy Attorney General Nicholas deB. Katzenbach's appearance in a Commission executive session.

Carr said, "... we were assured, both privately and in public statements, that ... laboratory findings, etc., would be made available to the State of Texas ..."

Katzenbach expressed the Department's desire to make public "scientific examinations of evidence", including "ballistics tests".

From this lie, which I believe constitutes another perjury, Williams proceeded to another that is an enormous deception so transparent it is incredible that even a judge in the Department's hip pocket would be content to leave it as a record he accepted:

The release of raw data from such investigative files ...

*See. pp. 603-4.

316

would seriously interfere with ... important law enforcement responsibilities ... could lead, for example, to exposure of confidential informants; the disclosure out of context of the names of innocent parties; ... possible blackmail; and, in general, do irreparable damage; ... create a highly dangerous precedent ... /Emphasis added/

All this from simple, well-known, non-secret laboratory testings of minute particles of clothing and metal? Involving no names, no informants?

Exposure of confidential informants? Blackmail?

And after a controlling decision in the United States District Court in Baltimore (Wellford v. Hardin, 315 F. Supp. 175 (1970)) that "Purely factual reports and scientific studies cannot be cloaked in secrecy ..."?

This same Department of Justice unsuccessfully defended in that action.

It is only because the results of spectrographic comparisons show that the official accounting of the assassination is both false and was known to be false that it has to be and has been suppressed.

Assistant United States Attorney Robert M. Werdig's response to Fensterwald's question, what law was being enforced, was semi-hysterical and non-legal, "that there must be some law enforcement purpose" (transcript of hearing of November 16, 1970, in Civil Action No. 2301-70, p.11) - even if it doesn't exist and cannot under the law, it has to, somehow.

To this he added (pp.11-2):

... because there wasn't any statutory explication of the crime, that there wasn't any law, natural or human, to our basic society that wasn't violated ...

There was every kind of "law" except real law. Or, there was no law.

If John J. Sirica could sit still for Williams' repetitious perjury, this citation of nonexistent "natural or human" law as a substitute for also nonexistent statutory law, could accept and rule favorably to the government on the citation "there must be some law enforcement purpose" when none existed, none was known to exist, none was in any way possible, need there be any doubt of his qualification to be chief judge of that federal court when it came time for the Nixon-Agnew-Mitchell-Kleindienst (and yes, Burger) administration to appoint a new one? With such stellar qualifications, required he any other?

That action is now under appeal.*

At that time we will have new evidence discovered after Sirica's decision. So it can be understood, I introduce it with a reflection of Commission staff misgivings about the proof that identical bullets accounted for all the firing and that one could have had a career like nothing in mythology or science fiction, the Hollywood spectacular of Bullet 399. It should be understood that, unless all fragments recovered from any source except the governor are provable as causing the explosion of the President's head and all traces recovered for analysis from the clothing and the Governor's wrist are identical with Bullet 399, the whole official story is destroyed. And if the FBI knew this not to be the case and withheld its proof, aside from the culpability reflected, the historical magnitude of which I leave to the reader's own estimate, there is apparent reason for all this suppression, including of the spectrographic and other tests and of access to the clothing in any kind of evidentiary form.

In referring to the staff apprehensions, it is, I think, necessary to remember the tight rein Rankin held on all his lawyers. All letters to Hoover or the FBI of which I know were signed by him and required his advance approval. He did not permit asking all the staff wanted to be asked of the FBI. Requests were frequently modified and

*See Part 4.

317

their scope restricted. However, his control was not as firm when staff members had personal contact, as Melvin Eisenberg did with Special Agent John F. Gallagher, the spectrographer, on March 16, 1964.

(Further meaning may be imparted by recalling from the first part of this book the two Eisenberg April memoranda on the conferences to determine when what shots hit whom.) *

Of those technical questions Eisenberg asked, to which Hoover responded in his March 18 letter (CD525,20H1-2), the fourth is most relevant here. Hoover's restatement of the question and his answer are:

> 4. Would neutron activation analyses show if a bullet passed through the hole in the front of President Kennedy's shirt near the collar button area and also if a bullet passed through the material of his tie? Neutron activation is a sensitive analytical technique to determine elements present in a substance. During the course of the spectrographic examinations previously conducted of the fabric surrounding the hole in the front of the shirt, including the tie, no copper was found in excess of that present elsewhere in undamaged areas of the shirt and tie. Therefore, no copper was found which could be attributed to projectile fragments.

To this he added the letter's concluding sentence:

> It is not felt that the increased sensitivity of neutron activation analyses would contribute substantially to the understanding of the origin of this hole and frayed area.

In what will follow, the recounting of my Civil Action No. 2569-70 and efforts to get meaningful pictures of the damaged areas of shirt front and tie, this response will be of increased significance. Translated from Hooverese into plain English, what this says is that the damages were not caused by any bullet or fragment of bullet. Had either been, there would have been traces of cooper from the bullet jacket, as was said to be the case with the holes in the back of the President's garments.

How, then, was this damage caused? It was not caused by a bullet exiting or entering.

And what happened to the bullet alleged to have entered the back? The official stories are that X-rays show no bullet in the body although both post-Commission panel reports on the pre-Commission X-rays show fragmentation, which in itself rules out Bullet 399 as the cause.

And what caused the wound in the front of the President's neck if spectrography rules out 399, no telltale traces of it or any other bullet remaining on the clothing where it is claimed to have exited?

The reason for suppressing the spectrographic analyses are pretty clear, as is the need for all the lies up to and including perjury and the suppression of what has to this point here been exposed for the first time and what will follow.

Hoover's concluding sentence seems to say that there is no need for making any neutron-activation analyses, and this was a pennypinching investigation. But in the context of the real meaning of the answer to the question, it means much more. It means that since spectrography proves this damage was not from a bullet, neutron-activation will do no more than confirm the spectrographic analyses and prove all over again that the "solution" to the crime and the Report are monstrous fakes.

There is no innocence for the silent Eisenberg, who was soon abandoned by Dr. Light, as noted earlier, over the same evidence, or for any of the others involved in these areas. Least of all can there

*See pp. 55ff.

be for Specter, who converted all this chicanery into a successful political career. If the members could not be expected to know this, a number of staff lawyers had to - including Rankin.

It did not stop here, however. Because of the deliberate confusion built into the files and their excessive bulk, none of us researching them has been able to reconstruct all of the deviousness, including with the so-called "science". However, Paul Hoch has found that some neutron-activation testing was done. It is reported in an unpublished July 8, 1964, letter from Hoover to Rankin.* Even for Hoover, that old master of official semantics, it is a remarkable performance. This deals with the lead.

Here is the first paragraph:

As previously reported to the Commission, certain small lead metal fragments uncovered in connection with this matter were analyzed spectrographically to determine whether they could be associated with one or more of the lead bullet fragments and no significant differences were found within the sensitivity of the spectrographic method.

First of all, he avoids saying which of the many fragments were compared with which. Let us assume that he really means a comparison between fragments recovered from the bodies and the fragments of bullets recovered from the car, the only known sources of such fragments. Aside from whatever he may or may not mean by "significant", what he may or may not regard as "significant differences", any differences dismember the Report. If the spectrography showed the possibility of common origin, all the wily old dissembler need have said - and he does know his business - is very simple: "This analysis shows the possibility of common origin." Or, if he wanted to expand a bit, "These spectrographic analyses of the composition of the samples compared prove they could have come from the same bullet."

This is the requirement for any other evidence or part of the Report to be considered at all.

If Hoover did not say something like this, there is only one reason for it: He knew he did not dare! He knew the proof was to the contrary.

There is also something quite important and missing. The test reported was no more than comparison of unidentified fragments with "one or more of the lead bullet fragments", also unidentified. Now, how about that fragment from Connally (Specimen C9)? It had to be compared not with any fragment but with Bullet 399, from which the Report says it came. If it did not, then on this basis alone the whole Report is false. Without the FBI reporting this comparison and its results, there is every reason to presume that this required comparison shows the Connally fragment did not come from Bullet 399, hence the omission. This is not carelessness, not by a long shot, coming from the man who practically invented the FBI business.

To simplify this, one of two things: At best, the spectrographic analyses do not confirm the official story and at worst, they disprove it.

His second paragraph reads:

Because of the higher sensitivity of the neutron activation analysis, certain of the small lead fragments were then subjected to neutron activation analyses and comparisons with the larger bullet fragments. The items analyzed included the following: C1 - bullet from stretcher; C2 - fragment from front seat cushion; C4 and C5 - metal fragments from President Kennedy's head; C9 - metal fragment from the arm of Governor Connally; C10 - metal fragments from rear floor board carpet of the car.

First of all, if not until after the Commission had expected to have completed its work, there was neutron-activation testing. Until now, this was a state secret. There is no reference to it in all the

*See p. 608.
                                    319

Commission's publishing. It was avoided like the plague in all testimony and the Report itself. This also can be no accident.

Second of all, Hoover reports insufficient testing. There is none of the clothing, for example. And of the two fragments from the front seat and the scrapings from the windshield, Hoover reports testing of one fragment alone. This, with the limitation to "lead" in both paragraphs, refers to a sample taken from the previously described "Q2" fragment, "Q3" being a piece of copper-alloy jacket only. Or, additional and more significant omissions when considered with the absence of any reporting of any neutron-activation testing of the clothing: There was none of the jacketing of this fragment or of Bullet 399, and copper traces were found on the back of the President's shirt and coat.

"The items analyzed" by Hoover do not include those three fragments said to have been recovered from the back seat of the limousine, Commission Exhibit 840. The reason may have been established when Howard Roffman ordered a photograph of these fragments from the Archives so he could study them. However, the picture sent him showed only two fragments, not three.

When he raised questions, the Archives acknowledged "it appears that one of the fragments is missing ... We have made a search for the missing fragment but have not found it and must assume it was not transferred to us with the others."

If we strip the polite officialese to stark fact, this means the FBI did not give the missing fragment to the permanent repository of evidence in the Archives. If the FBI was and remains silent - and this is not its only infidelity with the most quintessential of the evidence - it does not persuade that this now-missing fragment is in any way helpful to the scientific analyses as interpreted by Hoover or to the fiction presented as an official Report. All three of these fragments must have the same origin as the two said to have been found in the front seat, for they are all said to have been part of what was recovered from the single bullet said to have exploded in the head.

With all of these limitations and disqualifications of any genuine scientific testing, all the clear effort to avoid the reporting of disproof of the whole sorry fabrication foisted off on the entire world, what does Hoover say? This is his third and last paragraph:

While minor variations in composition were found by this method, these were not considered sufficient to permit positively differentiating among the larger bullet fragments and thus positively determining from which of the larger bullet fragments any given small lead fragment may have come.

The cat is out of the bag again!

"Positive differentiation among the larger bullet fragments" was not the purpose of the test. It was to establish common origin of all the "larger bullet fragments", plus all others except C9, the one from Connally, a basic requirement of the Report. Without this, no Report, merely a gruesome official lie. The same is true if C9 cannot be tied to C1, Bullet 399.

Nor was the question one of "determining from which of the larger bullet fragments any given lead fragment may have come".

The Report is also based on the absolute necessity for all five fragments from the car, plus the sweepings from the windshield, the sample from the curbstone and all fragments from the President's head, however many there were, all having come from this one exploded bullet.

From whatever one larger fragment of bullet any of the fragments from the President's head may have split off also is not the question, nor is it possible to answer this irrelevant question.

By not asking the right question, Hoover is able to lie and kid himself into believing he is not lying. He asks what he knows is the wrong question so that he can give an irrelevant answer and avoid the right question and the destructiveness of the right answer.

There is only one reason for all this, only one reason for Hoover to have avoided the obviously right question, "Did the head fragments come from the bullet of which the car fragments are part." It is because he cannot say "yes".

And if he cannot say "yes", if he has to go through all this FBI gobbledygook which may in the past have convicted God knows how many innocent, it is not because he does not know the right answer to the right question. It is because he cannot face either question or answer.

There is no end to the cuteness of that old cutie Hoover. But there must be an end to exposing them, for book after book could be written on just this, the deceits so often masterful, the semantics that, though heavy-handed and awkward, did succeed, perhaps easier because his victims yearned to be skinned.

One more here cannot be ignored. It is that verbal gem cut with such skill and care, that sparkler about "minor variations in composition". Variation in composition is negative proof, one of the purposes of the tests. Variation in composition proves no common origin and disproves the Hoover and the Commission Report "solution" to the crime. If the fragments are, as required to be by the official fabrications, all from a single shot to the head except the Connally fragment, which must come from Bullet 399, then in each case there has to be no variation in composition. Hoover sought to circumvent this by saying the variations are "minor".

If in either case there is variation, end of Report and Hoover is a cunning faker.

To say there are "minor" variations is to say a woman is only a little bit pregnant.

Unless the metal from Connally has the same composition as Bullet 399, poof! and the Report is up in smoke.

If there is any variation in the lead composition of everything else - the erroneously accounted for fragments removed from the President's head, the fragments found in the car, the scrapings from the windshield, the traces from the curbstone - all other lead of which there is any relic - then this Report has to be the biggest official lie in official history. All this lead must be of exactly the same composition or it cannot be claimed that the fatal bullet was fired from "Oswald's" rifle.

So, what all of this must mean is that the suppressed scientific tests disprove the conjecture substituted for the fact that is basic to any consideration of any other evidence and proves the falsity of the Report and the "solution" to "the crime of the century", the assassination of the President.

No innocence, again. None for the indestructible master of deceit, Hoover. None for any of the Commission lawyers who saw these reports.

And ample reason for and explanation of why the medical evidence I was able to obtain had to be withheld from the Commission. Suppressing these laboratory tests dovetails perfectly with suppressing all the most important medical evidence.

Hoover is beginning to slip. He underestimated Nixon, whom he apparently regarded as a fellow unchanger, another to whom the passing of time means nothing. Or, his spies inside the White House, intelligence and/or analysis failed him. Here is part of the aging autocrat of the FBI's pronunciamento in the June 1971 issue of the Veterans of Foreign Wars Magazine, under the title "Mao's Red Shadow":

Red Chinese intelligence in the United States, as compared with Soviet Russia's, has a major handicap in that Peking is not recognized diplomatically by this country nor is it yet a member of the United Nations. This deprives the Red Chinese of a legal base from which to operate spies.

And for a real zingy close:

The shadow of Mao Tse-tung can be seen and felt in the
United States today. We can expect the subversive danger
to grow as time passes. The only way to meet it is to be
prepared.

This is about as close as anyone has ever come to calling Nixon
a "Comsymp" or inventing the no less mellifluous "Maosymp" to describe
the President who, almost immediately upon publication of Hoover's age-
less wisdom, began secret negotiations with the man of the red shadow,
supported his country's entry into the United Nations, and negotiated
an invitation to visit it.

What it required of Hoover besides diplomacy can be imagined for
he had planned a mass reprint of his major statement of United States
policy as he thought it should be. When he discarded the reprint notion, he let it be known it was "for budgetary reasons". This was
indeed a great budgetary sacrifice for the man to whom the unstinting
taxpayers provide a reported five armored limousines stashed around the
country in the cities he prefers to visit, that avid follower of the
bangtails.

30. THE "NEW SCIENCE" PLUS THE "NEW SCHOLARSHIP"

EQUALS THE NEW EVIDENCE

Another omission is consistent with the scientific mumbo jumbo about the lack of copper on the front of the shirt and the tie. I pursued it in federal court in Civil Action No. 2569-70, after long and unsuccessful effort to get from the Archives a single clear or meaningful picture of any of the President's clothing showing any of the damage.

That effort cannot be reported in full here, not even in detailed summary, for it is, in one set of court papers alone, longer than a long book. In this suit I was my own lawyer. James Lesar made helpful suggestions with the Complaint, the document that sets forth what is sought and why it is a matter of legal right.

As with the "Memorandum of Transfer", it involves the President's family and their GSA contract. Because the family of a President was enmeshed in and made to seem responsible for the legally and normally unacceptable, I had to apply strictures and restraints upon myself not to become an adjunct of the continuing federal effort to transfer responsibility to the family.

In every way possible, the government tried to make it seem that suppression is required of it by this contract and the law. Both are false. The truth is that the contract requires exactly the opposite.

Off and on, when it was possible, I tried to make arrangements to study the damage to the clothing. This resumed when the transfer to the Archives was announced the first of November 1966. I then had a conference with the Archivist who has since retired, Dr. Robert Bahmer. From then on the Archives never acknowledged - even in court - having possession of the clear pictures it was required to provide me.

As my collateral work produced substantiation of what had been but a strong suspicion, I renewed these efforts. They were always frustrated by the Archives. However, as I continued to press, they finally admitted that they did have shirt pictures not published. The uselessness, the deliberately poor photography represented in all the Commission's published pictures of all the clothing - all done for it by the FBI - had compelled the Archives to have its own competent laboratory photograph the shirt.

To those who know the FBI from Hoover's adulation and self-adulation subsidized by the use of FBI personnel to help friendly writers or to do work that bears his name, from the omnipresent newspaper and electronic publicity and from the TV show, the professional incompetence of the pictures of the President's clothing with which he bewitched the overly-busy old fuddy-duddies of the Commission and their staff which was capable of consuming and holding down what no jackal could retain will seem beyond belief. That the following description is not exaggerated can be checked by those whose local libraries hold the 26 volumes, where these pictures of the clothing, Exhibits 393-5, appear on pages 23-7 of Volume 17.

That this is not exceptional, not special treatment reserved for the President's clothing, can be checked by a larger number of readers. In WHITEWASH, on page 208, I reproduce the FBI-Commission picture of Oswald's shirt, described in the testimony as "striped". I have made a careful examination of this shirt. It also has a gold fleck worked into its grass-weave pattern. It glitters in the light. After proper application of the FBI's consummate photographic skill, this shirt appears to be solid black, which is no mean science. Those who have the Bantam book, The Witnesses, prepared by The New York Times, will find this black-on-black rendering of Exhibit 673 on page 53 of the exhibits.

In its earnest desire not to disturb the people or the press in its Report, the Commission omitted these advertisements for the more subtle and lesser-known spe.ialties of the FBI under Hoover. Nor do the FBI's pictures of the President's clothing appear in the mass edition of the Report by Bantam, in which all the photographic exhibits from the Report are inset between pages 344 and 345. The front view of the shirt and a view of the tie do appear in The Witnesses, on page 3 of the exhibits. In these mass sources the fidelity of my description can more readily be ascertained than from the 26 volumes, which very, very few people have ever seen or can see, a condition in no sense troubling to the government, which arranged it that way by making them hard to obtain and the cost of getting them, $76.00.

With some of the best evidence, can there be a better reason for omission from the 900-page Report?

Parenthetically, those who do have the Bantam edition of the Report may want to look at the center picture on the inside front cover, a picture also not in the Report. It is an official picture of an official reconstruction of the crime. In this reenactment, the President's rear nonfatal wound had to be located well down on his back, not in his neck, for it even to seem to be possible that one bullet transited him and then struck Connally in the back. At that, it is the wrong place on Connally's back, makes impossible the bullet's alleged subsequent cavorting through and out of his body and its devilment of his extremities, and for even this disproof of the official story to be reconstructed, the angle has to be and is shown as ever so much flatter than the Report says. This reenactment is clarified by the addition of dotted lines to show the conjectured path of the mythical bullet and large white dots on the backs of the men representing the victims.

In Volume 17, the President's jacket is shown in front and back views on pages 393 and 394, the FBI's perfection in photography internally identified as "C29". In both pictures the coat is solid black, which in real life it is not. No bullet hole is visible. None is marked.

These pictures may have some value as Hoover's Rorschach inkblots but not as evidence.

Front and back views of the shirt, Exhibit 393, follow. It is FBI C32. This apotheosis of Kodakery is, even for this FBI, a new zenith. Not only is no damage of any sort identifiable or marked in either view, it is completely invisible with magnification on the front. Those who know where the hole in the back is, with care and magnification can locate it. But there is no way of distinguishing it from any of similar photographic blemishes. To the uninitiated, finding this hole is like a treasure hunt in which there are no treasures. Now, this shirt in its real life is triple-striped, the stripes being in sets of three. There is no way of learning this from the published pictures, where the FBI has succeeded in fusing all three sets of stripes into a single blurred stripe, apparently setting its camera out of focus to do it.

FBI C31, the tie, Exhibit 395, is last. Color is no less skillfully altered, it seeming to be black. A paler simple pattern can be detected. It is here alone that the FBI, with its photographic wizardry, failed to obliterate every characteristic, including color, every detail. Not only does the existence of a pattern show, but it can be seen that the tie was cut off, for the knot is still tied. What cannot be seen is any hole in the tie. Thus, the FBI rubbed off on innocent Exhibit 395, the unoffending tie, a bit of the magic of Bullet 399, which is required to have transited the knot in departing the front of the President's neck, else the Report and all that means is an evidentiary house of cards.

However, the FBI was equal to this challenge when it faced it squarely. That we shall come to in a few pages with one of the officially unpublished samples of its unexcelled skill and science, its unequaled ability to do what it considers necessary with evidence.

After obtaining some of the medical evidence in the foregoing chapters, I renewed pressure on the Archives to get to see something besides the FBI's demonstrations of its disappearing-act photographic accomplishments. I wanted to examine evidence, not black-on-white pictures. It was then, for the first time - and this was the spring of 1970, more than five years after the Report was issued and four years after my first request - that the Archives admitted it had made shirt pictures in its own photo lab.

When I examined the shirt pictures, I had some questions. In answering one of them under date of April 16, 1970, the Archivist added this sentence:

We do not furnish copies or enlargement of these photographs for the same reason that we do not take special photographs of the clothing for researchers - to avoid any possible violation of the agreement with the Kennedy family.

He is a liar. For those who take offense, brace yourselves: I am soon going to call him and prove him a perjurer, as I have in court, without protest or pro forma denial.

The truthful part is where he says what he will not do. He will not voluntarily do anything that does not perpetuate suppression of evidence. The lie is in saying it is required by the Kennedys. The fact is that this contract is specific in requiring that he do take exactly these kinds of pictures for researchers, as I forced him to acknowledge in court.

I tried. I really tried in every way I could, with compromises and with letters to the government's representative on the Kennedy estate, Burke Marshall, who is supposed to serve the opposite role. I made a dozen written efforts with the Archivist, all a painful waste of time. Although this is one of the more innocuous of many redundant examples of how the government sought to blame the Kennedys for the suppression of some of the best evidence of how the most famous Kennedy was killed, the alternative was to risk causing them needless added pain and to risk validating the government's spurious claim that the Kennedys did contract suppression. The last thing I wanted to do, despite their silence, is add to this pain.

Two provisions of this contract are exactly opposite Rhoads's representation of them. The "Appendix A materials" include the clothing, described in this appendix to the contract as "Clothing and personal effects of the President". They are listed by their official Warren Commission exhibit numbers, "Commission Exhibit Nos. 393,394, 395" (p.7). In stipulating that there be access, Section I(2) reads, "Access to the Appendix A materials shall be permitted only to:". There follow two categories, "(a)", certain officials, and "(b)" is:

> (b) Any serious scholar or investigator of matters relating to the death of the late President, for purposes relevant to his study thereof. The Administrator shall have full authority to deny requests for access, or to impose conditions he deems appropriate on access, in order to prevent undignified or sensational reproduction of the Appendix A materials. The Administrator may seek the advice of the Attorney General or any person designated by the Attorney General with respect to the Administrator's responsibilities under this paragraph I(2)(b).

GSA provides unclear, rexeroxed copies only.

This fits me. There is no doubt that I am both a "serious scholar" and an "investigator into matters relating to the death of the late President",* certainly by far the most prolific. The only basis on which I can be denied is by proving it would be to "prevent undignified or sensational reproduction".

My intentions were exactly the opposite. The reason I needed other pictures is because those made available are inadequate and not capable of any but "undignified or sensational" use. They are useless for scholarship. To clarify this legal point, in writing I asked the Archivist and Marshall to show me how any except distasteful use was possible with pictures they were only too anxious to supply at a cost of $1.50 each (later inflated to $2.00), or how in any extreme interpretation they invent, they could possibly allege undignified or sensational intentions when my requests were limited to the area of damage only. This means requests for pictures as small as a half-inch square, the largest being the distance between the tabs of a shirt collar of the day when these were narrow and short. Of course, neither could or did meet the challenge of the contract. That unofficial adjunct of the Justice Department, Marshall, said he left this entirely to the Archivist, and the Archivist declined to respond.

The Archives' official and readily-available pictures show nothing but blood and gore. They hide the damage. I wanted pictures which show the damage to the garments, not the blood with which they are drenched.

The contract does have a provision by which I could be denied permission to examine the actual clothing, but then limited to a showing that I would damage them. It is Section III:

(1) In order to preserve the Appendix A materials and the Appendix B materials against possible damage, the Administrator is authorized to photograph or otherwise reproduce any of such materials for purposes of examination in lieu of the originals by persons authorized to have access pursuant to paragraph I(2) or paragraph II(2).

There was no possibility that I could damage the clothing with my eyes, but I was denied permission to see the clothing so I could specify the few pictures I wanted taken. This provision requires that as an alternative, the only contractual alternative. By "photographs or otherwise", the Archivist is required to provide what "any serious scholar or investigator" considers that he requires for purposes of his study.

Moreover, the Archives' own regulations, a copy of which they did not supply me or the court and denied the existence of to someone else I had request them (I had obtained a copy of a copy from another source, an Archives use in court half a continent away), places a further imposition on the Archivist. These are and were titled "Regulations for Reference Services on Warren Commission Items of Evidence." There are five.

The second declares, without any ifs or buts, "Still photographs will be furnished researchers ... Copies will be furnished on request for the usual fees." (Emphasis added.)

The last part of the fifth reads:

To the extent possible, photographs of these materials /i.e., those not to be touched/ will be furnished to researchers as a substitute for visual examination of the items themselves. In the event the existing photographs do not meet the needs of the researcher additional photographic views will be made. A charge may be made for unusually difficult or time-consuming photography. Photographs reproduced from existing negatives or prints will be furnished

* The FBI says so. See p. 425.

326

for the usual fees.

So, not only did the Kennedys require exactly the opposite of suppression, specifying, rather, full and free access to those doing legitimate research, but this and other Archives regulations require the providing of copies of the pictures at my cost. For this purpose I have maintained a non-interest-bearing deposit account at the Archives for six years.

When I had made so many requests, all turned down, I finally appealed under the regulations. Consistent with undeviating practice and in violation of the law, the appeal was ignored. Not until several months had passed in silence did I file the complaint in this suit. Thereafter, I did hear from the appeal. It was turned down in language calculated to make it seem that I had neither appealed nor had my requests been rejected. That whole business is so Orwellian, it is best not to confuse the reader with all the detail. But to give a bit of the flavor, the rejection of the appeal admitted that identical pictures had been taken for the Columbia Broadcasting System and would be shown to me. After the end of the last working day before my last response to government arguments was due in court, I received another letter saying this was a lie, that no such pictures had been taken for CBS!

In response to one set of my court papers, Assistant United States Attorney Robert M. Werdig certified to the court that he had served on me copies of allegedly attached exhibits, as the law requires he do. He had not. And he did not - not in response to three requests. By the time he finally got around to it, it was after the original time I had for response had expired. It took half of that time for what he did send to reach me. To this day he has never supplied a full copy of one of the exhibits, which will mean more to lawyers than to laymen.

Because the law requires that I begin with a request and pursue it through the channels of appeal, and that I had complied was already recorded and documented in the complaint, among the many obvious reasons for Werdig's not sending me these attachments to his argument until after I had completed my response is an affidavit by the Archivist. It is not out of character with the rest of the record in this case, at its most decent, merely deception and misrepresentation. Because of the legal requirement imposed upon me that I request and be rejected, his ninth paragraph is perjurious. He swore I

had never specifically requested permission to examine the above-mentioned articles of clothing, nor has he specifically requested permission to photograph the above-mentioned articles of clothing. Consequently, the National Archives and Records Service has never denied such requests.

In hasty response I sent the court copies of many letters of exactly the kind Rhoads swore neither I nor he had written. The total thickness of the copies of such things I filed in this case is not much less than an inch, and some of these were tissue copies. The documentation is abundant.

If, as I believe, charged in papers filed with the court and think I proved beyond reasonable doubt, this is perjury - it is false and could not be more material to what was at issue, the requirements of a perjury charge - then an additional crime is involved, subornation of perjury. He who gets another to commit perjury himself commits this crime of subornation of perjury. So, whoever in the legal departments of the Archives or GSA approved this affidavit, and someone in the Department of Justice, which filed it and should have known it to be false, suborned perjury.

Again I ask, who watches the watchman, who prosecutes the criminal prosecutor, when we have a "law-and-order" administration whose biggest accomplishment seems to have been to move crime from "in the streets" into the halls of justice, the offices of government?

There was, in the end, a hearing. Werdig assured the judge that the Archives would take the pictures I had, indeed, requested. He had an assistant general counsel of GSA there to agree. When I tried to read the regulations requiring that they also provide me with copies, without which I could not make any comparison with those pictures I had or consult an expert criminalist and a world-famous forensic pathologist, as I had already arranged, Judge Gerhard Gesell banged the gavel and dismissed the case. The government, by promising to take and show me the pictures I asked for, conned an overly busy judge who is not even required to hold a kangaroo-court hearing but can act on the papers filed alone - and does not even have to read them! This is only one of the problems faced in suing the government when it is all-powerful, immune in criminal activity and appoints and promotes judges.

There is a strange twist to this case for which I digress, believing it not as irrelevant as it may seem. Within a few days, Judge Gesell heard the government's case against The Washington Post for publishing what became known as "The Pentagon Papers". In his ruling against the government and in favor of the Post, a real power in Washington, which I am not, Gesell used language from my complaint. He may, in fact, not have been aware of it.

During the course of all these years of trying to get copies of the not-suppressed pictures, I got all that photographic rubbish with all that gore, every unhidden copy. This includes what is identified as FBI Exhibit 60. It is not published by the Warren Commission and the only copy in its files is made from a printing negative. This means that the fine photoengraving dots required for printing, invisible to the naked eye, dominate the picture on enlargement and negate enlarging.

What examination was possible showed dirty work at the FBI crossroads. It is a composite prepared for the Commission and is faked. I neither mince words nor exaggerate. It is faked in two different ways. This much I knew by studying it and comparing it with other pictures I had by then.

For trying to get a photographic rather than a lithographic copy - the Archives said they had none - I managed to pick the right psychological moment.

With his own bull-headed help, I had just exposed Kleindienst as one of the greater liars in an administration in which they are not scarce, a distinction not even Barry Goldwater's personal contribution to integrity in government could relish and no Deputy Attorney General of the United States should. This was in my successful suit to get those Ray extradition records he had confiscated from the British court. And I had whipped him. Considering what I presume they think of me and my work, this should not have caused any celebrations in his swank suite. So, instead of asking him for a copy of FBI Exhibit 60, for which he would have referred me to the Archives and then there would have been this hassle about the ruinous photoengraving dots, I merely asked him for the part that shows the shirt collar. And instead of going through the whole rigamarole, filing their Freedom of Information forms, sending a check and all the formalities, I just wrote him a letter.

(Now, for some reason, although I do not think it figured in Kleindienst's decision to send this to me, which he did, and promptly, the Department of Justice seems not to like my checks. Somebody does not want even to cash them. Two checks accompanying later Freedom of Information requests, written in December 1970, were not cashed until July 16 and 20, 1971. The Mitchellisti have short tempers. Somebody tore up the second one. Yup, into little pieces. The surprising thing is that it cleared. It was not Scotch-taped together neatly, nor was it complete. Two pieces are missing.)

As soon as I got this picture, I wrote right back and asked for two more parts of FBI Exhibit 60.* The speed with which Kleindienst sent them to me, and the fact that he even sent me 8 x 10 prints instead of the small 3-5/8 x 4-1/2 of the first one, almost made me sorry I had not asked for the remaining parts. I did not then believe that I needed them. With what I have since found to be the case and with

*See pp. 597-8.

the magnification clear prints make possible, I now wonder if there could have been something unexpected that I thus may have missed.

Better yet, the second two prints were original prints, not copies or copied from a file print. They bear proof of this.

When the second man in the Department of Justice (not counting Martha) learns the results of his first decency, it may be his last.

Before describing this and other pictures, let me repeat the official story, that Bullet 399 entered the back of the President's neck to the right of the midline and just above the curve of the shoulder, went downward through his neck, striking no bone, and exited through the shirt at the point where the collar is buttoned and through the tie. If this is not true, it is all a ghastly charade. Pictures alone can tell whether or not this is true.

Pictures are worth thousands of words and are more graphic than any words.

More, as by now may be understood, I seek to make the accurate historical and legal record to refute the shameful official lie of this Report, one hope being that before it is completely impossible to do anything about it there will be an official effort to solve the crime and punish the guilty, if all still live.

What I have already presented shows that everybody involved had to know that this Report was false.

Chalk one up for J. Edgar Hoover, the FBI, the military, and those on the Commission with guilty knowledge - all who failed to do what their jobs required of them. Till now they have gotten away with it.

Because they did not then seem essential to my purposes, I did not ask for pictures of the jacket. I am without doubt that there is no hole in the front, I have no interest in the blood and brain-matter on it, and there is no reason not to believe the hole in the back is where described. With the softer material and coarser weave of the jacket, I then believed the outlines of the hole in its back would not help materially.

The Archives copies of the published prints of both sides of the shirt, Exhibit 394, are like a magnificent sample of a used butcher-shop rag. The only certainty is the abundantly clear display of blood. On the back this stain is wider at the top and becomes more dense as it runs down the shirt. Eventually, it completely obliterates the pattern. This, however, is no boon to research. In that eight-inch width of photographic print, under a strong lens, with good light - and if you know where to look - there is what can be taken as the bullethole. It is about 1/16-inch wide, or less than one percent of the width of the picture. Not exactly an investigator's dream of evidence he can use.

There is one thing to be said for the photographic print rather than the printed copy: although even in this size the fact that each stripe is made up of three stripes is not visible to the unaided eye, with a good magnifying lens, if one knows this to be the fact, one can make it out. With an eight-power lens it is fairly clear, despite the poor exposure of the film during photographing or copying.

My copy, the Archives noted on the back of the print, was an enlargement of a file copy.

The front, similarly labeled, is also out of focus. By "enlargement" is meant a rather small increase in size, much less than double. This is a very small magnification, not what is usually termed an "enlargement".

The distribution of blood, in no way helpful to any part of any official story, is the same front and back. In the front it completely hides the stripes, therefore, would seem to be more concentrated. In both cases, it is markedly heavier on the President's left side. This cannot be attributed to its flow after he fell over, for it also runs down his shirt, front and back. Had it pumped out after he fell over,

329

its path would be _across_ the vertical pattern, not _down_ it, from top to bottom. The blood on the shirt actually runs well down the left sleeve, something that officially is neither mentioned nor accounted for.

The collar is buttoned. The one place there is _no_ sign of blood is where the bullet is said to have emerged, the fuzziest part of a picture of pronounced fuzziness.

The inside of the back of the close-fitting collar - his shirts were tailored - is heavily saturated with blood. With the shot allegedly _below_ the collar in the back - six inches below - well, Isaac Newton wrote the law against that. And how the saturation would be so much heavier on the inside than the outside if it dripped down from the head wound escapes me. One of the reasons these things seem to remain mysteries and are unexplained is because in this investigation to end all investigations - remember those impressive statistics, Hoover's answer to everything being statistics - they were never looked into. Neither reported nor investigated. With all those inquiries into all officially deemed essential evidence, ranging from Oswald's pubic hairs to Ruby's strippers, there was hardly time for the cause of death, real study of it and what relates, like these pictures and the better ones not available. One reason is succinctly put by Mankiewicz.

It is generosity to describe these pictures as disclosing and containing no evidence that can be used in support of the Report for they show no evidence all - except what was ignored and refutes the Report. The damage to the front of the shirt is invisible. Not even a good 10-power German engraver's lens can bring it out.

By far the best is the picture of the tie, which seems out of focus and not properly exposed. This picture, like that of the front of the shirt, is printed the wrong way on the photographic paper, thus diminishing the amount of tie that can be shown. Not all of it is shown. There are two marks that can be the damage. Both are fuzzy. Considering that a bullet, allegedly responsible for a Niagara of blood on the shirt, is said to have come through one of them, it is remarkable that _neither_ is tainted with _any_ blood.

The first trace of what may be taken as blood is well below the know and, if it is blood, without doubt, was caused by the spray when the head exploded.

The knot is perfect. It is without possibility of doubt that the tie was cut off beginning up against the left side of the knot, as worn.

When, in response to my extended complaints, the Archivist bestirred himself and made me a further "enlargement", it was only three-fifths larger and about that much more indistinct. What I know to be the hole in the back of the shirt measures less than an eighth of an inch and everything is paler. And this was not sent to me until the month _after_ I filed the suit.

Not much bait for abandoning it.

Later, when I saw the Archives photographer, 30-year veteran government employee Elmer H. Griffith, all of whose work for me and all of which I know is of top professional quality, I asked him how it came to pass that these pictures are so far below very poor amateur quality when his were always so fine. He told me they are all FBI pictures.

This is not to say the FBI cannot take good pictures or that they cannot print or enlarge them properly. FBI Exhibit 60 - one left out of the GSA-family contract - if not the best, is good, clear photography.

That the only available clear picture is omitted from the contract is hardly coincidence. Whether or not he was of a Mankiewicz bent of mind, I do not think Marshall was responsible. I think he merely rubber-stamped what government lawyers had prepared. But the fact is that there was no other good picture of which we could know, what is in the Memorandum of Transfer being a state secret, the new category of official evidence in the official investigation of a Presidential assassination.

330

My first examination of FBI Exhibit 60 disclosed possible reasons for its elimination from the tabulation in the contract. As I told Kleindienst during his period of short-lived aberration, when he did his job the legal, not his customary, way and made public information available to the public, one reason may be susceptible of innocent explanation. I did not report the other, for innocence in it is not possible.

FBI Exhibit 60 consists of four different, overlaid pictures. A little less than the top two-thirds is of the back of the shirt. In the upper left-hand corner and taking up a little less than 10 percent of the entire montage is an enlarged inset of the hole in the back of the shirt. It is sharp and clear although enlarged to more than five times the size of the unclear "enlargement" provided by the Archives. It could have been enlarged more, but I doubt the FBI wanted that. It is about a seventh the width of the enlarged inset.

What immediately attracted my attention to it is that, when I examined the hole in the shirt itself to which there is a white line drawn from the inset hole, the outlines of the two did not coincide. With the confusion and lack of detail imposed by the lithographic dots, and much smaller than any of the Archives prints as is this picture of the shirt, the difference in clarity is still so great that, where one cannot make out even the shape of the hole in the Archives pictures (also by the FBI), in even the smaller representation of this hole in FBI Exhibit 60, the outlines can be made out.

And, <u>it is not the same as the hole in the inset!</u>

Ah, the conspiracy chicks this can hatch!

I studied and I studied and I thought and I thought. How could this possibly happen, FBI reputation being what it is and all that?

Finally, I had a hunch, and it worked out - without proving any possible conspiratorial inference is wrong.

That fabled FBI precision, its great care with evidence and Hoover's insistence upon perfection as he conceives perfection as he dominates all from his elevator chair behind his throne-desk notwithstanding, the inset in his Exhibit 60 is printed upside down!

Not that there was any need of this "error", any more than there was for an exhibit digesting and interpreting - and carefully distorting - the picture evidence for the Commission.

Government photographic skill is such that an enlargement of this quarter-inch hole in the shirt itself could have been clear if blown up to the size of a wall in a high-ceilinged room. An impartial FBI would have given an impartial Presidential commission clear large prints of the evidence and no more. An impartial commission would have accepted no more.

It is Hoover's proud boast that he does not interpret. Aside from interpreting in this exhibit, the only other thing he did is <u>mis</u>interpret.

What the reason was for printing the inset hole upside down I do not know. The FBI is not paying for newspaper space to advertise the reasons for those "errors" Hoover pretends it does not make. Given the lack of need for making the montage, it is less easy to assume this is nothing but simple, careless, uncharacteristic-for-the-FBI error. Especially when this interpretation, not presented as more than conjecture, is possible:

The shot is supposed to have come from the President's rear and to his right. This suggests that the point of initial impact might have the sharper cut in the cloth. In reality, this sharper edge is in the left-hand side of the shirt. But with the FBI reversal of the only clear picture of this hole, the sharp margin then appears on the right, suggesting validity in the official story, that the shot came from that side.

The bottom section of FBI Exhibit 60 consists of two more insets, the one on the right slightly the larger. It is of a view of the front of the President's collar limited to exactly what I had been trying without success to get from the Archives. In it, the collar-button is open, the button and the button-hole clearly visible. The thoughtful FBI marked each of the two slits in the cloth with white arrows. Otherwise, they might have been overlooked. They are not holes.

As I studied this picture, two things became pretty obvious. The slits do not seem to coincide and certainly are not identical. If caused by the same exiting perfect bullet, they had to coincide and had to be virtually if not actually identical. And, having in younger years fired bullets into almost everything, the slits themselves - not holes but slits - were like no bulletholes I recall. They are entirely unlike that on the back of the shirt. At 2,000 feet a second, a bullet punches its way through something. It does not slip and slide through. Consultation with experts confirmed this.

Hence, my interest in this definitive picture, the first for which I am indebted to Kleindienst's temporary co-existence with the law.

As of this writing, having disposed of one rifle, I still possess two rifles and two handguns. I have never seen any bulletholes like slits and was immediately convinced they are not, in fact, bulletholes at all.

I do not play tricks with the reader. This is no subject for literary devices. Nor do I pretend that I had not earlier developed a theory as soon as I thought about the lack of spectrographic traces of bullet on the front of the shirt and the tie. Absence of Commission questioning on the point fortified this belief. It is one of the items of key evidence into which the Commission had to have inquired - and did not.

When the President was wheeled into the emergency room in Dallas, those doctors had a major crisis situation with which to deal. They did not have time to think of unbuttoning buttons, the task of nurses. They had cut off the tie, without any doubt, and in so doing preserved essential, irrefutable evidence. But when, with desperate speed, they started to open the collar with a scalpel, the close-fitting shirt left insufficient space to work the knife without danger of injury to the front of the neck. So, after starting to cut off the shirt, it was unbuttoned at the top. That simple. That obvious.

When I wrote Kleindienst to thank him for the clear photographic print of this inset and to tell him of the error for which there might be innocent explanation, I also asked for photographic rather than offset prints of the back of the shirt and the enlarged inset. With these it was possible to be certain that the inset was printed upside down and I so informed my benefactor, in writing, leaving a record in the Department's files as in my own of possibly innocent error - if the FBI wants to boast of its carelessness and incompetence. I have no objection should they so decide, for there remains what cannot be innocent, not just FBI "incompetence".

That is the lower left-hand corner inset of the tie. It is as vital as evidence as my comment in the preceding paragraph notes. Before addressing this picture, I feel the reader is entitled to assurances that I am not off on an anti-FBI kick with constant references to its seeming incompetence, its pervading carelessness, its domination by its noble leader.

Hoover started preempting the investigation long before, as he swore, Lyndon Johnson asked him to do it. His agents participated in the first interrogation of Oswald when, to his and their knowledge, it was illegal. There was no federal jurisdiction, no right to spend federal money without warrant. The time it took the agents to get to this first interrogation indicates they first checked it with Washington, which is precisely the sworn FBI testimony in the King assassination. SOP in the FBI-SOG, as they call it. Standard operating procedure, check with "Seat of Government". No lesser designation of Hoover, nothing simple and descriptive would suit him. Headquarters could not be referred to internally as "HQ" or "HQFBI". Only "Seat of Government" is appropriate for the man who so considers himself and, in so many ways, really is.

Here are a few samples of this noncareless "carelessness".

Although jurisdiction rested with the Secret Service, the FBI had already been to Klein's Sporting Goods in Chicago, preempted the Secret Service, and so thoroughly intimidated everybody at Klein's that nobody would talk even to the Secret Service. (Chicago Secret Service Report of November 23, 1964, File #CO-2-34030; WHITEWASH II, p.39).

When it was necessary to make it seem possible that Oswald was on the sixth floor of the Texas School Book Depository Building to be able to fire those shots, which, like the illustration with the rifle, is relevant to the suppressed evidence here considered, the FBI had redundant evidence of its impossibility and of its unlikelihood, all carefully hidden. A secretary, Mrs. Carolyn Arnold, who saw Oswald, was interviewed by the FBI. It then reported her as uncertain whether she had really seen him and placed the time at "a few minutes before 12:15 PM" (CD5:41), which allowed just enough time for what he is alleged to have had to do. But what Mrs. Arnold actually said is that this was "at about 12:25 PM" (CD706(d)). There has been no complaint since I published this suppressed evidence in 1967, no allegation it is misrepresented in any way (PHOTOGRAPHIC WHITEWASH, pp.74-6;210-1).

Time after time the same and worse happened in New Orleans, where the FBI went to some pains to hide indications of CIA involvement in Oswald's past. To this I devoted major parts of OSWALD IN NEW ORLEANS, also in 1967, with no single complaint, official or unofficial, registered to date.

Time after time the FBI reported the opposite of what witnesses said and failed to report what they did say. It made countless harassing visits in the guise of interviews (not written up) to witnesses who persisted in telling the truth as they knew it.

One of the best illustrations of this also shows how the FBI could get away with it. The Commission's lawyers covered them or went along with them. In WHITEWASH II (pp.71-92) I tell the story of what happened to Arnold Louis Rowland, a young man with an incredibly accurate memory of observations uncongenial to the FBI and the Commission. He saw someone other than Oswald in that window and other men, armed and in other windows of that building. The FBI made seven undenied "interviews" in an unsuccessful effort to get Rowland to change his story. And when his wife, whose testimony supported his, sought to change a factual error in the transcript of her testimony, Assistant Counsel David Belin not only did not permit it, but on the very same page made a stylistic change in the wording of one of his questions. Today, Belin, an affluent lawyer, calls those who cannot condone suppression and lies when a President is killed "sensationalists". For a lawyer to condone FBI lying and intimidation of witnesses is not wrong. Topsy-turvy world.

So, I am not just making cracks at the FBI. I am citing a small part of its record, a record that I think proves without peradventure the alterations in the evidence cannot be assumed to be because the FBI is sloppy, careless or does not know what it is doing.

One of the best possible examples of this is the picture of the tie in FBI Exhibit 60.

This photography is entirely unlike the FBI's in the Commission's exhibits. It is quite clear. The exposure and printing of the print are perfect. Each minor part of the small patterns in the design of the tie is visible to the naked eye. George Eastman would have been proud of this example of competent photography.

It is also a prime example of the heavy-handed Hoover/FBI subtlety. This is the one picture in FBI Exhibit 60 that has a legend ("Nick exposed white lining of tie"). This legend is added to hide the deliberate corruption of the evidence. And the immediate purpose of this deliberate corruption of evidence by the FBI was to deceive the harried members of the Commission and delude the staff.

The intent is made clear by the propaganda caption added to the bottom of the printed version of FBI Exhibit 60 furnished to the Commission. It reads:

View of the back of President Kennedy's shirt, with close-up of bullet entrance hole. Lower two photographs show projectile exit hole in collar and nick in right side of tie.

Here the wily Hoover at once indoctrinated and slipped, for he did say, unequivocally, that the holes in the front are "projectile exit holes", something he cannot and did not even try to prove and something that is contrary to all the credible and all the suppressed evidence. The "nick" is suggested, here and before the Commission, to be where the bullet grazed the tie in leaving, consistent with an unquestioning acceptance of the official "line", that the bullet was supposed to be going from the President's right in back to his left in front.

In actuality, the damage to the tie falsely attributed to a bullet was at the extreme left-hand edge of the knot as the President wore it, shown in CE395, exactly coinciding with where, I think without question, those desperate nurses tried to cut the collar loose. There is no doubt in my mind that the slight damage to the tie was from a scalpel, not a bullet, the only rational explanation of all the lies, distortions and suppressions herein documented from what was so carefully suppressed. Nor can there be any doubt the FBI knew this and knew it exculpated Oswald, proved a conspiracy, or both. In itself, this dismembers the Warren Report.

The FBI-Hoover solution was simple. And this, too, is not just a crack at Hoover. He did swear that there was "no substantial evidence of any type that would support" the possibility of a conspiracy, not "any scintilla of evidence" of any conspiracy. He added, "I have read all the requests ... from this Commission, and I have read and signed all the reports that have come to the Commission" (5H98-9).

So, what the FBI did to eliminate this "substantial evidence" of a conspiracy was to rearrange the tie before taking this fine, clear photograph of it. That tiny "nick", virtually invisible and undetectable without advance knowledge in the pictures Hoover gave the Commission for publication, is moved from the extreme edge of the knot to right smack dab in its center. And thus the nonexistent hole made by the bullet that never touched the tie catches the eye and suggests that this bullet did, indeed, go through the tie and left a hole in so doing.

The FBI has skills for every purpose. They can be masters of deceit. Whether the inset picture of the hole in the back of the shirt was presented wrongly to the Commission in this predigestion by an innocent accident may be a question. I think it was not, that it was deliberate. But the rearranging of the tie simply cannot be accidental. That is both the destruction of evidence and the manufacture of evidence. If there is no law against it, there certainly should be.

What makes this all the more culpable is the lack of required explanation. The FBI removed a piece of tie cloth from this "nick" for spectrographic analysis. This picture shows the tie after removal of that sample! Now if this was a "nick" to begin with - and remember, all those medical people in Dallas had seen the tie - the only way it could become a hole is by the removal of the hanging piece for spectrography. And only the FBI could have done that.

With all these pictures and all these needless captions, why not a picture of this quintessential evidence "before and after", the custom, before the FBI took its sample and after it did? And a caption to explain how much cloth was removed, even a picture of the sample taken?

That, however, would have killed the whole frame-up at the outset.

There is no reason to believe that any fabric was missing from the tie until the FBI took its sample. The small size of the present nick makes anything else virtually impossible. Prior to sampling, there

was never any hole in the tie. In any event, it was not in the <u>middle</u>
but on the extreme edge. By this rearranging of the evidence that disproves the official line, Hoover made it possible to argue, as the Commission did, that in brushing the edge of the knot the bullet took a
piece of fabric with it. For the hasty viewer or the unthinking, he
posed fake evidence to suggest that the bullet went through the center
of the knot, with the lining showing in the picture because the tie had
been moved so much in taking it off, handling, examining and photographing.

With all that propaganda and conjecture and worse in the unnecessary caption, was there no room for the simple statement a piece of fabric had been taken from the tie for analysis? Can the absence of this
explanation be unintended or innocent?

When it is recalled that this composite picture is from the
report the President ordered from Hoover and was supposed to make public, <u>without</u> any Commission, none having been decided upon by then, it
becomes even more culpable. Further bearing on this, the printed copy
of the FBI report does <u>not</u> identify this mockup as "FBI Exhibit 60", a
later designation by the Commission. It is labeled merely "Exhibit 60".

In my view, there is no innocence in the reversal of the hole in
the shirt, either. This I base not only on faith that the FBI does know
and understand the simplest elements of the FBI business, a faith I do
have in it. I base it upon those two other clear original pictures
"Law-and-Order" Kleindienst gave me in his aberrant, single compliance
with the Freedom of Information Law. They also are part of FBI Exhibit
60.

One is a <u>full</u> picture of the <u>entire</u> back of the shirt. It is
carefully arranged on a wire hanger. This is to say <u>at least</u> one hanger. There are two other similar projections from the top of the shirt,
one on each side of what is unmistakably a hanger. Magnified ten times,
the one on the left as one looks at the picture, which is the same as
the President's left side, seems to be a thin, fuzzy, twisted twine.
I cannot identify the one on the right, which may be photo lab carelessness. Nor can I with positiveness say anything else about them other
than this: They were not needed to support the shirt. Nothing but conjecture is possible, this having been the way it was officially arranged.
But I can conjecture about the FBI's use of the needless.

Ordinarily, a shirt placed neatly upon a hanger hangs straight.
In this case the FBI went to some pains to have the shirt <u>not</u> hang
neatly. For reasons we cannot know, the FBI and the Commission having
been silent about it, the FBI also arranged for the shirt not to be
placed evenly on the hanger or hangers. The left side of the shirt is
pulled to the front, in this view from the back, to the end that part
of the left side is invisible in this picture.

The hanger is not the only proof the shirt was hanging. Shadow
from artificial illumination all around the shirt also proves it. That
there was special lighting for special effect is also visible, especially
at the bottom where the shadow is blackest. Lighting for this picture
was from both sides with concentrated added lighting from a little to
the left and right of the shirttail if the greater shadow there has
significance.

There are several points at which the FBI, for whatever reason,
has arranged for indentations in the cloth to pucker toward the body
side. The deepest, an impossible one without some device for holding
the cloth in defiance of gravity, is to the left of the center of the
shirt and perhaps ten inches below the shoulder band, causing a deep
fold from that point to the bottom of the tail. This fold needlessly
hides a great deal of the fabric of that side of the back of the shirt.
The pucker in the shirt is shaped like an "L" on its side, running to
the left armpit laterally and a matter of a few inches downward at about
what would be the center of the shirt had it been properly and evenly
arranged in hanging.

The left arm of the shirt is grotesquely arranged with a fold, also impossible without something rigid, like wires, to deform it. At a point impossible to identify with precision but above the elbow, the sleeve suddenly turns <u>upward</u>, away from the camera, for several inches, and then droops downward again. The upper portion, from the shoulder down, seems to be extended to the outside by something rigid, inside the shirt and therefore invisible.

One of the consequences of this deliberate deforming of the view of the shirt is to diminish the amount visible and the distribution of blood on the fabric. What remains I still cannot explain in terms of any of the available evidence, even that which is here brought to light for the first time.

The nonfatal wound is said to have been on the right side. There is alleged to have been no defect of any kind in the skull on the left side. The President wore a jacket and thus shielded the shirt against staining from the outside. <u>But almost all the blood is on the left side of the shirt</u>!

For a very large area the shirt is solidly stained with blood, no speck of the fabric not being covered with it. From the center of the shoulderband to down onto the sleeve to well down on the left side it is <u>all</u> blood. This also extends to the top of the collar on the left side. And there is a long, wide path of blood running downward from the center and leftward, how far and how concentratedly being masked by the fold formed by this special hanging. What is visible extends to close to the waistline. We cannot know whether the fold hides blood still lower.

Whereas there is very little blood on the right sleeve, the left has large blotches in a number of concentrations, including the cuff. And the right side of the back is free of blood save for a comparatively small area around the hole and a few small blotches to the right of it.

From the official story, and with the shirt protected from the outside by the jacket, it seems impossible to explain how there could have been this enormous amount of blood all on the <u>left</u> side when the wound described as minor was on the <u>right</u> and when <u>all</u> of the blood had to have come from the under side of the fabric, from the President's body. This amount of bleeding from the inside and the wrong side at that would seem impossible from the minor wound of the official evidence or the official interpretation of that evidence. This blood ran down from a point to the left of center, not the right, and from a point that would seem to have had to be very high on the back.

It is another unexplained mystery, another omission in the investigation and testimony, another obvious element of evidence suppressed instead of addressed.

The acknowledged hole in the back of the shirt is visible to the naked eye as the only pale point in the enormous bloodstain. Its proportions, as well as an irregular hole that is roughly rectangular can be measured, are two to one. It is twice as wide as it is high. On the enlargement, it is about 5 mm wide and 2-1/2 high as measured through the middle in each direction. It is where it coincides with every bit of uncontaminated, uncontrived, nonmanufactured evidence, fairly far down on the back, so far below the visible shoulderband that it could not possibly have worked its way up high enough to have been caused by a wound in the neck. Because of this special FBI hanging, it appears somewhat to the left of where it really is.

Is any further explanation required for the "professionalism" of the photography by the FBI for the Commission in which nothing of value is visible, or of the Commission's selection of those unclear pictures of the shirt, not this clear one?

In this picture of the back, there is no doubt at all that the sharp edge of the bullethole is on the left, not the right. There may not have been any sharp edge to the hole before the sample was removed for spectrography. Without the lithographic dots to obscure it, the outline is made particularly clear by the blood-saturation of the cloth up to and including the edges and the contrast provided by the white background seen through the hole. Where there is irregularity, individual fibres can be isolated on magnification.

There are typed legends at the bottom centers of the second and third pictures Kleindienst gave me. They are evidence that Kleindienst gave me originals from the files, not copies made of what was there. Each legend is a small piece of white paper affixed with magic tape. Each is not in the print. Each is attached to it.

The first reads, "Portion of Exhibit 60 showing the back of President John F. Kennedy's shirt."

The second print is of the uncropped inset, the full 8 x 10 print of the enlargement that was cut down in size for the inset. Its legend reads, "Portion of Exhibit 60 showing enlarged view of hole in President John F. Kennedy's shirt."

In every way the FBI could arrange it, this enlarged view, like the original from which it comes (there is a difference in exposure and tones, but kinks and twists in the fabric are identical) is designed to suggest that the cloth is forced away from the lens, from the viewer, as though by a bullet going in that direction. This cannot be an accidental contrivance. Without interference the cloth would hang straight and limp. It took some doing to arrange the humps and creases to make this hole project inward, but the science of the FBI was equal to that challenge.

This close-up is a remarkably clear picture. The weave of the fabric is visible through the blood. The wave in the fine lines of the triple-stripe vertical pattern is apparent to the unaided eye. Even wisps of individual fibres are quite visible, more so with simple magnification. The magnification of the enlargement makes more obvious the thoughtful care with which the ever-loving FBI arranged for all the unnatural, gravity-defying ridges, rills, humps and hollows in the cloth of the shirt that was suspended from the top by one or more than one wire hanger or other devices.

From the top, I said, and that is true of the original. But a special Orwellian concept of science was invoked, in this instance with some carelessness, by the photographer, photographers or others.

The carelessness lies in enlarging a sufficient area to include the bottom part of the shoulderband and the seam by which it and the back of the shirt are attached to each other. This piece of shoulderband is masked out of the enlargement as it is cropped in FBI Exhibit 60. But if one holds this 8 x 10 enlargement with the shoulderband up, as it belongs, the legend is upside down!

What the somebody in the FBI did was just reverse the enlargement, with the shoulderband to the bottom instead of the top, then add the legend. In the laboratory, naturally, whoever made the composite did not have to have someone standing over him telling him to do wrong. All he had to do was read. If that laboratory agent could read English, his error could not have been arranged to be more automatic!

Ah! the new science of the FBI! How more "scientific" can it get when it investigates the assassination of a President?

And the new scholarship of the Archives!

The concern of the Archivist that there be neither "undignified" nor "sensational" use of pictures of the clothing becomes more comprehensible when appraised by the new "science" of the FBI and the pictures short-time-helper Kleindienst gave me.

"New science" plus "new scholarship" equals new perspective.

Or, that for which the professional sycophants and apologists have for so long been clamoring, new evidence.

Now they have it, but not quite all.

Will there now be a new attitude?

31. HUMPTY-DUMPTY EVIDENCE, or WHEN TO LOSE IS TO WIN

Kleindienst sent me these pictures July 6, 1970, the month before I filed suit for others.

From the moment I received them, I have kept these pictures in the envelopes in which they came, indulgence of small superstition. The picture of the collar is quite small for the large manila envelope in which it was mailed without backing or protection of any kind. Yet it reached me without crease or bent edge. The 8 x 10s, similarly without protection, also reached me in perfect condition and without postage. Kleindienst did not use a regular Department of Justice franked envelope, and his secretary added no stamps. She merely typed his title, the name of the Department and the city in the upper left-hand corner of a plain brown manila envelope and thus it came, sure, fast and undamaged.

Remarkable, considering what usually happens to my mail!

If anything new was required to establish the need for the most careful and detailed study of the evidence in the clothing, these pictures and the deceptions practiced in them by those many masters of deceit, no one having the capacity of carrying this off alone, these pictures were more than sufficient.

With respect to these pictures, my intentions, the law and the contract, there never were and there now are no serious questions. Were my interest gore, it was already and superabundantly sated. The contract requires proof of the intent to make "undignified" or "sensational" use as the basis for government claim of the right to deny access, that being the sole judgment specifically vested in the Archivist. Nothing but pictures susceptible of only such use were published by the Commission. The need for further study of the evidence in the clothing has been apparent from the moment the Report appeared, if one is making any kind of study that can, in the words of the contract, be termed "serious". Contradictions and conflicts in the not-suppressed pictures alone are enough to require the study of additional pictures. The alterations made in the evidence by the FBI are a further basis for added study of views not available.

In court, there was no allegation I intended any undignified or sensational use. None was ever made anywhere by the government, verbally or in writing to me or in papers it filed in court. If it ever planned to make this spurious claim, my unanswered challenges to both Rhoads and Marshall eliminated any desire to confront me on that basis. The judge did not let me finish my verbal argument on the law and regulations and had either not read or ignored my citation of these requirements of the contract in the prehearing papers. Once the government told him it would take pictures for me and let me see them but were precluded by the contract from giving me copies, he went for it and banged the gavel.

Prior to this, in arguing with Rhoads that the need to study other pictures exists, when he could not understand that I was taking this to court, he forgot his earlier-quoted misinterpretations of the contract in which he said they do not and cannot take pictures for research. The custodian of the nation's treasure in records and those who counsel him have instant improvisations for each required misinterpretation, the better to suppress and to deceive themselves into the

338

belief they are not suppressing.

I had written him that there are no adequate views of the damage to the knot.

Considering that my first written request for pictures was in June 1966 and that he had steadfastly maintained the contract prevented the taking of pictures for research, perhaps I should have felt a sense of accomplishment when, after no more than four years and two months, the Archivist, under date of August 19, 1970, said he could take pictures showing this damage but would not give me prints. After I filed suit, he wrote me again, under date of September 11, saying he could make further pictures.

He did not. My opinion of him will be higher if he regrets this for the rest of his life.

But what happened to his legal misinterpretation already quoted, his four-months-earlier ruling of April 16, 1970, that, because of the contract, "we do not take special photographs of the clothing for researchers"?

Too bad he argued and refused to for so long and, after saying he would, did not. Some are now impossible!

The hearing and the in-court promise to take the pictures I need was on June 15, 1971. The next morning I mailed a simple list of four pictures I wanted taken for me, saying I would not ask for more than my research indicated I needed:

1. A side view of the knot of the tie, taken from the wearer's left and showing nothing but the knot. As of my last knowledge, there was no such picture.
2. A view of the back of the knot from as close to 90 degrees as presents no problem for the photographer.
3. A picture of the back of the damage to the front of the shirt, showing nothing but this damage, hence making, as in the other cases, as large as possible a negative.
4. A picture of the tie in place underneath the collar, with the collar button buttoned, showing no more than the complete shirt tabs in width, going a little above the collar and however far below it would come with the greater dimension of the film in the same plane as the collar.

These are simple pictures, modest requests and, if the official accounting of the assassination were in any sense tenable, pictures that should have been taken and published to begin with. . I knew in asking for these pictures that the government would not and could not possibly comply, that being the real reason for the suppression and the only reason for all the dirty tricks in and out of court. I saw absolutely no possibility that the fourth, in particular, would ever be taken, for any picture showing the slits in the shirt-front covered by the tie and no coinciding hole in the tie is the living death of the whole seamy, sordid, sickening rotten mess like nothing in our history.

The same day I initiated efforts to appeal Judge Gesell's dismissal of the suit without a hearing on the merits.. That there be no dispute as to any material fact is prerequisite for this decision, and that requirement, abundantly, the government did not meet, as it had not met other requirements for his decision to be correct.

Predictably, Rhoads did not reply. I waited more than three weeks and on July 10 wrote the judge a letter saying the government had not kept its in-court promise, sending a carbon copy to Rhoads.

That did it. Rhoads replied July 15 saying the pictures would be ready for my "examination in two or three days".

I did not press him. I waited a week, until July 22, before going to see them and then telephoned as soon as I got to Washington, giving several hours' notice before appearing.

Had I not written Judge Gesell, I would never have seen the pictures when I did. Although he ruled against me, and I think erroneously,

Judge Gesell is anything but a rubber stamp for the government. Rhoads and every other official knows this. Marion Johnson, the man in immediate charge of that archive, was on vacation. With any choice, Rhoads would have delayed this until Johnson returned.

Mike Simmons was the only other one, and Mike goes right down the middle. He has no axe to grind and has never shown any interest in doing anything except living and working in strict conformity with the regulations. I have never known him ever to do anything to delay or impede research in any way.

We met in a better-lighted second-floor room next to the guarded "search" rooms used for certain kinds of research, including into the Warren Commission materials.

Those pictures taken earlier to which I have been promised access do not include any of the knot, no doubt because I made specific request for that and the Archivist changed his interpretation of the contract to say he could do it, implying he would.

The three manila envelopes Simmons had were all marked "NOT TO BE COPIED FOR ANYONE". The prints themselves had no identification on them, so as he handed me each one I asked him to number them.

The first two, marked 1 and 2, are of the tie, front and back. The envelope is labeled "Picture of Front and Back of Tie". The pictures are brilliantly clear. The back of the tie is entirely unmarked. There is no hole in or through it, thus no bullet thataway!

Goodbye, Warren Report!

Once again, "Who killed the President?"

The "nick" is just as clear, as is the underlying lining. The lining is entirely undamaged. And, this is the "nick" after FBI removal of a sample of unknown size for spectrography. There is no way of knowing if it was any more than an almost-invisible slit before the FBI took this sample. The very small size of the present hole seems to eliminate any other possibility. This is not and cannot be a bullethole. Nobody could ever have looked at it and believed it was.

The knot, however, no longer exists!

The tie in which the knot was imperishable evidence entrusted into the care of the Archivist for "preservation" - the same Archivist who claims that the Kennedy family felt he is, according to him, more secure than any other repository available to it - now has only tainted, destroyed evidence! Humpty-dumpty evidence!

What better kind of "evidence" can there be for the official investigation of the murder of a President, especially this President?

He is dead, anyway, is he not? Nothing can bring him back to life, can it?

Cannot put Humpty-Dumpty together again, that tie-knot the way it was again, or bring John Kennedy to life again. It all works out.

I asked Simmons about this. He was baffled. He said Rhoads had written me a letter about it. And he had heard Rhoads and Johnson discussing how this impossible thing could possibly have happened, each perplexed and without knowledge. They said.

There are too many things we do not know to assess blame beyond all question, although it must be done. We do not know, for example, if the evidence was ever examined when accepted and signed for. Yet we do know that, after getting the clothing, the Archives did take some pictures, those of the FBI being photographic monsters.

Once the "impossible" does happen, all the impossible seems to become possible and the "possible" may be impossible.

Can the Archives have been unaware if the knot had been untied before it got possession of this irreplaceable evidence?

Careful examination of that hoked-up FBI tie picture in its

Exhibit 60 can lead to the belief it was then untied. I am pretty certain it was. But can the Archives have accepted, without protest or record, a knotted tie that was unknotted, knowing, as everyone there did, that the tie in evidence was a knotted tie, the knot being its evidentiary part? *

It seems impossible that the knot could have been untied and Johnson, at least, not know it. Aside from examination that should have been made on acceptance and when pictures of the clothing had earlier been taken, this tie was twice the subject of litigation herein reported. Rhoads did, in writing, knowing I was going to court, promise to take pictures of the knot. Johnson drafts these letters for him. Could they have written they would take pictures of a knot they knew did not exist? And have all this wash out in court?

Not likely.

What of the untied knot when the tie was in FBI possession?

The FBI did not have to take the knot apart to see if metal was imbedded in it. Visual examination would have disclosed no more than a cut on the side. But, if anyone suspected metal might be inside, there was always X-ray, which would show it. It is more sinister if, by some remote chance, metal was discovered, for that is entirely unreported and any metal in that knot is still another of the many total and complete disqualifications of the Warren Report and the whole "solution" to the crime all over again.

Unless the FBI lied, the contrary is true. All the President's clothing was subjected to X-ray examination and more, the FBI keeping to itself whatever other examinations it made. If one could but dredge thoroughly that evidentiary morass in the Commission's ignored and misrepresented files, there is almost no nugget of truth that cannot be sifted from it. Keeping the original still secret, the reason I have to sue, the FBI did provide secondhand or more remote proof. It is in Dallas FBI File No. 100-10461, Commission File Number 205, the last sentence on page 154:

> X-ray and other examination of the clothing revealed no additional evidence of value.

Whatever the FBI may regard as "evidence of value", this means one of two things:

> There was no metal, in the knot of the tie or anywhere else; or
> The FBI found metal and is hiding the fact.

For even this FBI, this Hoover, the second is impossible to believe.

With Jesus speaking only to Hoover and Hoover speaking only to God, mere mortals have less way of knowing than the Presidential Commission, which learned from the great one no more than he felt it was good for them to know. So, with this the most extensive criminal investigation in man's history, once again we can only conjecture about the knot. What seems like the most probable explanation is that the knot was untied for the FBI's fake Exhibit 60 picture, when the ultimate disposition of the clothing was unknown but the FBI was the official repository of all the official exhibits (including the missing fragment from CE840). This is not publicly known, but it was the case. Hoover knew it. The FBI kept the originals and automatically provided the Commission with a minimum fixed number of photographic copies. This secret is in two of the Commission's unnumbered files, GAI FBI and INV 5. On March 12, in a memorandum on "procedure" to the staff, Rankin concluded:

> 3. The originals of all Commission exhibits are
> to be kept in the custody of the FBI. The
> FBI will make three (3) photographs of each
> exhibit for our use. One set of photographs
> should be given to Mrs. Eide for use by the
> Commissioners, one set should be placed in

*Knotted when examined by Clark panel.

341

the file., and the third set should be kept
by the p..son who prepared the exhibits.
Attached to this memorandum is a copy of a
letter which was sent to the FBI in connection with first 145 exhibits. Attorneys who
have be. . ... .re.i.i. .or identification
of exhi... . in any ..r.icular deposition
should .. ... for the exhibits to be
picked .. by the Bureau and filed with
the Co...ission exhibits, and should
address . request in writing to the FBI
for photographs of the exhibits in
accordan.. with the procedure set forth
in the a...ched letter. These requests
should ... channeled through Mr. Willens.
Each ate. ..y should also prepare a list
of such Commission exhibits with a phrase
describin. each item which should be placed
with Commissioner's set and in the file set.

(As best I can decipher this, it reads:

The originals of all Commission exhibits are to be kept in
the custody of the FBI. The FBI will make three (3) photographs of each exhibit for our use. One set of photographs
should be given to Mrs. Eide for use by the Commissioners,
one set should be placed in the files, and the third set
should be kept by the person who prepared the exhibits. Attached to this memorandum is a copy of a letter which was
sent to the FBI in connection with first 145 exhibits. Attorneys who have been responsible for identification of exhibits in any particular deposition should arrange for the
exhibits to be picked up by the Bureau and filed with the
Commission exhibits, and should address a request in writing
to the FBI for photographs of the exhibits in accordance with
the procedure set forth in the attached letter. These requests should be channeled through Mr. Willens. Each attorney should also prepare a list of such Commission exhibits
with a phrase describing each item which should be placed
with the Commissioner's set and in the file set.

Note that this means Specter should have had a complete, personal set of all the exhibits with which he worked, including all
pictures of the clothing.)

As was customary, the President being (safely) dead anyway, the
copies of these memos are largely illegible. If there is a slight error in transcription, the transcriptions are still faithful. There are
two vertical pale stripes running down these pages, in their true Archival condition. This obliterates much. But with the President dead,
the military divested of its secrets, the FBI in firm possession of its
secrets, why not pinch pennies, why not have unclear copies? Why telephone for service on the Xerox machines? Would not bring JFK back to
life again to be less "careless" in the record-keeping, would it?

Also leaving no doubt that the FBI was to be the repository of
all the exhibits is the attached, similarly-blemished carbon of Rankin's
letter to Hoover: It reads:

We would like . series of photographs of the Commission
exhibits prepared in t.. same manner as the enclosed photograph,
that is, with a title at the bottom showing the Bureau inventory
number and the Commission Exhibit Number. We would like three
photographs of each ex...it, including photographs of each exhibit
which is itself a photograph. Photographs of clothing should be
in color, photographs of other items should be in black and white.
Except in the case of Commission Exhibit No. 111 (FBI Exhibit
No. 324), where an exhibit contains more than one page, a photograph should be taken of each page.

Not all Commission exhibits have been returned to the Bureau. As additional exhibits are returned, photographs should be made in accordance with the above instructions.

(This reads, as best I can decipher it:

We would like a series of photographs of the Commission exhibits prepared in the same manner as the enclosed photograph, that is, with a title at the bottom showing the Bureau inventory number and the Commission Exhibit Number. We would like three photographs of each exhibit, including photographs of each exhibit which is itself a photograph. Photographs of clothing should be in color, photographs of other items should be in black and white. Except in the case of Commission Exhibit No. 111 (FBI Exhibit No. 324), where an exhibit contains more than one page, a photograph should be taken of each page. Not all Commission exhibits have been returned to the Bureau. As additional exhibits are returned, photographs should be made in accordance with the above instructions.)

"Photographs should be in color," this letter says. Of Oswald's clothing there are color pictures. I have examined and bought copies of them. But were there a single one of any of the President's clothing in color, after more than five years the Archives had failed to show me one, despite all my efforts, inquiries, letters - even after I filed suit for copies of these pictures.

Back to the tie. Having untied it, what was to keep the FBI from tying the knot again? The knot could have been untied and retied by the FBI, knotted when the Archives got it and, to the best of anyone's knowledge, still knotted the last time anyone on the Archives staff saw it.

Were this the case, how could it have become unknotted again?

That is where it gets hairy. All this special material is kept in a special safe to which only two people had the combination, Rhoads and Johnson. And that safe is inside a locked area that, in turn, is automatically secured by a combination-lock, stout metal door whenever the door is closed. A powerful spring keeps that outer door closed unless it is held open.

If, as I am willing to, we assume that neither of these archivists did the deed or deliberately made it possible for another to do it, what possibilities remain?

And who would want to destroy any evidence of the murder of a President, anyway? Why? Had not these honorable men decreed Oswald the lone assassin? And was not Oswald also safely dead?

Why destroy evidence, then?

The one certain answer is a negative answer: not because it supported the official lone-dead-assassin myth.

If it did, the government would have done everything short of buying prime TV time to show it. Instead, they went to court to suppress it.

So, who else could have done it?

This means, with no Archivist collusion, getting into a closely-guarded building after hours, without attracting suspicion and getting around inside it without attracting attention or triggering alarms. This is much more complicated than it seems, because there is nowhere in the world as weird a layout as in the Archives Building. No stranger could safely make his way around at all. The special area in which the Warren Commission materials are locked is hard to find. In the front of the building, or the Pennsylvania Avenue side (the only entrance used), there is no floor coinciding with the one on which it is located. In the back, or Constitution Avenue side (where the entrance is kept closed), this room, 6W3, is on a floor that is the equivalent of halfway between the mezzanine and second floors at the front. In the back, that is the sixth floor.

343

Wild, man! But for real. Just finding it is no job for an amateur James Bond. You have to know where it is, then how to get there. And, unless it was someone who could get into the building with all the doors closed and then frustrate all the security measures, it would have to have been done after the regular working day but before the after-dark Archives official closing at 10 p.m. Johnson and Simmons work the day shift. They are not there during the night hours to blunder into an intruder.

If there are candidates who could do all this, they would also have to know both combinations or be able to pick both locks and, if they are alarm-protected, not trigger the alarms.

This is beyond even the fabled skills of the fabled SMERSH. Only a federal spook could pull it.

Thus, it seems that if this evidence was destroyed beyond reconstitution _after_ it reached the Archives and without either Rhoads or Johnson doing it or being involved in letting it be done, it could _only_ have been done by a federal agent or agents.

Why should _who_ have wanted this evidence destroyed?

The question is self-answering.

Rhoads' letter of July 21 reached me July 23. I replied the same day. He is Joe Cool. All this did not trouble him a bit:

> We have found that at some time in the past the knot in President
>
> Kennedy's necktie was untied. We have therefore prepared photo-
>
> graphs of both the front and the back of the tie in the knot area.
>
> The photograph of the front of the tie shows the "nick" or dam-
>
> aged area. We have also prepared the photographs of the inside of
>
> the damaged area of the collar of the shirt and front of the collar
>
> with the tie under the collar. The last of these photographs, of
>
> course, does not show a knot.

Rhoads is the original unflappable "scholar". No concern at all. None of the plaint of the Song of Solomon's maiden who had lost her virginity, the purity of which he had boasted in court.

Thus is the vineyard of national integrity kept in the era of political assassinations.

Because he had "no sorrow, no regrets, no apologies, not even the slightest expression of concern", because he reported no investigation to see how this happened, I asked "if you intend to conduct an investigation and, if you do, when can I expect to know its results."

When Rhoads responded August 13, he still had no regrets, no sorrow, no apologies, not the slightest expression of concern. And he made no mention of any investigation, started or planned.

There is little comfort in knowing how much experience the government's spooks have in investigating themselves. The Report of the Warren Commission is one of hundreds of examples in which the result never varies.

Simmons' next envelope is marked "CE394 - Portions of Back and Cuff of Sleeves". The print Simmons marked "3" is of the back of the shirt. It does not show the shoulderband so there is no way of knowing which side is up. I asked to be informed which side is which, but when

Rhoads wrote me three weeks later, he studiously avoided answering. There is a "good" reason.

The print numbered "4" is labeled "cuffs", but it seems to be too short for cuffs and too rounded on the points for the collar, but it is. On the back of the shirt as measured on this picture, the shoulderband is two inches high at the shoulder and, as best as can be measured at the collar, which hides part of it is about 2-3/4 inches. This is a one-for-one picture, meaning it was taken actual size. I determined this by laying my scale on those in the picture. They exactly coincide.

Print "5" is marked, "CE394 - Portions of Front of Collar, Shirt and Tie." As Rhoads said, there is no knot, so my graphic purpose in requesting this picture can never again be served. Moreover, with the tie laid over the damaged area of the outer section of the shirt front, all the damage to the shirt is hidden, and there was no way of knowing whether the slits coincide (I believe they do).

Print "6" is the back of the coat, CE393, with the flap of the collar apparently folded under so that in-the-picture-rulers permit measurement. With this precisely testified to by the FBI, it discloses nothing new except that they did not lie - much. As this picture is posed, the hole is from about 4-5/8 to 5-1/8 inches from the collar seam, or almost 1/2 inch long. It extends to the right of the vertical seam for a quarter inch beginning at 1-3/4 inches.

Print "7" is CE394, the back and front of the shirt. Somehow - more magic? - this hole has been enlarged to a half-inch from top to bottom, beginning at the 5-1/2-inch mark. With no seam in the middle, the ruler is placed at the right seam. From there to the beginning of the hole, it is over 8-3/8 inches, the hole being about 3/8-inch wide.

The print marked "8" is of the front of the collar, with a piece of white cardboard laid on the opposite side. None of the white shows through the slits. They are not holes.

By having rulers in the pictures, as I had begun with Bullet 399 years earlier, actual measurements are unaffected by the reduction or enlarging possible in photographing and printing.

In "7", picture of the hole in the back of the shirt, it appears that more cloth has been removed from the shirt, changing the dimensions and proportions. One of the reasons genuine research requires copies is so that such questions need not exist. If all the original tests were genuine, there would seem to be no need for any further tests.

After all the depressing experiences of years of investigating the assassinations and living with all the official dishonesties and trickeries, discovering this new destruction of the most important evidence and the lack of official concern or embarrassment about it was a numbing experience. After knowing it had happened, it still seemed impossible that the United States Government could permit this to happen. Can it be possible that a federal agency would promise a federal judge it would make suppressed public information in the form of public evidence at the crux of the official investigation of the assassination of a President available to a writer and either know it could not do what it promised the judge or be so complacent when it learned it could not; that irreplaceable evidence of this unique essentiality had been destroyed and no responsible official knew how so unheard-of a thing could have been accomplished or by whom or for what purpose? Or not care?

Was it not more suspicious when this promise made in court was not fulfilled for so long? Taking these few pictures required but minutes, yet none were taken, not until after my complaint to the judge. Believing, as I have come to believe and as the record abundantly proves, that one of Rhoads' primary principles of Archival management is to delay and impede my investigations and research, could it possibly be that he and the government just do not give a damn about their pledges in court or the evidence they store?

When the destruction of evidence became apparent, with this added delay after long years of delay, is it reasonable to believe there is or can be innocence in it or in the Archives or inside the FBI?

These perplexities beset me, interfering with my concentration on the pictures and their mute evidence. Some of the pictures were confusingly identified, some not taken. So, when Simmons reported that Johnson would return from vacation the following week, I asked that the pictures not taken be taken, that the existing questions be clarified, and that I be informed so I could return for continuing examination of the evidence of the clothing.

32. "THE PLACE OF JUSTICE IS A HALLOWED PLACE"

While I was trying to fit together the pieces of this photo-graphic puzzle, two things coincided. Rhoads wrote on August 13 to say, in his usually self-serving formulation, that the Archives had finally taken the pictures for which I had asked. And I remembered that I had forgotten and found in my files - the above-quoted Rankin March 12 memorandum and its specification that the FBI make color pictures of all clothing exhibits for the Commission. Color could show what black-and-white might not.

Early the next morning after Rhoads' letter came, I drove to Washington and at 10 a.m. again was examining clothing pictures.

Walking from the parking lot to the Archives, I passed the architect's concept of the main entrance to the Department of Justice, which is the building to the west of the Archives Building. Both are between Pennsylvania and Constitution Avenues. Seventh Street separates them. Over Justice's massive metal doors, carved into the marble, are words the perfection in appropriateness of which immediately struck me: "The Place of Justice Is A Hallowed Place." Inappropriateness lies in the fear by government of the people, against whom these enormous doors are barred. Only the smaller, easier-to-control entrances to the "Place of Justice" may now be used.

While looking at the pictures, all black-and-whites, I engaged Johnson and Simmons, both of whom watched my examination in Room 201, in conversation about the colors of the President's clothing. It was apparent they had seen the garments. The coat, they said, is gray. The tie is two shades of blue, the shirt white with the stripes alternately blue and brown. It was thus evident that they had examined the clothing, which bore on the existence of the knot in the tie when they had seen it.

Examination of the pictures of the inside of the collar, made to my request with thorough professional competence, did disclose a few new facts of evidentiary value.

It is even more clear that the slits could not have been made by a bullet. The fraying of the fabric is regular, on the edge of the cut. These loose threads flopped over the other edge while the picture was being made. It is not a regular fraying as one would expect from the rupturing by a 2,000-foot-per-second violence. In this picture the "slit" is clearly a cut, not a hole. When the cloth lies flat, there is no width to the damage, no material missing, nothing punched out by the bullet. The edges lie against each other.

There is less blood inside the collar-band than on the outside of the fabric, not consistent with the bloodstains coming from the body side. Where the sides of the shirt overlapped in wearing, no blood.

The dead giveaway of the fabrication that this is where the magical bullet must have exited, according to the official story, is the nonmagical, mute evidence of the slit on the left side. The irregular, zigzag mark of a cutting blade is visible with an engraver's lens no more powerful than the 10-power miniature I carry. More proof of cutting developed later.

The second picture of the inside of the collar was taken this time with what I had asked to see in mind. It shows the entire flattened

347

collar from the front. Not important as evidence, except as it bears on the point that the shirt did fit snugly, did not bag loosely, was, really, a tailored shirt, is the label showing it was made for the President by "Charles Dillon, Shirtmaker, 444 Park Ave., N.Y." Here again, on the button side, it is obvious that the fraying of the fabric is from the left, the cut stopping at the seam above it, where the material is fortified by the seam. The material on the buttonhole side in this picture is creased and shows nothing. Although a few blotches of blood are visible under the button, most of the blood is, inconsistently, on the wearer's left side.

Reexamination of the pictures of the front and back of the unknotted tie, assuming it to be approximate life-size, which with other pictures proved to be the case, showed the width is 2-1/4 inches. If this is not the actual size, the measurements I made of the "nick" will be in proportion. The "nick" measures 5/16 inch in length. Its width varies from 1/32 inch to 3/32 inch - after FBI removal of the sample. This is hardly a bullethole. There is but a single stain on the tie, on the outside and directly under the "nick". The stain is about 1-1/4 inches long, egg-shaped and Johnson confirmed it is blood, again sign of personal examination. The left edge of the damage, looking at the picture of the tie, or the right edge as the President wore it, is a straight cut.

My impression that the entire character of the hole in the back of the shirt has been changed by the removal of more fabric is fact. I confirmed it by reexamination, tracing and measurement on the enlargement made for me, the one marked "3" by Simmons. This is much greater than actual size because of enlargement, but the proportions show the significance.

Whereas in the original FBI Exhibit 60 pictures I got from Kleindienst this hole is roughly rectangular, suggesting the shape of a map of the United States without the lower peninsulas, about twice as wide as it is high, it now is in the opposite proportion. Maximum measurement from top to bottom is 1-1/16 inches. Width varies from 7/16 inch at the top to 1/4 inch at the bottom.

Someone took a relatively big bite out of this.

Who, J. Edgar, demon investigator, protector of the evidence?

I traced this hole on the thinnest sheet of paper available in that office. Then I traced the same hole on the picture taken from the other side. The enlargements differ in size and some of the ends of the threads alter the outline slightly, but the proportions show the identical alteration since the original photography. Here the size is 7/16 inch by 3/16 inch, as close to exactly the same as examination of frayed fabric permits.

To be absolutely certain, although I can almost draw the original hole with my eyes closed from study of the enlargement in FBI Exhibit 60, I traced this hole from the picture of the back of the jacket, Exhibit 393. It is roughly 1/4 inch wide there and about 5/16 inch high. With such a small hole, the tracing I made cannot be 100 percent faithful, but it is close enough. By use of this engraver's lens, I could see clearly that it is from the top that the sample was removed for spectrography. From both left and right sides, neither the outer extremity of the approximately round original hole, cuts were made upward. The one on the left goes a trifle higher, making the connecting straight-line cut diagonal, from left to right.

Long before discovering this additional destruction of evidence, this new tampering with the clothing, I sought to learn the standard practices in handling and preserving evidentiary materials the character of which must be altered for required scientific testing.

All testimony about the damage to the clothing should have been based upon the appearance of the damage prior to FBI-wrought changes in its appearance. Hoover knew this, as did every agent and lawyer involved, in the FBI and on the Commission. Thus, there is no such evidence in the Commission's files, no single case of anyone testifying on the basis of it, no single reference to the taking of these required evidentiary photographs in all the evidence and all the files I have combed.

There is no more respected or dependable a forensic medical expert than Dr. Cyril Wecht, one of the few who, in order to better qualify for his role in this field, took the time to study the law and qualify as a lawyer. He is both forensic pathologist and lawyer. I asked Cyril what the standard, accepted practice is when samples are to be removed for spectrographic analysis. He confirmed his own belief by consulting his criminalist in the Allegheny County Coroner's office in Pittsburgh, Pennsylvania, Darrell Collom. Collom is also experienced and respected, a frequently published expert in his discipline.

Collom told me that, prior to the removal of any samples, the evidence must be carefully photographed, with close-up views of the areas from which samples are to be removed, before they are removed.

On learning the proper standards and procedures, I asked Kleindienst for access to copies of those pictures the FBI had to have taken prior to taking any samples from any of the President's clothing for any analysis. It required but three months and 20 days for Kleindienst to respond to this simple request, no doubt because the law and his Department's interpretation of the law require "promptness" in responding to requests for what the law calls "public information".

Richard the Law-and-Order-Minded abandoned his good-guy role. He did not say the FBI took no pictures of this kind. In fact, he confirmed that it had. He again invoked the inapplicable provision of the exemptions covering "investigatory files compiled for law enforcement purposes". And he said "I cannot grant your request", which is false to begin with because, even if the exemption did apply, the Department is authorized to waive it and has on other occasions.

As we have seen, there is and was no law-enforcement purpose in any of this investigation, Hoover himself so swearing.

What makes this by-then customary use of raw power to suppress more troubling than the suppression itself is that all of the testimony before the Commission dealt with the clothing and the numbered exhibit photographs of the clothing taken after removal of the samples for testing. Or, after the character of the evidence testified to had been altered. Kleindienst himself had given me copies of some of these pictures He could not simultaneously hold that he could and could not give me prints of identical pictures under the same provision of one law.

What he thus did is confirm that the pictures entered into evidence and the pictures of which he did supply copies were taken after removal of the samples. But he refused to let me see any pictures of any of the clothing taken before the FBI changed the character of their evidence. These still-suppressed pictures would, of course, show the nature and shape of all the damage prior to FBI alteration.

Can Kleindienst have a more persuasive reason for this illegal suppression of evidence? And does it not also protect Hoover?

Typically, of course, that famous investigator who considers himself the Seat of Government did not give the Commission copies of the pristine evidence nor did he testify to the condition of this evidence before he permanently changed its character, the change that, while required for proper scientific analysis, just also happened to make what was not bullet-damage seem like it, change without which the forged fiction of the Report would not have been dared.

This removal of fabric, the amount taken never described by the FBI and never talked about by the Commission, could account for all the fabric missing from the tie precisely as Dr. Richard Bernabei's experiments in taking a similar sample from a duplicate of Bullet 399 show that the crater of metal, the minute amount missing from the base of the exhibit, could account for the very small amount of metal missing from that part of the bullet.

What is absent in both instances is what the Warren Report, the "solution" to the crime and the reputation of the FBI cannot survive: before and after pictures and an exact accounting of the size and weight of the samples removed. Without knowing this, were the standards that obtain in courts of law to be applied, it would have to be assumed that all the missing material, in each case, can be accounted for by the FBI's sample-taking.

With expert witnesses like Shaneyfelt and Frazier and experienced lawyers like the Commission's, these omissions in the evidence cannot be regarded as mere oversights. All knew the requirements of evidence and all knew the absence of this information meant they were framing evidence, which is what these pictures do show. With the bullet, as we have seen, Frazier did not even tell the Commission he had removed any lead. Not until he was cross-examined in New Orleans did he ever admit this publicly. Meanwhile, the Archives acknowledged to Howard Roffman that a small piece of the base of the bullet broke off and is, therefore, not shown in pictures of the base.

It is fair to say that the FBI arranged for it never to be known if any of the fabric of the tie was missing when the tie reached the FBI, just as it arranged for it never to be known if any of the metal other than what is scored off the sides by the rifling in firing ever was missing from Bullet 399.

Thus, I had to trace the new pictures of the holes as I restudied them, to make the best record I could of the alterations in the evidence made by the FBI and to establish and compare the condition of this damage as of that day with what it had been at the time the indistinct pictures were entered into the Commission's evidence.

All these tracings are here reproduced so the reader can see for himself and understand fully the totality of federal dedication to the preservation and most faithful official representation of this, among the most important and probative evidence of the crime.

When all of it - 100 percent - has been contaminated while in federal care - and where no untainted pictures are available, can there have been more touching concern for the President or for the preservation of the evidence of how he was killed?

At this point I engaged Johnson in conversation about the unknotting of the tie, expressing my belief that neither he nor Rhoads, the only two with the combination to that inner lock, had motive for undoing the knot. Speaking for himself, he assured me he had not done it. We then talked about when he had last seen the knot and he said he did not remember ever making an examination of it. He recalled the promise to me, in writing, to take the pictures of it I had requested. (He drafts most of Rhoads' letters on the Warren Commission materials. He also admitted preparing the Rhoads affidavit that I regard as perjurious, but said it was thereafter gone over by the lawyers.) He agreed that, had that promise then been kept, the false promise would not have been made in court and a false official record of the existence of the knot as of the time of the June 15 hearings would not have been made.

Tracings of holes in back of JFK's clothing from pictures of different sizes, supposedly unaltered and made by one bullet.

Johnson was evasive about when he examined what clothing. Although to me alone he had drafted numerous letters about this clothing, particularly this tie, which can and I think does undo the entire "solution" to the assassination, he claims no recollection of ever having examined it. However, his recollections of minor details of the tie itself and of other garments is clear and proved accurate.

This clothing was not given to Evelyn Lincoln in spring of 1965 but it was, according to what Tom Kelley told me, included in the "transfer".

On this point, Johnson is correct. The list of what the FBI transferred to the National Archives pursuant to Clark's Executive Order of October 31, 1966, includes "FBI Exhibit No. C-26-C28,C30,C33-C36,

Clothing and personal effects of President Kennedy." Despite all the official falsifications in court when I sued for access to this evidence, the government not only denied it was evidence and hence I was not entitled to access - even though the family-GSA contract describes it by its official Warren Commission exhibit numbers - it was never officially described as anything but evidence.

The question I raised in court remains unanswered. How could one set of exhibits, in this case clothing, be transferred to the Archives under restrictive conditions of an alleged contract dated October 29, 1966, and two days later be transferred to the National Archives on the specific order of the Attorney General and without such restrictive conditions?

It seems apparent that the FBI was in constant possession of this clothing from the first save when it was used before the Warren Commission, when it surely was closely guarded. Nor is there any doubt about when the FBI got its hooks into this evidence. Paul Hoch has supplied me with copies of pages 153 and 154 of the Commission's File 205. These are a paraphrase report bearing the initials of Special Agent Robert F. Gemberling, who collated evidence in Dallas. It is Dallas FBI File 100-10461. It is here quite relevant as it is to some of the foregoing. *

As was customary with the more significant proofs, the Commission's files contain the least legible copies possible.

And as is too frequently the case, the word of the FBI and the Department of Justice is untrue, frightening when one considers the number of Americans convicted and jailed on their word alone.

It will be remembered that the most frequent and always-false explanation given for denying suppressed evidence is that it is exempt under the law as part of an investigatory file compiled for law enforcement purposes. All investigatory files are not exempt. Only those compiled to be used in enforcing a specific law. In the case of my suit for the spectrographic analyses, this was the false claim already recounted.

The original reports of their studies were never permitted outside the FBI. Even the President's Commission, in Hoover's view, could not be trusted with the real evidence, the real test results. He gave the Commission paraphrases and invalid interpretations instead, thus controlling what it could and did think and know. So, the Commission had this paraphrase it elected to suppress.

That begins with the unequivocal statement that "Under date of December 5, 1963, the FBI Laboratory advised Honorable JAMES J. ROWLEY, Chief, United States Secret Service ... as follows concerning an examination requested by communication of November 23, 1963:"

Or, the Secret Service requested the "examination" made by the FBI. Now, it was not then a federal crime to kill a President and the Secret Service in this instance was without any law-enforcement purpose or capability. In plain English, here is new proof that the government lies in claiming the evidence is part of a law-enforcement file and thus can be suppressed.

Under "Specimen:" 10 items are listed, preceded by these words: "Evidence personally delivered by Special Agent Orrin Bartlett on November 23, 1963."

Bartlett was the FBI's "liaison agent with the Secret Service, in the FBI laboratory", according to Frazier's testimony (3H435). Bartlett's first delivery to the FBI laboratory of evidence earlier supplied by the Secret Service was in Frazier's possession in the FBI laboratory the night of the assassination (5H67). This first delivery includes the since-disappeared bullet fragment recovered from the limousine.

Now, for the Secret Service, not for law-enforcement purposes, what did the FBI laboratory "examine"? Fourteen different pieces of the President's clothing, identified by FBI Numbers Q19 through Q29.

* CD205:153. See p. 599.

These include "Q21-Q22 Trousers and coat", "Q24 Necktie" and "Q25 Coat".

Although the time is not here specified, the date is, and that is the day after the assassination. From that day until it was delivered to Johnson, the FBI had possession of the clothing.

Under "Results of examination", while the FBI is incomplete and indefinite, in some areas it is explicit. Of the holes in the back of the coat and shirt, the subject of the first paragraph under this heading, it does locate them consistent with the foregoing measurements. What it fails to do, while giving measurements to locate the holes, is to give the more important information, the information here quite relevant. It omits the dimensions of either hole, the essence of the evidence. It does not even describe their shape. However, it does tell a lie, the concluding sentence of this paragraph: "These holes are typical of bullet entrance holes."

Here, perhaps, there is also reason for the restriction to secondhand evidence, for when the man who made the examination spoke in his own name, Frazier swore that he could not say from his examination of these same holes whether they were of entrance or exit.

So soon was the FBI engaging in its new science, propaganda by laboratory reports. The next paragraph, which also begins with a lie, carries this propaganda forward:

"The evidence bullets submitted in this case are clad with copper metal." Now either the plural, "bullets", is a lie, or everything else relating to bullets and ballistics is. The single submitted bullet is famous 399.

The next sentence reads: "Spectrographic examinations of the fabric surrounding the holes in the back of the coat and shirt revealed minute traces of copper."

The inference is obvious: Oswald's alleged bullet, jacketed with copper, left its traces on the edges of the holes. But this would be true of any and every copper-jacketed bullet. What this report fails to say and therefore must be assumed it could not possibly say is that the composition of the copper examined from all samples is identical. This is not said, therefore, the reasonable presumption is that it is not said because it cannot be said. But unless it can be said and proven, the evidence is that Bullet 399 did not deposit those copper traces on the clothing. *

Next the slits in the shirt are described, in this case also with propaganda. Their measurements and locations are given, and the cuts become, by FBI semantics, "holes", which they are not. This word is used for a lie that is soon enough made explicit. First reference is to "a ragged slitlike hole". In the second sentence, the description of "slit" is dropped and these cuts become "this hole". The same false description, the identical words, also begin the third sentence, "This hole has the characteristics of an exit hole for a projectile."

And that, too, is a deliberate lie. It is not a hole, has no such characteristics, and it is impossible, as a matter of scientific fact, for a 2,000-foot-per-second bullet to cause such damage.

Even Frazier, from his New Orleans testimony, can be cited to show this is a lie. There, in answer to a question for which I had prepared Oser (transcript p.166), he described these slits as "... it was fairly regular rather than being irregular. It was an elongated slit in the cloth. It didn't have side tears coming out from the slit /sic7."

Frazier was so contemptuous of the prosecution in New Orleans he flaunted this description of a cut, not of the rupturing caused by a bullet. **

In this report we also have more FBI magic. The same bullet that took material with it and left real holes in the back of these garments, took no fabric with it, left no holes in the front. And then in its subsequent turnabout career through Governor Connally, it took so much material from his jacket into his wrist the doctors were immediately

*See pp.428,441,446.   **See 5H61.

able to identify that material as mohair.

The next sentence - do not lose faith in your semper fidelis FBI - is the one that answers our immediate question about the knot and when it was known still to be tied: "A small elongated nick was located in the left side of the knot of the tie, Q24, which may have been caused by the projectile after it had passed through the front of the shirt."

The reader will note, for I have omitted nothing in quotation, that there is yet more FBI magic, a bullet that deposits copper in the back of clothing but discriminates against the front of clothing, leaving no traces there. Here the laboratory is not quoted as saying there are copper traces on either the shirt front or the tie and, indeed, there are none. By avoiding any mention of this alleged caprice of Bullet 399, to which all other pixie characteristics were officially attributed, by not saying there are no metallic traces on the front of the shirt or the tie, the FBI simply skirts the evidence that again proves it lies.

There remains this other evidence of official FBI lying already cited.

If that bullet transited the front of these garments, capricious as its character may have been, there are laws of science, and it violated them - or it did not make this damage - for there are no metallic traces. Not any, no matter how minute in quantity.

Again an FBI lie, this time a silent lie, this time in one of the first reports to reach and influence the Commission. Remember, the Commission never had the spectrographic analyses. There was no secret from the very first that neither the cuts in the front of the shirt nor the cut in the tie bore any traces of the passage of a bullet. Again, Frazier acknowledged this, without Finck-like evasion, in New Orleans. When asked another of the questions for which I had prepared Oser (transcript p.183), he admitted that he "found traces of copper on the fibres in the area of the" holes in the rear of the garments, Frazier said only "No, sir," when asked, "Did you find such copper traces on the front slits ... of (the) shirt and tie?"

In this Dallas FBI report, however, and in its false description of the "elongated nick", and where there is another lie, there is also the fact, the clue we seek. The lie is in saying that a bullet that came right through the center of the shirt at the collar, at the collar button, could have caused a "nick" at the left extremity of the knot. One need not be a scientist or an FBI "expert" to understand the impossibility of this. Especially not if it came almost straight through the President's neck and then, undeflected, entered the governor to the right of this knot, under the governor's right armpit, the official story. Here also the reader should note, there is no FBI gobbledegook about this "nick" having the "characteristics" of anything attributed to a bullet. The reason is not because the FBI would not say what is not true, for it did in these other cases. It is because even this FBI would not stretch this misrepresented cut in the lefthand edge of the knot that far in its unending misrepresentations.

But, as of this time, as of the completion of the FBI "examinations", the tie is still described as having its knot in these words, "located in the left side of the knot of the tie".

Can anything be more reprehensible than the destruction of official evidence when only officials are in a position to destroy it? Can there be a crime of which this can be more true than the murder of a President, or a situation in which it can be less pardoned than the official investigation of that crime?

So, our effort to trace the possession of this clothing begins with the beginning of the FBI's deliberate misrepresentation of the character and meaning of the evidence, the beginning of its framing of evidence and solution. This shows that the FBI did, immediately, have and keep possession of all the President's clothing.

As official evidence, it, like all the other official evidence, belonged in the possession of the FBI. Until when? I asked, and Johnson gave a vague answer, the fall of 1966. Until the time of the Attorney General's executive order? I asked, and he said "Yes." When I asked if it then was boxed or otherwise protected, he again evaded by saying that he, personally, had made the transfer from the FBI building and there was an enormous amount of material. (The latter point is true.) I did not press him.

There was also the later time, when the 1968 panel studied it, that this evidence was handled. Getting it for them was Johnson's job. If the knot had been undone before this clothing passed into the Archives' and Johnson's personal custody, those eminences of the sciences selected for their dedication to and knowledge of medico-legal requirements and, of course, personal integrity, are and were silent on the vital point, as was their internationally-known attorney, Bruce Bromley, whom I had met in the 1930s when he represented a private detective agency whose brutalities against workingmen were being investigated by the Senate committee of which I was part.

Under "Clothing" in this panel's inventory of what it examined are all three pieces, coat, shirt and tie. If the knot was then undone its silence is culpable and a self-description to which no word need be added.

The panel is less unequivocal about this than might be expected of such experts in forensic medicine and the law (p.14). On the one hand, their inventory, while listing these three items of clothing, does not list any of the pictures of this clothing. Briefest of the three short paragraphs on the clothing is the few words beginning "Tie (CE395)"

In the front of the component of the knot of the tie in the outer layer of fabric a ragged tear about 5mm in maximum diameter is located about 2.5 cm. below the upper edge of the knot and to the left of the midline.

The minor point here is the transparent deception in referring to the "diameter of a very narrow nick - as narrow as 1/32" - the obvious intent being to suggest roundness, and that to suggest a hole. The precise measurements have heretofore been set forth and it should be without doubt it is plain crookedness, not science, to suggest a "diameter" to a narrow, vertical flaw. When it was on the extreme left-hand edge, designating it "to the left of the midline" is an identical and deliberate misrepresentation.

Unless this is taken as a description of the untied knot, where the damage is near the middle. Especially with the opening words placing this misrepresented "tear" as "in the front component of the knot". Of course, "front" suggests what the propagandists guised as scientists wanted believed, that a bullet came out there. It can be taken to mean that the tie was flat, not knotted.

If it does seem that the panel is describing a still-existing knot, it is not beyond question. With its record, what is in this paragraph being enough to prompt dubiety, the panel's words can be taken either way. If it covered the untying of the knot, it is hardly the only wrong this panel sought to hide.

The record being adequate and corrupt in all the necessary fine detail, I saw no need further to embarrass Johnson. Instead, I asked for access to the color pictures taken for the Commission by the FBI at Rankin's direction. Johnson was visibly reluctant, hemmed and hawed, and I said I would prefer not to make another trip or again to have to establish my right to access to the official evidence in court. These are, I reminded him, the official copies of the official evidence, so no hocus-pocus about the contract, which could not cover the exhibit pictures the FBI took for the Commission on its orders and as part of the FBI's official Commission role.

Without further protest he and Simmons went for them, the only other relevant comment being the thinking-aloud, that these pictures are stored in more than one file.

354

Exhibit 393, the jacket, is also identified in the print as FBI C29. While it is fairly clear, it is far from color-perfect. Its technical flaw bears on a significant evidentiary matter. The two purposely-unclear representations of these pictures in black and white published by the Commission (17H23-4) had always fascinated me because I could not pinpoint the need for making the entire thing so black. That of the front (p.23) can be determined to be of the front only by the slightest shadow at the lapels, so slight as to escape detection without careful study, and because the lower edges of the opening project a bit lower and become visible against the white background. I also had always wondered about the whitish marks on the left side (the President's right) and the opening up of the opposite sleeve to show its paler lining.

Quite opposite to the total blackness of this perfection in FBI police science as officially published, the jacket is not of solid color or even black. It is gray, with the appearance of a linen-like weave when color picture is examined with a lens. It is a fine material that this FBI photography succeeds in altering. The gray it makes blacker and the whitish, fine flecks alternating with the gray in the weave are de-emphasized.

Two spectacular revelations are the seeming absence of blood on the lining of the back of the jacket, or very little of it, this pinnacle of FBI photographic skill leaving which unclear, precisely where the shirt is so saturated with it, and the extent of the cuts in the fabric. What this means is that, even with the President lying on his back at Parkland, his shirt had absorbed the blood and it had not, not at least by what the FBI leaves visible, stained the lining. I asked Johnson to check this. He agreed with me. Yet faint reddish stains are visible on both sides of the front of the jacket. In this picture the lining seems dark purple. Johnson says it is blue.

Distinguishing shades of blue can be difficult in black-and-white, but it should present no problem with color photographs. The tie provides a good illustration of this. Its colors cannot be ascertained except in the color shots. It is of a dark blue body, with the pattern a lighter, bright blue.

If we can safely assume that the FBI's best experts - do they have or would they use inferior experts when a President is assassinated? - have the competence of the average snapshotter, we have to wonder about the reason or reasons for this punk work. We do not have to wonder any more about why the government would not take pictures for me until compelled to do so and will not let me have prints for the study of an impartial and competent forensic pathologist like my friend Cyril Wecht and a scientifically conservative-minded criminalist like Darrell Collom.

Although the printed picture does show some cutting of the garment, it is not nearly what the color picture discloses. The jacket was cut from the lapel to the left armpit, then down the sleeve and to the cuff. On the right side, there are cuts in the cloth up from the right pocket to the armpit and from there diagonally downward to the opening of the jacket.

The blood that shows (the FBI arranging for it to be faint) is on both shoulders.

The FBI reserved its greatest skill for the pictures of the shirt (CE394, 17H25-6 and FBI C32).

In the view of the back, there here was no need to use a hanger and other devices. The shirt lies flat on a white background. The dispersal of blood is as I noted above, but with the shirt lying flat it is even more apparent that the solid staining goes farther to the left, or wrong side from the official story, than can be seen in the picture of the hanging garment. Again the FBI arranged for a shortening of the left sleeve by making a fold in it when arranging the shirt for the taking of the picture. And, although this is the view from the back, they then further contorted the sleeves so that, in both front and back views, the openings at the cuffs show. With the left sleeve the button is visible. In color, the further down the center of the back the blood went, the darker the stain, indicating greater concentration.

As the FBI posed the front, it is another bit of magic, a magical shirt, with cuffs opening front and back! Here both buttons can be seen in even the printed copy and without magnification. Charles Dillon's carelessness in making the President's shirt, having the left sleeve shorter than the right - according to the FBI, that is - is more exaggerated. But the real perfection in the rearranging of evidence lies in what in the printed picture is made to seem to be a lateral shadow and crease. It runs from the outside of the right armpit downward, zigzag toward the opening of the shirt that is here buttoned and then only slightly upward to the same point on the left sleeve. In the color picture the real direction and extent of this cutting are apparent. It is a massive cut from one side to the other.

It thus becomes obvious that, without being disrobed, the President was first treated in the emergency room exactly as he was rolled in on the stretcher. The distraught doctors, in their urgent need for speed, did only that which was required of them, rush to begin the impossible effort to save him.

The only reasonable explanation of the pre-FBI treatment shirt-front and tie damage is that the nurses first loosened the tie, as its original picture shows happened, cut it off, making a slight slice in the knot against which they made this cut. The President was a neat dresser. On the FBI's C32, which is the Commission's Exhibit 395 (17H27), the wider, outer end extends almost twice the distance from the knot as the shorter end. When they started cutting open the tightl fitting collar, they realized their knife was striking flesh, that the could not safely cut off the collar. They then unbuttoned it, leaving the small cuts where they had made this effort.

And the wound in the front of the neck had to have been above the collar line.

Thus, there remained no bullet traces on any of this fabric. No bullet hit there. The wound had to have been above the collar.

All the Dallas doctors were thoroughly intimidated prior to thei Warren Commission testimony - in fact, before the Commission took any testimony and before it received its copy of the autopsy report. One of the subtler, little-noted and now forgotten reports of this appeared in The New Republic dated December 28, 1963. Magazines appear before their publication dates and, of course, are written still earlier. Thi article clearly states that the Dallas doctors had said the anterior neck wound came from the front, was a wound of entry. It then reports how their "reversal" was procured: "Two Secret Service agents called on the Dallas surgeons and obtained the reversal. (No officials had questioned the doctors until that visit.) They did so by showing the surgeons a document described as the autopsy report."

The totality of official misrepresentation of all initial observations of this as an entrance wound may, after the lapse of so much time, be difficult for the reader to comprehend. Two new citations may here reflect this and illustrate the magnitude of the job faced by thos who rewrote the script of the assassination through the medical testimo

For afternoon papers of November 24, 1963, UPI was still reporti out of Washington that "Staff doctors at Parkland Hospital in Dallas sa only that the sniper's bullet pierced the midsection of the front of hi neck ..."

And as late as 1969, when retired Dallas Police Chief Jesse Curr published his own attempt at self-justification (JFK Assassination File he used neither "ifs" nor "buts". That long after the official line ha been laid down and stuffed down so many throats, Curry - who was there - at Parkland - wrote with commendable candor, "Dr. Perry examined the throat wound and assessed it as the entrance wound." (p.34)

The intimidation reported by The New Republic succeeded, but at that early stage only part of what would have to be covered up was understood by the officials responsible for the covering up. The rest fell to Specter, who did it by the nature of and the omissions from his questioning. Naturally, nobody told the members of the Commission what was being prefabricated for their signatures. Sometimes, in an effort to learn and to understand, the members participated in the questioning of the small percentage of the witnesses who testified before the Commission itself. One of these rare cases is here quite relevant.

Dr. Charles James Carrico, then but 28 years old, is the physician who first attended the President in the emergency room. His March 30 testimony immediately preceded that of Perry. Dulles interrupted the Carrico questioning to try and learn exactly what was being testified to about this anterior neck wound (3H361-2).

"Will you show us about where it was?" he asked.

Carrico showed by placing his hand on his own throat while speaking, his rejoinder ending, "this was a small wound here".

To this demonstration of "here", Dulles responded, "I see. And you put your hand right above where your tie is?" (Emphasis added)

Carrico confirmed with a "Yes, sir".*

Although those who drafted the Report for the Commission deliberately ignored this and the members, of whom only five were present to hear this, seem to have forgotten it, the doctor who first saw the President, the only one who saw him before the clothes were attacked so the President could be treated, placed the front-neck wound above the knot of the tie.

Perry did not get to the emergency room until the clothing had been removed (3H377).

Again it was a member, McCloy, not Specter, who asked what had to be asked, "Was he fully clothed?"

"Not at the time I saw him," Perry testified, adding that Carrico and the nurses had removed the clothes, "which is standard procedure."

Carrico had been well briefed on the official problem and prior to any of this cited testimony Specter twice tried to lead him around what he really saw and what really happened (3H359). Careful to avoid asking how, a question he never asked, Specter put it this way the second time: "What action, if any, was taken with respect to the removal of President Kennedy's clothing?"

"As I said," Carrico responded, "after I had opened his shirt and coat I proceeded with the examination and the nurses removed his clothing as is the usual procedure."

Prior to this Carrico had volunteered only that "we" had "opened his shirt, coat," to listen "very briefly to his chest".

Not until after Dulles blundered into the truth Specter sought to hide did Specter get a chance to try and again obscure what Carrico's testimony means, that the wound was above the collar and tie. He asked, "Was the President's clothing ever examined by you, Dr. Carrico?" When the doctor said "No", Specter asked, "What was the reason for no examination of the clothing?"

This was not a stupidity, for Specter well knew that Carrico had first been too busy and then had left the emergency room. Carrico understood what was expected of him and avoided the pitfall, that never-asked-never-answered question, how the clothing was removed:

Again in the emergency room situation the nurses removed the clothing after we had initially unbuttoned to get a look at him, at his chest, and as the routine is set up, the nurses removed his clothing and we just don't take time to look at it.

All the members of the Commission knew and at this point all the record shows is that the nurses disrobed the President. But earlier,

*Confirmed personally to me. See pp.381-2.

357

on March 21, in Dallas, with no member of the Commission present, Specter questioned Margaret M. Henchcliffe (6H139ff.). She was the first medical person to see the President:

Well, actually I went in ahead of the cart with him and I was the first one in with him, and just in a minute, or seconds, Dr. Carrico came in.

She followed this (6H141), after describing long experience with gunshot wounds in her emergency-room duties, by identifying this front-neck wound as one of "entrance".

When Specter tried to get her to say it could have been an exit wound, she insisted she had never seen an exit bullethole that looked like this one. When he pressed her further, all he got was her recitation of her expertise with gunshot wounds. Eight of her 12 years of nursing experience had been in emergency rooms in a city where gunshot wounds are common. She is one of the few courageous witnesses.

It is she who made the record of when the President was disrobed, not until after he was pronounced dead, after all the medical procedures had been completed:

Well, after the last rites were said, we then undressed him and cleaned him up and wrapped him up in sheets ... (6H141).

Three days later, again with no member of the Commission present, Specter questioned Nurse Diana Hamilton Bowron (6H134ff.). She is one of those who wheeled stretchers out to the limousine, of the first medical people to see anything (6H136). In fact, in an emotional moment, Mrs. Kennedy pushed Nurse Bowron away when the nurse attempted to assist in getting the President onto the rolling stretcher. She was one of the first three in the emergency room.

Consistently, Specter avoided the question of what happened to the President's clothing. However, she volunteered it in answer to another question, "Miss Henchcliffe and I cut off his clothing" (emphasis added) so treatment could be started.

Specter had not expected to call her as a witness. He improvised this for other reasons and she agreed to waive the customary written advance notification (6H134-5). He knew what to avoid and tried to. She had, as had other medical personnel, submitted written reports to their superiors (21H203-4). Beginning with "I was the first person to arrive on the scene with the cart", she recounted the same explanation of how she and Nurse Henchcliffe removed the President's clothing.

With this background, some of Specter's other and also-proficient practice of Orwell's memory-holing is especially in point. Having so carefully avoided all reference to the cutting off of the President's garments and the obvious cutting of the collar, misrepresented as bulletholes in the face of evidence all of which is contrary, he proceeded to forget the other relevant and existing evidence, in all elements and aspects faithfully copied by the Clark 1968 panel.

Specter knew the autopsy surgeons removed a tissue sample from the back for closer laboratory study. He also knew none had been removed from the wound in the front of the neck. He knew better than to believe that malarky about the autopsy doctors not knowing there had been a front-neck wound at the time they had the body before them. He just avoided calling one of the in-Dallas witnesses who knew, Burkley, and did not ask the others who also were at the autopsy. Burkley and the Secret Service agents knew of this front neck wound. There is no reason to believe that, if Humes and his associates did not recognize it, none of those who had seen it and also knew of it from the conversation and activities in Parkland did not volunteer it or that the Navy doctors did not ask - particularly because they pretended not to know what happened to the bullet they said entered from the rear. Nor is there any reason to believe Burkley, the military man and physician, did not tell them all he knew.

At the Navy hospital, two "sections", or samples, were removed from the edges of two wounds. Specter knew this. He entered the proof, CE391, in evidence. It is the Humes supplemental autopsy report, forwarded by Galloway to Burkley December 6.

Expediently, it just happens that this original, too, has disappeared. Tom Kelley tells me the Secret Service does not have it. The Archivist says he does not even know of it and related items: "We do not know of an original of Commission Exhibit 391 or any memoranda, letters of transmittal or appendages to this exhibit ..."

Specter, however, and not only because he entered it into evidence, did have a copy of this supplementary autopsy report. It is one of 16 items Rowley sent Rankin under da.e of March 13, prior to Specter's taking of the autopsy testimony. The Secret Service identification is Control 1221. Opposite that number in the listing is the one reference to any routing of any of the 16 items within the Commission, "Mr. Specter has". It was not only automatic, for he had to have it, but we have this proof that he did, from the Commission's File 498.

This supplementary report is short, two pages. There are interesting items, some of which can add more confusions, like the entry after a listing of seven sections "taken for microscopic examination", under examination of the brain. This follows:

During the course of this examination seven (7) black and white and six (6) color 4x5 color negatives are exposed but not developed (the cassettes containing these negatives have been delivered by hand to Admiral George W. /sic/ Burkley).

Or, still more photographic confusion and obfuscation.

Then, under "skin wounds":

Sections through the wounds in the occipital and upper right posterior thoracic regions are essentially similar.

This means that slides were made of the tissue at the edges of these wounds.

They, too, are not accounted for. Kelley tells me the Secret Service does not have them. The Navy told me they have nothing at all. There is no Commission evidence, published or unpublished, other than this reference to the taking of the tissue-samples for study. As the Archivist confirmed, everything relevant has just disappeared.

Orwell again.

The thoroughness of the 1968 Clark panel is such that it does not list these slides in its inventory of evidence it examined.

And, what is here most relevant, there was no section made of the wound in the front of the neck. Or, if it was made, it, too, was disposed of. It is not listed, not inventoried, not testified to.

Only when a President is assassinated and autopsied in a military hospital is what is done for a murdered Bowery bum not done.

And this just happens to coincide with the minimum need for a false, no-conspiracy, frame-up Report, avoiding all the missing and here recaptured "new" evidence about that wound from the front. Neither Oswald nor anyone else could have been in front and in back of the President at the same instant. This is just further proof that what was required to be done was not done, to protect the "solution" manufactured to achieve the predetermined end of the whole awful mess; and what was not helpful to it was ignored or misrepresented.

It was proper, not improper, that the President's clothing be cut. There was no alternative in the medically-required futility of trying to save the irreversibly-dead man who, had the impossible succeeded, would have been a human vegetable.

Only, why did the Commission and the FBI feel it necessary to try to hide this in the printed pictures?

Why did Arlen Specter, the experienced lawyer, then a former Assistant District Attorney of Philadelphia, a man who knows criminal evidence, find it necessary to avoid this in <u>all</u> of his questioning of <u>all</u> the medical witnesses, including those who made the cuts?

Not, certainly, in pursuit of that bragged-of only client, "truth"

Specter is the father of the Commission's bastard "single-bullet" baby, that illegitimate, "no-conspiracy", "lone assassin" offspring. He fought all the evidence and all those on the staff who disagreed to father it. (Remember again those Eisenberg April memos written after the pregnancy became visible in the March 16 autopsy testimony.) Until the moment of delivery, the Commission was a lady of easy virtue. Each of the silent members of the staff who had doubts and remains uncon-fessed is as guilty, as much a participant in this gangbang of history and justice. Each, in effect, restrained the arms and legs of the vic-tim as Specter indulged his guilty lust to sire this great lie.

To mix metaphors hermaphroditically, so to speak, this is per-haps the first time in official history that one man was his own whore and his own pimp. Though he had accomplices, the parthenogenic monster is Specter's.

And still again I dare him to sue me!

If he is man, not pimp/whore, I will read these words on the steps of his City Hall so he can sue me where he, made District Attorney and all-powerful by this foul deed, can have all advantage, leaving my fate to whatever lawyer will volunteer to defend me. By then there will be some.

ARLEN SPECTER HAD TO KNOW WHAT HE WAS DOING!

He can have no innocence.

He was in full charge of this part of the work, Francis Adams, his initial superior, having quietly left to return to his New York law practice rather than be part of this. (If we can respect Adams' depar-ture, what of his silence?)

Specter had to know the damages to the shirt front and tie were from a scalpel, not a bullet, and he nonetheless faked the entire mon-strous "solution". This freed and exculpated assassins, framed an in-nocent man, to legitimatize the illegitimate official account of the assassination of the man who had started a reordering of national pri-orities away from war and toward peace, toward the belated granting of part of their share of the national heritage to those so long denied it.

Were Arlen Specter the largest stockholder in war industries, he could no better have served the purposes history soon enough showed were served by this assassination.

For these purposes, the assassination required proper baptism.

Specter's holy water came from the foulest sewer.

And all the eminent nostrils smelled frankincense and myrrh.

Need one have more than a Mankiewicz' concern? Was not the President (safely) dead?

With the understanding imparted by this first examination of the until-now withheld pictures, the withholding of which was of sufficient importance to the government to force me to sue for access, what hap-pened to the tie is clear.

All the Borgias did not die in medieval days. There is a new breed.

All the Councils of Kings, the assassins of blighted antiquity, have not crossed the Styx. Their modern counterparts range from the Potomac and the Hudson to the Golden Gate.

Their successors flourish in Washington, D. C., the United States of America of the last half of the twentieth century, in the period between Hitler 1932 and Orwell 1984.

33. WAKETH THE WATCHMAN?

What is necessary is a wrap-up of what this means. To me, it means that in my original analysis of why the pictures and X-rays of the autopsy were not in the Warren Commission evidence, why, as the legally-required best evidence, they were not in the hands of the autopsy doctors when they testified, was both right and wrong. I was right in assuming they were not in evidence because they prove the preconceived decision of the government, embodied in the Warren Report, was a false one. I was wrong in believing that, if they were ever brought to light, they would have to be manufactures - fakes.

They may or they may not be. Or they may in part be genuine and in part fabricated. As of now, I think they are genuine. With the X-rays, we have a choice between destruction and removal. There is no doubt all the X-rays are not now present.

If I was right in seizing immediately upon the autopsy pictures and X-rays as the evidentiary jugular - and I was - how seriously I underestimated the federal capacity for dishonesty and corruption! Everybody involved in this evil is tainted. All the Commission members, all the lawyers then and still silent, all who knew better than they said and still did what they did. All who called for "new evidence", as though there were something wrong with that "old" evidence not suppressed, merely misrepresented. All who, calling for "new evidence", refuse to look at it when it is offered, and in my efforts alone there are many. All who sat on the "vote ja" bodies who affirmed the official fictions.

Above all, that old master of deceit, St. Edgar the Indispensable, and his many guiltily-involved subalterns; that crafty manipulator of the investigation and of the evidence; holiest of the holy - just listen to him - one does not have to ask him, he proclaims it! Self-portrayed a saint, the apostle of "law and order", he is, in fact, its enemy, the man who has presided over its end. It is past time to view the skeletons in his closet. One of them is that of the assassinated President.

There is no innocence. None for the silent clerks who shuffled the papers here exposed to public examination. None for those eminent lawyers of the Commission. None for the investigating agents. And none for that Uriah Heep, the great white father of the Pedernales who was so busily engaged in rewriting history while he was making it, or for his lackeys and lickspittles.

Silence, too, ought to be considered a crime against society when it is of the nature of what is herein presented. Or detachment from responsibility.

The also-assassinated Robert Kennedy had an apt twisting of Dante. His former associates quote him as fond of saying that "a special corner of Hell is reserved for those who in time of great moral crisis preserve their neutrality".

It is a truly remarkable coincidence that so many of our victims of political assassinations, men who took positions and expressed them with vigor, felt impelled to declare themselves on this point of public morality and nondetachment.

One of John Kennedy's formulations is, "A man does what he must, in spite of personal consequences, in spite of obstacles and dangers and pressures - and that is the basis of all human morality."

Midway between John Kennedy's assassination and his own, Dr. Martin Luther King, Jr., put it this way: "He who passively accepts evil is as much involved in it as he who helps perpetuate it. He who accepts evil without protesting against it is really cooperating with it ..."

In Abraham Lincoln's words, "If the end brings me out all right, what is said against me won't amount to anything. If the end brings me out wrong, ten angels swearing I was right would make no difference."

With this biblical suggestion, one might be reminded of St. Jerome: "If an offense come out of the truth, better is it that the offense come out than that the truth be concealed."

And so, to the silent as to the breast-beaters, both equally guilty, I say that, if your own consciences do not charge you, these assassination victims do. That special corner of Hell should be reserved. A man does do what he must. He who accepts evil is part of it. Let the angels swear. It is as Lincoln said, and so it must be.

Better the offense come out, the truth not be concealed.

It is the custom of nonfiction that the work be summarized at the end. As I began I conclude, with acknowledgment that I depart from the accepted norm. To repeat the bill of particulars set forth in the preceding pages would be to add great length and needless redundancy. If at this point the reader recalls but a fraction of what I have given him, he recalls more than enough; and the recollection cannot be pleasant, cannot make him proud of his government or his society and its institutions. There is no need to bludgeon him with repetition of a long, long list of misrepresented, suppressed or destroyed evidence, or to remind him what it means of the assassination, its investigation and the transgressions of so many, the named and the unnamed.

From my opening pages, nothing remained of the integrity of the "investigation" and those many associated with it, from the new President down. How could it have been an honest investigation when the conclusions and the final Report were outlined before hearings were held, before witnesses were heard, before what tangible evidence was considered at all was examined?

The enormity, the criminality and, I think one is now justified in saying, the conspiracy inside the federal government is like nothing in our history. In olden days such things were commonplace, when the murder of a king accomplished everything. In the modern era, in the more advanced countries, elective societies moved past the point where this was possible. With the king, the king was the state. With the President, he is the chief executive, the senior elective officer, the head of the state, the policy-fixer (at least, in theory), but he is not the entire state. Eliminating a president - killing him - would not capture the state for the murderers or those they served. So, what was accomplished by a regicide seemed impossible with the assassination of a president.

However, the elective societies also have grown, and the position of a president has, with this growth, altered. In theory, he still determines and establishes policies. In practice, with the proliferation of government and the altered complexion, complication and potential of international disputes and relations, he has become the captive of his advisers, each of whom has a vested interest in what the president knows, believes and does. If, in practice, a president is no longer able, with complete independence, to establish and enforce his own policies, a strong president can prevent what he regards as wrong policies from becoming national policies. If he has inherited or if he has himself instituted policies he later comes to believe wrong, he can do much to change them, whether or not political realities and the fractioning of political power in an elective society permits him to enforce those changes he wants.

When John Kennedy was killed, he had announced, and he had begun to bring into being, the most radical changes in American policy. They were contrary to those he inherited, contrary to what had been his. My book in preparation, TIGER TO RIDE, deals with this aspect of his murder.

When John Kennedy was murdered, his murder brought a new government into authority. When that government investigated his murder, it also investigated its own credentials, established its own legality and purity. Whether or not the people know the words, the old legal question was in everyone's mind, "Cui bono?" Who profits? The first, regardless of innocence, is the successor. Therefore, the investigation by the beneficiary becomes an investigation of himself.

This is not to say that Lyndon Johnson was part of the conspiracy that killed John Kennedy and made him President.

However, he was President, and he became President by that murder alone.

John Kennedy put it pretty well. He was manipulated into one crisis after another by those advisers he was powerless to control. After the first, the Bay of Pigs, he assumed full responsibility, even though what happened was neither his idea nor his desire. Full responsibility is the President's, he said, and publicly he assumed that responsibility. It could not be put more succinctly than by Harry Truman, who said, "The buck stops here."

The murder of a head of state - any head of state in any society or any kind of society - is always a time of great crisis for everyone involved - and everyone is involved. Even the ordinary faceless unknown, for it is their country, their futures, control of which is changed without their assent or participation. So, if what should not have happened did, in some cases this can be expected, in others excused.

Here is what happened when John Kennedy was murdered:

Federal police took possession of his corpse, by force, over the opposition of local authorities, in open violation of local law. For practical purposes, this means in violation of all law, for only local law then applied.

Federal police immediately removed that body from the only legal jurisdiction, the only place the law could work, seek his murderer. For practical purposes, this meant they preempted Texas law, trials, investigations.

Federal authorities, while pretending that investigations were going forward locally, thus took control over the heart of any investigation, the most important tangible evidence of the crime, of how it was committed, of how many were involved, of what was the real cause of death - the autopsy.

Federal authorities immediately saw to it that no non-federal employees had any connection with or knowledge of the autopsy. More sinister still, all civilians were removed from and kept out of the autopsy room, save for four members of the federal police who were in attendance and the few whose duties required them to be present briefly. (An example is Secret Service Agent Clint Hill, called in after the examination was completed to take official note of the location of the wounds. He later testified the President was shot in the back, not the neck.) For practical purposes, the military had complete control over the autopsy examination and who could see any part of it. No civilian had anything to do with the autopsy or the report of the examination, the protocol. When a single civilian observer, and a competent, qualified one, Dr. Malcolm Perry, was consulted by phone and told the autopsy chief surgeon the President was shot from the front, and when he included this in the protocol, someone in the military mysteriously expunged this and substituted different words, eliminating from the autopsy as turned in by the doctors the statement that the President had been shot from the front.

The President had a military autopsy. The military violently opposed those changes in policy he had initiated. Bearing in mind that these changes in policy were, in fact, not at all to military liking, it is perhaps pertinent to recall some of what we have seen of what this military autopsy really meant, whether or not there is a direct relationship or whether one can be suspected:

The autopsy was so deficient it made solution of the crime improbable if not impossible, certainly more difficult, from the very first moments.

Under military orders, what was required to be done was not done. Thus, essential and required fact was not adduced and was not available - never was nor can be.

The path of the so-called nonfatal bullet, assuming there was but one, was not traced through the body because of direct military order that it not be done even though as a matter of law and regulation it had to be done.

Required pictures were not taken, do not now exist, or both.

Required X-rays that were taken only after protest that they had not been made were secreted by the military but were not delivered to the civilian part of government and today have no official existence.

Evidence immediately known and in contradiction to what as instantly became the official fiction, the false solution to the crime, was suppressed by the military.

The so-called nonfatal bullet had fragmented, which eliminated any possibility that Bullet 399 was this bullet. This meant at least another, if not an entirely different kind of bullet - one not at any time admitted or accounted for - was used in the assassination. In turn, in and of itself, this is irrefutable proof of conspiracy, whether or not of Oswald's innocence.

With only military "experts" participating in the "autopsy", all were promptly threatened into silence, first verbally and then in writing, to the end that there could not, without the most severe consequences, be any questioning of the official lie thereupon certified as official truth and fact by any of those present.

Only thus was it possible to mislocate the wounds, in the back and in the head, and to misrepresent the wound in the front of the neck, which had to have been one of entrance, one Oswald could not have caused, one that could not have come from any shot from the rear. The truth about any one of these official lies destroys the larger official lie of the "solution" to the crime.

And the military death certificate, suppressed until this book, certifies that the so-called nonfatal wound was much too low to permit the official explanation of its cause. Yet every military mouth has been closed, if not from complicity, by threat if not fear.

This death certificate is false or the military witnesses are perjurers, all of them - Humes, Boswell and Finck, the latter also in the New Orleans trial. In any event, these military witnesses committed perjury before the Warren Commission on more than this wound.

The moral guilt of the silent is not less.

With this brief encapsulation of the military autopsy, can it be assumed that it was without purpose, or that the purpose was unrelated to announced and commenced changes in policy?

The charade of an investigation of the murder was a federal game. There were no other players. Federal police manipulated the information that reached the federal lawyers who did the work for the federal Commission. When Texas began its own investigation, it was frustrated at every turn, bamboozled, cajoled, deceived and misled by the federal

364

investigation. Federal power saw to it that no single proceeding of the investigation was public. Federal authorities saw to it that witnesses spoke to no one, thus foreclosing the press from sources of information that might later contradict the decision of the federal investigation. In practice, this meant federal power saw to it there would be no other investigation, and that to the degree possible, all sources of information would be stifled.

Federal officials, directly and indirectly part of the investigation, carefully corrupted the press and the public mind with carefully planned "leaks" of "secrets", each calculated to precondition the national mind to accept the coming, unacceptable, federal conclusions.

Federal power saw to it that no other side would be presented, not even in secret federal hearings. When seriously damaging information contrary to federal preconceptions and predeterminations could not be avoided, it was suppressed or destroyed - by federal personnel - when it could not be misrepresented. The fact of destruction is now beyond question. It involves most of the tangible evidence essential to the autopsy and to any solution to the crime.

Federal power, then, seized control over everything connected with the murder and its solution and coming (federal) explanation.

Let us now return to that federal parody of medicine and the law, the so-called autopsy of the murdered President. That it was unacceptable in any court of law, at best incompetent, at worst conspiratorial and accredited by apparent perjury, is amply set forth above.

That autopsy and the still-existing attendant proofs have never been examined except by federal eyes.* The federal (military) doctors swore their testimony before the federal Commission, which prayed and willed it into a pretense of fact and suppressed what jeopardized it, both testimony and documents.

(One little-known aspect of this is the suppression by the Commission of the account of the closest eyewitness of the President's wounds. There was only one close eyewitness, the widow. First, the Commission delayed taking her testimony, then it restricted those who could hear it, and it wound up, on its own, expunging every word she said about those wounds. My persistent efforts to get access to this account of the wounds, and nothing else of that suppressed testimony, under any conditions and restrictions imposed by federal suppressors - and the suppression itself is impermissible - has been frustrated by federal power to frustrate since the spring or summer of 1966. It can not be because the widow's description of the wounds - I emphasize the only close eyewitness account before changes were possible in their appearance and the only close eyewitness account of where they struck, how they looked and what they did - supports the official explanation that it is and has been suppressed.)**

To this date, there has never been any federal criticism of the autopsy, examination or report, of the investigation by federal agents and the federal Commission, or of the resultant Report. Everything and everybody were perfect. By the time the purloined pictures and X-rays of the autopsy were restored to government possession, there had been considerable criticism of all federal activity, first in minor-magazine articles and then in books, of which the first on the Commission was WHITEWASH. It and those that followed, with the collateral attention they got, pinched the government in its until-then quiescent conspiracy nerve. In total, there was suddenly considerable unofficial attention to the deficiencies of the investigation and its reporting.

So, first federal power got the film, of which it had cunningly divested itself, back under federal control. With the power of the government to command publicity and the willingness of a servile press to award it, for a short while, this calmed criticism. Then WHITEWASH II appeared and showed that, instead of quieting suspicions, the operation on the return of the film, when considered in the total story of the autopsy, actually raised new questions without answering any of the existing ones. The numbers, for example, did not add up.

*See Epilogue **See pp. 386-7.

As the first step in frustrating exposure of the evil it had wrought, federal authority had the autopsy doctors say what could not possibly be true, that they authenticated the pictures and X-rays of the autopsy. Meanwhile, a number of sycophantic articles in major magazines, inspired books and TV specials appeared, temporarily restoring federal tranquillity. They confused but did not convince the people.

Then, with the realization the story still did not hold together, the Department of Justice got the autopsy doctors together again to say again, this time in a report, that they had studied their pictures and X-rays and this film proved their autopsy report correct. No reasonably intelligent person can read this report with any knowledge at all of the fact and credit it. The Department knew this report would not, in itself, stand examination. It also was self-serving. The only reason this film was not shown to an impartial panel of genuine experts is that it proved beyond doubt that the solution to the crime was a monstrous lie.

Meanwhile, beginning with the Attorney General himself, the very day of the Senate hearing on his appointment, when he was Acting Attorney General, there was a super-colossal campaign of federal inspiration against Garrison. It was at this juncture that the Attorney General convoked his special panel.

Having no immediate need for the reports of his two panels, the Attorney General sat on them - until two new crises arose together. These are his departure from office (translation, "Control of the situation") and Garrison's subpena action. When Judge Halleck set January 17 for the hearing, there remained but one day of work before the new administration came in. January 17 was a Friday, the last full day of the Johnson administration and of Clark's tenure. The next day of work was Monday, January 20, Inauguration Day.

This history narrows the focus on what we have examined, two junior-grade Warren Reports Clark did not dare release until compelled. They are federal reports, part of the federal record here outlined.

Now, if by any chance of a flexible imagination, these two reports could by slightly honest men be said to endorse in any way either the autopsy or the Warren Reports, there is no chance the Acting Attorney General would have suppressed them or released them under circumstances that precluded any examination by the press or his opposing lawyers. His transgressions against legal courtesies are pretty glaring, when he pulls the kind of cute capers only the federal government can get away with. He would not for nothing risk so antagonizing the judge who would render the verdict.

The two reports say they show the autopsy and Warren Reports are correct. But each, separately, proves both wrong, and wrong beyond improvisation, patching or restoration. They are Humpty-Dumpty reports by a Chicken Little Attorney General who blew his cool when a single cloud passed over. Only desperation enticed the Attorney General to let anyone see them. He gambled no one would do what I have done.

Each of the panels certifying its report endorsed the autopsy and Warren Reports lied. Each had to know it was lying. Each engaged in the cheapest kind of literary pot-boiling to accomplish dishonest ends.

Each knew the ends and understood the dishonesty. When the autopsy doctors acknowledged, no matter how indirectly, that there was metal in the President's thoracic region, they knew its significance, knew Humes had sworn directly the opposite, and each of the other two, also under oath, certified his testimony. Humes' testimony is that all three autopsy doctors examined the X-rays during the autopsy - particularly the one showing the metal - with the assistance of the radiologist - and that they show no missile anywhere in the President's body. Unless the government conspired to fake the X-rays, this is perjury. It is actionable. But that action must be initiated by the Department of Justice for which the report was made and by which it was released, the Department of Justice that endorsed it, the Department of Justice whose operating personnel is unchanged by the change in administration.

When the panel, again with the most skillful indirection and misdirecting understatement, slipped in the few words that there were bullet fragments in the same area, it also knew what it was doing. If it didn't, it had no business doing anything. It therefore knew that it was destroying the autopsy and Warren Reports beyond repair. And when the panel located a head wound so very far from where the autopsy doctors placed it - from the same X-rays, unless there was this conspiracy within the government to fake the evidence of the President's murder and how that government came into dominion - it knew it was lying when it said its study supported the two previous reports.

Unless it did not work at all, it also knew it was protecting perjury, the very perjury upon which all of subsequent history pivoted. The perjury of the autopsy doctors is dual: In their false swearing and false documentation on the so-called non-fatal wound and in their false swearing about and mislocating of the shot in the head. Truthful testimony about either precluded the possibility the Warren Report could have suggested one man was the assassin. This means that truthful testimony about either proved what the government demanded not be proved, that there was a conspiracy to murder John Kennedy.

Every bit of contrary evidence since then has been fashioned by the government. It might influence or change what people and other governments believe. But it does not change the fact:

JOHN KENNEDY WAS KILLED BY A CONSPIRACY!

Now, for the first time, we have credible evidence of a conspiracy inside the government. Whether or not part of the conspiracy to kill may be a question. There should no longer be a question about the "whitewash", the "cover-up".

Until Clark blew his cool, I had believed the unexplained wrongs might be attributed to pressures and unresisted temptations within the government. What, in his final moments of ultimate desperation, the Attorney General himself gave us, eliminates this possibility. It just is beyond belief that all these things are innocent, nothing but coincidence:

That the panel of doctors told the same lies about the same things;
    That they ignored the same evidence;
    Misrepresented the same evidence;
    Misinterpreted the same evidence the same ways;
    Ignored the same missing pictures;
    Ignored the fact that pictures are missing;
    Ignored, for all practical purposes with the panel and completely with the original doctors, the fact that X-rays are missing;
    Ignored, completely with the original doctors and for all practical purposes with the panel, that the single crucial front-head X-ray was unexplainedly twice burned;
    Lied, in making no clamor, deceived by their silence, and led the world to believe that all the pictures and X-rays are genuine and present - still exist - and that they "support" the earlier reports they actually demolish;
    Twisted and tortured the language to make it appear they were saying what they did not and then concluded the opposite of what their own work proved;
    Were silent for all the many months after their studies, making themselves willing partners of suppression.

The federal government still suppresses vital evidence of the murder. What it does not suppress it has destroyed - and this includes all the tangible evidence, none of which now exists in its original form or exists at all!

Engaged in (if, indeed, it did not engineer) an illegal contract with the executors of the estate of the murdered President to enable it to suppress the pictures and X-rays, the most crucial evidence. The

property given away was federal property, beyond the authority of any
one to give away. It could not, in any event, have been part of the
estate, for that is created the moment of death. The pictures and X-
rays are not part of the murdered President's estate. The law under
which this spurious deal was made is not, in any event, applicable.
And, because everything prior was illegal, the government could not
invoke its own contrived illegalities to cloak its own illegal act with
the semblance of legality.

These are but some of those many things that cannot be condoned
or accepted that are part of the federal conspiracy involved in its
investigation if not in the murder of President John F. Kennedy.

"The crisis in credibility" has become a common phrase in American political life. Gradually, over the years - save on one subject,
assassinations - it has become an accepted representation of reality.
The American people and the world question the credibility of official
statements of the American government. The phrase became popular - and
appropriate - under the Johnson Administration.

It is, rather, a crisis in integrity. The government lies.

The President lies.

Years after he became President only because John Kennedy was
assassinated, few, not only the sophisticated, do not consider LBJ a
liar. The same is true of his successor, the "Tricky Dick" and "Dirty
Dick" Nixon who also became President only because John Kennedy was
killed.

As recently as the time of John Kennedy it would have been considered scandalous to talk of a president as a liar. When Lyndon Johnson became President, Presidential lies became cocktail-party jokes.
It required only a few bullets and a few years. The difference between
Johnson and Nixon lies in the difference in the manner of the men.
Johnson was all piety and Nixon all seriousness. But both lied non-
stop, blatantly and repeatedly, their bigger lies on the more vital
questions.

Reporters could be heard to groan, "Oh, that liar!" but their
papers and radio and TV were too polite to use the ugly word. This is
the Emperor's Clothes reality of American journalism of the era of political assassinations without which all of history would have been
different, without which so many uncountable hundreds and hundreds of
thousands of human beings would be intact, not killed - blown apart,
burned to death or shot - or assassinated.

Finally, thanks to the willingness of the young to do the unpopular and become themselves unpopular, an outcast generation to their
elders, the total lie of Viet Nam became an accepted fact, yet for years
the undeclared war there continued, despite Richard Nixon's campaign
lie that got him elected, that he had a secret plan to get us out. His
getting us out began with increasing the number of Americans fighting
and dying there. It continued by spreading it to other lands and with
an enormous escalation of the bombing and slaughter of innocent civilians, largely women, children and old men. When even the most stub-
bornly blind of the military could no longer avoid the reality, that
no investment of American lives could end the determination of the Vietnamese to control their own lives and country and there was less danger
to the President who sought change, the withdrawal of Americans from
that America-ravished land became Richard Nixon's issue of the coming
campaign, and instead of doing what he could have done, just gotten out,
he scheduled withdrawal into a campaign issue.

With Johnson it was the reverse. He pretended that the last
thing in his mind was open involvement. It is Barry Goldwater who was
the warhawk. LBJ, platitudes pouring from his pious mouth, swore that
no American boys would go to Southeast Asia to fight a war Asian boys
should fight. And all the time he was preparing for just that - as
soon as the election was over.

The two cases cannot be separated. It is the murder of the

President that made what happened in Viet Nam possible, beginning with the sanctification of the Johnson succession. We would have had neither the Johnson succession nor its policies without this murder. And without the sanctification, without the whitewashing of the murder, there would have been such turmoil that the change in policy would not have been dared.

Kennedy learned and switched to peace. Johnson benefited and made the war.

The military and its defenders played the key role, if in no other way by making a fake solution to the assassination harder to avoid, a task promptly taken over by its civilian friends in government, beginning with the new President.

This is the story of America's Reichstag Fire.

If it is not to bring about in the United States what came to pass in Germany, what the Germans did not do we must do.

First, we must inform ourselves - all of us. Then we must make ourselves heard.

Then there must be - we must insist upon - a full, free and completely public official investigation, by a body with the power to punish such crimes as perjury and the disposition to do it.

Until then, the United States may remain a powerful and a wealthy country. But it will not be the land of the free.

Nor the home of the brave.

EPILOGUE

Lack of popular interest was, far and away, the reason most commonly given by publishers for rejection of WHITEWASH, probably the world's most rejected book. It was not true, as the subsequent best-selling first underground edition proved beyond doubt. But what a commentary it is on publishability in the era of political assassination when a President can be killed, that assassination is investigated by a Presidential Commission, and the first book analyzing the work of that Commission is "unpublishable"!

By the time the first part of this book was completed, and it was several times rejected for the same alleged reason, it still was not true that there was no interest in the subject. By the time the last part was done, however, it may well have been the fact that the market-place prospects of any serious work on the subject were, indeed, dim by normal publishing standards. After WHITEWASH there were several serious works. One, that by Sylvia Meagher, is an exceptional work. There was also an outpouring of junk and literary thievery on the anti-Commission side; and many insupportable and incompetent works of open or disguised sycophancy in favor of the government. It is tragic that no single publisher had the interest or concern to commission a work plumbing the literary morass of what was officially hidden. Many competent investigative reporters engaged in newspaper, magazine and book writing were available. The wealthy houses fight for cheap sensation. Several offered advances against royalties that went into six figures for literary scrimshaw in support of the official mythology on political assassinations.

The glut was enough to convince concerned publishers, of whom there remain a few, that books on this subject can no longer pay their own way. There seems to be none willing to risk financial loss in order to bring to light officially-suppressed facts about how and why the President was killed and about how his murder was investigated.

Indeed, there is reasonable ground for suspecting that some of the most disreputable works were designed to kill interest. One is an extravagant work of unprecedented libel, meticulous in its pseudoscholarship, expertly written and edited, put together in an operation so vast and costly that I have traced those engaged in it to eight different countries. There is no doubt that those connected with intelligence operations of the United States and France at the very least were behind Farewell America and a movie of the same title, the aborting of which I was able to help in a small way. It was the book to end the credibility of all books on assassinations.

Incredibly, its excesses fascinate the intelligent but unthinking marginal paranoids among those genuinely concerned about these assassinations, even though the book itself cannot survive consideration of its content.

Thus it was that, upon completion of POST-MORTEM, I was overjoyed at an offer to pay for printing it as another "underground" book, for the cost exceeded what I may yet mortgage.

The offer came from a younger but mature man who seemed deeply troubled by the accident of birth into great wealth, a man who displays apprehension over the state of society. It was accompanied with what was also pleasing, an offer to edit and contract the work for sale in the $5.00 range and to seek commercial sponsorship for the condensation. It is the small-sized book that has greatest commercial appeal, and simplified writing enhances that. We both felt that no contraction of such sensational evidence could, by itself, be accepted without the backstopping of the fully documented original and I, at least, wanted the entire work to be available, if only for history, institutional and scholarly use.

Once we agreed, he started changing the conditions, first by requiring simultaneous appearance of both editions. He shifted gradually to where he, equipped with no more than a reading of some of what had been published, would constitute himself what he conceived himself, a subject-expert and accomplished investigative-reporter, competences not acquired by birth into wealth, and would interview those who in his view had knowledge of the fact. He would incorporate their versions in the book.

His first new condition meant that if he did not do an acceptable job of editing and shortening the book or if for any other reason he did not or could not find a publisher willing to print it, no version would ever be printed. The second meant interminable delay and wrangling, inordinate added length to an already overlong book, and involved evidentiary and factual judgments that, as he soon established, were beyond his capabilities. Those whom he said he intended to interview are one of the less active members of the Warren Commission, a former cabinet member, and some of the staff counsel. In his mind, the fact of his wealth and Establishmentarian name would open all doors. People who, as he told himself, would not speak with me would speak with him. When I asked what any could say that could in any way alter fact, he had no answer. Somehow, there is magic in wealth and family name, and it overcomes all. The one answer I did get is that he did not expect them to fall to their knees and beg for mercy. That I had written those involved and asked them to confront fact, and that all had refused, appeared to have no meaning to him.

As a compromise I proposed that, after the entire work was printed and nothing could frustrate that, each of those he wanted to say whatever it is he imagined they would or could say would be given a copy and asked for a statement. I agreed to incorporate any defamation of me, no matter how false, vile or irrelevant. He agreed but soon backed out.

It became apparent that what he really had in mind was an unrecognized ego indulgence to be financed by his wealth, that he wanted to convert the entire work into what he wanted to believe, not what the fact says, and that, despite his self-concept, he lacked understanding of some of the most basic evidence - or did not want it presented.

His final offer began, "I shall pay you $10,000 for whatever use you please, in return for the right to produce my own book on the assassination using your materials ... You will therefore give me a waiver to use any copywritten /he meant copyrighted7 material from POST MORTEM ..."

Not even a whore _sells_ her body. She merely rents it for temporary use.

This insulting offer was later hedged with conditions no self-respecting writer could consider, such as that I would "not be allowed, however, to come out with" any version of this book "within a year of the time you receive the $10,000". No time for payment was set. He kept changing conditions as he put them on paper. The last began with the stipulation that the agreement would not be entered into "until after I have completed my PhD thesis" and was then qualified by "Indeed, if my thesis is successful enough, I may not want to enter into this agreement at all."

These conditions combine into all wealth could do to delay indefinitely, if not totally suppress, this book. The final words say all that need be said about dedication and purity of motive: If his

371

thesis earned the fame for which he yearned, he need spend no more in its pursuit.

During our last personal discussion, which ended with his blurting out, "I have never been so put down in my life," a rather strange formulation, he finally admitted that he was off on a "get Kennedy" kick. Robert and Edward had not behaved as he conceived that he would have had his brother been assassinated, hence he had strong objections to the chapter "Hades, Not Camelot". He was flabbergasted when I said, "O.K., leave it out of the condensation." His "put down" confession was preceded by a point-by-point analysis of his emotions vis-a-vis the attitudes of the surviving Kennedys.

This concession did not satisfy him. He was determined to conduct and incorporate prejudicial, angled, anti-Kennedy interviews, the net result of which would have been to provide a means for those really guilty of the suppressions to attribute them to Senator Edward Kennedy alone. It was a basic condition that to me is an obscenity and a corruption of the history of one of the turning points in American history.

What began with hope ended with new frustration. Between the beginning and the end of this affair, an enormous amount of time was wasted for my wife and me. It was a painful, exhausting experience.

All of this preceded the end of the five-year period specified in the GSA-family agreement after which the most carefully prescribed access to the evidence itemized in the contract could be granted. Only those without requisite knowledge of the relevant evidence could qualify. This is a strange and unbecoming provision, even though it does specify the required scientific credentials with care and precision.

The misuse to which this provision could be put and the attractiveness of this misuse to those of power in the government, who also have every personal reason for fixing guilty responsibility upon others, had troubled me for a long time. I feared the inevitability of another corruption of fact, another framing of the innocent and of history, another obstacle to the establishment and acceptance of truth. When I had in my possession enough of this "new evidence" that is not new, merely suppressed and misrepresented, I saw a use for it that promised prevention of further trifling with reality, suffering to the innocent and the false fixing of blame. I proposed to a seriously concerned forensic pathologist who, more than merely holding impeccable credentials, is a brilliant, articulate, responsible man that he and I might do together what neither of us could do alone, "break" the case in a proper forum. In more than a year he had not replied. Meanwhile, insofar as I could, I kept him abreast of the results of my investigations.

When I wanted a technical expert to use in my suit for pictures of the clothing, I asked the pathologist to serve as this expert. His first response was, "I hope I will be able to testify for you in my fields of expertise ... I shall try to obtain testimony from a competent criminalist." Pursuant to this encouraging offer, I kept him as informed as I could of the result of that investigation. His comments glow from the pages of a correspondence that grew to book-thickness, representing considerable time and effort, enough for the writing of another book. But by the time of the hearing in that suit, he was so busy making money he could not do all the things that yielded him a more-than-comfortable income; therefore, he would not be my expert witness. So, unable to afford a lawyer and having to act as my own, I was also without the technical expert upon whom I had depended.

Throughout this period, sandwiching a request for a free copy of FRAME-UP, he set forth endless encomiums, like "I certainly admire your tenacity and perseverance"; "your perseverance and tenacity are truly remarkable"; "it is unfortunate for all of us that you are not a man of independent wealth!"; "I hope that you achieve the judicial breakthrough that is needed in order to begin to unravel this whole mess"; "I realize that you are doing this by yourself and on a shoestring, and I admire you for your tenacity and perseverance"; "we all need a breakthrough /referring to the potential of the suit7 for substantive and psychological reasons!"; "if this case is ever to be re-opened and re-evaluated, it will be due to the continuing efforts of a few people like yourself, who refused to leave the truth obscured and buried"; "you certainly have put in a formidable amount of time and effort in this tragic and almost unbelievable affair, and I only hope you meet with some success in the future".

These and other unsolicited but pleasing praises characterize the correspondence. They hardly substitute for the simple scientific thing I requested, a selection from standard scientific texts on the capabilities and limitations of spectrographic analyses and neutron-activation testing. I preferred a selection by the trained, professional mind rather than my own, to assure that the sources quoted would be the most dependable. Promised often, I never got it. Yet it represented no more work than asking a secretary to xerox a page or two from office texts - and he has three offices, for each of three deservedly successful professional careers, as independent consultant, professor and coroner. In response to the previous reminder, dated August 21, 1971, there was commiseration, "I am truly sorry that you are into this thing so deeply and do not have the necessary financial backing and other resources required to permit your pursuing everything in timely and appropriate fashion. Somehow, I hope you can get a break." To this nonresponse I wrote on September 12, "Much as I appreciate your kind wishes and expressions of sympathy, to solicit these was not the purpose of my 8/21. Quite some time ago you promised to get ... from standard sources exactly what can and cannot be done with, by and through spectrographic and neutron-activation tests so my writing could be accurate and could cite them."

There was never any response. This was six weeks before access could be granted under the contract to pathologists and others in related fields of science and technology.

Without telling or consulting me, and despite this long correspondence in which there is constant quest for the results of my investigations into the field in which he had been unwilling to invest any of his own well-paid time, he had applied for access under the contract. He was willing to do so little work that, rather than ask the Archives for a copy of that contract, back in 1968 he had asked me for a copy of it and I bore the nominal cost of providing it.

Thus, the nonproductiveness of this long correspondence had a reasonable explanation, as did his disinterest in a joint project that might "break" the case. He knew the contents of both of the earlier parts of this work, having read them, and of much of the last, having asked and been told the new fact. He had been infected by the bug that leaves so many of those disagreeing with the official account of the assassination with an insatiable yearning to be the one, the only one, who does "break" the case.

With him, two things are different: He had done no original work or research and had contributed to none; and he, as could any pathologist, stood to gain an enormous professional reputation from it, he more than others because he also has a private consulting business.*

Whether or not selfish motive was conscious and deliberate, and the brief record cited can be interpreted as providing an answer, that is not what so deeply troubled me about his nonhelp in even the simplest matters and his secretiveness when he knew that I alone had made the detailed study and done the great amount of work embodied in this book. My earlier work, in any event, was by far the most exhaustive on this aspect of the case. That he was discussing and counseling with the uninformed and not with me made me apprehensive for many reasons, one of which is that, should he gain access to the materials covered by the contract, he would be under-informed and perhaps misinformed as well.

However, my greatest worry was the probable further burying of truth and the corollary, the exculpation of the guilty and the victimizing of the innocent that would be the most likely result of what could be anticipated to be the great publicity that would accompany his examination of this material.

_____
*Malpractise. Doctors can't advertise.

Were he to emerge from his examination and be silent, the purposes of the examination would be nullified and it would then be incumbent upon those in control to permit another to make the examination and issue a statement.

Were he to emerge and say what he well knew in advance he would say, that "his" examination shows the Warren Report to be wrong and the crime is unsolved, in his and other eyes he would be heroic. But those really responsible for the false solution and the suppression would be exculpated. They are the ones who command the major media attention. All have prepared self-justifications for immediate production. I have possessed some for years. And because of the auspices and the wording of the contract, this would, inevitably, be interpreted as saying and meaning that the survivors of the President and they alone were responsible for the false solution to his murder and the suppression of the evidence. To me, this would be the ultimate obscenity and another tragedy.

When my suggestion that he think this through was without meaningful response, I decided that, if possible, this new tragedy had to be avoided.

It could be arranged for others, including sycophants, to see this evidence and say what officialdom wanted said, and of that we could do nothing. But for a man of such unquestionable professional credentials to be the one to say the official story is false would have put the entire affair in a different context and would have made the most spectacular propaganda success for the guilty.

While I felt the prospects of his getting access were not good, such is my low estimate of the bureaucratic imagination and intelligence, I also felt it was a risk that should not be run, particularly when, as the reader by this time can assess for himself, there was little likelihood that anything not already produced by my investigation (and this to his knowledge) would result.

The difference, aside from his new fame, would be in making a hero of Hoover and a villain of the last remaining Kennedy male.

When I presented the problem to a Senator who had been a long-time friend, as a wise and experienced politician he required no explanations. He saw the potential immediately. He said he had known Burke Marshall for a long time and would take it up with him. Soon I got the message that under no circumstances would Marshall permit any access.

Then there was the Princeton University conference on the FBI, where, strangely, in the context of Hoover's unsecret hatred of all Kennedys and Marshall's responsibility for their integrity as representative of the executors of the President's estate, Marshall appeared as Hoover's defender. His defense received national attention. A participant in that conference left with no doubt at all that Marshall would not grant any access to this evidence he controlled.

Thus assured, wrongly, as will become apparent, that another falsification of fact had been avoided, I turned to other work. I left on a long trip to a number of cities, including Dallas. There, on the morning of December 1, 1971, I interviewed three Parkland Hospital doctors then available who had taken part in the emergency treatment of the President.

I had interviewed Perry on an earlier trip. To the credit of all, despite the fact that my views had been well-publicized and, in fact, had been repeated on local television just a few days earlier, not one objected to being interviewed. All the interviews were in their offices in the attached school of medicine. Before summarizing these interviews and in fairness to these men, I remind the reader of the unenviable position in which all had been placed and of the pressures, already detailed, to which all had been subjected.

In confidence I respect, one I will not name told me of a first-person account by a Navy doctor present at the autopsy, a fact hidden in all records.

It was deer season in Texas. Some of those I interviewed outside the hospital had just returned from trips to hunting country, some were about to leave. Perry had sought deer and antelope the previous week. He and his family are fond of the meat. Hunting is a form of exercise he enjoys. They had not had good luck. His 11-year-old son had the only chance at a deer, a bad shot, so they bagged none.

This led us into a discussion of hunting, rifles, ammunition and the effects of various kinds of ammunition, designed for different purposes. As with many men who really enjoy hunting. Perry is an expert on ammunition. In common with many hunters and gun hobbyists, he handloads his own ammunition. In connection with this writing and that on the King assassination, I have made a study of rifles and ammunition, have consulted various experts, standard literature and criminalists, and I believe that Perry is much more expert in these areas than most doctors in other parts of the country. It has been my opinion that there are few cities in the country in which the assassination could have been committed where the witnesses could have been as helpful to any sincere investigation because of their knowledge of wounds, weaponry and ammunition.

This, too, is a secret in the official investigations. Neither the Commission nor the FBI was interested. Their interests lay in the other direction, in hiding. Perry's amateur expertise is one of these secrets, through no fault of his.

Most of this is Arlen Specter's fault. I found Dallas officials who developed intense personal dislike for him and the manner of his "investigation". Specter knew what to do to keep what he wanted out of the official evidence. One new example of this is Allan Sweatt, then Chief Criminal Deputy in the sheriff's office. Sweatt was responsible for the immediate taking of statements from eyewitnesses. He handled all the pictures immediately known about. But Sweatt was not a witness before the Commission, was not the subject of any FBI interrogation in the Commission's evidence. Specter used Sweatt's polygraph room to conduct the Ruby lie-detector test. He used polygraph "experts" whose credentials are considered dubious in Dallas. The first thing Specter did was to chase Sweatt, an authentic expert, from his own office. Sweatt was not present when Ruby was questioned.

So, if there are inadequacies and errors in the testimony of the doctors and if, as I believe, in some cases it crossed the line into criminality, the responsibility is Specter's. The doctors deserve sympathy and sympathetic understanding of the position in which all had been put. All were under inordinate pressure. Perry is but one example. He is but one of the many with technical knowledge valuable (if not, indeed, essential) to any thorough and honest investigation whose expertise was hidden from the members of the Commission and its record, secret and published.

The first doctor available was Charles Carrico, by then on the surgery teaching staff. He confirmed all I have written that relates to him and what happened in his presence and added that which Specter did not want and had not asked for.

Carrico was the first doctor to see the President. He saw the anterior neck wound immediately. It was above the shirt collar. Carrico was definite on this. The reader will remember that Dulles had blundered into asking Carrico to locate that wound when Specter failed to probe this essential matter. It is not by accident or from stupidity that Specter did not ask this fundamental question. The only qualification Carrico stipulated in my interview is that the President's body was prone when he saw it. However, when I asked if he saw any bullet holes in the shirt or tie, he was definite in saying "No". I asked if he recalled Dulles' question and his own pointing to above his own shirt collar as the location of the bullet hole. He does remember this and he does remember confirming that the hole was above the collar, a fact hidden with such care from the Report. Although there is nothing to dispute it in any of the evidence and so much that confirms it, this had to be ignored for in and of itself it means the total destruction of the lone-assassin prefabrication. So it, too, was memory-holed.

According to Carrico, the doctor who was there and under whose supervision it was done, the clothes were cut exactly as I report. In emergencies, speed is essential. Clothing is cut to save life-precious split-seconds. Practice was not to take time to undo the tie but to grasp it, as he illustrated with his own, and cut it off close to the knot. The knot is not cut. The customary cut is made where there is but a single thickness of necktie. With a right-handed nurse, what happened with the President's tie was inevitable. In this cutting, a minute nick was made at the extreme edge of the knot. Because of the danger of injury to the patient, the collar button and the top of the shirt are unbuttoned, and that is what the pictures of the President's shirt show did happen in this case. Trained personnel did exactly what they are trained to do, what they do instinctively. Because these medical personnel are trained to do what they automatically did in this case, Specter had no interest in it. His interest was in the case he framed.

I asked Carrico what Specter <u>did not dare</u> ask, the simple question whether, in his opinion, and based on <u>his</u> experience in emergencies, the nick on the knot and the slits in the collar were made by the nurses, not by a bullet. Carrico considers it unlikely. He saw neither the nick in the tie nor the cuts in the shirt before the nurses started cutting.

Was any other examination made, I asked him. He said that he followed standard procedure, running his hands down both sides of the back without turning the body over. The purpose is to ascertain if there is a large wound. If there is, it can be felt through clothing.

If Carrico, an honest, straightforward man, spoke so openly with me, I have no doubt that he would have been no less informative with any and all official investigators, had they - <u>any</u> of them - truth for their client.

From Carrico's office in Room 208, I went to the sixth floor, where Drs. Robert N. McClelland and Perry have offices opposite each other. McClelland was in, Perry was then not. McClelland was pleasant, greeting me cordially. I asked him about his contemporaneous statement, that "the cause of death" was "a gunshot wound of the left temple" (R527) He does remember it and began an apology by saying "it was a total mistake on my part". His explanation is that "Ginger", Dr. Marion T. Jenkins, called the spot to his attention. McClelland seemed genuinely disturbed about this. He was bitter that the New Orleans assistant district attorneys had asked him about it and self-satisfied with how he talked them out of calling him as a witness - by telling them he would swear it had been a "total mistake".

I asked him why he never corrected this alleged mistake, especially when he was deposed and Specter, having avoided it with obvious care, asked him instead if there was anything he had said that he wanted to change or anything he wanted to add (6H39).

McClelland had no answer. So I asked him how he knew it was, in fact, a "total mistake". He then shifted to this position: "I don't know that it wasn't and I don't know that it was." We both realized this was a far cry from his opening, "it was a total mistake," for almost immediately, and without vigorous questioning, he was admitting openly and without leading questions that it might not have been any kind of mistake. A bit embarrassed, he formulated still another position, "I presume it was a wrong assumption."

He was anxious to complain about Garrison and his assistants, and I listened to a long, bitter and irrelevant diatribe, which seemed to satisfy him. When he ran down, I asked how he would or could now account for such an error, if error it was. He then conjectured it was a spot of splattered blood. Perhaps an experienced surgeon and a professor of surgery cannot tell the difference between a bullet hole of entrance to which he attributed the crime of the century and a spot of blood. I found it not easy to believe. So I asked him how he came to realize that perhaps he was in error. That, it turns out, was not anything he had seen or of which he had personal knowledge, but the autopsy report taken around and shown by the federal agents! It was not in the autopsy report so it was not true, regardless of his own professional observation and opinion.

There was another obvious question and I asked it: Had he, Jenkins, or anyone else wiped this alleged spot to see if it was no more than a spot of blood or to see if it was a bullet hole when all knew there would be an inquest which would have to establish the cause of death? His answer was simple, direct and unequivocal: "No."

I reminded him that Jenkins also had testified to the existence of this left-temple wound. McClelland had no explanation.

Jenkins was not available. His second reference to this under oath was remarkably detailed and precise in locating the alleged wound in the left temple (6H51). This followed immediately upon an off-the-record "discussion" with Specter, the content of which Specter described as "on a couple of matters which I am now going to put on the record" (6H50). With regard to Jenkins' professional belief and observation of the carefully described and oriented left-temple wound, Jenkins testified, "you have answered that for me". This is one way of conducting an "investigation", with the lawyer telling the expert witness what to say and believe.

Thus it is clear, regardless of whether the doctors' observations were correct or in error, on what could have been a vital element of the evidence, the only doctors who have personal knowledge have no basis for denying their immediate, competent, professional and unsolicited observation, that there had been a left-temple wound of entrance and that it was the likely cause of death. Instead, they were told by Specter and by federal agents what to say and believe and what not to say or believe.

When I left Room D614A and walked across the hall, Perry was in.

He is a warm, friendly man, inclined to smile pleasantly while talking, with what appears to be justified pride in his and his institution's professional accomplishments. While he remembered me and my belief that the official account of the assassination is wrong, he was not reluctant to be interviewed. His recollections of the great events in which he had been caught up are, and for the rest of his life will be, sharp. From my interviews with him, I am without doubt that, had he not been subjected to powerful and improper pressures, there would have been no word he would have said that would not have been completely dependable.

From time to time embarrassment showed. He began defensively, going back to the anterior neck wound. He does not deny telling the press that it was one of entrance. He does say that he has been given a tape of one of his interviews in which he hedged the statement by saying it was, to a degree, conjectural. Most doctors, under those circumstances, great urgency, the President as the patient and without their having turned the body over, would have said something like "appeared to be" in describing the wound as one of entrance. While superficially maintaining the position in which Specter put him under oath, of saying he did not really know whether the wound was of entrance or exit, Perry readily admits that Humes correctly understood him to describe it as a wound of entrance. He also admits that federal agents showed him and the other doctors the autopsy report before their testimony.

As I led him over those events and his participation, what he did and the sequence, he recalled that he first looked at the wound, then asked a nurse for a "trake" (short for tracheotomy) tray, wiped off the wound, saw a ring of bruising around it, and started cutting. In describing the appearance of the wound and the ring of bruising, he used the words, "as they always are". Pretending not to notice the significance of this important fact he had let bubble out, I retraced the whole procedure with him again. When he had repeated the same words, I asked him if he had ever been asked about the ringed bruise around the wound in the front of the neck. The question told the experienced hunter and the experienced surgeon exactly what he had admitted, one description of an entrance wound. He blushed and improvised the explanation that there was blood around the wound. I did not further embarrass him by pressing him, for we both knew he had seen the wound clearly. He had twice said he had wiped the blood off and had seen the wound clearly, if briefly, before cutting.

The official representation and that of an unofficial apologist to which we shall come would have us believe that bruising is a characteristic of entrance wounds only. This is not the case. The reader should not be deceived on this or by Perry's admission that there was bruising. Exit wounds also can show bruising. One difference is that exit wounds do not have to show bruising. That in this case there was bruising by itself need not be taken as an expression of Perry's professional opinion that it was a wound of entrance. The definitive answer is in those words he twice used, quoted directly above, "as they always are". It is entrance wounds only that always are of this description. Thus, Perry had said again and in a different way that this was a shot from the front. In context, this also is the only possible meaning of what Carrico had said.

In the official version, the President's nonfatal and all of Connally's wounds were caused by the same bullet. We discussed them. Perry was called in on the Connally surgery "by the boss" because he is an expert on arterial injury. When the other doctors noted the location of the thigh wound, they feared the possibility of proximity to an artery. One would never know this from Specter's questioning of any of the doctors or from any of the reports of federal agents. There is no reason to believe it is because of the reluctance of the doctors to speak freely.

Because of the reason for which he had been called in, Perry made careful observations of that wound as he made his examination. The hole was much too small for a bullet to have caused it. He said that from his examination of the X-rays, the fragment was relatively flat and could not have been deposited by a whole bullet that then backed out. He showed me with his fingers that the fragment was less than a half-inch under the skin and that it had gone about three to three and a half inches after penetration. This near-the-skin trajectory alone is more than enough to invalidate the entire official story. Because he saw no danger to any artery, Perry did not remove this fragment. This, he said, is the usual practice. He volunteered that, had the fragment been there from an unremembered childhood accident, it would have presented no hazard to Connally. I asked, had there been such a childhood accident, would it not have left a scar? Perry said the fragment was so thin it need not have.

Gradually, as we discussed his observations, Perry came to realize that he was providing a professional destruction of the official story. So, when we were discussing the Connally thigh wound, I reminded him that the official police account, written at the time of the crime and quoting the doctors, had said the same thing, that this wound had been caused by a fragment.

He then volunteered on this point that the X-rays showed fragmentation in Connally's wrist. When I quoted Shaw's and Gregory's testimony that there was more metal in the wrist than can be accounted for as missing from Bullet 399, Perry nodded his head in agreement.

Perry was not unwilling to express criticism of the autopsy doctors. Humes had told Specter that the bruise on the President's pleura might have been caused by Perry's surgery. Perry was affronted by the suggestion. He said they never cause such bruising in tracheotomies in adults and are exceedingly careful to avoid it in the smaller bodies of children. When Perry learned of this bruising, he had wondered if the cause was fragmentation. If he then had no way of knowing it, on the basis of my "new evidence", that today does seem to be the most reasonable explanation.

The autopsy doctors were wrong in attributing the chest incisions to subcutaneous emphysema. The way Perry said this, it was as though he were saying, "Any child should know that." Perry, personally, had asked for these incisions. They were for a "closed chorostomy". This is irrelevant except as a professional opinion on the competence of the Bethesda doctors.

Having learned what Specter suppressed, that Perry is an amateur expert in ammunition, I discussed other evidence that Specter suppressed, the pattern of fine fragmentation in the right front of the President's head as disclosed without explanation in the panel report. Perry was without doubt that this could not have been caused by a jacketed, military bullet. The reader should remember that, under the terms of the Geneva convention, military ammunition is encased in a hardened jacket for "humanitarian" reasons, to prevent just this kind of fragmentation in human bodies. Military ammunition is designed to avoid explosion of the bullet in the body, for a clean transiting of the body. This is not the case with hunting or "varminting" ammunition, that is, a bullet designed for the humane killing of pests or undesirable animals.

Perry's opinion is that the fine fragmentation and its pattern in the right front of the head alone could be the end of the Warren Report. As he thought about this "new evidence" on the wounds, Perry said that, from his experience, the panel description of the pattern of fragmentation is consistent with what he would expect from a "varminting" round. It is the opposite of the behavior of a military round, which is supposed to prevent this.

To illustrate his point, which is not his alone, Perry described the explosion of a varminting bullet on a recent hunt, when he had shot a prairie dog. The damage in each case was similar. The inference is that the massive damage to the President's head could have been caused by an entering bullet. Other amateur experts, like Dr. Richard Bernabei, had already told me this.

All his colleagues hold the highest opinion of the county coroner, Dr. Earl Rose, who was avoided with such official diligence that his name is not once mentioned in all the testimony. Rose objected vigorously to the kidnapping of the corpse. It was his responsibility, under the only obtaining law, to perform the autopsy. All the doctors agreed that, had he done it, the questions and doubts that now exist would not.

After the interview I discussed the "new evidence" with Perry, inviting him to come and see it for himself. I described the reporting of medical fact by the Clark panel, then quoted the death certificate. He said that if the government could do such things he would be terrified. I told him, "Then you should be terrified."

Were one inclined to be terrified about those things which have become normal with government and cannot be tolerated in any kind of decent society, there would be no end to terror on this subject.

Another case is one more illustration of the official misuse of the Kennedy name. It happened when I was away in early May of 1972. During this absence, I received an undated letter from Rhoads. He had declassified "the one page of Mrs. John F. Kennedy's testimony ... that had been withheld ..." He enclosed a copy.

There were many pious speeches in the "Top-Secret" executive sessions of the Commission about calling the widow. There was always the pretense of concern for the feelings of the bereaved. It had finally been decided that the chairman and Rankin would question her at her 3017 N Street, Northwest, Washington residence, in the presence of the then Attorney General, Robert Kennedy. This was postponed until the time the Commission expected to have its work completed, hardly the proper or appropriate time for interviewing the only close eyewitness to the fatal shot. A witness with her knowledge should have been one of the first called and one of those most closely examined.

But finally, at 4:20 p.m. on Friday, June 5, 1964, it came to pass.

It was so brief and superficial that, as printed, the whole thing requires less than three pages (5H178-81). When the formalities are eliminated and if one considers everything else relevant, the relevant is about two pages. Including formalities, it took exactly ten minutes, no more. It was all over at 4:30.

Mrs. Kennedy was looking directly at her husband when his head exploded. The Commission suppressed the relevant frames of the Zapruder film (as I exposed in WHITEWASH II). It pretended to make a typographical error, saying that Life had supplied a series ending with Frame 334. But simple arithmetic with a J. Edgar Hoover letter told me that Life had been asked for and had supplied nine additional frames, through Frame 343. The Commission suppressed them from its printed record. It was not because of the indescribable horror felt and shown by the widow as she saw the terrible thing from inches away, not because of official sensitivity about her feelings, that these frames were not published. It is because they, too, contradict the official account of the fatal shot and raise doubts about the nonfatal injuries.

Her husband's head did explode in her very face.

At the point where, from the printed transcript, it appears she was about to describe this, the Commission, with seeming honesty, inserted "/Reference to wounds deleted/".

This is a deliberate and multiple lie. Mrs. Kennedy made no specific reference to any wounds. Not here and not elsewhere. Rankin saw to that, it being his obligation to take testimony from her, not schmalz, to ask her about the wounds, not avoid it.

So, he did avoid it. The question to which she responded was not about wounds. It is, "Do you remember Mr. /Clint/ Hill /her Secret Service Agent/ coming to try and help on the car?"

And this one acknowledged is not by any means the only change in her testimony. As a matter of historical record, I here reproduce the entire page.

6815

Mrs. Kennedy. I don't remember anything. I was just down like that.

And finally I remember a voice behind me, or something, and then I remembered the people in the front seat finally, or somebody knew something was wrong, and a voice yelling, which must have been Mr. Hill, "Get to the hospital," or maybe it was Mr. Kellerman, in the front seat. But someone yelling. But just down holding him. I was trying to hold his hair on. But from the front there was nothing. I suppose there must have been. But from the back you could see, you know, you were trying to hold his hair on, and his skull on.

Mr. Rankin. Do you have any recollection of whether there were one or more shots?

380

Mrs. Kennedy. Well, there must have been two because the one that made me turn around was Governor Connally yelling. And it used to confuse me because first I remembered there were three and I used to think my husband didn't make any sound when he was shot. And Governor Connally screamed like a stuck pig. And then I read the other day that it was the same shot that hit them both. But I used to think if I only had been looking to the right I would have seen the first shot hit him, then I could have pulled him down, and then the second shot would have gotten Governor Connally. But I heard Governor Connally yelling and that made me turn around, and as I turned to the right my husband was doing that. He was receiving a bullet.

This can be compared with the printed page.

As there are changes not indicated in the published transcript, so also do they serve specific purposes, not merely to delete the non-existent "reference to wounds". They are not whimsical. This trickery with the sworn testimony is to protect the predetermined official mythological "explanation" of that assassination from its destruction by the widow. Because she was the widow, was the closest eyewitness, that destruction, at the time the Report was released, might well have been total and permanent.

My efforts to gain access to even an edited and censored "reference to wounds" by Mrs. Kennedy go back six years from the time, a month after its declassification, Rhoads sent me the withheld page. My first letter asking for it was written June 26, 1966. Although I was not then aware that lying is the way of official scholarship, the response had a generous supply of what now, clearly, are lies. To use more polite language is to deceive the reader and history. Two excerpts should suffice:

> The manuscript transcripts of testimony of witnesses among the records of the Commission are withheld from research because they contain matter deleted in the published Hearings for the reason that the Commission considered publication to be in poor taste or the information to be irrelevant to any facet of the Commission's investigation (Hearings, Vol. I, p. v.).

* * *

> The National Archives merely has custody of the records of the Commission and can make available only those records that have been cleared for research use. I should like to emphasize that it is our policy, and has consistently been our policy to provide access to researchers on a basis of complete equality.

The irrelevant comprises most of the published hearings. What is "in poor taste" is and always has been readily available, much of it published. Repeatedly I have had to be my own censor in masking what is in poor taste and the defamatory, such as allegations of homosexuality, in using the unrestricted. And even if a few of Mrs. Kennedy's graphic words might be misinterpreted as in poor taste, that is the nature of spontaneous testimony, as it is its importance. In any event, it is neither why her words were edited nor encompassed by the inserted description of what was suppressed.

The representation that the "Archives merely has custody of the records of the Commission and can make available only those records that have been cleared for research" is the most deliberate kind of duplicity and entirely misrepresents the reality, as the reader should remember. The Archives had and exercised the right and obligation to declassify the Commission's own records. It is only the records of other agencies that have to be "cleared for research" from outside the Archives. The Archives used its legal responsibility for political purposes, to suppress, and for propaganda, not for scholarship. Cases have been cited and we shall resume with one in what follows.

With the recounted history and with the month's delay in sending this one page to me, I was suspicious. I found myself wondering if it could be only by accident that this page was sent the first time I was working away from home in six months. Could it be no more than happenstance that I would be getting it in a flood of other accumulated mail and at a time when I would be deeply preoccupied with different work? Consistent with these doubts is the absence of a date of the letter, the only case I can remember in a truly enormous correspondence.

So, I made a word-by-word comparison of the suppressed page with the printed representation of it. Prior to any indication of any change, I found one that seems significant and, like all the others, is not in any way indicated in the published, altered version.

In the first sentence of the first of the two longer paragraphs, the published version has but two seemingly minor changes. The word "finally" was shifted. It alters completely what she was saying. It is made at best ambiguous when it was unequivocal. It is made to seem that she, or "a voice behind me" or "somebody" undescribed "finally knew something was wrong". And the tense is changed to make it seem that her recollection is of the time of her testimony, not the very instant of the crime. "Remembered" is changed to "remember". In saying what she actually said, "and then I remembered the people in the front seat finally" reacting, she is not criticizing the Secret Service agents but saying there was a longer interval between the time of the first shot and the time of reaction, "finally". She carried this further in the next paragraph, which confirms the unwelcome Connally and Kellerman testimony, meaning that the first shot was much earlier than officially admitted.

Rankin was typically cagey and misleading in his formulation of his question. He did not ask her how many shots she heard. Instead, he put it this way, attempting to influence her response: "Do you have any recollection of whether there were one or more shots?"

One of the changes appears to be legitimate. Mrs. Kennedy's use of "that" is meaningless without description. It was changed to what seems accurate. What the court reporter should have included in the transcript but did not was added. Her recollection is faulty, as this shows, because it had been changed by what "I read the other day". There was, of course, no interest in what she had read. The changed recollection is what officialdom desired. Thus, she is made to say what the existing pictures prove quite wrong, that she did not turn "to the right" until "my husband was doing this /indicating with hand at neck7". She turned much earlier. This is what the rest of the testimony on this suppressed page says.

She did not hear the first shot. And, what "made me turn around was Governor Connally yelling." This is what Connally and his wife swore to, that they had heard the first shot, as he could not if it had

hit him. Bullets do travel faster than sound. Connally remembers his
reaction to knowing the President has been hit and remembers being hit
separately and later. The Commission could not accept his testimony
and conclude as it did, so it did not accept his attestation, his
wife's, or this entirely confirmatory testimony by Mrs. Kennedy.

Skipping the remainder of that sentence for a moment, to present
it in proper context, the next, as edited and published, reads, "And
Governor Connally screamed." It is not considerations of good taste
that inspired censoring of the rest of that sentence. The accomplished
intent is to hide the clarity of her recollection and testimony and the
emphasis she placed on Connally's "scream" causing her to turn. She
described how he "screamed", "like a stuck pig". She emphasizes this
again toward the end of the paragraph, "But I heard Governor Connally
yelling and that made me turn around ..." She began the paragraph in
the same way, what "made me turn around was Governor Connally yelling".
Three times in the same paragraph she testified that what made her turn
around was not awareness of a bullet having been fired, but Connally
"yelling" and screaming "like a stuck pig".

And without having heard the first shot, how many were there?
What did she volunteer before Rankin's dishonest question designed to
persuade her to testify to fewer shots than she knew? She testified
there were four! There was the one she did not hear, the one that
made Connally yell; and "I remembered there were three."

Delay in questioning her, the manner of questioning her and
whatever she "read the other day" had the inevitable and intended effect. They "confused" her. As with Zapruder, whose recollection of
reality was changed from the uncongenial to the official, and as with
so many others, she was conditioned. As if her suffering were not
enough!

And the poor woman, treated like Pavlov's dogs, wound up thinking her clear recollection was wrong when it was not. She could not
understand how she could remember what was officially verboten until
"I read the other day that it was the same shot that hit them both"!
She, Governor and Mrs. Connally and the distraught and dedicated Kellerman, 100 percent of the close witnesses on this evidence, were correct. But correctness was not the desire of those who boasted "truth
is our only client". So incorrectness became correctness.

Just like Orwell said, only 20 years early.

Her distress is further reflected in another changed sentence.
She did not mean she wanted the Governor killed. What she actually
testified to is, "But I used to think if only I had been looking to the
right I would have seen the first shot hit him, then I could have pulled
him down, and then the second shot would have gotten Connally."

What her unaltered testimony really says and means, because she
had turned to the right before Frame 210, the first point at which the
Commission claims the President could have been hit, is that, if she
had been aware of the first shot, if she had heard it, instead of reacting to Connally's yelling, she might have saved the President from
being hit by the fourth and fatal one, from the only one she saw hit
("He was receiving a bullet").

The reader need not wonder about what was removed at the point
the Commission says "/Reference to wounds deleted/". It includes a
further reference to lack of immediate awareness or reaction "in the
front seat". But no reference to any wound, no description of any,
the purpose for which the closest eyewitness should have been questioned. In both versions, the honest and the altered, there is the
incomplete sentence not referring to Connally but a later time and
voice, "But someone yelling". In the published form, between this and
the bracketed insertion, there is only "I was just down and holding
him down", which is not what she testified. Her authentic words are,
"But just down holding him. I was trying to hold his hair on. But
from the front there was nothing. I suppose there must have been. But
from the back you could see, you know, you were trying to hold his hair

383

on, and his skull on."

Part of the skull had disappeared, as we have seen. Her intentness on having the President's head seem intact, which is understandable, may explain what happened before the head was exploded and "I was just down and holding him down": her unrecalled venture onto the trunk of the car, where Clint Hill may well have saved her life, almost at the cost of his own. Hill's belief, that she was trying to retrieve a piece of skull, makes as much sense as anything else. Subconsciously, in what must have been the most excruciatingly painful reliving, and emotionally, in agonized words that seem incoherent, she said more than the Commission wanted said.

"But from the front there was nothing" can mean that there was no flap of hair and skull for her to press back into an intact head. Two pieces were missing. The Commission was not anxious for this to be known, witness suppression of the Harper reports I discovered, and the continuing suppression of those pictures of the piece of skull. "From the back" here, I believe, means the piece of skull, from the back of the head.

The understandable repugnance comes through unintendedly in her depersonalizing of what she did, substituting for the personal pronoun: "you were trying to hold his hair on, and his skull on." There was no "you". She alone suffered that greatest of agonies.

Yet in a sense this subconscious misspeaking was apt. In a very real sense it was appropriate for her to formulate a charge against the Commission she had no reason to make, that it was "trying to hold his hair on, and his skull on", where there was none. And where all officialdom had to know there was none.

Figuratively and literally, this is true. Characterization of men who would do such a thing when a President is assassinated - and misuse his widow for such a purpose - is unnecessary. It is not necessary to attribute motive, either, for at this point there can be but one, and it is obvious.

Mrs. Kennedy did confirm that the President had been shot much earlier than the government could acknowledge and still pin a bum, no-conspiracy rap on Oswald and history. She did confirm the unwanted but unavoidable testimony of both Connallys and Kellerman, which also mean precisely this. She did remember it in a way irrefutably confirmed by the existing and misrepresented film - all of it that captured that scene. And what she testified she did is confirmed by this film and by all the testimony about what she did (WHITEWASH II, part III).

So her testimony had to be suppressed and distorted. This was a nobility of purpose and purity of soul to which the involved officials all could and did rise.

And it is all consistent with that medical evidence that had been suppressed and what this book now brings to light. That confirms her. So, she was distorted and suppressed, it was pretended that her testimony was edited for "taste" only, and the Report could issue. Had her testimony not been rearranged and suppressed, this could not have been dared.

If Malcolm Perry was not "terrified" before, he well might be now.

It came as somewhat of a surprise when, shortly after returning home, I learned that, contrary to what I had been told was Burke Marshall's assurance, he was granting what from the first seemed like exclusive access to the materials covered by the contract to a far-out character, the only one seeking access precluded by that contract.

Fred Graham phoned me on Thursday, January 6, telling me frankly that he wanted to "pick" my "mind about the Warren Commission Report. I am on very short notice trying to pull myself together as to minor detail and I can't recall what was said about it. And that is, it had to do with President Kennedy's brace. And his Ace bandage."

This told me whose tea leaves he was reading, for only one gypsy is on that white cloud.

"Here's why I'm asking about it," Fred continued. "They are finally going to, in the next few weeks, open up some of the material to pathologists. And they are accepting requests from pathologists who want to look at it."

"Are you a pathologist?" I asked. That he did not anger does not surprise, but what he volunteered did.

"No, I'm not a pathologist, but they will let people like me, not like me but they will let people who are not pathologists, who they consider have a legitimate reason, commission a pathologist to go and study the stuff. And they say that they don't limit to pathologists who represent people who agree with the Warren Report. In fact, Burke Marshall, who's in charge of this for the Kennedy family, assumes that anyone who wants to look into it does not agree with the Warren Report."

"Does not agree with the Warren Report"? Both Graham and Marshall knew better. But the first part was true. I am without doubt that there was then a plan to let Fred and the Times have access to this "stuff". That includes what the Archivist had personally sworn in court he could let nobody see when I sued for pictures of the clothing.

Fred was aware that the only one then approved was the only non-pathologist and the only known apologist among four medical applicants. He indicated as much in saying, "I'm not sure he's really going to act on this. This is just what he says. He is reserving the right to approve each one on a person-to-person basis."

Translation: Marshall, to Graham's knowledge, had rejected the applications of the three pathologists and approved the application of the only non-pathologist.

Fred was calling the applicants to ask what they wanted to see. One told him, "One of the things I want to see is the brace and the Ace bandage he was wearing because ... that's apparently what kept him from falling over after he was hit the first time."

This fingered the doctor even more and confirmed my previous belief that, with the assassinations, he is a witch doctor. If the President's brace could not keep him from sitting, it could not keep him from falling. And did not. He "fell over" in about a second after the so-called fatal shot, which is pretty fast. Having had lower-back trouble myself since 1939 and from long experience with a variety of such braces, I explained both points to Fred.

"Well, now, here's what the doctor told me. He said that the Ace bandage was wrapped around Kennedy's crotch ... over the brace to anchor the bottom of the brace ... passed through his crotch, around a buttock, back through the crotch, around the buttock, in a figure-8 pattern ... I can see no reason for this except to anchor a corset."

I explained that the Ace bandage could give mild support to the very bottom of the spine as no brace that permitted sitting could and that the one thing it was not needed for was to anchor the brace. Braces come equipped with soft, between-the-legs straps to keep them from riding up as the wearer moves.

Fred understood. I offered to show him an unpublished picture of the brace the President was wearing. "I see," he said. "Just imagine how tough it was talking around with an Ace bandage wrapped around your, uh, through your crotch and around your - Well, now, what I want to get at, and I think you have virtually answered it ..."

As our conversation continued I warned Fred that he had been "used" before in such an arrangement and was about to be used again. He wanted to know how, and I told him the story of the GSA-family contract, with its consequences. (We returned to this topic in a later conversation.) In confidence, I offered him access to my unprinted material, that which is in this book, to prepare him for questioning whoever saw the material.

"Well, now, if I'm gonna talk to, uh, when these people start going through," he started. I said, "If they do." He corrected me, "When they do. He's gonna let them see it." I asked who Marshall had decided to let see what. "Well, I don't know what. /It was "the material subject to that agreement."7 He says he has decided to open the material. Now, whether he is being selective, well, I don't know."

As we talked, he got a little defensive, for I knew from his first words what was afoot, although he did not realize it. "... they are letting pathologists, they say, doctors, anyway, go in there and look at these things ... what should I ask them when they get through?"

That, I said, depends on whom he questions.

"Well, the first one's gonna be Dr. John Lattimer."

Lattimer is a well-known urologist, a science that progresses no higher in the body than the navel and a man whose poorly-hidden politics derive their inspiration from Belmont, Massachusetts. I had been in correspondence with him and had copies of his scanty and irrelevant and meaningless work on the assassination of the President. It is sickeningly sycophantic and, like his politics, at no point in contact with reality.

So, I told Fred, "You should be familiar with the record he has to defend," and to this end I offered him my file, an offer he did not accept. I warned him to expect nothing but propaganda, a forecast as accurate and as easy as the prediction that the sun would rise.

When I asked the names of the other medical applicants, Graham repeated, "Lattimer is the only one who has been given permission." Of the other three, Cyril Wecht, John Nichols, a Kansas pathologist, and Forrest Chapman, Wayne County, Michigan, medical examiner, "Marshall says it /permission7 has not been denied, but it hasn't been granted, but it hasn't been granted or denied because, he says, he hasn't focused his mind on it yet." That Marshall had not "focused his mind" is beyond dispute unless one casts him in an evil role. But that without "focus" he had given access to the one man specifically excluded by the contract he signed also is beyond dispute. Perhaps it requires something other than "focus" to accredit the one who could not be accredited.

Fred did know enough to say of Lattimer, "... Here's what's gonna happen: ... He is gonna say it supports the conclusions." I agreed. So, Fred asked, "Well, in talking to him, though, how can I ask him questions about it that might uncover his apologetic, uh, position?"

Again I offered my files, without acceptance. Reading them, knowing some of what had been published and having enough experience in life to get into college should have been more than enough. The fact is that the average teenager should have been equal to that very easy task without reading anything.

Graham, who would not examine what I offered him, said, "I'm in the dark about how intelligently to debrief someone like Dr. Lattimer after he sees the stuff because I don't know where the residual flaws are." He forgot he had reviewed Inquest and WHITEWASH. I encouraged him to speak to Wecht and gave him each of Cyril's numerous telephone numbers. So, Fred said, "Well, listen; we'll keep in touch, and I'll get to Wecht. That's a good idea."

A short while later I thought of something I should have told Fred and phoned him. He then told me he knew when Lattimer was going to see the material but in his own interest could not tell me. This is true. It would have risked throwing away a "scoop", even though I knew enough to do that, had I the intent. Not entirely consistent with what he had said earlier, Graham admitted of Lattimer, "Now, I have a feeling that Lattimer was given the go-ahead for this because he is, as you say, an apologist, and, you see, his reaction will get more public notice than Wecht." This is to admit that the press is a partisan, not a reporter.

"Let's leave it," Fred said. "I'll have a talk with you, as I said. You'll - in the course of things, I'm gonna write a piece about some of this, and then we'll put our heads together and see where we stand then; okay?"

Our heads did not get together. He did write a "piece". As he then knew, Lattimer was to be at the Archives the next day, a Friday. As Fred later told me, he knew (even before Lattimer knew) that Lattimer was getting what amounts to exclusive access to this long-suppressed material, what amounts to a private copyright on public information if Lattimer had the knowledge, ability or courage to exploit it.

Graham's "exclusive" appeared on Sunday the ninth, beginning on the front page. Not knowing when what would happen but anticipating that it involved still another violation of the regulations, I immediately wrote the Archivist and the appeals officer of GSA. In time, both reacted. It took the Archivist two weeks. He responded first.

Considering that it was an international scoop and on a subject so long so controversial, the editors of the Sunday Times, with all the space they have, did not play it as long or as hard as they could have. They gave it about 50 column inches, including the most modest headlines. About a third of this space was devoted to two illustrations. One is a sketch, Exhibit 385; the other, a photograph of unintended appropriateness, Lattimer pointing to his head.

One more willing to conceive of conspiracies might take a sinister view of Fred's writing. No one knowing the fact can call it honest, in intent or in formulation. There are clear departures from normal journalistic practice. There is studied but artificial "objectivity". This includes the straight and unquestioned presentation of what Fred knew was not true, and what he had to know was not credible, not even rational. We discussed this later. One willing to consider him a devious man intent upon preservation of all the falsehoods in the official account of how the President was assassinated would have little difficulty believing he had used me as a sounding board to eliminate in advance as much as possible of the error inevitable in anything the under-informed and over-opinionated Lattimer could and would say.

The story opens with what, from our earlier conversation, has to be considered a nonaccidental misstatement, that it is "the family of the late President" which "has not begun to let interested medical specialists /sic7 see the items."

In no proper sense is Lattimer a "medical specialist". His field is one totally detached from the medical evidence of the assassination, the President's urinary system not being involved in any way. And as Fred himself had told me - in fact, as the contract specifies - it is Marshall, and not the family, who made the decision. Marshall is the representative of the executors of the estate, which is not even the same thing as saying he represents the family.

Lattimer is then described as a "physician" rather than a urologist, which makes it less inconceivable that he should be the first and then only one to see this evidence. It also hides what Fred knew, that the contract precludes his having access under any circumstances. This is followed by the gross exaggeration, again not possibly accidental, that Lattimer has "written and lectured extensively about the assassination". There is absolutely nobody in the world who had done either and done less of either. And in no case is any of it relevant. It begins with the assumption of the total infallibility of the Report.

The impossibility that then follows is what achieved international attention, Lattimer's assertion that the pictures and X-rays, of which he neither meant nor mentioned the important ones, "'eliminate any doubt completely' about the validity of the Warren Commission's conclusion that Lee Harvey Oswald fired all the shots that struck the President."

Relatively minor after this is the glaring omission, also well known to Graham and to everyone at the Times, that Oswald also had to have inflicted a total of five wounds on Governor Connally.

387

No dishonesty on such a subject is minor except in relation to other points. However, the "conclusion" in question is on page 19 of the Report. It reads, "The shots which killed President Kennedy and wounded Governor Connally were fired by Lee Harvey Oswald." (Emphasis added.) Neither Graham nor Lattimer could have checked and missed this. Nor could either have honestly avoided the "missed" shot, which was fired and caused a slight wound to James Tague. The Commission's and Lattimer's conclusion is that Oswald fired all the shots that were fired, not just those "that struck the President", Lattimer's understatement.

No matter what magical powers are attributed to these misrepresented pictures and X-rays, and no matter what scientific skills and expertise are attributed to the expert on some body wastes and nothing else, it requires no medical training, none in the law, which Graham has, no experience as a reporter, nothing except a modicum of common sense to know that no pictures or X-rays, separately or combined, can show who fired what shots.

I wrote Fred, Marshall and Lattimer asking how this could happen. The closest thing to a response was Fred's: "Let's don't beat that to death." When I asked him how he could possibly write this, he called that a "loaded question". But the simple fact, comprehension of which does not require even ownership of the poorest camera ever made, is that Lattimer and Graham knew and had to know this to be falsehood, not even respectable mythology.

Neither they nor the Times editors who handled the story were troubled or asked any question. Nor did any other editor of whom I know. Suddenly there was no wire-service copy editor, no rewrite man, no proofreader, no editor in the entire country who could ask the simple question, "How can this be?"

Those familiar with my work know I have felt from the beginning that, without the collaboration of the suddenly uncritical press, this shabby farce of a Report on a fake inquest could never have been foisted off on the survivors and the people. So, to the degree possible, I have undertaken to collect press accounts. Most stories were lifted from the Times.

And most headlined this falsification. Here are some examples:

Philadelphia Inquirer: "Oswald Sole Assassin, Doctor Says"

London Daily Express: "'No Doubt' That Oswald Killed Kennedy"

Washington Post: "Expert Says Oswald Alone Shot JFK"

Newsday: "JFK Data Points to Oswald: Doctor"

Berkeley (California) Gazette: "The JFK Assassination: 'It Was Oswald'"

Dallas Morning News: "JFK Photos Uphold Verdict, Doctor Says"

Daily News (New York): "Sees Kennedy X-rays, Backs Warren Study"

Long Island Press: "X-rays Confirm Oswald Was Alone, Medic Says"

Omaha World: "Shots Fatal to JFK Were All Oswald's"

Norwalk (Connecticut) Hour: "X-rays End Doubt, Avers Expert"

These headlines are not an unfair representation of what the papers got from The New York Times and other wire services. The first paragraph of UPI's story says, "Lee Harvey Oswald alone fired the fatal shots," even though Lattimer had no interest in the cause of death and is not quoted on it except to call one picture "horrible". Reuters gave its international subscribers this in its first paragraph, "Lee Harvey Oswald fired all the shots which struck and killed the President." AP's lead said, "'Eliminate any doubt completely' ... that Lee Harvey Oswald shot all the bullets that hit President Kennedy." All quoted Lattimer. This is what he said. And were it true, as it cannot be, it still does not prove the Report correct.

Graham said that there were "65 X-rays, color transparencies and black-and-white negatives", which, as the reader now knows, is not accurate and not complete. Of these, he said what he knew is false, because I did tell him of the parts of this and my other work which prove otherwise, "...because the Kennedy family guarded them so closely that they were not allowed to be seen even by the members and staff officials of the Warren Commission." Over and above what I told him, he knew this to be false. As a lawyer, if not also as a reporter who wrote much on the subject, he knows there was no way in the world this evidence could have been denied the Commission had it wanted or even asked for it. And, as I have now established, Commission and staff did have it.

If this was not enough for the "get Kennedy" cabal inside the executive branch, what followed helped: "It has been officially explained that the photographs were suppressed to avoid anguish to the family." Not so. It is the unofficial self-defense of those responsible. To twist the shiv he added a later paragraph reading, "Shortly after the assassination, the autopsy pictures and X-rays were given to the President's brother, the late Robert Kennedy, then the Attorney General. On Oct. 29, 1966, they were placed by the Kennedy family in the National Archives ..."

No single statement here quoted is true. It was not "shortly after the assassination", nor was it even shortly after the end of the Warren Commission. It was the year after the Commission ceased to exist and the second year after the assassination. They were not "given to the President's brother" but to Evelyn Lincoln, at the National Archives, for a branch of the National Archives, the Kennedy Library. Until then, the Secret Service had them, as here shown for the first time. On October 29 they were not "placed by the Kennedy family in the National Archives" for they were already there. And it was not "placement" but transfer of legal title, whether or not in all cases held.

Lattimer's ignorance and self-justification are then retailed as fact: "The Warren Commission might have made a stronger case if the staff personnel who prepared its report had had access to the pictures and X-rays." In fact, they did.

If nothing else, Graham's failure to "keep in touch" or "put our heads together" led him to accept one of Lattimer's deliberate dishonesties, the deliberateness of which will become apparent, that the "distinctly downward angle" of the so-called rear, nonfatal shot, was "more than was shown by the schematic drawings released by the Warren report". These drawings, as Lattimer knew, are not the basis of the Commission's conclusion, right or wrong. They are his straw man, his creation for self-glorification, for an immature attempt to validate his own earlier published and permeating error. The Commission's conclusions are based on other evidence, including testimony, as he was to admit to a later questioner.

"... the pictures show that the front hole is considerably lower than the one in the back" is one way of not saying there exists no picture of the hole in the front from the front, the only one that can really show it. Lattimer admitted this, too, when questioned by an impartial reporter.

"... photographs of the rear wound show 'what appears to be a circular bruise which is typical of wounds of entry,' he said." Now, what kind of doctor is it who cannot be sure of a bruise when he sees it in full color? But more importantly, bruising can also occur in wounds of exit, although atypical, while it is typical of wounds of entrance. And there was what he fails to mention, bruising of the front hole.

"Third, the X-rays prove that the front and rear holes were made by the same bullet ... left two tiny flakes of metal and air in the tissues along the path between the holes."

There is no path shown by the X-rays, and the fact is, bullet tracks through soft tissue are not discernible in X-rays. There is no innocence in admission of the presence of metal. However he describes this, it is guilty knowledge on Lattimer's part if he knows any of the evidence on which he, without false modesty if by false pretense, presents himself as an expert.

"Dr. Lattimer was also allowed to see other items that have been shown to only a few persons but have not been absolutely hidden from nongovernment experts. These include the President's bloody and bullet-ridden clothing ..." Graham knew this was false, knew that Rhoads had sworn in court that he was prohibited from doing this, and that I had sued for access and been denied it for this reason.

He then got to the invention unique to Lattimer about which Fred had telephoned me. He handled it other than Lattimer had as quoted by every other source, saying that the brace and bandage appear "to have little importance in the slaying but gives a revealing insight into the discomfort Kennedy suffered". Attributing it to Lattimer, not to me, Graham then said of the bandage, "Its purpose was to help support the lower spine." This is opposite to what Lattimer says, which is "that it could also have kept him upright after he was hit by the first bullet, so that he was exposed to the second". This is also what Lattimer had decided in advance and no viewing of the objects themselves can address.

Quoting Lattimer again (he did everything except discover America and invent sex), "His finding that a round from such a weapon would penetrate 47 inches of pine wood ..." This is not Lattimer's; it is the uncredited work of John Nichols. And it is irrelevant to what happens in flesh and bone. All valid experiments prove the 6.5 bullet, whether or not used in the assassination, could not penetrate the bodies as it is alleged to have done. Lattimer knows nothing about the work in the field if he does not know that. It was never accomplished by any expert for the government and CBS admitted it could not duplicate the alleged degree of penetration through flesh.

Of the Clark panel report, Lattimer pontificated that, because it is in "technical language", it "understated the extent to which the items corroborate the Warren Report". As Fred had said, "let's not beat that to death."

Perhaps something pricked Graham's conscience for even his mention of me, for what reason I do not know, is not accurate. After correctly quoting me in the last paragraph as categorizing Lattimer as no more than "an apologist for the Warren Commission", Fred had me asking a question I could have asked but did not, "What does a urologist know about bullet holes in human bodies?" What actually happened is that, after speaking with Wecht, as I had urged, Fred quoted him to me as asking only, "What does a urologist know about bullet holes?" I am confident Cyril did not have in mind bullet holes in tin cans, targets, tree-trunks or anything like that. So, I told Fred that Cyril must have meant, as a forensic pathologist would and in the sense of forensic-pathological interest, in human bodies, as studied for medico-legal purposes.

CBS alone of the TV networks went for Lattimer and his propaganda. I would not think of suggesting that there is any connection between this and CBS's own record in its still-exceptional four hours of prime time in support of the official version. But with this Friday story written on Saturday and printed by the competition Sunday morning, CBS was not content to feature the story Sunday night on TV and all day on radio. It was one of the few filmed items fed the entire network Monday morning, the only "second day" story of which I know. Not even the Times, whose "beat" it was, ran a follow-up. When CBS goes, it goes big. It also gave Lattimer a press conference Sunday night. For that only one of the better studios would do, the "CBS Reports" studio. This is the true impartiality in "news" - giving it to all the competition.

CBS's competitors/guests got little they did not read in the Times. Some were even less questioning than Graham. The Long Island Press, for example, had no question when Lattimer said what the Warren Commission could not, which bullet did what. Of the "first" bullet and its allegedly steeper downward angle? How did Lattimer learn that? "He said he reached the conclusion after inspecting X-rays and the suit, shirt and tie worn by the President." Now, even for so eminent a scientist and open-minded an "investigator" as Lattimer, this is no mean feat. It is impossible for the X-rays to show the points of entrance and exit in soft tissue. The rear holes in the shirt and jacket are inches lower than the alleged point of exit in the front of the neck. There is no cloth in the front of the jacket to show where a bullet could have gone out. In even Lattimer's version, the trajectory from back to front on the shirt is consistent with those computerized at Cape Kennedy, befitting a moon shot, not a "distinctly downward angle". The tie? Need one consider more than Lattimer's silence about what has happened to it?

There is as little limit to Lattimer's "science" as there is to the credulity of an unquestioning press. Example: "I know from my own experiments that Oswald was a perfectly competent marksman." With Oswald dead long before the beginning of these "experiments"? The Marines, who trained and then tested the living Oswald, rated him a "rather poor" shot. Lattimer improved on the Marines. He used the ghost of the dead Oswald in his experiments to prove him "a perfectly competent marksman". Is there any other way to prove Oswald's rifle capabilities "experimentally"?

Before seeing the X-rays, according to UPI, Lattimer "had doubts about certain points". In Newsday's formulation, this "removed previous reservations he had" about the Report. "He had had some reservations before" is the way the Daily News put it. AP was consistent: "removed previous reservations." One of thse alleged doubts - and I say "alleged" after going over all of Lattimer's few writings on the assassination - is given in Lattimer's own words by Robert Wetherington in the Daily News: had the President been "struck down by a single assailant".

Or, did Oswald alone do the dirty deed?

This is what Fred Graham smoothed out in that headline-making paragraph, the "doubt" not previously "eliminated", whether "Lee Harvey Oswald fired all the shots".

In his featured appearance on CBS TV's morning news the next day, Lattimer opened with the contrived confession that "I think we've all sort of had a feeling of insecurity about whether the Warren Commission was really telling the truth" and a generality about "fact" that in his opinion "would show up on these photographs and X-rays". Having seen them, he presented not one such "fact". He reported only what he had earlier written and wanted believed, whether or not true. It is a virtuoso display of inadequate knowledge of the evidence, limited understanding of the Report, plus deliberate misrepresentation of what that Report does say. For this exalted, scientific purpose, he invented what he had not told Graham or what Graham had been too shrewd to print:

"... I think that the most immediate and obvious thing, point of interest, that I observed was the fact that the one-bullet track that was alleged, y'know, to have gone into the back of President Kennedy's neck and then come out the front and then gone on through Governor Connally, was, indeed, in a position where it seemed much more believable than I had been led to believe by the drawing which was in the Warren Commission Report."

The drawings, as we have seen, are his favorite contraption. What to him is "more believable" is not evidence he saw in this autopsy film. He neither saw nor could see that one bullet had entered the back, or the President's neck, exited the front, and then done all that damage to Connally.

CBS's David Culhane asked if his conclusion after seeing the autopsy film is "that the Warren Commission saying that there was one assassin is true", which is pretty good cue-feeding. Lattimer responded in his longest single uninterrupted answer. It contains no single reference to any of this long-withheld evidence he had just seen. First he said "yes", then added, "I think there's no credible evidence for other assassins and there's plenty of evidence that the rifle that Oswald had did, indeed, fire this bullet ..."

This is not and cannot be in the autopsy film, nor can it in any way be proven or reflected or even suggested by that film. Lattimer expanded on this, falsely and without interruption, working himself up to where he even said, "nobody argues about it." A more total and deliberate falsehood is impossible.

Then he went into "three empty cartridges". These are not in the material covered by the contract, what he had just seen. His ignorance of them is so great that all he could say of them is that they "conform to the type used by Oswald". With no less precision and without ever having been to the Archives, he could have said this of millions and millions of cartridges. Lattimer then referred to what does not exist and what he had not seen, "his handprint on the rifle". This also is not covered by the contract. From this, he launched into a really zany invention calculated to argue that planting the bullet was impossible (a later expansion on this device is more quotable), again, not from what he had just seen.

If "there was nothing to indicate a transverse bullet passage", neither is there a responsible critic who ever said the President had been shot from side-to-side. Having created a new straw man, Lattimer shot him down: "and, of course, again, this is one of the things that people have conjectured."

People also conjectured a shot had been fired from the front, a vagrant truth from Lattimer. Of this he said, "I, myself, sat on the box where Oswald fired from," a falsehood made more explicit in a later talk-show appearance and an impossibility, for that box was immediately removed and was never returned. Continuing with what is irrelevant to his alleged "examination" of this precious evidence made possible just for him, he alleged that, having gone onto the grassy knoll and the railroad trestle, "I can't see how any skilled marksman would assume such a position". This is to say that no "skilled marksman" would prefer a level, straight-on shot when he could elect a difficult, through-a-tree, steeply downward angle at a target moving in an "S" pattern and away. No duffer does not know better. He rambled along with embellishments of this fantasy until even CBS had to interrupt him. But not one word of this "new evidence" did he, even by accident, utter for the CBS audience.

Culhane fed him more lines that added up to only Oswald firing. "Right. Exactly," Lattimer told him. Lattimer then launched into the pretense that he had been his own devil's advocate and sought what was contrary to his and the Commission's view. That really turned him on. He got so carried away with his newest fiction that he said, "And after spending the entire day /his emphasis/ going over these things with a fine-tooth comb, backward and forward and plaguing the poor men at the National Archives to re-run and re-view and 'let me see it again' and 'here's something I didn't register the first time' /sic/ which they all did with great patience, which they all did in a locked room, and so forth, I couldn't find anything wrong."

After this, all CBS could say is, "It's now 16 minutes before the hour." I can say more.

He did not, despite his emphasis, spend "the entire day" in that "locked room and so forth". It was, according to the Archivist, a total of only four hours.

Now what is he - what can he be - talking about, plaguing those "poor" people to "re-run", "backward and forward", what "didn't register the first time"? This cannot describe individual sheets of film, whether transparencies, prints or X-rays. It refers to movies. No movies are in this sequestered material!

This is a remarkable self-revelation by Lattimer, a disclosure that he had never done the most basic research, what numberless young people have done to get an understanding of how the President was killed. He did not until then study the Zapruder film or other movies? What more does it take to be accredited as a real expert to Burke Marshall, or to the Archivist, custodian of the film and keeper of the records on it?

Despite his eminence in medicine and the high position he holds at Columbia University, Lattimer is not really very bright. As late as the end of 1968, which is _five years after the assassination_ and after he had published what he had to say on the subject, he admitted to Sylvia Meagher that he "did not even see the motion picture to which you refer", Zapruder's.

So, when at long last somebody had a chance to look at the deep secrets, Burke Marshall's pick looks at old movies, talks about what he did not have to have permission to see, like the movies, rifle and cartridges, none of which had been hidden or are covered by the contract, and has still no single word of fact for the people on what the suppressed evidence he alone could see proves of how their President was killed.

It is almost awe-inspiring how Lattimer can talk about nothing except the preconceptions of his own under-informed and over-opinionated mind - and with _that_ makes the international front page.

Lattimer is less than a model of precision. Forgetting the fundamental requirement of the Report, that one bullet inflicted _all_ seven nonfatal injuries, blithely blabbing away about it, "this bullet", he conceded that it could have hit "maybe just Connally alone". As the reader by now knows, in itself, this means at least a fourth shot and a conspiracy, whether or not Oswald was part of it.

This is opposite to what Graham and the _Times_ reported and everyone else repeated without question.

That night Lattimer appeared on the Long John Nebel Show in New York. (Jerry Policoff taped and transcribed it.) Here he repeated, "I was able to sit on the actual box in the actual window." This is another way of saying, "I believe whatever pops into my mind."

He began by saying his interest in the JFK assassination was triggered by an existing interest in that of Lincoln, "and it was so striking that the two events were parallel in so many ways." How much more "striking" a "parallel" can there be than conspiracy in Lincoln's and no conspiracy in JFK's, his view?

When there was criticism of the Warren Report, why this was "to my amazement"; in fact, criticism of the government "was very upsetting" to him. Thus, the Lattimer concept of a free, representative society. And "parallels".

But, he claims, even after the completion of his "research" (which actually consisted of no more than rifle practice with his sons), "I must say that I had considerable doubts," and these related to the possibility of whether more than one shooter was involved.

He then told Nebel, as he had told others, that "the rear hole ... is quite far above the front hole".

(Of course, he saw no "front hole", as the reader knows. On January 24 he was questioned by a competent reporter, Art Kevin, of Radio Station KHJ, Hollywood, California. Kevin got him to admit of the front wound, "It is no longer visible as such.")

Aside from this, necessary to keep his stuff from being laughed off the pages of the medical journals in which it had appeared, "the other thing I looked for, uh, to try and be sure, uh, that, uh, what I presumed to be correct was indeed correct was, uh, any sign that a bullet might have traveled through President Kennedy's body in a transverse direction ... from the side."

In his quest for self-justification, from his own words, two things only interested him, _neither_ having to do with the cause of death, determination of which is the purpose of the autopsy and the purpose for which the film he saw had been exposed.

Lattimer was honest and direct on one point: He is utterly and completely unqualified in pathology. This all his appearances do confirm, as does everything he had written. He describes what he calls his "capabilities" thus: "I was on the spot and that I am able to fire

393

the rifle, uh, in, you know, demonstrations."

By "on the spot" Lattimer does not mean at the time of the crime. Like millions of other Americans, he went to Dallas. And he can fire a rifle. How many Americans, by Lattimer's self-certification, are not as least as expert as he? They are in the millions!

Oh, Lattimer is indeed a very special expert. He has, he says, Oswald's Marine "rifle scorebook", "which demonstrates that he was a thoroughly competent marksman ... able to score 48, 49 of a, out of a possible 50 points." This is a very special score, for Oswald never did anything like that kind of shooting, as the Marines certified to the Commission (19H16-8). At his very best, Oswald did no better than what is expected of "most Marines". And the last time he was tested, he was, by grade alone, a "rather poor 'shot'". When it is considered that he was at the very bottom of the lowest grade, it can be understood how really lousy a shot Oswald was. What this invention establishes is not Oswald's but Lattimer's "capabilities".

Lattimer babbled on like a polluted stream. There was none of the clear water distilled from his examination of this precious evidence, not here as not anywhere else. Nothing but his preconceptions and the bland assertion that the Report is right because it says it is right and he is right because he says he is. Evidence and relevance are below his science.

However, his explanation of the "proof" that Oswald was the lone assassin is worth direct quotation:

"Uh, I see no possible way that anyone could have fired a bullet into a bale of cotton, let's say 10 feet thick, uh, recovered the bullet - you know, it takes you hours to find a bullet like that when you're digging it out - run around to where they anticipated that Kennedy and Connally might be, broken through the security guards, and deposited the bullet where it might be found. That ... this is just foolish to think that this could be done. Therefore, I think that there's no doubt at all that Oswald, uh, fired that bullet. I guess that's pretty conclusive to me."

Foolish it is. Thinking it is not. Conclusive it might be, on Lattimer's rationality as well as his claimed firearms expertise. It is not necessary to tote any 10-foot bales. A variety of means are used for the immediate recovery of test bullets, not 10-foot bales of cotton; such things as mattresses and watertanks. But who says that if there had been a conspiracy it would have been of the rabidly insane only? Of those who would await completion of the crime before preparing false evidence about it? Or who would await the coming of "security guards" in so enormous a hospital with so many entrances - and employees - before getting the bullet inside the building.

This is a medical dimwit so dull he cannot even invent reasonable fiction. What compelled him to invent it at all when he was supposed to be talking about this quintessential evidence he had just seen remains a mystery, as it does that anyone in any element of the media did not once ask, "But tell me, doctor, what does the evidence you saw show? Of what does it consist? How does it address the cause of death?" And many other such simple and direct statements that would not have been lacking on the other side or on any other subject.

Lattimer followed this fairy tale with another of his positive statements, again entirely unrelated to what he had seen or to the subject of the interview: "Oswald shot a policeman, Officer Tippit, uh, without any doubt." More, these "bullets that he fired into Officer Tippit undoubtedly came from the gun that was found on Oswald when they captured him." This is perhaps the most scientific representation yet of the FBI's statement that it could not make any ballistics connection between that pistol and any bullet recovered from Tippit's body (R172).

This is a good time to examine Lattimer's care in his research.

Four and a half years after the assassination, after his writing that we will examine, he asked Sylvia Meagher, "Do you know anything about the location and nature of the fatal wounds of Officer Tippit? I have not had time to dig for this, but if you should happen to come across any description of the wounds or data as to where I might find it, I would certainly appreciate this."

If Lattimer read the Report, he found the 20 pages on the Tippit shooting (156ff.) entirely other than he represents. He would not have found this essential data in it. Perhaps Lattimer would not find this strange. I did, so I did the obvious thing. I went to hhe Archives and bought the Tippit autopsy. For pennies I got it with an assortment of related Secret Service reports. So, what kind of "expert" is Lattimer, what kind of work has he done, when first he has his conclusions, then he confesses his ignorance, ignorance of the most elemental kind of research, and by then has not yet learned that all he had to do was write a letter to the Archives?

What can be "without any doubt" to him becomes comprehensible.

One could write a long study of the puerile scrivenings to which this man has appended his name. Because of the importance of his medical position, one might also hope that in medicine his methods and understanding are other than they are about assassinations.

More than anything else, his integrity, too.

Let us first address all those alleged doubts about Oswald being the lone assassin, whether there could have been a conspiracy, continuing, as Lattimer put it, until he saw this material covered by the contract.

In the Journal of the American Medical Association dated October 24, 1966, his opening sentence reads, "Had it not been for a pair of remarkable coincidences, the assassin, Lee Harvey Oswald, would not have been able to kill President John F. Kennedy." There is no equivocation here, no troubling doubt, none of the later-contrived false pretense to justify his getting access to this evidence. It says Oswald was the lone assassin. That, in fact, is precisely the wording of Morton Mintz's review in The Washington Post of two days later: "It was Oswald and Oswald alone who killed the President."

Here also Lattimer addresses that which he sought to find justifiable in this evidence, his weird notions about the brace and bandage he had emphasized to Graham:

"The unfortunate consequence of this arrangement was that after he had been struck by the first bullet, he did not topple or crumple forward or laterally where he would have been out of sight."

For this reason only, one of the "remarkable coincidences" Lattimer loves, was the President killed.

Lattimer's October speech to the International College of Surgeons appears in the December 1968 issue of International Surgery. Here he "validates" the single-bullet theory - none of those later-alleged doubts - by a simple and unscientific confusion: between the number of fragments (by his incomplete and unscientific count) and their weight.

All the competent doctors testified that there was more metal missing from 399 than could be accounted for in Governor Connally's body alone. Aside from what was not accounted for, such as the metal in his chest, what was washed out at the hospital and what could have fallen out, there was no acknowledgment of the fifth of what could be claimed to be missing from it, automatically removed by the act of firing, and of the weight of the two samples removed for spectrographic examination. The latter two factors can and probably do account for 100 percent of what can be alleged to be missing from Bullet 399. But there is no doubt that all the doctors described it as impossible and inconceivable for this bullet to have caused those seven nonfatal wounds, leading to the Specter substitution of a hypothesis described earlier.

In each and every case, these doctors were talking about the amount of metal, not the number of fragments. So, Lattimer got a similar bullet, squeezed it in a vise, which cannot be compared with what happens in firing, took what he squeezed out and, using laboratory equipment, sliced it into 41 tiny pieces. From this he concluded the utterly irrelevant, that the "four fragments which the Warren Commission contends ... are by no means excessive since these experimenters were able to slice 41 fragments" from the piece they squeezed out.

It did not trouble Lattimer and sons that bullets do not get laboratory-sliced in hitting a human, that the alleged bullet was designed to prevent what he did with his slicer, and, worst of all, that until this very moment it has not been connected with either victim.

Some people slice baloney. Lattimer prefers leads. It is all the same.

If either of these unworthy trivialities can be called serious writing, the stuff with which Lattimer touted himself and the uncritical press anointed him expert, it exhausts his "serious" writing on the JFK assassination. By even these standards the rest of his stuff is peripheral. Medical World News of December 12, 1969, rehashed his baloney science, adding a picture of Lattimer standing by his own sketch of what he then alleged happened with this single bullet. What is labeled as "bullet path" is up to a 45 degree downward angle. The rest of the disqualification need not concern us. This is already too much. But it surely does account for his straw man of the Report's "drawing". The Report is explicit enough in the text, which is not subject to such interpretations as Lattimer distorted. Rightly or wrongly, it says (p.106), "the probable angle through the President's body was calculated at 17°43'30"."

So, with a 100 percent error coming from not having even used his basic sources to begin with, and with that imperishably preserved in this medical journal, Lattimer's fabrication in his appearances is comprehensible, as is his gross misrepresentation of what he alleges to have seen. He compounded this in his press conference with a new deceptive sketch, pictures of which were distributed nationwide by both AP and UPI. In it he shows what he falsely represents as the Commission's trajectory, the one he describes as "too parallel", or almost flat, and the one he says he "saw" without the front hole any longer existing! Thus he exploited the Kennedy name and the national integrity in the futility of trying to validate his compulsive foolishness in Medical World News. It troubled him naught that he now placed the bullet higher than it could possibly have been by any account, in the neck itself, as his own words repeatedly did.

Although he seems to resent it, Lattimer is not held in awe by the entire medical world. The March 17, 1970, issue of the same publication carries two mildly critical letters. Part of his reply is more appropriate elsewhere. None of it is factual or credible on this point. And on those later-invoked alleged lingering doubts and uncertainties, "experiment as I will, I am unable to discredit the Warren Commission data on these points." He repeats that Oswald is the lone assassin.

The earliest and longest of Lattimer's writing was presented to the annual meeting of the Medical Society of the State of New York, on February 14, 1966. Publication was in the society's Journal dated July 1. With what was not intended as levity, it is titled "Similarities in Fatal Woundings of John Wilkes Booth and Lee Harvey Oswald". I do not want the reader to wonder whether I ridicule without reason, so I do not keep it secret that, albeit with typical subtle anti-Semitism, Lattimer says that Jack Ruby without doubt killed Oswald. The "similarity" begins with the concession that Booth may have been a suicide! Other "similarities"? Booth was shot with "a percussion-cap weapon", .44 caliber, Oswald with a .38 modern bullet; Booth got it in the neck, Oswald in the gut; both were "shot down deliberately" (even if Booth were a suicide?) and "while in the glare of bright lights provided by their captors /the TV crews held Oswald captive?/ and by persons acting against orders or against the law". Perhaps it is best that we not seek an order to Ruby not to kill Oswald, fragile as these "similarities" are!

But the real killer, the self-assassin in this case, is Lattimer's own concluding words, his purple-passionate best.

It may give perspective and insight into the man to quote the language with which he pretended to dismiss the excellent work of Sylvia Meagher, a work with which, like a number of others, Lattimer can not coexist. He faulted her first for "the vigor and extreme enthusiasm with which", as he saw it, she "subscribed to the campaign against the Warren Report". Unable to find defect in her "unique and valuable documentation in the field of documentation of the Report", which is hardly a rational description of her destruction of it, he expressed a personal preference for what to him is "an unvarnished manner, rather than too much emotion or bias".

His own concluding words in the Medical World News letter, naturally, to his taste, "unvarnished", without "emotion or bias", are:

Oswald showed what the educated, modern-day, traitorous guerrilla can do among his own people - working with religious-type conviction, willing to lay down his life, but proposing to kill as many anti-communists as possible. Oswald was devious, skilled at his business, and amazingly cool.

How better portray a man who had not completed high school and could not spell simple words than "educated"? How better describe one who hated both Russian and American Communists than "traitorous guerrilla" and all that?

Or what better a self-portrait of the man of reason, science and pure research, as he described himself to the International Surgeons, "uninvolved"?

If anyone could find this better way, Lattimer is that man. It is in his "summary" of the "similarities" in the Oswald and Booth killings:

While both shootings may well have been the work of excited men in attacking what they considered to be a national enemy, there are many sophisticated observers who regard this point as being unduly naive. They believe that since both accused presidential assassins were active enemy sympathizers (Booth for the Confederacy and Oswald for the Communists)33,34 and since both shootings took place during an era of large-scale undercover operations, psychological persuasions, philosophic rivalry and intelligence activity, that both men may have been silenced as part of a larger design.

The two footnotes are falsehoods that bear on Lattimer's rationality, the politics he tries to hide, and his honesty. The first reads, "Oswald renounces his U.S. citizenship;" the second, "Oswald pledges allegiance to USSR." References are to the 26 volumes which say no such thing. Oswald was careful not to revoke his citizenship and not to pledge allegiance to the USSR. Why else did the State Department bring him back, advancing all costs? If Lattimer did not know this, he knows nothing.

This is the polite variant of the extreme of the radical right, the parallel of the anti-Semitic verbosity of "Rubenstein" for the man who changed his name to Ruby, an irrelevancy, at best. It is consistent with membership in several superpatriotic groups among the many to which this joiner belongs. It is not consistent with the kind of man to whom one would expect either the Kennedys or the man who acts in their name, Burke Marshall, would entrust his honor or theirs. One can only wonder how Marshall dredged him up. Marshall refused to say when I asked him a series of relevant questions. Instead - and apparently unaware of the offers made by the government - to Graham and repeatedly to me, he parried by saying, "I am not aware that you have the medical qualifications necessary," no more.

That Lattimer does not "have the medical qualifications necessary" under the contract concerned neither Marshall nor Lattimer, who bragged that he does not. And in response, if it can be called a response, to the pertinent questions I asked him, Lattimer contented himself with this:

> The only way I can answer your many questions will be by sending you reprints, so that the record will be kept straight. I will do this as soon as they become available, which will, incidentally, be quite a while.

If ever!

Lattimer and those of his twisted political view of life and events have the subtlety of a back-alley fishmonger hawking aging wares. I learned this of him earlier when, in response to a few pointed questions about the drivel he had written, he thanked me for the "enthusiasm" of my letter - and said nothing else. They love flattery, live on and for it, imagine it when it does not exist, and cannot abide the asking of any question. With this previous experience, I had a young friend write him from a university. It was a sycophantic letter couched in the polite cliches of those of Lattimer's apparent politics.

Instead of the brief paragraph of nonresponse to a writer - and he did undertake public responsibilities in first seeing this evidence and then giving it international misrepresentation - he gushed right back to the student with three single-spaced typewritten pages!

I asked that he be asked the source of his Bircher-style quotation of "many sophisticated observers", continuously phrased in the plural. With 34 footnotes for the rest of the cruel joke on history, no source was cited.

This "they", all these "sophisticated observers", it turns out, are John Kingsley Lattimer: "this was only my own characterization." The purity and honesty of this dedicated man!

Those "large-scale undercover operations", "intelligence activities" and plain gibberish of the time of the assassination, November 1963? They refer to "the intelligence activities surrounding the Cuban crisis". As attributed to Castro, this is the fiction of the political paranoiacs. If reference is to the time of the Bay of Pigs, that was two and a half years earlier. If it is intended to refer to the missile crisis, that was more than a year old. And if there was any significant Cuban intelligence activity in the United States at either time, what was J. Edgar Hoover doing?

Not dreaming he was really writing to me, for the letter he was answering did not bear my name, the great Lattimer addressed this question of the conspiracies he had invented and ascribed to others for all the world as though he had never written as he had. He actually presumed that Oswald and Ruby were both "Communists" and both members of the same cell:

> I have been able to uncover no evidence of any conspiratorial groups. In fact, the severe instability of both Oswald and Ruby would have worried me to death, if I was their "cell" leader.

Were this not enough, he appended a "P.S.": "Were you aware of the similarity of A. Hidell and A. Hitler, as an indication of who he admired?" /sic/

Leave it to Marshall's man Lattimer to come up with two new kinds of "Communists", Hitler-"admirer" Oswald and H. L. Hunt-fan Jack Ruby!

The reader need not pant in anticipation. There was, indeed, a Communist cell in Dallas. It had six members. Four of these were spies. For whom they spied - and I know - is immaterial.

But none of the four spies nor either of the two nonspies was Oswald or Ruby.

And anyone who does not or will not swallow this acknowledged fabrication is, naturally, "unduly naive"!

How did Lattimer get selected when he was without the qualifica-

398

tions stipulated by the contract, being neither a pathologist nor from a related field of science or technology?

"I am happy to report that I do not know the Kennedy family, do not know Mr. Burke Marshall and was totally surprised to discover that I was the only one authorized to view the materials."

"Happy" not to know those awful "liberals", the Kennedys or Marshall?

Might one wonder if they, too, are now as "happy"?

There is a becoming modesty to the man: "I can only assume that my publications on the Lincoln and Kennedy matters, involving actual research /i.e., squeezing and shaving bullets, no more7 might have influenced Mr. Marshall in my favor, rather than those who have done no actual experimentation and have done their 'researches' while sitting on the seat of their pants."

Lattimer has yet to learn what others have done. Except for John Nichols, whose irrelevant work Lattimer stole, from the news reports. That 47 inches of pine through which Lattimer said he fired a bullet? Before Marshall made him famous, in earlier writing he acknowledged it was Nichols' work - and 48 inches.

On that single-bullet hang-up: He stuck with the drawing as the Commission's "conclusion" for what else can he now do, although he does know it is not? He professed to have been "in some doubt" until he saw this "new evidence".

Unlike the panel and all others, including, when he forgot, himself, he avoided embarrassing questions about measurements and said, "It was not possible to measure photographs the way one would measure the body." Especially not when they have a scale given! Thus he avoided "your question about the exact angle of inclination". Then he set his straw man of "drawings" afire: "The discussions in the text of the Warren Commission Report are infinitely more detailed and analytical than the drawings."

What about the other end of this "angle of declination", the front neck wound and those pictures "not possible to measure"? Well, "the exit hole in the front, it had been cut across by an incision 6.5 cm. long, which was gaping open about 1/5 cm." These are pretty exact nonmeasurements.

With no picture of this throat wound, he seems to have thought he could say, with safety if not with integrity, "There was no sign of any circumferential bruise around this area." (This is opposite to what Perry told me.) Why was this existing bruise nonexistent? "... the band of his collar held the skin in place and did not permit it to stretch with the bullet... This is only conjecture, but it is certainly true that the collar band of the shirt supported the area of exit."

"Certainly true"? When there is no evidence that any bullet exited through the collar and the evidence placing it above the collar is uncontradicted? First, magic bullets, now magic collars and magician/doctors.

How does he prove the Warren Report right about the head wound, the cause of death? It was "considerably higher than shown". Or, being wrong makes the Commission right.

"As you know, frame 313 of the Zapruder movie shows the fragments of the skull going forward ... without any doubt ..."

This frame shows a multi-directional spray of soft tissue, no more. What is "without any doubt: is that the first recovered piece of skull was to the left, not the front; another also was to the left, where Harper found it the next day; and still another was testified to by Secret Service Agent Clint Hill, who saw it going backward.

Was Lattimer just the man Burke Marshall was looking for? I cannot speak for him and he will not speak for himself. I would have no reluctance in speaking for Diogenes, who carried a lantern about, day and night, in search of an honest man.

The closest thing to a response was a telephone call from Fred Graham. I understood him to say he was calling to make partial answer and that he would write in full when he could. He first feigned surprise that I expected answers and then admitted this had to be the case because I did not read the questions to him, merely responded to what he said. At that he said enough.

Of the back brace and bandage? "In this talk with me very early in the game he mentioned the brace and the bandage and then later, in our conversation after he saw the stuff, he didn't want to talk about the brace." That was also after Fred's talk with me about them. It is what probably accounts for Fred's writing four of his 26 paragraphs about it.

When he claimed to have wanted to be prepared to question Lattimer and had not accepted my offer to see the evidence of this book or Lattimer's writings, he said of the latter, "Well, I have 'em." It turned out that he had less than the insignificances I have cited. That did not keep him from writing that Lattimer "has written and lectured extensively".

He said, "There are no sinister circumstances involving my article at all." Restricting this to how he got onto it, what he says is completely in accord with normal newspaper practice. An editor had kept his story on the contract in the "tickler" or futures file. When the five years were up, it automatically came to that editor's attention. He asked Graham to look into it. But there is a fascinating co-incidence. Several months had passed, by Fred's own account. Marshall had not acted on any of the requests. He wrote Lattimer the very day Fred reached Marshall, which was "as soon as Marshall hit New Haven, coming back from the Virgin Islands, right after the first of the year. ... I got him on the phone the first day and he said, 'Why, yes, as a matter of fact, I today', about that time, 'wrote a letter to Lattimer telling him that he could go. But I haven't made up my mind about the other three.' So, I called Lattimer and actually got him before he got the letter."

A less generous opinion could be that Marshall decided on the one sycophant only when he knew that kind of account would get the enormous prestige of the _Times_ behind it, plus the many papers to which it syndicates and the considerable collateral attention that could be expected.

Thus, to Fred, who was unwilling to defend the accuracy of his story, there was not "any kind of design". Of my advance prediction that he would be "used", he acknowledged, "You said that."

He then sought to defend himself against this by saying that "I talked to you and I talked to a couple of others, and I tried my best to get them, you and them, to ... warn me against anything to look for." I had, of course, and had offered proof.

He defended his writing in these words: "It was a story that was interesting to a lot of people and got a good play and from a newsman's point of view it was a good story."

True, all too true, unfortunately.

From time to time we got to the substance of the story. I asked if he remembered that Lattimer said "from the very beginning that he had doubt about Oswald being the assassin until he saw these pictures and X-rays"? Graham agreed, "Yeh." I read him some of what is quoted above, what he had said he did have, Lattimer's writings. Fred did not think he did have Lattimer's letter to _Medical World News_, which is something less than an answer.

The matter of the unquestioning quotation of Lattimer declaring the impossible as unquestioned fact came up when I asked about Fred's failure to consult an independent authority if he did not trust his own judgment on something as glaringly false as this, "one of the norms."

"Well, I talked to Wecht," he protested.

"After speaking to Lattimer and before writing the story?" I asked.

He had.

"And did you ask Wecht, 'Can pictures and X-rays show who fired the bullet'?"

"Well, that's a pretty loaded question, now, Harold."

"It's a loaded question because that's a loaded story. You know that pictures and X-rays can't show who fired the bullet."

Fred found it expedient to shift back to my letter asking the questions. I had raised the question of professionalism with him, as I did again in another letter, with no response.

What would he or the Times do about the reporting of the impossible as fact and on such a subject? "Well, listen, I'm - obviously, I'm not and can't do anything about that. That's what the man said ..."

Next to the last thing he said was the "let's don't beat that to death" plea. Last was "O.K., and I'll keep in touch."

No man likes being used or even accused of it. Fred did not, either, so he felt called upon to explain the leak of the GSA-family contract to him. I have no trouble believing his account.

"Well, it's possible that back then they could very well have let that out by their own choice, and I'll tell you how that happened. I called Rhoads, the Archivist ... for something, and damned if I know what triggered my call to him, but when I called him he said I was trying to pump him about the terms. I think - something had happened about that time that made it relevant, what the precise terms of this thing were. And Rhoads said, 'Mr. Graham, you are the first person to inquire since the Freedom of Information Act went into effect.' He said, 'I feel that since that statute is in effect, I can now no longer conceal the text of the contract.' So, he said, 'If you want it, come and get it.' And I hotfooted it right over and got it..."

Strange, this selective federal dedication to the law and "freedom of information". It applies only to the uninformed, those with a predisposition to be uncritical, to think a story is a story, as long as it gets a good play. And to the larger media which have become, in effect, an unofficial arm of government.

If we believe Graham's account of how he got an "exclusive" on the contract so long after I had asked for it and been refused, how can one explain Rhoads' failure to abide by his own regulations? He did not supply it to me when the law went into effect, and that was many months before he told Fred to ask for it. How interpret the "explanation" to me, that it was denied to prevent sensational or undignified publicity? That is precisely what the government wanted. And what it got from Fred - put just the way the executive branch desired.

(At the time the government fed the exclusive use of the GSA-family contract to Graham, Dr. Robert Bahmer was Archivist, Rhoads his assistant. Bahmer retired quietly after my strong protest over this palpable propaganda by his agency. His letter of alleged explanation to me was actually written by Marion Johnson. There is no reason to believe Bahmer had any personal knowledge of what was done in his name.)

While I did not break Fred's confidence, immediately after his first call I wrote letters to Marshall, Rhoads and Robert Q. Vawter, the GSA official to whom appeals are made under the Freedom of Information law. My letters were written on January 6, the day before the regulations and the contract were flagrantly violated with Lattimer. These letters would not have passed through all the channels of bureaucracy until after violation, after Lattimer had seen the "stuff". And after Rhoads had, in my opinion, again made a perjurer of himself in

401

my suit, where he had sworn that under the contract he could not let anyone see any of the clothing.

I had caught him dead to rights. I was entitled to what I sued for. Rhoads knew it, I knew it, the United States Attorney knew it - everyone except the judge knew it. After the trial I made lengthy and usually ignored efforts to get dated copies of all the regulations.

These law-and-order folks with their great dedication to "freedom of information" then did what was prohibited.

First, after my suit, they had changed the regulations that required the taking of pictures of three-dimensional evidence for researchers to exempt the clothing. Under this change, the clothing was to be sequestered. But then came my letter of the sixth coinciding with Graham's story of the ninth in which he reported that Lattimer had been given "the President's bloody and bullet-ridden clothing", inaccurately described as "not absolutely hidden". The ninth was a Sunday, with the government closed. So, on the tenth, these "Regulations for Reference Service on Warren Commission Items of Evidence", were still again revised, with this language added to the previous revision on the clothing: "except those researchers whose applications to examine the X-rays and photographs relating to the autopsy of President Kennedy are approved by the Kennedy family representative."

This could not have been changed before it was, could it, that being the first day of business? But at least the Archivist did record his violation and his guilty knowledge in his attempt at ex post facto sanctification.

There was another dirty little deal cooking with Graham and the Times to let them have access by proxy. So, again caught, the Archivist wrote me on January 21 pretending to make the same offer to me: "If you will select a pathologist or any other qualified person and secure approval of his application by the Kennedy family representative, we shall be pleased to show the autopsy material and the clothing to him." Picture of Burke Marshall, hero of Chappaquiddick, opening those pearly gates for me!

They sure were anxious for me to be party to this vile game. Vawter wrote me on February 8 reminding me of their pretendedly friendly offer. None of this evidence of the killing of a President should be used improperly, for sensational or undignified purposes. The keepers of the memory hole do nothing else with it. Faithful to that scheme, they attribute their motive to those who will not be and have not been involved in such rottenness.

Their objective is clear to those who will but look: to exculpate the guilty, to blame the innocent, to assure that what was once called Camelot but was not becomes an ever-burning hell.

With their power, with their unquestioning allies of the press, with the witting or unwitting connivance of those whose crime is silence, they may yet succeed.

But not with my help.

THE NEW "NEW EVIDENCE"

Then, in the fullest turning of the wheel, there was Watergate.

With Watergate there was a dramatic change in the national consciousness, a mass skepticism questioning the integrity of the official diktat. This meant that the people were now more willing to believe the truth I had long proclaimed and proved, that an official whitewash had deliberately and knowingly denied them the true story of a President's murder. It also meant a new opportunity for exploitation by those whose professed dedication to the truth is really a facade for their unique blend of self-promotion, unfounded sensationalism and paranoia. They have been aptly tagged "conspiracy theorists" because they deal not with fact but with theory unsubstantiated by fact, theory, so preposterous and impossible that its mere consideration would shame rational, mature individuals. These, to whom the national media has devoted ample coverage, have received notoriety and handsome fees for wild attacks on the CIA, FBI and others in an evergrowing cabal. In reality, they have been the foremost servants of those agencies.

The New York Times' December 1974 disclosure of illegal domestic activities by the CIA made Congressional investigations and further revelations inevitable. To preempt Congress and weaken the impact of the coming exposures, President Ford appointed an investigatory commission of his own, headed by Vice President Rockefeller. The question of CIA involvement in assassinations both foreign and domestic was sure to be raised amid the new revelations. And with the threat of a further coming-apart of the official account of the JFK assassination - an account in which Ford shared responsibility as a Commissioner - Ford could anticipate dire political results. Ford's record on the Warren Commission spelled possible trouble during the campaign in which he would seek election to the presidency to which he had been appointed. To serve his ends, which were opposite the ends of truth, Ford personally selected David Belin to conduct the Rockefeller Commission's investigation. As a staff lawyer for the Warren Commission, Belin had personally suppressed exculpatory evidence placing Oswald away from the scene of the crime in both of the crimes of which he was accused. As a private lawyer, Belin was compulsive and outspoken in his unfounded defense of his and the Commission's integrity. As Ford's CIA "investigator," he was an insurance policy against harmful disclosures. Unless Ford wanted to expose himself and destroy his candidacy, there can be no doubt that he desired and sought no investigation.

The conspiracy theorists whose theories contemplate CIA involvement in everything short of original sin played into Belin's and Ford's hands. One of the inevitable consequences of all their irresponsibilities and indecencies was to set up a new whitewash for the Rockefeller Commission. There was and could have been no beneficiary other than those agencies that, when needing investigation and cleansing, were exculpated by these excessive and baseless charges against them. The conspiracy theories served the agencies in the same way that "black books" sponsored by intelligence agencies do, by building public sympathy for them, by setting up straw men easily knocked down.

This same dredging of the same muck threatens to frustrate Congressional investigation of the real scandal, the official whitewash. And the national media continues to devote attention to the

403

irresponsibles and their craziness while avoiding the continuing but
unheralded serious research, the facts and documentation so destructive of the official mythology and integrity.

My quest for evidence, as partly recounted in all the earlier
books incorporated into this volume, has continued, amid the spectacle
of corrupt government hiding and perpetuating its crimes, aided in
its pursuit by unlikely and unwitting allies, its most outspoken
enemies.

The measure of meaningful opposition to these destructive traits
of government is not its loudness or the amount of newspaper copy promoting it. The government cannot be held to account for its many
abuses unless they are exposed truthfully and fully. Exposure is not
voluntary. Corrupt government does not voluntarily confess its sins.
What follows is a chronicle of my most recent efforts to force disclosure - and an exposition of the contents and meaning of that which
was so reluctantly given me from the secret vaults in which it was
hidden for over a decade.

One of the results of my first suit (C.A. 2301-70) for the
suppressed spectrographic analysis was a backfire into the face of
suppressive government.

Freedom of information, an inherent American tenet, is a fiction with all administrations. The 1966 law to assure this freedom
had been converted into a license to suppress by the Johnson and Nixon
administrations through the courts. Congress, however, was disturbed
by all this corruption and its results. In 1974 it amended the law
(WHITEWASH IV,pp.123,167ff). The first of four cases cited as requiring the amending of the "investigatory files" exemption of the Freedom
of Information Act (FOIA) is my C.A. 2301-70, in which the court rewrote the law to deny me the spectrographic analysis (Congressional
Record, 5/30/74,p.S9336). The language of Senator Edward M. Kennedy
during the Senate debates is explicit, "to override the court decisions ... on Weisberg against United States .. the impact and effect [of the amendment] ... would be to override those particular
decisions." The House-Senate Conference Report on the amended FOIA,
Rep. No. 93-1380, officially expresses the intent of Congress. It
goes to great lengths to make explicit that records concerning scientific tests employing nonsecret processes are <u>not</u> exempt from disclosure as "investigatory files" (pp.12-3).

President Ford had a vested interest in continued suppression
and new suppressions that all administrations want to be possible.
His veto of the amended FOIA was overwhelmingly overridden.

The new law became effective February 19, 1975.

Once the FOIA was amended, the government dared not resort
again to raw power alone to continue its suppressions. Congress had
spoken with explicitness in overriding President Ford's veto. So the
government needed a new kind of hanky-panky. It needed judges sympathetic to it to obtain decisions with which it and the courts could
rewrite the law and veto the will of the Congress. Strategy and tac-
tics both had to change.

The new official approach to the problem presented by the new
law was apparent to those who analyzed what the government did and
did not do in C.A. 2052-73, my suit for the long suppressed executive
session transcript of January 27, 1964. Before Jim Lesar, my lawyer,
could appeal the decision, the government decided to give me that
sensational transcript. All 90 pages are printed in facsimile in
WHITEWASH IV. This happened while Congress was deliberating amendments to the FOIA and when all readings were that the amendments
would be passed.

The government then reached a basic decision, evolving a new
approach: Continue to stonewall as long as possible and then, in the
last minute prior to the filing of a suit, surrender what it had suppressed for more than a decade, law or no law.

The January 22, 1964, executive session transcript is one example.* Another is the Memorandum of Transfer mentioned earlier.≠ Lesar renewed my request for this document and others related to it on March 15, 1975. The Archives rejected the request. We appealed administratively on March 31, a necessary prerequisite to filing in court. A copy of the memo was mailed to me under date of April 15. This was pretty speedy action, speeded, no doubt, by the potential for misuse once suppression was ended.

Physically, the Memorandum of Transfer is like few, if any, others of official nature. In all of history, there are few, if any, of its character and content.

It is not on any letterhead;
It is not typed by a real typist;
It contains no explanation of the reasons or needs for the "transfer;"
It does not identify the role of the recipient of that which it transferred, thus does not say to whom the transfer was really made;
It transfers what, with minor exceptions only, was not Kennedy property and was federal property;
This includes those that are Navy records, required by Navy regulations to have been preserved by the Navy.

A more sinister setting-up of the Kennedy survivors for responsibility for suppressions for which they were not responsible and which were outside their power could not have been contrived by guilty officialdom.

The memo's date, April 26, 1965, is of particular interest, if only by coincidence. WHITEWASH, the first book on the subject, was then making its way around New York publishing houses, some of which were later identified as CIA publishers. It was long before there was any controversy generated by any assassination book.

What was accomplished by this transfer for which there was no need was a means of hiding all this evidence.

All those many listed documents the Warren Commission did not have and the Archivist claimed not to have were included. After this, the Archivist could say that he did not have them. Because the Commission did not have them, the special archive of the Commission's files did not hold them.

This, however, is not the full story.

Mrs. Evelyn Lincoln, the assassinated President's former personal secretary, had an office in the Archives building. She was there not as the personal representative of Robert or any other Kennedy. She represented the Kennedy Library.

And the Kennedy Library, like all other Presidential libraries, is under and controlled by the Archivist of the United States.

The Archives did have these records when it professed not to have them.

There was never the remotest possibility the disclosure of these records could embarrass any Kennedy. The only scandals they could trigger would have been over governmental indecency and suppressions.

Unless otherwise used, the medical records themselves were properly subject to withholding under the permanent exemptions of the FOIA. But the record of the transfer of these records is nowhere exempted from disclosure by that law.

This transfer was a device to suppress evidence that destroyed the false solution to the assassination.

To create a situation in which at any time and in any way the resultant suppression could be attributed to the family of the President transcends the obscene.

*See pp.467-72. ≠ See pp. 558-9.

The characterization is no less deserved because this was but another step in the careful plan begun during the days of the Commission and advanced by it. The Commission understood this need and recognized its own situation. Prior to its first hearing, in utmost secrecy, it confronted the realities of what Hoover and the FBI were doing to the Commission and the possibilities of any real investigation of the JFK assassination. By the time of its January 22 executive session, called to consider how it would face reports that Oswald had been a federal informant, it could no longer hide from itself the certainty that Hoover was determined to see to it that there would be no real investigation and how he would see to it.

On January 22 the Commission was well aware of what it was admitting about itself, too. Dulles spelled it out at the end: "I think this record ought to be destroyed." (Seven years ago I obtained "proof" that "this record" was "destroyed.")

What escaped destruction was the stenotypist's tape, as Paul Hoch detected.

When it was certain that we were taking those steps required before filing suit, the tape, according to a later Archives explanation, was sent to the Pentagon where a stenotypist transcribed most of it.

There are a few wrong words in this transcript. Names are misspelled. The voices and the people were strange to the transcriber. Sometimes there is a confusion between Warren and Rankin, both of whom are represented by the letter "A."

From context (pp.11-2), it is without question that Rankin began this spelling-out to the members, that "the FBI is very explicit that Oswald is the assassin ... explicit that there was no conspiracy, and they are also saying in the same place that they are continuing their investigation. Now in my experience of almost nine years [he had been Solicitor General] it is hard to get them to" state a conclusion with an airtight case. "They claim they don't evaluate, and it is uniform prior experience that they don't do that [evaluate]. Secondly, they have not run out all kinds of leads" bearing on conspiracy. "But they are concluding that there can't be a conspiracy without these being run out."

Dulles agreed that the FBI had not done this investigating and from the many FBI reports he had seen confirmed that each disavows any "conclusions."

Rankin continued, "Why are they so eager to make both of these conclusions ... such a departure." He returned to the question of conspiracy when he again mentioned the report of Oswald having been an informant. He said that he and Warren had discussed it and agreed "that if that was true and it ever came out and could be established, then you would have people think that there was a conspiracy to accomplish this assassination that nothing this Commission or anybody could dissipate."

Boggs lamented, "You are so right." Dulles moaned, "Oh, terrible." Boggs then found the "implications of this are fantastic." Dulles described them as "Terrific." (pp.11-2)

If there had been a conspiracy, it was the sacred task of this Commission to establish the proof. It was supposed to investigate and report all the facts. Instead, it did exactly what it attributed to Hoover.

Consistent with this, in the session five days later, Rankin raised the informant question, not in terms of investigating, come what may, but as a "dirty rumor," with the Commission's obligation, "it must be wiped out." (WHITEWASH IV,p.48)

There was no innocence, no intention ever to investigate.

There was no doubt about what Hoover and the FBI were doing to the Commission:

406

"They would like to have us fold up and quit," all agreed January 22 (pp.12-3).

"This closes the case" is the way Boggs put what the FBI was forcing on the Commission. "Yes, I see that," Dulles agreed. Rankin spelled it out bluntly: "They found the man. There is nothing more to do. The Commission supports their conclusions and we can go home and that is the end of it."

Dulles again agreed, as did Boggs. Ford, who participated in other portions, here was silent.

This is the very point (p.13) at which the need to destroy unprecedented admissions, confessions and recognitions was agreed to.

It took me eight years to break this suppressed transcript out of the vaults. The reason is not that alleged as a coverall justification, "national security." Without any doubt it was to hide this confession that the Commission never intended to investigate, that Hoover and the FBI were determined to keep them from investigating, and they knew and accepted this. In this acceptance the Commission made its decision. If there had been no other influence on the Commission and its work, this alone was enough to control both. And we are back at our own beginning, with conclusions first.

These are the same reasons other evidence is suppressed. Nobody in power really gave a damn if any Kennedy might be embarrassed by the ending of suppression on the Memorandum of Transfer. When I obtained and used it, there was no suggestion of any embarrassment. The real reason was to hide official cupidity. That is precisely the reason these scientific tests had to be suppressed at all costs.

By any standard, popular, historical or legal, the January 22 transcript is one of the most revealing and candid of sordid government secrets. The full text appears here for the first time.* The reader can judge this for himself.

"The Place of Justice ..."

My renewed effort to obtain the reports or results of the spectrographic and neutron activation analysis began with a formal request of December 6, 1974. The Justice Department referred it to the FBI. On December 19, FBI Director Clarence Kelley wrote to me, "We are attempting to identify and locate the documents."

We gave Kelley a month and a half before Jim Lesar started the steps prerequisite to filing suit, beginning with a letter to then Deputy Attorney General Lawrence Silberman. It was clear the government was going to continue to stonewall. This had been apparent from Kelley's letter, pretending that there was any need to "identify" or "locate" what I had requested, documents so well identified and located as of the time of my prior suit for them that the FBI could swear that their release would virtually destroy federal law enforcement.

A decade earlier, Hoover had personally promised the Warren Commission, under questioning by then Representative Ford, that the FBI's records on the assassination would be better preserved than Kelley today maintains (5H99-100):

I think it is essential that the FBI investigate the allegations that are received in the future so it can't be said that we had ignored them or that the case is closed and forgotten.

After another Ford request for further reassurance,

Well, I can assure you that so far as the FBI is concerned the case will continue to be an open investigation for all time... information ... will be thoroughly investigated ... we have the record ...

Ford's next question ended with, "the authority to conduct this

---
*Pp. 467-62.

407

investigation it is not an investigation with a terminal point. It is an authority that goes on indefinitely?"

"Very definitely so," the man sometimes called the world's best file clerk guaranteed the man to become President through all of this.

But with the files left by the world's best file clerk, the "records" that would be kept forever in the investigation that had no "terminal point" under "an authority that goes on forever," Kelley could not find this most basic of all evidence?

Another part of the reason is that the FBI had already sworn to having collected and studied all these "documents" in the affidavit by Special Agent Marion E. Williams in C.A. 2301-70 (WHITEWASH IV, pp.175-6,187-8). If the FBI of the fabled record-keeping had these files in the suit only recently before the Supreme Court, why would they have to launch a new search for them? What was the problem in "identifying the documents?" How many murders of Presidents had the FBI investigated in recent years? How many tests of these kinds had it performed when Presidents were murdered?

It was the same way with the Atomic Energy Commission's work on the assassination investigation. AEC has since been divided up. This part is now the Energy Research and Development Administration. ERDA was another stonewaller. Their initial response was an outright lie: They claimed to have nothing. The neutron activation analysis had been done at its Oak Ridge plant but nowhere in the entire atomic-nuclear establishment was there so much as a scrap of paper! They said. This incredible AEC letter follows in full:

UNITED STATES
ATOMIC ENERGY COMMISSION
WASHINGTON, D.C. 20545

OCT 16 1974

James H. Lesar, Esquire
1231 Fourth Street, S.W.
Washington, D. C. 20024

Dear Mr. Lesar:

This is in response to your September 19, 1974, letter to Mr. Bender requesting copies of any tests which the Atomic Energy Commission performed for the Warren Commission or any person or agency acting for it in connection with the investigation into the assassination of President Kennedy.

The AEC's Oak Ridge National Laboratory (ORNL) did provide technical support to the Federal Bureau of Investigation in the performance of neutron activation analyses on the paraffin casts from the right hand, the left hand, and the right cheek of Lee Harvey Oswald. The results of these analyses are discussed in the testimony of FBI special agent John F. Gallagher set forth in "Hearings Before the President's Commission on the Assassination of President Kennedy," Volume XV, pages 746-52. Neither AEC nor ORNL prepared any report on the results of these analyses.

No other tests such as you described were performed by AEC or at any AEC facility.

Sincerely,

Bertram H. Schur
Associate General Counsel

There was other fruitless correspondence with Department of Justice lawyers, from the top down. We knew what to expect. What we did not expect is what compliance with the law required: Production of scientific proof that the FBI faked an investigation of the assassination of the President and faked "proof" that Oswald had been the lone assassin. Enough of this proof dealing with the bullets, fragments of bullets and objects struck by them, is in the earlier portions of this book. Until the FBI was ready to confess to this, in some ways a more heinous crime than the assassination itself, we knew it would not deliver this evidence.

We knew, as certainly as one can know anything, that neither Frazier nor the FBI was about to confess that it and he had faked the entire "investigation" and "solution" of the assassination by hiding the fact that Frazier had taken all the metal missing from Bullet 399 and then pretending that this lead he personally removed is the lead recovered from Connally's body. We did expect it would go through the motions of giving me this suppressed scientific evidence because of the specificity of the legislative history of the amending of the law. In effect, Congress ordered the FBI to give me this evidence.

What we were not fully prepared for is the degree to which government lawyers and the judge would lend themselves to what, for ordinary citizens, are serious crimes, crimes these same lawyers prosecute and for which judges mete out jail sentences.

What has come to be the way of life in government and come to be accepted by the courts was later neatly summarized by Meg Greenfield of The Washington Post's editorial staff. In an article dealing with the excesses of intelligence agencies (CIA: Reality vs. Romance, 8/13/75), she addressed the fact and the consequences of official secrecy. One may or may not agree with her opinion, "I do not think that excessive secrecy in these matters represents nearly so great a threat to the public's right to know as it does to the perspective and judgment of those who live in the world of secrets." Long experience, more than a decade of it on this subject alone, leaves no doubt that this "excessive secrecy" has been a constant "threat to the public's right to know." This same experience is, however, affirmation of her observation, "The first and foremost danger of excessive secrecy is that it corrupts the people who hold the secrets."

In all the FOIA suits I filed and in all cases where I received without suing what I would have filed suit for, there was corruption. In every case there was "excessive secrecy." The two are inseparable.*

There will be less of both when the press begins to report these lawsuits and the corruption that taints them all. In this case, despite its history of being partly responsible for the changing of the law and being the first filed under the new law, in itself normally the cause of journalistic interest, from the time of its filing through the district judge's decision, there was never a reporter in the courtroom.

In fact, those other individuals and groups who profess so great an interest in the law at no time had a single spectator present.

Excessive complacency of the press protects excessive secrecy in government that is the generator of corruption.

Despite the false swearing of the FBI through Williams in the earlier case and the contentment of that judge with the transparent false swearing, there was nothing secret about what I sought except the results, those final reports of the tests. There are no details about the tests themselves that cannot be learned in almost any library. As rapidly as these tests are developed to even further perfection, that also is published, in books and in specialized journals. The processes and their uses are taught in schools. For this there are texts, for the chemistry and physics departments and for such specialties as criminalistics.

A relatively recent text, 1973 third edition of Fundamentals

* See pp. 610-22.

of Criminal Investigation, by Charles E. O'Hara, illustrates how long these processes have been not been secret and their potential. (O'Hara is a professional police official and lecturer in police science at Western Reserve University. The book is published by Charles C. Thomas, Springfield, Illinois.)

His treatment of "Spectrographic Analysis" beginning on page 719 reports,

The spectroscope has been in practical use over a century. The spectrograph (a spectroscope with an arrangement for recording on film ...) has been employed in chemical analysis for some fifty years. ... possible to analyze minute fragments of a gram. ... an extremely rapid means of accomplishing the analysis and provides a permanent photographic record of the findings.

In the "Illustrative Cases" that follow, O'Hara evaluates the precision of this test by comparison with fingerprints (pp.722-3). It is possible that, in the spectroscopic examination of substances containing impurities, "finding two identical batches ... may be even smaller than finding two human fingerprints exactly alike." His evaluation is that "such a coincidence is far beyond the leeway of reasonable doubt."

"Neutron activation analysis" he describes (p.725) as "measuring the wavelength and intensity of radiation given off by substances" made radioactive when "subjected to a stream of neutrons. These measurements serve as qualitative and quantitative determination of the constituents ... and as means of unique identification. The method is a non-destructive, ultra-microanalytical tool of extreme sensitivity." [Emphasis added]

So sensitive and dependable are these tests that O'Hara describes one of the past, the case of a man picked up "three blocks from" where a woman coming out of a subway had been assaulted "from behind by an assailant who clapped his hand over her mouth .... The woman had not seen the man's face." But "Spectrophotometric analysis showed that ... a red smear on the palm of his left had was from the woman's lipstick." (p.723)

The techniques are well-known and well-used. Even when the FBI was virtually in its infancy. In A. Lucas' Forensic Chemistry and Scientific Criminal Investigation, published by Longmans, Green 40 years ago, under "projectiles" there are cases of acquitting accused police and watchmen by use of this analysis (pp.265-6). O'Hara (pp. 721-2) reports the exculpation of a policeman who actually killed a man in a hit-and-run chase because spectroscopy proved the officer's claim "that the bullet had ricocheted from a nearby automobile" when he fired a "warning." The fatal bullet, recovered from the victim, actually retained a tiny trace of paint. "Spectrographic analysis of this minute sample of the paint established that it was identical with the paint on the car, thus verifying the patrolman's story."

Prior to the sophistication now reached in neutron activation analysis, a 1953 text, Crime Investigation, by Paul L. Kirks, Professor of Biochemistry and Criminalistics at the University of California at Berkeley (Interscience Publishers, New York and London), says, "The Spectrograph is nearly the ideal instrument for the study of identities of metals and metals in turn come near to being ideal evidence for the spectrograph. ... the most outstanding [use] is in metal analysis ... When the plate is developed all spectra have identical development and will be strictly comparable regardless of other conditions."

When the nonsecret literature on the nonsecret tests is almost rhapsodic about what they can do, can one believe that the FBI is not skilled in these tests and in the most complete and acceptable manner of conducting them? When they have for decades been so "superior" for metals, particularly bullet evidence, and have repeatedly saved the lives of policemen, does one believe the nation's leading police force is not ultraproficient in these definitive police methods, prepared to use them not only to convict but to exculpate any of its own agents and other police in time of need?

The Journal of Forensic Science, which certainly the FBI receives, has carried definitive articles in recent years. One reported study conducted "under a research contract with the Division of Isotope Development of the United States Atomic Energy Commission ... and the Office of Law Enforcement Assistance of the United States Department of Justice" (Vol. 16, No. 3, July 1971) begins, "It has been shown that neutron activation analysis (NAA) can be used to determine a number of impurity and alloying elements - especially antimony - in bullet lead with very good accuracy, precision and ease."

A second supported "by the National Research Council of Canada ... through an agreement with the Department of the Solicitor General of Canada" (Vol. 18, No. 1, January 1973) concludes that "It is clear that for the several kinds of ammunition studied, there was a substantial variation in the trace element content between samples of different manufacture, and the different ammunition variations could have been clearly distinguished from each other." This is to say that bullets of different manufacture are "clearly distinguished from each other." The same is true of different batch mixes of a single manufacturer.

The study emphasizes in its title what all the readily available literature stresses, the importance of trace elements in these tests. It is "Studies of the Trace Element Content of Bullet Lead and Jacket Material." In the commonly available ammunition, 12 different components were found, not counting the impurities that also are vital in both processes and in making positive identifications and eliminating the possibility.

The Missouri Law Review (Vol. 37, 1972) has a study on "Neutron Activation Analysis." Its evaluation of the degree of perfection and certainty and of the requirements of evidence is headed "Degree of Certainty Required of Expert Testimony." It goes into cases in several jurisdictions. They hold that these tests can be definitive and the results can be stated positively.

In State v Holt the conviction was reversed because the expert testimony on NAA results was not expressed with the proper degree of certainty. The expert witness testified that "the samples are similar and are likely to be from the same source." The Ohio Supreme Court concluded that such testimony should have been based on reasonable scientific certainty that the samples came from the same source.

This is the capability of NAA and how the courts interpreted it.

"The enthusiastic use of NAA by a number of federal government agencies has been influential in increasing the use and acceptance of NAA evidence in federal and state courts," the law review study continues, attesting also to the knowledge of and skill in the proper performance of NAA by these federal agencies. In crime the FBI is first among these federal agencies.

Perhaps one of the reasons the Warren Commission did not want these test results - nowhere in its Report is there mention of NAA - is another statement of both capability and the requirements of proof as well as the essence of preparation of these test results:

Reliable statistical interpretation is the crux of meaningful evaluation of NAA results and the inferences drawn therefrom. For example, two samples which have nearly identical trace element concentration do not necessarily have common origin.

This is followed by explanation of the "firm statistical basis" that "must be acquired."

This kind of relevant quotation could be continued indefinitely. It is all excerpted from what several inexperienced students obtained from their libraries. If college students can find this literature, there is no doubt it is not unknown to the venerated FBI.

The FBI, however, gave neither this kind of information nor the results of its tests or final reports to the Commission, all of whose lab services it performed. Instead, Hoover wrote it on March 18, 1964, alleging that, for its purposes, NAAs are valueless. His letter (20H1-2) concludes, "It is not felt that the increased sensitivity of neutron activation analyses would contribute substantially to the understanding of the origin of this hole and frayed area."

(Even for the past master, this was quite a semantical exploit, as we have seen and will see further.)

On its part, the Commission made no demands. Yet all this Commission's members were lawyers. Several had been prosecutors. There were many former prosecutors on its large legal staff. Some were still on the Justice Department payroll. Specter, whose area this was, had been an assistant district attorney. He became Philadelphia's district attorney. Spectrography and NAAs were not unknown to any of the many who made no demands and have since been silent - except in the protestation of purity of purpose and performance.

Hoover, who discouraged NAAs and provided no formal results or anything more than pseudo-scientific gibberish, certainly knew better. Perhaps best: He saw to it that the Commission had no meaningful test results. It was not Hoover's timidity. He could be quite forward. He recommended to the Commission that it interview Russian defector Yuri Nosenko, who was in the CIA's hands, not Hoover's. Without asking anyone, Hoover made the arrangements and then notified the Commission of it, knowing neither it nor the CIA wanted the Commission to interview Nosenko. Neither wanted Nosenko's evidence, which both suppressed.*

Most Americans believe that when there is a lawsuit there is a formal proceeding, with witnesses who are examined by the lawyers on one side and cross-examined by those on the other. Cross-examination, in our legal belief, is the greatest machine for the discovery of truth.

This, however, requires live witnesses on the witness stand. There, as all TV viewers know, if there is false swearing, it is a serious crime for which, under the law, witnesses are punished. Some, anyway.

In not one of my FOIA suits was there such a hearing.

The 1966 law was rewritten in court without a single witness being heard. That may have been repeated in this new suit.

In all these cases there was official lying. I believe that in each it was the felony of perjury. It was by affidavit, not live. It was by a unilateral statement sworn to before a notary public./

One cannot cross-examine a piece of paper.

No official of any rank - and they ranged from FBI agents to agency heads - was even asked by a single judge if he had sworn falsely. Naturally, not one was punished. All received rewards for their false swearing, usually success in its purposes: Defeating the law and its intent and sometimes perpetuating suppressions.

When in the earlier suit for these tests an appeals-court panel ordered this kind of hearing and directed the judge on remand to give me a full opportunity to explore the improprieties attributed to the FBI, the Department of Justice demanded and received a review by the entire appeals court and had this overturned.

It could dare let itself be looked at in a court of law.

Only one judge showed any offense. He threatened Jim Lesar and me - not the perjurer, who didn't even bother to deny it.

This, not what is on the tube and in the movies, is the way it really is.

Even when there was the greatest interest in the JFK assassina-

*See pp. 427-9. /See pp. 610-22.

tion in a decade, when the Congress was talking about investigating it.

It ought to be transparent that, if these tests supported the official explanation of this "crime of the century," the government would not wait to be sued to make them public. It would advertise them by every available means. Particularly in this new case, with its legislative history precluding the spurious claim that it would ruin the FBI, endanger law enforcement and even disclose the identity of informants and expose details of peoples' personal lives (WHITE-WASH IV, pp.187-8).

Instead, the government resisted by every means, from lying to stonewalling.

If this suppressed, basic evidence was ever to be made available, we had no choice but to sue again.* What is called the "complaint," setting forth the facts, was filed February 19, 1975. Attached were items of evidence ranging from my first request to Hoover on May 23, 1966, to the ERDA falsehoods to an affidavit by me.

A month and two days later the government asked for an extension of time, after which they were granted another. Why they needed time when there had been the first suit and there had been months to prepare for this one is not for the reasons given. Finally, on Friday, May 2, there was the first "calendar call" when the judge was to inform himself on the status of the case. What he learned is that the government had not complied and did not and could not give him evidence of compliance, even in the form of affidavits. In order to establish fact - under oath - we filed what are known as "interrogatories" to be answered by the FBI and ERDA. The judge, tolerant as he was of noncompliance after a decade of effort and two and a half months of Nixonian stonewalling, held that the government could respond under oath to these questions in the form of affidavits. Ultimately, it filed affidavits. Not one was responsive. Or truthful.

The judge was John H. Pratt. His most recent claims to fame were ruling that the FBI could engage in electronic surveillance without court sanction and being overruled by the appeals court (Post, 6/24/75).

Pratt then gave the government more time, until Wednesday, May 21, when he scheduled the next calendar call. Again the government had not complied and had not provided the affidavits he had ordered. Again he was patient with the government, tolerant of its stonewalling.

That day the government did provide one affidavit - just as the judge was about to walk into the courtroom. (Our response was for me to allege and prove in an affidavit that the government's affidavit was false, that it attested to compliance when, to the knowledge of the affiant, there was not compliance. We attached a series of documented proofs. In what is known as a "motion to strike," we asked that this false affidavit be expunged from the record. Judge Pratt never ruled on it and never intended to from the notice he posted outside his courtroom for the next and last hearing.)

Rather than chastise the government or utter a word of complaint, Pratt gave it still more time to file the ERDA affidavit.

When, despite repeated promises to us and to the most patient of judges (patient when the government was deficient), ERDA still had not responded, on June 12 we filed a motion for the production by ERDA of what was required of it and one against the FBI for what it was still suppressing. In order to assure that there would be a full and complete record, as full and complete as not being allowed to give and take testimony permits, we filed motions to compel answers to the unanswered interrogatories and to postpone the next calendar call and stay all proceedings until there was the promised compliance and a resolution of the unanswered questions of false swearing.

Still again, Pratt did nothing to require compliance, respect for the law or in the end even schedule any of our motions for hearing.

* C.A.226-75.

Six days later the government filed an "Opposition" opposing all of this. With it, finally, an ERDA affidavit.

Twelve days later, on June 30 and under the most unusual circumstances, it filed in court a motion to dismiss the suit on the ground of compliance. Attached was another affidavit by the same FBI agent. Michael Ryan, an Assistant United States Attorney for the District of Columbia, delivered all of this by hand and after the end of the working day to Jim's home. With it was a fat envelope of more than 400 entirely uncollated and unidentified papers the source of which was not indicated. This was five times the volume of papers that had been turned over to me all the times the government had sworn it had given me everything, had sworn to "compliance."

The reason for this exceptional personal service became clear while we were trying to make sense out of all that unidentified paper, no two sheets of which were attached together, papers the government itself said candidly in its motion had no relationship to what I sued for. It was to cut down the time we had. Preparing to answer all of this was not easy. I had drafted an affidavit Jim was going over, to eliminate what he considered not relevant and to put it in proper form. He also had legal research to do and other cases to handle.

Ryan's personal delivery was the end of June 30, which was just before the long Fourth of July holiday weekend. The afternoon of July 8, Pratt's clerk phoned Jim and told him the judge wanted all our responses the next day. Jim's legal research went by the board. With the distance between us eaning a 120-mile trip, we got part of the planned affidavit executed and Jim did the best possible in filing our Opposition.

We did not have until the next calendar call set for July 15.

When we got to the entrance to Judge Pratt's courtroom that day, we knew what was up. The only motion he had before him according to his posted notice was a two-part one including one never filed! The bulletin board read, "Motion to Dismiss and Protective Order." A protective order is an order to silence, a gag. It is a direction to keep your mouth shut on penalty of punishment by the court.

This and the motion to dismiss were both aimed against me.

The judge was considering nothing else.

Not proof of noncompliance, not proof of perjury.

He was going to consider only throwing out the case and gagging me.

Ryan insisted prior to that hearing that he had nothing to do with and no knowledge of any protective order.

Details of the hearings and what evidence I did obtain follow.

This chronology of the case, the state of "freedom of information" when the Department of Justice is opposed to it and willing to and capable of doing anything to frustrate it, and when it has a judge favorable to it and of unhidden prejudice, are helpful to understanding this evidence and how the government and the courts really work.

The judge never mentioned that protective order. He did dismiss the case as moot, ruling that whatever he meant by partial compliance is full compliance.

As of that minute, the government had not delivered a _single_ record called for in the complaint, not a _single_ paper I sued for.

Noncompliance could not have been more complete. It was _total_.

And until this moment that a federal judge posted notice of a gag rule against a writer who dared sue for suppressed evidence in the JFK assassination is totally unreported.

However, there is that beautiful inscription over the main entrance to the Department of Justice building, "The Place of Justice is a Hallowed Place."

This is the entrance barred to the public in recent years.

The "Results" and the "Reports"

Jim and I went to the hallowed place March 14, without a tape recorder, our March 6 request "that we - and the Bureau - be allowed to tape record the conference" having been rejected by Ford's new "Mr. Clean," Attorney General Edward H. Levi. By him and Kelley, to whom Jim addressed the identical request the same day. We went there knowing the only reason not to have a record of a conference is to be able to create a dispute about what was agreed to. We also knew that there was no need for any conference, so we had every reason to suspect this to be the FBI's intention.

We knew they would have to give me something. There is a rarity in the amending of the law. In effect, it ordered the FBI to give me the tests results and reports I sought. In effect, the FBI had said it had them in refusing them in the first suit and by its predictions of the alleged dire consequences of releasing them.

It seemed obvious that if the FBI wanted to end discontent over the account of the JFK assassination, all it had to do was to produce these results and let the world see that the FBI had done what it had to do, done it well, and that these scientific tests of exquisite fineness proved the FBI and the Commission had been correct and truthful.

This suit provided the ideal opportunity and, with the language of the Congress, a dramatic setting. All the FBI had to do was line up its evidentiary ducks in a row and let the world see the truth.

With the Bureau as well as the CIA under strong attack, this was the best of times. Unless it was the worst of times.

We had no doubt which. There had been this same need all those years and all those years the FBI had fought and refused. If the results supported the official story, they would never have been kept secret. The FBI would not now take the hangout road merely because Congress had passed a law. There is a clear record extending into this case that laws are for others, not the FBI.

We were escorted into the office of Thomas H. Bresson, whose FBI title is Freedom of Information Officer. An officer FBI Agent Bresson is. He has a fine big office, and a fine large desk. But "freedom" and "information" are foreign to our experience with him.

Frazier and Special Agent John W. Kilty, whose function we were never told, also awaited us.

The need for this conference, we were informed, was to resolve alleged differences between us. "Semantical," no more, they said, hinging around what I meant by "results" and "final reports." What I seemed to have in mind is other than they did.

And, they said, other than they had in their files!

In starting the whole wearying and costly process all over again on November 27, 1974 - and the FBI and Department of Justice know how wearying and costly it can be and do their best to make each more so - I had used language that seemed specific and intelligible enough:

The Department saw fit in this previous case to make misrepresentations to the courts. I therefore want it to be clear that I sought and now seek only the final, scientific reports on these tests. Not raw materials, not laboratory work, only the conclusions as embodied in the full report, or the report itself.

In an effort to cover the rawness of what he did in dismissing the case as moot on July 15, Judge Pratt actually pretended I had not asked for the neutron activation analyses (Transcript,p.10). The language of this initiation of the suit would be specific enough to most non-Department of Justice people: "similar neutron activation testing, whether or not by the FBI, of these same objects and materials, namely," followed by the list of them all. "Here also," it concluded, "my request is for the complete report only."

As my lawyer, Jim's request of ERDA "under the provisions of the Freedom of Information Act [5 U.S.C. 552]," the beginning of all of this with that agency, was for

copies of any tests which the Atomic Energy Commission performed for the Warren Commission or any person or agency acting for it ... including but not limited to any spectrographic or neutron activation analyses which were made on the bullets, bullet fragments, clothing, automobile parts, medical specimens, curbstone, or any other objects ... the reports on the results of such tests, not the "raw data" on which they are based.

ERDA was codefendant with the Department of Justice in this action. Could it possibly have taken a federal judge five months to learn that there was this pretended defect in the suit? Is it possible that the government would not have detected this defect if it existed?

How hallowed can a place of justice be, be it a courtroom in which a judge is a partisan or the Department of Justice in which the representatives of the Attorney General pretend they cannot understand common words like "results" of tests and "reports" on them?

The judge finally admitted that we had in fact sued for the NAAs but the FBI never admitted that they had what I would call either "results" or "reports."

Frazier carried the ball on this. In fact, he was the only one of these three FBI agents who even pretended to know anything about it. All questions of fact were referred to him by the others.

Is not the purpose of conducting these tests to compile results and report them? I asked.

Yes, it is, Frazier agreed. And they had done it.

Well, that's what I want, I told him.

That's the problem, he responded. We don't have them in the form in wh ch you appear to believe they exist.

How do they exist?

In the communications sent to the Warren Commission.

Only that?

Only that.

Didn't somebody need a compilation of all the tests, results, figures computed and recorded, all those decimals of parts per million of so many different lab specimens with which to inform Mr. Hoover?

No, Frazier said, they had the raw material, as I call it, the results as they call it, and from this they prepared the information Director Hoover needed.

If that wasn't enough to bring Ananias back to life, it should have made Baron Munchausen envious.

When Frazier and his agent associates had prepared as unequaled a lie as this one or the FBI had phonied its investigation of the assassination of a President to this degree, running all the risks that exposure entailed, it was fruitless to fly into that stone wall. Instead, I asked for copies of all of Hoover's communications with the Commission on this.

Here Bresson took over.

The FBI can't do that, he said. It is all publicly available at the Archives and we could get it there. The Archives was not party to the suit. The agency of what the law calls paramount interest was the Department of Justice. But they would not provide copies of what they said I sued for when they were supposedly attempting an out-of-court settlement. In fact, they did not even provide a list of what they

416

included as these communications that supposedly were their "reports" on these most detailed and elaborate of studies.

(We made repeated verbal and written requests of the Archives. Well after the beginning of hearings, it provided nothing, then it sent us some but not all of these records. In five months, as of the day of the judge's decision, we did not have all of them.)

There was no point in arguing "reports" any further on their turf. How about "results," I asked. Oh, yes, that they had - a stack of bound files halfway between Frazier and me as they had the chairs arranged prior to our arrival.

Frazier then undertook to describe these "results" as they, not the dictionary, define results. They were the handwritten notations made during the examinations of the various specimens.

Isn't that "raw material?" I needled him. And wouldn't the whole FBI crumble into ruins if they gave me any of that?

This, of course, is what FBI Agent Marion Williams had sworn to.

No, it really isn't "raw material," the unembarrassed Frazier said. It is the "results" from which the "reports" which are letters that include no results were drafted.

For a decade I had been pursuing those things suddenly converted into scientific "reports." There is none that can be called a "report" of any kind. It is a very large exaggeration to call them even an intelligible expression of opinion.

I quoted some of their language. Frazier squirmed a little, but he insisted those were "reports" - the only reports. And what they were offering me as a substitute for the "results" is this raw material that suddenly was not raw material because it now suited the purposes of the FBI not to call it raw material. It is raw, some invisible, some illegible, some nonexistent.

Frazier displayed a folder of the spectroscopy. It was not very large, so I asked for a copy of the whole thing. I asked about the NAAs and Kilty reached over and took the top and much thicker folder off the stack. I looked at that stack and worried about the cost of copying all of it if it was not what I wanted. I said I would go over it and pick out the pages I wanted.

You can't do that, Bresson said.

That is the law and it is and has been the Department's practice, I told him.

The law does not require citizens to buy copies of the public information. It grants the right to buy copies. The law grants access, which means the right to examine public information.

Bresson was firm. I could see nothing. They would provide copies but I could see nothing. How would I know what I was getting, whether or not it is what I want? I wouldn't, he said. When I argued not only the law but the cost of buying copies of what I didn't want, he was indifferent and impervious. I could have nothing or I could wind up paying for perhaps thousands of pages of records I did not want. In the FBI there is no in-between.

Jim's remonstrations as a lawyer and his citation of the law made no difference.

Finally I asked how many pages we were talking about and the cost per page. The expert on "freedom of information," the man charged with making copies of the public information available to the public, Bresson, did not know the xeroxing charge. Kilty appeared to be more helpful. He held up a bound folder and estimated it was perhaps a hundred pages.

Rather than engage in further fruitless argument, I said I would pay for it, go ahead and copy it. All the NAArecords that were neither "reports" nor "results" but I was to consider "results."

No, they could not tell me how long the copying would take.

We left wondering if this would be the most of the least productive of meetings.

The FBI could not have been more forthright in letting us know it had not done the required work on this most basic of evidence with the tests that are so definitive in their potential and nonsecret as processes. There was no "semantical" difference. They had not done what is required in these absolutely essential tests (remember the language already quoted, that a "firm statistical basis .. must be acquired") or they were lying. I had asked Frazier if all the statistics on each and every one of all the tests of all the specimens had not been tabulated and he had said it was not done and was not necessary.

The performance of the tests requires the listing of all the elements of the dozen substances tested in all the many items of evidence. What extraordinary memories these FBI agents have to remember all the "results" and not have to record them! Not even those made when Oswald was alive and to be tried? The first day's work alone involved thousands of figures. Was an agent, Frazier or any other, going to take the witness stand and under oath testify from memory on all those thousands of numbers? After Oswald was killed, there was Commission testimony, other tested evidence and the further, NAA testing. Individual sheets of this work hold hundreds of figures - and there were scores of sheets.

What a claim for the FBI's intellectual endowment! There were hundreds of tests. Some were and had to be done over and over. So detailed are the measurements that they are expressed numerically in parts per million. All these specimens to be tested for a dozen elements to parts per million and the figures on each after being replicated did not have to be put on paper in a single large comparison where the agents, Hoover, the Commission and then the world could see them?

The one claim not inherent was to having invented a brain-wave computer by which the FBI laid telepathic printouts in Hoover's and the Commission's minds.

The personal risk in this for Frazier was as great as an FBI agent can run. Loyalty to the Bureau, high as it may have been, may not have been all his motive for as large a lie as an FBI agent can tell. Frazier himself was under oath on this, before the Commission. He had sworn to the submission to him of a "formal report" by Spectrographer John F. Gallagher and that "I prepared the formal report of the entire examination." More, that both of these formal reports are "part of the permanent record of the FBI." (5H67)

Frazier may have taken a chance I would not remember this, but it would be a risky chance because, if he swore falsely to the Warren Commission or swore opposite to this testimony in a court of law, he was in trouble - perjury. It was also risky because judges should know enough about these tests to know they cannot be done without the extensive measurements being recorded and then tabulated and then interpreted.

Whether the FBI was stonewalling or lying, given a fair shake in court before a fair judge, we felt that this alone could end the long national agony over the cover-up called an investigation of this lingering trauma.

A decent, concerned federal judge ought be outraged that the FBI had not done its work when investigating the assassination of a President and ought want to know why. So also ought a decent federal judge find it beyond tolerance if the FBI lied about it and still suppressed the "results" or "reports" that proved its so-called investigation was a deliberate fraud, a whitewashing of the crime and the exculpation of the criminals.

Can anything as monstrous as either alternative be conceived?

There is no other choice. The FBI did or did not do what was required of it or it did or did not lie about it.

If these lies were to be repeated in court, they would be a felony, perjury. They would be the most "material" of lies because, with a supposed out-of-court settlement offered after filing of the complaint, the central issue was of compliance. Once the suit was filed, for it to be dismissed there would have to be this assurance of compliance to the court.

We learned fast enough that a federal judge praising Kleindienst for his Watergater's perjury was not unique. Judge Pratt's only outrage was that citizens were using this most democratic of laws passed by the Congress and that we would dare allege and repeatedly prove official perjury. (July 15 transcript, pp.12,14,19)

When we left that strange meeting, wondering whether we were in 1984 or going Through the Looking-Glass with Alice in Wonderland, we also knew that the FBI and the Department of Justice had deliberately contrived nonexisting "differences" and could not assume they had no purpose. This contrivance was known all the way to the top. When under date of March 17 Mary C. Lawton, Deputy Assistant Attorney General, Office of Legal Counsel, responded to Jim's March 6 letter to Attorney General Levi, she wrote,

I understand that your differences with the Bureau will be discussed with it in a meeting scheduled for March 14, 1975 [sic]. I trust that the meeting will resolve any misunderstandings regarding what kinds of documents Mr. Weisberg desires to obtain pursuant to the Freedom of Information Act.

This is both Alice and Orwell. She wrote the letter in advance of the meeting, when we had expressed no "differences with the Bureau," and simultaneously three days after the meeting without reference to it.

We did not assume that the Attorney General or his Office of Legal Counsel had any less understanding of what "reports" or "results" mean any more than we assumed they had any good reason to assume these "differences" in advance.

We did assume that they all knew what they were doing and we knew enough to have no doubt that it was not and could not be honest.

Whether or not we articulated it, we both then knew that we were once again on our way to the Supreme Court with no apparent means of paying any of the costs and with more than we could expect to do without this added major taking of time.

Seventeen days later Kelley wrote Jim a one-sentence letter:

I am enclosing 17 pages of materials described in my letter to you dated March 26th, plus five pages of documents relating to the curbstone examination which your client, Mr. Weisberg, has requested.

At the bottom he noted "Enclosures (6)."

Twenty-two pieces of paper were stapled together in six sets. Of these not fewer than eight were pages I had obtained from the Archives, those same records Bresson said they would not give me and I would have to get from the Archives. When it suited his purposes, he provided them. This reduced the actual information to 12 pages.

Of these, two were a "Laboratory Work Sheet" to which a page of notes was stapled. The "Specimens submitted for examination" were one, "Q188, Bullet from Edwin A. Walker's residence." Because I had not asked for this and when offered it said I did not want it, this reduced the sheets of paper they provided that could have been included within my request to 10.

(I was not interested in chasing that Walker ghost. The Dallas police identified the bullet fired at General Walker as of a different caliber. This lab sheet does not give or suggest the caliber. However, testing this bullet gave the FBI a chance to prove the allegations that

Oswald fired this shot. That they did not use the opportunity does not persuade that they had proof or even a smell of it.

(The attached sheet, not fully legible, shows that this bullet was run spectrographically. Eleven chemical ingredients are identified in columns headed by their symbols. Q188 was compared with both the "copper jacket" and the "lead alloy" of Q1, Q2 and Q3. These are the "magic bullet," 399, and the two fragments recovered from the front seat of the limousine. Except for these lab identifications, there is not a single figure on the entire sheet. Instead, in a 12th and undescribed column, two sets of capital letters are recorded, "VG" four times and "G" seven times. This is neither the form nor the result of a real spectrographic analysis, which requires the "firm statistical base" that "must be acquired." Rather does it seem to indicate the degree to which it might be claimed that Oswald shot at Walker.

(Written in at the bottom of the lab sheet form is a similar columnar breakdown, without a single figure. Eight chemical elements are noted for Q188 and Q2. Whatever is meant by the unexplained symbols used instead of numbers, in three of the eight cases they are different. If any conclusions can be drawn from this, they have to include the impossibility of the Walker bullet having been the same as those allegedly used in the assassination.)

Two of the remaining 10 pages attached to a sheet referring to Rankin's request by letter of April 9, 1964, relate to Governor Connally's clothing. By the simple process of repeated rexeroxing, these are rendered largely illegible. They are for samples Q566-9, Connally's suit coat, trousers, shirt and tie. (No underwear and his name is spelled "Connelly.")

This evidence did not reach the FBI lab until April 9, four and a half months after the crime. The front sheet, where it can be read, under "result of examination" says, "The coat, trousers, shirt and tie were microscopically examined. No foreign deposits of metal were found on the cloth surrounding the holes in the coat, trousers and shirt."*

Was there a spectrographic analysis not indicated under "results?" Yes, the symbols for two are on the final page. They are completely negative. No proof a bullet or bullets struck Connally's clothing.

In these remaining 10 pages there was at least relevance.

Two, attached to the carbon of a Hoover letter so unsecret I had quoted the original more than 10 years earlier in WHITEWASH, relate to the curbstone. We will deal with them separately.

In part, the "result of examination" written in on the lab sheet for President Kennedy's clothing is meaningful and states a real conclusion. In part, it fudges. X-ray and spectrographic examinations were made. The specimens were all of his clothing plus a comb and a handkershief, Q19-29, inclusive.

These papers are not the work papers of a spectrographic examination.

Here again the copies were made as indistinct as possible.

The deceptive part is, "Spectro of fabric around hole in back of Q25 shirt and Q22 coat record traces of copper."

In the official version these deposits - not of copper but of a copper alloy - have to have been left by Q1, Exhibit 399, the magic bullet. It was examined spectrographically. In the absence of a statement that the deposits on the coat and shirt were from this bullet or at least could have been from this bullet, the only reasonable interpretation is that the tests did not show either to be true. As the cited court cases show, this would have been totally exculpatory in a trial and on this basis alone there was an unsolved crime.

What also destroys the whole official account is "Spectro of fabric around hole in Q-24 tie and near button at neck of shirt (front) no traces of copper or lead. Nothing sig." This is part falsehood.

* See p. 45, 605.

There was no "hole" in Q24, the tie. The sketch does show one - through and through, exactly as a faked picture was contrived to make it appear.

That there are "no traces" of the passage of any bullet or any fragment of a bullet is of no significance to FBI Agents Frazier and Heiberger is in itself significant. It is proof that these damages, as we have already seen from other evidence, were not caused by a bullet. And it means that they and others in the FBI knew it from the very first and from then on knew the whole official story was false.

From this moment on there was no innocence and there was deliberateness and there was deception and in any decent society with any system that can be called "justice" it should be criminal and it should be punished.

Here again we have evidence of conspiracy - to hide the truth and protect the assassins.

And so many - involved and with knowledge - joined in that awful crime of silence!

These three agents report that two sets of spectrographic examinations were run, yet there is no single figure given for any chemical element.

Sketches of the rear of the jacket and shirt show that hole to be, respectively, 5-3/8" and 5-6/8" from the tops of the collars and 1-6/8" and 1-1/8" to the right of center. What is not identified but appears to be the dispersal of blood on the back of the shirt shows it to be mostly to the left of center, from the top of the collar well onto the left sleeve and down to where it joins the body of the shirt. There is a further downward projection in the center. It goes almost halfway to the tail. This pattern of blood is not consistent with an injury on the right side only nor from one to the right side of the head only.

Figures are recorded on the remaining pages. They do not include all the "specimens submitted." Attached to the examinations by Agents Frazier, Stombaugh and Gallagher of Q1-15, inclusive, noted as "received" on "11/22/63" are references to Q2, Q4, Q5, Q9, Q14 and Q15 only. What is missing is significant and meaningful. It reflects instant knowledge of what had to be suppressed to palm off the predetermined story.

Most important of all is the absence of any reference to the magic bullet, Q1; to the whole one found in the rifle, Q8; to the copper jacket fragment found in the front of the car, Q3; and to the two shell casings or empty cartridges immediately taken from the Dallas police, Q6 and Q7.

Yet as a result of this testing, Hoover immediately - the next day, November 23 - assured Curry and later the Commission that these were tested. The first item under "results of examination" is "The bullet Q1." All the other projectile-related specimens are included.

However, this Hoover report is scientifically meaningless because it says nothing. It is not even good propaganda to represent as the scientific "results of examination" no more than "The bullet, Q1, is a 6.5 Manlicher-Carcano rifle bullet. Specimen Q1 weigh 158.6 grains. It consists of a copper alloy jacket with a lead core." (p.2) This is neither the "results" of nor a "report" on spectrographic examination.

Naturally, the clothing is not included and there is nothing to show an effort to connect the "copper traces" from the clothing with Bullet 399 (24H262-4).

With Q3 entirely of jacket metal, copper, not lead, omitting it is consistent. There is a reason we will come to for the omission of any reference to the analysis of these two empty shells.

Three sheets remain of the 22, not one of which is responsive to the request of the suit and the requirements of the law. They are the only ones on printed tabular paper. They are different in appearance, character and seemingly handwriting. Except that Q1 has been added, they have the identical omissions.

They have no source, no signature, no name written in, no conclusions stated, and they omit all but two of the chemical ingredients to have been tested.

The first page, headed "Antimony Determination," also notes "60 days," which does not suggest spectrographic but does suggest NAA testing. The continuation on the second page is headed "Antimony Determination in Lead Specimens." Q15 is omitted from the last page, headed "Silver Determination."

Whether or not done properly, it gives the appearance of "acquiring" at least some kind of "statistical base." With so many of the identified elements omitted, it could hardly be the requisite "firm statistical base."

The experts can argue the meaning of variations of from an average low of 534 parts per million (ppm) of antimony in the Q2 fragment to a high of 697 ppm in the magic bullet, Q1. (The range of individual samples is from 515 to 750.)

Similarly, the silver in Q1, the whole bullet, averages significantly higher than that in any of the tested fragments, 9.40 ppm compared with an average of 7.93 for Q2.

The previously-quoted Canadian government-supported study reported in the Journal of Forensic Sciences shows silver to be present in bullet jackets. However, whatever agency performed whatever testing this is or is part of and for whatever purpose, the jacket portion, Q3, still again is not included. Nor for the last time, either. The FBI shunned Q3.

Like an evidentiary sore thumb, there is no reference to Q8, the whole, unfired bullet, Commission Exhibit 142. There is until now secret scientific proof that it is quintessential in these tests.

Were these not enough, there were many other evidentiary omissions in what Kelley and the FBI represented to be all the scientific tests.

If this is the FBI's spectrographic work, murder by gunshot ought to be the safest crime in the country.

Whether by stretching the most generous imagination this can be called spectroscopy at all - any part of it - it is not complete. It does not include the spectroscopy known to have been done and, one of the reasons for this made-up FBI need for the "conference," does not include the NAAs.

When we complained about the omission of the NAAs, the FBI had the gall to say I did not ask for them. This was the first request. It was repeated in every subsequent formulation, in writing and in the complaint. One of the benefits to the FBI in refusing to permit a record to be made of this "conference" is that we have no record of that long exchange on the NAAs and the argument over whether I would be able to examine them as the law says.

Does one wonder that, when the case was assigned to the judge who tried to give the FBI the legal right to electronic surveillance without court order, the FBI dared pull these dirty tricks, including perjury? Or that the judge undertook to make it appear that we had not actually asked for the NAAs when the entire record is to the contrary?

Inadequate as they are, this batch of mixed-up papers it took a decade to get proves that the decision to cover up was made almost instantly and that what was necessary to the cover-up was done instantly.

By themselves, far short as they are of anything that can be called real spectrographic examination as the FBI is equipped and able to perform this test, they constitute still another disproof of the official account of the murder of the President.

They prove again that the FBI and so many lawyers knew exactly what they were doing - and that what they were doing, no matter how they justified it to themselves, was wrong. Legally, ethically and morally wrong.

Yet these are the very people on whom society depends to uphold the law.

This, with new evidence, is still another part of their record.

Through the Looking-Glass

Despite its best efforts, daring, corrupt and successful as they were, the FBI could not completely avoid giving me more "new"eevidence.

That it dared be corrupt, that it could be successful, gets to the overall sweep of this work. This is not a whodunit. In court, in this series of books, in research and investigation, this is a broad study, centering around political assassinations, of how government and the other institutions of society functioned and malfunctioned during and after these dramatic and dangerous events.

In every assassination there was greater trauma because government and the other institutions of society failed. Those failues become a new danger to free society. If these kinds of things can happen when a President is killed, when can they not happen?

So, while it may seem redundant to tell the same story with new evidence, if there is to be as complete a record as can be made, for history and for learning and reform in the present, these repeated failures, especially of the police agencies, lawyers and the courts, require reporting.

FBI agents are not all lab men, like Frazier. Most are lawyers. In this kind of lawsuit, lawyers of the Civil Division of the Department of Justice are involved. The Office of the United States Attorney - again lawyers - handles or participates in the court work.

Forget for a moment how terrible it is that a President is assassinated and, instead of investigating it to the degree possible, the government covers up and hides evidence and thus protects those who really committed the crime.

Consider how the lawyers and the courts functioned more than a decade later.

Theoretically, the federal judiciary is independent. In practice, it is composed largely of former executive-branch lawyers. Advancement of judges is decided by executive-branch favor. Nomination and promotion are by the executive. Within my experience, the judiciary is predisposed in favor of the government. It tolerates what ought be intolerable. An extreme manifestation is the praise of Richard Kleindienst for his Watergate felony by the judge who described it as an excess of loyalty.

How the system worked in this case, what actually happened in court, does more than show how the government gets away with crookedness. It explains how so many would seem to risk so much. Those who did these wrongful and unlawful things are the enforcers of the law. They expected and expect no punishment. Who prosecutes the prosecutor?

Capsuling this record also serves to indicate how much more suppressed evidence there can be and must be and why it can remain suppressed.

The first hearing, a calendar or "status" call, was May 2. Assistant United States Attorney Michael J. Ryan opened it with "I have been advised by my clients [the Department of Justice and ERDA] that the request of plaintiff [me] in this matter has been fully complied with and that they are now in the process of preparing an [sic] affidavit to that effect." He promised it for the third working day thereafter and "would be filing a praecipe dismissing this matter."

Jim told the judge, without Ryan's denial, that "the documents which we have been given so far themselves refer to other documents which come within the request, which we have not been given." He followed this with specifications and with details of official falsehoods. He asked that truth be established in the usual way, under oath, by interrogatories we had filed. The judge suggested to Ryan, "In your affidavit why don't you come to the outstanding matters of the interrogatories ... If the answers to the interrogatories are covered in an affidavit I assume that would be satisfactory ..." (Transcript,p.10. Hereafter references are to the page of each day's transcript.)

It was window-dressing when Pratt said, "These affidavits are on personal knowledge" (p.10) and "can state categorically that everything in the way of a test that they have made has been submitted." Ryan agreed (p.11). He asked for a fourth delay and was given three more weeks.

Pratt displayed prejudice in closing the hearing with this nasty crack (p.12):

15	THE COURT: I assume, Mr. Weisberg, at least for
16	the time being has other means of support, doesn't he, Mr.
17	Lesar?
18	MR. LESAR: Well, his financial circumstances are
19	not good, but that is a situation which I don't expect to
20	change in any event.
21	THE COURT: Good enough to hire you.
22	MR. LESAR: He has had my services without any fee.
23	THE COURT: All right. Okay. May 21. If you

The next status-call hearing began May 21. Just as Pratt walked into the courtroom, Ryan handed Jim and me a single copy of the affidavit Kilty had sworn to eight days earlier. It identifies Kilty as a lab agent "in a supervisory capacity." The one purpose served by this newest dirty trick, holding back the affidavit for a week - one of their regular dirty tricks - was to make it impossible for us to rebut it on the spot.

Ryan misrepresented Kilty as having "the best personal knowledge of the FBI's files" on this subject (pp.2-3). But neither he nor Kilty ever said what files Kilty searched. One of the oldest of the dirty tricks is to search the wrong files and avoid the right ones. The most obvious of the many evidentiary and factual deficiencies here is that, without first-person knowledge, Kilty has no way of knowing whether he "reviewed" all the work. There is, in fact, reason to believe that the major file was kept elsewhere (5H67).

About ERDA, which supplied no affidavit in any response to the interrogatories or the judge's order, Ryan said, "I have been after the agency for the last several days ... and I was assured that it was on its way ... they promised it would be here this morning. I don't have it yet" (p.3). That affidavit "would be in my office today or somebody will hear about it" (p.4).

Nobody heard. This ERDA affidavit was not executed for another 20 days. It was not filed for another month and a half, on June 18. But nothing the government did or did not do bothered Pratt.

Kilty's affidavit was not "made on personal knowledge," the requirement, Jim noted. He gave "proof that other tests were conducted which have not been made available to us." Pratt asked him to tell Ryan about them. Jim had, at the previous hearing. When he started to explain, all he got out was, "Well, the fundamental problem --" when Pratt cut him off with "we are not going to make a cause celebre out of this case ... not going to go through a lot of confrontation and so on" (p.5).

This, of course, is one way of dealing with official perjury.

Pratt repeated, "I think you ought to tell Mr. Ryan and so on" and Jim managed to get out, "Your Honor, I did --" before Pratt cut him off still again with "I am not going to make debating points in this with me [sic]" (p.5). Pratt persisted

Pratt persisted in rewriting the law. In its wisdom Congress, having had its own experiences with official suppressions and lying, placed the burden of proof of compliance on the government. Pratt by-passed this requirement of the law by telling Jim, "it seems to me in good conscience it is up to you to tell Mr. Ryan" (p.5). Finally (pp.5-6), he let Jim remind him that Jim had done this at the previous hearing. Jim added new specifics. Confronted with another sworn FBI statement that was here proven false, Pratt repeated still again, "you ought to tell Mr. Ryan about it" (p.6). All Jim could do is repeat that he had. He also told the judge that the burden of proof was not on us and that if we told the government all we knew it was withholding, it would get away with suppressing all else (p.7).

Pratt was impervious. Jim pointed out that Frazier had first-person knowledge and could have supplied an affidavit while Kilty did not even pretend first-person knowledge. Confronted with proof, Pratt said no more than "I accepted Mr. Ryan's representation that Kilty knows more about it than these other people" (p.8). "These other people" happen to be the ones who actually performed the tests!

All of this book is a Byzantine account dealing with what we can hardly believe of the less civilized past. Nothing in it, certainly not in any of the litigation, is farther out than the government's endorsement of me as an expert - the preeminent expert. When it could not entirely ignore my proven charges of perjury against it and tried to have them expunged ("motion to strike"), with the question what was in the FBI's own files, it actually filed a document suggesting that I know more about the subject than anyone in the FBI:

In the motion to strike (pp. 2-3), plaintiff also alleges the

existence of certain documents which he claims have not been

provided by the F.B.I. In a sense, plaintiff could make such

claims ad infinitum since he is perhaps more familiar with events

surrounding the investigation of President Kennedy's assassination

than anyone now employed by the F.B.I.

Ryan followed with a big speech on the FBI's "good faith effort" while admitting that in "prior cases ... the Government had withheld this information ..." (pp.8-11).

Jim followed with other specific proofs of official lying on the central - really only - issue, compliance (pp.11-3), and asked again that the interrogatories be answered under oath to resolve the existing questions, the legal norm. Pratt refused, adding, "I have read your interrogatories. I have a little bit of the feeling that they were somewhat oppressive, but maybe that is what you intended them to be" (p.13). His response to his obligations as a judge when he had this repeated proof of the misuse of the courts and the law and of false swearing was more unhidden prejudice, "I have the feeling

that this Freedom of Information Act case takes on some of the conspiracy theory risen concerning the Kennedy assassination. It's part
of the same thing. I mean, somebody is hiding something" (p.14).

When Jim reminded the judge that the record held confirmed
lies on just this point, the very judge who then and thereafter made
it impossible and always ignored it replied, "Okay, nail them to the
mast on that" (pp.14-5).

There was no end to Pratt's flaunting of prejudice, such as
saying we preferred going to trial, with all the costs and trouble
that means. Simultaneously, he was frustrating Jim's effort to avoid
trial while still getting the law lived up to (p.17). Pratt's clear
intent was to prevent a trial at which it would all hang out while
seeing to it that the government's noncompliance was protected. He
ignored the proof totally. He then added another provision to his
rewriting of the law: "I would like to suggest that substantial compliance might well be a basis for mooting this case. In other words,
you may be able to nitpick and come up with this item or that item
... It is not going to bother me ..." (p.19).

Not content and not able to dismiss with the record we had
made, the judge actually apologized to Ryan for it: "I'm sorry, too,
but you have a redoubtable adversary, as you know, Mr. Ryan." Ryan
muttered one word about me, "Persistent." Pratt added, "I will bet
you are glad you don't have him in every case" (pp.19-20).

And with that he gave the government "a little over four weeks"
more, until June 20, to comply with the law it had twice sworn falsely
to him it had complied with (pp.19-20). Not without adding further
evidence of preconception and prejudice: "I don't know whether we
can accomplish anything further by prolonging this" (p.21).

One can sympathize with the problems of a judge whose purpose
is to see to it that evidence remains suppressed, the law violated
and violators go unpunished because they are officials when the hearings he holds merely produce more proofs of this criminality and he
has to work his way around them. Especially when he wants to replace
Congress and rewrite the law.

The next hearing was on July 15, not June 20. Ryan took up
the first third with a speech about the fullness of official compliance and the honesty of official intentions. He had supplied another
evasive Kilty affidavit contradicting the first and one by ERDA Associate General Counsel Bertram Schur, together with those hundreds of
uncollated and unidentified papers. While admitting "that the burden
of proof is on the government under the Freedom of Information Act"
(p.4), Ryan simultaneously sought to avoid it by claiming that we had
not told him what was still withheld. We are supposed to tell him
what is in FBI files! The lie and the intent to lie could not have
been more deliberate (pp.4-5). I had ticked this off to him personally in the courtroom at the end of the previous hearing. With vigor
that made him stutter, Jim later confronted him on this (p.17) without apology from Ryan or interest from the judge. The second Kilty
affidavit pretends to explain it away. Ryan argued what he described
in the judge's own hinted words as "substantial compliance" in his
motion to dismiss the case, with what is directly opposed to the law,
that "a presumption of validity attaches to the actions of a federal
agency." In that motion he voluntarily described all he had delivered
as "documents not understood to be within plaintiff's request." In
simpler language, this means that by giving me what I had not requested, the government complied with the law and did not have to give
me what I had asked for and proved it did have (pp.2-7,17).

This also came up in a different expression because we established that "plaintiff has not received a single page of the documents
which he requested under the Freedom of Information Act." Ryan's nonresponse beginning with "we have great difficulty when faced with a
statement like that" does not deny or refute it. He argued that what
I had not asked for is what I had asked for. He could not refute
Jim's accurate citation of the legislative history of the law. The

Congress _did_ say the government's word cannot be taken without proof! The judge tried to help out Ryan a bit in his illogical nonresponse by again calling me a conspiracy theorist (p.3-7).

Jim came right to the point in declaring "there is a factual issue in dispute here, and that is whether or not there has been any compliance at all with Mr. Weisberg's request for the final reports on the tests made which he has requested. We have not been given any such final reports, but there is no under-oath, first-person statement stating that those reports do not exist. We have not been provided even with some of the documents which the government has attempted to substitute for the final reports" (pp.7-8).

Pratt did not interrupt him until Jim said that the record proves "the government has persistently stalled in this case."

"Stalled in this case?" Pratt protested. In this he made his intention clear: "This suit was only filed five months ago, and here you are having a resolution of it right now."

Actually, the matter was then ten months old. What Pratt was saying is that compliance or no compliance, law or no law, regardless of proof, he was about to throw out the case with his own protest at being embarrassed. He here became government co-counsel, even trying to argue that we had not asked for the NAAs.

NAA requests are in a _third_ of the paragraphs of the complaint. Three of the four attachments are on it. All earlier hearings dealt with it without Ryan raising any question. The Kilty affidavits attest to this particular request as does attached correspondence from Director Kelley. There was no basis for this question. It served only to interrupt Jim's presentation and to try to throw him off balance and interfere with his thinking.

It took three pages (9-11) before Pratt backed off, "Yes, I see that... All right."

He followed this with (p.12) his own manner of getting around the sworn proof before him of perjury in the FBI's affidavits. The government did not refute or even address it. Pratt threatened that we could be sued for making and proving these charges:

```
10    THE COURT:  Well, you not only say they lack

11    good faith, but you say the record conclusively demonstrates

12    that both affiants lied.

13         You and Mr. Weisberg bandy about these materials

14    with considerable ease and are very quick to impugn motives.

15         MR. LESAR:  Well, I think we have provided the

16    Court with considerable --

17         THE COURT:  If you were not in the context of a

18    courtroom, you might get yourself faced with a lawsuit.

19         MR. LESAR:  We will be making the same statements

20    out of court, and I have no fear there will be no lawsuit.

21         THE COURT:  You mean you have no fear there will

22    be a lawsuit.
```

Pratt again backed off. Jim reminded him that one FBI agent, Kilty, had filed two affidavits, each directly contradicting the other on material points.

In the first affidavit Kilty swore that there was neutron activation analysis on the clothing, windshield and curbstone:

7. With regard to the interrogatories submitted by Mr. Weisberg, the affiant states that the FBI Laboratory employed methods of elemental analysis, namely neutron activation analysis and emission spectroscopy. Neutron activation analysis and emission spectroscopy were used to determine the elemental composition of the borders and edges of holes in clothing and metallic smears present on a windshield and a curbstone.

But in the second Kilty swore exactly the opposite, that spectroscopy had been used on this same evidence and that "NAA was not used in examining the clothing, windshield or curbing:"

8. Concerning plaintiff's allegation that, although NAA testing was conducted on the clothing of President Kennedy and Governor Connally, he has not been furnished the results of this testing: further examination reveals emission spectroscopy only was used to determine the elemental composition of the borders and edges of holes in clothing and metallic smears present on a windshield and a curbstone. NAA was used in examination of certain metal fragments, and plaintiff has already been furnished material relating to these examinations. NAA was not used in examining the clothing, windshield, or curbing.

While these are not his only false swearings, nothing could be more material. Kilty proved Kilty swore falsely about it. One of his sworn statements is false. The other proves it. In what Kilty had given us, I had found the record of NAAs on the windshield sweepings, identified by the FBI as Q15. Kilty swore there was no such NAA testing. Jim waved this "page which refers to specimen Q-15" proving "that the test was conducted" (p.18). It also proved perjury.

All Pratt could do is ask, incredulously, "You got that from the government, did you?" (p.18)

With this Pratt ended the hearing, ruling, "I am satisfied that there has been a good-faith effort on the part of the government, and that the government has complied substantially with its obligations under the Freedom of Information Act. Accordingly, I am going to grant the government's motion to dismiss this matter as moot." He added that we could go "to the Court of Appeals, and you may have some gentlemen there who will tell me I am wrong. They have done that before." Indeed, they had, as in the case where Pratt sought to give

438

815

XP.

ATE   OPER.

USTOMER

HG. NO.

RAD. POS.

2144   OUT 2144 t 20

DETECT   VOLTS

GEOM   ABS

CHAN SECT   1   2   3   4

AMP   ZERO

GAIN

TIME   BG

Δt_L Δt_C

the FBI powers to conduct illegal electronic surveillance not granted by law. Now he went so far as to say "I think the government has been oppressed" and that "in relying on Mr. Kilty for two affidavits" and on ERDA for another "they did all they were required to do" (p.19). Having recommended and praised perjury, he rewarded it by adjourning court.

The ruling was absurd. Kilty proved Kilty swore falsely and that is all the government had to do to win. Before this judge, anyway.

Once again we had gone through the legal looking-glass in which up is down and wrong is right, guided by a judge who was for all practical purposes part of the executive branch, a judge determined to perpetuate suppressions by rewriting the law.

"Judges throughout the United States are afraid to enforce the law," Attorney General Levi said in a Voice of America broadcast a few days later (Post,7/26/75). The day it was reported I wrote the Attorney General asking him to enforce the law against perjury and to inquire into whether his subordinates suborned this perjury.

The reply, signed by Rex E. Lee, Assistant Attorney General, Civil Division, the division involved in this very suit, said only that the charge was "rejected by the Court." Ignored would have been more accurate. But this, as Lee preferred not to understand, is exactly what Levi had inveighed against, judges not enforcing the law.

There is a difference. Levi was not talking about Watergate crime, not about crimes over which he and his predecessors presided, sometimes ordering it. Not about white-collar crime or all the federal abuses of law and citizens' rights. He was back with Nixon taking crime off the streets. He was four-square with Nixon, Mitchell, Kleindienst and all the others moving crime from the streets into government and by his authority protecting all of it.

If Levi were not the kind of man who could utter these sanctimonies straight-faced; if he were not the kind of man who considers stealing a loaf of bread criminal and official subverting of the law ethical, he would not have been appointed to administer justice. Not with all the charges that could still be made and tried hanging over from Watergate. Not after accounts of all the other crimes by the CIA and the FBI began coming out.

The conduct and record of government lawyers is not what Chief Justice Warren Burger had in mind when he told the American Bar Association convention August 5, 1975, that "one of the most crucial problems of our profession and of the courts in particular" is "an almost complete lack of judicial or professional regulation of members of the bar, and this has lead to a great tolerance for misbehavior and misconduct that brings the system of justice into disrepute..." (NYTimes 8/6/75).

But would it not be nice if it were!

It is closer to what FBI Director Kelley told the same bar convention three days later (Post 8/10/75), "We [sic] must be willing to surrender a small measure of our liberties" (whatever he means by "small" and "liberties") in order to "preserve" them.

How else did the "Sieg Heil!" and the "Duce!" cries start more than four decades earlier?

Surrendering any "measure of our liberties" is not as reversible as being a little bit pregnant.

From the foregoing as well as what follows, it should not be inferred that the FBI does not prize its good name as well as its own liberties, given and taken. Nay, nay, nay - a thousand times nay! Nor is it reluctant to enter suit to protect and defend its name, even to exercising a proprietary right over the alphabet. There is nothing - but nothing - the FBI will not do to uphold its name and its ownership of the alphabet with it.

Thus it sued an established French clothing manufacturer, Fabrication Brill International, for marketing such garments as evening dresses under Brill's own initials, FBI.

On August 12, 1975 (Post 8/13/75) the FBI lost in federal district court in Washington.

John Pratt was not the judge.

And there was no "protective order."

Nagging Coincidences in Hiding Evidence

During this writing, on August 14, Los Angeles Superior Court Judge Robert Wenke ordered a test-firing of the pistol with which Sirhan Sirhan supposedly killed Robert Kennedy (Post 8/15/75). By then there was proof that all the known damage and all the known bullets had not been traced exclusively to Sirhan. There was reason to believe that this could not be done. Wenke responded to a number of suits, including by Paul Schrade, a member of Kennedy's campaign staff and a victim of the shooting, by former Congressman Allard Lowenstein, and by Sirhan, represented by Barry Gold (Post 8/15/75).

That Lowenstein had been conducting his own inquiry into the RFK assassination was first widely publicized in December 1974. The responsibility of his approach earned favorable comment.

On August 20 it became known that "some of the evidence" had "disappeared or been destroyed." This included two "bullet-marked ceiling panels" where three bullets hit. Dion Morrow, the city attorney's representative, was quoted as saying "There were no X-rays of the ceiling panels, and the panels were destroyed in June of 1969." The reason? "There was no place to keep them - you can't fit ceiling panels into a card file." Reuters also quoted Morrow as saying "the left sleeve of Kennedy's coat disappeared" before the Sirhan trial in 1969 (Post 8/21/75). According to UPI the same day Morrow described all the missing evidence as "not of great significance."

Evidence that does not fit in card files or file cabinets is commonplace. Most police departments are prepared to and do handle large items of evidence. Trucks and autos and people who provide evidence are not destroyed. To my knowledge Los Angeles has special provisions for evidence that does not fit into small cabinets.

X-rays, also commonplace in murder cases, do.

The next day Morrow provided a further explanation. In the words of Robert Meyers (Post 8/22/75), "The two ceiling panels, X-rays of the panels and records of the X-rays were all regarded as nonevidentiary material."

The major press covered the meeting of the Los Angeles City Council the morning of August 21. However, it did not cover the police commission's meeting that afternoon with Acting Los Angeles Police Chief Daryl Gates the witness. Jeffrey Kaye of Zodiac News Service, most of whose clients are college radio stations, was there. Zodiac's story was distributed the next day, condensed by Jon Newhall.

Kaye reports that the ceiling panels were destroyed under an order drawn up June 27, 1969. This order included the also-destroyed doorjambs and spectrographic analyses prepared by the police criminalist, DeWayne Wolfer. X-rays of the ceiling panel were made but "cannot be located." Gates swore that Wolfer's spectrographic analysis also had disappeared.

Among the other inexplicable disappearances of evidence Zodiac reported is that of several doorjambs. The early morning of that assassination AP syndicated a picture of police pointing to what looked like bullet holes in one doorjamb. With Sirhan's pistol holding eight bullets only, and eight bullets not able to account for all the known wounds plus the holes in the ceiling panels, the destruction of these would-be bullet holes in the doorjambs, obviously vital evidence in the crime, becomes even more suspect.

Zodiac reports that these added destructions also took place in June 1969 when the evidence was required to be preserved for appeals and possible reversals and new trials. In Sirhan's case all the evidence had not been used, evidence that could be incriminating or exculpatory, essential to either the prosecution or the defense.

The prosecution would destroy evidence it had not used if it could convict Sirhan on retrial only because in the most spread-out of large cities there was no place to store it?

That the evidence could have been exculpatory and would jeopardize the prosecution is more easily believed.

The same and other accounts make it clear that there had been no examination of the spectrographic analysis said to have been made and that no NAAs had been made.

Can it be believed that incriminating evidence would ever be destroyed in a crime of this magnitude, one in which from the first there had been serious and wide-spread questioning and doubts about conspiracy? In the trial Sirhan's lawyers saw fit to plead him guilty. From the first others insisted he was not the only shooter and that there had been a conspiracy.

Besides what I knew I had in my files, how familiar it seemed! How exact a parallel with what did happen in the JFK and King assassinations. What had just, in fact, happened in C.A. 226-75, where the FBI alleged it did not have the reports of the scientific tests, where autopsy X-rays disappeared and there are questions about the pictures. Where the knot on the tie was undone when it was evidence and after all the testing on it.

Remember Rankin's quoted letter not written until February and his definition of the "scene" of the crime? So Elm Street, in perfect condition, was repaved and the background needed for photointelligence was destroyed. This includes fixed and permanent evidence for photoanalysis like the places witnesses said bullets struck the street and the sign over which Zapruder filmed. The repaved street had new and different stripes painted on it. Once the sign was moved, no precise reconstruction was possible.

My published work on this dates to 1965 and 1966. (Dozens of references in WHITEWASH and WHITEWASH II. The charts alone in WHITEWASH II, pp.243-6, show the different number and location of the road stripes.)

The many parallels in the James Earl Ray case, in which I am the defense investigator, include denial to the defense of access to evidence needed for his defense, the disappearances of entire boxes of it, and the total absence of any of the many FBI lab reports, especially of spectroscopy and NAAs. Particularly noteworthy is FBI Agent Frazier's false swearing about the ballistics evidence, that

431

identification with a rifle was impossible (FRAME-UP, esp.p.506).
When I examined the remnant of bullet Frazier swore was a whole bullet, it was so obvious to the naked eye that this fragment could be
identified with a rifle that I arranged by phone for a criminalist
with whom I had not previously spoken to examine that evidence and
testify. He testified contrary to Frazier. He was not cross-examined
on this testimony. It was not rebutted. Neither Frazier nor any
other FBI agent appeared in court to uphold either his integrity or
that of the FBI.

Can it be only coincidence that in the three major political
assassinations there are the same inexcusable and totally unnecessary
violations of the integrity of identical and similar evidence when
the FBI is involved in all three?

What was in my files alone on the Robert Kennedy assassination
relates closely to the recounted and to-be-recounted history of C.A.
226-75 and to the conduct and attitudes of Judge Pratt.

In the Sirhan case all the shots are sworn by Frazier's Los
Angeles police counterpart to have been fired from Sirhan's pistol.
But the evidence, once independent experts could examine it, identi-
fied all the shots as having come from an entirely different pistol.

What happened to this other pistol? It was destroyed by the
Los Angeles police. Here is the police teletype on it:

```
112570 1810
OCS 1410
N CII 503 OCS
SO SAN ANA
ATTN SGT ADELSPERGER/ID SGT
11-25-70 1808 PST
REUR 68 OCS DATE

BUR FILES REVEAL A .22 CAL IVER JOHNSON SERIAL H18602 REPORTED
DESTROYED 7-00-68 BY PD LOS ANGELES CR 67 021065
NO WANTS

CII PROPERTY IDENT UNIT MC GILLIVARY AM/RM
```

What proves Sirhan killed RFK, according to District Attorney
Joseph P. Busch (who died on June 27 amid the new controversy)? As
reported by the Los Angeles City News Service on October 18, 1971,
Busch said that the test "bullets were compared with the bullet removed from the sixth cervical vertebra of Senator Kennedy." This is
the base of the neck. The fatal shot to the brain entered the mastoid, fragmented and was not identifiable. Bush cited proof that
Sirhan had shot, not that he had killed.

And now, what about this destruction and/or disappearance of
evidence in June 1969? Well, the previous month there was a secret
conference ostensibly for the purpose of guaranteeing that this did
not and could not happen. Actually, it was to try to connive some
legal-appearing basis for denying access to the evidence as much as
possible.

This secret gathering of May 15, 1969, was in the chambers of
Assistant Presiding Superior Court Judge Charles A. Loring. (Sirhan
was convicted less than a month earlier, on April 17.) Judge Herbert
V. Walker, who handled the Sirhan trial, was with him. So were Robert
A. Houghton, Deputy Los Angeles Chief of Police and chief of detec-
tives in the Sirhan investigation; Deputy District Attorney David
Pitts; Emery Hatcher, Chief Deputy, County Clerk's office, with Peter
Talmachoff, chief of its criminal division; and another clerk, Mrs.
Alice Nishikawa. One side only - the prosecution. There was no rep-
resentative of Sirhan's defense.

Quotation of the transcript here is rearranged by the subject
discussed.

As with the Warren Commission and all those prejudicial advance leaks to propagandize for that Report's acceptance:

DEPUTY CHIEF HOUGHTON: We had a meeting ... in which the District Attorney requested that we were to use ... investigative files ... which constituted, in his terms, red herrings in the case. Now there were about fifteen or sixteen of such categories and five of these received some publicity. (p.7)

* * * *

MR. PITTS: ... but nobody asked for that stuff [psychiatric statements] in the courtroom and yet it was released ... I have some misgivings because it was not in evidence. (pp.16-7)

The Commission and the FBI began with a predetermined conclusion. These judges were as impartial. The prosecutor was not concerned about the requirement of the canons of the bar, that his primary responsibility is not to convict but to see to it that justice is done:

JUDGE LORING: ... Suppose the Supreme Court should, through inadvertence, order a reversal here. Is there anything going to be investigated ... if there is going to be a press release ...
JUDGE WALKER: It would be a question to this extent. If the Supreme Court does so, in all likelihood it would not be within at least two years and possibly three.
JUDGE LORING: The damage, if any, would have been done. ... I just did want to raise the question and ask if you had considered if there should be a reversal and what effect this is going to have.
JUDGE WALKER: ... you possibly couldn't get this thing up on appeal before two years. I am hopeful that the nature of the court will change by then.
MR. PITTS: It is going to create a substantial problem. No matter how far it is in the future, if it is reversed. ... the Legislature is going to have to talk their heads off about it and I don't know anything you can do. (pp.29-31)

"Solving" the crime with a no-conspiracy solution, typical of all three cases, required withholding evidence, another characteristic of all three. So, here, too, it was done:

DEPUTY CHIEF HOUGHTON: Well, the [police] photos I am talking about [medical, pre-autopsy] were not introduced into evidence. (p.4)

* * * *

MR. PITTS: We used a very minimal of photos because, after all, it wasn't an issue anyway, no controversy. (p.4)
JUDGE WALKER: I know Alice has kept track of it. It is not going to be any problem to figure it out. (p.4)

* * * *

JUDGE WALKER: Anything not in evidence, I don't see why we have to make it available. (p.17)

* * * *

DEPUTY CHIEF HOUGHTON: ... The total investigation files are in great detail. ... we interviewed a lot of people and you never knew who they were going to talk to. I am sure some of it will leak out. The majority of it has not. ... It is all in written form, about 50,000 pieces of paper, and the final report to the Chief consists of nine volumes ... (pp.18-9) ... all the evidence we have in our system, I would say easily is 4,000 items. (p.22)

* * * *

JUDGE LORING: Well, I think the answer to the people who want to hear the tape ... they will have to supply their own electrical energy. (p.23)

Going along with this was the recognition that, with appeals pending, some of the evidence had to be kept intact and secure. Not for justice but to prevent a "mess," a bad public reaction. All the evidence was not discussed with specific identification. In even a meeting of this kind, the police and prosecution did not trust the judges to know of all of it. Only enough for them to understand and meet the political problem. There is, for example, no mention of the two ceiling panels or the X-rays of them, or of the scientific tests, although FBI materials are included:

JUDGE WALKER: These exhibits were extremely valuable and they are going to go up on appeal and to have them mutilated or even some of them, it is going to be very bad and I think particularly if they are not in packages. (p.4)

* * * *

JUDGE WALKER: ... we have got these bullets, we have got the gun ... What I am trying to do is set something up ... so they are not mutilated or lost or anything else, because it is easy for these exhibits to get lost in your office and everybody is in a mess. (p.5) ... but we have got the coat, we have bullets, we have got expended shells, unexpended and so forth, which are physical.

JUDGE LORING: Well, I think they could be put in some kind of a plastic or cellophane container ...

MR. PITTS: To be realistic about it, there aren't going to be many people who want to look at these bullets anyway. What can they do with it?

DEPUTY CHIEF HOUGHTON: I don't think that is the problem. ... I think you could store the bullets, however you want to store them or for how long ... Then you could say they are in permanent storage, whatever you want to say. Now as to the coat, I agree with Judge Loring ... I think you might be able to put that in a bag ...

JUDGE LORING: You would probably want to preserve that in some kind of container in any event ...

JUDGE WALKER: How about the bullets, guns [emphasis added] and other physical things? (pp.12-3)

* * * *

MR. PITTS: ... the physical things other than papers ... that they are viewed upon Court order for good cause shown, period.

JUDGE WALKER: You are talking about the coat and shells again?

MR. PITTS: Right, every bit of it ...

DEPUTY CHIEF HOUGHTON: Could I make a comment here? Off the record. (Discussion off the record.)

JUDGE WALKER: Well, I think we have got it pretty well in mind now. It is up to me, along with the cooperation of the rest of you, to work out a proper order. (pp.23-4)

* * * *

MR. PITTS: ... There should be some kind of security precautions enforced so far as the Clerk's Office is concerned ...

MR. HATCHER: With all of our precautions, they might destroy something ... (p.31)

The session opened with and was dominated by the need to keep secret all the evidence possible, where people could either not see it or could under great difficulties only. Where copies could not be denied, it was decided to charge 50 cents a page for them. It was agreed that this exorbitant charge would discourage interest. Prosecutor Pitts made this grim joke: "Those who aren't satisfied with

434

the facilities available can bring their own equipment." Clerk Hatcher protested, "Oh, no, no." To which Pitts rejoined, "No comment." (p.31)

With the defense absent and with secrecy expected, as with the Warren Commission executive sessions, the intent to keep all the evidence as secret as possible and as difficult to get at when secrecy was not possible is not hidden. Among friends only limited hiding was necessary:

JUDGE WALKER: I am willing to seal these subject to order of court, and I think I can put it on some kind of ground. I am going to look at it and find myself some ground and do it. (p.2)

* * * *

JUDGE WALKER: Anything that went into evidence I don't think we can take a chance on sealing. (p.4)

* * * *

DEPUTY CHIEF HOUGHTON: ... we have done a lot of investigating of cases which were not subject to testimony ...
MR. PITTS: ... They asked for interviews and interviews they got, but when it came down to embodying conclusions of investigative personnel ... Material of that kind I abstracted from the file.
DEPUTY CHIEF HOUGHTON: In other words, what you did, you must have done it earlier to block it out ... because some of that was built into some of these interviews.
MR. PITTS: No, it wasn't built into the Q and A, and I gave you that which purports to be questions and answers.
DEPUTY CHIEF HOUGHTON: We got a lot of actually what was a summary of interviews, not Q's and A's.
MR. PITTS: Yes ... Where possible the stuff was not made a matter of record. (pp.6-7)

* * * *

DEPUTY CHIEF HOUGHTON: We have got all of those [files] plus some others ... of some significance, not materially significant, other than those that they asked for on discovery ... They might have Virginia Teresa and that might have been marked.
MR. PITTS: I don't think so.
DEPUTY CHIEF HOUGHTON: Some of it had not reached the press ... nobody knew it except us, the District Attorney and the FBI ... (pp.7-8)

* * * *

JUDGE WALKER: ... How about the search warrant?
THE CLERK: That is only for identification.
JUDGE WALKER: Okay, fine.
DEPUTY CHIEF HOUGHTON: Which search warrant?
JUDGE WALKER: Well, the one nobody had.
DEPUTY CHIEF HOUGHTON: For the car? We had two ...
The first search warrant was never material. It was the wrong car. That was a Chrysler.
JUDGE WALKER: There was one I didn't want to put in evidence because of the affidavits attached to it.
THE CLERK: He never asked it to go into evidence ...
MR. PITTS: There was the search of the DeSoto [Sirhan's].
DEPUTY CHIEF HOUGHTON: It never came in issue?
MR. PITTS: It never came up so we never put the search warrant in evidence. (pp.9-10)

* * * *

MR. PITTS: ... with respect to the restrictive order ... do you want an affidavit or an order prepared by someone?
JUDGE WALKER: Well, you can make up an affidavit or an

order for my signature ... I can't very well make an affidavit ... I don't know whether we need an affidavit. Could-
n't you just simply prepare an order? I think there should
be something in the record that supports my order, and now
whether it is a good legal support or is not is another
question.
    JUDGE LORING: Couldn't you recite an examination of the
photographs, discovery material of such a nature and so
forth, otherwise it would serve no useful purpose.
    MR. PITTS: That's what I had in mind.
    JUDGE WALKER: I will do it that way but you will have
to help me ... (p.11)

                              * * * *

    DEPUTY CHIEF HOUGHTON: ... the files of this investiga-
tion should be separate from all the other files and they
will be under lock and key and there will be a minimum distribution of keys. At the moment there are three. ... one
I will have. ...
    MR. PITTS: Nielson has one, and who has got the other?
    DEPUTY CHIEF HOUGHTON: Captain Brown. We are going to
isolate the files ... (p.32)

    The end of it all was almost as Dulles ended that January 22,
1964, executive session, with Judge Walker saying, "I don't think we
will have this written up at this time for distribution." (p.33)

    Like the Warren Commission, those who were supposed to be im-
partial, the judges, were partisans. They did what they wanted to
do, not what justice required. Like that order for which Walker would
find "some kind of ground ... whether it is a good legal" order. They
feared the decision could be reversed because the trial was not fair
but were assured that Nixon would alter the complexion and views of
the Supreme Court in time for the remade court to support them.

    They were aware that the physical evidence had to be preserved.
Nobody raised any questions of space for storage and there was space,
described as bays, in which the evidence could be kept in "packages"
and "containers," the clothing in plastic bags. Along with this were
what could be taken as hints that some might be destroyed.

    Whether or not this was the intent, it is what happened - the
very next month! But as with the Warren Commission, it took persist-
ence and diligence by those later seeking truth to expose the destruction of evidence.

    With this destruction of evidence there was the plan for with-
holding it "under lock and key."

    This characterizes the police, the prosecution and the courts
in all three major political assassinations.

    It is anything but justice or the quest for truth or decency
in society and government.

    It is a close duplication of the FBI's suppression of these
scientific tests, not doing what was required in them and then making
access as difficult as possible to what little it would let out, law
or no law.

    Pratt did "put it on some kind of ground." He did "find myself
some ground and do it." He did not worry about "good legal support"
and he was openly contemptuous of the appeals court.

    Nixon had already remade the Supreme Court by then.

                          More "New" Evidence

    Those hundreds of pages of thousands of figures Ryan gave us
that we had not asked for do have values, values obvious since September 27, 1964. Their values are why they are suppressed in the Warren
Report. One is clear in the last testimony in the 26 appended volumes

                                 436

that appeared two months later.

I did not seek them or the raw material of those tests only because I could not pay for them.

In its desperation to protect the judge acting as its agent, the government had to deliver something that in its allegations would appear impressive. What they gave today is less significant than what I sued for.

If exculpating Oswald were the major question, after more than a decade I'd have found some way of paying for these records and would have sought them. To report that they do exculpate Oswald is to report the simple fact. That is why they, too, had to be suppressed. Broader and deeper issues became more significant with the passing of the years and the changes time brought. Oswald's remarried wife told their children their father was the lone assassin. There is the abstract question of justice. But there remains this unsolved crime and this kind of malfunction of all our institutions.

My earlier suits ended the decade of suppression of those TOP SECRET executive-session transcripts in which the Commission was horrified over the possibility that Oswald had served a federal agency and deliberated how to "wipe it out." Thereafter the major interests benefitting from belief Oswald was innocent are these agencies. For others concern should be about the state of the country as a consequence of all of these now unquestionable abuses and subversions.

Most of those hundreds of pages are the raw material of the testing of the paraffin casts the Dallas police made of Oswald's hands and face to determine whether he could have fired a pistol and a rifle or handled one that had been fired (15H749). The tests do not prove that either did happen. They are capable of proving that either could have happened. They are capable of proving that neither did. Other common substances can leave the same deposits as residues from gunfire. The absence of deposits is exculpatory.

These paraffin tests were subjected to neutron activation analysis. They show deposits on the hands, which need mean no more than that Oswald handled any of the many ordinary materials that can leave the invisible traces NAAs pick up. This means that he could have fired a pistol, not that he had. There is no similar evidence on his cheek. The tests given me show that in seven "control" cases where others fired a rifle this evidence was left on the cheeks. This was the last problem the Commission addressed in what began as a whitewash and turned into a coverup.

An authentic expert was the Commission's very last witness. FBI Spectrographer John F. Gallagher was not called until September 15 (15H746-52), when the Report was already set in type. He was called in such haste that the transcript opens with an apology for it. His testimony, taken in complete secrecy, is a brief six and a half pages, not enough for the beginning of an introduction to the testimony he could and should have given.

In this record of intended dishonesty there is no greater abomination, no more repugnant abandonment of any standard of honesty or decency. No more completely definitive self-exposure of the deliberateness of the falsification of the actualities of the assassination and of all of history to follow. He could and should have testified about all the evidence for which I sued. He was asked about and testified to none of it.

Counsel Norman Redlich asked Gallagher (15H747) "are you familiar with any neutron activation analyses which were conducted in connection with the assassination of President Kennedy?" Gallagher's response was limited to "Neutron activation analyses were conducted at Oak Ridge National Laboratory, Oak Ridge, Tenn., on the paraffin casts from the right hand, and left hand, and the right cheek of Lee Harvey Oswald."

Here Redlich interrupted. He did not ask if any other neutron activation testing was done. Gallagher did not volunteer that it was. In his effort to make it appear that Oswald did fire a weapon, Redlich slipped in asking Gallagher two questions we shall see are self-incriminating. Redlich wanted and got affirmative answers to "with regard to the rifle cartridges, did you examine the cartridges which were actually found on the sixth floor ..." followed by, "And did you determine that the elements barium and antimony were present ...?"

This was deceptive questioning intended to frame a case against Oswald. Redlich kept out of the record that the other evidence, including these shells, had been submitted to NAAs. But he could not and did not get Gallagher to say that Oswald had fired any weapon (15H750). Gallagher did testify that "there are common commercial products which do contain" the same chemical elements (15H750). They are "found in a variety of common substances" and "are not specific."

These "common objects" as listed by Hoover (20H1) begin with what Oswald spent all day handling on the job, "printed paper and cloth" - books. Among others are "paint, storage batteries, rubber and matches." If any guilt attaches to Oswald from this testing, it is that he did the job he was paid to do, handle books.

When the cast of the cheek was studied, there were greater quantities of these traces on the wrong side of the cast, the side away from the cheek, than on the cheek side itself. This is what the papers given me prove and Gallagher swore to (15H751).

Redlich went on to become Assistant Corporation Counsel of New York City (under Rankin as Corporation Counsel). Then, in 1975, he became dean of the New York University Law School. With these qualifications, he failed to ask Gallagher if there had been comparative testing made on subjects who had fired and handled weapons. The papers given me establish repeated tests of this kind and that in each case the readings were much greater than any from Oswald. Redlich also failed to ask Gallagher a single question about Gallagher's own work on the spectrographic and neutron activation examinations of all the other evidence - all those dealing with the crime itself. All these results are contrary to the official and preordained "conclusions" of the "investigation."

There is and there can be no innocence here. Redlich concluded it with a feeble effort to hide his questionable conduct. He asked Gallagher if they had had a brief prior discussion and if in the testimony they had covered all they discussed (15H752). This is to say that they had connived in advance to eliminate what neither the FBI nor the Commission wanted known.

The Commission had to delay calling Gallagher until after its work was entirely over except for problems like this and those posed by Senator Russell's disagreement (WHITEWASH IV,pp.21-2,97,132,208). What Redlich did was as dangerous as it was unconscionable. Nobody dared go into the actual results of any of the tests. And the earlier nitrate testing on the paraffin casts made by the Dallas police also yielded exculpatory results (R560).

This deliberate hiding of the truth was already in the Report at the time of Gallagher's testimony, which should have been the earliest taken by the Commission rather than the very last. The deception is furthered under "Expert Examination of Rifle, Cartridge Cases and Bullet Fragments" where the Report says that these "were all subjected to firearms identification analysis by qualified experts" (R79). These were neither all the tests nor the essential ones.

That this testing was limited and was not definitive also is hidden. At no time and in no way was the Commission or the FBI ever able to link all the bullets and fragments to the common origin that is a precondition of any investigation or conclusions by either. If these fragments did not have common origin, the entire "solution" on this basis alone is a deliberate fraud.

The Report and the 26 volumes completely omit these tests -

even mention of the fact of the NAAs being performed except on the paraffin casts.

Buried in Appendix X - not in the text - is the subsection "The Paraffin Test." After what could not be avoided, itemizing some of the common substances that do leave deposits like those from firing a weapon or handling one that has been fired ("tobacco, Clorox, urine, cosmetics, kitchen matches ..."), the Report admits "A positive reaction is, therefore, valueless in determining whether a suspect has recently fired a weapon." (R561) It fails to state the obvious corollary, that the absence of traces is exculpatory. It quotes not Gallagher but another agent as saying that he "would not expect to find any residues on a person's right cheek after firing a rifle." This instead of the known evidence that in all the control testing these residues were deposited!

It was easier to suppress these tests and the fact of their being made.

Were this not enough, the Report then calls the paraffin tests "unreliable." Is that why the tests were made?

It concludes this section (R562) with a distorted version of the Oak Ridge paraffin testing without here or elsewhere mentioning Gallagher's name or the controls run in those tests, controls exculpating Oswald.

It says only paraffin casts were tested at Oak Ridge! (R562)

All this addresses more than fact, more than dishonesty. It is a clear representation of intent. The intent to foist off on an anguished people a fake solution to the assassination of the President could not be more apparent. Why else lie and hide and pull all these Watergate-like dirty tricks in secrecy and then contrive an Orwellian Report that was known to be absolutely false?

Despite all the perjury and stonewalling, the FBI could not avoid delivering more and completely definitive evidence. It includes what Redlich and Gallagher contrived to suppress about what both mentioned, those empty rifle shells. It includes the real story of the so-called "missed" bullet. It includes tests required to have been done with NAAs. If there were no NAAs, it is only because the results were known and proved the opposite of what was wanted.

When Hoover died Nixon became the first President to appoint another FBI Director. His choice, his own hack, L. Patrick Gray, turned out to be a felon, one of Nixon's stable of felons. As FBI Director, Gray personally destroyed irreplaceable Watergate evidence, then lied about it. The last of his contradictory versions under oath was televised before the Watergate committee August 3 and 6, 1973 (Hearings,pp.3449ff).

Clarence Kelley, the man Nixon felt best qualified to succeed a Gray, did not serve an apprenticeship under Hoover. Enough of those who learned the Hoover way from Hoover remained in the FBI.

Once we nailed the FBI in its lying about what was requested in my suit, it had no choice but to pretend to comply - in its terms rather than with what I actually sued for. In a letter of April 10, 1975, Kelley claimed full compliance with the delivery of what he represented as all the NAAs. He listed them. The invisible touch of the ghost of Hoover swirls around Kelley's actual words intended to say "full compliance" without actually saying it, which would have been the grossest and most deliberate of lies:

"It is considered that" these new pages, he wrote Jim, and "that already furnished to Mr. Weisberg, responds fully to his FOIA request." (Not one paper I had asked for was ever delivered.)

The operative word here is "considered." Who "considered" what? The FBI lied and Kelley lied. They hide this from themselves with semantics, whatever anyone may attribute to "considered." This is the kind of FBI trickery that puts the innocent in jail.

Here is what Kelley's letter, semantics aside, actually represents as 100 percent of the FBI's neutron activation analyses:

Commission Exhibit Number	Laboratory Number	Description
CE 399	Q1	Bullet from Stretcher
CE 567	Q2	Bullet fragment from front seat cushion
CE 843	Q4, Q5	Metal fragments from President's head
CE 842	Q9	Metal fragment from arm of Governor John Connolly
CE 840	Q14	Three metal fragments recovered from rear floor board carpet

On April 10, 1975, Kelley was the one person who, above all others, had every reason to know or be able to learn the total inadequacy of this list of what NAAs were required.

This list refers to less than all the evidence the FBI collected the first day only. It excludes the complete bullet found in the rifle, Q8; the fifth fragment found in the car after its return to Washington, Q3; two of the three empty rifle shells found in the TSBD, Q6 and Q7; the sweepings from the windshield, Q15; and the President's clothing, especially the jacket, tie and shirt, Q22, Q24 and Q25.

Including evidence collected later would make a long list. Of these items the curbstone, Q609, is of major importance.

ERDA's affidavit, like Kelley's letter, is couched in Hoover-like semantics, falsely representing the extent of the NAA testing by the AEC. Schur swore that the only tests conducted were "neutron activation analyses on the paraffin casts from the right hand, the left hand and the right cheek of Lee Harvey Oswald and on bullet fragments;" and that "no other tests were performed by or for the AEC on behalf of the Warren Commission."

While swearing to the AEC's having done no other testing, Schur was simultaneously turning over to me proof of this other testing, including on the various shells, the windshield and Bullet 399.

In restricting himself to "fragments," Schur was consistent with the lie in the seventh paragraph of Kilty's second affidavit, misrepresenting the extent of my request to "material concerning metal fragments only." Kilty had made the identical misstatement in paragraph 4 of his first affidavit, limiting what "Mr. Weisberg requested" to "a. Specific spectrographic and neutron activation material ... representing reexaminations of the metal fragments ..."

In each and every case what is omitted is absolutely vital to any case against Oswald.

If the omitted Q3 fragment was not part of a bullet that included Q2, the three fragments making up Q14 and the two fragments identified as Q4 and Q5, then Hoover, Frazier, Gallagher and others in the FBI knew within 24 hours and on this evidence alone that the entire "solution" was fraudulent. If all these were not from a single bullet, then there had to have been at least a fourth bullet. This means at least two shooters. That means conspiracy.

(Do not forget that the receipt for what we are to believe is both Q4 and Q5 is for "a" missile. Two tiny fragments are "a" missile?)

All these pieces of bullet and 399 (Q1) itself must be not
less than consistent with the unlisted complete bullet found in the
rifle, Exhibit 141 (Q8).

Indispensable to any official version of the assassination is
that Q1 have deposited on JFK's clothes invisible but readily detectable traces of precisely that copper alloy jacketing Bullet 399. Unless spectroscopy proved that the traces on the back of JFK's clothing
are those that could have come from 399, on this added basis all those
involved know the official account is a cruel hoax.

For what reason other than certain knowledge that this was not
true would the FBI omit this NAA testing?

We know the related falsehoods, not accidental falsehoods,
about the damage to the front of JFK's clothing. No bullet caused
any of it. It was easier to lie about it, to manufacture a case that
all the many manufacturers knew was false. It was easier to fake
pictures, as the FBI also did.

So, Kelley lists no NAAs on any clothing. (There is no official evidence that the cleansing of Connally's clothing did or could
have removed all traces.)

When the sweepings from the windshield are required to have
the same source as the missing Q3 and Q2, Q4, Q5 and Q14, can it be
believed that the head of the FBI did not know the indispensability
of NAAs on Q3? But Q15 and Q3 are not here.

That neither the FBI nor ERDA provided any results of any
testing on Q3 does not mean that Q3 was not tested. ERDA came up
with no single reference to it in the work it did for the FBI. The
FBI, however, provided a worksheet tabulating not NAA results but
conditions of the tests. This tabulation identifies the samples and
certain details about them.

It includes the testing of Q3. But no test results, no identification of any components and, of course, no statistics. Not even
symbols.

	249	153747	2433	245377	2'	27.66	.752
b	249	252,477	8400	244077	2'	27.65	.752
c	457	30,565	1050	29,515	1'	17.2	.8375
d	3.7?	24,920	819	24,101	1'	17.27	.8368
Q3	.023	925	462	463	1'	19.56	.8177
S	3.74	40770	7,750	39420		27.75	.751
		38,144	1365	36779	2'	29.37	.739
La	12?	133,050	5180	127876	2'	27.88	.750
Lb	21.4	218,156	7700	210056	2'	27.95	.750
Lc	1.22	14481	616	13,865	2'	26.57	.7602

The facsimile reproduction from the FBI's NAA papers leaves no
doubt that Q3 was tested. Why does the government swear it was not?

There is also the indispensability of NAAs on all four shell
casings. Kelley lists none.

How can we explain such a letter from the FBI Director?

Fairness to Kelley requires a flashback to the government's
Opposition in C.A. 226-75. We had asked for an affidavit from one

441

with personal knowledge, not one who claimed to have merely consulted unidentified files in unidentified FBI offices. Among these we had named Frazier. Others are Gallagher and Williams but this does not exhaust the list. This is what Ryan then filed:

Plaintiff alleges in his motion to strike and attached affidavit that the Kilty affidavit is deliberately deceptive, not based upon personal knowledge, and should have been made by Special Agent Robert A. Frazier who plaintiff believes is still an active agent with the F.B.I. Laboratory. Defendants respectfully inform counsel and the Court, however, that Special Agent Robert A. Frazier retired from the F.B.I. on April 11, 1975 after thirty-three years, ten months and three days service, and that supervisory Special Agent Kilty is the most knowledgeable active service Special Agent to give this testimony on behalf of the F.B.I.

Frazier had been through the Warren Commission ordeal. He had been FBI-man enough to perjure himself. He was unafraid when subpoenaed to testify in New Orleans. When we met him in that March 14 meeting, he seemed hale and hearty. He looked younger than I. Given the well-known clean living Hoover demanded of his agents and the absence of disability retirement, why should so hale and hearty an agent as Frazier, one who knew what others allegedly did not of this most major of crimes, take his retirement on April 11?

What is unusual about April 11?

One thing only: It is the day after April 10. And April 10 is the day, if he had not learned earlier, that Kelley suddenly came face-to-face with all this hanky-panky.

This did not inspire Kelley to beat his breast and bare all.

But it _is_ the day before all of a sudden Frazier returned to private life. Coincidence, perhaps. But the odds against coincidence "after thirty-three years, ten months and three days" do seem a bit long.

(Frazier's continuing ability to walk, talk and sign his name means he still could have executed an affidavit. As could Gallagher and many others. And as a judge other than Pratt, _any_ judge with concern for the minimum requirement of legal evidence, could have insisted. Kelley did not see to a first-person affidavit, from Frazier or anyone else.)

Frazier's retirement does not diminish Kelley's letter's import. If Frazier's departure is connected, Kelley's offenses are magnified. It means Kelley learned the truth about the past, learned what then and there was afoot and became part of it.

Innocence is the one human quality that does not taint any part of this account.

Particularly not with Kilty and with the legion of FBI agents and lawyers and those in the Civil Division, the United States Attorney's office and elsewhere in the Department who, through connection with and knowledge of Kilty's false swearing, had personal knowledge

442

of its cause and meaning. Any knowledge was guilty knowledge. Subsequent tolerance and silence joined them in this same awful crime.

Virtually everything Kilty attested to was false. Where it was not, it was deceptive. If to those not fully informed the evidence we provided was not enough for full comprehension, what Kilty himself swore to that these agents and lawyers went over was enough. He sw re both ways about the same thing - directly contradicting himself - on the material.

Kelley does run the FBI. If any public servant cannot in good conscience do what is demanded of him, the respected tradition of public service requires resignation. This is not uncommon and it did happen shortly after Judge Pratt's decision. The man who quit had been close to Kelley. He quit on the kind of principle we are considering.

Kelley brought William D. Ellingsworth to Washington with him to be his top FBI press aide. In Kansas City Ellingsworth had been a reporter and then Kelley's press assistant when Kelley was police chief.

In quitting the FBI, Ellingsworth told the Associated Press (Post 8/27/75), "They wanted a public relations program. I wanted a public information program. ... I never got the opportunity to be open."

The buck stops with the boss, Kelley.

Kelley cannot have failed to know of the essentiality of comparisons in composition of the lab specimens not included in his April 10 list. He had to know that this list is limited to less than the specimens collected immediately. He had to know that it eliminated all specimens obtained later. And he had to know that at the very beginning these minima have to have been established for there to be any reason for continuing on the initial, basic and unvarying assumption of Oswald's solitary guilt:

The jacket and the core of the whole bullet have to have been compared with all the other listed specimens and those collected later, like the curbstone.

The same is true of Bullet 399, Q1, and the three empty shells, not just the first two that he omits in his list.

Q3, the bit of copper from supposedly the exploded bullet, has to have been included, not always excluded.

The copper alloy in Q2, Q3, Q1 and the whole cartridge, Q8, have to have been compared with each other. So does the clothing. No clothing is listed.

All five specimens Kelley lists contained lead alloy, the trace elements of which have to have been compared and results, as with the copper alloy, tabulated.

Then there are Q15, the sweepings from the windshield, and the curbstone. There are others but this is a long enough list.

There is only one reason Kilty swore falsely about the testing of these sweepings, the clothing and the curbstone: The results destroy the prefabricated case.

But from the unrelenting pressure we kept on the FBI, it could not avoid letting out a little more of this "new" evidence. It did not include relevant communications.

It had a reason for refusing copies of the correspondence relevant to these tests and to the suit in which it substituted these kinds of records for the final results and reports.

It knew what it had; it may or may not have known what the Archives had; and it certainly did not want to enable us to further perfect the record against it.

It does not really take much. No matter how much more there

443

is – and it has to be a large volume – it is not necessary to use all I have for the purpose of establishing the attitude and the record of the FBI and the Commission and the collaboration of ERDA.

ERDA, then AEC, began excited by the prospect of using its science and labs in the ex poste facto conviction.

From the content of the first of this series of documents, it is clear there are earlier records still suppressed. The problem is Hoover did not want done what AEC wanted to do. He knew the inevitable result of precise testing he did not control would be disproof of what he had decided. On December 11, 1964, two days after Hoover formalized his decision, in CD1, Paul C. Aebersold, Director, Division of Isotope Development, wrote Herbert J. Miller, then chief of the Criminal Division. Aebersold recalled several weeks of discussion "with various persons in your agency" about "what additional light nuclear activation might shed." This assistance was offered "within less than 24 hours of the assassination." It included "our laboratories experienced in obtaining criminalistics evidence ... We believe it is not too late to outline what may yet be done."

Translation: That offer was not accepted by Hoover.

Several words require the emphasis added to other of AEC's opinions: "... it may be possible to determine by trace-element measurements whether the fatal bullets [sic] were of composition identical to that of the purportedly unfired shell." This "unfired bullet" is Q8, the bullet missing from Kelley's listing of what was subjected to NAA.

"If the same batch of ammunition was used in the sniper bullet fired at" resigned ultra-rightist General Edwin Walker, "the method might show a correlation."

This did not tempt NAA on Q8. The "Walker" bullet, Q188, was tested. There is no official allegation it shows the remotest "correlation." In fact, that this testing was done is suppressed from the Report.

"Other pieces of physical evidence in the case, such as clothing ... might lend themselves to characterization by means of their trace-element levels."

Hoover knew better than the AEC. No NAAs on the clothing.

The Commission also knew better – than to fight with Hoover.

The AEC did "not wish to appear to be intruding in the investigation" but "we wish to indicate our eagerness ... Our work leads one to expect that the tremendous sensitivity of the activation analysis method is capable of providing useful information that may not be otherwise attainable."

This, of course, stated the problem. Hoover did not want what the AEC offered. He did not regard attaining the unattainable as "useful." He did not want even more definitive answers to questions he did not have to ask.

Apparently not in response to this generosity, a letter drafted by Willens for Warren's signature was sent on January 2, 1964, to then AEC Chairman Glenn T. Seaborg. For all the world as though AEC was part of Interpol, it asked "from your agency all information relating to Lee Harvey Oswald ... and Jack Ruby ... as well as other information which you may believe to be relevant to our investigation."

Not surprisingly, Seaborg replied immediately that "we have no record of either of these individuals." But "we are, however, in cooperation with the" FBI lab on "a very sensitive method of trace element analysis ... may be of any value in further corroborating [sic] evidence already in hand by the" FBI. "This work is being done at our Oak Ridge National Laboratory ..."

January 7 Rankin sent Hoover a copy of Aebersold's letter asking "your advice regarding the feasibility and desirability of taking

444

advantage of this offer."

AEC's offer was for metal testing, the bullets, fragments and objects allegedly struck by them. Hoover's January 10 response reported how "well acquainted" the FBI lab was with this "analytical technique." He confirmed that with the AEC "work is already in progress applying this technique to certain phases." He promised to report "the results of these analyses when they have been completed."

From the available record this never happened. But it is significant that he used two plurals, "phases" of the investigation and "analyses." In C.A. 226-75, the government alleged in court that as of this time only the paraffin casts were being tested.

Kilty's oaths were as free as the wind. Here is what he swore to when the FBI needed his oath:

6. Concerning plaintiff's allegation that, although the date of all the neutron activation analysis (NAA) documents furnished him is May 15, 1964, there is an indication that this technique was already being utilized as early as January 10, 1964: the earlier NAA, the quote from Mr. Rankin in Paragraph 27 of plaintiff's affidavit to the contrary notwithstanding, was conducted upon paraffin casts taken of Lee Harvey Oswald's hands and cheek. Plaintiff requested NAA material concerning metal fragments only. No neutron activation analysis of the metal fragments was made prior to May 15, 1964.

More incredible is it that the government made these claims when it was simul aneously turning over proof they were false. The ERDA papers disclose tests dated in January 1964, in addition to those on the paraffin casts.

However, there is no doubt how the Commission understood what the FBI was doing. Here is what Rankin told it January 27, from the executive-session transcript reprinted in full in WHITEWASH IV (p.103):

Now, the bullet fragments are now, part of them are now, with the Atomic Energy Commission, who are trying to determine by a new method, a process that they have, of whether they can relate them to various guns and the different parts, the fragments, whether they are a part of one of the bullets that was broken and came out in part through the neck, and just what particular assembly of bullet they were part of.

They have had it for the better part of two and a-half weeks and we ought to get an answer.

More explicitness on the testing of the individual fragments and the purpose to determine the bullets from which each came - exactly the Aebersold/AEC offer - is not possible.

(If Rankin mislead the Commission, as the government now alleges, then the government lays the worst indictment yet against the
Warren Commission. Rankin's remarks show he and the members knew
these tests could exculpate Oswald. Yet long before May 15, as we
have seen,* the Commission had concluded Oswald was guilty and had
outlined its Report.)

On March 10 Hoover wrote one of his masterpieces posing and
answering the wrong issue./ He lumped hands and face together:
"casts from the hands and cheek" and said the examinations of the
deposits "could not be specifically associated with the rifle cartridges."

He was careful not to take the cheek cast and the rifle cartridges, as he should have. If he had, he could not have deceived as
easily. He would have had to say what in the end the Commission had
to work its way around, that the NAAs on the cheek were proof that
Oswald had not fired a rifle.

When gilding his lilies, Hoover was not one to spare the gilt:
"No characteristic elements were found by neutron activation analyses
which could be used to distinguish the rifle from the revolver cartridges."

The question was not one of "characteristic elements" that are
common to both varieties of ammunition. Nor did anyone have to "distinguish the rifle from the revolver cartridges" by "neutron activation analysis." For anyone with the most rudimentary knowledge, the
partly-closed eye is more than enough to make this distinction without
a meaning. The average gun buff can do this with his eyes closed, by
feel alone.

Hoover could not have addressed anything more completely irrelevant nor could he have done it more impressively or successfully.

This was followed by the previously reported meeting between
Commission Counsel Melvin Eisenberg and FBI lab expert Gallagher in
which Eisenberg managed to avoid asking for copies of any results
while asking general questions about what could cause similar chemical deposits. Hoover's March 18 letter (CD 525) is the response in
which he told the Commission what, in non-Hoover English, means that
Bullet 399 did not cause the damage to JFK's clothing: "It is not felt
that the increased sensitivity of neutron activation analysis would
contribute substantially to the understanding of the origin of this
hole and frayed area." This could be true only if Hoover already had
proof that 399 caused the damage or had not. If he had proof that it
did, it is one secret he would not have kept.≠

By this time four months had passed and the Commission, which
then expected to issue its Report in less than three months, still
did not have any real information from its chief investigator, Hoover,
on this most basic of all the evidence required for any Oswald-lone
assassin/no conspiracy conclusion. Describing the attitude of the
staff of eminent lawyers as timid is a great kindness. The Commission
members' awareness of what Hoover was doing to them is as unhidden as
it was secret in its until-now suppressed January 22 transcript# in
which it recognized that Hoover's purpose was to box them in and limit
what they could say and find to what he wanted. So, by March 18, the
wily old master manipulator had all the readings he needed on what he
could - and did - get away with.

Redlich, who wound up guiding Gallagher around all the meaning
in the paraffin-cast NAAs and ignoring all else, correctly understood
the real situation. On July 1 he wrote Dulles about "the proposed
Readers Digest article" and "with reference to the neutron activation
analysis." The second of his four numbered points, each of which
would have been exculpatory in a trial, is "There is no basis for concluding that he [Oswald] also fired a rifle." The "also" is propaganda because in his first point Redlich said of Oswald's having fired
a pistol and what the NAAs show, "this is by no means certain." His

* See Ch. 1. / See p. 625. ≠ P. 318.
# See pp.475-87, especially pp. 485-7.

446

last point refers to what Hoover said March 18, "that barium and antimony are found in a variety of substances" and does not mean a pistol was fired or even handled.

Calling the situation and attitude of all these eminent and powerful men pathetic falls short, far short, of what is established by this partial record on the NAAs alone. These were the Chief Justice of the United States, powerful Senators, the former CIA head and the man later to be President. Their staff went on to become district attorneys, judges, law school deans and the heads of other commissions. Yet in the end they were in total ignorance and only mildly curious about some aspects. This is tragically, painfully and informatively clear in Eisenberg's plaintive September 5 memo to Redlich on "Neutron Activation Analysis."

September 5, 1964

M E M O R A N D U M

To: Norman Redlich

From: Melvin A. Eisenberg

Subject: Neutron Activation Analysis ✔

The following questions should be asked of the FBI:

1. A description of the neutron activation test. ✔

2. When the test was performed on the paraffin cast. ✔

3. How much barium and antimony were found on the cast.

4. Were any significant elements of other than barium and antimony found?

5. How rare are barium and antimony as compared with nitrates or other oxidozing agents which can cause a reaction to the paraffin test?

6. Were barium and antimony found on both sides of the paraffin cast of the cheek?

7. If so, doesn't that indicate that the casts were contaminated so that the whole test was worthless?

8. What is the meaning of the statement in the letter from the FBI that there was more barium and antimony on the cast than might normally be expected to be found on a person who had not fired a weapon. Does this mean that there were more barium and antimony than would be present on a person's hands even if he had handled some of the items listed in the letter from the FBI setting forth items containing barium and/or antimony? If not, what is the validity of the statement?

By September 5 the Report was written. Yet the Commission lacked even "A description of the neutron activation test," did not know "When the test was performed on the paraffin cast," had no idea of the quantities of elements detected or which ones were and was stretching for an excuse to say the tests were worthless. At that late date there is no single word on the record about the really important testing, on the bullets, fragments and objects they allegedly struck.

Not a <u>single</u> word with the Report already written, a Report from which all of this is totally suppressed!

No innocence here, either.

None anywhere. From the very first moment the AEC knew the score. In Seaborg's response to the letter written for Warren on January 2, he actually said that the NAA results would be "transmitted to Mr. Rankin by the Federal Bureau of Investigation." (The stamped date is illegible. If so many of these documents were not too unclear, more would be reproduced in facsimile. One of the predominating characteristics of the available copies of these precious files is their illegibility. They are often made from very poor carbon copies or have been repeatedly xeroxed to make them indistinct.)

Nobody - <u>nobody</u> at all - opposed Hoover. Not the commissioners, not their staff, not the head of the AEC, not anyone who worked on any test or knew any of the results, not even an uncowardly clerk. He had the "results" but gave <u>nothing</u> to the Commission. In all the years since there has been not one peep. No leak in a government virtually run by leaks and a press cultivating them.

Had any one member of the Commission staff, any of these lawyers well into outstanding careers, former prosecutors and judges-to-be, done his job these secrets would not have remained for a writer and unpaid lawyer to seek through courts that also want suppression. Judge John A. Danaher had said it all in the first suit, that the law on "freedom of information" as he saw it "forfends against appellant's proposed further inquiry into the assassination of President Kennedy." Unaware of or not caring about the incongruity, he concluded in capital letters, "REQUIESCAT IN PACE." (Decision No.71-1026)

It appears that all those who failed deliberately do rest in peace. It also appears that the ghost of Hoover has come back in Kelley's body because Kelley has and suppresses to the degree he can all this proof so entirely opposite the FBI's and all official accounts of the assassination of President Kennedy and its turning the world around.

"Highly dangerous" to the FBI, its total ruin is what the FBI swore in the first suit would be the result of letting me have the results and final reports of these scientific tests. Other than Williams and the government's lawyers intended, this is true. Or should be.

As this danger relates to these test papers, those I obtained, those missing or not performed and those still suppressed, the underscoring added to Aebersold's letter states the hazards: from the NAA's "tremendous sensitivity;" its capability of proving "identical composition;" and the reemphasized importance of "trace-element measurements." The indispensability of measurement of those elements present in most minute proportion is also underscored by all the scientific literature.

We have seen that in the measurements of the lead alloy that were made - not in a <u>single</u> instance including all the chemical elements - rather than yielding "identical" measurements, the NAAs show wide variations between samples of evidence that must have common or "identical" origin for there to have been any basis for the predetermined conclusion of no conspiracy and Oswald as the lone assassin.

This was, as the quoted scientific and forensic literature also indicate, perhaps more important for the jacket material. The test papers refer to it as copper. It actually is a copper alloy.

Yet in no single sheet provided by the FBI is there any measurement of the composition of the copper alloy in Q1, Q2 or Q3, described in the initial FBI lab records as "a portion of the base section of a copper alloy rifle bullet ... from which the lead core is missing."* (CD5:163) Q2 and Q3 were found the day after the assassination in the front seat of the President's car. Between them they weigh 65.6 grains (CD5:163) or if from one bullet were more than

---

*See p. 604.

40 percent of it.

This same initial report says "it could not be determined whether specimens Q2 and Q3 are portions of the same bullet or are portions of two separate bullets."

By means of neutron activation analysis, this determination is possible.

In solving the crime it was essential. If there was more than one bullet from which both these two fragments and the three of lead only identified as Q14 from the rear-seat floor and Q4 and Q5, lead fragments from JFK's head (those called "a missile" by the FBI) came, then on this basis alone there was a conspiracy and still unsolved is the assassination of the President. All these fragments plus the Q15 sweepings about which there was the perjury have to have come from the one bullet that exploded in the President's head in all official versions of the killing.

There is a long discussion of this in the last two chapters of WHITEWASH. The situation is identical with Bullet 399, which has to have caused all seven nonfatal injuries. The FBI and the Commission were aware of this. In one form it came out when Dr. Robert Shaw testified that there was no proof of what hit Connally "and we still do not know which bullet actually inflicted the [sic] wound on Governor Connally." When Dulles asked, "Or two bullets" as the cause of Connally's wounds only, Shaw's response was, "Yes; or three." (4H109)

With this the actuality, the indispensability of the evidence, and with the FBI's swearing that there had been no NAA on the windshield when in fact it and ERDA both supplied proof that there had been, how account for there being this omission in what the FBI supplied?

In all that ERDA supplied on the NAAs, this essential information on Q3 is entirely missing. It is a glaring omission in Kelley's April 10 letter. Does anyone believe that either the head of the FBI or the AEC's experts about whom Aebersold boasted were unaware?

No official account permits anything other than Q2 and Q3 to have caused the damage to the windshield. Both were parts of the jacket - again copper alloy. And now there is no Q15 testing claimed under oath? It is omitted in what the head of the FBI represents in response to a lawsuit as all of this testing?

Even all this is an understatement because in one of those few pages of supposed spectrographic results Q2 and Q3 were both listed under the symbol for copper. There was no numerical representation of whatever that test may have shown. There are symbols, plus signs. They are not the same for Q2 and Q3.

This table dated December 12, 1963, is the only reference to the copper in Q1, Q2 and Q3 in what the FBI swore are the full spectrographic analyses. Hoover's November 23 report to the Dallas

449

prosecutorial authorities includes no single figure on any element in the copper samples. This was contrary to the basic requirement specified in <u>all</u> the cited scientific literature.

(The significance of the omission of all statistics becomes even greater with performance of NAAs. Just how sensitive NAAs can be is reported in <u>Scientific Evidence in Criminal Cases</u>, by Andre Moenssens, Foundation Press, Page 397: "The extreme sensitivity of NAA allows it to identify some elements in concentrations as low as one ten-millionth of a microgram." With elements "less sensitive to detection" the concentration need be no greater than "five millionths of a gram." The "Limitation of Detections in Micrograms" varies within minuscule limits only. For antimony it is 0.0009, barium 0.005, copper 0.0002. These are quantities so ultra-minute they can hardly be conceived and cannot be seen.)

Remember the FBI's failure to test for human residues and how durable these residues are?* If we add to this fairly convincing proof that all involved knew they were putting together a fraudulent explanation of how the President was killed, then question how these fragments got into the car and then recall that the car was at times unattended and was washed, is it unreasonable to ask if it never occurred to any of the hundreds of official investigators that perhaps this evidence was planted?

These investigators had many reasons to ask this question and solid reasons for believing it. More follow.

Copper alone poisoned the investigation and the investigators.

Why else no NAAs on the President's clothing when the jacket of 399 only can have left traces according to the official accounts?

It is admitted that there was spectroscopic examination of the clothing. There is a sheet dated 11/25/63 headed "JFK Coat & Shirt." There is not a single figure on it. There are symbols relating to the back holes and again they are not identical. And no traces on the front of the shirt and tie?

No official questions? Only perjury?

The copper in the empty shells was no less poisonous.

Three were found near that sixth-floor window under circumstances so strongly suggesting they had been planted that the FBI went to some trouble to make it appear they could have been found where they were as a result of their having ricocheted off the cartons of books on ejection from a rifle. (WHITEWASH,p.34) There was also that entire cartridge Aebersold said the AEC was so "eager" to work on. Two of these empty casings, Q6 and Q7, were flown to Washington immediately with the whole one, Q8.

<u>Not one is referred to in any of the spectrographic results given me and sworn to as complete.</u>

Spectrographic examinations <u>were</u> made. The one document we could ever get the FBI to say embodied its "results" and "report" is the published five-page lab "report" sent Dallas Police Chief Curry November 23 (24H262-4). It says there was spectroscopy and it has "results of examinations." The only "results" of spectroscopy read, "specimens Q6 and Q7 were identified as having been fired in this [K1] rifle." This is neither the result of spectroscopy or truth, as Hoover himself said June 2 in a letter to Rankin that holds other intelligence.

Naturally enough, there are no "results," real or imagined, on Q3.

Nor in these full and complete spectroscopic "results" <u>any</u> mention of the third empty shell Hoover sent Agent Vince Drain to get from Curry in the middle of the night (7H404). This shell is identified as C38 (26H449).

How there could have been the carelessness that follows is not

*See pp. 95-9.

450

easily explained. Perhaps it is because what Ryan hand-delivered to
Jim after the end of the working day went directly to him from ERDA
and did not pass through FBI hands. Whatever the explanation, the
added proof of FBI perjury is minor compared with the evidence.

In the middle of the hundreds of entirely uncollated pages are
two headed "Materials Controls" and "Samples from L.H.O." The latter
relates to the paraffin tests.

The care and precision with which these tests are done is indicated in the "Materials Controls" sheet where the measurements of
barium in milligrams is carried to the fourth decimal and in the
paraffin testing to 0.0316.

There was this same care and precision - and carelessness -
with the sandwiched page. It is headed "Cartridges" but it refers
to four empty shells.

The first two are Q75 and Q77. They are Tippit-killing evidence.

The next two are Q6 and Q7. Each is described identically as
"Rifle (powder from inside)" of tests for barium (Ba) and antimony
(Sb). Aebersold said the "tremendous sensitivity" of the "activation
analysis" could pick up the tiniest "traces of antimony and barium
(from the bullet primer)." He said NAAs would pick up "gunpowder
residues."

While barium and antimony are not the only components of gunpowder, this test for them shows the "tremendous sensitivity." It is
in microgrms.

To fully appreciate the significance of these figures, remember
that Aebersold also said that "by trace-element measurement" it could
be determined "whether the fatal bullets were of composition identical
with that of" the unfired one, the always-missing Q8.

CARTRIDGES		Ba/Sb micrograms	Sb. micrograms
Q75	Powder scr... (....... ...)	...	...11
Q77	Powder scrape from ... (R + P)	.....	...01
Q6	Rifle (powder from inside)	31.79	6.62
Q7	Rifle (powder from in...	44.35	7.42

Rather than showing "identical" composition, these tests record large differences. The column headed "Ba/Sb" shows 4.8 for Q6
and 5.9 for Q7. The differences under "barium micrograms" are between
31.79 and 44.35. Under "Sb micrograms" these differences are between
6.62 and 7.42. In percentages, these come to 21, 39.35 and 12.1,
respectively.

Maybe the FBI of the fabled memory and the telepathic computers
with the brain-wave printouts could keep the thousands of figures in

451

mind and not require the tabulations required of mortals performing the same tests, but is there any magic to make differences of 40 per cent "identical?"

If these otherwise undescribed figures on this one sheet lost among so many uncollated hundreds of sheets represents measurements of weights of the samples examined, then there remains what in any ordinary sense is a significant difference. It is in the proportion of each ingredient rather than the weight. This difference is between 4.8 and 5.9. Depending on how calculated, this is 19 percent or 23 percent.

What cannot be without significance is that even when repeatedly challenged, when case after case of known withholding, false swearing and perjury was laid against the FBI in court records, it not only did not supply this, which it had in files easily located, it lied still again. It had this paper and, inevitably, countless others. It had them in files easily identified. Seaborg's letter said the AEC would give the FBI everything. After that, the record in this suit is that the FBI did the work at Oak Ridge with AEC facilities.

Comparison of what I received from the FBI and ERDA proves beyond doubt that each had papers called for by their interpretation of this suit and withheld them. The FBI provided worksheets ERDA withheld. These worksheets show the conditions of specific tests for which no results in any interpretation were provided. We have examined one significant example of what ERDA provided that the FBI withheld.

Why anyone would want to withhold the results - any results - of scientific tests dealing with how and by whom a President was killed is a question to which each can provide his own answer. That both agencies were not honest is fact.

Could these fantastic FBI memories retain what was not tested and had to have been in any real investigation?

Does it make any real difference whether the FBI committed perjury, assisted by the Department of Justice and the judge or whether it did not perform the most essential of tests when a President was assassinated?

It does make a difference that the FBI did not provide this sheet in what Judge Pratt held to be "compliance" while he made speeches about how proper and necessary questions "burdened" the poor FBI.

And it does seem that, despite his anxiety not to, poor Aebersold, while saying "we do not wish to" did "appear to be intruding in the investigation."

But neither Aebersold nor the AEC "intruded" into the "investigation" of this and another quintessential of a no-conspiracy/Oswald assassin "solution." There the FBI's own fact "intruded."

Eisenberg did not do very well with the scientific tests but he did try to press the unpressable Hoover about ballistics tests. On June 2 Hoover wrote Rankin that "pursuant" to what he described as Eisenberg's "informal request" of May 15, 1964, "examination was conducted on the C6, C7 and C38 cartridge cases and the C8 cartridge to determine if they had been loaded and extracted from the C14 rifle more than once." (26H449-50)

(The C and Q identifications are of the same evidence as handled differently by the FBI. C14 rifle is also K1.)

It turns out that C6 "had been loaded into and extracted from a [sic] weapon at least three times." That "the extractor and ejector marks" on all four items of evidence "do not possess sufficient characteristics for identifying the weapon which produced them." That "there are also three sets of marks on the base of this cartridge case which were not found on C7, C8, C38 or any of the numerous tests obtained from the C14 rifle." But "one set of marks" on C6 "was identified as having been made by the magazine follower" of the rifle.

C7 "had been loaded into and extracted from a [sic] weapon at least twice." One set had been traced to the chamber and one "to contact with the bolt." Of these marks only Hoover said he could not say whether "one or two loading operations" caused them.

Having said this and having said that it had been "loaded into and extracted from a weapon at least twice," Hoover also left unexplained the second certain use of this casing in a rifle - apparently a different rifle - about which he said nothing at all.

There were two sets of marks on C8, one of which was "not identified with the C14 rifle" for reasons about which Hoover only conjectured. Another rifle again?

There were marks on C38 meaning "it had been loaded into and extracted from a [sic] weapon at least twice." Because Hoover explains this only by saying "it was not possible to determine whether the two sets or marks which were identified were produced by one or two loading operations in the C14 rifle" he raises too many questions.

If there were at least two loadings and unloadings into a weapon and it was possible that the only marks "identified" could have been a single loading and unloading of this rifle, what about marks not identified and that "at least" second loading and unloading?

Hoover again raises and leaves unexplained the possibility of a second rifle.

In each case there were multiple loadings and unloadings and in each case the clear and unaddressed possibility of another rifle is raised and is not answered.

This also addresses the honesty and purposes of what Hoover wrote Curry, quoted above (24H262-4), at a time when Oswald was not yet murdered and would be brought to trial where Curry was chief of police.

None of this immediately available information was told to Curry, from whom the evidence was seized.

Hoover included "Firearms - Spectroscopic - Microscopic Analyses" as three of the "Examinations requested." He has under "Results of Examinations" in the matter of "ASSASSINATION OF PRESIDENT JOHN F. KENNEDY" only what we quoted above where clearly it is not the results of spectroscopy yet is represented as the results of all the examinations. When he said of Q6 and Q7 only and about this assassination only that they "were identified as having been fired in this rifle," his intent is deception of the prosecution - a frame-up. He knew November 23, 1963, what he was finally forced to admit elliptically in this buried letter of June 2, 1964: All the bullets had been chambered more than once, with strong suggestions of in another rifle. Yet he told Curry that all were used in the assassination.

Hoover knew this was false. His June 2 letter is an admission that he did not know when those cartridges were fired. Combined with the other suppressed evidence Hoover and the rest of the FBI and the Department of Justice fought so hard to continue suppressing, there is the question that has to be faced: Were these empty shells planted?

Hoover did know it was possible. There is no other reason for his deceptions, semantics, stonewalling, not making the required tests and resisting all to the bitterest of ends.

The other "intrusion" the FBI hid to the degree possible has to do with these same scientific tests on the curbstone struck by the missed shot. This shot is indispensable to the Commission's account of the three shots it permitted. James T. Tague was wounded by a spray of concrete from where a bullet hit the curb at the diagonally opposite end of Dealey Plaza. As Hoover found it expedient to account for the assassination in his definitive report without mention of the wound the President was known to have had in the front of his neck, so also did Hoover prefer to omit this missed shot in that five-volume report, CD1.

Hoover could stonewall the Commission but it could not stonewall itself. It had to acknowledge this missed shot and the wounding of Tague. Its published evidence is summarized in WHITEWASH beginning on page 156.

The Report itself quotes the immediate police broadcast by Patrolman L. L. Hill, "I have a guy that was possibly hit by a ricochet from the bullet off the concrete." (R116) Tague's slight cheek injury was reported by Deputy Sheriff Eddy R. Walthers (7H547,553). Walthers was photographed examining another spot struck by a bullet not included in any official accounting. He also found the spot near where Tague was standing "where it appeared that a bullet had hit the cement," as the Report (R116) put it. At the same point it quotes Tague, "There was a mark. Quite obviously it was a bullet, and it was very fresh." Tom Dillard, a newspaper photographer, and James Underwood, a TV news director, both took professional pictures.

From the Commission's records it appears that it paid no attention to this damaged curbstone until July 7, 1964, when it asked the FBI to conduct an investigation. The pressures causing this included a June 11 memo from Specter urging that Tague and Virgie Rachley (Mrs. Donald Baker) "be deposed on where the missing bullet struck."* The FBI produced nothing except the account of misadventures reported in a letterhead memorandum dated July 17. (21H474)

The FBI's Dallas office pretended not to be able to find this photographed spot or any "nick": "The area of the curb at this point for a distance of ten feet in either direction was carefully checked and it was ascertained that there was no nick in the curb in the checked area, nor was any mark observed." It suggested that "there have been numerous rains, which could have possibly washed away such a mark and also that area is cleaned by a street cleaning machine ... which could also wash away such a mark."

Underwood had previously told the FBI "he could not be positive the mark was made by a ricocheting bullet" and Dillard "was of the opinion the mark very possibly could have been made by a ricocheting bullet and that it had been recently made." (21H472ff.) Here the "mark observed and photographed" is located "at a point twenty-one feet and eleven and one-half inches east of the point where Main Street passes under the triple underpass."

So Shaneyfelt was sent down. The rains and the street-cleaning machines appeared to stay away. August 5, he got Dillard, Underwood and their photos and returned with a piece of curbing. Shaneyfelt found it exactly where the pictures showed.

Hoover sent the Commission one of his semantical masterpieces August 12. (21H475-7) Shaneyfelt testified September 1. Although the FBI had taken the steadfast position with Jim and me that it would not give us copies of any communication, they wanted us to have a carbon of what had been printed by the Commission and, masking out a large part of the upper right corner, they gave us a xerox attached to two other sheets of paper.

FBI accounts did do what the rains did not. They diminished this visible place where a bullet hit to a nick then a mark and finally, after the Hoover/Shaneyfelt operation, into no more than a smear.

Hoover also had to account for what the rains and street cleaner left for him to deal with. Fact forced him to conjecture. His conjecture in this case was too much for the Commission. In the end, however, the problem was the Commission's. Because Hoover did not give it what I obtained in this suit, he eased their burden and saved his own face.

The appearance of precision is in Hoover's letter: "This mark was located and was found to be 23 feet, 4 inches [not "twenty-one

*See p. 122.

454

feet and eleven and one-half inches"] from the abutment of the triple underpass" on the south side of Main Street. "Assuming that a bullet was shot from the [easternmost] sixth floor window of the TSBD "struck the curb ... at the location of the mark ... and assuming that it passed directly over the President" it would have been "at approximately frame 410" of the Zapruder film. This is 97 frames after "the fatal shot ... frame 313 ... represents a lapse of time of 5.3 seconds ... Based on a direct shot ... this bullet would have passed over the center of Elm Street at an elevation of about 18 feet from the street level."

Assumptions, primarily, of Oswald's guilt. The basic approach is not to investigate. Why else presume the shot could have come from nowhere else?

Insanity also is presumed. Why else would a lone assassin, looking through a telescopic sight with his alleged magnified and clear view, fire at his victim _after_ seeing the top of his victim's head blow off? And is it not insane to wait approximately as long after the fatal shot as the entire assassination took in the official account to fire again for no purpose?

Also assumed is the firing of two remarkably accurate shots, both hitting the target, followed by one so wild it was high over the victim and impacted twice as far away as the victim was or 260 feet past him. (21H483)

The "mark" is reduced to a smear in Hoover's description of the lab work on the curbstone: "Small foreign metal smears were found adhering to the curbing section within the area of the mark. These smears were spectrographically determined to be essentially lead with a trace of antimony. No copper was found."

This is his full representation of all the scientific testing.

These communications represent the rewriting of the field reports in Hoover's "SOG" as he called FBI headquarters, "Seat of Government." In the past comparison between the field and the headquarters reports has shown the latter to be quite opposite to what the former say. If there is no reason to assume this is true with the curbstone, it is true that the distances given are not identical and the description of the lab work is meaningless.

In both documents greatest and repeated emphasis is placed on the alleged absence of even a "nick" where the bullet hit. This was the beginning of the FBI's creation of another magic bullet like 399.

Given the facts Hoover gave the Commission, the first consideration in any real investigation would not have been that the shot came from an impossible point of origin. It should have been investigation of another point of origin.

Instead, Hoover undertook to argue and explain. In doing this he put his monkey on the Commission's back. He knew better than anyone else that the Commission was hung up on a no-conspiracy/Oswald assassin line. He knew also that it was not about to fight with him. And he knew its schedule. Delaying even the pretense of an investigation until the Report was about to appear left the Commission no flexibility. It would not start all over again and admit all its work was invalid.

In short, he knew he could get away with just about anything.

Even the blood of poor James Tague, little of it as flowed. How account for it? Hoover did not need "all great Neptune's ocean" to "wash this blood clean from my hand." Tague's blood was a seemingly incarnadine stain on the no-conspiracy/Oswald assassin preconception. With dictatorial control over the FBI and the certainty he could manipulate the Commission, Hoover did for himself in his lifetime what all the seas did not do for Macbeth. Hoover's soap was semantics, his bathroom the FBI labs.

Shakespeare's end was Hoover's beginning. His "out" of the

"damned spot" is in what we have seen of CD1, his definitive report. His absolute control made it possible. In that briefest mention of how the President was killed, Hoover accounted for all three alleged shots without mention of the "missed" one.*

On August 12, 1964, Hoover was not embarrassed by having said on December 9, 1963, in CD1 that Connally was hit by a separate bullet, one that did not hit Kennedy. He ignored it, too, in a masterpiece of semantics that begins with an "assumption" for which there was no basis and is opposed to the investigative need:

Assuming this mark was made by a fragment of a bullet from the assassin's rifle, the evidence present is insufficient to establish whether it was caused by a fragment of a bullet striking the occupants of the Presidential limousine, such as the bullet that struck the President's head, or whether it was a fragment of a shot that may have missed the Presidential limousine.

There are other possibilities. Evidence is not "insufficient to establish" that it could not have been "caused by a fragment of a [sic] bullet striking the occupants" of the car. Bullet 399 made its mysterious appearance not on Main Street but in the hospital. The fragments that remained after the explosion of the fatal shot did not have the energy required to get them out of the car and if they had the simple laws of physics prevented any one from going all the way to where this curbstone was hit and having enough strength left to make even a "smear." That side of the President's head, 100 per cent of the evidence proves, was intact. A fragment of this bullet striking that curbstone would have had to go all the way around the world first and after 25,000 miles reverse itself 180°. To make the trip this fragment would have had circumnavigational capability and precision like nothing ever launched at Cape Kennedy (then Canaveral). If it somehow maintained its original muzzle velocity this trip would have required about 200 hours. Even with the energy and intelligence and capability of reversing itself in thin air, is this not asking a bit much of any bullet, even one to which Hoover imparted his greatest magic? Especially if it had to be a week later for its rendezvous with destiny?

But the Commission headed by a chief justice and including the man now President of the United States had no questions and printed the fable without comment.

Hoover tried to keep himself free and clear with other options. Having "assumed" that the damage to this curbstone originated with "the assassin's rifle," meaning Oswald's, he ended his discussion of what he intended to be taken as the results of spectroscopy with the conclusion, "Therefore, this mark could not have been made by the first impact of a high velocity rifle bullet."

This, too, is semantics and is meaningless. The so-called "bullet from the assassin's rifle" was not of high velocity. Hoover's own expert, Frazier, swore that it was of low velocity. (3H14) Hoover knew it. Twice its muzzle velocity is not uncommon. So any conclusions based on the known falsity of "high velocity" are null. One of these is that "the damage to the curbing would have been more extensive if" this "high velocity" bullet had not "first struck some other object."

Hoover managed to omit the known distance from his letter. He also managed to avoid mentioning whether or not there was anything other than air between the alleged sniper's lair and this point of impact. Well, there was only air. Not even a tree. Here the absence of copper is poisonous, and the spectroscopy proved it. Hoover's way of getting around this was to say that it "precludes the possibility that the mark on the curbing section was made by an unmutilated military-type full metal-jacketed [sic] bullet ..." (He had trouble with that copper. Bullets are of metal, cores and jackets both.)

Of the unmentioned possibilities that remain in even Hoover's

*See pp. 74-5.

version there is a soft bullet. One without a full, hard jacket. Instead, he seemed to go for another alternative in language that provided him a means of saying he had not meant this interpretation, that it "could have originated from the lead core of a mutilated metal-jacketed bullet" of the "assassin's" type. In the next paragraph he added that, with all these presumptions of which there is no evidence, the damage to the curb "would have been much more extensive."

In turn this has to be comprehended in terms of Hoover's description of the "damage" as no more than a "smear" and certainly, absolutely, positively, not even a "nick."

If one could "mark" a concrete curbstone with a common pin, "the damage to the curbing would have been much more extensive" than a "smear."

This is Hoover at his semantical best.

There was nothing but air between the presumed assassin and the allegedly nondamaged curb hundreds of feet away. What remained? A ricochet? Not from the car or any of its occupants, as we have seen. There was also nothing else from which a bullet fired from that TSBD window could have ricocheted and inflicted the damage that was other than a smear a matter of inches only above the street surface.

To Hoover's knowledge there were a number of other reported impacts of bullets on the street and sidewalks. He and the Commission pretended they were imaginary. (The accommodating Dallas authorities had repaved the street.) Because sidewalks are not paved, one remains. (WHITEWASH II,pp.37-8,106,131)

The laws of physics and geometry preclude Hoover's limited conjectures. So does the actuality before this "damage" was downgraded progressively from "mark" to "smear."

At no point and in no way in this and the other relevant documents cited did Hoover rule out another - a different - kind of bullet or the obvious possibility of another point of origin. He had reason to believe the latter possibility. (WHITEWASH II,pp.36-8,106,131,167) His semantics begin with the stipulation of an assumption, not a statement of fact. Where he got to what he represented as the results of spectroscopy, he said "The absence of copper precludes the possibility" of "an unmutilated military-type full metal-jacketed bullet." He left open the unmentioned possibility of a soft bullet or a different kind while implying the impossible as the only possible cause.

The impossible is also that to which he restricted himself in what he represented as the final results, the total yield, of spectroscopy. His rightful heirs intended going no further in response to my FOIA suit.

In the masking of a large part of the upper righthand corner of the one lab page more than the fraudulent representation, "internal communications," was hidden. The name of the agent or agents who performed the test, part of "examinations requested by" and of "Examinations requested" are collectively memory-holed. If there are any "Results of Examination" that is the one - the only - blank part of the form.

What the FBI and the Department of Justice through Kilty swore is 100 percent of all the scientific testing and all the results is at the top of the next page.

This work sheet is explicit in describing the particular test made, "Jarrell-Ash," but includes no single measurement, analysis or comparison. Obviously, there had to be a comparison between the traces from this curbstone and all the other lead recovered from all the other specimens. The absence of this has to be taken as proof that the results were uncongenial to the predetermined conclusion.

Bearing on the utter meaninglessness of the statement that the smear showed no more than "lead with a trace of antimony" is Hoover's

E6

609 ~~Request for location and examination of mark on curbing at assassinu site~~ Piece of curbing.

Small foreign metal smears (see attached for location) were run spectrographically (Garrett-Ash.) & found to be essentially lead with a trace of antimony - Could be bullet metal. No copper observed.

March 13 response to a Commission question about "items in common usage which contain antimony." Among 14 itemized "common objects" other than a bullet that could have caused this "smear" Hoover lists type metal, lead alloys, paints and storage batteries.

Nobody knew better than Hoover that bullets have lead alloys containing other components, not just antimony. The whole purpose of the test was to identify, measure and compare all these components, especially trace elements. That would have been one way of proving the official story or at least proving it was not impossible. Hoover did not take that way. The only apparent reason is that he knew he dared not.

If there had been as little as a single part in each millionth part of that "smear" that held any other substance, as bullets do, the test would have disclosed it. Because he did not, there is no reason not to believe that this smear was not made by some stray paint, a broken storage battery or a thrown piece of type metal.

Unless the "smear" was too tiny and mechanical blending of its elements was too imperfect.

This possibility is eliminated by the lab's attached sketch:

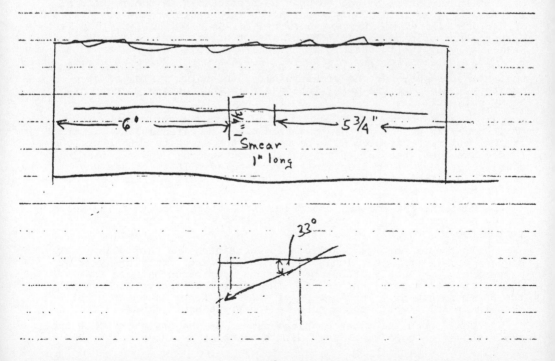

It shows the smear to be regular in shape, 1-3/4 inches high and 1 inch wide and to be almost in the center of the piece of curbing, side to side and top to bottom.

But the bullet itself, with the copper jacket which is a major part of it, was only a mite longer than an inch and a mere quarter of an inch thick. Remove that jacket and the lead is tinier. How could so thin a cylinder make a rectangular smear an inch and three-quarters in the wrong or vertical dimension? And an inch the other way?

It could not. And the specimen was not too small. Samples almost microscopic in size are adequate for testing.

Then there is the second sketch, showing the direction that Hoover described as "a general direction away from" the building.

This sketch depicts and specifies a 33° angle.

At this distance - about 600 feet - from that sixth-floor window the angle alone eliminates both a direct hit from that window and a ricochet that could have caused any injury to Tague regardless of how that injury was caused.

Hoover gave none of this to the Presidential Commission for which he was, supposedly, chief of investigations. Instead, in this letter he told it that "From a microscopic study [not provided in the litigation after we pointed out this language] this lead object ... was moving in a general direction away from the Texas School Depository Building."

It required a nonexistent "microscopic study" to determine, among other things, direction? Here is what Kilty swore to and Judge Pratt accepted:

3. Concerning plaintiff's allegation that he has not been given the "spectrographic testing" of "small foreign metal smears on a piece of curbing": the Laboratory work sheet which was previously furnished plaintiff and from which he quotes is the notes and results of this test. A thorough search has uncovered no other material concerning the spectrographic testing of the metal smear on the curbing.

4. Concerning plaintiff's allegation that he has not been given the "microscopic study" referred to at the bottom of page two of an August 12, 1964, letter from J. Edgar Hoover to J. Lee Rankin, which letter has also been furnished plaintiff: a thorough search has uncovered no additional documents concerning a study of this type.

Palpably these are false swearings. Hoover swore that the FBI would never close its investigation and would investigate every new claim or charge. (5H99-100) In making a liar of Hoover, Kilty and the FBI swore there is no substantiation now for any of this. There is a reason.

Is there anything - a bullet or anything else - that leaves any building going in any direction by any means that is not "moving in a general direction away from" it?

Would this not have been true of a shot at the moon?

But what Hoover said is proven false by this lab paper and sketch. Hoover was careful not to give them to the Commission. They were produced for the first time anywhere in this suit. They appear here for the first time anywhere.

Much as this Commission sat still for, it surely could not
have accepted a 33° angle as that made from a height of 60 feet to a
point about 600 feet away.

Worse still, the sketch shows the alleged path to be <u>toward</u>,
<u>not away from the building</u>!

As you look at the sketch the building is to the east, the
left. It shows the alleged shot coming from the west, the right.

And at a distance of a little over 20 feet it would have had
to originate from somewhere inside the solid concrete of the triple
underpass!

Is there any wonder Kilty swore that this is the <u>entire</u> "microscopic examination," that there is no other record?

What a microscope!

In concluding his nonreport to the Commission Hoover employed
another masterpiece of Hooverese, saying, "A photograph of the mark
of the curbing before removal and a photograph of the curbing after
removal" were attached. He did upgrade the smear to a mark on the
"before" photo, but he does not say it is on the second. Here he
neither deceived nor lied. He merely tricked. They provide still
more for the spirit of the departed Hoover and the consciences of the
living to contend with.

It is alleged repeatedly that, in the language of the FBI's
July 17, 1964, memo on this (nicely titled "<u>LEE HARVEY OSWALD</u>") that
"It should be noted that no nick or break in the concrete was ob-
served." (21H474)

Then why <u>did</u> poor Tague bleed, little as his cheek bled?

There are two possible answers, both completely destructive of
the official story, either requiring a new, full and completely public investigation that should include the FBI.

Shaneyfelt used a print made from the TV movie film of James
Underwood and a print of the still picture Tom Dillard took with his
Mamiyaflex 120. (21H473) The files of the Warren Commission abound
in tributes to the photographic skills of the FBI. There are color
pictures with no color and pictures of cut clothing arranged to hide
the cuts. But this sequence of pictures is one not easily surpassed
in this subtle FBI art.

Underwood gave the FBI his entire reel of film, countless
frames. (CD1395:34) Shaneyfelt then selected a single frame. It was
cropped and enlarged, eliminating much. Then it was processed to
make it even grainier and less distinct. If Underwood had a poorer
frame than this the FBI converted into a still, he had nothing fit to
air and nothing that could have been comprehensible when aired.

The challenge by the Dillard picture was greater. Dillard provided two prints. (CD1395:35) He had taken two clear, professional
pictures, as one would expect of an experienced news photographer.
The FBI's answer was simple and direct: over-expose one picture and
make it more contrasty, by special paper or other means. The result
is a picture that is another tribute to the FBI's obfuscatory art.

However, despite all this effort and considerable talent with
pictures and with words, <u>both</u> pictures <u>do</u> show physical damage - not
just a mark or a smear. In each the size can be judged from other
objects, fingers and a ball pen. The shading that could not be completely eliminated from the Underwood frame shows that flaking of the
concrete radiated away from the hole it and the Dillard picture both
show.*

Once the FBI turned over a nonspectrographic analysis and
called it their complete spectrographic analysis; a nonmicroscopic
examination and described it as their microscopic examination; claimed
it had not made neutron activation tests on what honesty of intent and
perfecting of evidence required; and told all the other official

*See pp. 608-9.

460

falsehoods, I had the Archives photographer make pictures of the existing curbstone. They show what is described after my examination reported in the first part of this book.* After nine years the difference in shade is still visible, the difference in texture can still be felt and the hole shown in the Underwood and Dillard pictures has not reappeared.

One might conjecture that the FBI dug up the wrong curbstone section. However, there are marks that indicate Shaneyfelt got the right piece. The alternative is that sometime between the assassination and the FBI's belated and forced quest about eight months later, the hole was patched. Whatever is true, the "mark" or "smear" that officially is not even a "nick" actually was a hole, as the pictures show, and the FBI and the Commission staff knew it.

Consistent with this apparent intent to misrepresent, to make the false story appear to be within possibility, are the deficiencies of this sketch. It is drawn to appear to be flat, as without special indications one would assume. It is made to appear as a right-angle view of the curbstone, with lines representing the street level and the top drawn in. It does locate the "smear" from side to side, where no evidentiary purpose is served. It does not orient the "smear" from top to bottom. Here the dimensions are needed. Without them it is impossible to determine if the FBI, on being challenged about this sketch, would claim that the top of it is really the back of the top and that they have portrayed three dimensions while indicating only two. Without a contorted explanation like this the sketch shows the "smear" about midway between top and bottom, where it was not.

C.A. 226-75 is going to be appealed as this is written. What higher courts will rule and whether or not, if so ordered, the FBI will deliver what it and the ERDA still suppress is uncertain. What it could not avoid surrendering, what this suit did yield after almost a decade of fighting for it - this "new" evidence - is totally destructive of the official account of the assassination of our President. Countless people of all ranks and stations within the FBI, the Commission, ERDA and elsewhere in government were and are aware of these gruesome falsifications of the crime and of subsequent history.

This is the most basic evidence. In a criminal proceeding it would be the beginning of an investigation. When JFK was killed it was totally suppressed. In a court of law it would have acquitted the only accused.

There is no part of this evidence that stacks, none that was treated honestly by the FBI, the Department of Justice or the Commission. There was, there is, there can be no innocence. All this evidence is tainted. Hoover and FBI agents faked to give it a meaning it does not have, a meaning the other evidence yielded by these years of private, personal inquiry prove it cannot and does not have.

So many knew! So many know! All are silent!

Why anyone connected with the official investigation of the assassination of a President would lie - from the Director of the FBI to any agent under him - is a question that perplexes only the uninformed or those unwilling to believe what is beyond question. It is and has been the practice. In this suit there was no single official communication, written or verbal, that was not controlled by lies. There was no single paper filed in court, no verbal representation made to the judge, that was not tainted by falsehood. Some of it was perjurious.

The FBI had to be really uptight about the JFK assassination and these scientific tests in particular to run the risks perjury entails. It had to expect every judge on every level would be tolerant of a felony that undermines the courts. It had to assume that the major media will continue to ignore or suppress what would normally be newsworthy and the subject of further, independent journalistic inquiry. Or it is running great risks to buy time. If this, from

*See pp. 57-8.

461

what, for what? Not in innocence.

This is not the FBI we have read about in the inspired books.
It is not the FBI glorified on radio and TV. It is the real FBI.

It is Hoover's FBI but not Hoover's alone.

It is Kelley's FBI but not Kelley's alone.

It is your FBI - the one you have, the one you will continue
to have.

Unless something is done to cleanse it.

It cannot be cleansed without punishment of its criminals.

When criminals enforce the law crime is enshrined.

When criminals investigate the assassination of a President
the assassination is and remains unsolved. Their corruption engenders
the wildest conjectures. These conjectures serve then to give public
exoneration to the corrupters. The cycle is frightening and has the
most frightening potential.

Without this, that the FBI could fake evidence when it investigated the assassination of a President and persist in the fake for
more than a decade, in court and under oath, is terrifying enough.
That this was done is now beyond question.

Why?

The Bell Still Tolls

In concluding WHITEWASH II: The FBI Secret Service Coverup
nine years ago, I permitted myself the first expression of the passion
I have not since then hidden from the reader. (pp.230ff.) If this
kind of open expression of deep feeling strongly held is not welcome
among those who dictate literary acceptability and success, it is the
obligation of the author in fairness to and honesty with the reader
on a subject like and having the consequences of this one.

That epilogue to that earlier book begins with the question:
"What can one say at the end of a book like this? What can one say
about the society that makes it possible, the government that does
what it documents, and the press ... Of the silent ...

It continues, saying that "The late President had such friends
he had no need of enemies;" that he "had declared his intention of
changing" national policy: that for him there was the dubious epitaph
of "the autopsy unworthy of a Bowery bum" while leaving us "the shame
of this unsolved murder ... With that award no decent American can
live in honor and without fear."

It concludes (pp.241-2) with an account of my earliest efforts
to obtain these suppressed scientific tests. I had before then begun
the decade of effort this book represents incompletely despite its
size. An adequate record of all that work and its evidentiary yield
cannot be bound within one set of covers. It is no less impossible
to summarize this mass of evidence, this proof of ceaseless official
suppressions, lies, distortions, and even new criminal acts, perjury
and its subornation.

There was reason for fear nine years ago. There is more reason
for fear now. In the intervening years we reaped the bitter harvest
of the sowing of thorns in the assassination itself and in the official "investigation." Those intervening years brought us other assassinations, Viet Nam, Watergate, unprecedented national disenchantment,
its expression in unprecedented violence, and have us on the brink of
international and domestic economic and political chaos. They have
brought us a tremendous increase in authoritarianism and a situation
conducive to its acceleration.

These were inevitable with what this book documents.

The ensuing years and the fruit of the long toil in the evidentiary vineyard magnify this emotion and the fear first expressed

nine years ago.

There was no Blondel when John Kennedy was consigned to history with this dubious epitaph of a fake inquest by those who, without it, could not have brought us the Southeast Asia adventure Kennedy had avoided and sought to end, those 50,000 of our own best and youngest killed and so many more of theirs; so many, many more scarred and marred forever; The Watergate in its fullest meaning; the rot of the inner cities and of spirit; and the permanent bankruptcy from the total waste of those countless billions the waste of which has brought us to what can be the brink of financial disaster and the beginning of a newer and more repressive authoritarianism.

Without this assassination and those that followed and without the corruption of all the subsequent proceedings that never met traditional legal standards and requirements, we would not now be treading barefoot on this sowing of new thorns from the harvest of the old.

Cry out in pain, fellow citizens.

In anguish and sincerest anger in a clamor for cleansing that must be heeded lest your cries turn to despair when it is too late.

Ask not for whom the bell tolls.

It does toll for you, especially the younger of you who will live longer in its endless din.

Who does not learn from history is doomed to relive it.

There is a special corner of hell reserved for those who in time of moral crisis do preserve detachment and silence, Bobby Kennedy's personal modification of Dante.

There is a time and a place for everything.

There are times that try men's souls. This is and has been one.

There are lights in the belfry.

Let the word go forth that henceforth we will not have this. Otherwise, friend and foe will be alike.

We now have more to fear than fear itself. In 1984 words have no meaning, are unheard.

The official account of the JFK assassination and the Warren Report were never credible. The respect in which the members of the Commission - picked with such consummate political cunning by LBJ - were held made people and the major media believe in advance that its work would be honest. The mass of the Report when it was issued defied the digesting of the most honest reporter with a deadline to meet. This was even truer of those massive 26 volumes for which no reporter had the required background.

There was a pretense that it could be believed, a pretense fostered by the uncritical media already corrupted by systematic leaks by the old master, Hoover, and others.

To reasonable people the analysis of the Report alone in WHITE-WASH left nothing of consequence in the Report to be believed. There was a compulsive need to believe it.

Imagine it: The vaunted head of the FBI investigates the assassination of a President, devotes five large volumes to it and does not report all the shots known to have been fired or all the wounds known to have been inflicted!

Hoover knew from the very beginning and from the immediately available evidence that there had to have been more than one assassin, whether or not Oswald fired a shot. The evidence, not political theorizing, proves more than one assassin. More than one assassin means there was a conspiracy, and nobody in government was willing to face the awful, terrifying meaning of a conspiracy to kill a President.*

What Hoover knew many others in the FBI and Department of Justice knew and have known. The Commission recognized this situation and its own, accepted both and then accepted the contorted Report in which it sanctified the turning around of the world.

This book recounts parts of a much larger personal investigation in which others, like Jim Lesar and Howard Roffman, were of considerable help when they could be. That one man could, despite enormous resistance, develop all this "new evidence" is less a tribute to him than an indictment of others. It is an indication of what officials could and should have done but, having refused to, then sought to make the doing impossible for others. New felonies became the norm. Courts accepted them or became part of them.

All fact and evidence combine to compel the same question, what can one say at the end of a book like this? What can be said that can justify all these wrongdoing officials who suppressed all this proof that the official "solution" to the most subversive of crimes in a country like ours was false and, when foisted off on the trusting and grieving people, was known to be false?

Can there be justification for what becomes a new crime, in some ways a more terrible one than the assassination itself?

With the passing of time there can be no undoing. More time will have to pass before we can know if there will now be a cleansing of this ugliness and if this weeping sore can be healed.

With the ticking minutes the bell tolls.

It tolls mourning and it warns.

What distinguishes this book is that it represents the results of a conscious search for the "new evidence" official apologists have always protested is necessary for the Report not to be credited. That always was and remains a false claim. Somehow, probably the ultimate tribute to Lyndon Johnson's political shrewdness in selecting the members of his Commission, they were imputed powers of perfection our basic doctrine refuses the most exalted, our judges. We assume judges will err and we have machinery for correcting their error. We have come to accept that when a President has a problem he cannot address in any other way, he appoints a commission to study it. He selects those he can expect to do what he wants, they work in secrecy, then issue what he wanted issued all the time and lo! it becomes instant truth, not subject to testing of any kind. The Warren Commission set the pattern.

But I doubt any administration will again permit the records of any such commission to be in any degree available to another investigating devil loving the scripture of truth and willing to fight for it. The reason for this search for the missing evidence was other than the satisfaction of the unthinking and making their irrationality seem reasonable. There was never anything wrong with the "old" evidence that was so ignored and misused. It meant and said other than represented, thus the demand for the "new." But it was incomplete in the Commission's files.

The most vital of this "new evidence" that is new only because the Commission did not want it is evidence the Commission did not have and evidence it did have and merely lied about. To the reader unwilling to believe or shocked by the evidence, it may appear this word "lie" is used loosely. It is not. There is here, often in facsimile, positive proof of the fact and of intent. The Commission's lack of access to the autopsy film is a convenient example. It was never denied this film and it did have it. Yet since then there have been the companion lies, that it was denied this evidence and that the murdered President's family denied it.

Where the word "perjury" is used, it is used in literal fidelity to fact. Perjury is false swearing to the material. These false oaths were witting, deliberate and material.

One may argue over motive in these incredible transgressions against truth and in the denial to the people of the "best evidence" in the assassination of their President and its subversion of our

464

entire system of supposed self-government. About intent there now is not and there cannot be any question. This official intent is apparent in those of the formerly suppressed executive sessions here reprinted, some for the first time. (While these conclusions were being written, Jim and I filed another FOIA suit for the remaining suppressed executive session transcripts, C.A. 75-1448.) The Commission <u>knew</u> it had had the autopsy film, <u>knew</u> there was an official certificate of death, <u>knew</u> the name of the authority who certified to it and <u>knew</u> it had to have him and his papers as evidence before it. More so because Burkley was the one medical man present in both the Dallas emergency room and at the autopsy. The Commission also knew of the existence of his papers. It did not have to make the safe assumption that they existed. My leads in this long quest for them were the Commission's own papers, among the very first I located almost a decade ago in the ransacking of its evidentiary quicksand of generally uncollated files.

There can be no genuine argument over whether or not the Commission should have had the ballistics/scientific-test evidence it did not have and I had to sue to get part of - part that is more than enough. There could not have been any real investigation without it. Yet <u>all</u> the results of <u>all</u> the tests are <u>totally</u> missing from this Commission's files and consideration. And when in its ultimate extremity it could not avoid taking testimony from one of these experts, it used him for dishonest purposes and adduced from him <u>not a single word</u> about <u>this</u> evidence. Intent is unhidden.

In the course of this work I have provided accounts of how the Commission deliberately avoided the evidence it did not want that was thrust upon it. The reading it was given unsolicitedly on Connally's X-rays is an example. It did not want what disputed its preconception so it persisted in demanding copies until it got copies to which no interpretation was attached. The Dallas doctors themselves were abused in a similar manner, forced to say other than they knew and had said - when their President was killed and they were essential witnesses.

Following first exposure of this official falsification of the official account of how our President was killed in my first book, those that followed and the attention all received, resuscitation of the official Report was needed. Instead of regarding itself as a hallowed place, the Department of Justice convened panels of compliant experts who managed, by secrecy and semantics, to say that this official account was truthful while discussing overwhelming proof that it was not.

There is no end to this, the volume of this "new evidence" is so great. There is no end to proof that all involved in all the falsifications were witting.

In a sense this book goes further and does more than would be required in a court of law. No defense counsel would be required to work with adverse witnesses only, witnesses all preconditioned to oppose him. He would not be required to sue for evidence. And he would have cross-examination available. His need would be to cast reasonable doubt, no more, to acquit.

In this case, no more to indict. There is more than reasonable doubt.

This evidence is totally destructive of the official case.

The indictment is more than of the Commission and its staff; more than of the compliance executive agencies; more than of the dominating authoritarian, Hoover. It is an indictment of the flaws in the society that made it possible and made years of accrediting the false solution to the terrible crime an urgent need.

Society requires that this be cleansed or society as we have from childhood had it described to us is not and cannot be free and healthy.

Reasonable consideration of this story as a murder mystery ended with the issuance of a Report that did not tell the people what happened, how it happened and why. If a private investigator cannot come up with answers to all the questions left by the official investigation and its Report, there now is no doubt that nothing we have been told about the _fact_ of the assassination itself was true.

This is so overwhelming the actuality that, as we have seen, the official account does not even locate the President's wounds where they were. On this most basic evidence there is naught but knowing falsehood.

From the time of the Report the real question has been of society - the society in which this can happen and the society that will be if there is not now what rectification is possible.

Terrible as it is that a President can be killed and that crime remain unsolved, it is more horrible still that the governments that came to power as a result of that assassination persist in all the same false pretenses about it and insist on public belief of all those falsehoods. It is more frightening that government can persist in these lies about the crime than that the crime itself could happen.

Dangerous as it is to any concept of freedom that a President can be killed and all of representative society overthrown with bullets, it is even more dangerous that government, in calm deliberation, can first create and then continuously sanctify a falsification of the crime and the deepest of subversions it represents.

We decide now what the future holds, what kind of society we can have. We decide by inaction as we can by action.

We are now at an end that must be a new beginning.

W. WARREN,
    Chairman
RICHARD B. RUSSELL
JOHN SHERMAN COOPER
HALE BOGGS
GERALD R. FORD
JOHN J. McCLOY
ALLEN W. DULLES

J. LEE RANKIN,
    General Counsel

January 11, 1964

MEMORANDUM FOR MEMBERS OF THE COMMISSION

Attached is a Progress Report which the Chairman asked

me to prepare and distribute.   J. Lee Rankin

- 4 -

These materials and those yet to arrive will be reviewed by the staff
as quickly as possible.

Mr. Rankin and I have given further thought to the organization
of the work of this Commission in line with the thoughts expressed at
the last meeting. I think it would be desirable to commence by dividing
the substance of the work into approximately six areas. Any such
division at this point, of course, must necessarily be tentative. I am
enclosing as Appendix C a tentative outline prepared by Mr. Rankin
which I think will assist in organizing the evaluation of the investigative materials received by the Commission. This outline divides the
work into the following six areas: (1) Assassination of President
Kennedy on November 22, 1963; (2) Lee Harvey Oswald as the Assassin of
President Kennedy; (3) Lee Harvey Oswald: Background and Possible
Motive; (4) Oswald's Foreign Activity (Military Excluded); (5) Murder
of Lee Harvey Oswald by Jack L. Ruby; and (6) Security Precautions to
Protect the President. As the staff reviews the materials, the outline
will certainly undergo substantial revision, and I hope that all members
of the Commission will advise Mr. Rankin of any suggestions they wish to
make regarding this outline.

Simultaneously with this effort, of course, high priority is being
given to preparation for taking the testimony of Mrs. Oswald and any
other witnesses which the Commission believes should be interviewed under
oath in the near future. One member of the staff has been reviewing all
the interviews of Mrs. Oswald and related material in order to prepare
adequately for this interrogation. I anticipate that the results of his
work will be submitted to Mr. Rankin next week for approval and the
testimony of Mrs. Oswald can be taken later in the month. The FBI has

- 5 -

been requested to conduct a complete background investigation of the
Paines. Similar investigations will be requested of other people in
Dallas and Fort Worth who associated closely with Oswald and his family.
The proposed interview of Mrs. John F. Kennedy will be discussed with
the Attorney General during the next week.

As of 1/11/64, the Commission had done no investigation and had merely been reviewing
reports it had received from other agencies (Rxi-xii). The FBI, in its famous report
of 12/9/63 (CD 1) had concluded Oswald alone was guilty but the Commission had yet
to do a single thing to confirm the FBI finding and had grumbled about its inadequacy
at their 12/16/63 executive session (WHITEWASH IV, pp. 139-40). Yet the Commission
organized its work on the premise that Oswald was indeed guilty, as area (2) of the
"tentative" outline makes clear. Why else would "high priority" be given to taking
the testimony of Marina Oswald, who was a witness to nothing remotely connected with
any basic fact of the assassination. Marina's was the first testimony taken, during
the first week in February. Mrs. Kennedy, who was the closest witness, was not questioned until June, long after her memory may have faded.

I. Assassination of President Kennedy on November 22, 1963 in Dallas

    A. Trip to Texas - Prior to Assassination

        1. Initial plans for trip
            a. relevant dates
            b. itinerary
            c. companions
            d. motorcade to luncheon
            e. other

        2. Events of morning of November 22
            a. arrival at airport - time, etc.
            b. motorcade - crowds, time, etc.

    B. Assassination (based on all available statements of witnesses, films, photographs, etc.)

        1. Shots
            a. number of shots fired
            b. time elapsed during shots
            c. direction of shots
            d. location of car at time

        2. Postures and apparent injuries to President Kennedy and Governor Connally
            a. President Kennedy
            b. Governor Connally

    C. Events Immediately Following the Shooting

        1. Treatment at hospital
        2. Activities of Dallas law enforcement
        3. Return of entourage to Washington
            a. President Johnson's trip to airport
            b. trip of Mrs. Kennedy with body of late President to airport
            c. swearing-in

        4. Removal of President Kennedy's body to Bethesda Naval Hospital
        5. Removal of car to Washington - condition and repairs

    D. Nature and Extent of Wounds Received by President Kennedy (based on examinations in Dallas and Bethesda)

        1. Number of individual wounds received by President Kennedy
        2. Cause of death
        3. Time of death
        4. Evaluation of medical treatment received in Dallas

---

    This "Tentative Outline" was attached to the 1/11/64 Warren progress report. It is an explicit statement that no real investigation was intended and that the Commission merely anticipated substantiating the FBI Report. Its revelations of the Commission's prejudices and failures abound. Section I (B), dealing with the basic facts of the assassination, was to be "based on all available statements of witnesses, films, photographs, etc." Yet many crucial witnesses were completely ignored and many avoided until just before the Report was printed. Also, the FBI and the Commission did everything they could to keep as many pictures as possible out of the record, returning most without even keeping copies. This is documented in PHOTOGRAPHIC WHITEWASH. Note also section I (D), which contemplates an "evaluation of medical treatment received in Dallas," at best an irrelevancy, but makes no provision for "evaluation" of the quality of the autopsy, the source of the most basic information about the wounds. How could the Commission rely on the autopsy findings unless it assured itself they were dependable and based on a proper autopsy by qualified pathologists? As later documents reveal, the Commission had grave doubts about the autopsy findings but did nothing to dispel them.

II. Lee Harvey Oswald as the Assassin of President Kennedy

A. Brief Identification of Oswald (Dallas resident, employee of Texas School Book Depository, etc.)

B. Movements on November 22, 1963 Prior to Assassination

    1. Trip to work
      a. time
      b. package
      c. other significant facts, e.g. any conversations, etc.

    2. Entry into Depository
      a. time
      b. package
      c. other significant facts

    3. Activities during morning
      a. nature of his work
      b. location of his work
      c. other significant facts

    4. Movements immediately prior to 12:29 p.m.

C. Movements after Assassination until Murder of Tippit

    1. Presence within building
      a. location
      b. time
      c. encounter with police
      d. other relevant facts

    2. Departure from building
      a. time
      b. direction of movement
      c. other relevant facts, e.g. crossing police line, etc.

    3. Boarding of bus
      a. time and place of boarding
      b. duration of ride
      c. other relevant facts, e.g. dress, appearance, conversations, etc.

    4. From bus to taxi
      a. time and place
      b. distance and route of cab
      c. time to destination
      d. other relevant facts obtained from cab driver or other witnesses or sources

- 2 -

Had the Commission followed this outline based on the preconceived conclusion, it would have done the opposite of what it intended. If it was supposed to investigate Oswald's "Movements immediately prior to 12:29 p.m.," II(B)(4), why did it never question Mrs. Carolyn Arnold, the Depository employee who saw Oswald on the first floor just before 12:29, at the same time that other witnesses saw the "gunman" on the sixth floor? See PHOTOGRAPHIC WHITEWASH, pp. 210-11. Why also did it totally suppress Mrs. Arnold from the Report and the printed evidence?

5. Arrival at rooming house
   a. time
   b. actions within rooming house
   c. departure and direction

6. Route until encounter with Tippit
   a. time
   b. distance

D. Murder of Tippit

   1. Encounter of Oswald and Tippit
      a. time
      b. location

   2. Evidence demonstrating Oswald's guilt
      a. eyewitness reports
      b. murder weapon
      c. autopsy and ballistics reports
      d. paraffin tests
      e. other, e.g. statements (if any)

E. Flight and Apprehension in Texas Theater

   1. Movement until entry into theater
      a. time
      b. actions, e.g. reloading weapon
      c. other relevant facts, e.g. recovery of jacket

   2. Apprehension in theater
      a. movements of Oswald in theater
      b. notification and arrival of police
      c. arrest of Oswald
      d. removal to station

F. Oswald at Dallas Police Station

   1. Interrogation
      a. time, manner and number of interrogation sessions
      b. persons present
      c. persons responsible
      d. results

   2. Other investigation by Dallas police
      a. line-ups and eyewitness identification
      b. seizure of Oswald's papers
      c. other

   3. Denials and other statements by Oswald

   4. Removal to County Jail on November 24, 1963

   5. Killing of Oswald by Ruby

- 3 -

The one thing the Commission dared not include in its Report is that which it knew
was necessary, II(C)(6), the time it would have taken Oswald to get from his rooming-
house to the site of the Tippit murder. According to the official account, he had
11-12 minutes to do this. David Belin took 17 minutes, 45 seconds to walk the same
route (6H434). Likewise, the Report is silent on the witness who proved the murder
occured even sooner than the Commission was forced to admit. See p.493. II(D)(2)
is a candid revelation of the Commission's desire for "evidence demonstrating Oswald's
guilt" in the Tippit murder, but of all the factors listed, none supported such a
conclusion, and some were exculpatory, hence suppressed, as with the "paraffin tests."
See pp. 437ff.,446ff.

G. Evidence Identifying Oswald as the Assassin of President Kennedy

1. Room of Texas School Book Depository identified as source
   of shots

   a. eyewitness reports
   b. trajectory of shots
   c. evidence on scene after assassination
   d. other

2. Oswald placed in Depository (and specific room?)
   a. eyewitness reports
   b. fingerprints on objects in room
   c. facts reviewed above

3. Assassination weapon identified as Oswald's
   a. discovery of rifle and shells
   b. obtaining and possession of gun by Oswald
   c. whereabouts of gun on November 21 and November 22
   d. prints on rifle
   e. photographs of Oswald and rifle
   f. General Walker ballistic report.

4. Other physical evidence
   a. clothing tests
   b. paraffin tests

5. Prior similar acts
   a. General Walker attack
   b. General Eisenhower threat

6. Permissible inferences from Oswald's:
   a. flight from Depository
   b. statements on bus
   c. murder of Tippit

H. Evidence Implicating Others in Assassination or
   Suggesting Accomplices

1. Evidence of shots other than from Depository?
2. Feasibility of shots within time span and with use of telescope
3. Evidence re other persons involved in actual shooting
   from Depository
4. Analysis of all movements of Oswald after assassination
   for attempt to meet associates
5. Refutation of allegations

- 4 -

This section borders on the pathetic. The Commission never traced the "trajectory of shots" because all information was contrary to shots from the sixth floor window. The "eyewitness reports" did not do what the Commission here admits it wanted them to: "Oswald placed in Depository." Even the Report admits this (R145-6). Whoever wrote this outline so sure of Oswald's guilt was so ignorant of the fact as to suggest that Oswald might be placed in a "specific room," when in reality the sixth floor is all open space and is at no point divided into rooms. The Commission wanted "assassination weapon identified as Oswald's" but never investigated whether this really was the "assassination weapon" at all; it deliberately avoided all relevant evidence on this point---the spectrographic and NAA tests. It likewise had to suppress the exculpatory results of the AEC's NAA tests with the paraffin casts which did not "identify" Oswald as the assassin, as was alleged here. If it is a "permissible inference from Oswald's flight from Depository" that he was the assassin, what inferences are permissible from the fact that the Commission suppressed evidence that Oswald did not "flee" the Depository but left calmly and probably stopped to direct reporters to phones in the building (CD 354)?

III. Lee Harvey Oswald: Background and Possible Motive

    A. Birth and Pre-school Days

        1. Family structure (death of father; statements of persons who knew family; interviews of mother, brother, and members of family)

        2. Where family lived (statements as to childhood character of Oswald from neighbors who recall family and child)

        3. Standard of living of family (document factors which would have bearing upon development)

    B. Education

        1. Schools (reports from each school attended regarding demeanor, grades, development, attitude to fellow students, activities, problems, possible aptitude for languages, sex life, etc.)

        2. Reports of fellow students, associates, friends, enemies at each school attended

        3. Reports from various neighbors where Oswald lived while attending various schools

        4. Special report from juvenile authorities in New York City concerning Oswald

           a. report of case worker on Oswald and family
           b. psychiatrist who examined him, treatment and results, opinion as to future development

    C. Military Service

        1. Facts regarding entry into service, assignments, stations, etc. until discharge

        2. Reports of personnel from each station regarding demeanor, character, competence, activities, sex life, financial status, attitude, etc.

        3. Report on all activities while in Japan

        4. Report and document study of Russian language
           a. where and when
           b. books used
           c. instruction or self-taught
           d. any indication of degree of accomplishment

- 5 -

XERO
COPY

XERO
COPY

The outline continues past page 5, but it is apparent from this that the real focus of the "investigation" was to come up with "possible motives" to explain why Oswald did what could not be proved. The detail of this part of the outline, especially as compared to the sketchy nature of the outline which was to guide the investigation of the basic facts of the crime, leaves little doubt that as of this early point in the investigation, much more effort had been devoted to assembling the story of Oswald's life than to establishing the fundamental issue whether Oswald was in fact the assassin. This is one way to begin a totally impartial investigation.

January 11, 1964

MEMORANDUM FOR: Mr. Howard P. Willens

FROM: Charles N. Shaffer

SUBJECT: Information Failure

Today, I was at the Justice Department and Assistant Attorney General Miller furnished me with the two attached letter-head memoranda dated December 19 and December 30, 1963, which were received from the Bureau in due course and which obviously are pertinent to the work of this Commission.

At the moment we are in no position to finally evaluate the content of either. I am morally certain that neither of the above have been transmitted to Mr. Rankin as they properly should have been. Accordingly, I am disturbed that the Bureau is conducting investigation and not furnishing us with the results.

Knowing the Bureau as we do, I suggest the matter be informally discussed with their representative in contact with the Commission. In this way, the matter can be corrected with the least amount of friction.

Noted and talked with Mr. Malley about this on 1-14-64.

J. F. R.

Rankin may have "noted and talked with Mr. Malley" about this "information failure," but the problem was never solved. Eight days later Rankin complained to the Commission that the FBI had "not run out all kinds of leads in Mexico or in Russia." See p. 485. At their 1/27/64 executive session, the Commissioners agonized over how they could possibly go to Hoover for information on whether Oswald had been an FBI informant. See WHITEWASH IV. In both subtle and obvious ways, Hoover largely determined the parameters of the Commission's investigation. For example, when he said no NAA testing of the slits in President Kennedy's shirt (Gallagher Ex. 1), there was none. He dared not consent to any further testing which could conclusively wreck his solution of the crime.

Of this untenable investigative situation, the Report says: "Because of the diligence, cooperation, and facilities of Federal investigative agencies, it was unnecessary for the Commission to employ investigators other than the members of the Commission's legal staff" (Rxiii). Unless the legal staff had nuclear reactors in their homes which they could use to perform the tests Hoover vetoed, the Commission lies in saying "it was unnecessary" to seek independent investigators.

January 15, 1964

MEMORANDUM FOR MR. J. LEE RANKIN

FROM: Howard P. Willens

SUBJECT: Conversation with Mr. Malley

I called Mr. Malley this morning to ascertain whether or not the copies of the two supplemental reports received yesterday had been distributed by the FBI to members of the Commission. The answer was negative and I have taken steps to distribute the reports.

Subsequently Mr. Malley called me to discuss his conversation with you yesterday regarding the FBI report dated December 17, 1963 regarding the allegation by Mr. White regarding a meeting with Oswald in San Francisco on or about September 1, 1963.

Mr. Malley asked me whether you intended to write a letter to the Bureau asking that all such reports be submitted to this Commission. He went on to say that the report was not really as important as it might appear upon an initial showing. He said that the only reason this report was distributed to the Department was that it mentioned the Nazi Party. He suggested that prior to the writing of any such letter to the Bureau he would like to sit down with you and discuss the matter in greater detail. For example, he stated that the Bureau's Dallas office alone has compiled a report of 300 pages listing threatening remarks, complaints, etc., which the Bureau considers insignificant. He suggests that if any general request is made there will be no convenient stopping point and all these matters will be referred to the Commission. He suggests that this course of action would only serve to divert the Bureau's investigative manpower and the staff of the Commission.

He also suggested that many of the requests that we have been making of the Bureau could be handled informally by telephone from members of the staff to him rather than by correspondence. He suggests that the correspondence route only serves to complicate the matter. I suggest that you, Mr. Shaffer and I discuss this matter and then have a further

discussion with Mr. Malley.

This is an indication of how the Commission handled its "information failure." The FBI was the Commission's chief investigator, but this memo suggests who was really running the investigation. Quite simply, the FBI wanted to decide what did and did not get into the Commission's hands. It did not even want the Commission's requests to be a matter of record, but rather preferred to have all requests discussed in person. Imagine the horror that information "which the Bureau considers insignificant" might "be referred to the Commission"! The real question always was, who decides what is significant? Malley makes it clear the FBI wants to make these kinds of decisions, and he invokes the absurd justification that to have it otherwise "would only serve to divert the Bureau's investigative manpower."

Gentlemen:

I called this meeting of the Commission because of something that developed today that I thought every member of the Commission should have knowledge of, something that you shouldn't hear from the public before you had an opportunity to think about it. I will just have Mr. Rawkin tell you the story from the beginning.

Mr. Rawkin: Mr. Wagner Carr, the Attorney General of Texas, called me at 11:10 this morning and said that the word had come out, he wanted to get it to me at the first moment, that Oswald was acting as an FBI Undercover Agent, and that they had the information of his badge which was given as Number 179, and that he was being paid two hundred a month from September of 1962 up through the time of the assassination. I asked what the source of this was, and he said that he understood the information had been made available so that Defense Counsel for Ruby had that information, that he knew that the press had the information, and he didn't know exactly where Wade had gotten the information, but he was a former FBI Agent.

That they, that is, Wade before, had said that he had sufficient so that he was willing to make the statement.

Ford: Wade is?

A: The District Attorney.

Ford: Carr is the Attorney General.

Boggs: Right, of Texas.

Rawkin: I brought that to the attention of the Chief Justice immediately, and he said that I should try to get in touch with Carr and ask him to bring Wade up here, and he would be willing to meet with him any time today or tonight to find out what was the basis of this story. I tried to get Carr

MORE

This transcript of the Commission 1/22/64 executive session was not prepared until 1975 when the Archives located the reporter's notes and sent them to the Pentagon for transcribing. Records I had earlier discovered indicated that all records of this session had been destroyed at the Commission's order. "Mr. Rawkin" is actually J. Lee Rankin. "A" appears to refer to Warren as well as Rankin. "⌐" appears to be

and he was out campaigning in Texarkana and so forth, and so it took us quite a while to get back to him and talk to him. I just got through talking to him and he told me the source of the information was a member of the press who had claimed he knew of such an agency, that he was an undercover agent, but he now is coming with the information as to his particular number and the amount he was getting and the detail as to the time when the payments started. Wade said he as well as him did not know the name of the informant but he could guess who it was, that it was given to his assistant, and he was sure that he knew, and he said he was trying to check it out to get more definite information. Carr said that he could bring Wade in some time the first of the week, but in light of the fact that it was this man of the press and that they did not think it would be broken by the press immediately, although there had been all kinds of stories down there but Carr said there were some 25 to 40 different stories about this being the case admonishing the press themselves, but this was the first time that he got something definite as to how they were handling it or how it could be handled by himself. But I was concerned of an undercover agent. He thought that the press would not bring the story without some further proof, and they are working on that now, he said. So he thought that if he brought Wade back on Monday or Tuesday, that that would still take care of any major problem. When he first told us, he said the press had it and he was fearful because he hadn't even gotten this from Wade. He got it from another man that the press would bring it before we could know about it and the Commission would be asked all kinds of questions without having information about it. Now he said Wade told him that the FBI never keeps any records of names.

Mr. Boggs: Wade is the District Attorney for Dallas County?

Rawkin: That is right.

MORE

the last member identified. The Pentagon transcriber was not familiar with the Commission members or its work. There are minor errors and several blanks in this text.

Q: And the other man, Carr, is the Attorney General?

A: That is right.

Q: And the other people who have knowledge of this story?

A: He indicated that the press down there had knowledge of this story, and that the information came from some informant who was a press representative, and he, that is, Wade, could guess who it was but his assistant knew and he never asked him. They were trying to get more explicit information.

A: Lee, would you tell them?

Mr. Dulles: Who were you talking with when you got this information, Wade himself?

A: I was talking with Carr.

Boggs: There is a denial of this in one of these FBI records, as you know.

A: Yes.

Cooper: In this file we had yesterday, one of the lawyers for this fellow who claims to represent --

Boggs: Thornhill, I think.

Cooper: Oswald or one of them, Ruby, told about this, do you recall it, he said it was being rumored around.

Rankin: Yes, it was being rumored that he was an undercover agent. Now it is something that would be very difficult to prove out. There are events in connection with this that are curious, in that they might make it possible to check some of it out in time. I assume that the FBI records would never show it, and if it is true, and of course we don't know, but we thought you should have the information.

A: Lee, would you tell the gentlemen the circumstances under which this story was told?

A: Yes, When it was first brought to my attention this morning --

MORE

Rankin admits "I assume that the FBI records would never show" if Oswald had been an informant, yet the Report relies on nothing more than pro forma denials and an assurance that "Hoover has sworn that he caused a search to be made of the records of the Bureau," a search which somehow proved Oswald was never an informant. R327; WHITEWASH IV, p. 158.

Boggs: What time was this, Lee?

A: 11. 10.

Boggs: That is after the Ruby episode of yesterday?

A: That is right.

Q: Yes.

A: And Mr. Carr said that they had used this saying before the Court that they thought they knew why the FBI was so willing to give some of these records to the Defense Counsel, and they were   ing to the Defense Counsel being able to get the records and asking the Court to rule that they couldn't get them.

Q: That is, the District Attorney was?

A: That is right, and he said a number of these records were furnished by the Texas authorities, and that they should not be given up to the Defense Counsel, and that the reason he thought that they were so eager to help Ruby was because they had the undercover, that Oswald was the undercover agent and had the number of his badge and so much, he was getting two hundred a month and so forth, and that was the way it was explained as his justification to the Court as a basis for determining the records and that that was the excuse the FBI, the reason the FBI had for being so eager to give the records up. That is the way it was developed. Now Mr. Jaworski, who is associated with the Attorney General working on this matter was reported to you before, and

, story, I don't talk to Story about it but I did talk to Jaworski and he said he didn't think Wade would say anything like this unless he had some substantial information back of it, and thought he could prove it, because he thought it would ruin many in politics, in Texas, to be making such a claim, and then have it shown that there was nothing to it.

MORE

Mr. Jaworski, of Watergate Special Prosecutor fame, helped the Commission avoid any investigation of the Oswald-informant rumor he thought "had some substantial information back of it." The Commission never questioned the reporter, Lonnie Hudkins, who had written a story for the Houston Post concerning the "rumor." On 5/8/64 Jaworski wrote Rankin that since the Commission had "the testimony of the FBI agents," which was false in that most of the agents who could have recruited Oswald gave only affidavits and some were ignored totally, "as well as that of Marguerite Oswald," which did and could prove nothing, "I am wondering if it is really worth your effort to follow up on Hudkins." WHITEWASH IV, p. 146.

Boggs: No doubt about it, it would ruin many.

A: And Jaworski is an able lawyer, mature and very competent. We have complete confidence in him as a person. Now that is the evaluation of the situation.

Ford: He hasn't made any investigations himself?

A: No, he has not.

Ford: Was Wade or anyone connected with Wade?

A: No.

Dulles: Talking about Story, just a few minutes ago just telling him I wasn't going to be down in Texas, I had told him I was going to be down at the time, he didn't indicate that he had anything of any importance on his mind. Maybe he won't offer it to him obviously.

Rawkin: I don't know that it was even brought to his attention.

Dulles: I don't believe it was, now. Of course, he is not in the hierarchy.

A: Well, I think they were planning on telling the Attorney General and Jaworski.

Ford: How long ago did they get a feeling that there was some substance to the rumors that apparently had been -- I just assumed, and I didn't ask them that, that Carr called me and seemed to be in a matter of great urgency at 11:10 this morning, and that he was fearful that they would bring in the papers before we would even get to know about it, and that is the way he was talking and acting about it.

Cooper: He felt there was ... He didn't know the name of the informant?

A: No, he did not.

Q: What then would lead him to think it had substance?

A: Well, he said that the reason he thought it might have substance was because Wade had heard these rumors constantly, and his assistant had gotten

MORE

this information from the informant as to a definite bada number, and the amount and the date.

Cooper: How would you test this kind of thing?

A. It is going to be very difficult for us to be able to establish the fact in it. I am confident that the FBI would never admit it, and I presume their records will never show it, or if their records do show anything, I would think their records would show some kind of a number that could be assigned to a dozen different people according to how they wanted to describe them. So that it seemed to me if it truly happened, he did use postal boxes practically every place that he went, and that would be an ideal way to get money to anyone that you wanted as an undercover agent, or anybody else that you wanted to do business that way with without having any particular transaction.

Ford: There might be people who would see what was going on with that particular box, because the postal authorities do watch, they have means of watching in many places that no one could see. They can watch the clerks as to what they are doing in these boxes, and they can watch the individuals that are going in and out. They do that only when they have an occasion to be suspicious, but they might, in watching for somebody particularly, they might also see other things that they just have to note. That is a possibility.

Dulles: What was the ostensible mission? I mean when they hire somebody they hire somebody for a purpose. It is either. . . Was it to penetrate the Fair Play for Cuba Committee? That is the only thing I can think of where they might have used this man. It would be quite ordinary for me because they are very careful about the agents they use. You wouldn't pick up a fellow like this to do an agent's job. You have got to watch out for your

'MORE

Again, proof that the Commission was no innocent babe when it claimed to disprove the Oswald-informant rumor on the basis of pro forma denials and searches of "records." "A," who is probably Rankin, is "confident that the FBI would never admit it, and I presume their records will never show it." What better reason to accept the FBI's repeated denials and investigate no further?

Also, witness the spectacle of then Congressman Ford, now reputed to be such a "decent" President, a "Mr. Nice Guy." He knew in 1964 of surveillance by the postal authorities: they "do watch, they have means of watching in many places that no one could see." Apparently Mr. Nice Guy was then too busy passing defense appropriations to protect the people from the Russians to have done anything to protect the people from their own government.

agents. You have really got to know. Sometimes you make a mistake.

Ford: He was playing ball, writing letters to both the elements of the Communist parties. I mean he was playing ball with the Trotskyites and with the others. This was a strange circumstance to me.

Dulles: But the FBI get people right inside you know. They don't need a person like this on the outside. The only place where he did any at all was with the Fair Play for Cuba Committee.

Boggs: Of course it is conceivable that he may have been brought back from Russia you know.

A: If he was in the employ from 1962, September 1962, up to the time of the assasination, it had to start over in Russia, didn't it, because didn't he get back in February? When did he get back here from Russia?

A: I think it was February; February of this year.

Q: Of '62. Was it of '62?

A: Oh yes, that is right, it was '62.

Dulles: They have no facilities, they haven't any people in Russia. They may have some people in Russia but they haven't any organizations of their own in Russia.

A: Yes.

Dulles: They might have their agents there. They have some people, sometimes American Communists who go to Russia under their guidance and so forth and so on under their control.

Cooper: Of course there are rumors all around Dallas, of course the FBI is acquanited with rumors too.

A: One of the strange things that happened, and it may have no bearing on this at all, is the fact that this man who is a defector, and who was under observation at least by the FBI, they say they saw him frequently, could

                                                        MORE

walk about the Immigration Office in _____ Orleans one day and come out the

next day with a passport that permitt.. him to go to Russia. From my obser-

vations of the case that have come to us, such passports are not passed out

with that ease.

Dulles: Mr., I think you are wrong on that.

A: I could be.

Dulles: Because the passports are issued valid for anywhere except

specified countries. There is a stamp as I recall that says not good for

Communist China, North Vietnam, and so forth. For a long time they had on

the stamp not good for Hungary. But any American, practically any American,

can get a passport that is good for anywhere. An American can travel and

Russia is one of the countries that you can now travel to.

A: Well, maybe you can.

Dulles: You can get them quick.

A: I think our General Counsel and I both have some experience in cases

that have come before our Court which would indicate that that isn't exactly

the fact.

Dulles: I think in the State Department. . .

A: They have great difficulty, some of them, in getting a passport to

go to Russia.

Boggs: Particularly for someone who has any Communist . . . .

A: Oh, yes.

Dulles: Is there any evidence the State Department has that record in

the files? I don't think that record has ever turned up.

Cooper: They admitted there wasn't any.

A: What record, that he was a defector?

MORE

Apparently, one of the great services the former CIA head on the Commission, Dulles,
could render was to steer the investigation clear of the CIA. The Commissioners here
recognize what they later pretended was not true, that the circumstances under which
Oswald got his passports to and from Russia were extraordinary. Dulles tried to
pretend there was nothing unusual: "You can get them quick." He had to be politely
reminded, apparently by Warren, "that that isn't exactly the fact." The unmistakable
implication is that Oswald's relationship with the government was such that his passport applications would receive special treatment. Dulles tried to lead the Commission
off a trail that inevitably lead to the CIA. He needn't have worried since the
Commission did not bother to investigate.

Dulles: Yes, I don't think the State Department or in the Passport Bureau, there was no record. It didn't get down to the Passport offices. That is one of the things we ought to look into.

A: The State Department knew he was a defector. They arranged for him to come back.

Dulles: But it don't get   passport files or the passport records. They are issuing hundreds and thousands of passports. They have their own particular system.

A: Yes.

Dulles: They don't run around from time a man comes in. If they don't find any clue, and they don't according or our record here they don't find any warning clue in his file -- they should have a warning clue in his file but as I recall they don't.

Cooper: That is what they admitted, that they had not supplied the warning.

Dulles: And the Passport Office don't on its own ussually go around and inquire. They wait until it is assigned there. Then they follow it up.

Cooper: This ray be off the point a bit, but as I re-read the report, the chronology of the FBI checks on Oswald, they knew that he had gone to Texas. They learned from Mrs. Payne: they knew where Mrs. Oswalk was living. They talked with her. They knew where he was working.

Boggs: Sure. That is all in the file.

Cooper: I know that. I say they knew where he was working.

Boggs: I am sure you went over that material that we received a few days ago. You will find the report from the FBI dated back last summer, and months before that and then months after that, why some agent would make a report on it.

MORE

Cooper: Sure.

A. I think it was in October.

Rankin: They had a report on many, they had an agent go and see him
when he was in prison.

Boggs: In New Orleans?

A: In New Orleans.

Q: Right.

A. And he lied to them before the police. He said his wife was a Texas
girl, and he married her in Texas, and a whole string of stuff, and in Dallas
they had a report prior to that that was definitely contrary to it.

Boggs: The fellow Butler, who works for the profit organizations that
Dr. Oxnard heads to disseminate and tie Communist propaganda to Latin America, is the one who confronted him on the streets in New Orleans. I know
Butler. He is a very fine young man. It was . . . Butler says that this was
the first time that they established that he had been in Russia and that he
had defected at one time and then returned. You have that undoubtedly in your
files, that film, that tape that was made and borrowed in New Orleans?

A. Yes.

Boggs: Of course on that tape -- I listened to that tape -- he gives
the normal Communist line, reaction to everything.

A: That is right.

Q: The same old stereotyped answer?

A: Yes.

Cooper: How do you propose to meet this situation?

Boggs: This is a serious thing.

MORE

A: I thought first you should know about it. Secondly, there is this factor too that a   consideration, that is somewhat an issue in this case, and I suppose you are all aware of it. That is that the FBI is very explicit that Oswald is the assassin or was the assassin, and they are very explicit that there was no conspiracy, and they are also saying in the same place that they are continuing their investigation. Now in my experience of almost nine years, in the first place it is hard to get them to say when you think you have got a case tight enough to convict somebody, that that is the person that committed the crime. In my experience with the FBI they don't do that. They claim that they don't evaluate, and it is uniform prior experience that they don't do that. Secondly, they have not run out all kinds of leads in Mexico or in Russia and so forth which they could probably -- It is not our business, it is the very --

Dulles: What is that?

A: They haven't run out all the leads on the information and they could probably say -- that isn't our business.

Q: Yes.

A: But they are concluding that there can't be a conspiracy without those being run out. Now that is not   from my experience with the FBI.

Q: It is not. You are quite right. I have seen a great many reports.

A: Why are they so eager to make both of those conclusions, both in the original report and their experimental report, which is such a departure. Now that is just circumstantial evidence, and it don't prove anything about this, but it raises questions.   We have to try to find out what they have to say that would give any support to the story, and report it to you.

MORE

What a picture of the FBI diligence and reliability so touted by the Commission in its Report (Rxiii). The Commissioners knew that the FBI had reached its "very explicit" conclusion without having "run out all kinds of leads." This is the same FBI that was supposed to be the Commission's investigator and insisted that it, not the Commission, should say what information is "significant." (See p. 473). With the Commissioners well aware that the FBI was "so eager to make both of those conclusions" about Oswald's lone guilt, how could it possibly trust the FBI to make an impartial investigation?

Ford: Who would know if anybody would in the Bureau have such an arrangement?

A: I think that there are several. Probably Mr. Belmont would know every undercover agent.

Q: Belmont?

A: Yes.

Q: An informer also would you say?

A: Yes, I would think so. He is the special security, of the division.

Dulles: Yes, I know.

A: And he is an able man. But when the Chief Justice and I were just briefly reflecting on this we said if that was true and it ever came out and could be established, then you would have people think that there was a conspiracy to accomplish this assassination that nothing the Commission did or anybody could dissipate.

Boggs: You are so right.

Dulles: Oh, terrible.

Boggs: Its implications of this are fantastic, don't you think so?

A: Terrific.

Rankin: To have anybody admit to it, even if it was the fact, I am sure that there wouldn't at this point be anything to prove it.

Dulles: Lee, if this were true, why would it be particularly in their interest -- I could see it would be in their interest to get rid of this man but why would it be in their interest to say he is clearly the only guilty one? I mean I don't see that argument that you raise particularly shows an interest.

Boggs: I can immediately --

A: They would like to have us fold up and quit.

MORE

The Commission felt the implications of an Oswald-FBI connection were "terrible," "fantastic," and "terrific." That is probably one reason why Rankin five days later secretly called this "a dirty rumor that is very bad for the Commission,...and it is very damaging to the agencies that are involved in it and it must be wiped out insofar as it is possible to do so by this Commission." WHITEWASH IV, p. 48.

Here and on the next page the Commission really let the cat out of the bag. It knew quite well why Hoover was so insistent on his conclusion of Oswald's sole guilt: "They would like to have us fold up and quit." Boggs hit the mark when he said (p. 13)

Boggs: This closes the case, you see. Don't you see?

Dulles: Yes, I see that.

Rawkin: They found the man. There is nothing more to do. The Commission supports their conclusions, and we can go on home and that is the end of it.

Dulles: But that puts the men right on them. If he was not the killer and they employed him, they are already it, you see. So your argument is correct if they are sure that this is going to close the case, but if it don't close the case, they are worse off than ever by doing this.

Boggs: Yes, I would think so. And of course, we are all even gaining in the realm of speculation. I don't even like to see this being taken down.

Dulles: Yes. I think this record ought to be destroyed. Do you think we need a record of this.

A: I don't, except that we said we would have records of meetings and so we called the reporter in the formal way. If you think what we have said here should not be upon the record, we can have it done that way. Of course it might. . . .

Dulles: I am just thinking of sending around copies and so forth. The only copies of this record should be kept right here.

Boggs: I would hope that none of these records are circulated to anybody.

A: I would hope so too.

Rawkin: We also give them to you Commissoners. Now if you don't want them, those are the only ones who get them but Sides himself: off the record.

E N D

that the FBI's announcement of a solution "closes the case." How could the Commission dare investigate and run the risk of proving Hoover wrong? Hoover's position, so succinctly stated by Rankin was this: "They found the man. There is nothing more to do." And so it was that Hoover either discouraged or prevented any meaningful investigation suggested or requested by the Commission. That the Commission could be fully aware of this situation and still rely on Hoover as the chief investigator can mean only one thing: it never really intended an investigation.

MEMORANDUM   February 10, 1964

TO: Mr. Willens

FROM: Mr. Shaffer

        I have prepared the attached letter to Mr. Hoover for Mr.
Rankin's signature which furthers the correspondence represented by
Mr. Hoover's letter of February 7 to Mr. Rankin's letter of February 4.
I suggest that the attached letter be sent to Mr. Hoover not only
because of the reasons stated therein, but to facilitate independent
analysis of the Bureau's ballistic conclusions, should such be deemed
advisable. In this connection you might recall errors which occurred
in the placement of the 3 shots not only by the Bureau but by the
Secret Service as well.

Shaffer recognized a need to "facilitate independent analysis of the Bureau's ballistic conclusions." In writing to Willens, who was the Commission's liaison with the
Justice Department, he tempered his remarks with "should such be deemed advisable."
There was no question but that the ballistics information the FBI was feeding the
Commission warranted "independent analysis." For one thing, much of the information
was meaningless and suspect, such as in the cases of the spectrographic analysis and
the alleged bullet damage to the President's clothing. See pp. 599ff. The Commission
wanted no "independent analysis." Even where it had the FBI perform vital tests on
the bullets and fragments, it learned about the results of the tests through Hoover,
not directly from the FBI, and Hoover told the Commission only what he thought it
should know. See p. 607. This becomes quite culpable considered in the context that
the Commissioners were well aware that Hoover was, at the very least, a partisan; his
position was that the case was closed because he had solved it. He was bound to resist any investigation which threatened to wreck his solution, and the Commissioners
knew it. This awareness on the part of the members was reflected in the 1/22/64 transcript. It is also clearly expressed in the following excerpt from the 1/27/64 executive session transcript. Mr. Rankin brought up the point that the reconstructions by
the FBI and the Secret Service differed significantly:

        We have some differences between the Secret Service and the

FBI, we have location of their cars and where the shots were

and things where they differed as much as 17 feet, and we are

trying to find out how they could have that much difference be-

tween them, and there is an explanation. It isn't as bad as

that, because some of it is part of calculations.

        Mr. McCloy. Calculating their speed, I suppose.

        Mr. Rankin. That is right. And whether or not the first

shot occurred behind the sign or just as he came out from behind

the sign and matters of that kind.

        Mr. McCloy. I can see the difficulty with that. But on the

488

other hand, I have a feeling we are so dependent upon them
for our facts that it might be a useful thing to have him before
us, or maybe just you talk to him, to give us the scope of his
investigation, and as of that date, some of the things that are
still troubling us, and we will be able to ask him, for example,
to follow up on Hosty.

Mr. Rankin. Part of our difficulty in regard to it is that
they have no problem. They have decided that it is Oswald who
committed the assassination, they have decided that no one else
was involved, they have decided --

Sen. Russell. They have tried the case and reached a
verdict on every aspect.

Rep. Boggs. You have put your finger on it.

Mr. McCloy. They are a little less certain in the supp-
lementals than they were in the first.

Mr. Rankin. Yes, but they are still there. They have decided the case, and we are going to have maybe a thousand further
inquiries that we say the Commission has to know all these things
before it can pass on this.

And I think their reaction probably would be, "Why do you
want all that. It is clear."

Sen. Russell. "You have our statement; what else do you
need?"

Mr. McCloy. Yes, "We know who killed cock robin". That is
the point. It isn't only who killed cock robin. Under the terms

"Him" in the second line is Hoover. McCloy frankly admits how dependent the Commission
was on the FBI "for our facts." He suggests personally asking Hoover to help with "the
things that are still troubling us." Rankin, a good friend of Hoover's, recognized
the problem right away: The FBI had already decided Oswald alone was guilty and its
position was that no further investigation was necessary. The Commission's acknowledge-
ment of the problem marked the full extent of its response to the problem. It continued to rely on Hoover for virtually all its investigation, let him have his way when
he vetoed additional inquiry or held back information, and then praised his "diligence"
and "cooperation" in the Report.

FWHA and AS:mln

MEMORANDUM

January 23, 1964

TO: Mr. J. Lee Rankin

FROM: Mr. Francis W. H. Adams and Mr. Arlen Specter

SUBJECT: Statement of Objectives and Problems in Response
           to your Request of January 22, 1964

Our present objective is to assemble the
materials and prepare the comprehensive memorandum
referred to in Mr. Rankin's memorandum of January 13,
1964. Our memorandum will cover the subject matter
in the revised working outline of Phase I, which is
attached.

There is also attached a memorandum of things
to be done and some of the problems involved.

Attachments
(1) Revised working outline
(2) Memo of things to be done
    and problems

MEMORANDUM OF THINGS TO BE DONE AND SOME OF THE PROBLEMS INVOLVED

(a) Prepare a detailed chronology

(b) Prepare a working index of the evidentiary material.

(c) Secure from the FBI and consider the underlying documents and
    reports related to the rifle and shells. Since Mr. Ball and
    Mr. Belin are also covering this aspect, we shall work with
    them.

(d) Consider the survey of the scene made by the Secret Service,
    and arrange for additional surveys, including probably a contour
    map of the area.

(e) Consider the various reports on the reconstructions made by
    both the FBI and the Secret Service.

(f) Further viewing and analysis of the moving pictures of the
    actual happening and of the reconstructions.

See p. 85. All of the vital "things" Specter and Adams knew had "to be done" were
never done. Thus, in the context of what the Commission neglected to do, this memo
is explicit proof that the failure of the official investigation was other than innocent. The "underlying documents and reports related to the rifle and shells," which
presumably includes the bullets as well, were never "secured from the FBI." One phase
of those underlying documents, the spectrographic and NAA testing, was held so tightly
by the FBI I had to sue for them 10 years after Specter and Adams told the Commission
they must be "considered." Now the government swears it does not have the records
which its expert assured the Commission did exist and would be preserved. (5H69.
See also Part IV).

(g) There would seem to be a considerable amount of confusion as to the actual path of the bullets which hit President Kennedy, particularly the one which entered the right side of his back.

(h) It will be necessary to examine the windshield and try to determine whether the shots did any damage to the windshield.

(i) Consideration should be given to taking the sworn testimony of the bystander witnesses.

(j) Consideration should also be given to obtaining statements from Mrs. Kennedy, Governor and Mrs. Connally, Senator Yarborough, and President and Mrs. Johnson. A decision should be made by the Commission as to whether these individuals should be requested to give testimony, under oath.

(k) The Secret Service agents involved have all made statements of which we have copies. Consideration should be given to having each of these agents make such statements under oath.

(l) We are considering examining the scene of the shooting ourselves. If it is determined that statements should be taken from Governor Connally, perhaps this could be done at the same time.

(m) Consideration should be given to obtaining the camera to determine if the speed of the vehicles can be ascertained and the timing between shots from a review of the film.

(n) The FBI should obtain statements from certain bystanders, identified in prior reports, who have not been interviewed.

(o) Newspaper reports of November 22nd through the next few days should be reviewed to consider questions in the public mind and to determine whether there is any competent evidentiary basis for allegations of fact which differ from the Secret Service or FBI reports.

(p) Obtain expert opinions from medical personnel and professionals in weaponry field to explain the path of the bullet in President Kennedy's body.

(q) Obtain the transcript of the television interview by the doctors at Parkland Hospital on the evening of November 22nd.

(r) Ascertain whether the President was wearing a brace and undershirt.

---

with the official autopsy report in hand, what the Commission later represented as the definitive version of the President's wounds, so reliable that pictures and x-rays need not have been viewed to confirm its accuracy, Specter and Adams were plagued by a "considerable amount of confusion as to the actual path of the bullets which hit President Kennedy." The confusion was never resolved by the Commission, which simply chose to accept the version of the wounds which was indispensable to its preconceived conclusions. This considerable confusion is nowhere reflected in the Report, which falsely asserts that any confusion over the wounds was cleared up during the autopsy (R88-9).

However, the Report was forced to admit that "considerable confusion has arisen" because the Dallas surgeons who observed President Kennedy reported he was shot from the front (R90). The Report argues that the Dallas doctors were simply misquoted and that no real confusion exists. This brings in item (q) above, recognition of the need to obtain transcripts of what the Dallas doctors actually told the press about the front neck wound. Instead of doing this, however, Specter fabricated the story that the tapes and transcripts were unavailable because of cataloguing problems at the television stations. This was false. See WHITEWASH, pp. 169-70; PHOTOGRAPHIC WHITEWASH, chapter 7. Thus the Commission was able to twist what the doctors originally said.

Env. 1 no. 15
Connolly, John
Kennedy, John F.

MEMORANDUM

Green copy

January 30, 1964

TO: J. Lee Rankin

FROM: David W. Belin

SUBJECT: Oswald's knowledge that Connally would be
in the Presidential car and his intended target.

According to the Secret Service Report, Document No. 3, page 11,
the route of the motorcade was released on the evening of November 18
and appeared in Dallas newspapers on November 19 as shown in Exhibits
69 and 68 (Document No. 3 is the December 18 Secret Service Report).

In examining these exhibits, although the general route of the
motorcade is shown, there is nothing that shows that Governor Connally
would be riding in the Presidential car.

In determining the accuracy of Oswald, we have three major
possibilities: Oswald was shooting at Connally and missed two of the
three shots, the two misses striking Kennedy; Oswald was shooting
at both Kennedy and Connally and all three shots struck their
intended targets; Oswald was shooting only at Kennedy and the second
bullet missed its intended target and hit Connally instead.

If there was no mass media coverage that Connally would be
riding in the Presidential car, it would tend to confirm the third
alternative that Kennedy was the only intended target. This in turn
bears on the motive of the assassination and also on the degree of
marksmanship required, which in turn affects the determination that
Oswald was the assassin and that it was not too difficult to hit the
intended target two out of the three times in this particular situation.

In any event, I believe it would be most helpful to have the
FBI investigate all newspaper, television and radio reports from
November 18 to November 22 in Dallas to ascertain whether or not
in any of these reports there was a public announcement that Connally
would be riding in the Presidential car. If such public announcement
was made, we should know specifically over what media and when.

Of course, there is another element of timing: If Connally's
position in the motorcade was not released until the afternoon of
November 21, then when Oswald went home to get the weapon, he would
not have necessarily intended Connally as a target.

Finally, we would like to know whether or not there was any
release to the public news media that Connally would ride in any car
in the motorcade, regardless of whether or not it was the Presidential
car.

Thank you.

David Belin and Joseph Ball were responsible for putting together a case against Oswald.
The concern from the beginning was not to investigate who killed Kennedy but was simply
to make sure the evidence that couldn't be suppressed was tailored to the preordained
conclusion that Oswald alone was guilty. When Belin wrote this memo on 1/30/64, the
Commission had not called a single witness. The only relevant evidence it had was from
the FBI, which had already concluded Oswald was guilty. As Belin saw the alternatives
here, there was no room for any possibility other than Oswald firing three shots. See
p. 55.

AFFIDAVIT IN ANY FACT

THE STATE OF TEXAS

COUNTY OF DALLAS

BEFORE ME,_____Mary Rattan_____

a Notary Public in and for said County, State of Texas, on this day personally appeared._____

T. F. Bowley w/m/38 of 1424 Summertime Lane, 126 5965_____

Who, after being by me duly sworn, on oath deposes and says: On Friday November 22, 1963 I
picked up my daughter at the R. L. Thornton School in Singing Hills at about
12:55 pm.   I then left the school to pick up my wife who was at work at the
telephone company at Ninth Street and Zanga Street.   I was headed north on
Marsalis and turned east on 10th Street.   I traveled about a block and noticed a
Dallas police squad car stopped in the traffic lane headed east on 10th Street.
I saw a police officer lying next to the left front wheel.   I stopped my car and
got out to go to the scene.   I looked at my watch and it said 1:10 pm.   Several
people were at the scene.   When I got there the first thing I did was try to help
the officer.   He appeared beyond help to me.   A man was trying to use the radio
in the squad car but started he didn't know how to operate it.   I knew how and
took the radio from him.   I said, "Hello, operator.   A police officer has been
shot here."   The dispatcher asked for the location.   I found out the location
and told the dispatcher what it was.   A few minutes later an ambulance came
to the scene.   I helped load the officer onto the stretcher and into the ambulance.
As we picked the officer up, I noticed his pistol laying on the ground under him.
I then picked the pistol up and laid it on the hood of the squad car.   When the
ambulance left, I taken the gun and put it inside the squad car.   A man took the
pistol out and said, "He's with him."   He up and the officer, and I saw that
he wounds in it and he a shirt.   This man then took the pistol with him and got
into a car and drove off.   The police arrived and I told to a police sergeant
at the scene.   I told him I did not witness the shooting and after questioning
me, he said it was all right for me to leave.   I then went on to the Telephone
Company office at Ninth and Zanga.
                                                    T. F. Bowley

SUBSCRIBED AND SWORN TO BEFORE ME THIS 2   DAY OF _ December ___ .A.D. 1963

                            Mary Rattan
                            Notary Public, Dallas County, Texas

95-CF-473   11

David Belin claims that Oswald's guilt is demonstrated by taking the Tippit murder and
working backwards. Belin should know since he suppressed the evidence proving Oswald
could not have killed Tippit. The Report claimed that Tippit was killed at 1:15 because
Domingo Benavides reported the killing over Tippit's car radio "at about 1:16 p.m."
(R166). Yet Benevides had told Belin that another man had placed the call (6H449).
That man, T. F. Bowley, was never questioned by the Commission and is never mentioned
in the Report. This affidavit is published without comment at 24H202. Yet, if Tippit
were killed at 1:10, as Bowley swore, Oswald would have had no more than 7 minutes to
walk almost a mile to the scene of the crime, an impossibility of which Belin was well
aware. what better reason for Belin to ignore Bowley and pretend the killing took place
later?

493

MEMORANDUM

To: J. Lee Rankin

From: Alfred Goldberg

RE: Proposed Outline of Report of the Commission

1. Pursuant to our discussion of March 3, I am submitting the attached preliminary draft of a suggested outline for the Report of the Commission. It is, of course, incomplete, but it may serve as a point of departure for development of a more definitive outline.

2. Since this report is intended for the public, it should aim to achieve the maximum of clarity and coherence through the use of simple, straightforward language. The report should be thoroughly documented by full citations to the Commission's records.

3. Part III, Analysis of Basic Questions, is the heart of the report. It should present the evidence relating to each question, weigh it, and arrive at a firm answer wherever possible. Part IV, Analysis of Theories and Rumors, should be relatively brief because it will deal with the great variety of theories, hypotheses, and rumors surrounding the event. This part should demonstrate that the Commission was fully aware of these questions and took due notice of them. To explore these questions in detail would give them much more than their due.

6. The President's Executive Order directs that the Commission address itself to two events - the assassination of President Kennedy and the "subsequent violent death of the man charged with the assassination." Part I, The Assassination, should cover the period from the decision to make the trip to Dallas through the return to Washington. It is probably desirable to include an introductory section, as indicated, on Presidential Journeys. The murder of Oswald is properly the

-2-

subject of Part II, immediately following the account of the assassination of the President.

7. If the attached outline of Part I, The Assassination, is satisfactory as a starting point, it is possible to begin drafting Sections A-D. The facts relating to these sections are relatively well-established and the controversial aspects - primarily the operations of the protective services—will be dealt with in Parts III and VI. I am prepared to begin work on these four sections at your direction.

1 Inclosure

With none of the expert testimony taken, none of those "considerable confusions" even close to resolution, and indispensable scientific and ballistics tests not yet done, the Commission was already outlining its Report. How Rankin and the staff could know what the Report should say before any investigating was done is not explained here. Obviously, the conclusions were reached in advance of the "investigation." The contemplated "Analysis of Theories and Rumors" should be brief, it was felt, because all that was really necessary was to demonstrate that the Commission "took due notice" of rumors. This is an apt if unintended characterization of how the Commission dealt with its dirtiest rumor---that Oswald had been a government informant. Goldberg, apparently anxious to put his historical skills to work, felt "prepared to begin" drafting the sections setting forth the basic facts of the assassination before any such facts were in evidence! Such was the commitment to the truth. See p. 112.

PROPOSED OUTLINE OF REPORT

(Submitted by Mr. Redlich)

I. Statement of Objectives and Standards (Mr. Rankin)

(The Report should start with a brief statement setting
forth the Commission's view of its objectives and standards
used to achieve them. It is important to clarify the
Commission's position as a fact-finding body and to indicate
wherein our findings differ from a judicial determination
of criminal guilt.)

II. Brief Summary of Major Conclusions (Redlich and Willens)

(The purpose of this section is to provide the reader with
a short statement of our major conclusions without having
to read through the entire document.)

A. Basic Facts Concerning Assassination of President Kennedy
   and Shooting of Governor Connally

B. Identity of the Assassin

C. Conclusions Concerning Accomplices

D. Conclusions Concerning Motive

E. Ruby's Killing of Oswald and Conclusion as to Possible
   Link to Assassination

III. The Assassination - Basic Facts (Adams and Specter)

A. Physical Setting

   1. Description of Motorcade

   2. Description of Area where shooting Occurred

B. Shooting

   1. Number of Shots

   2. Medical Effect of Each Shot

   3. Point from which shots fired

This proposed outline of the Report was submitted by Norman Redlich the week after
Goldberg submitted his, referred to in the previous memo. The two outlines are virtually identical. (I have presented Redlich's because it reproduces more clearly.) Each
reveals the degree to which the conclusions were prefabricated.

The idea of having a summary section which could spare readers the task of reading
the Report was accepted by the Commission as a device really to keep reporters from
reading the Report when it was released. Chapter 1, Summary and Conclusions, was used
as a press release and was reproduced in full by several newspapers upon publication
of the Commission's 888-page Report.

4. Statistical data

    a. Elapsed time of shooting

    b. Distance travelled by Presidential Car

    c. Speed of car

    d. Distance travelled by each bullet

5. Events Immediately following Shooting

    a. Reaction of Secret Service

    b. Trip to Parkland

    c. Events in Parkland

    d. Trip to Love Field

    e. Return to Washington

IV. <u>Lee H. Oswald as the Assassin</u> (Ball and Belin)

(This Section should state the facts which lead to the conclusion
that Oswald pulled the trigger and should also indicate the
elements in the case which have either not been proven or
are based on doubtful testimony. Each of the factors listed
below should be reviewed in that light.)

A. Identification of Rifle as Murder Weapon

B. Oswald's Ownership of Weapon

C. Evidence of Oswald Carrying Weapon to Building

    1. Fake Curtain Rod Story

    2. Buell Frazier's Story

    3. Possible Presence in Paine's Garage on Evening of
       November 21, 1963

D. Evidence of Oswald on Sixth Floor

    1. Palm Prints on Carton

    2. Paper Bag with Oswald Print

The only part of Section IV not accepted by the Commission was its only decent suggestion, that the prefabricated prosecutorial presentation "also indicate the elements in
the case" not proven or "based on doubtful testimony." Had the Commission done this,
it would have exculpated Oswald. The easier alternative was to hide and lie about what
was unproved or doubtful. When this outline was written, the Commission had taken no
testimony on any of the points alleged to prove "that Oswald pulled the trigger," and
it was never able to substantiate any of these points, especially "Identification of
Rifle as Murder Weapon." The only evidence which had the slightest chance of making
such identification even feasible was the spectrographic and NAA tests so studiously
avoided by the Commission.

E. Eyewitness Testimony

F. Oswald After Assassination - Actions in Building

G. Oswald After Assassination - Actions up to Tippit Shooting

H. Shooting of Tippit and Arrest in Theatre

   1. Eyewitnesses

   2. Gun as Murder Weapon

   3. Oswald's Ownership of Gun

I. Statements After Arrest

J. Prior Actions

   1. Walker Shooting

   2. Possible Nixon Attempt

   3. Practice with Rifle

K. Evidence of any Accomplices in Assassination

L. Appraisal of Oswald's Actions on November 21 and 22 in Light of Assassination

   (This will be a difficult section, but I feel we must face up to the various paradoxical aspects of Oswald's behavior in light of his being the assassin. I suggest the following items for consideration.)

   1. Did He Have a Planned Escape?

   2. Why did he pass up the Opportunity to get money on November 21 when he returned to Irving?

   3. Discussion with Marina about getting apartment in Dallas

   4. Asking fellow employee, on morning of November 22, which way the President was coming.

Again, the Commission could prove none of these points. The outline is expectably silent on any evidence exculpatory of Oswald, such as that placing Oswald away from the scenes of both crimes with which he was charged. If Redlich felt " we must face up to the various paradoxical aspects of Oswald's behavior in light of his being the assassin," (paradoxical indeed that this assassin could be in two places at once!), the Commission did not agree. It never "faced up" even to the meager considerations listed under item "L."

V. Possible Motive (Jenner, Liebeler, Coleman, Slawson)

A. Brief Biographical Sketch of Oswald (Fuller biography in Supplement)

B. Any Personal Animosity Toward Kennedy or Connally

C. Do his Political Beliefs Furnish Motive

D. Link to Domestic Left-Wing Groups

1. Fair Play for Cuba

2. Communist Party

3. Conclusions to be drawn from such links

E. Link to Right-Wing Groups

F. Possible Agent of Foreign Power

G. Possible Link to Underworld

VI. Killing of Oswald by Ruby (Hubert and Griffin)

A. Facts of the Killing

1. Actions of Ruby starting with November 22

2. Description of Events on November 24

B. Discussion of Possible Link with Assassination of President Kennedy

C. Other Possible Motives

1. Brief Biographical Sketch (Fuller Sketch in Supplement)

2. Ruby as Self-styled Patriot, Hero, Important Man

3. Possibility of Ruby being Mentally Ill

SUPPLEMENT TO BE PUBLISHED WITH REPORT.

A. Visual Aids To Help Explain Main Body of Report (All Staff Members Concerned)

B. Organization and Methods of Commission (Willens)

C. Security Precautions to Protect Life of President (Stern)

   1. What Was Done on This Trip

   2. Broader Recommendations in This Area

     (I recognize that this area has been the subject of extended discussion and it might be desirable to move this section into the main body of the Report)

D. Detailed Facts About President's Trip up to Assassination (Adams, Specter, Stern)

E. Biography of Oswald (Jenner, Liebeler, Coleman, Slawson)

F. Biography of Ruby (Hubert and Griffin)

G. Oswald Relationships with U.S. Government Agencies (Redlich, Stern, Coleman, Slawson)

H. Discussion of Widely Circulated Theories (Redlich and Eisenberg)

I. Other Important Documents We May Wish to Publish As Part of Supplement, I suggest the following:

   1. Autopsy Reports

   2. Summary of Testimony of Experts on Physical Evidence (Eisenberg)

   3. Charts and Other Data Presented by Experts (Eisenberg)

   4. Reports of Medical Examination on Governor Connally

   5. Report of FBI and Secret Service on Location of President's car at Time of Shots (Redlich and Eisenberg)

WDS:mfd:23 Mar 64
MEMORANDUM   March 23, 1964

TO: J.'Lee Rankin

FROM: W. David Slawson

SUBJECT: Comments on Dr. Goldberg's Proposed Outline of the
           Report of the Commission

 1. I think that it is obvious that our report
should be documented as thoroughly as possible. When the
Commission itself has interviewed a witness, or when a staff
member has interviewed a witness, the written record of the
interview will usually solve our documentation problem. However, there are many instances where this will not be
practical. For example, the Mexican trip concerns all sorts
of routine information as to when a paycheck would probably
have arrived at a certain post office, what the usual procedures are for keeping records in the American and Mexican
Immigration Offices, the fact that a photograph which
purports to be of a passenger manifest on a Mexican busline is
in fact just that, etc. In most of these instances I see no
harm in referring directly to the FBI or Secret Service report
involved and permitting the report itself to be published as
part of the public record. In a few situations the report may
have to be "sterilized," i.e., references to the office or the
name of the special agent or a few other sensitive words
deleted. A more difficult problem will be the use of those
reports which involve statements by informants. Anyway, I
believe that we might begin to explore this problem with the
FBI and the Secret Service now. If these two agencies are
going to take a strong stand against making any reports at all
public, we may be faced with the job of gathering all kinds of
routine testimony, duplicating what is already in this report,
on our own, and if we have to do this, we should know it soon.

 3. I think we should consider adding a section
which would contain refutations of all the various factual
misconceptions that have attained notoriety since the
assassination. I have in mind here such things as the so-called
"fact" that there exists a photograph showing Lee Harvey Oswald
standing on the sidewalk outside the TSBD Building at the same
moment as the presidential car is driving by. Many of the
magazine articles that spin out theories that Oswald was an
FBI agent, or that he was an agent of the "communist Jewish
conspiracy," obtained their apparent plausibility because they
are based on such "facts" as these that are not facts at all.
I mention this because I do not think that Part IV, Analysis
of Theories and Rumors, as presently conceived by Dr. Goldberg,
would cover factual misconceptions, and it is, after all, the
facts rather than the theories that must be set straight in the
public's mind, because if given the proper facts the public
itself in the long run will probably not be misled by wild
theories.

2

See p. 112.

500

MEMORANDUM FOR THE RECORD

FROM: Melvin A. Eisenberg

SUBJECT: Conference of April 14, 1964, to determine which
          frames in the Zapruder movies show the impact
          of the first and second bullets.

On April 14, 1964, a conference was held to determine
which frames in the Zapruder film portray the instants at
which the first and second bullets struck.

Present were: Commander James J. Humes, Director
of Laboratories of the Naval Medical School, Bethesda,
Maryland; Commander J. Thornton Boswell, Chief Pathologist,
Naval Medical School, Bethesda; Lt. Col. Pierre A. Finck,
Chief of Wound Ballistics Pathology Branch, Armed Forces
Institute of Pathology; Dr. F. W. Light, Jr., Deputy Chief
of the Biophysics Division at Edgewood Arsenal, Maryland,
and Chief of the Wound Assessment Branch of the Biophysics
Division; Dr. Olivier, Chief of the Wound Ballistics Branch
of the Biophysics Division at Edgewood Arsenal; Messrs.
Malley, Gauthier, Shaneyfelt, and two other unidentified
agents of the FBI; Messrs. Kelley and Howlett of the Secret
Service; and Messrs. Redlich, Specter, and Eisenberg of the
Commission staff.

A screening was held of the Zapruder film and of
slides prepared by LIFE from the film. Each slide corresponded with a separate frame of film, beginning with frame 171.
The consensus of the meeting was as follows:

(a) The President had been definitely hit by
frames 224-225, when he emerges from behind a sign with his
hands clutching at his throat.

(b) The reaction shown in frames 224-25 may have
started at an earlier point—possibly as early as frame 199
(when there appears to be some jerkiness in his movement)
or, with a higher degree of possibility, at frames 204-06
(where his right elbow appears to be raised to an artificially
high position).

(c) If the reaction did not begin at 199 or 204-06,
it probably began during the range of frames during which
the President is hidden from Zapruder's camera by a sign,
namely, frames 215-24.

cc: Mr. Rankin   Mr. Belin
    Mr. Willens ✓   Mr. Specter
    Mr. Redlich ✓   Mr. Eisenberg
    Mr. Ball

2

(d) The President may have been struck by the
first bullet as much as two seconds before any visible reaction
began. In all likelihood, however, the maximum delay between
impact and reaction would be under one second, and it is
possible that the reaction was instantaneous. Putting this
in terms of frames, the President may have been struck as
much as 36 frames before any visible reaction is seen.
If the visible reaction begins at 199, the President may
have been struck as early as 163; if the visible reaction
begins at 204-06, he may have been struck as early as 168-170;
if the visible reaction begins while the President is behind
the sign, he may have been struck as early as 179-188.

(e) The velocity of ... bullet ... ... been little diminished by ... ... Therefore, if Governor Connally ... in the path of ... ... it would have struck him not (probably) ... ... he sustained in his chest cavity. ... ... this occurred are provided by the ... ... recovered from Governor Connally's ... ... to have penetrated a wrist and (?) ... ... not hit Governor Connally, it ... ... but apparently did not. ... ... bullet ... ... the Governor's stretcher does not appear to have penetrated a wrist, if he was hit by this (the chest) bullet, he was probably also hit by the second bullet.)

(f) If Governor Connally was hit by both the first and second bullets, it is impossible to say ... ... at that point, or by what point, he had been hit by the second bullet.

(g) Governor Connally seems to slump down at frames 224-226, and may be reacting to a wound at that point. (If so, it would be a wound from the first bullet.)

(h) Governor Connally seems to begin showing an expression of anguish around 234. If he was hit with two bullets, this expression may have resulted from his chest wound.

(i) After Governor Connally straightens up at frames 224-225 he starts a turn to the right. As a result of this turn, at no time after frame 235 was Governor Connally in a position such that a bullet fired from the probable

5

site of the assassin would have caused the wound in the chest cavity which Governor Connally sustained--that is, after frame 235, the Governor presented a side view to the assassin rather than a back view."

(j) It is not possible to say whether prior to 235 Governor Connally was ever in a position such that one bullet could have caused the five wounds he sustained.

(k) As in the case of the President, Governor Connally could have consciously felt his two wounds before he begins to react, but the maximum likely time interval between hit and reaction is one second, and the reaction may have been instantaneous. The likelihood of an instantaneous reaction is particularly great in regard to the wrist wound, since pain is usually felt more quickly in a limb than in the torso.

_____

*/ Mr. Specter disagrees with this, and feels the Governor was in position to receive the chest wound up to 240.

_____

Paragraph (e) understates the truth in saying that bullet 399 does not appear to have penetrated a wrist. However, it states untruth in describing 399 as "the bullet recovered from the Governor's stretcher." Arlen Specter tried to but could not prove that 399 had any connection at all with Connally's stretcher at Parkland Hospital (6H129-43). Yet, the Commission's entire case rested on the joint assumptions, among others, that 399 wounded not only Connally's wrist but his fifth rib and left femur and the President's neck, and fell out of the thigh wound and onto the stretcher carrying Connally.

Mr. Rankin

April 22, 1964

MEMORANDUM FOR THE RECORD

FROM: Melvin A. Eisenberg

SUBJECT: Conference of April 21, 1964, to determine
           which frames in the Zapruder movies show
           the impact of the first and second bullets.

On Tuesday, April 21, 1964, a conference was
held to determine which frames in the Zapruder film portray
the instants at which the first and second bullets struck.

     Present were: Dr. F. W. Light, Jr., Deputy Chief
of the Biophysics Division and Chief of the Wound Assessment
Branch of the Biophysics Division at Edgewood Arsenal, Maryland;
Dr. Olivier, Chief the Wound Ballistics Branch of the Biophysics
Division at Edgewood Arsenal, Maryland; Dr. Joseph Dolce,
Consultant to the Biophysics Division at Edgewood Arsenal;
Dr. Charles F. Gregory and Dr. Robert Shaw of Parkland Hospital,
Dallas, Texas; Messrs. Gauthier, Shaneyfelt, and one other
unidentified agent of the FBI; and Messrs. Redlich, Specter,
Belin and Eisenberg. Later in the proceedings, Governor and
Mrs. Connally, Mr. Rankin and Mr. McCloy joined the conference.

     A screening was held of the Zapruder film and of
slides prepared by LIFE from the film. Each slide corresponded
with a separate frame of film, beginning with frame 171.
The consensus of the meeting was as follows:

     (a) The President had been definitely hit by
frames 224-25 when he emerges from behind a sign with his
hands clutching at his throat.

     (b) After Governor Connally straightened up at
frames 224-26 he starts a turn to the right. As a result
of this turn, at no time after frame 236 was Governor Connally
in a position such that a bullet fired from the probable
site of the assassin would have caused the wound in the
chest cavity which Governor Connally sustained--that is,
after frame 236 the Governor presented a side view to the
assassin rather than a back view. 1/

_____

1/ Mr. Specter disagrees.

(c) In many frames up to 250, the Governor's
wrist is held in a position which exposed him to the type
of wrist wounds he actually received.

(d) After viewing the films and slides, the
Governor was of the opinion that he had been hit by frame
231.

(e) The Governor stated that after being hit, he
looked to his right, looked to his left and then turned to
his right. He felt the President might have been hit by
frame 190. He heard only two shots and felt sure that the
shots he heard were the first and third shots. He is
positive that he was hit after he heard the first shot,
i.e., by the second shot, and by that shot only.

In a discussion after the conference Drs. Light and
Dolce expressed themselves as being very strongly of the
opinion that Connally had been hit by two different bullets,
principally on the ground that the bullet recovered from
Connally's stretcher could not have broken his radius
without having suffered more distortion. Dr. Olivier
withheld a conclusion until he has had the opportunity
to make tests on animal tissue and bone with the actual
rifle.

If the conference of April 14 was destructive of the case being fabricated against
Oswald, the conference of April 21 was worse, as Eisenberg's memo reveals. See p. 56.
Of course, it was nothing new that wound ballistics experts could not accept as fact
that 399 had struck a wrist; it is common knowledge and experience that even jacketed
bullets do not cause such substantial bone damage and suffer no distortion. All the
expert testimony before the Commission was to this effect. But consider what this
conference says of the Commission's investigation:

—Dr. Dolce, who "was very strongly of the opinion" that 399 "could not have"
caused the wrist wound, was never called to testify before the Commission. The Report and the published evidence are silent about his strong dissent from this finding
essential to the government's case;

—Dr. Light, who agreed with Dr. Dolce, did testify before the Commission but was
never asked why he felt 399 could not have wounded the wrist. In response to Specter's
hypothetical question, Dr. Light indicated that the passage of a single bullet through
the two victims was a possibility based on the circumstances outlined by Specter (e. g.,
that 399 was found on Connally's stretcher!). Specter even had the audacity to ask
Light, "And what about that whole bullet [399] leads you to believe that the one bullet
caused the President's neck wound and all of the wounds on Governor Connally?" Light's
reply was polite but firm: "Nothing about that bullet. Mainly the position in which
they were seated in the automobile." (5H95). Thus Dr. Light's expert opinion was kept
carefully kept out of the record;

—Dr. Olivier's tests, in anticipation of which he withheld an opinion at this
conference, produced nothing but mangled, distorted bullets (CE's 853, 856, 857).
Specter never asked Olivier if 399 could have done what the official theory demands
and emerged in such perfect condition;

—Nothing was done to investigate the suggestion of the wound ballistics experts
that Connally might have been hit by 2 separate bullets, a possibility incompatible
with the lone assassin finding. Particularly helpful in this area might have been
the spectrographic and NAA tests so arefully kept out of the record.

This memo takes criticism of Specter's Commission work out of the realm of "Monday
morning quarterbacking." Specter knew the fatal flaws in his theory at the very time
he was trying to build a record in support of that theory; he knew what scientific
tests had to be done, which experts had to be called. He ignored the flaws, ignored
the tests and ignored the experts and devised a solution to the crime he had to know
was impossible.

And can it be regarded as anything less than culpable that, with a record like
this, especially a suppressed memo of a secret conference like this, the authors of
the Report could write: "All the evidence indicated that the bullet found on the
Governor's stretcher could have caused all his wounds"? (R95).

FD-302 (Rev. 1-3-59)

FEDERAL BUREAU OF INVESTIGATION

Date ___11/29/63___

1

NOV 30 1963

The following copy of an X-ray negative was received from Mr. JACK REYNOLDS, Administrator, Parkland Hospital, on November 29, 1963, which reflected an x-ray of the left thigh of Governor JOHN G. CONNALLY, which was taken on November 22, 1963.

Dr. JACK REYNOLDS furnished the following letter which accompanied this x-ray negative which is set out as follows:

"SUPPLEMENTARY REPORT DESCRIBING IN DETAIL THE APPEARANCE AND LOCATION OF A SMALL METALLIC DENSITY SUPERIMPOSED ON THE SOFT TISSUE SHADOWS OF THE MEDIAL ASPECT OF THE LEFT THIGH OF GOVERNOR JOHN G. CONNALLY ON FILMS DATED November 22, 1963.

"AP and lateral films of the distal portion of the left thigh were obtained and include the distal portion of the shaft and the region of the knee. One film is in the AP projection and the other the lateral projection with the direction of the beam from medial to lateral and the film lying adjacent to the lateral aspect of the thigh.

"No fractures are seen. A few punctate and linear densities are seen on the film but these are inconstant, and appear on one and not the other and therefore are interpreted as artifacts.

"There is, however, one density which remains constant on both films and appears to lie beneath the skin in the region of the subcutaneous fat in the medial aspect of the thigh. By measurements on these films, without correction for target film distance and object film distance, this small density lies 15.2 cms. above the distal end of the medial femoral condyle on the AP film and, on this film, lies 8 mms beneath the external surface of the skin. It is 6.25 cms medial to the femoral shaft. On the lateral film, the center of this small metallic density lies 15 cms above the distal end of the medial femoral condyle. It lies 4.9 cms posterior to the skin of the anterior surface of the thigh and it is superimposed on the shaft of the femur. In relation to the femur, the density is superimposed on a point 1.5 cms posterior to the exterior of the anterior cortex.

Commission No. 5

on ___11/29/63___ at ___Dallas, Texas___   File # ___DL 89-43___

by Special Agent ___VINCENT E. DRAIN/atd___   Date dictated ___11/29/63___

(5)

2

DL 89-43

        "The shape of this density is irregular but is
roughly oval. Precise measurements are difficult but it is
estimated that the greatest length in the AP projection is
about 3.5 mms and the greatest width about 1.3 mms.

        "Measurements of the density in the lateral projection
reveal the greatest length to be about 2 mms. and the greatest
width to be about 1.5 mms. The long axis of the metallic
object is oriented generally along the axis of the femur."

        This copy of an X-ray negative was delivered to
the FBI Laboratory on November 30, 1963.

    Among the many things about which the Commission went to great efforts to learn
as little as possible are the metal fragments left behind in Governor Connally's
wounds. If 399 did not wound Connally, the official solution to the assassination
cannot be true. But, in addition to the fact that its lack of deformation precludes
its having wounded Connally, 399 presented the additional problems that it was at most
a mere 2 grains below average weight for such a bullet and of all its surfaces, only
the base end could have deposited fragments---the rest of the bullet is obviously
intact. Thus, every fraction of a grain of metal left in Connally imposed an additional burden on the already untenable tasks demanded of 399.

    This FBI report quoting the x-ray reading provided by Dr. Reynolds was suppressed
from the Commission's printed evidence. See p. 82. If the size of the metal fragment
embedded in Connally's thigh bone, the femur, is accurately recorded here, this alone
establishes that 399 could not have wounded Connally. The picture of 399's base end
reveals no surface from which such a large fragment could have come. See p. 602.
What better reason could there have been for the Commission to ignore this report?
If Reynolds' measurements be criticized for their failure to make adjustments for
distortion, then what is to be said of the Commission which failed to get an adjusted
reading, even with these x-rays in hand? (CE's 694-696).

    The Report pretends there was no metal left in Connally's chest, an unlikely
proposition since the bullet shattered and stripped away 10 cm. of the fifth rib.
However, when Arlen Specter deposed the Parkland doctors in Dallas before some of
them were flown to Washington to testify before the Commission, he was told that post-
operative x-rays of Connally's chest revealed "a small fragment remaining." This was
the observation of Dr. Tom Shires, who was in charge of Connally's post-operative care
(6H111). Dr. Shires was not among those later called to repeat his story before the
Commission and Specter, for all practical purposes, buried the information and investigated no further, not even to get a competent reading of the post-operative chest
x-rays.

    The history of the metal fragments in Connally's wrist indicates that the famed
federal investigators cannot count. CE 842 consists of two lead fragments removed
from the wrist wound during the initial surgery. Yet page after page of FBI reports
refer to these two fragments as one (CD5:152-6). Hoover's lab report to Dallas Police
Chief Curry on November 23 refers to this as a "metal fragment." (24H 262). The FBI
Supplemental Report, CD 107, states that "one [fragment] was recovered from Governor
Connally's arm." With the doctors and the x-rays at its disposal, the Commission
could only further obfuscate the record. With needless imprecision the Report states:
"An x-ray of the Governor's wrist showed very minute metallic fragments, and two or
three of these fragments were removed from his wrist." (R95). Presumably the Commission
could count: two fragments were removed. Presumably, also, the Commission could
identify the x-ray to which it referred and count the fragments depicted therein. A
lateral pre-operative x-ray of the wrist seems to show at least five fragments scattered
in the wound (CE 690). A post-operative x-ray, one taken after the two fragments were
removed, seems to show at least two more remaining (CE 692).

    Such was the scientific precision with which the Commission developed the basic
facts of the assassination.

AUTHORIZATION FOR POST-MORTEM EXAMINATION

In the event authorization for post-mortem examination is obtained by letter, telegram, or mechanically recorded telephone call, paragraphs 1 and 2 shall be completed by hospital authorities and the letter, telegram, or memorandum confirming telephone call of authorization attached to this form for permanent file.

NAME AND LOCATION OF HOSPITAL	DATE
U.S. Naval Hospital, Beth...	22 November 1963

1. You are hereby authorized to perform a complete examination on the remains of

John F. Kennedy
(Name of deceased)

Authority is also granted for the preservation and study of any and all tissues which may be removed. This authority shall be limited only by the conditions expressly stated below:

Signature of witness _[signature]_

Signature (Mrs) JOhn F. Kennedy
(Person authorized to consent)

Address _____

Address White House

Washington, D.C.

Authority to consent Wife

The performance of the autopsy specified above is approved.

Signature R.O. CANADA CAPT MC USN

Title Commanding Officer

Date 22 November 1963

PATIENT'S IDENTIFICATION *(For typed or written entries give: Name—last, first, middle; grade; date; hospital or medical facility)*

REGISTER NO.	WARD NO.

AUTHORIZATION FOR POST-MORTEM
Standard Form 522

From the official archive of a president's murder, this is the clearest copy available of the autopsy authorization. Line 2 should read: "You are hereby authorized to perform a complete post-mortem examination on the remains of..." This authorization destroys many of the official myths. Clearly, if the authorization is to be part of the "permanent file" and "authority is also granted for the preservation" of all tissue removed for study, then the photographs and x-rays taken during the autopsy, government property, are also to be a part of the permanent file and not subject to claims of ownership by the family of the deceased. See pp. 101-2. Also, if the authorization includes "a complete" autopsy, there can be no excuse for the failure to dissect the putative bullet path through the neck. Dr. Finck's apology for this fundamental failure is thus rendered invalid. See pp. 235-6.

[Handwritten notes by Dr. Humes]

...on conversation, ï Dr. ......

Bloody ai◯g ......
upper mediastinum

Only a few mm in
size 3 - 5 mm.

...... of Cal.
wall of the trachea...
no missile in the wound.

Dr. Malcolm 1-5050
4115 Park Lane
Dallas 20, Tex.
FL 2 - 5548
Home

Off. in Med. School
Dept. of Surgery
Dr. Adkins
Dr. Malcolm Perry ...... H Hume

This page of notes taken by Dr. Humes during phone conversations with Dr. Perry in Dallas on November 23 marks the beginning of the original copies of a set of autopsy papers in the Commission's evidence, CE 397. However, the Commission had only Xerox copies of these originals, and never saw or tried to see the originals themselves. After years of effort, I was able to force the Secret Service to release them to the Archives. See pp. 249ff. At once the reason for suppression was obvious: the originals bear the initials, signature, and endorsement of George Burkley, the President's physician. The Xerox used by the Commission apparently was made in the short interval before Burkley marked the papers. (He has made no marks on the above sheet.)

The above notes reveal that Perry told Humes the wound in the President's throat was "only a few mm. [millimeters] in size 3-5 mm." Perry had cut this wound in half to perform a tracheotomy on the President; Humes claimed that the bullet wound was not visible to him at the autopsy by virtue of the tracheotomy incision. However, with the information he got from Perry, Humes knew this throat wound, called an exit wound in the autopsy report, was actually smaller than the entrance wound on the back, a virtual impossibility. Humes originally described the throat wound as an entrance or "puncture" wound in his final draft of the autopsy, a description mysteriously altered in the typed copy. See p. 2 of the holograph.

508

A63.272   Kennedy, John F.

Date of birth __ __ 1917
Date of death 11/22/63
Hour of death 1⁰⁰ pm CST Dallas, Tex.
Hour of autopsy 8 pm EST Bethesda, Md.

<u>Clinical Summary</u>

According to available information the deceased,
President John F. Kennedy, was riding in an open
car in a motorcade during an official visit to
Dallas, Texas on 22 Nov. 1963. The president
was sitting in the right rear seat with Mrs.
Kennedy seated on the same seat to his
left. Sitting directly in front of the
president was Gov. John B. Connally of
Texas and directly in front of Mrs. Kennedy
sat Mrs. Connally. The vehicle was moving
~~at approximately twenty miles per hour~~ down
an incline into an underpass that leads
to a freeway route to the Dallas Trade Mart
where the president was to ~~give~~ deliver an address.

GGB   Three shots were heard and the president
fell forward ~~to the floor of the vehicle~~

The final written draft of the autopsy report begins here. Note Dr. Burkley's initials
"GGB" in the lower left hand corner. These appear again on the last page of the holograph. They are missing from the copy of the holograph published by the Commission
in CE 397. See pp. 249ff. Note also the unprofessionalism and propaganda of the
"Clinical Summary." Humes had no way of proving that three shots were fired. He also
records what is demonstrably false—that "the president fell forward," consistent
with a rear shot but inconsistent with the facts.

509

bleeding from the head. (Governor Connally was seriously wounded by the same gunfire). According to newspaper reports (Washington Post Nov. 23, 1963) B.J. Jackson, a Dallas Times Herald photographer, said he looked around as he heard the shots and saw a rifle barrel disappearing into a window – on an upper floor of the nearby Texas School Book Depository building.

Shortly following the wounding of the two men the car was driven to Parkland Hospital. In the emergency room of that hospital the president was attended by Dr. Malcolm Perry. Telephone communication with Dr. Perry on Nov. 23, 1963 develops the following information relative to the observations made by Dr. Perry and procedures performed there prior to death.

Dr. Perry noted the massive wound of the head and a second, puncture wound, of the low anterior neck in approximately the midline. A tracheotomy was performed by extending the latter

---

In the last full sentence on this page, Humes reports that Perry noted a "puncture wound" of the anterior neck. This is the one use of the word "puncture"---always used by Humes to denote "entrance"---not stricken through in the holograph. The holograph indicates no revision here. But here is how the final typed copy of the autopsy report reads (CE 387): **Dr. Perry noted the massive wound of the head and a second much smaller wound of the low anterior neck in approximately the midline. A tracheostomy was performed by extending the latter wound. At this point**

Who authorized this alteration? Why? The Commission had no interest in answering such questions and left them unanswered to this day. See p. 150.

wound. At this point bloody air was noted bubbling from the wound and an injury to the lateral wall of the trachea was observed. Incisions were made in the upper anterior chest wall bilaterally to combat possible sub-cutaneous emphysema. Intravenous infusions of blood and saline were begun and oxygen was administered. Despite these measures cardiac arrest occurred and closed chest cardiac massage failed to re-establish cardiac action. The president was pronounced dead approximately thirty to forty minutes after receiving his wounds.

The remains were transported via the presidential plane to Washington D.C. and subsequently to the Naval Medical School, National Naval Medical Center, Bethesda, Md., for post-mortem examination.

<u>General Description of Body</u> The body is that of a muscular, well-developed and well-nourished adult caucasian male measuring 72½ inches and weighing approximately

170 lbs. There is beginning rigor mortis, minimal dependent livor mortis of the dorsum and early algor mortis. The hair is reddish-brown and abundant, the eyes are blue the rt. pupil measuring 8 mm. in diameter, the left 4 mm. There is edema and ecchymosis of the inner canthus region of the left eye lid measuring approximately 1.5 cm in greatest diameter. There is edema and ecchymosis diffusely over the rt. supra-orbital ridge with abnormal mobility of the underlying bone. (The remainder of the scalp will be described with the skull.) There is clotted blood on the external ears but otherwise the ears, nose and mouth are essentially unremarkable. The teeth are in excellent repair and there is some pallor of the oral mucous membrane.

Situated on the upper rt. posterior thorax just above the upper border of the scapula there is a 7 x 4 mm. oval ~~puncture~~ wound. This wound is measured

Note the striking out of "puncture" in the last line. Here Humes was describing the entrance wound in the back.

5

to be 14 cm. from the tip of the rt. acromion process and 14 cm. below the tip of the rt. mastoid process.

Situated in the low-anterior neck at approximately the level of the third and fourth tracheal rings is a 6.5 cm. long transverse wound with widely gaping irregular edges. (The depth and structures of these wounds will be further described below.)

Situated on the anterior chest wall in the nipple line are bilateral 2 cm. long recent transverse surgical incisions into the subcutaneous tissue. The one on the left is situated 11 cm. cephalad to the nipple and the one on the right 8 cm. cephalad to the nipple. There is no hemorrhage or ecchymosis associated with these wounds. A similar clean wound measuring 2 cm. in length is situated on the antero-lateral aspect of the ~~right~~ left mid arm. Situated on the antero-lateral aspect of each ankle is a

---

At the top of the page, Humes locates the back wound in terms of highly mobile and variable orientation points, the mastoid (behind the ear) and the acromion, the tip of the shoulder. Unless the length of the neck and the position of the body at the time of measurement is known, these measurements locate nothing. The normal fixed reference point, a particular vertebra, is omitted. See pp. 38, 304, 308-9.

recent 2 cm. transverse incision into the sub-cutaneous tissue.

There is an old, well healed 3 cm. McBurney abdominal incision. Over the lumbar spine in the midline is an old, well healed 15 cm. scar. Situated on the upper antero-lateral aspect of the rt. thigh is an old, well healed 3 cm. scar.

Missile Wounds

1. There is a large irregular defect of the scalp and skull on the right invading chiefly the parietal bone but extending somewhat into the temporal and occipital regions. In this region there is an actual absence of scalp and bone producing a defect which measures approximately 13 cm. in greatest diameter.

From the irregular margins of the above scalp defect tears extend in stellate fashion into more or less intact scalp as follows:

a) From the right inferior temporoparietal margin anterior to the lt. ear to a point slightly above the tragus.

b) From the anterior parietal margin anteriorly on the forehead to approximately 4 cm. above the rt. orbital ridge

c) From the left margin of the main defect across the midline antero-laterally for a distance of approximately 8 cm.

d) From the same starting point as (c) 10 cm postero-laterally.

Situated in the posterior scalp approximately 2.5 cm laterally to the right and slightly above the external occipital protuberance is a ~~lacerated wound tangential to the surface of the scalp~~ measuring 15 X 6 mm. In the underlying bone is a corresponding ~~puncture wound through both tables of~~ the skull which exhibits ~~beveling of the margins of the bone when viewed from~~ the inner ~~aspect of the skull.~~ Clearly visible in the above described long skull defect and exuding from it is ~~lacerated~~ brain tissue which on close inspection proves to represent ~~the~~

Humes twice omitted the word "puncture" on this page, once actually replacing it with a word of entirely opposite meaning, "lacerated."

the major portion of the right cerebral hemisphere. At this point it is noted that the falx cerebri is extensively lacerated with disruption of the superior sagittal sinus.

Upon reflecting the scalp multiple complete fracture lines are seen to radiate from both the large defect at the vertex and the smaller ~~puncture~~ wound at the occiput. These vary greatly in length and direction the longest measuring approximately 19 cm. These result in the production of numerous fragments which vary in size from a few millimeters to 10 cm in greatest diameter.

The complexity of these fractures and the fragments thus produced tax satisfactory verbal description and are better appreciated in photographs and ~~x-ray~~ roentgeno- grams which are prepared.

The brain is removed and preserved for further study following formalin fixation.

Received as separate specimens from Dallas, Tex. are three fragments of skull bone which in

---

Here Humes admits the indispensability of at least the x-rays of the President's body. The complexity of the head wound taxes "satisfactory verbal description" and is better depicted in the x-rays.

aggregate roughly approximate the dimensions of the large defect described. At one angle the largest of these fragments is a portion of the perimeter of a roughly circular wound presumably which exhibits ~~beveling~~ of the outer ~~table~~ and estimated to measure approximately 2.5 to 3.0 cm in diameter. Roentgenograms of this fragment reveal minute ~~particles~~ of metal in the bone at this margin. Roentgenograms of the skull reveal multiple minute metallic fragments along a line corresponding with a line joining the above described (~~frontal~~) ~~occipital~~ ~~parietal~~ wound and the Lt. supra-orbital ridge. From the surface of the disrupted Rt. cerebral cortex two small irregularly shaped fragments of metal are recovered. These measure 7 x 2mm & 3 x 1 mm. There are placed in the custody of agents Francis X. O'Neill Jr. and James W. Sibert of the Federal Bureau of Investigation, who executed a receipt therefor (attached)

2. The second wound presumably of entry is that

Note the precision and assurance of these pathologists. If their findings were so certain, their autopsy so thorough and competent, why did they feel constrained to add the qualification "presumably" before their designations of wounds as those of entry or exit? If this is a token of how sure they were of their conclusions, then they were not even prepared to state with assurance that the President was shot from the rear!

CIC

described above in the upper rt. posterior thorax. Beneath the skin there is ecchymosis of sub-cutaneous tissue and musculature. The missile path through the fascia and musculature cannot be easily probed. The wound of exit was that described by Dr. Malcolm Perry of Dallas in the low-anterior cervical region. As described by Dr. Perry the wound measured a "few millimeters in diameter" however it was extended as a tracheostomy incision and thus its character is distorted at the time of autopsy. However there is considerable ecchymosis of the strap muscles of the rt. neck and of the fascia about the trachea adjacent to the site of the line of the tracheostomy wound. The third point of reference in connecting these two wounds is in the apex (supra-clavicular portion) of the rt. pleural cavity. In this region there is contusion of the parietal pleura and of the extreme apical portion of the rt. upper lobe of the lung. In both

---

The wound seen by Dr. Perry is here referred to as one "presumably of exit," with "presumably" added as an afterthought, again, hardly a demonstration of scientific precision or confidence in the official autopsy findings. Humes also omits the measurement he obtained from Perry, "3-5 mm.," and thus omits from the autopsy report the fact that the supposed entrance was larger than the supposed exit.

instances the diameter of contusion and ecchymosis at the point of maximal involvement measures 5 cm. Both the visceral and parietal pleura associated overlying these areas of trauma.

<u>Incisions</u> The scalp wounds are extended in the coronal plane to examine the cranial contents and the customary "Y" shaped incision is used to examine the body cavities.

<u>Thoracic Cavity</u> - The bony cage is unremarkable. The thoracic organs are in their normal positions and relationships and there is no increase in free pleural fluid. The above described area of contusion in the apical portion of the rt. pleural cavity is noted.

<u>Lungs</u> - The lungs are of essentially similar appearance the rt. weighing 320 Gm the left 290 Gm. The lungs are well aerated with a smooth glistening pleural surfaces and grey-pink color. A 5 cm dia. area of purplish red discoloration and increased firmness to palpation is situated in the apical

Under "Incisions," Humes describes how the body was taken apart, including what amounts to peeling away the scalp and removing brain, and slicing open the entire thoracic and abdominal cavity with a huge "Y" cut to examine and weigh the organs. He does not explain why, having so mutilated the body as any autopsy requires, he did not also dissect the supposed bullet path in the neck, also an indispensable requirement. See pp. 235-6.

portion of the rt. upper lobe. This corresponds to the similar area described in the overlying parietal pleura. Incision in this region reveals scanty hemorrhage into pulmonary parenchyma. Heart. The pericardial cavity is smooth walled and contains approximately 15 cc of straw colored fluid. The heart is of essentially normal external contour and weighs 350 Gm. The pulmonary artery is opened in situ and no abnormalities are noted. The cardiac chambers contain moderate amounts of post-mortem clotted blood. There are no gross abnormalities of the leaflets of the cardiac valves. The following are the circumferences of the cardiac valves: aortic 7.5 cm, pulmonic 7 cm, tricuspid 12 cm, mitral 11 cm. The myocardium is firm and reddish-brown. The left ventricular myocardium averages 1.5 cm in thickness, the rt. ventricular myocardium 0.4 cm. The coronary arteries are dissected, are of normal distribution and smooth walled and elastic throughout.

<u>Abdominal Cavity</u>. The abdominal organs are in their normal positions and relationships and there is no increase in peritoneal fluid. The vermiform appendix is surgically absent and there are a few adhesions joining the region of the cecum to the ventral abdominal wall at the above described old abdominal incisional scar.

<u>Skeletal System</u> - Aside from the above described skull wounds there are no significant gross skeletal abnormalities.

<u>Photography</u> - Black and white and color photographs are ~~prepared~~ depicting of significant ~~findings~~. Exposed but undeveloped

<u>Roentgenograms</u> - Roentgenograms are ~~prepared~~ made of the entire body and of the separately submitted three fragments of skull bone. Developed routinize —

<u>Summary</u> Based on the above observations it is our opinion that the deceased died as a result of two ~~separate~~ penetrating wounds inflicted by high velocity projectiles fired by a person

as persons unknown. The projectiles were fired from a point behind and ~~toward~~ at ~~slightly above the~~ ~~region~~ ~~of the~~ ~~of the~~ ~~of the body at the moment of impact.~~ The observations and available information do not permit a satisfactory estimate as to the sequence of the two wounds.

The fatal missile entered the skull above and to the right of the external occipital protuberance. A ~~small~~ portion of the projectile traversed the cranial cavity in a posterior-anterior direction (see lateral skull roentgenogram) depositing minute particles along its path. ~~The A~~ portion of the projectile made its exit through the parietal ~~bone~~ on the right. ~~The two wounds~~ carrying with it portions of cerebrum, skull and scalp. The two wounds of the skull combined with the force of the missile produced extensive fragmentation of the skull, laceration of the superior sagittal sinus and of the rt. cerebral hemisphere.

The ~~second~~ ~~other~~ missile entered the rt. superior posterior thorax above the scapula ~~to the right of the midline~~ and traversed the soft tissues of the supra-scapular and supra-clavicular portions of the base of the right side of the neck. The missile produced contusions of the rt. apical parietal pleura and of the apical portion of the rt. upper lobe of the lung. The missile contused the strap muscles of the rt. side of the neck, damaged the trachea and made its exit through the anterior surface of the neck. As far as can be ascertained this missile struck no bony structures in its path through the body.

A supplementary report will be submitted following more detailed examination of the brain and of microscopic sections. However it is not anticipated that these examinations will materially alter the findings.

In addition it is our opinion that the wound of the skull produced such extensive damage to the brain as to preclude the possibility of the deceased surviving this injury

---

The "Autopsy Descriptive Sheet" which should follow this page as reproduced in the official sequence has been reproduced earlier in the book. It is a single sheet of notes and markings on two sides, certainly not the full extent of the autopsy notes but all that is officially available. See pp. 310-11.

U. S. NAVAL MEDICAL SCHOOL
NATIONAL NAVAL MEDICAL CENTER
BETHESDA, MARYLAND 20014

In reply refer to

24 November 1963

C-E-R-T-I-F-I-C-A-T-E

I, James J. Humes, certify that I have destroyed by
burning certain preliminary draft notes relating to Naval
Medical School Autopsy Report A63-272 and have officially
transmitted all other papers related to this report to
higher authority.

J. J. HUMES
CDR, MC, USN

accepted and approved this date

George G. Burkley
Rear Adm MC USN
Physician to the President

This is the original of Humes' certificate that he burned a draft of the autopsy report.
It is not the same as the copy printed by the Commission, 17H48, which does not include
the handwritten approval of Dr. Burkley. Indeed, what can be said when the President's
physician certifies that he accepts and approves the burning of evidence in the crime!
See p. 261.

This certificate has led to the myth, propagated by Arlen Specter, that Humes
burned his autopsy notes. "The record is plain," Specter told U.S. News and World
Report, 10/10/66, "that there had been a series of notes taken by Dr. Humes at the
time of the actual performance of the autopsy which had been destroyed." Specter
knew better, since he put this certificate (absent the Burkley endorsement) into evidence and had it confirmed by Humes (2H373). As the certificate on the next page
makes clear, the "autopsy notes" were preserved. What Humes burned he alternately
described as "preliminary draft notes" (above) and "that draft" of the autopsy report
later revised, (2H373).

Having been assured by Humes that the first draft of the autopsy report had been
destroyed forever by burning, Specter asked not a single question, not even the simple,
indispensable question: Why? On this the Commission's record is barren. Specter,
however, would like the public to believe otherwise. He now claims Humes "explained
his reasons (for burning) fully before the Commission"---in his testimony.

U. S. NAVAL MEDICAL SCHOOL
NATIONAL NAVAL MEDICAL CENTER
BETHESDA, MARYLAND 20014

In reply refer to

24 November 1963

C-E-R-T-I-F-I-C-A-T-E

I, James J. Humes, certify that all working papers
associated with Naval Medical School Autopsy Report A63-272
have remained in my personal custody at all times. Autopsy
notes and the holograph draft of the final report were handed
to Commanding Officer, U. S. Naval Medical School, at 1700,
24 November 1963. No papers relating to this case remain in
my possession.

J. J. HUMES
CDR, MC, USN

Received above working papers this date.

J. H. STOVER, JR.
CAPT, MC, USN
Commanding Officer, U.S. Naval Medical School
National Naval Medical Center

Accepted and approved this date

George G. Burkley
Rear Adm MC USN
Physician to the President

This, an original copy, also bears the endorsement of Dr. Burkley absent from the copy
published by the Commission. Here Humes makes explicit that he never burned any notes
made during the autopsy. "Autopsy notes and the holograph draft of the final report"
were preserved and given to Capt. Stover on November 24. Stover must have received
all autopsy notes because Humes specifies that "all working papers" of the autopsy were
in his possession until the transfer to Stover, after which "no papers relating to this
case remain in my possession." With this transmittal, the mysterious story of the missing autopsy notes begins. See pp. 145, 261.

NATIONAL NAVAL MEDICAL CENTER
BETHESDA 14, MARYLAND

25 November 1963

From: Commanding Officer, National Naval Medical Center
To: The White House Physician

Subj: Autopsy protocol in the case of John F. Kennedy, Late President
      of the United States

1. Transmitted herewith by hand is the sole remaining copy (number
eight) of the completed protocol in the case of John F. Kennedy.
Attached are the work papers used by the Prosector and his assistant.

2. This command holds no additional documents in connection with
this case.

3. Please acknowledge receipt.

C. B. GALLOWAY

This letter and the receipt which follows are from CD 371, although neither appears
in the Commission's published evidence. When Specter introduced the autopsy papers,
CE 397, into evidence, he stated for the record that CE 397 "is the identical document"
marked CD 371 "for our internal purposes." (2H373). However, the two documents are
not the same because the printed exhibit omits these two pages. Suppression accomplished
many purposes, among them making it impossible to trace the chain of possession of the
vital autopsy notes.

Many pages of notes made by all three pathologists during the autopsy were preserved and must have been delivered to Dr. Burkley on November 25. Dr. Humes transmitted all papers in his possession to Admiral Galloway on November 24, and here
Galloway claims to transmit all papers he has, retaining none. Burkley in turn gave
everything he got from Galloway to the Secret Service on November 26, as the following
receipt executed that day reveals. And there the trail ends. The Commission's records
include but one sheet (two sides) of notes, none of which were made by Humes. See
pp. 102-5, 247-8, 251-6. The one sheet published directly contradicts the autopsy
findings on a quintessential point, the location of the back wound. One can only guess
what the suppressed notes reveal. And one cannot avoid asking why the Commission,
charged with evaluating all facts relating to the assassination, did not obtain or
publish the missing autopsy notes, and suppressed the receipts documenting their chain
of possession. See p. 50.

TREASURY DEPARTMENT

WASHINGTON 25, D. C.

CO-2-34030

Protective Research Section
November 26, 1963

Receipt is acknowledged this date, Nov. 26, 1963, of the
following items from Dr. George G. Burkley:

One piece of bronze colored material inadvertently broken
in transit from casket in which body was brought from Dallas.

One letter - Certificate of Death of John F. Kennedy - State
of Texas - dated Nov. 22, 1963,

One carbon copy of letter dated November 26 from Commanding
Officer, U. S. Medical School, concerning law and regulations
regarding confidential nature of the events.

One receipt dated Nov. 22, 1963, for bed sheet, surgical
drapes, and shroud used to cover the body in transit.

One receipt dated Nov. 22, 1963, regarding a carton of
photographic film, undeveloped except for X-rays, delivered
to PRS for safekeeping.

An original and six pink copies of Certificate of Death
(Nav.Med.N)

One receipt from FBI for a missile removed during the
examination of the body.

One letter from University of Texas South West Medical
School including report from Dr. Clark and summary of their
findings of treatment and examination of the President in
the Dallas County Hospital. Said letter of transmittal states
that three carbon copies have been retained in that area.

One copy of autopsy report and notes of the examining doctor
which is described in letter of transmittal Nov. 25, 1963 by
Dr. Gallaway.

Transmittal Letter and 7 copies of the above item (autopsy report)

Authorization for post mortem examination signed by the Attorney
General and dated Nov. 22, 1963.

Robert I. Bouck

The Commission failed to publish this receipt even though it is supposed to be included
as part of a published exhibit, CE 397. The reason is obvious: had it been published,
questions would immediately have arisen as to why none of the items included in the
list are a part of the Commission's evidence. That the Commission did not obtain these
items, readily available to it, is proof that it did not seek the most basic evidence
of the crime. The Navy death certificate alone is destructive of the entire official
solution to that crime. See pp. 102, 307-8.

UNITED STATES GOVERNMENT

Memorandum

U. S. SECRET SERVICE
File No. CO-2-34,030
DATE: March 13, 1964

TO : Mr. J. Lee Rankin, General Counsel
President's Commission on the
Assassination of President Kennedy

FROM : James J. Rowley, Chief
U. S. Secret Service

SUBJECT: Secret Service Reports

There is forwarded herewith reports covered by
Secret Service Control Numbers 193, 621, 874, 973,
1181, 1184, 1187, 1199, 1203, 1205, 1221, 1222, 1224
and 1225.

There is also attached a classified document receipt
from Mr. John J. McCloy.

Attachments

- Commission Exhibit No. 391

6 December 1963

From: Commanding Officer, U. S. Naval Medical School
To: The White House Physician
Via: Commanding Officer, National Naval Medical Center

Subj: Supplementary report of Naval Medical School autopsy No. A63-272,
John F. Kennedy; forwarding of

1. All copies of the above subject final supplementary report are forwarded herewith.

J. H. STOVER, JR.

6 December 1963

FIRST ENDORSEMENT

From: Commanding Officer, National Naval Medical Center
To: The White House Physician

1. Forwarded.

C. B. GALLOWAY

The supplemental autopsy report, CE 391, was not forwarded to the Commission until
3/13/64. It is identified by its Secret Service Control Number 1221. The report was
forwarded to the White House on 12/6/63, and there is no record of when the Secret
Service got it. Surely, however, it was always available to the Commission, which
avoided it until three months after it was written. The autopsy doctors testified
only three days later, 3/16/64, and Specter had already interviewed Humes and Boswell
the day before he received this report. The transfer to the White House included only
"all copies of the...final...report," according to Stover's memo, and there is no accounting for drafts or notes related to it.

/221

1r/6/63

SUPPLEMENTARY REPORT OF AUTOPSY NUMBER A63-272
PRESIDENT JOHN F. KENNEDY

PATHOLOGICAL EXAMINATION REPORT   No. A63-272   Page 1

GROSS DESCRIPTION OF BRAIN: Following formalin fixation the brain
weighs 1500 gms. The right cerebral
hemisphere is found to be markedly disrupted. There is a longitudinal laceration
of the right hemisphere which is para-sagittal in position approximately 2.5 cm.
to the right of the of the midline which extends from the tip of the occipital
lobe posteriorly to the tip of the frontal lobe anteriorly. The base of the
laceration is situated approximately 4.5 cm. below the vertex in the white matter.
There is considerable loss of cortical substance above the base of the laceration,
particularly in the parietal lobe. The margins of this laceration are at all
points jagged and irregular, with additional lacerations extending in varying
directions and for varying distances from the main laceration. In addition, there
is a laceration of the corpus callosum extending from the genu to the tail. Exposed in this latter laceration are the interiors of the right lateral and third
ventricles.

When viewed from the vertex the left
cerebral hemisphere is intact. There is marked engorgement of meningeal blood
vessels of the left temporal and frontal regions with considerable associated
sub-arachnoid hemorrhage. The gyri and sulci over the left hemisphere are of
essentially normal size and distribution. Those on the right are too fragmented
and distorted for satisfactory description.

When viewed from the basilar aspect
the disruption of the right cortex is again obvious. There is a longitudinal
laceration of the mid-brain through the floor of the third ventricle just behind
the optic chiasm and the mammillary bodies. T his laceration partially communi-
cates with an oblique 1.5 cm. tear through the left cerebral peduncle. There are
irregular superficial lacerations over the basilar aspects of the left temporal
and frontal lobes.

In the interest of preserving the
specimen coronal sections are not made. The following sections are taken for
microscopic examination:

    a. From the margin of the laceration in the right parietal lobe.

    b. From the margin of the laceration in the corpus callosum.

    c. From the anterior portion of the laceration in the right frontal lobe.

    d. From the contused left fronto-parietal cortex.

    e. From the line of transection of the spinal cord.

    f. From the right cerebellar cortex.

    g. From the superficial laceration of the basilar aspect of the left temporal
        lobe.

/221/

In its fresh state, the brain is very difficult to handle at an autopsy because of the
fragile nature of the tissue. The usual practice is to "fix" the brain in a solution
which makes it firmer, thus easier to examine and dissect. Here, for no apparent reason, the brain was not dissected. A standard requirement in any medico-legal autopsy
is the slicing of the "fixed" brain into coronal sections. The absence of that procedure here is one of many inadequacies of the autopsy. The official record is unen-
lightening, and does not even specify when the examination of the brain occurred or
when this report was written.

PATHOLOGICAL EXAMINATION REPORT   No. A63-272   Page 2

During the course of this examination seven (7) black and white and six (6) color 4x5 inch negatives are exposed but not developed (the cassettes containing these negatives have been delivered by hand to Rear Admiral George W. Burkley, MC, USN, White House Physician).

MICROSCOPIC EXAMINATION:

BRAIN: Multiple sections from representative areas as noted above are examined. All sections are essentially similar and show extensive disruption of brain tissue with associated hemorrhage. In none of the sections examined are there significant abnormalities other than those directly related to the recent trauma.

HEART: Sections show a moderate amount of subepicardial fat. The coronary arteries, myocardial fibers, and endocardium are unremarkable.

LUNGS: Sections through the grossly described area of contusion in the right upper lobe exhibit disruption of alveolar walls and recent hemorrhage into alveoli. Sections are otherwise essentially unremarkable.

LIVER: Sections show the normal hepatic architecture to be well preserved. The parenchymal cells exhibit markedly granular cytoplasm indicating high glycogen content which is characteristic of the "liver biopsy pattern" of sudden death.

SPLEEN: Sections show no significant abnormalities.

KIDNEYS: Sections show no significant abnormalities aside from dilatation and engorgement of blood vessels of all calibers.

SKIN WOUNDS: Sections through the wounds in the occipital and upper right posterior thoracic regions are essentially similar. In each there is loss of continuity of the epidermis with coagulation necrosis of the tissues at the wound margins. The scalp wound exhibits several small fragments of bone at its margins in the subcutaneous tissue.

FINAL SUMMARY: This supplementary report covers in more detail the extensive degree of cerebral trauma in this case. However neither this portion of the examination nor the microscopic examinations alter the previously submitted report or add significant details to the cause of death.

J. J. HUMES
CDR, MC, USN, 497831

1221

Under "SKIN WOUNDS" only microscopic tissue sections from the margins of the two posterior wounds "presumably" of entry are described. The "coagulation necrosis" said to be depicted on these tissue slides is a sure sign of a bullet's entrance. However, there is no explanation why tissue sections were not taken from the margins of other wounds, including surgical incisions, especially the tracheotomy incision which still bore traces of a bullet wound and could have been microscopically tested.

Dr. Humes testified that "Dr. Boswell, Dr. Finck and I convened to examine the brain" after fixation (2H355). Yet Humes was the only one to affix his name to this report; presumably, he was the sole author. The Commission sought no explanation why the other doctors did not participate in the writing.

RESULTS OF AUTOPSY ON JOHN F. KENNEDY

On November 23, 1963, an autopsy was performed on the body of former President JOHN F. KENNEDY at the National Naval Medical Center, Bethesda, Maryland. A total body X-ray and autopsy revealed one bullet hole located just below shoulders to right of spinal column and hand-probing indicated trajectory at angle of 45 to 60 degrees downward and hole of short depth with no point of exit. No bullet located in body.

A second bullet entered back of head and thereafter emerged through top of skull. Two metal fragments removed from brain area, the first 7 x 2 millimeters and the other 3 by 1 millimeters in size.

The above two metal fragments were turned over to Agents of the FBI for delivery to the FBI Laboratory.

A piece of skull measuring 10 by 6.5 centimeters had been flown in to Bethesda from Dallas hospital and this disclosed minute metal fragments where bullet emerged from skull.

With respect to the bullet hole located in the back, pathologist at National Naval Medical Center was of the opinion this bullet worked its way out of the victim's back during cardiac massage performed at Dallas hospital prior to transportation of the body to Washington.

With respect to this situation, it is noted that Secret Service Agent RICHARD JOHNSON turned over to the FBI Laboratory one 6.5 millimeter rifle bullet (approximately .25 caliber), copper alloy, full jacket, which he advised was found on a stretcher in the emergency room of the Dallas hospital to which the victim was taken. JOHNSON was unable to advise whether stretcher on which this bullet was found had been used for the President.

The above information was received by communication from the Baltimore Office, dated November 23, 1963.

149

This is what FBI Agents Sibert and O'Neill reported on the day after the autopsy, one day before the final autopsy report was completed. While they were reporting the fact that no outlet for the <u>back</u> wound could be found at the autopsy, Dr. Humes was learning (for the first time, he says) that there was a bullet wound in the front of the neck that had to be accounted for. (The first line of this communication is in error. The autopsy was conducted on the evening of November 22.) See p. 76.

At approximately 3 p.m. on November 22, 1963, following the
President's announced assassination, it was ascertained that
Air Force One, the President's jet, was returning from Love
Field, Dallas, Texas, flying the body back to Andrews Air Force
Base, Camp Springs, Maryland. SAs FRANCIS X. O'NEILL, JR.
and JAMES W. SIBERT proceeded to Andrews Air Force Base to
handle any matters which would fall within the jurisdiction
of the Federal Bureau of Investigation, inasmuch as it was
anticipated that a large group of both military and civilian
personnel assigned to the Base would congregate at Base
Operations to witness the landing of this flight.

Lt. Col. ROBERT T. BEST, Director of Law Enforcement and
Security, advised the President's plane would arrive at
5:25 p.m. Subsequently, Col. BEST advised that the plane
would arrive at 6:05 p.m.

At approximately 5:55 p.m. agents were advised through the
Hyattsville Resident Agency that the Bureau had instructed
that the agents accompany the body to the National Naval
Medical Center, Bethesda, Maryland, to stay with the body
and to obtain bullets reportedly in the President's body.

Immediately agents contacted Mr. JAMES ROWLEY, the Director
of the U. S. Secret Service, identified themselves and made
Mr. ROWLEY aware of our aforementioned instruction. Immediately
following the plane's landing, Mr. ROWLEY arranged seating
for Bureau agents in the third car of the White House motorcade
which followed the ambulance containing the President's body
to the Naval Medical Center, Bethesda, Maryland.

On arrival at the Medical Center, the ambulance stopped in
front of the main entrance, at which time Mrs. JACQUELINE
KENNEDY and Attorney General ROBERT KENNEDY embarked from the
ambulance and entered the building. The ambulance was thereafter driven around to the rear entrance where the President's
body was removed and taken into an autopsy room. Bureau
agents assisted in the moving of the casket to the autopsy
room. A tight security was immediately placed around the
autopsy room by the Naval facility and the U. S. Secret Service.
Bureau agents made contact with Mr. ROY KELLERMAN, the
Assistant Secret Service Agent in Charge of the White House
Detail, and advised him of the Bureau's interest in this matter.

On __11/22/63__ at _____Bethesda, Maryland_____ File # _____89-30_____

by __SAs FRANCIS X. O'NEILL, JR.;__ _____ Date dictated __11/26/63__
　　JAMES W. SIBERT : dfl

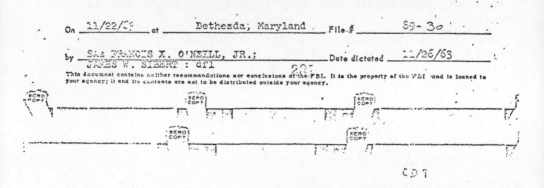

CD 7

This is Sibert and O'Neill's report on their observation of the autopsy. It was not
published by the Commission, and is contradictory of many vital elements of the official
case. See pp. 24, 42.

He advised that he had already received instructions from Director ROWLEY as to the presence of Bureau agents. It will be noted that aforementioned Bureau agents, Mr. ROY KELLERMAN, Mr. WILLIAM GREER and Mr. WILLIAM O'LEARY, Secret Service agents, were the only personnel other than medical personnel present during the autopsy.

The following individuals attended the autopsy:

Adm. C. B. HOLLOWAY, U. S. Navy, Commanding Officer of the U. S. Naval Medical Center, Bethesda;

Adm. BERKLEY, U. S. Navy, the President's personal physician;

Commander JAMES J. HUMES, Chief Pathologist, Bethesda Naval Hospital, who conducted autopsy;

Capt. JAMES H. STONER, JR., Commanding Officer, U. S. Naval Medical School, Bethesda;

Mr. JOHN T. STRINGER, JR., Medical photographer;

JAMES H. EBERSOLE;

LLOYD E. RAIHE;

J. T. BOZWELL;

J. G. RUDNICKI;

PAUL K. O'CONNOR;

J. C. JENKINS;

JERROL F. CRESTER;

EDWARD F. REED;

JAMES METZLER.

During the course of the autopsy, Lt. Col. P. FINCK, U. S. Army Armed Forces Institute of Pathology, arrived to assist Commander HUMES in the autopsy. In addition, Lt. Cmdr. GREGG CROSS and Captain DAVID OSBORNE, Chief of Surgery, entered the autopsy room.

Major General WEHLE, Commanding Officer of U. S. Military District, Washington, D.C., entered the autopsy room to ascertain from the Secret Service arrangements concerning the

Note the extensive list of military personnel present at the autopsy. In fact, the only civilians allowed in the room were the FBI and Secret Service agents. With all the doubts surrounding the autopsy and the nature and location of the wounds, only three of the medical personnel in attendance were called to testify before the Commission. The failure to call Dr. Burkley (here misspelled "BERKLEY") is particularly significant since he was in the motorcade during the assassination, present with the President at Parkland Hospital, in attendance at the autopsy, certified that the President was shot in the back, and transmitted the missing autopsy notes to the Secret Service. An obviously vital witness, he is not even mentioned in the Report. See Chapter 28.

transportation of the President's body back to the NAV.....
RMC CHESTER H. BOYERS, U. S. Navy, visited the autopsy ....
during the final stages of such to type receipts given by FBI
and Secret Service for items obtained.

At the termination of the autopsy, the following personnel
from Gawler's Funeral Home entered the autopsy room to
prepare the President's body for burial:

    JOHN VAN HAESEN
    EDWIN STROBLE
    THOMAS ROBINSON
    Mr. HAGEN

Brigidier General GODFREY McHUGH, Air Force Military Aid
to the President, was also present, as was Dr. GEORGE B....,
U. S. Navy.

Arrangements were made .. for the performance of the autopsy
by   . the U. S. Navy and Secret Service.

The President's body was removed from the casket in which it
had been transported and was placed on the autopsy table, at
which time the complete body was wrapped in a sheet and the
head area contained an additional wrapping which was saturated
with blood. Following the removal of the wrapping, it was
ascertained that the President's clothing had been removed
and it was also apparent that a tracheotomy had been performed,
as well as surgery of the head area, namely, in the top of
the skull. All personnel with the exception of medical
officers needed in the taking of photographs and X-Rays were
requested to leave the autopsy room and remain in an adjacent
room.

Upon completion of X-Rays and photographs, the first incision
was made at 8:15 p.m. X-Rays of the brain area which were
developed and returned to the autopsy room disclosed a path
of a missile which appeared to enter the back of the skull
and the path of the disintegrated fragments could be observed
along the right side of the skull. The largest section of
this missile as portrayed by X-Ray appeared to be behind the
right frontal sinus. The next largest fragment appeared to
be at the rear of the skull at the juncture of the skull bone.

The Chief Pathologist advised approximately 40 particles of
disintegrated bullet and smudges indicated that the projectile
had fragmentized while passing through the skull region.

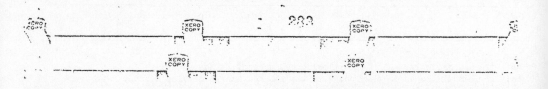

Nowhere is there an explanation of why it was "apparent" that "surgery of the head
area" had occurred, a falsehood. The Commission sought no explanation. Nor was the
Commission interested in ascertaining how these FBI agents could know it was "apparent
that a tracheotomy had been performed" when Humes' story is that he had to wait until
the following day to learn that.

During the autopsy   inspection of the area of the brain,
two fragments of metal were removed by Dr. HUMES, namely,
one fragment measuring 7 x 2 millimeters, which was removed
from the right side of the brain. An additional fragment of
metal measuring 1 x 3 millimeters was also removed from this
area, both of which were placed in a glass jar containing a
black metal top which were thereafter marked for identification
and following the signing of a proper receipt were transported
by Bureau agents to the FBI Laboratory.

During the latter stages of this autopsy, Dr. HUMES located
an opening which appeared to be a bullet hole which was below
the shoulders and two inches to the right of the middle line
of the spinal column.

This opening was probed by Dr. HUMES with the finger, at which
time it was determined that the trajectory of the missile
entering at this point had entered at a downward position of
45 to 60 degrees. Further probing determined that the distance
travelled by this missile was a short distance inasmuch as the
end of the opening could be felt with the finger.

Inasmuch as no complete bullet of any size could be located in
the brain area and likewise no bullet could be located in the
back or any other area of the body as determined by total
body X-Rays and inspection revealing there was no point of
exit, the individuals performing the autopsy were at a loss
to explain why they could find no bullets.

.. call was made by Bureau agents to the Firearms Section of
the FBI Laboratory, at which time SA CHARLES L. KILLION advised
that the Laboratory had received through Secret Service
Agent RICHARD JOHNSON a bullet which had reportedly been found
on a stretcher in the emergency room of Parkland Hospital,
Dallas, Texas. This stretcher had also contained a stethescope
and pair of rubber gloves. Agent JOHNSON had advised the
Laboratory that it had not been ascertained whether or not
this was the stretcher which had been used to transport the
body of President KENNEDY. Agent KILLION further described
this bullet as pertaining to a 6.5 millimeter rifle which
would be approximately a 25 caliber rifle and that this bullet
consisted of a copper alloy full jacket.

Immediately following receipt of this information, this was
made available to Dr. HUMES who advised that in his opinion
this accounted for no bullet being located which had entered

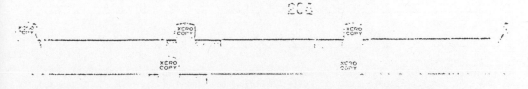

Sibert and O'Neill, like all the other witnesses who saw the rear non-fatal wound,
first reported it was located in the President's back, not in his neck as the autopsy
doctors were later to misrepresent. The thoroughly unprofessional nature of the
autopsy is characterized by Humes' sticking his finger into the tiny back wound, an
opening purported to measure 7 by 4 mm. What better way to destroy the character of
the wound?

the back region and that since external cardiac massage had
been performed at Parkland Hospital, it was entirely possible
that through such movement the bullet had worked its way
back out of the point of entry and had fallen on the
stretcher.

Also during the latter stages of the autopsy, a piece of the
skull measuring 10 x 6.5 centimeters was brought to Dr. HUMES
who was instructed that this had been removed from the President's skull. Immediately this section of skull was X-Rayed,
at which time it was determined by Dr. HUMES that one corner
of this section revealed minute metal particles and inspection
of this same area disclosed a chipping of the top portion
of this piece, both of which indicated that this had been
the point of exit of the bullet entering the skull region.

On the basis of the latter two developments, Dr. HUMES
stated that the pattern was clear   that the one bullet had
entered the President's back and had worked its way out of the
body during external cardiac massage and that a second high
velocity bullet had entered the rear of the skull and had
fragmentized prior to exit through the top of the skull.
He further pointed out that X-Rays had disclosed numerous
fractures in the cranial area which he attributed to the
force generated by the impact of the bullet in its passage
through the brain area. He attributed the death of the President
to a gunshot wound in the head.

The following is a complete listing of photographs and X-Rays
taken by the medical authorities of the President's body.
They were turned over to Mr. ROY KELLERMAN of the Secret
Service. X-Rays were developed by the hospital, however,
the photographs were delivered to Secret Service undeveloped:

    11 X-Rays
    22 4 x 5 color photographs
    18 4 x 5 black and white photographs
    1 roll of 120 film containing five exposures

Mr. KELLERMAN stated these items could be made available
to the FBI upon request. The portion of the skull measuring
10 x 6.5 centimeters was maintained in the custody of Dr.
HUMES who stated that it also could be made available for
further examination. The two metal fragments removed from
the brain area were hand carried by SAS SIBERT and O'NEILL
to the FBI Laboratory immediately following the autopsy and
were turned over to SA KURT FRAZIER.

285

The Commission's published record nowhere reflects that Dr. Humes felt it "clear" as
of the night of the autopsy that the bullet entering the back had not exited. Instead,
the Report asserts that Humes fully traced the bullet path through to the front of the
neck and had his hypothesis "confirmed" when he learned of the front neck wound the
next day from Dr. Perry. "Further exploration during the autopsy disproved that theory"
of a short penetration by the bullet in the back (R88). The authors of the Report had
to know this was false, and perhaps this is why Sibert and O'Neill were never called
to testify.

    Note also Kellerman's assurance that the pictures and x-rays were available to
the FBI, contrary to the official fiction.

AS:mln

MEMORANDUM

March 12, 1964

TO: Mr. J. Lee Rankin

FROM: Arlen Specter

SUBJECT: Interview of FBI Agents Present at Autopsy

On March 12, 1964, I interviewed Special Agents Francis X. O'Neill and James W. Sibert in my office from approximately 10:00 a.m. to 10:45 a.m.

SA O'Neill and SA Sibert advised that the autopsy surgeons made substantial efforts to determine if there was a missile in President Kennedy's body to explain what happened to the bullet which apparently entered the back of his body. They stated that the opinion was expressed by both Commander Humes and Lt. Col. Finck that the bullet might have been forced out of the back of the President's body upon application of external heart massage. They stated that this theory was advanced after SA Sibert called the FBI laboratory and talked to SA Killion who advised that a bullet had been found on a stretcher at Parkland Hospital. SA Sibert relayed that information to the doctors.

SA O'Neill and Sibert advised that they did not recall any discussion of the theory that the bullet might have been forced out of the body by external cardiac massage until after SA Sibert reported the finding of the bullet on the stretcher; however, neither agent could conclusively rule out the possibility that such a hypothesis was advanced prior to that time, but each expressed the opinion that he thought that theory was expressed after information was obtained about the bullet on the stretcher. SA Sibert advised that he made no notes during the autopsy. SA O'Neill stated that he made only a few notes, which he destroyed after his report was dictated. SA O'Neill advised that he is sure that his notes would not have shown when the Doctors expressed the thought that the bullet might have been forced out by external heart massage, in relation to the time that they learned of the presence of the bullet on the Parkland Hospital stretcher.

I also questioned SA Sibert and SA O'Neill about their interviews of ASAIC Kellerman and SA Greer on the portions of the FBI report which Kellerman and Greer have repudiated.

SAs Sibert and O'Neill stated that they interviewed SAs Kellerman and Greer formally on November 27, 1963, and talked to them only informally at the autopsy. SA O'Neill stated that he is certain that he had a verbatim note on Kellerman's statement that the President said "Get me to a hospital" and also that Mrs. Kennedy said "Oh, no." SA O'Neill stated that he was

---

Although the Commission never spoke to Sibert and O'Neill, Arlen Specter did---off the record. From the unpublished files, this is his account of his conversation with them. See pp. 76ff.

sure those were direct quotes from Kellerman because O'Neill used quotation
marks in his report which indicated that he had written these precise words
in his notes, which notes have since been destroyed after the report was
dictated. SA O'Neill noted that Mr. Kellerman did not repeat that language
in the interview of November 27, 1963, and that in the later interview
O'Neill took down what Kellerman said without leading or directing him in
any way.

I also asked the two Special Agents about the language in their
reports that Greer glanced around and noticed that the President had
evidently been hit and thereafter got on the radio and communicated with
the other vehicles, stating that they "desired to get the President to the
hospital immediately." SAs O'Neill and Sibert advised that to the best of
their recollection SA Greer told them just that, but they probably did not
make any notes on those comments since their conversation with Greer was
an informal one at the time of the autopsy and they did not have an
opportunity to make extensive notes in accordance with their normal interviewing procedures.

Dictated from 11:45 a.m. to 12:00 noon

A fundamental issue in the Commission's investigation was the quality of the autopsy and the integrity of the autopsy findings. Especially if it was later to plead that
it could not vouch for the complete accuracy of the findings because it could not verify them with the pictures and x-rays (a fiction exposed in this book), the Commission
was under an added obligation to take testimony from all the witnesses at the autopsy
to learn what really happened, and to see if the accounts of the three pathologists
could be corroborated. This was Specter's area of investigation, and he had already
noted in his Jan. 23 memo, reproduced at pp.480f, that there was "considerable confusion"
about the path of the bullet in the President's back.

Specter knew that agents Sibert and O'Neill were present for the entire autopsy.
Here he represents them as emphatic that the pathologists "made substantial efforts"
to find out what happened to the bullet that entered the back. No witness, including
Sibert and O'Neill, had any recollection of the pathologists theorizing on any basis
other than a short penetration into the back. There is simply no evidence the doctors
believed or established otherwise at the autopsy. what really happened, according to
all the evidence, is that the doctors were convinced there was no through-and-through
path in the upper thorax, but, once the body was out of their hands on November 23,
were confronted with the front neck wound to explain. It was at that point, not at
any point during the autopsy, that the doctors began thinking in terms of a continuous
path.

The Report's account of this is one which Specter had to know was false having
spoken to Sibert and O'Neill. The Report states that the doctors "rejected a theory"
of short penetration during the autopsy. The official representation is this: "In
the earlier stages of the autopsy, the surgeons were unable to find a path into any
large muscle in the back of the neck," a difficulty which "further exploration during
the autopsy disproved." (R88). The Sibert-O'Neill report (p. 4) is clear that the back
wound was not even discovered until "during the latter stages of this autopsy," and
all the evidence suppressed by the Commission proves that no "further exploration during the autopsy" was able to disprove the finding of a short penetration.

AS:mln

March 12, 1964

TO: Mr. J. Lee Rankin

FROM: Arlen Specter

SUBJECT: Interview of Autopsy Surgeons

On the afternoon of March 11, 1964, Joseph A. Ball, Esq., and I went to Bethesda Naval Hospital and interviewed Admiral C. B. Holloway, Commander James J. Humes and Commander "J" Thornton Boswell. The interview took place in the office of Admiral Holloway, who is the commanding officer of the National Naval Medical Center, and lasted from approximately 3:30 p.m to 5:30 p.m.

Commander Humes and Commander Boswell, along with Lt. Col. Pierre A. Finck, who is currently in Panama, conducted the autopsy and Admiral Holloway was present at all times. They described their activities and findings in accordance with the autopsy report which had been previously submitted as Commission Report #77.

All three described the bullet wound on President Kennedy's back as being a point of entrance. Admiral Holloway then illustrated the angle of the shot by placing one finger on my back and the second finger on the front part of my chest which indicated that the bullet traveled in a consistent downward path, on the assumption that it emerged in the opening on the President's throat which had been enlarged by the performance of the tracheotomy in Dallas.

Commander Humes explained that they had spent considerable time at the autopsy trying to determine what happened to the bullet because they found no missile in the President's body. According to Commander Humes, the autopsy surgeons hypothesized that the bullet might have been forced out of the back of the President on the application of external heart massage after they were advised that a bullet had been found on a stretcher at Parkland Hospital.

Dr. Humes and Dr. Boswell were shown the Parkland report which describes the wound of the trachea as being "ragged", which they said was characteristic of an exit rather than an entrance wound. Dr. Humes and Dr. Boswell further said that it was their current opinion that the bullet passed in between two major muscle strands in the President's back and continued on a downward flight and exited through his throat. They noted, at the time of the autopsy, some bruising of the internal parts

This memo proves that Specter knew what he and the Commission represent as the truth is really false. See pp. 85ff.

of the President's body in that area but tended to attribute that to the tracheotomy at that time. Dr. Humes and Dr. Boswell stated that after the bullet passed between the two strands of muscle, those muscle strands would resist any probing effort and would not disclose the path of the bullet to probing fingers, as the effort was made to probe at the time of the autopsy.

He requested that Dr. Humes and Dr. Boswell prepare or have prepared drawings of the consequences of the shots on the President's body and head, and they also elaborated upon the facts set forth in their autopsy report.

Dictated from 11:30 to 11:45 a.m.

Lawyers are taught to use words carefully and with precision. Thus, when Specter had this memo rolled back into a typewriter to add that the wound "on President Kennedy" was a "back" wound, that is precisely what he meant, not a "neck" wound or a wound "in the back of the neck." The bullet which entered the back was travelling at a downward angle, meaning it could not possibly have followed a straight course and exited from the front neck, which would be above, not below the level of the rear wound. Such a bullet going all the way through would have emerged from the chest, as Admiral Galloway (misspelled here as "Holloway") clearly demonstrated to Specter. Specter unabashedly admits Galloway "illustrated the angle of the shot by placing one finger on my back and the second finger on the front part of my chest." Yet Specter knew there was no bullet wound to the chest. He simply ignored this gross refutation of the official version of the crime and pretended the back wound was a neck wound. Even at that, Galloway revealed the totally speculative nature of the autopsy, supposed to be a model of scientific precision, when he characterized the "tracing" of this considerably confused bullet path as an "assumption."

Furthermore, it is apparent from this memo that Humes and Boswell confirmed the Sibert-O'Neill account so opposed to the account in the Report: the doctors during the autopsy could not explain what happened to the bullet causing the back wound and did not then have reason to believe that this bullet had exited through the front of the neck. Specter is specific that the bullet's path through certain musculature represented the doctors' "current opinions" as distinguished from their opinions at the time of the autopsy. He is even clearer when he writes: "They noted, at the time of the autopsy, some bruising of the internal parts of the President's body in that area but tended to attribute that to the tracheotomy at that time." So, what remains of the official fiction of the Report that the doctors during the autopsy interpreted this internal bruising as conclusive indications of a bullet's passage?

Had Specter and the Commission been honest, they would have had to report that no bullet path could be found for all the time that the doctors worked on the President's body, but that one was "assumed" only after the body was out of their hands and they were left with a new wound to explain. And for this "assumption" to be even tenable, the back wound had to be raised several inches to become a neck wound.

A charge of this magnitude is serious indeed. As this memo shows, however, Arlen Specter knew what he was doing.

November 25, 1966

On November 21, 1966, Mr. J. Edgar Hoover, Director,
Federal Bureau of Investigation, received a letter from a newsman
expressing concern over the rash of books, articles and statements which
are "creating confusion and doubts about the validity of the findings of
the Warren Commission regarding the assassination of President Kennedy."
The newsman said that one of the "conflicts" concerned the alleged variance
of the results of the medical examination of the President's body, recorded
in FBI reports dated December 9, 1963, and January 13, 1964, and the
official autopsy report.

The newsman said he would appreciate any comment
Mr. Hoover would make concerning these matters.

The newsman requested that Mr. Hoover prepare a statement regarding the alleged conflict between information reported by the
FBI and the autopsy report.

By letter dated November 23, 1966, to the newsman,
Mr. Hoover said he shared the concern of the newsman regarding the
criticisms of the Warren Commission's findings. He pointed out that
while the critics had every right to state their views, they "should show
more regard for the facts on record. They have ignored certain facts,
misinterpreted others, and expressed pure speculation as truth."

If the reason this Hoover press release is so hard to read is not typical, it does illustrate the Department's and Bureau's attitude toward bringing out the truth and facing their own pasts. When twice the time permitted by law for response to my FOIA
request (p.545) passed, I appealed unsuccessfully to Ford's personal selection as Attorney General. Having to invoke the law to get a copy of a published press release
after nine years of effort is bad enough. It is worse that the Department again violated the law to assure free information it opposed. There is vindictiveness. There
is also embarrassment. Hoover's self-serving propaganda cannot survive the simple
analysis that follows. Is it the "critics" who "'should show more regard for the
facts on record.?'"

The Warren Commission and its findings concerning the assassination of President Kennedy currently are being severely criticized. The conclusions of the Commission, especially its conclusion that Lee Harvey Oswald acted alone in the assassination, have been openly challenged.

In support of their speculations, some of the critics allege, among other things, that there is a "conflict" between portions of two FBI reports and the official autopsy report regarding the wounds found in the President's body.

While there is a difference in the information reported by the FBI and the information contained in the autopsy report concerning the wounds, there is no conflict. The FBI reports record oral statements made by autopsy physicians while the examination was being conducted and before all facts were known. The autopsy report records the final findings of the examination.

Briefly, this is what happened. The autopsy was conducted at Bethesda Naval Hospital on the evening of November 22, 1963. Two

---

By 1966, with the publication of WHITEWASH proving that the FBI had "solved" the assassination on the basis of a version of the shots quite different from the Commission's, there had erupted a national controversy. The FBI stated in its report of Dec. 9, 1963 and again in its supplemental report of January 13, 1964 that the first shot did not exit from the President's body, and that Governor Connally was hit by a separate bullet. This, if true, would negate the single bullet theory and prove the existence of at least two gunmen---conspiracy. So, the heat was on Hoover to explain how he could have contradicted both the autopsy report and the Warren Report. See p. 66.

Hoover begins with the assurance that a conflict is not a conflict, that the FBI made no pretense of reporting anything other than "oral statements" made during the autopsy and not any "final findings." This is simply not true. The December 9 report states: "Medical examination of the President's body revealed that one of the bullets had entered just below his shoulder...that there was no point of exit, and that the bullet was not in the body." The prosecution-like FBI report draws the inference that 399 caused this short wound and fell out in Dallas. For Hoover it did not matter that a bullet travelling at 2,000 feet per second cannot possibly stop short after penetrating two inches of flesh. The January 13 report, written a month after the official autopsy report was in the FBI's hands, repeats this version of what "medical examination" revealed.

... Agents were present. They reported that Dr. James J. Humes, chief autopsy surgeon, located what appeared to be a bullet hole in the back below the shoulder and probed it to the end of the opening with a finger. The examining physicians were unable to explain why they could find no bullet or point of exit.

Unknown to the Agents, the physicians eventually were able to trace the path of the bullet through the body. On the morning of November 23, 1963, Dr. Humes contacted doctors who treated the President at Parkland Hospital in Dallas, Texas, the previous day and confirmed his assumption that a tracheotomy had been performed using a bullet hole in the front of the neck as the point of incision.

The information reported by the Agents present during the autopsy was summarized on page 18 of the FBI report dated December 9, 1963. Meanwhile, the clothing worn by the President when he was shot was examined in the FBI Laboratory. This examination revealed a small hole in the back of his coat and shirt and a slit characteristic of an exit hole for a projectile in the front of the shirt one inch below the collar button. A nick on the left side of the tie knot, possibly caused by the same projectile which passed through the shirt, also was noted.

- 2 -

Hoover is correct in stating that the FBI's source of autopsy information for the December 9 report was agents Sibert and O'Neill. He is probably also correct in his assumption that what occurred on November 23, the day after the autopsy, was "unknown to the agents." He is wrong, as we have seen, in stating that "the physicians were able to trace the path of the bullet through the body." Wrong, at least, as the word "trace" is commonly and properly used. The doctors guessed, or, to use Galloway's word, "assumed" the bullet path when they no longer had a body on which to "trace" it.

Hoover next pretends that this Sibert-O'Neill information was innocently incorporated into the December 9 report, but that the FBI really knew better after examining the President's clothing and finding some sort of "exit" slit in the front of the collar. First, the FBI examination of the clothing was conducted on November 23, as is revealed by CD205, page 153, reproduced in this appendix at p. 599. So, if the clothing revealed an exit for the back wound, the FBI had ample time to reflect this in the December 9 report, which it did not. Second, the clothing examination did not reveal an exit for the back wound. According to FBI Agent Frazier's testimony, the FBI had no idea what "exited" from the shirt at that point, if anything at all.(5H61).

Hoover's non sequitur in his first paragraph on p. 3 of his statement is unequaled in this whole sorry case. First, he claims that the unexplained shirt slits "clearly

These findings clearly indicated the examining physician's observation that the bullet penetrated only a short distance into the President's back probably was in error. Since this observation had been included in the FBI report of December 9, 1963, another reference was made to it in the report of January 13, 1964, in conjunction with the laboratory findings to point up this probability.

The FBI and the Warren Commission each received a copy of the official autopsy report on December 23, 1963, from Secret Service following a specific request for this document. Since the FBI knew the Commission had a copy of the official autopsy, its contents were not repeated in an FBI report.

Recently the charge has been made that the FBI altered the film of the assassination taken by Abraham Zapruder. This is totally false. The FBI never had the original Zapruder film in its possession—it was purchased by a national magazine. The FBI obtained a copy of the original uncut film and reproduced this for the Commission which since has turned it over to National Archives.

At the direction of President Johnson, the FBI conducted a prompt, intensive, objective and thorough investigation of the assassination. The results of this investigation were accurately reported to

- 3 -

indicated" that the short penetration theory was incorrect. Of course, if this was so "clear," the December 9 report was culpable in reporting otherwise. That the short penetration could be reported as fact in the January 13 report, after the FBI knew the "final findings" of the autopsy, is even more culpable. How does Hoover get around this? "Since this observation had been included" in the first report, "another reference was made to it" in the second! Hoover then pretends that since the second report also describes the clothing examinations it therefore would "point up this probability" that the short penetration was erroneous. Hardly. As before, the short penetration is presented as a fact established by "medical examination." The shirt slits are described with no statement as to what caused them; their relation to the holes in the back of the clothing is not even stated. But to Hoover, this was enough to make it apparent to anyone that the FBI was really saying there was a complete, back-to-front penetration.

Such was Hoover's contribution to correcting the already pitiful official record on the assassination.

the Warren Commission. Not one shred of evidence has been developed to link any other person in a conspiracy with Oswald to assassinate President Kennedy. All available evidence and facts point to one conclusion--that Oswald acted alone in his crime.

Mr. Hoover sent the newsman the attached statement and stated, "I am speaking only for the FBI, not for any other agency or group involved in any phase of the inquiry into the assassination of President Kennedy."

Route 12
Frederick, Md. 21701
September 6, 1975

FOIA Request
The Deputy Attorney General
The Department of Justice
Washington, D. C.

Dear Sir:

This is my request under the Freedom of Information Act for a copy of an FBI press release. I make it pursuant to the suggestion of the FBI's Freedom of Information Officer, Mr. Thomas H. Bresson, who says it can be obtained no other way.

This public statement by then FBI Director Hoover received extensive public attention when it was issued. My request for a copy was made at that time, was repeated thereafter, and in the nine subsequent years I have not received a copy.

The form of this news release was that of a four-page statement by Mr. Hoover dated November 23, 1966, attached to a letter in response to a supposed inquiry from the reporter to whom it was addressed two days later.

I use this formulation because by the most remarkable of coincidences it is an official answer to charges I had not made publicly but were included in a book, the copy of which I had not yet delivered to my printer. Other copies were outside my personal possession, in the possession of others in the media.

If a difficulty in locating this public statement persists within the Department, it can be identified by the New York Times story reporting it.

Sincerely,

Harold Weisberg

CC: Mr. Thomas H. Bresson
FBI Director Clarence Kelley
Attorney General Edward Levi

When my lawyer, Jim Lesar, asked FBI Freedom of Information Officer Bresson for a copy of Hoover's press release, he was told to file a Freedom of Information Act official request for it. No wonder the FBI wails that it is swamped with FOIA requests!

From: CAPT J. H. STOVER, Jr., MC, USN
        Commanding Officer
        U. S. Naval Medical School

To: Roy H. Kellerman
        Assistant Special Agent in Charge
        United States Secret Service

The following items of photographic material were placed in the custody

of Mr. Roy H. Kellerman, Assistant Special Agent in Charge, United

States Secret Service, 22 November 1963 at the Morgue, U. S. Naval

Hospital, Bethesda, Maryland:

    (a) 8 graphic film holders (4 x 5) containing 16 sheets of exposed

Ektachrome E3 film

    (b) 6 graphic film holders (4 x 5) containing 12 sheets exposed

Portrait Pan film

    (c) 1 roll 120 Ektachrome E3 exposed film.

To my personal knowledge this is the total amount of film exposed on

this occasion.

It is requested the film holders be returned or replaced.

                           J. H. STOVER, Jr.
                           CAPT, MC, USN
                           Commanding Officer
                           U. S. Naval Medical School

John T. Stringer, Jr.
(Photographer)

Floyd A. Rabe
HM2/USN

Rec. by: Roy H. Kellerman
U.S. Secret Service
11-22-63

The autopsy photographs were taken on government property by government personnel. As
the receipt shows, they were immediately turned over to the Secret Service, keeping
them in government hands. Item (a) has been changed from 8 to 11, item (b) from 6 to
9. The two signatures above Roy Kellerman's are those of John T. Stringer, Jr., Naval
Photographer, and Floyd A. Rabe, "HM2, USN." See pp. 270-75.

From: Commander John H. EBERSOLE, MC, USN, 495535/2100
Acting Chief of Radiology, United States Naval Hospital, National
Naval Medical Center, Bethesda, Maryland

To: Roy H. KELLERMAN, Assistant Special Agent in Charge United States
Secret Service

1. The following number and types of X-ray films were taken this date.

Eight (8) 14 X 17 inch X-Ray film

Six (6) 10 X 12 inch X-Ray film

John H. Ebersole
John H. EBERSOLE
Commander, MC, USN
Acting Chief of Radiology
USNH, NNMC, Bethesda, Md.

Rec. by Roy H. Kellerman
U. S. Secret Service
11-22-63

This almost illegible receipt for the x-rays was retyped by the Navy and certified by
Galloway and Stover. "Three (3)" 10 X 12 inch x-ray film was listed before being
changed to "Six (6)." The retyped text follows.

22 November 1963

From: Commander John H. EBERSOLE, MC, USN, 495535/2100
Acting Chief of Radiology, United States Naval Hospital, National
Naval Medical Center, Bethesda, Maryland

To: Roy H. KELLERMAN, Assistant Special Agent in Charge United States
Secret Service

1. The following number and types of X-ray films were taken this date.

Eight (8) 14 x 17 inch X-Ray film

Six (6) 10 x 12 inch X-Ray film

/s/ John H. EBERSOLE
John H. EBERSOLE
Commander, MC, USN
Acting Chief of Radiology
USNH, NNMC, Bethesda, Md.

Rec. by Roy H. Kellerman (s/s)
U. S. Secret Service
11-22-63

547

Mr. GERALD A. BEHN, Special Agent in Charge, White House Detail, United States Secret Service, was interviewed at his office and advised that during the President's visit to the State of Texas, then Vice President JOHNSON would always arrive at the next city to be visited ahead of the President and would join the party awaiting the President's arrival. This was accomplished by the use of two Jets; Air Force I, which carried the President; and Air Force II, carrying the Vice President. On departing from a city, Air Force I would first take off followed by Air Force II which would thereafter pass Air Force I in flight, cruising at a faster speed, thus allowing the Vice President to arrive prior to the President and be with the greeting party.

Mr. BEHN was questioned concerning the section of the President's skull, which was brought to the National Navy Medical Center at Bethesda, Maryland after the autopsy was in progress. He advised that this section, which was measured by the Doctor performing the autopsy as being 10 x 6.5 centimeters, was found in the Presidential car on the floor between the front and rear seats. He further related that two fragments of bullets had also been found in this vehicle in the front of the car and that the windshield had been cracked by the impact of one of these fragments.

BEHN was likewise questioned concerning the location of a bullet which had been found on a stretcher at Parkland Hospital in Dallas and which had been turned over by the Secret Service to an Agent of the Federal Bureau of Investigation for delivery to the FBI Laboratory. He stated that on learning of such a bullet being found at the Dallas Hospital he inquired of a group of his Agents who had returned from the Dallas trip on the night of November 22, 1963, and Secret Service Agent RICHARD JOHNSEN produced this bullet which had been handed to him by someone at the hospital who had stated that it was not known whether or not the President had been placed on the stretcher where the bullet was found.

On 11/27/63 at Washington, D.C.   File # BA 89-30

by SAs JAMES W. SIBERT & FRANCIS X. O'NEILL, Date dictated 11/27/63
   JR.;mk

This document contains neither recommendations nor conclusions of the FBI. It is the property of the FBI and is loaned to your agency; it and its contents are not to be distributed outside your agency.

BA 89-30
JWS:FXO:mk
2

Mr. BEHN advised that the undeveloped photographs and x-rays made during the course of the autopsy conducted at the National Naval Medical Center, Bethesda, Maryland, are in the custody of Mr. BOB BOUCK, Protective Research Section, United States Secret Service and could be made available to the Federal Bureau of Investigation on request.

Within five days of the assassination the Secret Service had possession of the autopsy pictures and x-rays and was holding them under no restrictions. The FBI could have seen them simply by making a request. The Commission was no different, and it had subpoena power if its "request" were denied, which it was not. See p. 104.

Admin

MEMORANDUM

April 30, 1964

TO: Mr. J. Lee Rankin

FROM: Arlen Specter

SUBJECT: Autopsy Photographs and X-Rays of President John F. ...

In my opinion it is indispensable that we obtain th... ...
...d x-rays of President Kennedy's autopsy for the following re...

1. The Commission should determine with certainty ...
...hole came from the rear. Someone from the Commission shoul... ...
...films to corroborate the autopsy surgeons' testimony that the ...
...the President's back and head had the characteristics of poin...
...ew of the doctors at Parkland Hospital in Dallas observed t...
...the President's back or the small hole in the lower portion o...
...ith all of the outstanding controversy about the direction o...
...there must be independent viewings of the films to verify te...
...has come only from Government doctors.

2. The Commission should determine with certainty ...
...hole came from above. It is essential for the Commission t...
...udy the location of the bullet wound on the President's b...
...the angle may be calculated. The artist's drawing prepared ...
(Commission Exhibit #385) shows a slight angle of declinatio...
...hard, if not impossible, to explain such a slight angle of d...
...the President was farther down Elm Street than we have hard...
...Before coming to any conclusion on this, the angles will hav...
...lated at the scene; and for this, the exact point of entry ...

3. The Commission should determine with certainty ...
...ther variations between the films and the artist's ...
...Commission Exhibits Nos. 385, 386 and 388 were made from t...
...the autopsy surgeons as told to the artist. Some day ma...
...compare the films with the artist's drawings and find a signif...
...which might substantially affect the essential testimony and c...
...conclusions. In any event, the Commission should not rely on ...
...alone, especially in view of the statement in the autopsy report
Exhibit #387) that:

"The complexity of these fractures and the fragment...
produced tax satisfactory verbal description and are ...
appreciated in photographs and roentgenograms which ...
prepared."
                        - 2 -

When Inspector Kelly talked to Attorney General ...
...probably did not fully understand all the reasons f...
... According to Inspector Kelly, the Attorney General ...
...ordically decline to make them available, but only wa...
...led that they were really necessary. I suggest that ...
...it to the Attorney General its reasons for wanting t...
...assurance that they will be viewed only by the absolut...
...er of people from the Commission for the sole purpose ...
(or correcting) the artist's drawings, with the films not ...
...art of the Commission's records.

This memo destroys the official story of the unavailability of the pictures and x-rays.
They were not denied to the Commission by Robert Kennedy, who could not have denied
them had he wanted to. It also reflects the great doubts Specter had about the autopsy
but now denies. See pp. 121, 129.

549

Five, Autopsy Pictures of President Kennedy.

Mr. Rankin. The staff feels that we should have some member

of the Commission examine those pictures. We have a very

serious problem in the record now that Dr. Humes testified,

as you recall, that the bullet in his opinion probably passed

through the President and then through Governor Connally. And

we now have the testimony of Governor Connally that that couldn't

have happened. He is certain it didn't happen. And that the

bullet that struck him is one that did not hit the President.

We also have some drawings of President Kennedy which are

reconstructions by the men that participated in the autopsy.

And these men have not seen those pictures of the autopsy, but

they had those drawings made, and we don't know whether those

drawings conform to the pictures of the autopsy or not.

Now, I thought we could avoid having those pictures,

possibly avoid those pictures being a part of our record, because

the family has a strong feeling about them, and I think we should

respect it insofar as can possibly be done, and carry out

the work of the Commission -- because they don't want the

President to be remembered in connection with those pictures.

That is their basic thought.

I know that the Commission would like to respect that and

not have them in any way become a part of the records which the

public would get to see.

But I do feel that a doctor and some member of the Commission

should examine them sufficiently so that they could report

to the Commission that there is nothing inconsistent with the

This and the following pages are from the transcript of the Commission's executive
session of 4/30/64, the same day Specter wrote the previous memo advocating viewing
of the pictures and x-rays as "indispensable." With Specter taking this position,
Rankin had to take the matter up with the Commission. Throughout this discussion,
for reasons unexplained, the members and Rankin pretend that the Commission did not
once have these autopsy materials, contrary to the fact. WHITEWASH IV, pp. 102, 133.
Rankin clearly admits of the drawings on which the medical testimony was based, "we
don't know whether those...conform to the autopsy or not."

33   other findings in connection with the matter in those pictures.

In that way we can avoid any question that we have passed

anything up that the Commission should know or that we haven't

tried to take advantage of information that should be available

to us.

Mr. Dulles. Would the people who have made the pictures

have access to these photographs, also -- because they would

be the best ones to tell, as to whether the pictures were

consistent with the drawings they made.

Mr. Rankin. Well, they were made, as I understand it, under

the supervision of the doctors conducting the autopsy. And so

they just have never been developed because of the family's

wishes. And I think that the Attorney General would make them

available now -- although they were denied to us before because

he said that he didn't think there was a sufficient showing

of our need. But upon a showing now, I think that he would

recognize the need and permit that limited examination.

And then I feel that in dealing with the Attorney General,

however, we should make it plain to him that if the member of

the Commission who examines them, with the doctor, feels the

whole Commission should see them, that there would be that

reservation -- because I don't know what might appear to some

member of the Commission or the doctor in connection with them.

Mr. McCloy. There is this element. In the record there

is an indication by the doctor that there was a certain -- he would

---

Rankin was shrewd. He knew the pictures and x-rays were evidence "that should be
available to us," and he knew that questions would arise if the Commission failed to
make use of them, the best of the medical evidence. But he and the Commissioners
had known, since the executive session of 1/27/64, that they had an autopsy picture
which showed a bullet wound in the back, contrary to the later drawings. See p. 312.
Rankin lied in saying the pictures "just never have been developed because of the
family's wishes." The Secret Service has certified that the pictures were developed
on November 27, 1963. See p. 274. Likewise, there is no evidence that Robert Kennedy
had earlier denied the pictures to the Commission, and even if he wanted to, he was
powerless to do so.

34   prefer to have the pictures -- see the view of the pictures in

connection with the charts that he was representing to us.

There was a certain little note of minor inadequacy in connection

with the chart which we had, without the pictures.

Mr. Dulles. Which doctor was that?

Mr. Rankin. Humes -- you remember it was the doctor that

made the autopsy.

Mr. Dulles. Out at Bethesda?

Mr. Rankin. Yes.

Mr. Dulles. Yes, I remember that.

As I recall the testimony, I think it was the doctor from

Dallas --

Mr. Rankin. Dr. Gregory.

Mr. Dulles. The one who said that the bullet -- I under-

stood he said might have passed through the President's throat

and then through Connally. But I didn't think he said that he

thought it did. I think he said he thought it might have.

Is that correct?

Mr. Rankin. That is right.

Mr. Dulles. Could have.

Mr. McCloy. I thought the chief testimony on that came

from the Bethesda doctor. I remember he said, 'I think I could

show you this better on the photographs than I could through

these charts."

Mr. Rankin. That is right.

McCloy truly understates the case in saying that Humes had made "a certain little
note of minor inadequacy" of the drawings over the actual pictures. In fact, Humes
repeatedly stressed the inadequacy of the drawings as well as his "humble verbal descriptions" on which they were based. WHITEWASH, pp. 181-3. Of course, the whole
purpose of making a photographic record is precisely for this type of evidential use,
so that imprecise verbal descriptions, inherently suspect, need not be relied on.

35

The Chairman. Well, I think you can work that out, Lee, to do that, but without putting those pictures in our record. We don't want those in our record.

Mr. McCloy. Certainly not.

The Chairman. It would make it a morbid thing for all time to come.

Mr. Rankin. Is that effort to proceed in that manner, without having them in the record, and having an examination by the doctor and one of the members of the Commission satisfactory then?

The Chairman. Only for verification purposes. Yes, I think that would be all.

Mr. Dulles. By the doctor and a member of the Commission.

Mr. McCloy. Oh, yes, you would need a doctor present to interpret it to you.

The Chairman. All right.

This transcript destroys the many myths about the Commission's "decision" not to view the pictures and x-rays since they were felt to be corroborative evidence. Rankin asked for approval of the project and Warren gave the go-ahead: an autopsy surgeon (Humes) and a Commission member were to view the autopsy pictures "for verification purposes." Without a doubt, the Commission recognized the need for such an examination But it never took place. Rankin never arranged the examination ordered at this April 30 session, and there is no record as to why.

Former Commission member John J. McCloy commented on this to CBS News in 1967 and quite unintentionally revealed the extent of the Commission's failure. "I thought that he (Warren) was really going to see them, but it turned out that he hadn't," McCloy said. What could possibly be meant by "it turned out"? The Commission, in theory, was in charge; it was responsible for making things happen. The failure to examine the autopsy pictures, recognized by the Commission as a necessity, had to have been someone's responsibility. McCloy pretended he had no responsibility as a Commissioner, as if he had no control over things that "turned out" not to have been done, no obligation to see to it that such thing were done.

In a further perversion of truth, McCloy told CBS News that the pictures "were then in the hands of the Kennedy family." No photographic materials of the autopsy were in Kennedy hands at any time, least of all during the Commission's life when the Secret Service had possession. For the full text of McCloy's comments, see p. 300.

In connection with the Specter memo which follows, consider Specter's comments to U. S. News and World Report, 10/10/66:

Q: Why were all the pictures not shown?

A: Because the Commission decided that it would not press for those photographs, as a matter of deference to the memory of the late President and because the Commission concluded that the photographs and x-rays were not indispensable.

The photographs and x-rays would, in the thinking of the Commission, not have been crucial, because they would have only served to corroborate what the autopsy surgeons had testified to under oath.

If there is any more total refutation of these lies by Specter it is Specter's own memos and the Commission's deliberations of April 30.

MEMORANDUM

May 12, 190?

Mr. J. Lee Rankin

Arlen Specter

: Examination of Autopsy Photographs and X-rays of President Kennedy

The the autopsy photographs and x-rays are made certain to determine the following:

1. The photographs and x-rays confirm the precise location of the entrance wound in the back of the head depicted in Commission Exhibits 3?? and 388.

2. The photographs and x-rays confirm the precise location of the wound of entrance on the back of the President as depicted in Commission Exhibits 385 and 386.

3. The photographs and x-rays confirm the portion of the President's skull which was disrupted by the bullet when it exited as depicted in Commission Exhibit 388.

4. The characteristics of the wounds on the back and on the back of his head should be closely in the photographs and x-rays to determine for certain whether they are characteristic of entrance wounds under the criteria advanced by Doctors Finck, ????, Boswell, Gregory, ??, Perry and Carrico.

5. The films and x-rays should be viewed in ???? with Commission Exhibit ??? (a photograph of the frame of the Zapruder film immediately before the showing the head wound) or Commission ???? (the frame of the Zapruder film showing the wound) to determine for certain whether the angle of declination is accurately depicted in Commission Exhibit 388.
　　　　　　　　　　　- 2 -

It ?? not that we have a court reporter ????? Mr. Shaw after the x-rays and photographs to put on the record.

1. Any changes in the testimony or the like required by a review of the x-rays and films, and

2. Corroboration of the portions of the testimony which may be confirmed by the photographs and x-rays.

_____
Specter was sure that the "indispensable" examination was to take place. See p. 122, 130.

554

Inquiries have been received concerning the handling
and disposition by the Secret Service of certain X-ray
and photographic films relating to the autopsy performed
at the National Naval Medical Center, Bethesda, Maryland,
in connection with the assassination of President John F.
Kennedy.

The X-ray films were used for the briefing of the
Warren Commission's staff on the autopsy procedure and
results. None of the films are presently in the possession
of the Secret Service. Every item of tangible evidence
which the Secret Service possessed relating to the assassination of President Kennedy was made available to the
Warren Commission. All such evidence was either turned
over to the Commission during its life, or turned over to
the National Archives following the termination of the
Commission's activities, or placed in the custody of
individuals designated by the late President's family,
as appropriate.

Truth succombed to necessity after attention was focused on the deficiencies of
the Presidential autopsy. Until a false pretense was officially decided upon, the
lie that the Commission had never had access to the pictures and X-rays of the
autopsy, the Secret Service told inquirers part of the truth, as in this statement.
This particular Xeroxed copy was handed Paul Hoch, of Berkeley, Calif., at Secret
Service headquarters in Washington by Special Agent Jack Werner on Tuesday, June 21,
1966. In acknowledging that "The X-ray films were used for the briefing" of the
Commission's staff, the Secret Service failed to acknowledge the rest of the story,
that it also used the pictures for the same purpose. Then-Inspector Tom Kelley
showed them to Arlen Specter, as Specter admitted to Richard Whelen, biographer
of Joseph P. Kennedy, and U.S.News and World Report (WHITEWASH II, pp. 105,109).
The last sentence is evasive and deceptive. The Secret Service gave copies to
the National Archives, keeping originals. It was long after this statement was
drafted and issued that I forced it to give the Archives one of the original
copies of the autopsy, of which the Archives, until then, had none. Nor does
this statement cite any legal authority for giving the property of the United
States Government to "individuals designated by the late President's family as
appropriate." What this language probably means is that a member of the family
or someone designated to act for it "designated" one member, the late Robert F.
Kennedy, as "appropriate".

April 22, 1965

Dear Dr. Burkley:

This will authorize you to release to my custody all
of the material of President Kennedy, of which you
have personal knowledge, and now being held by the
Secret Service.

I would appreciate it if you would accompany this
material personally and turn it over for safekeeping
to Mrs. Evelyn Lincoln at the National Archives.
I am sending a copy of this letter to Mrs. Lincoln
with instructions that this material is not to be released to anyone without my written permission and
approval.

Sincerely,

Vice Adm. George G. Burkley
Physician to the President
The White House
Washington, D. C.

cc/Mrs. Evelyn Lincoln

Note the careful phrasing of Robert Kennedy's letter, kept secret by the Archives until
this year. Far from being a source of embarrassment to any surviving Kennedy, this is
destructive of the government's version of how vital evidence, property of the federal
government, got into private hands. Robert authorized the release to his custody of
only "material of President Kennedy...now being held by the Secret Service." This does
not say "material relating to President Kennedy," or "material of President Kennedy's
autopsy." By its terms its reference is specific: that which had been the personal
property of the late President. Obviously, the brother, as a private citizen, had no
authority to order the "release" to his "custody" of anything more, especially government property such as the autopsy pictures and x-rays. If it were Robert's intent to
authorize the release of the pictures and x-rays, then the resulting transfer would
have all the legal validity as if he had authorized release of the liberty Bell.
   It is most likely that Robert Kennedy himself did not write this letter, and any
notations indicating the real author or the typist are either absent or masked on this
copy.

April 26, 1965

Mrs. Evelyn Lincoln
National Archives
Washington, D. C.

Dear Mrs. Lincoln:

In accordance with authorization dated April 22,
1965 from Senator Robert F. Kennedy, the items on the
attached list relating to the autopsy of the late
President John F. Kennedy are herewith transferred to
the Archives for your custody, and in accordance with
the instructions contained in Senator Kennedy's letter.

Yours sincerely,

George G. Burkley
Vice Admiral, MC, USN
Physician to the President

Witnesses:

This letter by Burkley gives the game away. Robert Kennedy's "material of President
Kennedy" has been changed to "items...relating to the autopsy of" President Kennedy.
Thus, what was transferred was not what Robert authorized to be released to his custody.
It is obvious that Burkley and Kennedy, neither of whom possessed or had authority over
the pictures and x-rays, were being used. The sole purpose of this transaction was to
suppress evidence and misplace blame for it.

1. One broken casket handle

2. Envelopes numbered 1 to 18 containing black and white negatives of photographs taken at time of autopsy

3. 7 envelopes containing 4 x 5 negatives of autopsy material

4. 5 envelopes containing 4 x 5 exposed film containing no image

5. 1 roll of exposed film from a color camera entirely black with no image apparent

6. Envelope containing 8 X-ray negatives 14" x 17"; 6 X-ray negatives 10" x 12"; 12 black and white prints 11" x 14"; 17 black and white prints 14" x 17"; all negatives and prints pertaining to X-rays that were taken at the autopsy

7. 36 8" x 10" black and white prints - autopsy photos
   37 3 1/2" x 4 1/2" black and white prints - autopsy photos
   27 color positive transparencies 4" x 5"
   1 unexposed piece of color film

8. 27 4" x 5" color negatives of autopsy photographs
   55 8" x 10" color prints of autopsy photographs

9. 1 plastic box 9 x 6 1/2" x 1" containing paraffin blocks of tissue sections
   1 plastic box containing paraffin blocks of tissue sections plus 35 slides
   A third box containing 84 slides
   1 stainless steel container 7" in diameter x 8" containing gross material
   3 wooden boxes, each 7" x 3 1/2" x 1 1/4 , containing 58 slides-- blood smears taken at various times during life
   Complete autopsy protocol of President Kennedy (orig. & 7 cc's) - Original signed by Dr. Humes, pathologist
   Letter of transmittal of autopsy report (orig. & 1 cc)

   Office Memoranda from James K. Fox to SAIC Bouck Nov. 22, 1963, concerning the processing of film in the presence of Lt.(jg) V. Madonio, USN (orig. & 2 ccs)

   Orig. memo from Lt. Madonia to J. K. Fox, U. S. Secret Service, White House, Special Officer, dated Nov. 22, 1963, concerning receipt of certain films and prints and the processing thereof (Orig. & 1 cc)

This is the long-suppressed Memorandum of Transfer. See pp. 166, 288, 405.

Certificate of destruction of preliminary draft notes on protocol
of autopsy (1 cc signed by Dr. J. J. Humes)

Orig. & 1 cc and one xerox reproduction of memo from Comdr. John H.
Ebersole, M.C., U.S.N., Acting Chief of Radiology, to Roy H.
Kellerman, ASAIC, U. S. Secret Service, regarding X-ray films
dated 11-22-63.

Thermofax reproduction of memo from Francis X. O'Neill Jr., Agent
FBI, and James W. Sibert to Capt. J. H. Stover, Commanding Officer,
USN Medical School, regarding receipt of missile, dated 11-22-63.

1cc of letter dated Dec. 5, 1963 from SAIC Bouck to Capt. J. H. Stover,
Jr., MC, USN, concerning graphic film holders.

2 page memo from Captain Stover, MC, USN, Nov. 22, 1963 to Roy H.
Kellerman concerning receipt of photographic material.

George G. Burkley
George G. Burkley
Vice Admiral, MC, USN
Physician to the President

Witnesses:

Robert I Bouck
Special Agent Inspection
Edith E. Duncan

Received April 26, 1965 in Room
#09, National Archives, Washington,
DC. from Dr. Burkley and Robert
Bouck.

Evelyn Lincoln

October 29, 1966

Honorable Lawson B. Knott, Jr.
Administrator of General Services
Washington, D. C.

Dear Mr. Knott:

The family of the late President John F. Kennedy
shares the concern of the Government of the United States
that the personal effects of the late President which
were gathered as evidence by the President's Commission
on the Assassination of President Kennedy, as well as
certain other materials relating to the assassination,
should be deposited, safeguarded and preserved in the
Archives of the United States as materials of historical
importance. The family desires to prevent the undignified
or sensational use of these materials (such as public display) or any other use which would tend in any way to dis-
honor the memory of the late President or cause unnecessary
grief or suffering to the members of his family and those
closely associated with him. We know the Government respects these desires.

Accordingly, pursuant to the provisions of 44 U.S.C.
397(e)(1), the executors of the estate of the late President John F. Kennedy hereby transfer to the Administrator
of General Services, acting for and on behalf of the
United States of America, for deposit in the National
Archives of the United States, all of their right, title,
and interest in all of the personal clothing of the late
President now in the possession of the United States
Government and identified in Appendix A, and in certain
x-rays and photographs connected with the autopsy of the

late President referred to in Appendix B, and the Administrator accepts the same, for and in the name of the
United States, for deposit in the National Archives of
the United States, subject to the following restrictions,
which shall continue in effect during the lives of the
late President's widow, daughter, son, parents, brothers
and sisters, or any of them:

I

(1) None of the materials identified in Appendix A
("the Appendix A materials") shall be placed on public
display.

How the Kennedy family had any "right," "title," or legal "interest" in the autopsy
pictures and x-rays is not explained in this supposed transfer to the Archives. See
pp. 30ff.

(2)   Access to the Appendix A materials shall be permitted only to:

(a)   Any person authorized to act for a committee of the Congress, for a Presidential committee or commission, or for any other official agency of the United States Government, having authority to investigate matters relating to the death of the late President, for purposes within the investigative jurisdiction of such committee, commission or agency.

(b)   Any serious scholar or investigator of matters relating to the death of the late President, for purposes relevant to his study thereof. The Administrator shall have full authority to deny requests for access, or to impose conditions he deems appropriate on access, in order to prevent undignified or sensational reproduction of the Appendix A materials. The Administrator may seek the advice of the Attorney General or any person designated by the Attorney General with respect to the Administrator's responsibilities under this paragraph I(2)(b).

-2-

II

(1)   None of the materials referred to in Appendix B ("the Appendix B materials") shall be placed on public display.

(2)   Access to the Appendix B materials shall be permitted only to:

(a)   Any person authorized to act for a committee of the Congress, for a Presidential committee or commission, or for any other official agency of the United States Government, having authority to investigate matters relating to the death of the late President, for purposes within the investigative jurisdiction of such committee, commission or agency.

(b)   Any recognized expert in the field of pathology or related areas of science or technology, for serious purposes relevant to the investigation of matters relating to the death of the late President; provided, however, that no access to the Appendix B materials pursuant to this paragraph II(2)(b) shall be authorized until five years after the date of this agreement except with the consent of the Kennedy family representative designated pursuant to paragraph IV(2). For the purposes of this paragraph, the determination of whether such an expert has suitable qualifications and serious purposes shall be made by the Kennedy family representative. No access shall be authorized pursuant to this paragraph II(2)(b) during the lives of the individuals referred to in the second paragraph of this agreement for any purpose involving reproduction or publication of the Appendix B materials without the consent of the Kennedy family representative, who shall have full authority to deny requests for

-3-

access, or to impose conditions he deems appropriate on access, in order to prevent such use of the Appendix B materials.

III

(1) In order to preserve the Appendix A materials and the Appendix B materials against possible damage, the Administrator is authorized to photograph or otherwise reproduce any of such materials for purposes of examination in lieu of the originals by persons authorized to have access pursuant to paragraph I(2) or paragraph II(2).

(2) The Administrator may condition access under paragraph I(2)(b) or paragraph II(2)(b) to any of the materials transferred hereunder, or any reproduction thereof, upon agreement to comply with applicable restrictions specified in this agreement.

IV

(1) The Administrator shall be entitled to consult with the Kennedy family representative designated pursuant to paragraph IV(2), and to rely upon such representative's statements in writing as representing the views of the Kennedy family, in connection with the construction or application of this agreement in a particular case.

(2) The Kennedy family representative for the purposes of this agreement shall be *BURKE MARSHALL*. A successor representative of the Kennedy family may be designated in writing to the Administrator from time to time by Mrs. John F. Kennedy. In the event of the death or disability of Mrs. John F. Kennedy, any successor shall be designated by Robert F. Kennedy. In the event of the death or disability of both Mrs. John F. Kennedy and

-4-

Robert F. Kennedy, any such designation shall be made by Edward M. Kennedy. In the event of the death or disability of all three of them, any such designation shall be made by any adult child of the late President John F. Kennedy or by any of the late President's sisters, with the advice of other members of the family. Any representative designated hereunder will serve until a successor is designated.

V

This agreement may be amended, modified, or terminated only by written consent of the Administrator and the Kennedy family representative designated pursuant to paragraph IV(2).

VI

The Administrator shall impose such other restrictions on access to and inspection of the materials transferred hereunder, and take such further actions as he deems necessary and appropriate (including referral to the Department of Justice for appropriate legal action), to fulfill the objectives of this agreement and his statutory responsibility under the Federal Property and Administrative Services Act of 1949, as amended, to provide for the preservation, arrangement and use of materials transferred to his custody for archival administration.

.II

All duties, obligations and discretions herein conferred upon the Administrator shall inure to each holder of the office of Administrator of General Services from time to time, and to any official of the United States Government who may become successor to the functions of archival administration vested in the Administrator under

-5-

the Federal Property and Administrative Services Act of 1949, as amended. All such duties, obligations and discretions may be delegated to the Archivist of the United States, or to any successor to his functions of archival administration.

Please indicate your acceptance on behalf of the United States of America by executing the acceptance clause below.

Sincerely,

Burke Marshall, on behalf of the Executors of the Estate of John F. Kennedy

Accepted:

United States of America
by Lawson B. Knott, Jr.
Administrator of General Services

WRW

-6-

APPENDIX A

Clothing and personal effects of the late President, identified by the following exhibit numbers relating to the President's Commission on the Assassination of President Kennedy:

Commission Exhibit Nos. 393, 394, 395.

FBI Exhibit Nos. C26, C27, C28, C30, C33, C34, C35, C36.

APPENDIX B

1. Envelopes numbered 1 to 18 containing black and white negatives of photographs taken at time of autopsy

2. 7 envelopes containing 4 x 5 negatives of autopsy material

3. 5 envelopes containing 4 x 5 exposed film containing no image

4. 1 roll of exposed film from a color camera entirely black with no image apparent

5. Envelope containing 8 X-ray negatives 14" x 17"; 6 X-ray negatives 10" x 12"; 12 black and white prints 11" x 14"; 17 black and white prints 14" x 17"; all negatives and prints pertaining to X-rays that were taken at the autopsy

6. 36 8" x 10" black and white prints - autopsy photos
   37 3 1/2" x 4 1/2" black and white prints - autopsy photos
   27 color positive transparencies 4" x 5"
   1 unexposed piece of color film

7. 27 4" x 5" color negatives of autopsy photographs
   55 8" x 10" color prints of autopsy photographs

-7-

This is anything but an accurate or meaningful list of the autopsy pictures. From it the numbers of pictures of various sizes and kinds of film cannot be determined. There is no indication how many negatives were in an envelope. With the sad account set forth in the text, it must be assumed that this is no accident. It is consistent only with an effort to hide. The number of X-rays is given and proves that all the X-rays known to have been taken are not included. This proof of dirty tricks by the government and the representative of the executors of the estate of the murdered President seems not to have disturbed either. It should be noted that none of this was part of the President's estate, which is fixed by the moment of death. All this came into existence hours later. In addition, it was government property. It could not, legally, be given to anyone. The sole purpose of the "gift" was to get the film out of government custody, to provide an excuse for the government not to make it available for study by those cognizant of the fact of the assassination.

Report of Inspection by Naval Medical Staff
on November 1, 1966 at National Archives
of X-Rays and Photographs of Autopsy of
President John F. Kennedy

Beginning at approximately 2:00 p.m. on November 1, 1966

in Room 200-A of the National Archives Building, 8th and Pennsyl-

vania Avenue, Northwest, Washington, D. C., the undersigned

individuals jointly examined the items of photographic material

described below, which were represented to us by Dr. James B.

Rhoads, Deputy Archivist of the United States, to be the material

listed in Appendix B of a letter dated October 29, 1966 from Burke

Marshall, representing the executors of the estate of John F. Kennedy,

to the Honorable Lawson B. Knott, Jr., Administrator of General

Services. Each of us had participated on the evening of November 22,

1963 in the autopsy upon the late President Kennedy at the Naval

Medical Center, Bethesda, Maryland.

Upon inspection of this photographic material, we identi-

fied it to consist of X-ray and photographic pictures taken in the

course of the autopsy on President Kennedy, and we marked and

arranged the various items comprising such material as indicated

in the following descriptive list:

- 2 -

Part I - X-RAY MATERIALS

S" x 10" Negatives

(1)   Anterior-posterior view of the skull on 8 x 10" film, slightly

neat damaged, bearing the X-ray number 21296.

No sooner had the ink dried on the illegal contract by which the government shifted
blame for suppression onto the Kennedy family than the Archives was up to dirty tricks
with the Appendix B materials. This report, in which the participants miraculously
"identified" photographs they had never before seen, was used by the government to
propagandize what could not be true, that the autopsy doctors had "authenticated" the
pictures and x-rays. See pp. 25, 142, 147.

(2) A right lateral view of the skull on 8 x 10" film with two angle lines overdrawn on the film, the film bearing the X-ray number 21296.

(3) A lateral view of the skull on 8 x 10" film bearing the X-ray number 21296.

(4) X-ray of three fragments of bone with the larger fragment containing metallic fragments on 8 x 10" film bearing no X-ray identification number on the film.

(5) X-ray with three fragments of bone on 8 x 10" film, the larger particle containing metallic fragments *bearing no X-ray identification number on the film.*

(6) X-ray of three bone fragments on 8 x 10" film, the larger fragment showing metallic particles *bearing no X-ray identification number on the film.*

14" x 17" Negatives

(7) Anterior-posterior view of the abdomen on 14 x 17" film bearing the X-ray number 21296.

(8) Anterior-posterior view of the right shoulder and right chest on 14 x 17" film bearing the X-ray number 21296.

- 3 -

(9) Anterior-posterior film of the chest on 14 x 17" film bearing the X-ray number 21296.

(10) Anterior-posterior view of the left shoulder and left chest on 14 x 17" film bearing the X-ray number 21296.

(11) Anterior-posterior view of the abdomen and lower chest on 14 x 17" film bearing the X-ray number 21296.

(12) Anterior-posterior view of both femurs including both knee joints on 14 x 17" film bearing the X-ray number 21296.

(13) Anterior-posterior view of the pelvis. There is a small round density of myelogram media projected over the sacral canal. *bearing X-ray number 21296.*

(14) Anterior-posterior view of the lower pelvis, hips, and upper femurs. *bearing X-ray number 21296.*

Prints from X-Ray Negatives

Also identified were two prints of each of the above 8 x 10"
and 14 x 17" X-ray negatives and a third print of the X-ray numbered
8 above. During the course of our examination on November 1, 1966,
the back side of each of these prints was numbered with the numbers
assigned above in this report and each print was initialed by Captain
Ebersole with the letters "~~JEE~~ "JHE." 그 그

- 4 -

Part II - PHOTOGRAPHIC MATERIALS

4" x 5" Black and White Negatives with Prints

(1)   4 x 5" negative depicting the left side of the head and shoulders
(Two contact prints and two 8 x10" prints)

(2)   Similar view (Two contact prints and two 8 x 10" prints)

(3)   Similar view (Two contact prints and two 8 x 10" prints)

(4)   Similar view (Two contact prints and two 8 x 10" prints)

(5)   4 x 5" negative depicting the right side of the head and right
shoulder (Two contact prints and two 8 x 10" prints)

(6)   4 x 5" negative similar to number 5 (above). (Two contact
prints and two 8 x 10" prints)

(7)   4 x 5" negative depicting superior view of head (Two contact
prints and two 8 x 10" prints)

(8) 4 x 5" negative similar to number 7 (above). (Two contact
prints and two 8 x 10" prints)

(9)   4 x 5" negative similar to number 7 (Two contact and two
8 x 10" prints)

(10)   4 x 5" negative similar to number 7 (Two contact and two
8 x 10" prints)

567

(11) 4 x 5" negative showing posterior view of wound of entrance of

missile high in shoulder (Two contact and two 8 x 10" prints)

(12) 4 x 5" negative similar to number 11 (Two contact and two

8 x 10" prints)

(13) 4 x 5" negative showing anterior aspect of head and upper torso

including tracheotomy wound. Also discernible are two superficial

stab wounds on each side of the chest placed by the physicians in the

emergency room at Parkland Hospital, Dallas, Texas (Two contact

and two 8 x 10" prints)

(14) 4 x 5" negative similar to number 13 (above) except somewhat

closer view (Two contact prints and two 8 x 10" prints)

(15) 4 x 5" negative depicting wound of entrance in right posterior

occipital region (Two contact and two 8 x 10" prints)

(16) 4 x 5" negative similar to number 15 (Two contact and two

8 x 10" prints)

(17) 4 x 5" negative depicting missile wound of entrance in posterior

skull, following reflection of the scalp (Two contact and two 8 x 10"

prints)

(18) 4 x 5" negative similar to number 17 (above) with three contact

and two 8 x 10" prints

During the course of our examination on November 1, 1966,

each of the manila jackets containing the above-described negatives,

and the back of each of the above-described prints was initialed by

Dr. Boswell with the letters "JTB". Also, the backs of each of the

above-described prints were numbered in the numerical sequence of

(1) through (18) inclusive as assigned above in this report.

<u>Black and White Negatives - No Prints Available</u>

(19) 4 x 5" black and white negative, no print available, of basilar view of the brain

(20) 4 x 5" black and white negative, no print available, superior view of the brain

(21) 4 x 5" black and white negative, no print available, basilar view of the brain

(22) 4 x 5" black and white negative, no print available, direct basilar view of the brain

(23) 4 x 5" black and white negative, no print available, superior view of brain clearly depicting the extensive damage to right cerebral hemisphere

(24) 4 x 5" black and white negative, no print available, similar view to number 23 (above)

(25) 4 x 5" black and white negative, no print available, similar view to number 23 (above)

During the course of our examination on November 1, 1966, the numerical sequence (19) through (25) inclusive as assigned above in this report was placed upon the manila folders covering each of

- 7 -

these negatives and each folder was initialed by Captain Humes with the letters "JJH". Also at that time Dr. Boswell initialed each of these negatives using India ink with the letters "JTB".

<u>Color Transparencies, Color Negatives, and Color Prints</u>

(26) 4 x 5" color transparency with a 4 x 5" color negative and two 8 x 10" color prints of the right side of the head

(27) 4 x 5" color transparency with a 4 x 5" color negative and two 8 x 10" color prints, similar view as number 26 (above)

(28) 4 x 5" color transparency with a 4 x 5" color negative and two

8 x 10" color prints, similar view as number 26 (above)

(29) 4 x 5" color transparency with a 4 x 5" color negative and two

8 x 10" color prints of the left side of the head

(30) 4 x 5" color transparency with a 4 x 5" color negative and two

8 x 10" color prints similar to number 29 (above)

(31) 4 x 5" color transparency with a 4 x 5" color negative and two

8 x 10" color prints similar to number 29 (above)

(32) 4 x 5" color transparency with a 4 by 5" color negative and two

8 x 10" color prints of superior view of head .

(33), (34), (35), (36) and (37) -- 4 x 5" color transparencies with each

having a 4 x 5" color negative and two 8 x 10" color prints, all

similar view as number 32 (above)

- 8 -

(38) 4 x 5" color transparency with a 4 x 5" color negative and two

8 x 10" color prints of the missile wound high in right superior,

posterior shoulder

(39) 4 x 5" color transparency with a 4 x.5" color negative and two

8 x 10" color prints, same view as number 38 (above)

(40) 4 x 5" color transparency with a 4 x 5" color negative and two

8 x 10" color prints of the Anterior view of upper torso and head

showing tracheotomy wound

(41) 4 x 5" color transparency with a 4 x 5" color negative and two

8 x 10" color prints, similar view to number 40 (above)

(42) 4 x 5" color transparency with a 4 x 5" color negative and three

8 x 10" color prints of the missile wound in right occipital region

(43) 4 x 5" color transparency with a 4 x 5" color negative and two

8 x 10" color prints, similar to number 42 (above)

(44)   4 x 5" color transparency with a 4 x 5" color negative and two 8 x 10" color prints of the missile wound in posterior skull with scalp reflected

(45)   4 x 5" color transparency with a 4 x 5" color negative and two 8 x 10" color prints, similar view as number 44 (above)

(46)   4 x5" color transparency with a 4 x 5" color negative and two 8 x 10" color prints of the basilar view of brain

- 9 -

(47)   4 x 5" color transparency with a 4 x 5" color negative and two 8 x 10" color prints, similar view as number 46 (above)

(48)   4 x 5" color transparency with a 4 x 5" color negative and two 8 x 10" color prints, similar view as number 46 (above).

(49)   No color transparency but one color negative and two 8 x 10" color prints similar to number 46 (above)

(50)   4 x 5" color transparency with a 4 x 5" color negative and two 8 x 10" color prints of the superior view of the brain

(51)   4 x 5 color transparency with a 4 x 5" color negative and two 8 x 10" color prints similar view to number 50 (above)

(52)   4 x 5" color transparency with a 4 x 5" color negative and two 8 x 10" color prints similar view to number 50 (above)

During the course of our examination on November 1, 1966, numbers between (26) and (52) inclusive, as assigned above in this report, were placed upon manila folders each containing one color transparency and upon manila folders each containing one color negative and upon each of the above-described prints. Each of the manila folders and the back of each of the above-described prints was initialed by Dr. Boswell with the letters "JTB". There was no

571

manila folder with transparency numbered 49. The negative numbered 47 and the negative numbered 49 were both processed from the transparency numbered 47. We assume the negative (numbered 47) was taken by

- 10 -

the developer for the purpose of having a negative (of the transparency numbered 47) which did not contain the brush hair shown in the negative numbered 49 and to obtain better color intensity than is shown in negative numbered 49.

Part III - MISCELLANEOUS.

(1) Five 4 x 5" unexposed black and white film negatives, (each contained in a manila folder). We recall that these negatives were not exposed because, during the course of the autopsy referred to at the outset of this report, they were loaded into a camera as a part of a film pack but were never used to depict an image. They were unloaded without being used so that the camera could be reloaded with color film. This item is numbered as item three in Appendix B to the letter dated October 29, 1966 referred to at the beginning of this report. The reference to this item in that Appendix contains an apparent error, in that it describes these negatives as "exposed."

(2) One unexposed and not developed 4 x 5" Ektachrome film. We recall that this film was never exposed and therefore never contained an image, but was loaded into a camera as a part of a film pack and was unloaded without being used to depict an image.

(3) One unexposed but developed 4 x 5" Ektachrome transparency. We believe that this resulted from the unsuccessful efforts of the developer to portray any image contained on the film.

572

(4) One roll of 120 film (processed but showing no recognizable image) which we recall was seized by Secret Service agents from a Navy medical corpsman whose name is not known to us during the autopsy and immediately exposed to the light. This item is numbered as item 4 in Appendix B to the letter dated October 29, 1966 referred to above.

Upon completion of our examination, identification, marking, arrangement and listing of all of these photographic materials as described above, we left these materials with Dr. Rhoads. The X-rays and photographs described and listed above include all the X-rays and photographs taken by us during the autopsy, and we have no reason to believe that any other photographs or X-rays were made during the autopsy.

James J. Humes
Captain, M.C., USN
Nov. 10, 1966
date

J. Thornton Boswell, M.D.
Cdr. MC. USN (Ret.)
Nov 10, 1966
date

John H. Ebersole
Captain, M.C., USN
Nov. 10, 1966
date

John T. Stringer, Photographer
Naval Medical Center
Bethesda, Maryland
16 Nov 1966
date

The doctors are silent as to why Secret Service agents would have seized autopsy film from a Navy medical corpsman and exposed it to light, thus ruining it. This was a question striking at the heart of the integrity of the medical evidence never considered or resolved by the Warren Commission.

January 26, 1968

The Honorable Ramsey Clark
Attorney General
United States of America
Washington, D. C.

Dear Mr. Attorney General:

As you are aware, the autopsy findings in the case of the late President John F. Kennedy, including x-rays and photographs, have been the subject of continuing controversy and speculation. Dr. Humes and I, as the Pathologists concerned, have felt for some time that an impartial board of experts including pathologists and radiologists should examine the available material.

If such a board were to be nominated in an attempt to resolve many of the allegations concerning the autopsy report, it might wish to question the autopsy participants before more time elapses and memory fades; therefore, it would be my hope that such a board would be convened at an early date. Dr. Humes and I would make ourselves available at the request of such a board.

I hope that this letter will not be considered presumptuous, but this matter is of great concern to us, and I believe to the country as well.

Your attention to this matter will be greatly appreciated.

Respectfully,

J Thornton Boswell, M. D.

January 16, 1969

Statement of Burke Marshall

Since October 1966 I have acted on behalf of the Kennedy family as their representative in dealing with all matters and inquiries regarding the Letter Agreement of October 29, 1966 and the X-ray and photograph material relating to the autopsy of the late President Kennedy.

Last year, the Attorney General informed me that he had ordered the 1968 Panel Review and that it had been conducted. He described the contents of the panel's report.

I concluded that the report simply confirmed the autopsy report and saw no reason to concern members of the Kennedy family, and did not do so.

I have advised the Attorney General, in response to an inquiry from him, that I see no basis to object to the release of the report and no reason to do so.

I have since informed Mrs. Onassis and Senator Edward Kennedy of this matter and they have both asked me to say that they will have no comment to make on the report or its release.

The Justice Department released these pages in January 1969 along with its "panel" reports. Burke Marshall's semantics are a thing to behold. With counsel like this, the Kennedys need no adversaries. See pp. 137, 139.

The undersigned physicians performed the autopsy on the body of late President John F. Kennedy. In charge was James J. Humes, M.D., at that time Commander, Medical Corps, United States Navy, and Director of Laboratories, Naval Medical School. He was certified in 1955 by the American Board of Pathology in Anatomic and Clinical Pathology. Assisting him were J. Thornton Boswell, M.D., and Pierre A. Finck, M.D. Dr. Boswell at that time was a Commander in the Medical Corps, United States Navy, and Chief of Pathology, Naval Medical School. He was certified in 1957 by the American Board of Pathology in Anatomic and Clinical Pathology. Dr. Finck, a Lieutenant Colonel, Medical Corps, United States Army, was then Chief of the Military Environmental Pathology Division, and Chief of the Wound Ballistics Pathology Branch, Armed Forces Institute of Pathology, Walter Reed Medical Center. He was certified in 1956 by the American Board of Pathology in Anatomic Pathology, and in 1961 in Forensic Pathology.

The Surgeon General of the Navy advised Dr. Humes that the purpose of the autopsy was to determine the nature of the President's injuries and the cause of his death.

The autopsy began at approximately 8:00 P. M. on Friday, November 22, 1963, and was concluded approximately at 11:00 P. M. The autopsy report, written by Dr. Humes with the assistance of Dr. Boswell and Dr. Finck, was written on November 23 and the morning of November 24, and delivered by Dr. Humes to Admiral Burkley, the President's physician, on November 24 at about 6:30 P. M.

Dr. Humes was chosen to perform the autopsy because of the decision to bring the body of the late President to the Naval Medical Center in Bethesda, Maryland, where, as stated, he was Director of Laboratories.

At the direction and under the supervision of Dr. Humes, x-rays and photographs of the President's body were taken during the autopsy. The x-rays were examined that same evening. However, the photographs were not seen at that time. All x-rays and photographic plates were delivered that evening to Secret Service personnel. Dr. Humes and Dr. Boswell first saw the photographs on November 1, 1966, when requested by the Department of Justice to examine, identify, and inventory them at the National Archives. Dr. Finck first saw the photographs on January 20, 1967.

The undersigned physicians have been requested by the Department of Justice to examine the x-rays and photographs for the purpose of determining whether they are consistent

---

This undated, untitled report is the work product of the first of Ramsey Clark's panels. It abounds in brazen contradictions of the autopsy report and the circumstances of the autopsy. An extensive analysis appears in the text. See pp. 141ff.

with the autopsy report. Pursuant to this request, we met
after our regular work day, on January 20, 1967, at the office
of Dr. Robert H. Bahmer, Archivist of the United States,
where the x-rays and photographs were made available to us.
Our findings with respect thereto follow.

THE NECK WOUND

The Location

The autopsy report states that the "wound presumably of
entry" was "in the upper right posterior thorax". In non-
technical language, this wound was located low in the back
of the neck. Photographs Nos. 11, 12, 38 and 39 verify the
location of the wound, as stated in the report. Warren
Commission Exhibit 397 includes a drawing (Vol. XVII, p. 45)
which purports to show the approximate location of the wound,
and specifically states that it was 14 cm. (5-1/2 inches) from
the tip of the mastoid process (behind the right ear), and 14
cm. from the tip of the right acromion (the extreme tip of the
right shoulder bone). Photographs 11, 12, 38 and 39 confirm
the accuracy of these measurements. The drawing itself may
be somewhat misleading as to the location of the wound, making
it appear at a point lower than it actually was. No one
photograph shows both the wound at the back of the neck and
the wound in the throat, but by comparing Photographs 11, 12,
38 and 39 with the side views shown in Photographs Nos. 1-4,
inclusive, it is clear that Warren Commission Exhibits 385 and
386, which also depict the location of the neck wound, are
accurate. Photographs Nos. 26 and 38 show the wound in the
back of the neck to be higher from the horizontal plane than
the wound in the throat.

Entrance

Our finding, as stated in the autopsy report, that the
wound low in the back of the neck was an entrance wound is
supported by Photographs Nos. 11, 12, 38 and 39. They show
the edges of the wound to be inverted, regular and smooth.
At such a location and in such tissue these are the principal
characteristics of an entrance wound.

The Size of the Entrance Wound

The autopsy report states that the wound was 7 by 4 mm.
(0.275 inches by 0.157 inches); and Photographs Nos. 11, 12,
38 and 39 confirm the accuracy of this measurement.

With a new opportunity to locate the back wound in relation to a fixed orientation
point, the doctors simply repeat their original unorthodox and unreliable measurements.
They seem to retreat from Boswell's apology for "error" in the descriptive sheet by
claiming that the location of the back wound depicted on that sheet "may be somewhat
misleading." It evidently did not mislead Dr. Burkley, who verified it and independently located the wound in the same spot by means of a fixed reference point on the body.
The doctors also take the opportunity to proclaim that the drawings they had prepared
to illustrate the wounds for the Commission "are accurate." The drawings, CE's 385
and 386, are reproduced in the text at p. 309. As the documents there presented prove,
these drawings are entirely inaccurate in locating the back wound.

Exit

The autopsy report states that the "wound presumably of exit" was that described by Dr. Malcolm O. Perry of Dallas. This wound was used as the site of a tracheotomy incision, and its character thus distorted. Photographs Nos. 1-6 inclusive, 13, 14, 26-28 inclusive, 40 and 41 show the wound as being below the Adams apple.

It should be noted that the morning after the autopsy, Saturday, November 23, 1963, Dr. Humes telephoned Dr. Perry at the Parkland Hospital in Dallas. Dr. Perry was the physician who attended the President immediately after the shooting. Dr. Perry advised Dr. Humes that he had observed a missile wound below the Adams apple, and that the site of this wound had been used as the site of the tracheotomy incision. This information made it clear to us that the missile which had entered the back of the neck had exited at the site of the tracheotomy incision.

THE HEAD WOUND

Entry

The autopsy report states that a lacerated entry wound measuring 15 by 6 mm. (0.59 by 0.24 inches) is situated in the posterior scalp approximately 2.5 cm. (1 inch) laterally to the right and slightly above the external occipital protuberance (a bony protuberance at the back of the head). In non-technical language this indicates that a small wound was found in the back of the head on the right side. Photographs Nos. 15, 16, 42 and 43 show the location and size of the wound, and establish that the above autopsy data were accurate. Due to the fractures of the underlying bone and the elevation of the scalp by manual lifting (done to permit the wound to be photographed) the photographs show the wound to be slightly higher than its actually measured site.

The scalp wound shown in the photographs appears to be a laceration and tunnel, with the actual penetration of the skin obscured by the top of the tunnel. From the photographs this is not recognizable as a penetrating wound because of the slanting direction of entry. However, as we pointed out in the autopsy report, there was in the underlying bone a corresponding wound through the skull which exhibited beveling

---

Here the doctors introduce a new concept into forensic medicine. Information about the existence of a wound overlooked by the examining pathologist makes it "clear" that such a wound must be the exit point of another entrance of indeterminable penetration. The doctors avoid saying what about the front neck wound "made it clear" it was an exit wound, let alone the exit point of the back wound. This is characteristic of the unscientific and unprofessional nature of the official post mortem examination.

The pictures of the head must be truly miraculous if they show the entrance wound "slightly higher than its actually measured site," because the site was never "actually measured." The autopsy report says only that it was "slightly above" the knob of the head. With equal lack of precision, the doctors now say it was slightly higher than slightly above this point.

of the margins of the bone when viewed from the inner aspect
of the skull. This is characteristic of a wound of entry in
the skull.

Exit

The autopsy report further states that there was a large
irregular defect of the scalp and skull on the right involving
chiefly the parietal bone but extending somewhat into the
temporal and occipital regions, with an actual absence of
scalp and bone measuring approximately 13 cm. (5.12 inches)
at the greatest diameter. In non-technical language, this
means that a large section of the skull on the right side of
the head was torn away by the force of the missile. Photographs Nos. 5-10 inclusive, 17, 18, 26-28, 32-37 inclusive,
44 and 45 portray this massive head wound, and verify that the
largest diameter was approximately 13 cm. The report further
states that one of the fragments of the skull bone, received
from Dallas, shows a portion of a roughly circular wound presumably of exit which exhibits beveling of the outer aspect of
the bone, and the wound was estimated to be approximately 2.5
to 3.0 cm. (1 to 1.13 inches) in diameter. X-ray Nos. 4, 5
and 6 show this bone fragment and the embedded metal fragments.
Photographs Nos. 17, 18, 44 and 45 show the other half of the
margin of the exit wound; and also show the beveling of the
bone characteristic of a wound of exit. Photographs Nos. 44
and 45 also show that the point of exit of the missile was
much larger than the point of entrance, being 30 mm. (1.18
inches) at its greatest diameter. Photographs 5-10 inclusive,
32-37 inclusive, 44 and 45 show the location of the head wound,
and verify the accuracy of the Warren Commission drawings
(Exhibits 386 and 388, Vol. XVI, pp. 977 and 984) which depict
the location of the head wound.

NO OTHER WOUNDS

The x-ray films established that there were small metallic
fragments in the head. However, careful examination at the
autopsy, and the photographs and x-rays taken during the autopsy,
revealed no evidence of a bullet or of a major portion of a
bullet in the body of the President and revealed no evidence
of any missile wounds other than those described above.

Note the careful game with words under "NO OTHER WOUNDS." Dr. Humes' sworn testimony
is that the x-rays revealed no evidence of bullet fragments at any point in the President's body except the head. The official solution of the crime cannot stand unless
that testimony is true, for the bullet officially alleged to have wounded the neck,
399, is already impossibly burdened by the requirement that it have produced all of
Connally's wounds as well. Here the doctors say only that the x-rays reveal "no evidence of a bullet or of a major portion of a bullet in the body of the President" (as
distinguished from the head). What this peculiar language must mean, and as the
second panel later confirmed, is that there are indeed "minor portions of a bullet"
in the President's body, a negation of the official solution.

SUMMARY

The photographs and x-rays corroborate our visual observations during the autopsy and conclusively support our medical opinion as set forth in the summary of our autopsy report.

It was then and is now our opinion that the two missiles which struck the President causing the neck wound and the head wound were fired from a point behind and somewhat above the level of the deceased.

Our examination of the photographs and x-rays lasted approximately five hours, and at its conclusion the photographs and x-rays were returned to the Archivist of the United States.

_____
James J. Humes, M.D.

_____
J. Thornton Boswell, M.D.

_____
Pierre A. Finck, M.D.

Black is white, up is down, and the photographs and x-rays corroborate observations they dispute and conclusively support medical findings they conclusively destroy.

At the request of The Honorable Ramsey Clark, Attorney
General of the United States, four physicians (hereafter sometimes
referred to as The Panel) met in Washington, D. C. on February 26
and 27 to examine various photographs, X-ray films, documents and
other evidence pertaining to the death of President Kennedy, and
to evaluate their significance in relation to the medical conclusions
recorded in the Autopsy Report on the body of President Kennedy
signed by Commander J. J. Humes, Medical Corps, United States Navy,
Commander J. Thornton Boswell, Medical Corps, United States Navy and
Lieutenant Colonel Pierre A. Finck, Medical Corps, United States
Army and in the Supplemental Report signed by Commander Humes.
These appear in the Warren Commission Report at pages 538 to 545.

The four physicians constituting The Panel were:

(1) Carnes, William H., M.D., Professor of Pathology, University
of Utah, Salt Lake City, Utah, Member of Medical Examiner's
Commission, State of Utah, nominated by Dr. J. E. Wallace
Sterling, President of Stanford University.

(2) Fisher, Russell S., M.D., Professor of Forensic Pathology,
University of Maryland, and Chief Medical Examiner of the
State of Maryland, Baltimore, Maryland, nominated by
Dr. Oscar B. Hunter, Jr., President of the College of
American Pathologists.

This is the 1968 panel report released by Ramsey Clark in January 1969 to head off
Jim Garrison's efforts to have the pictures and x-rays produced in court at the trial
of Clay Shaw. See pp. 155ff. for extensive analysis.

Note the panel includes among its responsibilities to evaluate the photographic
materials in relation to the "medical conclusions" of Humes' Supplemental Report.
This the panel fails to do. The Supplemental Report is never again mentioned in this
panel report.

(3) Morgan, Russell H., M.D., Professor of Radiology, School
of Medicine, and Professor of Radiological Science, School
of Hygiene and Public Health, The Johns Hopkins University,
Baltimore, Maryland, nominated by Dr. Lincoln Gordon,
President of The Johns Hopkins University.

(4) Moritz, Alan R., M.D., Professor of Pathology, Case
Western Reserve University, Cleveland, Ohio and former
Professor of Forensic Medicine, Harvard University,
nominated by Dr. John A. Hannah, President of Michigan
State University.

Bruce Bromley, a member of the New York Bar who had been
nominated by the President of the American Bar Association and
thereafter requested by the Attorney General to act as legal counsel
to The Panel was present throughout The Panel's examination of the
exhibits and collaborated with The Panel in the preparation of this
report.

No one of the undersigned has had any previous connection with
prior investigations of, or reports on this matter, and each has
acted with complete and unbiased independence free of preconceived
views as to the correctness of the medical conclusions reached in
the 1963 Autopsy Report and Supplementary Report.

Previous Reports

The Autopsy Report stated that X-rays had been made of the
entire body of the deceased. The Panel's inventory disclosed X-ray

films of the entire body except for the lower arms, wrists and hands and the lower legs, ankles and feet.

The Autopsy Report also described the decedent's wounds as follows:

"The fatal missile entered the skull above and to the right of the external occipital protuberance. A portion of the projectile traversed the cranial cavity in a posterior-anterior direction (see lateral skull roentgenograms) depositing minute particles along its path. A portion of the projectile made its exit through the parietal bone on the right carrying with it portions of cerebrum, skull and scalp. The two wounds of the skull combined with the force of the missile produced extensive fragmentation of the skull, laceration of the superior sagittal sinus, and of the right cerebral hemisphere.

The other missile entered the right superior posterior thorax above the scapula and traversed the soft tissues of the supra-scapular and the supra-clavicular portions of the base of the right side of the neck. This missile produced contusions of the right apical parietal pleura and of the apical portion of the right upper lobe of the lung. The missile contused the strap muscles of the right side of the neck, damaged the trachea and made its exit through

---

The panel's first revelation is that the photographic record is incomplete. The missing x-rays are those of the President's extremities, ordered taken by Dr. Finck when he discovered that full body x-rays had not earlier been made. There is no accounting of what has happened to these x-rays.

the anterior surface of the neck. As far as can be
ascertained this missile struck no bony structures in
its path through the body.

In addition, it is our opinion that the wound of
the skull produced such extensive damage to the brain
as to preclude the possibility of the deceased surviving
this injury."

The medical conclusions of the Warren Commission Report (p.19)
concerning President Kennedy's wounds are as follows:

"The nature of the bullet wounds suffered by President
Kennedy * * * and the location of the car at the time
of the shots establish that the bullets were fired
from above and behind the Presidential limousine,
striking the President * * * as follows:

President Kennedy was first struck by a bullet
which entered at the back of his neck and exited
through the lower front portion of his neck, causing
a wound which would not necessarily have been lethal.
The President was struck a second time by a bullet
which entered the right rear portion of his head,
causing a massive and fatal wound."

Why the panel chose to evaluate the materials it saw in relation to these misnamed
"medical conclusions of the Warren Commission Report" is not stated. At best, this
was a meaningless exercise, since the passages quoted from page 19 of the Report say
even less than those quoted from the autopsy report and contain no specific descriptions
of the wounds which the panel could have used the photographs and x-rays to confirm or
dispute. Among the things avoided by the panel is the Commission's discussion of the
wounds at pp. 86-91 of the Report. Through this careful choice of "medical conclusions,"
the panel was able to misrepresent what its examination accomplished. That the pictures
and x-rays "support" this meaningless quoted section of the Report, as the panel concludes (p. 16), is thus meaningless in itself.

Inventory of Material Examined

Black and white and colored prints and transparencies

Head viewed from above
        #5(9JB), 8(7JB),, 13(8JB), 16(10JB), 32, 33, 34, 35, 36, 37

Head viewed from right and above to include part of face, neck, shoulder and upper chest
        #3(14JB), 4(13JB), 11(6JB), 12(5JB), 26, 27, 28, 40, 41

Head and neck viewed from left side
        #6(3JB), 15(4JB), 17(2JB), 18(1JB), 29, 30, 31

Head viewed from behind
        #7(16JB), 14(15JB), 42, 43

Cranial cavity with brain removed viewed from above and in front
        #1(18JB), 2(17JB), 44, 45

Back of body including neck
        #9(11JB), 10(12JB), 38, 39

Brain viewed from above
        #50, 51, 52

Brain viewed from below
        #46, 47, 48, 49

The black and white and color negatives corresponding to the above were present and there were also seven black and white negatives of the brain without corresponding prints. These were numbered 19 through 25(JTB) and appeared to represent the same views as #46 through 52. All of the above were listed in a memorandum of transfer, located in the National Archives, and dated April 26, 1965.

X-ray films.   (The films bore the number 21296 and an inscription indicating that they have been made at the U.S. Naval Hospital, Bethesda, Maryland on 11/22/63.)

Skull, A-P view
        #1

Skull, left lateral
        #2, 3

Skull, fragments of
        #4, 5, 6

Thoraco-lumbar region, A-P view
        #7, 11

Chest, A-P view
        #9

With all the controversy over the front neck wound, including whether traces of it were visible at the autopsy, photographs showing the front of the neck are of fundamental importance. Thus, nothing but deception and possible lies about them exist. Note the detailed inventory in the Humes-Boswell "authentication" report of 11/1/66. There, at pp. 5 and 8 are listed photographs depicting anterior views of the head and upper torso, including the tracheotomy wound (numbered 13 and 14 with initials "JB" and 40 and 41, with no initials). Yet here the panel describes these same numbered pictures as "head viewed from right and above to include part of face, neck, shoulder and upper chest." Thus, with all these inventories and all the official promises to "preserve" the record, there is no certain knowledge as to what photographs, if any, depict the anterior neck wound and with what degree of clarity.

Right hemithorax, shoulder and upper arm, A-P view
#8

Left hemithorax, shoulder and upper arm, A-P view
#10

Pelvis, A-P view
#13

Lower femurs and knees, A-P view
#12

Upper legs, A-P view
#14

Bullets

CE 399 - A whole bullet

CE 567 - Portion of nose of a bullet

CE 569 - Portion of base segment of a bullet

CE 840 - 3 fragments of lead

Motion picture films

CE 904 - Zapruder film

CE 905 - Nix film

CE 906 - Muchmore film

Series of single frames (215 through 334) from Zapruder film

Clothing

CE 393 - Suit coat

CE 394 - Shirt

CE 395 - Neck tie

Documents

The Warren Commission's Report and the accompanying volumes of
Exhibits and Hearings   (Study of these Documents was limited to
those portions deemed pertinent by The Panel.)

Examination of photographs of head

Photographs 7, 14, 42 and 43 show the back of the head, the contours of which have been grossly distorted by extensive fragmentation of the underlying calvarium. There is an elliptical penetrating wound of the scalp situated near the midline and high above the hairline. The position of this wound corresponds to the hole in the skull seen in the lateral X-ray film #2. (See description of X-ray films.) The long axis of this wound corresponds to the long axis of the skull. The wound was judged to be approximately six millimeters wide and fifteen millimeters long. The margin of this wound shows an ill-defined zone of abrasion.

Photographs 5, 8, 13, 16, 32, 33, 34, 35, 36 and 37 show the top of the head with multiple gaping irregularly stellate lacerations of the scalp over the right parietal, temporal and frontal regions.

Photographs 1, 2, 44 and 45 show the frontal region of the skull and a portion of the internal aspect of the back of the skull. Due to lack of contrast of the structures portrayed and lack of clarity of detail in these photographs the only conclusion reached by The Panel from study of this series was that there was no exiting bullet defect in the supra-orbital region of the skull.

Photographs 46, 47, 48 and 49 are of the inferior aspect of the brain and show extensive deformation with laceration and fragmentation of the right cerebral hemisphere. Irregularly shaped areas of contusion with minor loss of cortex are seen on the inferior surface of the first left temporal convolution. The orbital gyri on the left show contusion with some underlying loss of cortex. The sylvian fissure on the right side has been opened revealing a rolled-up mass of arachnoid and blood clot which is dark brown to black in color. The mid-temporal region is depressed and its surface lacerated. The peduncles have been lacerated, probably incident to the removal of the contents from the

Note the panel's detailed description of the entrance wound in the head as depicted in the photographs. The panel claims to have discerned a "penetrating wound" with marginal abrasion, capable of measurement. Yet when the autopsy doctors saw the identical pictures, they said a flap of skin obscured the penetration. They are explicit that the panel could not have seen what it claimed to see: "From the photographs this is not recognizable as a penetrating wound." See p. 3 of the autopsy doctors' untitled report.

cranium.

Photographs 50, 51 and 52 show the superior aspect of the brain. The left cerebral hemisphere is covered by a generally intact arachnoid with evidence of subarachnoid hemorrhage especially over the parietal and frontal gyri and in the sulci. The right cerebral hemisphere is extensively lacerated. It is transected by a broad canal running generally in a postero-anterior direction and to the right of the midline. Much of the roof of this canal is missing as are most of the overlying frontal and parietal gyri. In the central portion of its base there can been seen a gray brown rectangular structure measuring approximately 13 x 20 mm. Its identity cannot be established by The Panel. In addition to the superficial and deep cortical destruction, it can be seen that the corpus callosum is widely torn in the midline.

These findings indicate that the back of the head was struck by a single bullet travelling at high velocity, the major portion of which passed forward through the right cerebral hemisphere, and which produced an explosive type of fragmentation of the skull and laceration of the scalp. The appearance of the entrance wound in the scalp is consistent with its having been produced by a bullet similar to that of exhibit CE 399. The photographs do not disclose where this bullet emerged from the head although those showing the interior of the cranium with the brain removed indicate that it did not emerge from the supra-orbital region. Additional information regarding the course of the bullet is presented in the discussion of the X-ray films.

Examination of photographs of anterior and posterior views of thorax, and anterior, posterior and lateral views of neck (Photographs 3, 4, 6, 9, 10, 11, 12, 15, 17, 18, 26, 27, 28, 29, 30, 31, 38, 39, 40, 41)

There is an elliptical penetrating wound of the skin of the back

located approximately 15 cm. medial to the right acromial process,
5 cm. lateral to the mid-dorsal line and 14 cm. below the right
mastoid process. This wound lies approximately 5.5 cm. below a
transverse fold in the skin of the neck. This fold can also be
seen in a lateral view of the neck which shows an anterior
tracheotomy wound. This view makes it possible to compare the
levels of these two wounds in relation to that of the horizontal
plane of the body.

A well defined zone of discoloration of the edge of the back
wound, most pronounced on its upper and outer margins, identifies
it as having the characteristics of the entrance wound of a bullet.
The wound with its marginal abrasion measures approximately 7 mm.
in width by 10 mm. in length. The dimensions of this cutaneous
wound are consistent with those of a wound produced by a bullet
similar to that which constitutes exhibit CE 399.

At the site of and above the tracheotomy incision in the
front of the neck, there can be identified the upper half of the
circumference of a circular cutaneous wound the appearance of
which is characteristic of that of the exit wound of a bullet.
The lower half of this circular wound is obscured by the surgically
produced tracheotomy incision which transects it. The center of
the circular wound is situated approximately 9 cm. below the
transverse fold in the skin of the neck described in a preceding
paragraph. This indicates that the bullet which produced the two
wounds followed a course downward and to the left in its passage
through the body.

Examination of X-ray films

The films submitted included: an antero-posterior film of

With the chance to clear up perhaps the most nagging question, the location of the
back wound, the panel simply uses the same meaningless reference points from which to
make its measurements. It even introduces a new element of ambiguity by selecting a
physical feature unique to the President and perhaps visible only when the body was
in a certain position——"a transverse fold in the skin of the neck." No medical text
could possibly locate this non-anatomical structure, so there is no way to know what
the panel is describing.

the skull (#1), two left lateral views of the skull taken in
slightly different projections (#2 and 3), three views of a group
of three separate bony fragments from the skull (#4, 5 and 6),
two antero-posterior views of the thoraco-lumbar region of the
trunk (#7 and 11), one antero-posterior view of the right hemithorax,
shoulder and upper arm (#8), one antero-posterior view of the chest
(#9), one antero-posterior view of the left hemithorax, shoulder
and upper arm (#10), one antero-posterior view of the lower femurs
and knees (#12), one antero-posterior view of the pelvis (#13) and
one antero-posterior view of the upper legs (#14).

Skull: There are multiple fractures of the bones of the
calvarium bilaterally. These fractures extend into the base of
the skull and involve the floor of the anterior fossa on the right
side as well as the middle fossa in the midline. With respect to
the right fronto-parietal region of the skull, the traumatic damage
is particularly severe with extensive fragmentation of the bony
structures from the midline of the frontal bone anteriorly to the
vicinity of the posterior margin of the parietal bone behind.
Above, the fragmentation extends approximately 25 mm. across the
midline to involve adjacent portions of the left parietal bone;
below, the changes extend into the right temporal bone. Throughout
this region, many of the bony pieces have been displaced outward;
several pieces are missing.

Distributed through the right cerebral hemisphere are numerous
small, irregular metallic fragments, most of which are less than
1 mm. in maximum dimension. The majority of these fragments lie

---

If the panel is right in its observations in the third paragraph on the previous page,
the autopsy doctors lied in saying the front neck wound was not visible to them. The
panel explicitly states that the upper half of a wound seeming to be a bullet wound
was identifiable on the upper margin of the tracheotomy incision. Why this is "characteristic" of an exit wound the panel does not and surely could not say. But the
Commission never needed the pictures to know that part of the neck wound was visible
after the tracheotomy. Dr. Akin of Parkland hospital observed it and reported it to
Arlen Specter (6H65).

anteriorly and superiorly. None can be visualized on the left side of the brain and none below a horizontal plane through the floor of the anterior fossa of the skull.

On one of the lateral films of the skull (#2), a hole measuring approximately 8 mm. in diameter on the outer surface of the skull and as much as 20 mm. on the internal surface can be seen in profile approximately 100 mm. above the external occipital protuberance. The bone of the lower edge of the hole is depressed. Also there is, embedded in the outer table of the skull close to the lower edge of the hole, a large metallic fragment which on the antero-posterior film (#1) lies 25 mm. to the right of the midline. This fragment as seen in the latter film is round and measures 6.5 mm. in diameter. Immediately adjacent to the hole on the internal surface of the skull, there is localized elevation of the soft tissues. Small fragments of bone lie within portions of these tissues and within the hole itself. These changes are consistent with an entrance wound of the skull produced by a bullet similar to that of exhibit CE 399.

The metallic fragments visualized within the right cerebral hemisphere fall into two groups. One group consists of relatively large fragments, more or less randomly distributed. The second group consists of finely divided fragments, distributed in a postero-anterior direction in a region 45 mm. long and 8 mm. wide. As seen on lateral film #2 this formation overlies the position of the coronal suture; its long axis if extended posteriorly passes through the above-mentioned hole. It appears to end anteriorly immediately below the badly fragmented frontal and parietal bones just anterior to the region of the coronal suture.

Here we learn that the entrance wound in the head, never measured by the autopsy doctors who preferred to locate it merely as "slightly above" the occipital protuberance, was actually 100 mm. above that point. No silly millimeter here. That is 4 inches higher than the autopsy doctors made out, putting the wound high on the back of the President's head instead of near the hairline as the doctors swore to and depicted on drawings. This is how the panel "supported" the autopsy report.

The foregoing observations indicate that the decedent's head was struck from behind by a single projectile. It entered the occipital region 25 mm. to the right of the midline and 100 mm. above the external occipital protuberance. The projectile fragmented on entering the skull, one major section leaving a trail of fine metallic debris as it passed forward and laterally to explosively fracture the right frontal and parietal bones as it emerged from the head.

In addition to the foregoing, it is noteworthy that there is no evidence of projectile fragments in the left cerebral tissues or in the right cerebral hemisphere below a horizontal plane passing through the floor of the anterior fossa of the skull. Also, although the fractures of the calvarium extend to the left of the midline and into the anterior and middle fossae of the skull, no bony defect such as one created by a projectile either entering or leaving the head is seen in the calvarium to the left of the midline or in the base of the skull. Hence, it is not reasonable to postulate that a projectile passed through the head in a direction other than that described above.

Of further note, when the X-ray films of the skull were presented to The Panel, film #1 had been damaged in two small regions by what appears to be the heat from a spot light. Also, on film #2, a pair of converging pencil lines had been drawn on the film. Neither of these artifacts interfered with the interpretation of the films.

The panel's *non sequitur* could not be more apparent. It argues that one bullet must have wounded the head from the rear because no evidence of bullet damage on the left side of the head could be discerned. This ignores several obvious alternatives, such as a frangible bullet striking the right front of the head and exploding upon impact.

Note also the report of heat damage in two places on x-ray film #1. This damage was also mentioned by Humes and Boswell in their 11/1/66 report. Yet nowhere is there a description of precisely *what* region of the x-ray was burned. There is currently no way of knowing whether this damage might have hidden or been intended to hide evidence.

Neck Region: Films #8, 9 and 10 allowed visualization of the lower neck. Subcutaneous emphysema is present just to the right of the cervical spine immediately above the apex of the right lung. Also several small metallic fragments are present in this region. There is no evidence of fracture of either scapula or of the clavicles, or of the ribs or of any of the cervical and thoracic vertebrae.

The foregoing observations indicate that the pathway of the projectile involving the neck was confined to a region to the right of the spine and superior to a plane passing through the upper margin of the right scapula, the apex of the right lung and the right clavicle. Any other pathway would have almost certainly fractured one or more bones of the right shoulder girdle and thorax.

Other Regions Studied: No bullets or fragments of bullets are demonstrated in X-rayed portions of the body other than those described above. On film #13, a small round opaque structure, a little more than 1 mm. in diameter, is visible just to the right of the midline at the level of the first sacral segment of the spine. Its smooth characteristics are not similar to those of the projectile fragments seen in the X-rays of the skull and neck.

Examination of the Clothing

Suit Coat (CE 393) A ragged oval hole about 15 mm. long (vertically) is located 5 cm. to the right of the midline in the back of the coat at a point about 12 cm. below the upper edge of the coat collar. A smaller ragged hole which is located near the midline and about 4 cm. below the upper edge of the collar does not overlie any corresponding damage to the shirt or skin and appears to be unrelated to the wounds or their causation.

In describing the all too few x-rays of the "neck region" the panel demolishes the Warren Report and the integrity of the autopsy doctors' testimony. Humes had sworn there were no metallic fragments in the neck visible on the x-rays (2H361). 399 is clearly unfragmented, yet it had to have caused the neck wounds for the Commission's case to survive. Thus, the panel's statement that "several small metallic fragments are present" in the neck region, although lacking the detail and precision that might be expected from such eminences, is sufficient to prove that the Report and the autopsy findings on which it was based are irreversibly wrong.

<u>Shirt</u> (CE 394) A ragged hole about 10 mm. long vertically and corresponding to the first one described in the coat, is located 2.5 cm. to the right of the midline in the back of the shirt at a point 14 cm. below the upper edge of the collar. Two linear holes 15 mm. long are found in the overlapping hems of the front of the shirt in a position corresponding to the place where the knot of the neck tie would normally be.

<u>Tie</u> (CE 395) In the front component of the knot of the tie in the outer layer of fabric a ragged tear about 5 mm. in maximum diameter is located 2.5 cm. below the upper edge of the knot and to the left of the midline.

Discussion

The information disclosed by the joint examination of the foregoing exhibits by the members of The Panel supports the following conclusions:

The decedent was wounded by two bullets both of which entered his body from behind.

One bullet struck the back of the decedent's head well above the external occipital protuberance. Based upon the observation that he was leaning forward with his head turned obliquely to the left when this bullet struck, the photographs and X-rays indicate that it came from a site above and slightly to his right. This bullet fragmented after entering the cranium, one major piece of it passing forward and laterally to produce an explosive fracture of the right side of the skull as it emerged from the head.

The panel does not explain what a "linear hole" is. The damage to the front of the shirt cannot accurately be described as "holes." Two <u>slits</u> were found on the shirt at this point, and, as the photograph of them (reproduced at p.598) clearly reveals, they were of significantly varying lengths, the one on the button-hole side being considerably longer than the other. Thus, it is highly doubtful that the panel could have accurately measured both slits as being the same length, 15 mm.

The absence of metallic fragments in the left cerebral hemisphere or below the level of the frontal fossa on the right side together with the absence of any holes in the skull to the left of the midline or in its base and the absence of any penetrating injury of the left hemisphere eliminate with reasonable certainty the possibility of a projectile having passed through the head in any direction other than from back to front as described in preceding sections of this report.

The other bullet struck the decedent's back at the right side of the base of the neck between the shoulder and spine and emerged from the front of his neck near the midline. The possibility that this bullet might have followed a pathway other than one passing through the site of the tracheotomy wound was considered. No evidence for this was found. There is a track between the two cutaneous wounds as indicated by subcutaneous emphysema and small metallic fragments on the X-rays and the contusion of the apex of the right lung and laceration of the trachea described in the Autopsy Report. In addition any path other than one between the two cutaneous wounds would almost surely have been intercepted by bone and the X-ray films show no bony damage in the thorax or neck.

The possibility that the path of the bullet through the neck might have been more satisfactorily explored by the insertion of a finger or probe was considered. Obviously the cutaneous wound in the back was too small to permit the insertion of a finger. The

---

Note in the second paragraph that the panel's source of the information that the lung was bruised and the trachea lacerated was the autopsy report; this damage was not illustrated by any photographs the panel saw. The panel's inventory of photographs, as well as the inventory prepared by Humes and Boswell, lists no photographs of this internal damage. But this damage was photographed at the autopsy. In his testimony before the Commission, Humes described his examination of the chest cavity and the bruise atop the right lung, concluding: "Once again Kodachrome photographs were made of this area in the interior of the President's chest" (2H363). With the bullet path not dissected and nothing but doubt surrounding it, these are among the most vital of the autopsy pictures. Officially, they no longer exist, with no explanation for their destruction or disappearance. They may have been destroyed when Secret Service agents deliberately exposed a roll of film after the autopsy, but this is only speculation. Such is the state of the record of the murdered President's post mortem.

insertion of a metal probe would have carried the risk of creating a false passage in part, because of the changed relationship of muscles at the time of autopsy and in part because of the existence of post-mortem rigidity. Although the precise path of the bullet could undoubtedly have been demonstrated by complete dissection of the soft tissue between the two cutaneous wounds, there is no reason to believe that the information disclosed thereby would alter significantly the conclusions expressed in this report.

Summary

Examination of the clothing and of the photographs and X-rays taken at autopsy reveal that President Kennedy was struck by two bullets fired from above and behind him, one of which traversed the base of the neck on the right side without striking bone and the other of which entered the skull from behind and exploded its right side.

The photographs and X-rays discussed herein support the above-quoted portions of the original Autopsy Report and the above-quoted medical conclusions of the Warren Commission Report.

William H. Carnes, M.D.   Apr. 9, 1968
Date

Russell S. Fisher, M.D.   Mar. 28, 1968
Date

Russell H. Morgan, M.D.   Mar. 28, 1968
Date

Alan R. Moritz, M.D.   April 6, 1968
Date

Here the panel recognizes the need for dissection of the supposed path through the neck. Without dissection, there can be no certain knowledge about the bullet's path. The panel blandly assures "there is no reason to believe" dissection would have "significantly" altered the autopsy conclusions. Yet, how can there be anything but doubt when the relevant photographs are missing, when the necessary dissection was ordered not to be done by military authorities, when the Report misrepresents all the evidence about how the doctors guessed the bullet's path?

As with all the doubts it raises, the panel is worse than silent. It openly deceives. It could not possibly have done what its summary alleges, "support" the quoted conclusions of the autopsy report.

RUSSELL S. FISHER, M.D.
CHIEF MEDICAL EXAMINER
WERNER U. SPITZ, M.D.
DEPUTY CHIEF MEDICAL EXAMINER
CHARLES S. SPRINGATE, M.D.
ASSISTANT MEDICAL EXAMINER
RONALD N. KORNBLUM, M.D.
ASSISTANT MEDICAL EXAMINER
HENRY C. FREIMUTH, PH.D.
TOXICOLOGIST
PAUL SCHWEDA, PH.D.
ASSISTANT TOXICOLOGIST
JOHN T. MILLER, PH.D.
IMMUNOCHEMIST

THE MARYLAND POST MORTEM
EXAMINERS COMMISSION

WILLIAM J. PEEPLES, M.D., CHAIRMAN
ROBERT E. FARBER, M.D.
ROBERT H. HEPTINSTALL, M.D.
ROBERT J. LALLY
ROBERT B. SCHULTZ, M.D.

STATE OF MARYLAND
DEPARTMENT OF POST MORTEM EXAMINERS
OFFICE OF THE CHIEF MEDICAL EXAMINER
111 PENN STREET
BALTIMORE, MARYLAND 21201

March 4, 1970

Mr. Harold Weisberg
Coq d'Or Press
Route 8
Frederick, Maryland 21701

Dear Mr. Weisberg:

Once and for all, I have no working papers, drafts, etc. concerning the Panel
review of the Kennedy autopsy report in my possession. The Panel met in
Washington on February 26 and 27, 1968 and drafted its report on
February 27, 1968. I pulled this together in the next few days and submitted
copies to each member of the Panel, who edited them and returned them to me.
I correlated the edited reports and once again submitted them to the Panel
for final editing. Again the copies were returned to me and final copies
typed and submitted sequentially to each member of the Panel for his
signature. When all signatures were obtained I personally delivered the
original and five signed copies to Mr. Bruce Bromley and he subsequently
sent one copy to Drs. Carnes, Morgan, Moritz and myself and the original
was submitted to the Justice Department. I have not seen it since, but
am informed the copy released by the Justice Department was a photocopy of
our report without changes of any kind from our submitted copy.

In line with the agreement mentioned in the last paragraph of my letter of
February 19, 1970, Mr. Bromley and I, or I, independently, destroyed all
intermediate copies of the report.

With respect to the suit brought by New Orleans District Attorney
Jim Garrison, I submit that no members of the Panel either appeared in
Court in connection with this suit or submitted anything in writing.
If our original Panel report was submitted by the Justice Department I
suggest you correspond with them regarding that.

Finally, please be informed that this is the last correspondence of yours
that I intend to answer in regard to this matter.

Very truly yours,

Russell S. Fisher, M.D.
Chief Medical Examiner

RSF/vkh
cc: William Carnes, M.D.
    Russell H. Morgan, M.D.
    Alan R. Moritz, M.D.
    Mr. Bruce Bromley
    Mr. H. Richards Rolapps

The "agreement" to which Fisher refers was between all the panel members "not to maintain individual private files" of their examination because "it was felt that establishment of independent records...not in the custody of the Archivist might be judged
to violate" the contract by which the Kennedys "transferred" the autopsy materials to
the government. If this were the issue, destruction of all records was not the answer.
The records should have been turned over to the Archivist for preservation. With this
President's murder, destruction of evidence is the norm. See p. 221.

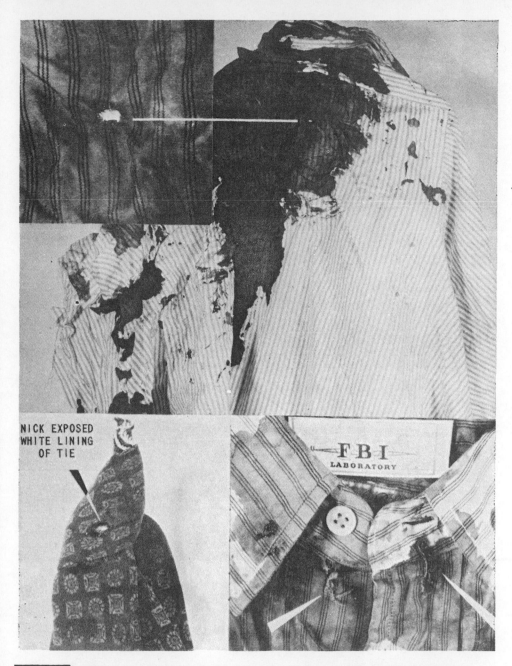

NICK EXPOSED
WHITE LINING
OF TIE

FBI
LABORATORY

This is FBI Exhibit 60, which the Commission did not dare print because it contains evidence destructive of its conclusions and its and the FBI's integrity. It is described in Chapter 30, beginning on p.328. The enlargement of the bullet hole in the back of the shirt was printed by the FBI upside down. The actual hole coincides exactly with the real location of this wound, which was lied about. The FBI even twisted the tie to make it appear that there was a hole in the center. Actually, this small nick was made with a scalpel and was on the very edge of the knot. It was enlarged with removal of a sample for scientific testing. The tests were suppressed because they proved no bullet hit the tie or shirt front. This combination of suppressed pictures alone proves that the President was not hit in the back of the neck but in the back and that the bullet hole in the front of his neck was above the shirt. Either is total disproof of the entire "solution."

This is an actual FBI print, not from the Warren Commission's files, obtained as described in Chapter 30, especially beginning on p.328. It has this caption typed on the back: "Photograph depicting portion of Exhibit 60." It is less clear as part of FBI Exhibit 60 (p.597) but in even that form shows much more than any picture the Commission dared print. In itself this picture, presented here for the first time anywhere, destroys the entire Warren Report and means the falsity could not have been accidental. It shows not bullet holes but slits. It also shows that when the shirt is buttoned they do not coincide and on this added basis could not have been made by a bullet. Note that the slit on the button side is entirely _below_ the neckband while that on the buttonhole side extends well up onto it. The FBI and the Commission both knew their representations were false. The Commission blundered into the truth separately when Dulles asked Dr. Carrico where the President's front neck wound was and Carrico told him it was _above_ the shirt. Carrico confirmed this to me when he also confirmed the obvious, that this damage to the shirt was done when the necktie was cut off by nurses under his supervision during emergency treatment.

Under date of December 5, 1963, the FBI Laboratory advised Honorable JAMES J. ROWLEY, Chief, United States Secret Service, Department of the Treasury, Washington, D. C. 20220, as follows concerning an examination requested by communication of November 23, 1963:

Specimen:

Evidence personally delivered by Special Agent Orwin Bartlett on November 23, 1963

Q19   Pair of black moccasin shoes
Q20   Pair of black socks
Q21 -- Q22   Trousers and coat
Q23   Belt
Q24   Necktie
Q25   Shirt
Q26   Handkerchief
Q27   Comb
Q28   Bandages and belt
Q29   White shorts

Results of examination:

Examination of the President's clothing revealed the presence of a small hole in the back of the coat and shirt. The hole in the back of the coat is positioned approximately 5 3/8" below the top of the collar and 1 3/4" to the right of the middle seam. The hole in the shirt back is located in the same relative area, being 5 3/4" below the top of the collar and 1 1/8" to the right of the middle. These holes are typical of bullet entrance holes.

The evidence bullets submitted in this case are clad with copper metal. Spectrographic examination of the fabric surrounding the holes in the back of the coat and shirt revealed minute traces of copper.

2
JL 100-10461

A ragged slitlike hole approximately 1/2" in length is located in the front of the shirt 7/8" below the collar button. This hole is through both the button and buttonhole portions of the shirt due to the overlap. This hole has the characteristics of an exit hole for a projectile. No bullet metal was found in the fabric surrounding the hole in the front of the shirt.

A small elongated nick was located in the left side of the knot of the tie, Q24, which may have been caused by the projectile after it had passed through the front of the shirt.

X-ray and other examinations of the clothing revealed no additional evidence of value.

The FBI report is from CD 205, pp. 153-4. It is more propaganda than science. It does not even report that the relevant bullets are jacketed with copper alloy, and fails to reveal how the composition of the "copper" on the coat and shirt compared with that of 399. Likewise, the shirt slits are not characteristic of a "projectile" exit but might be consistent with one, assuming the "projectile" were moving extremely slow. See p. 351.

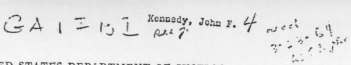

'FICE OF THE DIRECTOR

UNITED STATES DEPARTMENT OF JUSTICE
FEDERAL BUREAU OF INVESTIGATION

WASHINGTON 25, D.C.

March 23, 1964

By Courier Service

Honorable J. Lee Rankin
General Counsel
The President's Commission
200 Maryland Avenue, Northeast
Washington, D. C.

Dear Mr. Rankin:

Reference is made to your letter dated March 18, 1964, concerning the reasons for the opinion that holes in the clothing of President Kennedy were either "entrance holes" or "exit holes."

The hole in the back of the coat and the hole in the back of the shirt were in general, circular in shape and the ends of the torn threads around the holes were bent inward. These characteristics are typical of bullet entrance holes.

The hole in the front of the shirt was a ragged slitlike hole and the ends of the torn threads around the hole were bent outward. These characteristics are typical of an exit hole for a projectile.

A small elongated nick was present in the left side of the knot of the tie. This nick may have been caused by the projectile after it passed through the front of the shirt. No additional observations relative to the nick could be made due to the characteristics of the nick.

Sincerely yours,

J. Edgar Hoover

Hoover was hung-up on the clothes. The last thing he wanted was any additional inquiry which might blow the case for a lone assassin. That is why on March 18 he wrote the Commission disapproving NAA's on the shirt slits (Gallagher Ex. 1). See pp.318,446f. That same day Rankin persisted, seeking more detail on how the FBI had determined that the shirt slits were "exit holes." Hoover's response was a stonewall; he said little more than what he had already given the Commission, reproduced on the previous page. The slits were found to be exit "holes," he wrote, because the fibers "were bent outwards." When FBI Agent Frazier testified two months later, he contradicted Hoover. Frazier's testimony was cautious. The outward bend of the fibers was indicative of exit only "assuming that when I first examined the shirt it was---it had not been altered from the condition it was in at the time the hole was made" (5H61). This remains

600

UNITED STATES DEPARTMENT OF JUSTICE

FEDERAL BUREAU OF INVESTIGATION

WASHINGTON, D.C. 20535

November 26, 1969

Mr. Howard Roffman
8329 Blue Grass Road
Philadelphia, Pennsylvania 19115

Dear Mr. Roffman:

Reference is made to your letter dated
November 14, 1969, concerning the shape, size
and fiber characteristics of the slit in the
button line near the collar of President
Kennedy's shirt and the possible presence of
residues on this shirt in the area of this
slit.

Each of the above was considered in
the FBI Laboratory's examinations of President
Kennedy's shirt. These examinations, I assure
you, were thorough and inclusive and the
results are set out in the detail warranted
by the nature and physical condition and
composition of the shirt in the testimony of
Special Agent Robert A. Frazier in Volume V,
pages sixty through sixty-two, of the Hearings
before the President's Commission on the
Assassination of President Kennedy. In view
of this, it is the opinion of this Bureau
that further examinations would serve no useful
purpose; and, therefore, I regret that I am
unable to comply with your request.

Sincerely yours,

John Edgar Hoover
Director

an unproven assumption at best. The Commission, knowing how tenuous the determination
of "exit" was, had an obligation to employ NAA for a more certain answer. Instead,
the Report misquotes Frazier to make it seem he swore that the slits were the exit
point of the bullet which entered the back. The slits, Frazier swore, were "not specifically characteristic of a bullet-hole to the extent that you could say it was to the,
exclusion of being a piece of bone or some other type of projectile" (5H61). The
Report admits that the slits could not be proven to be a "bullet hole," but then falsely states: "The clothing worn by President Kennedy...had holes and tears which showed
that a missile entered the back...in the vicinity of his lower neck and exited through
the front of his shirt immediately behind his tie, nicking the knot of his tie in its
forward flight." (R91).

When Howard Roffman contacted the Archives in 1969 about having further, more
detailed examinations of the shirt slits made, he was referred to the FBI. Hoover's
response seems to say that any attempt to perfect the evidence beyond the miserable
state the Commission left it in would not serve a "useful purpose." To Hoover, Frazier's
testimony that he couldn't say what caused the shirt slits and couldn't even vouch that
the fibers had not been tampered with was all the "detail warranted" about this vital
evidence. This was an unintended but apt characterization of the fabled thoroughness
of the FBI's investigation.

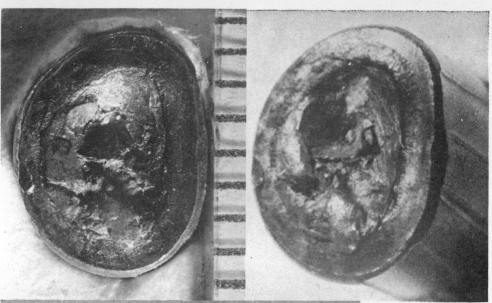

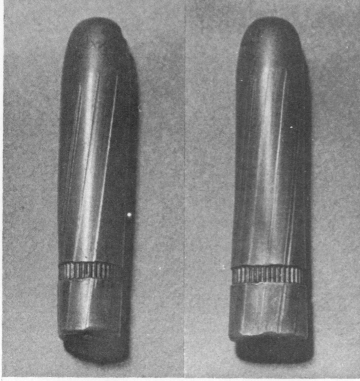

These are not
Commission or
FBI pictures.
They were taken
for this work.
They show that
all the metal
missing from
Bullet 399 was
removed by the
FBI (p.226),
which did not
tell the incur-
ious Commission
and joined it
in a deliberate
deception and
misrepresenta--
tion indispen-
sable to the
faked "solution."
The upper pic-
tures of the
base and the
left-hand one of the side clearly show the cutting off for testing of all the metal missing from this otherwise unscathed bullet. This is but one of the reasons the tests were suppressed
and I had to sue for them. They and these pictures destroy the
Report and Commission and FBI integrity.

Under date of November 23, 196   the FBI Laboratory,
fur   ed the following information to   . Jesse E. Curry, Chief
of   e, Dallas, Texas, Chief, U.S.   ret Service, and FBI,
D   , Texas:

"   :

"Evidence received from Special Agent Elmer L. Todd, Washington Field
   Office of the FBI on 11/22/63:

"Q1 Bullet from stretcher

"Evidence received from Special Agent Orin Bartlett of the FBI on
   11/22/63:

"Q2 Bullet fragment from front seat cushion
"Q3 Bullet fragment from beside front seat

"Evidence received from Special Agent James W. Sibert and Special Agent
   Francis O'Neill, Jr., of the Baltimore Office of the FBI on 11/23/63:

"Q4 Metal fragment from the President's head
"Q5 Metal fragment from the President's head

"Evidence received from Special Agent Vincent E. Drain of the Dallas
   Office of the FBI on 11/23/63:

"Q6 6.5 millimeter Mannlicher-Carcano cartridge case from building
"Q7 6.5 millimeter Mannlicher-Carcano cartridge case from building
"Q8 6.5 millimeter Mannlicher-Carcano cartridge from rifle
"Q9 Metal fragment from arm of Governor John Connolly
"Q10 Wrapping paper in shape of a large bag
"Q11 Suspect's shirt
"Q12 Blanket
"Q13 Bullet from Officer Tippit

"K1 6.5 millimeter Mannlicher-Carcano rifle, with telescope sight,
        No. C2766
"K2 Paper and tape sample from shipping department, Texas Public
        School Book Depository
"K3 .38 Special Smith and Wesson revolver, Serial No. V510210,
        Assembly No. 65248

"Evidence obtained by FBI Laboratory personnel during examination of
        the President's limousine:

"Q14 Three metal fragments recovered from rear floor board carpet
"Q15 Scraping from inside surface of windshield

"Also submitted: Photograph of rifle, K1
                  Finger and palm prints of Lee Harvey Oswald

"Results of examinations:

        "The bullet, Q1, is a 6.5 millimeter Mannlicher-Carcano rifle
bullet. Specimen Q1 weighs 158.6 grains. It consists of a copper
alloy jacket with a lead core.

_The original of this retyped report to Chief Curry was published by the Commission at
24H262. The FBI now pretends this represents the complete results of the spectrographic
analyses. See pp. 15, 516.

"Specimen Q2 is a portion of the core of a rifle bullet. Specimen Q2 weighs 44.6 grains and is composed of a portion of the copper alloy jacket and a portion of the lead core. Specimen Q3 is a portion of the base section of a copper alloy rifle bullet. Q3 weighs 21.0 grains and is composed of a section of the jacket from which the lead core is missing. It could not be determined whether specimens Q2 and Q3 are portions of the same bullet or are portions of two separate bullets.

"The rifle, K1, is a 6.5 millimeter Mannlicher-Carcano Italian military rifle Model 91/38. Test bullets were fired from this rifle for comparison with specimens Q1, Q2, and Q3. As a result, Q1, Q2, and Q3 were identified as having been fired from the submitted rifle.

"Specimens Q6 and Q7 are 6.5 millimeter Mannlicher-Carcano cartridge cases. They were manufactured by the Western Cartridge Company, East Alton, Illinois, as was the 6.5 millimeter Mannlicher-Carcano cartridge, Q8.

"Test cartridge cases obtained from the submitted rifle were compared with specimens Q6 and Q7. As a result, specimens Q6 and Q7 were identified as having been fired in this rifle. The bullet, Q13, from Officer Tippitt, is a .38 Special copper-coated lead bullet. Q13 weighs 156.6 grains and possesses the physical characteristics of 158 grain Western-Winchester revolver bullets. The surface of Q13 is so badly mutilated that there are not sufficient individual microscopic characteristics present for identification purposes. It

163

3
DL 89-43

"was determined, however, that the .38 Special Smith and Wesson revolver, K3, is among those weapons which produce general rifling impressions of the type found on Q13.

"The lead metal of Q4 and Q5, Q9, Q14 and Q15 is similar to the lead of the core of the bullet fragment, Q2.

The fabled scientific precision of the FBI cannot survive this ballistics report to Curry. As regards the spectrographic examinations, it says virtually nothing and fails to make the essential comparisons. The essence of the value of spectrographic analysis (a less sensative test than NAA, but still capable of detecting amounts of elements in parts per million) is to isolate all the minute quantities of trace elements in substances and develop precise statistical data about them to enable comparison with other substances for determination of common origin. With this potential, all we learn from this report is that the jacket metal was "copper alloy," the lead "lead." No bullet is composed of pure lead; rather some form of lead alloy is used. Yet this report identifies neither the alloy nor the elements and their quantities making up the alloy. Even though it identifies the copper as "alloy," it is silent on what elements are mixed with this copper to form the alloy. Thus, all information about trace elements, the nitty gritty of spectrographic analysis, is missing from this report.

Even with the meaningless data reported, some vital comparisons are not represented. No metal is compared with 399, although the lead fragments, Q9, are required to have come from the lead core of 399 for the official solution to be valid.

UNITED STATES DEPARTMENT OF JUSTICE
FEDERAL BUREAU OF INVESTIGATION

WASHINGTON 25, D.C.

April 16, 1964

By Courier Service

Honorable J. Lee Rankin
General Counsel
The President's Commission
200 Maryland Avenue, Northeast
Washington, D. C.

Dear Mr. Rankin:

Reference is made to your letter dated April 9, 1964, covering transmittal to the FBI Laboratory of Governor John Connally's coat, shirt, trousers and tie and requesting an examination of these items. The results of the examinations are set forth below.

For your information the coat has been designated C311 the trousers C312, the shirt C313 and the tie C314.

Nothing was found to indicate which holes were entrances and which were exits. The coat, shirt and trousers were cleaned prior to their receipt in the Laboratory, which might account for the fact that no foreign deposits of metal or other substances were found on the cloth surrounding the holes. Further, no characteristic position of the fibers of the cloth around the holes, which is one of the factors considered in determining whether a hole is an entrance or an exit hole, was found. The sizes of the holes in the clothing do not necessarily aid in this determination since a hole can be enlarged if a bullet strikes at an angle, sideways or partially sideways, or if it passes through a fold in the cloth. Also, if a bullet is irregularly mutilated, an entrance hole could be larger than an exit hole.

It was not possible from an examination of the clothing to determine whether or not all of the holes were made by the same projectile or projectile fragments.

Sincerely yours,

J. Edgar Hoover

Enclosures (14) - to Eisenberg

- 2 -

CR 827

With the Commission making such a priority of finding out why Oswald killed the President before finding out if he did, there was no time to make sure the evidence of Connally's bullet-penetrated clothes was preserved. The Commission did not arrange for examination of these items until more than four months after the murder, by which time their evidential value had been destroyed. Even then, there were no NAA's attempted to discovered if some metal traces remained after "cleaning." See pp. 124-6.

MEMORANDUM   GREEN   February 21, 1964

Copy

TO: J. Lee Rankin

FROM: Norman Redlich

SUBJECT: Assignments of Messrs. Redlich and Eisenberg

The areas in which Mr. Eisenberg is working are as follows:

1. Cataloging the evidence in the FBI's possession and the exhibits introduced into evidence in connection with the Marina Oswald deposition. (This involves obtaining translations, identification of photographs and books, and making up descriptive lists and cross-indexes.)

2. Working with me on the problem of studying assassination films to locate car position when bullets hit President Kennedy and Governor Connally.

- 2 -

3. Developing expert knowledge in certain areas of criminal investigation with a view toward assisting Messrs. Ball and Belin in the evaluation of the evidence concerning the assassination and related events. These areas, in the following order of priority, are: weapon identification; ballistics; paraffin tests; fingerprint and palm print evidence; handwriting identifications.

4. Mr. Eisenberg also considers it his responsibility to review the major underlying materials.

Two legal questions which you sent to us, dealing with the Commission's subpoena powers and the effect of an oath administered by the staff, have been assigned to Mr. Mosk.

P.S.

The difficulty of assigning priorities to our areas of work is best evidenced by the fact that since this memo was written I have been assigned the job of preparing the questions for James Martin which has assumed top priority over everything else.

In context, this outline of Eisenberg's work for the Commission is a revelation of how badly the Commission wanted to know nothing relevant to the assassination. Eisenberg was supposed to be "developing expert knowledge in certain areas of criminal investigation," including ballistics and paraffin tests---which were second and third in his list of priorities. Eisenberg treated these as such pressing priorities that seven months later, just before the Report went to press, he was getting around to suggesting that the FBI be asked what neutron activation analysis was and what it revealed about the paraffin casts taken of Oswald's hands and right cheek. His September 5 memo is reproduced at p. 447. The Commission never put a thing into its files about NAA's on the ballistics evidence, and also kept the spectrographic report out as well. But we should have sympathy, as Redlich begs in his P. S. It is so difficult to investigate the murder when James Martin, Marina's commercial representative, got "top priority over everything else."

UNITED STATES DEPARTMENT OF JUSTICE

FEDERAL BUREAU OF INVESTIGATION

Honorable J. Lee Rankin
General Counsel
The President's Commission
200 Maryland Avenue, Northeast
Washington, D. C.

WASHINGTON 25, D.C.

July 8, 1964

By Courier Service

Dear Mr. Rankin:

As previously reported to the Commission, certain small lead metal fragments uncovered in connection with this matter were analyzed spectrographically to determine whether they could be associated with one or more of the lead bullet fragments and no significant differences were found within the sensitivity of the spectrographic method.

Because of the higher sensitivity of the neutron activation analysis, certain of the small lead fragments were then subjected to neutron activation analyses and comparisons with the larger bullet fragments. The items analyzed included the following: C1 - bullet from stretcher; C2 - fragment from front seat cushion; C4 and C5 - metal fragments from President Kennedy's head; C9 - metal fragment from the arm of Governor Connally; C16 - metal fragments from rear floor board carpet of the car.

While minor variations in composition were found by this method, these were not considered sufficient to permit positively differentiating among the larger bullet fragments and thus positively determining from which of the larger bullet fragments any given small lead fragment may have come.

Sincerely yours,

J. Edgar Hoover

The Commission kept out of the Report and the evidence any indication that NAA's had been performed on anything other than the paraffin casts. This letter, buried in the Commission's files, represents the full record the Commission had relating to NAA's on any of the ballistics evidence. A more total abdication of the Commission's responsibility is hard to imagine. By January 1964 the AEC had informed the Commission that the increased sensitivity of NAA could be of great significance to the investigation. On January 27, Rankin told the Commission that the bullets and fragments were then with the AEC, that the "new process" had the potential of resolving some of the basic questions about the crime, and that the results were forthcoming (see p. 445). Now the government claims NAA's on 399 and the fragments were not run until May 15, 1964. Even if that is true, as it most likely could not be, it was not until July 8 that Hoover got around to giving the Commmission these sketchy, deceiving and imcomplete "results" of the NAA's. Had the Commission been conducting a real investigation, it would have been knocking down the AEC's doors to have those tests done fully and competently at the soonest possible point. Yet this belated letter from Hoover was unaccompanied by any documentation, does not include all the tests known to have been done (such as on Q15), omits any comparison of the various copper samples, fails to specify exactly which comparisons were made, and gives no indication who had decided the differences in composition were "minor" and why. It does not even include a single statistic. With this the Commission was entirely satisfied, asking no further questions, demanding no additional tests. See Chapter 29.

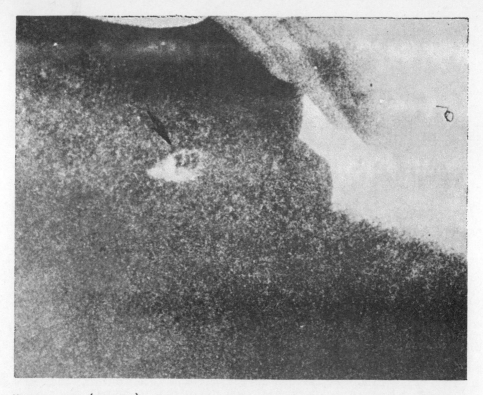

Underwood (above), Dillard curbstone pictures, FBI versions.

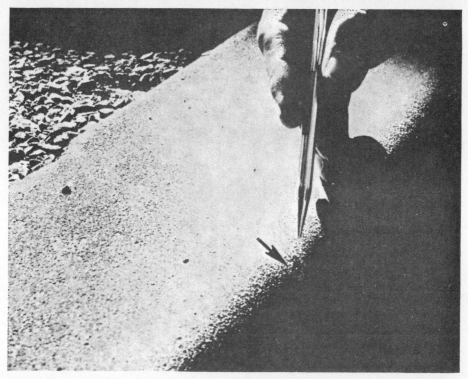

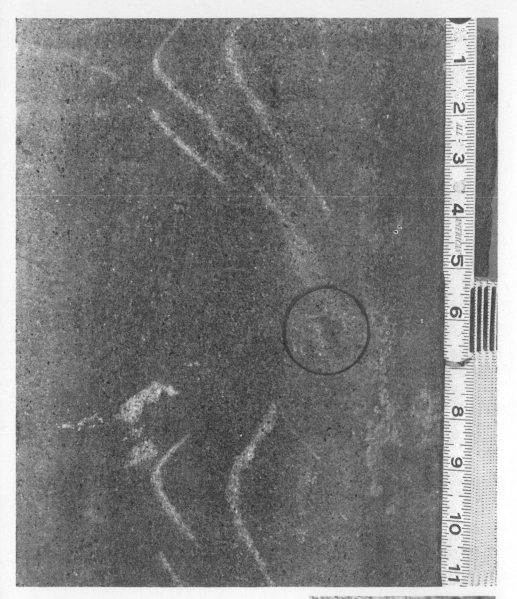

Curbstone as it exists in Archives
showing no bullet impact mark and
different, smoother texture at that
point. Compare with deliberately
poor FBI print of comtemporaneous
pictures, opposite. See text, especially beginning p.453. Smaller
picture is enlargement of "smear"
duplicating angle of Dillard's
picture, Shaneyfelt Exhibit 29-2.

UNITED STATES DISTRICT COURT
FOR THE DISTRICT OF COLUMBIA

HAROLD WEISBERG,

    Plaintiff,

  v.

UNITED STATES DEPARTMENT OF
 JUSTICE, and

U. S. ENERGY RESEARCH AND DEVEL-
 OPMENT ADMINISTRATION,

    Defendants

:   Civil Action No. 75-0226

FILED
JUN 5 1975

JAMES F. DAVEY
CLERK

AFFIDAVIT OF HAROLD WEISBERG

  I, Harold Weisberg, being first duly sworn, depose as
follows:

  1. I am an author. I live at Route 8, Frederick, Maryland.

  2. For the past eleven years I have devoted myself to an intensive study of political assassinations. I am author of five
published books on the investigation into President Kennedy's
assassination: Whitewash: The Report on the Warren Report;
Whitewash II: The FBI-Secret Service Coverup; Photographic Whitewash: Suppressed Kennedy Assassination Pictures; Whitewash IV:
Top Secret JFK Assassination Transcript; and Oswald in New Orleans:
Case For Conspiracy with the CIA. I have also written one book on
the assassination of Dr. Martin Luther King: Frame-Up: The
Martin Luther King-James Earl Ray Case.

  3. In the 1930's I was an investigator for and editor of the
record of a subcommittee of the Senate Labor Committee. After

---

This is one of several affidavits I filed in my suit for the results of the spectrographic and NAA testing, described in detail in Part IV.

Pearl Harbor I served in the OSS, where my primary responsibilities were as an intelligence analyst. I have also worked with the FBI and several divisions of the Department of Justice in connection with my work for the Senate Labor Committee or through my writing.

4. I have filed five Freedom of Information lawsuits and made numerous requests for information on the assassinations of President Kennedy and Dr. Martin Luther King. In each lawsuit which I have filed the government has responded with various degrees of dishonesty and deception, including perjury. I have been told repeatedly by government agencies that the records I sought did not exist and could not be disclosed where, in the end, they did exist, could be disclosed, and were given to me.

5. The most recent example of this is the transcript of the executive session of the Warren Commission held on January 22, 1964, where even the records say the transcript was destroyed. However, after I requested it under the new Freedom of Information Act, that transcript was given to me. [See Attachment A]

6. The first Freedom of Information Act suit I filed, Weisberg v. U.S. Department of Justice and U.S. Department of State, is a good example of the way in which dishonesty permeates the government's responses to my information requests. In that suit I sought the records used in the Bow Street Magistrate's Court in London, England to obtain the extradition of James Earl Ray. I had requested copies of these public court records from the Department of Justice after I learned that the official British copies had been confiscated by the United States from the Chief Magistrate's clerk and the Home Office. Deputy Attorney General Richard Kleindienst replied that the Department of Justice did not

have these records, and even if it did, they would be withheld as "investigatory files compiled for a law enforcement purpose."

7. Even after the State Department wrote that it had in fact retrieved these records, for all the world as though the Department of Justice did not have its own copies, and said specifically that they had been give to Kleindienst and we so wrote him, Kleindienst still maintained the same position.

8. Only have I could be stalled no longer and the case had been filed did Attorney General Mitchell suddenly, months late, pretend to rule on the appeal he had ignored, stating that I would be given the records I sought. I was allowed to inspect a list of the documents I wanted. I got some but not all. There then ensued a series of written assurances that what I had seen did not exist. After I returned to court, the Department of Justice suddenly found other than I had asked for, even other files than I had been shown. When the Department of Justice did not deliver all the documents I had requested by the time Chief Judge Curran had directed, I was awarded summary judgment.

9. One of the documents I requested was a copy of the file cover showing that this file, which contained only public court records, had been improperly classified, with a notation referring to the letter which I had received from the Department of State. After repeated written assurances of its nonexistence, I was finally sent a fabricated copy of the file cover. The file cover had been xeroxed and then cut up to omit what the Department of Justice wanted to suppress.

10. When Chief Judge Curran chided the government attorney, David Anderson, for noncompliance and gave the Department of Justice seven days to complete delivery of the requested materials,

Mr. Anderson filed an affidavit in which he falsely swore that he had given me what he had not. I asked for a photograph attached to affidavits submitted in evidence at the extradition proceedings which stated that this photograph of the scene of the crime represented what witnesses saw at the time the crime was committed. When this photograph was finally delivered to me--after I won summary judgment--it turned out that it was a staged photograph not taken at the time of the crime. Contrary to what these affidavits asserted, this was not a photograph of the evidence as found and the fact that the evidence was handled, rearranged and physically moved was also hidden. My own investigation, which located the actual, unstaged photographs, proved this.

11. In Weisberg v. General Services Administration, Civil Action No. 2569-70, the deception and misrepresentation was even more extensive, perhaps because I was pro se. In that suit I asked for pictures of certain of the Warren Commission evidence. I was told they could not be given to me under the terms of a contract which actually provided that photographs would be taken to avoid handling the objects themselves. When the case went to court, however, the government offered to take these pictures for me, and that was done. Before that, however, the Department of Justice produced an affidavit from the Archives in which he swore that I had not made the request, a prerequisite for my bringing suit. Yet the actual request had been put into the record by both sides and the rejection of it was put there by the government!

12. In Weisberg v. General Services Administration, Civil Action No. 2052-73, I sought disclosure of the transcript of the executive session of the Warren Commission held on January 27,

1964. The national Archives claimed that the January 27 transcript was exempt from disclosure because it was classified Top Secret pursuant to Executive Order 10501 and was part of an investigatory file compiled for law enforcement purposes. The Archives made no attempt to substantiate its claim to the investigatory files exemption and its answers to interrogatories admitted that the transcript had not been seen by any law enforcement official until at least three years after the Warren Commission went out of existence.

13. The Archives did attempt to substantiate its claim that the transcript was classified according to Executive Order by filing two affidavits, one by the Archivist, the other by the Warren Commission's General Counsel, Mr. J. Lee Rankin. Rankin's affidavit claimed that the Warren Commission had ordered him to classify the January 27 transcript pursuant to Executive Order 10501. I filed a counter-affidavit stating that this was false and attached documentary evidence proving it. Accordingly, Judge Gerhart Gesell ruled that the government had failed to show that the transcript had ever been properly classified. After Judge Gesell made his ruling the Archives "declassified" the transcript and, ignoring the transcript's exempt status as an "investigatory file", made it public. Once public an examination of its content showed that there never was any basis for its alleged classification.

14. The government's bad faith in these suits also pervades the history of my nine-year struggle to gain access to the spectrographic analyses. I initially requested the spectrographic analyses in a letter to FBI Director J. Edgar Hoover dated May 23, 1966. When there was no response, I filed suit for these documents on August 3, 1970. My request in that suit--Weisberg v. Department of Justice, Civil Action No. 2301-70--was for the final typed re-

ports of the spectrographic testing. At no time during the next four years of expensive and time-consuming litigation was I told that such final reports did not exist. That is, however, what the FBI now claims.

15. I have read the affidavit of FBI Special Agent John W. Kilty submitted by the Department of Justice in support of its claim that it has fully complied with my request for the reports of certain scientific tests conducted on items of evidence pertaining to the shooting of President Kennedy. I state catagorically that this is not a good faith affidavit and that the FBI has not complied with my request.

16. On February 19, 1975, I filed this suit for the spectrographic and neutron activation analyses and any other scientific tests performed on items of evidence relating to the shooting of President Kennedy. Six days later, in a response which ignored the filing of this suit but referred to a letter written by my attorney on January 15, 1975, Attorney General Edward H. Levi stated:

> Under these circumstances, Director Kelley felt constrained to defer final disposition of Mr. Weisberg's request, though the Bureau has proceeded with the task of identifying the requested materials. Some, which are clearly responsive, are contained in the National Archives and will be made available. [Emphasis added. For the full text of Mr. Levi's February 25 letter, see Attachment B]

17. In point of fact, this has not happened. The FBI has subsequently taken the position that it will not provide me with copies of any of these documents in its possession if the National Archives also has copies of them. Since I initially requested these documents from the FBI and Attorney General Levi promised to

provide them, I view the FBI's refusal to do so as evidence of a lack of good faith.

18. Because the FBI has refused to provide me with copies of documents which it says the Archives has, I have had to ask the Archives for copies. Although the Archives has stated to my attorney that all such reports in its possession are publicly available and I requested them nearly a month ago, the Archives did not provide them until after the May 21 hearing on this cause. [See Attachments F, G, and H]

19. After implying in his February 25th letter that the FBI does not have the final reports which were the subject of my 1970 suit for the spectrographic analyses, the Attorney General stated:

> There is . . . a great bulk of material which does not reasonably come within Mr. Weisberg's specification of "final reports". The Bureau is willing to discuss with Mr. Weisberg the nature of these materials to ascertain whether he is interested in having access to them.

20. By letter dated March 6, 1975, my attorney advised the Attorney General that I was willing to meet with the FBI to discuss the implementation of my requests but would prefer that both sides be allowed to tape record the conference. [See Attachment C] However, the FBI vetoed my suggestion that this conference be tape recorded.

21. Contrary to the assertion in paragraph three of the Kilty affidavit, the purpose of the March 14 conference was not to determine the scope of my request but rather to see if the FBI was going to implement it. At that conference, the FBI claimed there was a "semantical difference" between its interpretation of "final reports" and mine. The FBI claimed it had made no final reports comparing all the chemical components of each and every one of the various items of evidence tested and stating conclusions as to which ones could or could not have been of common origin.

22. Two weeks after I filed my 1970 suit for the spectrographic analses, FBI Agent Marion Williams executed an affidavit which stated that he had reviewed this file and that the disclosure of "raw data" contained in it would seriously interfere with the functioning of the FBI and in general "do irreparable damage". However, at the March 14 conference the FBI freely offered to give me this "raw data".

23. Contrary to what Agent Kilty asserts, I did not request the items which he specifies in the fourth paragraph of his affidavit. Rather the FBI offered to provide me with copies of unidentified batches of "raw data" which, however, the FBI would not permit me to examine. In order to save time and copying costs, I proposed that I examine all the spectrographic and neutron activation materials and select which documents I wanted copied. This suggestion was rejected out-of-hand by the FBI, which stated it would select the materials I was to be given.

24. I then asked for the FBI's estimate of how many pages of "raw data" they were offering me. To aboid squabbling over whether I had the right to select what I wanted copied, I asked for everything they had except: 1) the spectrographic plates, 2) nitrate tests, and 3) materials related to the slaying of Police Officer J. D. Tippit. The FBI gave me the Tippit materials anyway and charged me for them.

25. Paragraph four of the Kilty affidavit lists specific materials which Agent Kilty says I requested at the March 14 conference. This gives the false impression that I eliminated from my original request the neutron activation analyses and other scientific testing. I did not. I specifically asked the cost of the NAA materials and specifically ordered them. I have never

waived my claim to the neutron activation analysis (NAA) of the clothing of President Kennedy and Governor Connally as is sug- gested by the wording of paragraph 4-b.

26. Paragraph five of the Kilty affidavit refers to the ma- terials listed by Agent Kilty in paragraph four and then states: "All available data relating to the above consists of 22 pages also furnished Mr. Lesar by SA Bresson on March 31, 1975." Unless there has been destruction of evidence, this is false. For example, one of the documents given me is a partially masked copy of a letter from J. Edgar Hoover to Warren Commission General Counsel J. Lee Rankin. Attached to that letter is a laboratory work sheet which reports that "small foreign metal smears" on a piece of curbing "were run spectrographically (Jarrell-Ash)". I have not been given this spectrographic testing. Nor have I been given the microscopic study referred to at the bottom of page two of this same Hoover letter. Similarly, another document provided me refers to a lab report apparently dated "12/5/63". I have not been given that report either.

27. Nor has the FBI provided me with all the materials re- lating to the neutron activation analyses which were made. All of the NAA documents which I have been given bear a date of May 15. However, in his January 10, 1964, letter to Mr. Rankin, FBI Direc- tor J. Edgar Hoover stated:

> The FBI Laboratory is well acquainted
> with the analytical technique of neutron
> activation analysis. Through arrangements
> worked out with Dr. Glenn T. Seaborg,
> Chairman of the Atomic Energy Commission,
> work is already in progess applying this
> technique to certain phases of the current
> investigation. [Emphasis added. See
> Attachment D]

From this it is evident that NAA testing was performed long before the May 15 date on the documents which the FBI has given me. This is further corroborated by the reference to these tests made by Warren Commission General Counsel J. Lee Rankin at the Commission's January 27, 1964, executive session:

> Now, the bullet fragments are now, part of them are now, with the Atomic Energy Commission, who are trying to determine by a new method, a process that they have, of whether they can relate them to various guns and the different parts, the fragments, whether they are a part of one of the bullets that was broken and came out in part through the neck, and just what particular assembly of bullet they were part of.
>
> They have had it for the better part of two and a-half weeks and we ought to get an answer. [See Exhibit F to the Complaint]

28. In addition, I also have reason to believe that other NAA testing should have been done after May 15th. Yet I have not been given any NAA testing done after that date.

29. FBI Director Kelley's April 10, 1975, letter to Mr. Lesar, a copy of which is attached to the Kilty affidavit, states that the FBI has responded fully to my request for the spectrographic and NAA testing. Director Kelley's letter also lists the NAA-tested items on which I have been given "irradiation data and calculations". This list does not include NAA tests performed on the clothing of President Kennedy or Governor Connally. Yet Special Agent Kilty's affidavit states in its seventh paragraph that: "Neutron activation analysis and emmission spectroscopy were used to determine the elemental composition of the borders and edges of holes in clothing . . ." Because I have not been given any NAA testing of any clothing, Mr. Kilty's affidavit is false and deceptive. It also contradicts Mr. Kilty's and Director Kelley's assertions that the FBI has fully complied with my request for the NAA testing. I believe this court should address itself to the question of perjury.

30. Paragraph eight of the Kilty affidavit states: "The FBI files <u>to the best of my knowledge</u> do not include any information requested by Mr. Weisberg other than the information made available to him." [Emphasis added] Not only is this false swearing (see paragraph 29), but Mr. Kilty's affidavit does not establish that he is competent to make this determination in this and other respects. He does not state that he knows what these tests are or that he has personal knowledge of all the tests which were conducted. He does not even attest that he knows of and has searched all relevant FBI files. The fact is that the documents already given me refer to other documents and files obviously included within my request and to Mr. Kilty's knowledge not yet given to me. This is not the first time that the FBI, the Department of Justice and the United States Attorney have resorted to the shameful device of having the wrong man swear falsely in the hope of avoiding perjury and its subornation and with the clear intent of frustrating the law and the will of Congress.

31. Special Agent Robert Frazier does have personal knowledge of the tests which were performed. He testified before the Warren Commission in regard to the spectrographic analyses. He is still an active agent with the FBI Laboratory and was present at the March 14 conference. He is an official who could execute a proper affidavit. The use of the wrong agent to execute this affidavit is a bad faith ploy to avoid an affidavit by anyone with personal knowledge of the materials relevant to my request.

32. It is instructive here to recall the letter which the AEC's Associate General Counsel, Mr. Bertram Schur, wrote to my counsel last October 16. In that letter Mr. Schur flatly stated: "No other tests such as you described were performed by AEC or at

any AEC facility." Mr. Schur's statement was based not on personal knowledge but in reliance upon information "from the former
FBI agent who participated in the work described." After my lawyer provided Mr. Schur with proof that this was not true, he re-
tracted his statement. [See Attachment E]

33. The FBI deceived, stonewalled, and withheld information
from the Warren Commission. For example, FBI field reports were
re-written at Headquarters so as to state the opposite of what the
original field reports said, and the Warren Report relied upon and
reprinted the incorrect Headquarters' version.

34. At the Commission's January 22nd executive session,
General Counsel J. Lee Rankin noted the FBI's suspicious and
atypical behavior:

> A: I thought first you should know
> about it. Secondly, there is this factor
> too that a [blank space in transcript]
> consideration, that is somewhat an issue in
> this case, and I suppose you are all aware
> of it. That is that the FBI is very explicit
> that Oswald is the assassin or was the assas-
> sin, and they are very explicit that there
> was no conspiracy, and they are also saying
> in the same place that they are continuing
> their investigation. Now in my experience of
> almost nine years, in the first place it is
> hard to get them to say when you think you
> have got a case tight enough to convict some-
> body, that that is the person who committed
> the crime. In my experience with the FBI
> they don't do that. They claim that they
> don't evaluate, and it is my uniform prior
> experience that they don't do that. Second-
> ly, they have not run out all kinds of leads
> in Mexico or in Russia and so forth which
> they could probably--It is not our business,
> it is the very--
>
> Dulles: What is that?
>
> A: They haven't run out all the leads on
> the information and they could probably say--
> that isn't our business.
>
> Q: Yes.

13

A: But they are concluding that there
can't be a conspiracy without those being
run out. Now that is not [blank space in
transcript] from my experience with the FBI.

Q: It is not. You are quite right. I
have seen a great many reports. [See
Attachment A for full text of the January
22, 1964 transcript]

35. In the context of the foregoing affidavit which
addresses the court's statement that it takes the government's
word in good faith, I believe it appropriate respectfully to call
this court's attention to the agreed-to statement of former CIA
Director and Warren Commission member Allen Dulles: "I think this
record ought to be destroyed." [See Attachment A] At the January
27, 1964 executive session, Dulles stated that FBI Director J.
Edgar Hoover would lie about Lee Harvey Oswald's having had any
connection with the FBI. Mr. Dulles, expecting perpetual secrecy,
assured his fellow Warren Commission members at that same executive session that government officials do and should swear falsely
and that as Director of the CIA he personally might not tell the
Secretary of Defense certain matters. I also call attention to
Attorney General Levi's recent revelation that the FBI withheld
the existence of five "cointelpro" programs from five Attorney
Generals.

36. The FBI has not complied with my request for all of the
spectrographic and neutron activation analyses or other scientific
testing of the specified evidence. The pretense that it has is
made in bad faith and raises questions of misrepresentation, perjury and its subornation. For this, those responsible must be
called to account.

HAROLD WEISBERG

HAROLD WEISBERG,

        Plaintiff

                                Civil Action No. 75-226

        v.

UNITED STATES DEPARTMENT OF JUSTICE, et al.,

        Defendants

AFFIDAVIT

I, John W. Kilty, being duly sworn, depose as follows:

1. I am a Special Agent of the Federal Bureau of Investigation (FBI) assigned to the Laboratory Division of the FBI, Washington, D. C., in a supervisory capacity. This affidavit supplements my previous affidavit of May 13, 1975.

2. I have personal knowledge concerning the contents of Paragraphs 26-29, inclusive, of plaintiff's affidavit dated June 2, 1975, wherein plaintiff alleges numerous documents falling within his Freedom of Information Act (FOIA) request have not been furnished him.

3. Concerning plaintiff's allegation that he has not been given the "spectrographic testing" of "small foreign metal smears on a piece of curbing": the Laboratory work sheet which was previously furnished plaintiff and from which he quotes _is_ the notes and results of this test. A thorough search has uncovered no other material concerning the spectrographic testing of the metal smear on the curbing.

4. Concerning plaintiff's allegation that he has not been given the "microscopic study" referred to at the bottom of page two of an August 12, 1964, letter from J. Edgar Hoover to J. Lee Rankin, which letter has also been furnished plaintiff: a thorough search has uncovered no additional documents concerning a study of this type.

5. Concerning plaintiff's allegation that he has not been furnished "a Laboratory report apparently dated December 5, 1963": inasmuch as plaintiff has indicated he did not wish to receive our reports which are already available to the public, but rather the data compiled as input to these reports, this report

This is Kilty's second affidavit, which contradicts his first in the most material ways, as explained in Part IV. The notarization, removed to conserve space, was affixed 6/23/75.

was not furnished to him. This material is available to the public as Commission Document No. 205, pages 153-154.

6. Concerning plaintiff's allegation that, although the date of all the neutron activation analysis (NAA) documents furnished him is May 15, 1964, there is an indication that this technique was already being utilized as early as January 10, 1964: the earlier NAA, the quote from Mr. Rankin in Paragraph 27 of plaintiff's affidavit to the contrary notwithstanding, was conducted upon paraffin casts taken of Lee Harvey Oswald's hands and cheek. Plaintiff requested NAA material concerning metal fragments only. No neutron activation analysis of the metal fragments was made prior to May 15, 1964.

7. Concerning plaintiff's allegation that there may have been NAA testing subsequent to May 15, 1964: to prevent any further misunderstanding concerning NAA technique, it should be noted that the date written on the NAA documents furnished plaintiff refers to the date irradiation of the metal fragments was conducted. The compilation of other data appearing on these documents would have of necessity occurred after the date of irradiation.

8. Concerning plaintiff's allegation that, although NAA testing was conducted on the clothing of President Kennedy and Governor Connally, he has not been furnished the results of this testing: further examination reveals emission spectroscopy only was used to determine the elemental composition of the borders and edges of holes in clothing and metallic smears present on a windshield and a curbstone. NAA was used in examination of certain metal fragments, and plaintiff has already been furnished material relating to these examinations. NAA was not used in examining the clothing, windshield, or curbing.

9. FBI files, to the best of my knowledge, do not include any other information requested by plaintiff in addition to that previously furnished him.

John W. Kilty
Special Agent
Federal Bureau of Investigatic
Washington, D. C.

624

UNITED STATES DEPARTMENT OF JUSTICE

FEDERAL BUREAU OF INVESTIGATION

Honorable J. Lee Rankin
General Counsel
The President's Commission
200 Maryland Avenue, Northeast
Washington, D. C. 20002

WASHINGTON 25, D.C.

March 10, 1964

By Courier Service

Dear Mr. Rankin:

Reference is made to my letter dated January 10, 1964, advising that arrangements were made with the Atomic Energy Commission to process by nuclear analytical techniques items relating to the assassination of President Kennedy.

The paraffin casts from Lee Harvey Oswald were examined by neutron activation analyses at the Oak Ridge National Laboratories, Research Reactor Site, Oak Ridge, Tennessee.

These analyses were made to determine if the paraffin casts from Oswald which were made, chemically treated and washed by the Dallas law enforcement authorities, bear any primer deposits from the rifle cartridge cases found in the Texas School Book Depository Building following the President's assassination.

As a result of these examinations; the deposits found on the paraffin casts from the hands and cheek of Oswald could not be specifically associated with the rifle cartridges. Elements (barium and antimony) were found on the casts; however, these same elements were found in residues both from the above rifle cartridge cases and from the revolver cartridge cases which were fired from Oswald's revolver reportedly between the time of the assassination and the time of apprehension.

No characteristic elements were found by neutron activation analyses which could be used to distinguish the rifle from the revolver cartridges.

In view of the fact that the paraffin casts were not made until after the reported firing and handling of the revolver, no significance could be attached to the residues found on the casts other than the conclusion that barium and antimony in these residues are present in amounts greater than would be expected to be found on the hands of an individual who has not recently fired a weapon or handled a fired weapon.

Sincerely yours,

Commission Exhibit No. 2455

J. Edgar Hoover

See p. 446.

Subsequent developments, ranging from increased commercialization and self-promotion to a renewed campaign to blame the assassinated Robert Kennedy for CIA acts leading to the assassination of JFK, impel identification of these men. Crosby told me he was on the board of the African American Institute with Nicholas Katzenbach who, as Deputy Attorney General, represented the Department of Justice to the Warren Commission. It is Katzenbach who told the Commission at one of its first "Top Secret" executive sessions that Hoover was boxing it in with leaks to the press.

With or without Katzenbach's help, Crosby lobbied and pressured Burke Marshall to allow examination of the autopsy materials by prejudiced and incompetent "experts" whose blaming the Kennedy survivors for suppressions was inevitable. He also boasted to me of lobbying with a member of Senator Edward M. Kennedy's staff.

LBJ appointed Katzenbach to head an investigation of the CIA that was one of history's biggest coverups, as 1975's exposures proved. Checking this odd situation showed the African American Institute was a CIA front and had been for years. Among others with greater or lesser CIA connections and part of the JFK assassination story are Commissioner McCloy; federal judge Sarah T. Hughes, who swore in LBJ; and Leon Jaworski, who saw to it for the Warren Commission that the Texas Court of Inquiry he ran did nothing. (See WHITE-WASH IV, pp.14,39,47,146,153,157. He remained Watergate chief prosecutor just long enough to keep the grand jury from indicting Nixon, seeing to it that Nixon did not go to jail, and that the corporate fat cats who put up all the illicit money were let off with inconsequential fines.) Commissioner Russell had been in charge of the Senate's CIA "oversight." (See WHITEWASH IV, especially pp.21-2.)

With all the early allegations of CIA involvement, neither McCloy nor Jaworski should have had anything to do with any assassination investigation. Both helped assure that there was no real investigation, that there was the enormous coverup this book reports. Naturally, the bar association saw no conflict of interest when its top men were part of the same coverup while supposedly representing Oswald who, like Robert Kennedy later, had been assassinated and could not defend himself.

Wecht is one of those who believes that successful exploitation and commercialization of the subject gives him ownership and talking about it for fat fees makes him a genuine expert. To help him, he hired for his coroner's office staff Robert Smith who had been the so-called research director of the so-called Committee to Investigate Assassinations, a body that in years of work accomplished nothing. Smith then ghosted for Wecht, promoting Wecht.

While refusing to help with these FOIA suits and filing none of his own, Wecht repeatedly took full personal credit for all. In a May 5, 1975, press release, this included the memorandum of transfer and records I obtained by C.A. 226-75, "given to him" by the FBI "only a week ago." He added "regardless of what they show ... I shall say so." Since, silence on "what they show." He told the Pittsburgh Press (4/25/75) that "the bandwagon is getting a little crowded. ... Suddenly it's the thing to do and Cyril Wecht would like to take tickets." Why not? He has taken everything else. Preparing him to understand the autopsy materials required months of effort by others because Wecht did no original work and lacked knowledge and understanding of the evidence. What he told his briefers he had seen led one to exclaim that Wecht can't even read X-rays.

Coming exposes will prove the CIA withheld vast amounts of relevant data from the Commission and that the Commission knew it, knew the CIA would and did lie, and allowed the CIA to suppress those records which would embarrass it. (Instead of investigating the crime, the CIA investigated critics of the covering up. I have copies of some of its espionage on me.)

NOSENKO: THE GAMES HOOVER, THE FBI, CIA AND COMMISSION PLAYED

Little appreciated as it was then and in the ensuing years, essential to acceptance of the Report, particularly because of the absence of real proof and the presence only of disproof in the meaningful evidence, was prejudice against and hatred of Oswald. This need was met by building a false case of Oswald as pro-USSR and pro-Communist. All the credible evidence is to the contrary. Oswald hated the Russians and American Communists. (WHITEWASH pp.1,10,19, 72,119-23,137,149,192.) This propaganda line dominates the Report and the extensive conditioning campaign of "leaks" prior to its issuance. Its table of contents alone provides evidence. The entire last regular chapter dealing with the assassination (pp.375-424) is devoted to Oswald's "Background and Possible Motives." The preceding chapter allegedly on the alleged "Investigation of Possible Conspiracy" (none not involving him) has a separate 74-page section (R254ff) on "Background of Lee Harvey Oswald." Appendix XIII (R669ff) is 71 more pages on his "Biography." All of this and so much more just to make the anti-Communist Oswald appear to be a "Red" who could be accepted as a lone "nut" assassin.

Suppressing fact and truth was an early, major and endless problem. On the reality of Oswald, its confrontation with unwanted proof began 2/4/64 when a former KGB deputy section chief, Yuri Nosenko, defected to the CIA. Nosenko had had custody of the KGB's entire Oswald file.

With his life at stake if he lied, Nosenko talked. His story checked out. There is no mention of him or what he disclosed in the Report. Total suppression. I have obtained hundreds of relevant pages, seek more and will be writing about this separately. Nosenko told the CIA (not one report from which can be found in the Commission's files) and the FBI that the Russians actually believed Oswald was a "sleeper" or "dormant" American agent and had him and his mail under surveillance all the time he was in the USSR. Despite this, Oswald did not hide his dislike of the USSR. Marina's uncle, a colonel, begged Oswald "not to be too critical of the Soviet Union when he returned to the United States."

The Commission and its witting staff had to hide all of this. They and the Commission's successors have perpetuated secrecy to the degree possible.

The CIA could not deny the FBI access to Nosenko. FBI agents known to have interviewed him are Maurice A. Taylor, Donald E. Walter and Alekso Popanovich, beginning 2/26. The wily Hoover, knowing it would embarrass and compromise both the CIA and the Commission, arranged without being asked for Nosenko to offer to testify, the last thing the Commission wanted, and then put it in a letter.

The CIA people involved were under James Angleton, who, with others of them, was forced out as a result of the Watergate scandals. Typical of the continuing suppression is the withholding of the paragraph from David Slawson's 3/12/64 "TOP SECRET" memo on a CIA conference: "The first topic of conversation was Yuri Nosenko, the recent Soviet defector. A general discussion was held on this problem [sic] with the CIA's recommendation being that the Commission await further developments."

"Await" is the right word. The CIA stonewalled successfully. As of October 1975 I "await" response under the law to months-old requests for declassification of what never qualified for any classification, what Nosenko told the CIA about Oswald.

Slawson's colleague in this work is Ford's Secretary of Transportation, William T. Coleman, Jr. They put "TOP SECRET" classification on what the FBI did not classify at all and suppressed it all from their part of the Report.

It is a big secret but on 6/24/64 the Commission actually had Nosenko study some of its Oswald files. The day before it held an executive session. After not being able to get that transcript for eight years I filed suit on 9/24/75 (C.A.75-1448). Also on 6/24 this same pair wrote and classified TOP SECRET a memo to "The Commission" that begins by justifying their not questioning Nosenko, making no mention of the prior day's events or Nosenko's willingness to testify:

The Commission has asked us to prepare a short
memorandum outlining in what respects the information
obtained from Nosenko confirms or contradicts information
we have from other sources.

Nosenko's testimony to the FBI is the only information we have on what he knows about Lee Harvey Oswald.
(Commission Documents No. 434 and 451.) Perhaps more useful
information could be gained if we were to question Nosenko
directly, but it is unlikely. Nosenko told the representative
of the FBI who questioned him that he had given all the
information on Oswald he possessed.

They say Nosenko's only important knowledge was that Oswald
was not a KGB agent. That he was suspected by the Russians of being
an American agent was not important!

There can be no more classic example of Hoover's daring and
expertise in his own special brand of "dirty tricks." His unsolicited offer of Nosenko as a witness shifted all possible Commission
interest away from Hoover and reports Oswald had worked for him.
Hoover put his monkey on the Commission and CIA backs. The Commission saw irreparable destruction of its whole fabrication. The CIA
knew Dulles told the Commission the FBI had no agents in Russia (p.
481; WHITEWASH IV, pp.74-5).

Thereafter nobody ever crossed Hoover or raised any real questions about Oswald's possible FBI connections. Right after Hoover
started feeding them the Nosenko material, on 3/4/64, Coleman sent
his sidekick Slawson a news clipping reporting appointment of a CIA
official to be Deputy Assistant Secretary of State for Security.
"Bill" asked "Dave" if "the change came about because of the matters
we are working on."

"The matters we are working on" included Nosenko.

Eight days later they had that meeting with the CIA at which
they accepted what was suppressed in their memo, "the CIA's recommendation" to "await further developments." Rankin, Willens, Coleman,
Slawson, Stern and Griffin did not lay down the law to the stonewalling CIA. They did not invoke an unlimited Presidential mandate and
demand the information their job required or issue the subpoenas
Congress authorized. Not these stout hearts so determined on "disclosure of all the facts." Instead, they wheedled, which invited
Helms and the CIA to stonewall.

In Slawson's brave words they "pointed out to the CIA that we
had developed materials which might be of help to the CIA in assess-
ing the Russian situation, in particular the testimony of" Marguerite,
Robert and Marina Oswald and her business agent.

Even experienced spooks must have had trouble not bursting out
in laughter at this! What did Marguerite know "of help to the CIA"
from her practical nursing? Or Marina, the just-beginning pharmacist?
Robert from his Texas brickyard? James Martin from 15% of selling
Marina to whomever and however possible?

Imagine a Presidential Commission trying to bribe tough old
intelligence hands with trash like this! It gives a notion of the
character of the Commission's "investigation," why the best that can
be said of it is that it was a whitewash. And then having the gall
to stamp it "TOP SECRET," which means it could start a war!

There were "further developments," a few on Helms and the CIA
under him not limited to Watergate. The dirtiest kinds of dirty
tricks against Americans. If this Commission had done its work as
it was supposed to from what is in its files - holding the highest
security classification - it could have lead to exposure of these
dirty tricks, like killing Americans in drug experiments, intercept-
ing their mail and planning and pulling foreign assassinations. The
leads are there and I have them.

Does one suppose the Russians did not know that one of their
top man defected? Or what he could have said? What was of interest
to this Commission related to Oswald only, with not one word of it
secret from the Russians. Why stamp all this "TOP SECRET?" Only to

keep it secret from the American people, only to hide the kind of noninvestigation there was of the assassination.

This, of course, is but a partial record. It is enough to provide an "investigations" self-description. Once again it is the actuality, not the public pretense. One of the more disgusting parts of the coverup. More repugnant to any standard of decency and honor is what these characters actually planned to say of it in their Report. It, too, was classified for ten years. This boasting so opposite the truth is the first page of a section headed "DRAFT" from which I have eliminated only two illegible marginal notations:

In its investigation of Oswald's foreign contacts the Commission placed great reliance upon the Central Intelligence Agency and its information-gathering activities abroad. Also, the Commission received through the Agency information originating with defectors from the Soviet intelligence services on practices and procedures which would be applicable in the Soviet Union to a case like that of Oswald during his stay there. Some of the information furnished by the Agency, and most of its sources for that information, are of a highly confidential nature. Nevertheless, because it believes that the fullest possible disclosure of all the facts relating to the assassination of President Kennedy is of the highest importance, the Commission has included in this Report all the information, without exception, which it considered in coming to its conclusions, whether such information tended to strengthen or to weaken those conclusions. The only information which was not included in the Report, therefore, was either wholly irrelevant to any of the conclusions reached or was derived from sources which are known to be unreliable or whose reliability cannot be assessed at this time. In the latter case ... ... should later be proven to have been

Is it "wholly irrelevant" that the man the Commission intended to describe as the lone, pro-Russian assassin hated them? That they considered he was an American agent and kept him under surveillance? Or, because it is not "included in this Report" it is rather what was not "considered in coming to its conclusions?" Whichever, it defines "the fullest possible disclosure of all the facts relating to the assassination of President Kennedy."

This untold story is part of the past if not the credentials of our first unelected President and a member of his cabinet. If it does not say how we lost and got a President, it still says much.

comparison with notes, 255
draft, holographic, 252-3,255,
258,509-23,525
burning of, 184,209,220-1,
253-4,257,261,268,306
notes of, 54,102-5,145,237,247-
8,251-5,261,525-7
burning of, alleged, 37-8,103
134,144-5,160,253-4,257,261
268,524,559
missing, 533
receipt for, 248,250,525-7
preliminary, 253-4,261
rewritten, 257,508
supplemental, 158,200,218,252,
359,366,528-30,580-1,585,591
requirements of, 107,519
Review, Panels, 133-4,138-40,
146-52,154-215,217-22,246,255,
268-9,271,275,277,279-80,282-
4,300,318,354,358-9,366-7,379,
390,399,465,574-96
doctors, 146,148-9,155,160,
187,193-7,199-201,214,217-22
575-81
legal member, 187,209,214
misrepresentations, 583
pictures and X-rays, damage to
591; examination of, 565-73,
580-95; inventory of, 162-75
179,185,209,213,283,354,566-
79,581,584-5,594
report of, 134,138,152,155-69,
172-4,176-7,179-83,187-9,
191-7,199,201-4,206-9,211-6,
218-9,221-2,246,255,268-9,
277,282-3,300,318,366,379,
390,574-95
destruction of drafts, 222,
596
working papers, 218,220-1
testimony, vi,549,554,592
Autopsy manual, 235-6
Autopsy, Oswald, Lee Harvey, 7-8,
16,28,30,33,248,287
pictures, 16
Autopsy regulations, 106
Autopsy, Tippit, J.D., 8

Bahmer, Robert H., 18,147,248,323,
401,576
Bakeman, George, 72,534
Baker, Mrs. Donald (Rachley, Vir-
gie), 47,122,454
Baker, Marrion L., 89
Ball, Joseph A., x 81,86,490,492,
496,501,539,606
Ballistics, see under Evidence
Baltimore, Md., 133,218,223,317,
580-1
Baltimore Sun, 34-9,103
Bantam Books, 324
Barker, Eddie, 46
Barnum, 21,41
Barrett, Robert M., 53
Barson, Phillip, x
Bartlett, Orrin, 351,599,603
Bastard Bullet, The: A Search for

Legitimacy, 19,305
Battle, Preston, 291
Bay of Pigs, 363, 398
Behn, Gerald A., 46,104,276,548
Belin, David W., x,54-5,333,403,
470,490,492-3,496,501,503,606
Belmont, Alan, 485
Belmont, Mass., 386
Benavides, Domingo, 493
Bender, Mr. - , 408
Berkeley, see Burkley, George G.
Berkeley, Cal., 555
Berkeley (Cal.) Gazette, 388
Berkley, see Burkley, George G.
Bernabei, Richard, 349,379
Bertel, Numa, 133-7
Best, Robert T., 532
Bethell, Tom, 223,230
Bethesda, Md., x,29,33,66,71,113,
130,168-9,190,231,240,242,257-
8,266,271,276,304,379,468,501,
511,524-6,531-3,546-9,552,555,
565,573,575,584
Bethesda Naval Hospital, see Na-
tional Naval Medical Center
Billings, Richard, 47
Bishop, Jim, 239-40,242,244
Blackmun, Harry A., 313
Blondel, 463
Boggs, Hale, x,96,307,406-7,467,
475-9,481,483-4,486-7,489
Boleyn, Anne, 305
Bond, James, 344
Booth, John Wilkes, 396-7
Boston, Mass., 143
Boswell, J. Thornton, 34-8,40,42,
63,66,71,86-7,103,127,131,139-
42,144,146,148-9,153,158,167,
196,231,237,252,254,260-1,304-
5,309,312,364,501,528,530,533,
539-40,554,568-9,571,573,574-
6,579-80,584,591,594
request for study of JFK autopsy
pictures, 139-40,554
Bouck, Robert Inman, 102-3,250,265
274,276,302-3,527,548,557-9
Bow Street Magistrate's Court, 611
Bowers, Chester H., 72,270,534
Bowley, T. F., affidavit of, 493
Bowron, Diana Hamilton, 358
Boyers, Chester H., see Bowers,
Chester H.
Bozwell, see Boswell, J. Thornton
Bradlee, Benjamin, 238,240
Brennan, Howard Leslie, 118
Bress, David G., 135
Bresson, Thomas H., 415-7,545,618
British government, 227
Bromley, Bruce, 159-60,187,197,
220-2,581,596
Brookline, Mass., 308
Brown, Capt. -, 436
Brown, Edmund G. (Pat), 81
Bullets (JFK), 13,16-20,32,35,37,
41,44-9,51-3,55-8,62,65-8,73-
7,83-8,90-2,94-9,104,120,122-
5,127-9,131,152-3,163,169,171-
5,178-9,182-5,187-90,192-3,

8,421,423,425,431,440-1,456,
543,600-1,620
false swearing, Ray case, 431-2
Frederick, Md., 133,610
Freedom of Information law (5 U.S.
C. 552), v,vii,218,282,284,286
328,335,349,351,401,404-5,416,
419,421,425-6,428-9,545,620,
623
amendment of, vii-viii,404,409,
415,611
House-Senate Conference Report
No.93-1380, 404
lawsuits filed under, 246-7,313-
4,317-8,323,402,404,408,412-32
437,439,441-3,445,448-9,454,
457,459,461,465,490,610-22,626
false swearing in, 409,413,425
427-9,443,449,459,613-4,616-
20,623
transcript, 415,419
Freimuth, Henry C., 596
French Quarter, New Orleans, La.,
263-4
Friedman, John, 35
Friendly, Alfred, 64-5
Friml, Rudolph, 243
Fundamentals of Criminal Investigation, 409-10

GSA, see General Services Adminis-
tration
Gallagher, John F., 17-8,318,408,
418,421,437-40,442,446
Gallaway, see Galloway, C. B.
Gallatin, Tenn., 60
Galloway, C. B., 50,71,85-8,102,
104,113,127,236,244,248-9,251,
258,261,270,281-2,306,359,526-
8,533,539,543,547
Garrison, Jim, 3-4,133,136-7,144,
162,175,223-4,230,264,279,291-
2,366,376,580,596
investigation by, 3-4
Washington counsel, 133
Gates, Daryl, 431
Gauthier, Leo J., 501,503
Gavzer, Bernard, 82
Gawler's Funeral Home, 72,534
Geiselman, A. W., Jr., 34-5
Gemberling, Robert F., 18,24,351
General Services Administration,
30,140,284,286,327,387,401,560
Administrator, 560-5
Geneva Convention, 269,379
Germany, 369
Gesell, Gerhard, 328,338-40,614
Gilbert and Sullivan, 38,205,225-6
Goebbels [Joseph Paul], 3,183
Gold, Barry, 430
Goldberg, Alfred, x,112,494-5,500
Goldberg, Rube, 283
Goldwater, Barry, 328,368
Gonzales, Henry, 45
Gordon, Lincoln, 581
Government, U.S., v,vii-viii,2-3,
8-10,12-6,21-34,36,38-40,42,
47,49-51,54-5,62-3,69-70,78,

82,84,87,90,92,94-5,100-3,108-
10,112,114-6,118-9,122,125,128-
30,132-4,136-41,144-6,149,154-
6,159-61,163,168,170-2,175,178
181-2,184,188,194,197,199,206-
7,212-4,216-8,221-2,223,227,
230,245-8,255-6,263-4,267,273-
4,276,280-4,286-8,289,291-2,
295,299-300,304,306,313-4,316-
7,323-5,327-8,330-1,338-40,343
351,355,360-70,372,379,384,390
393,397,401-2,404,407,409,411,
413-4,416,423-9,436-7,441,445-
6,448,461-3,466,480,482,490,
549,555,560-4,596,607,612-4,
622
agencies, see individual listing
dishonesty of, vi-viii,412,426,
439-40,450,461,556,565,611,613
616,620,622
executive branch, vii-viii
property, 22.33.546,564
suits against, v,411,404
Graham, Fred, 140-1,168,273-4,291,
384-91,393,395,397,400-2
Grassy knoll, the, ix,48,109,392
Gray, L. Patrick, 439
Great Britain, 143,220,227
Home Office, 611
Greenfield, Meg, 409
Greer, William R., 73,77,146,206,
305,533,537-8
Gregory, Charles, 83,128,131,378,
503,552,554
Griffin, Bert W., x,498-9,628
Griffith, Elmer H., 330
Habana Bar and Lounge, 263-4
Hagen, Mr. -, 72,534
Haggerty, Edward A., Jr., 133,230-
4,237
Halleck, Charles W., Jr., 134-8,
142,155,162,189,216-8,220,223,
283,292,366
Hanes [Arthur], 291
Hannah, John A., 156,581
Hannon, Joseph M., 135
Harding [President Warren G.], 243
Hargis, Billy, 61
Harper, William Allen, 80-1,399
reports, 384
Harvard University, 155,581
Law Review, 112
Law School, 96
Harwood, Richard, 65-73,76
Hatcher, Emery, 432,434-5
Haseltine, Nate, 66
Hecht, Ben, 35
Heep, Uriah, 361
Heiberger, -, 421
Henchcliffe, Margaret M., 358
Henry VIII, 305
Haptinstall, Robert H., 596
Heren, Louis, 69
Hidell, A., 398
Hill, Clint, 305,363,380,384,399
Hill, L. L., 57,454
Hitler, Adolf, 281,360,398

639

Seaborg, Glenn T., 444,448,452,618
Search for Justice, A, 290
Secret Service, 1,4,9-10,24,27,41,
45-6,48-9,51-4,56-8,66-8,71-4,
77,81,86,88,101-5,109,111-2,
120-1,124,128,130,141,146,163,
177,189,200,203,206,214,228,
235,238,242-4,248-53,257,261,
265-6,270-1,274-7,282-8,302-3,
305,308-9,333,350-1,358-9,363,
380,382-4,389,395,399,488,496,
499,508,526-8,534,536,544,546-
8,551,553,555-9,575,599,603
  agents, 41,46,53,71,73-4,77,86,
  88,102-4,111-2,124,128,146,189
  200,203,206,235,243,250,265,
  270-1,274-6,302-3,305,356,358,
  363,380,382-4,399,491,501,531,
  533,536,548,555,573,594
    see also Behn, Gerald A.;
      Bouck, Robert I.; Greer,
      William R.; Hill, Clint;
      Howlett, John Joe; Johnsen,
      Richard; Kellerman, Roy H.;
      Kelley, Thomas J.; Moore,
      Elmer; O'Leary, William;
      Warner, Jack
  chief, see Rowley, James J.
  custodian of pictures and X-rays
    214,271,274-6,548,555
  files, 284,359
    CO-2-34,030, 528
  informers, 500
  interviews, 9
  Protective Research Section, 102
    249-51,276,527,532,548
  reconstruction, 48-9,54,228,488,
    490
  reports, 10,52-3,104,112,120-1,
    228,333,395,490,500,528
    (medical, under Autopsy, JFK)
    on JFK assassination, see
      under Commission, Files, No.
      3
  White House Detail, see Protec-
    tive Research Section
Segatelyan, Mikhail, 294
Seigenthaler, John, 290-2
Senators, 289,447
Shaffer, Charles N., Jr., 108,473-
  4,488
Shakespeare, [William], 455
Shaneyfelt, Lyndal L., 57,223-4,
  228-30,350,454,460-1,501,503
Shaw, Clay L., 133,137,155,223,279
  lawyers, 223,231-3,235,300
  trial of, 223-37,290,292,300,580
    596
Shaw, Robert R., 52,67-8,75-6,82,
  84,97,128,131,378,449,503,554
Shires, George Tom, 17,59,69,83-4,
  260,506,508
Shots, ix-x,14,16-7,22,28,44-5,47-
  9,51-8,60,65-6,68-9,74,77,79-
  82,86,89-90,92,103,105,108-9,
  113,118,120-3,127-30,137,153,
  171-3,181-2,205,212,219-20,

225-6,228,248,258,295-6,318,
  321,331,333,363-4,379-85,387-8
  463,468,488,490,492,542,549
  missed, x,49,51-2,54-8,65,77,89,
    92,113,120,122,153,172,295,388
    439,453-4,456,492
  number of, x,5-6,17,22,44,51-7,
    65-6,74,82,92,113,120-1,181,
    226,228,295-6,380-3,453,488,
    492,504,509,598
Sibert, James W., 24-5,42,50,71-4,
  76-8,86,103-4,146,169,206,248,
  266-8,271,273,275-6,278,305,
  517,531-2,535-8,543,548,559,
  603
  report of, 24-5,49-50,71-4,103-
    4,127,206,225,248,266-8,270,
    273,275-6,278-9,303,531-6,537-
    8,548
Silberman, Lawrence, 407
Simmons, John F. (Mike), 252,254,
  340,344,346-8,354
"Single-bullet" theory, 18-9,44-8,
  50-2,54-5,58,60,62,65,68-70,75
  79,82-4,86,91-2,94,99,113,120-
  3,125-6,129,199,212,224,247,
  360,395,399,542
Sirhan, Sirhan Bishara, 290,430,
  432
  car, 435
  lawyers, 431
  revolver, 430-2
  shots, 432
  trial of, 290,430,432
Sirica, John J., 246,314,317
Sixth-floor window, see under
  Texas School Book Depository
Slawson, W. David, x,112,498-500,
  627-8
Smith, Robert, 626
Smith and Wesson revolver, 603-4
Socialist Party, 7
Socialist Workers Party, 7
Solicitor General of Canada, Department of, 411
Solicitor General, United States,
  4,25,62,109,119-20,256,276,406
Song of Solomon, 251
Southeast Asia, 281,294,368,463
Soviet Union (see also Russia), 6-
  8,15,321,397
Sparrow, John, 294
Specter, Arlen, x,23,25,40,45-8,
  50-1,54-6,59-63,65,68-73,75-9,
  82-9,91-2,97,102,104,113,119,
  121-31,143-5,152,159,163,168,
  174,199-200,212,215,224,242,
  245,247,249-50,254,257,259-61,
  275,282,285,300,305,307,319,
  342,357-60,375-9,395,412,454,
  490-1,499,501-4,506,524,526,
  528,537,539,549-50,553-5,589
Spectrographic analysis, 13,16-20,
  95-6,99,124-5,171-3,204,226,
  246,313-4,317-9,334,336,340,
  348-9,351-3,373,395,404,407,
  412,416-7,420-2,428,438,449-50
  456-7,488,490,599,603-4,606-7,